Comparing Political Systems:
Power and Policy in Three Worlds

# Comparing Political Systems: Power and Policy in Three Worlds

SECOND EDITION

GARY K. BERTSCH

ROBERT P. CLARK

DAVID M. WOOD

1807 1982

JOHN WILEY & SONS
NEW YORK   CHICHESTER   BRISBANE   TORONTO   SINGAPORE

*Library of Congress Cataloging in Publication Data:*

Bertsch, Gary K.
    Comparing political systems.

    Includes index.
    1. Comparative government.      I. Clark, Robert P.
II. Wood, David Michael, 1934–            III. Title.
JF51.B48      1982      320.3      81-21863
ISBN 0-471-08446-8            AACR2

Printed in the United States of America

10 9 8 7 6 5 4 3

# PREFACE

This textbook is intended to introduce undergraduate students to the critical issues of power and politics in the world today. Although many outstanding scholars have addressed these topics in other books, considerable dissatisfaction still exists about the usefulness of the available textbooks for undergraduate instruction. Although we would be the first to admit that *Comparing Political Systems* does not fill all the deficiencies, we do feel that our book attempts to resolve some of the major shortcomings.

The first problem we faced concerned a unified conceptual framework. Emphasizing the critical forces of politics—the historical, environmental, and ideological setting in which policy making occurs, and the political organizations within which policy planning, decision, and execution occur—we take a straightforward policy approach. Simply stated we ask: What do political leaders and groups want to accomplish (*goals*)? What have they done and what are they doing (*actions*)? What are the consequences of their actions (*outcomes*)?

Second, we take a comparative approach to the study of these topics. Dividing the world into three primary groupings of nations—the Western democracies of the "First World," the Communist states of the "Second World," and the African, Asian, and Latin American states of the "Third World"—we emphasize cross-national comparison within each of the three "worlds" as well as comparisons between the First, Second, and Third worlds.

Since the book is divided into these three parts and is organized around common topics and chapters in each part, instructors have two basic alternatives in using the book. The instructor can take any one part (e.g., the Third World) at a time and focus on cross-national comparison within that particular world. After the book has been completed, the Conclusion will be of assistance in making comparisons among the three worlds. This approach may be desired by those who prefer to view politics within the three-world perspective. The alternative approach considers all three worlds simultaneously by taking common chapters (e.g., Chapter 3, "Political Culture and Socialization") from each of the three sections. This strategy emphasizes simultaneous cross-national and cross-world comparison and may be desired by those who prefer a more global approach.

Finally, we attempt to address some of the critical normative and empirical questions of political analysis. What *can* political systems do to enhance the opportunities for human dignity in the contemporary world? What *are* they doing and with what effects on the people? Most textbooks deal with political leaders, institutions, and processes without attempting to assess what these factors mean to rank-and-file citizens. Our book attempts to address this long-standing need.

Each of the three parts is also available individually in paperback from Wiley. Together they form a series based on the same framework and containing essentially the same materials as this volume. David M. Wood is the author of *Power and Policy in Western European Democracies*; Gary K. Bertsch of *Power and Policy in Communist Systems*; and Robert P. Clark of *Power and Policy in the Third World.*

We wish to ackowledge the invaluable contribution of the many individuals who assisted in the project and improved the contents in innumerable ways. We would particularly like to acknowledge the constructive reviews and sug-

gestions of many instructors who used the first edition. We would also like to thank those who reviewed the second edition in manuscript form. Both groups aided us in making considerable improvements to the text. For whatever deficiencies the book contains, we assume full responsibility.

GARY K. BERTSCH
ROBERT P. CLARK
DAVID M. WOOD

# CONTENTS

# GENERAL INTRODUCTION
## Politics and Human Values

Human values change from one culture to another, from one historical period to another. Yet, it seems to us that human beings spend a considerable part of their time worrying about, and trying to change, the condition of their lives. For some, the principal problem may be tangible or material—enough food to eat, proper clothing or shelter, adequate medical care. For others, unsatisfactory conditions may involve less tangible factors—education for themselves or for their children, the right to worship as they choose, permission to speak the language of their ethnic group. For still others, the major problem may be social—their acceptance by antagonistic groups, denial of their rights by others, a feeling of racial or ethnic inferiority.

Many aspects of human values also change. Consider the causes of human problems for example. Once nearly all people worried about poverty and its effects; now a growing number of people are concerned over the impact of industrial affluence. The remedies sought by people have changed, too. Traditional peoples often tried to solve their problems by placating threatening spirits; modern humans usually place their faith in science.

There is still another important change in the way people recognize, define, and deal with unacceptable life conditions. In earlier times, people were generally expected to cope with life's struggles as individuals or as members of small, informally organized groups, such as families,

clans, or tribes. Human problems were usually individual and private issues, not political and public ones. In recent decades, however, men and women the world over—from slums in Calcutta to factories in Moscow or to the farms of France—have looked increasingly to government to help them manage their lives and to overcome inadequacies in their conditions of life. (To say this is not to assert that governments always, or even usually, resolve these problems. Too frequently, governments have been part of the problem, not part of the solution.)

Most of the world's 167 or so independent governments are organized to respond to what their leaders perceive to be the foremost challenges facing their countries. On rare occasions, governments do fall under the control of irrational leaders who abuse their power and misuse their people for purely personal reasons. On the whole, however, governments attempt to deal with challenges that stem from problems their people face or from the conditions of human life in their country. Each of the world's governments has achieved a certain level of response to these challenges, a certain record of accomplishment in improving (or failing to improve) the condition of their people. No government solves all its country's problems immediately; none can fail for long and remain in power. All governments fall somewhere in between the two extremes of total success and abject failure. We intend to use this fact as a conceptual tool to study

1

and to explain differences in politics around the world.

This book is designed to introduce you to the comparative study of politics in three very different kinds of countries. Along the way, it poses two broad sets of questions and provides you with some information to help you formulate answers.

**1.** How do governments help people achieve what they value? What do governments do to resolve human problems? How well do governments accomplish their objectives? How can we measure and compare performance or achievement in so many different countries?

**2.** For what factors can we look to explain different levels of government performance? What difference does ideology or government structure make? Are political parties, interest groups, or mass communications important? Are constitutional freedoms crucial to enhancing human values or do they just get in the way of determined governments? Perhaps other factors not so clearly political are more important in determining the ability of governments to solve human problems—the wealth of the country, its natural resources, the level of education of its people, its level of industrialization, geographical location, historical background, and so forth. In short, does government matter to people and to human values? If so, how much and in what ways?

## WHAT DO PEOPLE WANT?

Before we can measure and compare the performance of governments, we must first discover what people want for themselves and, by derivation, what they want from their government. No matter how much of a particular service a government may provide, if that service is noxious to the citizenry, we could not rate that government's performance as high. Thus, in our formulation, political performance is directly linked to what people want—to the prevailing set of human values.

For many years, scholars from different fields of knowledge, including psychology,

sociology, political science, and economics, have studied what humans value in different cultural and economic settings.[1] To date, no one has developed a list of universal human values that is acceptable to all scholars in all cultures and that at the same time is precise and capable of being investigated empirically. Thus, in this book, we must work with a set of human values derived from criteria other than that provided by universal scholarly consensus.

To organize our inquiry into comparative political performance, we have decided to work with four human values: *power, respect, well-being,* and *enlightenment.*

We do not claim that our four values are universal or sacred, only that they are useful as an organizing principle to guide our work. They tend to be among the most important human values dealt with in a political context around the world, and they span the entire range of important values, from the inner needs of individuals to the public environmental requirements of social collectivities.

In addition, these four values reflect our normative concerns. We favor democractic power distributions, universal respect for all peoples, equitable distribution of the ingredients of well-being, and universal access to enlightenment. Of course, others have different priorities. The task of a political scientist is to blend the empirical foundations of one's discipline with one's normative concerns as a human being.

Simply placing labels on concepts, such as power and respect, does not tell us much about what people want or about how governments help them achieve these values. Each of the four values must be defined in some detail if we are to know what to look for in our inquiry. Yet, as we soon discover, each value may be interpreted differently in different countries or areas of the

---

[1] The literature on human values is extensive. The interested reader can begin with Hadley Cantril, *The Pattern of Human Concerns* (New Brunswick, N.J.: Rutgers University Press, 1966); Harold Lasswell, *A Pre-View of Policy Sciences* (New York: Elsevier, 1971); Abraham Maslow, ed., *New Knowledge in Human Values* (Chicago: Regnery, 1970); Gunnar Myrdal, *Value in Social Theory* (Boston: Routledge & Kegan Paul, 1958); Milton Rokeach, *The Nature of Human Values* (New York: Free Press, 1973).

world. Where it is necessary to do so, we point out major differences between the value definitions we develop here and those that prevail in other countries.

*Power,* the first human value, means the ability to influence the behavior of others. In a political context, power can be conceived as the capacity to change or infuence policy outcomes. If a handful of elites have complete power to determine policy decisions, policy outcomes will reflect their particular scale of values. The extent to which power is distributed among the broader population determines the degree to which the values of ordinary people are reflected in policy outcomes. Although most governments in their official self-justifications consider democracy an overriding political goal, few have been successful in distributing power democratically within their societies. As we will see, political realities do not always correspond with political ideals.

Because power is not only a value in itself but also a determinant affecting the allocation of other values, it is the most important. The American, French, and Russian revolutions were all fought to wrest power from an entrenched élite and to place it in the hands of deprived sections of the population. Power itself—and the ways in which it is wielded and distributed within a political system—is at the heart of politics.

Two aspects of power stand out and call for further discussion. On the one hand, all governments need to accumulate and consolidate sufficient power to be able to govern effectively. Without sufficient official power, governments cannot mobilize their armed forces to repel attack, spend money to meet the welfare needs of their people, or command the loyalty of a civilian bureaucracy. On the other hand, the distribution of power between citizens and government and among competing groups of citizens is also a pressing policy question in all nation-states. To varying degrees, rank-and-file citizens need to feel that they are able to influence the actions of their government, so, power must be distributed effectively between the people and their government. Further, many groups of citizens see the need to increase their power position with regard

to other groups in society. As the principal institution for distributing power in society, the government is responsible for attending to the needs of these people. The problem of power as a human value is double edged: (1) governments must acquire enough power to be able to govern and (2) the people must obtain enough power to influence their government and competing groups in society. In the case of governments that are solidly entrenched, the acquisition of power has already been accomplished, and the distribution of power is the dominant issue. Our discussion focuses principally on power distribution. Nevertheless, there are many governments in the world, primarily in the less developed regions, where the central problem is one of acquiring enough power to be able to meet the challenges of their society. Where necessary, then, our discussion shifts to an analysis of how governments in developing countries acquire enough power to become going concerns and to solve the problems that confront their people.

The second human value, *respect,* refers to the desire of most people to enjoy secure and supportive relationships with others, including (in our usage) political authorities. In our dealings with other people, most of us prefer to associate with those who respect our feelings and our ways of thinking, who encourage us to feel self-confident in their presence, who do not try to punish or abuse us for what we think or do, and to whom we give our loyalty and affection. There is a counterpart process in the political world that matters a great deal to both citizens and government alike. The different dimensions of respect—honor and prestige, respect for human rights, affection and loyalty—are all elements that contribute to the idea of community. Political community refers to a grouping of individuals who communicate, work together, and understand one another. Without a strong sense of political community, a political system will face excessive conflict and turmoil.

To enhance the development of community within a political system, respect must be accorded to all groups and individuals. If a particular race, ethnic group, or social class is not provided with respect through the laws of a country and if it is not allowed to vote or not accorded equal opportunities in education and employment, then, it is not likely to feel itself a part of a larger political community. Political systems characterized by discriminatory policies and actions tend to have societies divided by deep political cleavages—and these may sometimes express themselves in violent political conflict. The potential for violence is greater in countries where respect is not widely distributed.

Well-being, the third basic value at stake in politics, refers to the enjoyment by groups and individuals of income, goods, services, health, safety, and comfort. Although there seems to be a universal desire for increased well-being, ideologies and political systems hold different images of the proper distribution of wealth and other elements of well-being. *Capitalism* appears more individual oriented. Although attempting to provide equal opportunities, capitalist political systems allow individuals to achieve whatever levels of well-being are within their grasp. Thus, some individuals are able to accumulate great wealth and to enjoy an abundance of services, safety, and comfort. At the same time, certain individuals and groups live at the poverty level in these systems and suffer from crime, relatively poor health care, and social and physical deprivation. Capitalist belief systems remain ambivalent about these conditions and about inequality in general.

On the other hand, *Marxist* ideology and *Communist* political systems speak unequivocally in favor of more equitable distribution of well-being. They emphasize social equality and are willing to deprive the economically privileged of their wealth and shut off opportunities for material accumulation beyond a maximum standard. Marxism stresses the collective good over that of the individual and, although Marxism still has significant levels of inequality, it allocates goods and services and health and comfort more nearly equally than non-Communist states. Although environmental constraints have made it difficult for the leaders of some Communist countries, for example, China, to raise dramatically the level of well-being for the whole population, redistributive policies have made it

possible for the poorer classes to be above the level of abject poverty.

The term for our last value, *enlightenment*, is one with many different meanings, depending on whether one's focus is philosophical, historical, or educational. We define enlightenment as the process by which individuals learn about themselves and their world, whether by means of formal education, acquisition of information from the mass media, or transmission of informal social mores through family, peer group, or neighborhood.

Although educational opportunities in a given country are affected by economic factors, significant political choices must still be made. Education is an important means of overcoming economic deficiencies because human potential must be enhanced if economic development is to proceed.

Still, the choices to be made are not always obvious. Should quality education be guaranteed to all, regardless of race, social class, or ethnic origin? Should the objective be mass enlightenment or the development of an intellectual élite capable of giving leadership in the process of modernization? Here, too, the question concerns allocation of resources. How can resources be allocated to gain the maximum benefit to society? In some countries undergoing modernization, the choice has been to raise the general level of all groups in the population although this may be costly in terms of a de-emphasis on quality, élite-oriented education. Two Western capitalist countries, the United States and Great Britain, made quite different choices in this respect during their periods of rapid industrialization in the nineteenth century. Today, many British observers feel that their choice in favor of an élitist educational system was costly in view of the wide distribution of advanced technological skills now needed in modern industrial society. They compare their country unfavorably with the United States in this respect.

Enlightenment means much more than education. In many countries, the mass communications media are the subject of great controversy as they disseminate information that may be threatening to an incumbent regime. Many government leaders have controlled their nation's press or have expelled foreign journalists because of the threat they pose to their survival. Even in countries where the press is relatively free politically, questions concerning censorship, pornography, and the role of the press in trials and at times of crisis have come to the surface. Information, especially that broadcast through public channels, is not a free good and is usually subject to some controls in the name of the public interest.

Even cultural and ethnic learning—once thought intensely private matters beyond the reach of the state—have come under public scrutiny in many countries. In some nations, such as Iran or Spain, regional separatism is kept alive by informal means, despite official measures to suppress distinct languages and cultural traditions. In other nations, such as Belgium, Canada, and Yugoslavia, special regional sensitivities are protected by constitutional and other measures. In our highly politicized world, even one's innermost thoughts and modes of expression become the subject of public debate, if not of regulations.

Thus, we have developed our list of four important human values. From time to time, we refer to them collectively by the encompassing term, *human dignity*. Human dignity refers to a preferred state of being that many government leaders attempt to achieve through their allocation of power, well-being, respect, and enlightenment. Theoretically, the highest state of human dignity would be reached when a society received its preferred (ideal) mixture of values.

There are different conceptions of the term human dignity in today's world. Communist Party states adhere to a more collectivist conception, whereas those of Western Europe tend toward individualism. In this book, the concept carries with it the notion that each human being is considered an end in himself or herself and is not a mere instrument to enhance the values of some higher entity, for example, the state, a party, or a dictator. We obviously can not claim that all governments employ policies designed to maximize the Western concept of human dignity. A glance through a newspaper will uncover ex-

amples of governments that deny their people many, or even all, the values listed. The approach of each government in meeting its society's problems will differ, depending on the relative weight it places on such competing factors as dissent and conformity or on the rights of the individual and the rights of the collectivity. We strive in the pages ahead to be sensitive to the different concepts of human dignity in the world today; yet, we tend to emphasize personal standards as yardsticks against which to measure the performance of governments.

## THE FUNDAMENTALS OF POLITICS

Politics is the art of the possible. First, this means that there are social, economic, and cultural constraints that limit how far political leaders can go at any given time in correcting the deficiencies they find in their societies. Second, it means that there are choices open to political leaders and that the choices they make will have a crucial impact on the allocation of values within their societies. Politics *does* make a difference. We believe that there is no country in the world where decisions of political leaders could not bring about more nearly equal distributions of the four basic values outlined above. Yet, we are also acutely conscious of the caveat, "There is no such thing as a free lunch." Redistributive decisions in one realm will inevitably be costly in another. Thus, the decision to confiscate private wealth, for example, through a heavily progressive tax on personal income or through a levy on corporate income, will have the effect of reducing the pool of private savings that can be devoted to capital investment and, thus, to economic growth. But failure to redistribute may mean that the rich will get richer faster than the poor—society may become less egalitarian rather than more. These dilemmas face political decision makers in all parts of the world.

As we use the word, politics refers to the process by which certain values or things people want are distributed. We see politics as a process, that is a related set of public goals, actions, and outcomes. Political goals are what people hope to accomplish, the expressed objectives of political leaders, groups or ordinary citizens. *Actions* are decisions resulting in legislation, programs, or some other activity intended to achieve public goals. Outcomes are the consequences of political action. What results from the actions and what impact do they have on people? These results are the outcome of politics. Because the general result of all such sequences is policy, we will occasionally use the term policy process to describe these events.

The essence of the political process is the distribution of values. However, there are many other social institutions, such as schools, churches, businesses, and labor unions, that also distribute the things people want. What makes the political process of distribution different is its public scope and authoritative character.

Politics is a public process in the sense that it affects all the members of a population whether or not they agree with the outcome, have participated in the process, or, in fact, are even aware that a public decision has been made. The all-encompassing coverage of the political process distinguishes it from other social institutions whose impact is, for the most part, restricted to their members. Occasionally, to emphasize the fact that politics deals with the values of the public as opposed to private interests, we will also use the terms, public policy and public policy process.

Politics is an authoritative process because it involves the willingness of most citizens to abide by a policy even though they may not agree with its content. The authority of a regime to make policy for an entire population stems not only, and maybe not even primarily, from the justice or wisdom of the policy but also from the willingness of the people to attribute such authority to the regime. Such attribution may come from the way a decision is made as much as from the content of the specific policy.

This book examines and compares the political process that shapes the distribution of values in countries from all parts of the globe. Although élites and masses influence the making of public policy, they do so within the framework of regular and predictable patterns of behavior or institutions. Thus, our focus on the policy process

includes an examination of the political and governmental structures within which the power to make policy is located. Although we devote much discussion to explaining governments and their role in the policy-making process, we must cast our net broadly to include all actions relevant to the policy process. Thus, we often refer to political systems rather than to governments. Governments traditionally represent formal institutions (the executive, the legislature, etc.) and the political élites staffing them who are involved in the making of policy. Because of the nature of modern political life, only a minority of a society is usually directly involved in the determination of policy. These individuals are referred to as political élites; although they play crucial roles in the political process, they are not the sole participants.

The concept of political system is more inclusive than government and incorporates all individuals and institutions involved in the political process. For example, in explaining Soviet policy toward the West, one must understand the role of its formal governmental organs and political leaders. But that alone will not produce a complete understanding. The student of politics must also examine the influence of other, less formal factors, such as the military-industrial complex, political dissidents, and the flavor of international opinion. If this is true of the Soviet Union, then, it is likely to be even more true in the case of more open, democratic political systems in which there is a regularized pattern of interaction among government decision makers and groups representing different sections of the general population. For all political systems, we are interested in the influences that help shape policy, whether they are near to, or remote from, the actual policy makers. We are also interested in the consequences of the policies made for different groups within society. The political system includes the influences bearing on the policy makers, the impacts of their decisions on the public, and the resulting public reactions.

According to the *Political Handbook of the World: 1980*[2] there are today about 167 relatively

[2]Arthur S. Banks, ed., *Political Handbook of the World: 1980* (New York: McGraw-Hill, 1980).

independent, distinct, and self-governing political entities in the world. Each is organized as a national government and recognized by most of the other governments in the world as having the right to join the international community. Despite the wide variety of organizational forms represented by this collection of governments, the political goals pursued by the national leadership exhibit rather similar patterns.

The first goal of every national government élite is to preserve the nation as the principal acting unit. Scholars, philosophers, and ordinary citizens may debate the necessity, the desirability, or the feasibility of perpetuating the fragmentation of the globe into several hundred competing nations. However, the fact remains that the nation-state system is not on the wane even though for many reasons national units are frequently either too large or too small to attend to the problems of individual citizens. National political élites will defend with passion their right to remain in charge of the destiny of their people; the destruction of the colonial system was accompanied by the spread of the belief in self-determination for every ethnic group with a strong sense of self-awareness. Thus, the political system must see to it that the *nation* survives even at the cost of virtually every other goal.

Beyond the preservation of the nation, each governmental regime or political elite seeks its own institutional survival. Every government devotes a significant proportion of the nation's resources—often resources it can ill afford to spend—in pursuit of internal stability as well as in defense against rivals within its own boundaries. Political élites seek to concentrate power in their own hands, at least to the extent necessary to reduce the likelihood of violent upheaval or serious political discontinuity. Without power, the allocation of values promoting human dignity will not be accepted as authoritative by the population. In other words, internal *political stability* is a requirement for the orderly formulation and implementation of policy.

At the same time that élites struggle to preserve their nation—and themselves—intact they devote their energies and resources to the management of the dual processes of modernization and industrialization. Since the beginning of the Industrial Revolution (about 1750), political leaders in ever-increasing numbers have come to believe that human dignity can be significantly enhanced if, and only if, the social order is transformed from a traditional to a modern one, and the economy is transformed from an agrarian to an industrial one. The way in which each government responds to these challenges and manages these processes has much to do with the form the government takes, the shape of its public policies, and the level of performance it manages to achieve. Later, we will make more explicit how we intend to use this information to guide our search for a better understanding of the political process in many different political systems.

## TOWARD A BETTER UNDERSTANDING OF POLITICS: WHY AND HOW WE CLASSIFY NATIONS

The field of comparative politics is organized around the idea that we can understand better the political process if we can compare politics in one country (or set of countries) with politics in another. To compare nations, we need first to be able to classify them, to group them according to certain characteristics that we feel are important to understanding and explaining their similarities and differences.

In our case, we have elected to classify the world's political systems according to the way in which they are managing the processes of industrialization and modernization. Our classification scheme focuses on the policies governments adopt to deal with modernization and industrialization, the success with which they implement these policies, and the levels of performance they achieve in the process.

Since the beginning of the Industrial Revolution in England in the mid-eighteenth century, the undeniable wave of social change has been steadily in the direction of industrialization of the means of production, modernization of attitudes and modes of thinking, and development of political-system capacities. Although this process is very attractive to many people and promises to bring benefits to many different groups, the fact remains that industrialization has been stoutly resisted by some people in just about every country in which it has been proposed. This is because industrialization as a social process is never free, seldom cheap, and usually quite expensive—at least to some members of society. In one way or another, traditional, anti-industrial groups, such as peasants or landed aristocracy, stand to lose economically, psychologically, and politically from these changes; consequently, their natural inclination is to fight back and to resist change to the degree their resources permit. The nature of their resistance and the kinds of power available to modernizing élites to push through their changes go far toward determining the kinds of industrialization strategies adopted by reform-minded elites.[3]

Modernization of a society implies two separate, but closely related, processes.

1. At the psychological level, people must modernize their way of thinking, rejecting notions of fatalism, mysticism, and historical rigidity and embracing the more modern concepts of activism, science, historical causation, and the belief that a person can influence individual fate by an exercise of reason and skills. Modernization of the individual means increased educational opportunity and access to the network of mass communications. For society, modernization means a wider distribution of the value of respect. People come to value their own capacity to create a better world. They shed ancient taboos and inhibitions that had imprisoned thought. And they come to value this enhanced human capacity not only in themselves but also in others of their society.

2. At another level, society must be organized to enhance the physical and mental abilities of each person. Such organization requires the bureaucratization of task-performing institutions, the implementation of assembly-line and mass-production techniques, and the adoption of decision-making methods that emphasize rationality and systematic analysis. Thus, the improved knowledge, information, and skills of individuals can be mobilized to increase human productive capacity vastly.

Industrialization implies the increased application of technology to allow humans to manipulate the natural world to meet their demands and needs (and, not infrequently, to permit them to exercise power over others). Industrialization involves the discovery and application of techniques for transforming relatively inefficient energy sources into efficient ones, advances in materials processing, changes in transportation and communication technologies, developments in building and construction techniques, and many other related transformations. The result is a vast expansion of society's capacity to satisfy the human craving for greater material well-being. As the size of the pie of goods and services grows, all groups within society may potentially gain some share of the benefits.

The dual processes of modernization and industrialization have political implications that radiate in two directions from these revolutionary changes. On the one hand, political institutions must be transformed into modern agencies of change that are capable of guiding and directing the industrialization process where it has already been established and of initiating it where it has not yet begun. This process may cause a further accretion of power by political élites. On the other hand, the political system is called on to resolve the numerous social, economic, and psychological conflicts that arise from the very process of industrialization. New groups emerge that must be appeased in this process. In the long run, industrialization frequently brings with it a broadening of the distribution of political power.

To cope with the problems of industrial growth and modernization, government élites the world over have sought to increase their capabilities, their capacity for performing certain essential jobs that the unorganized and unaided citizens of the country cannot perform for

[3]Barrington Moore, Jr., *Social Origins of Dictatorship and Democracy: Lord and Peasant in the Making of the Modern World* (Boston: Beacon, 1966).

themselves. This process of improving a government's capabilities is referred to here as political development. These tasks call for extractive capabilities, such as the ability to tax income and to conscript young men and women for military service. They require that governments regulate the behavior of citizens by passing laws and punishing those who violate them. Thus, a strengthening of the law enforcement arm of the state is necessary. Government must have the power to remove resources (such as land) from one group and distribute them to another group.

But government leaders also find that they must develop the ability to sense what their citizens want from the political system so that their expanding needs and rising aspirations may be satisfied. Intermediary linkages between ordinary citizens and their political leaders must develop, whether these be legislative bodies, political parties, organized interest groups, electoral systems, the press, or whatever. And, finally, governments must generate and communicate symbolic messages to their people to satisfy the psychological needs of the citizens to trust the government and to have faith and confidence in its decisions. [4]

The strategy chosen by the political leaders to guide a nation through these difficult changes frequently emerges from a political process in which questions like these are asked and answered.

> Which government capacities or powers should be given priority? How should the overall mix of powers be blended together?
>
> Which institutions must be created and which eliminated to speed up the process of change?
>
> How rapidly and at what cost is development to take place?
>
> What kinds of social, psychological, and economic changes must occur for political development to take place?
>
> Which values—power, respect, well-being,

enlightenment—should receive top priority? Which groups should receive these values first?

Which groups in society should pay the costs of development?

The nations of the world can be classified according to how they answer these questions. The answers offered by developing countries, like India and Peru, differ markedly from those chosen by the Western European democracies, like France and Great Britain, and both of these differ from those of Communist Party states, like the Soviet Union and China. These answers constitute three separate and distinct strategies for political change. For shorthand purposes, we will label them the strategies of the First, Second, and Third Worlds, referring respectively to the industrialized democracies of Western Europe and North America; the Communist systems found primarily in the Soviet Union, Eastern Europe, and parts of Asia; and the less developed countries located primarily in the Southern Hemisphere—Latin America, the Middle East, Africa, and the southern zone of Asia.

## THREE POLITICAL WORLDS

Table I.1 illustrates how we have classified the 167 relatively self-governing states that are identified in the *Political Handbook of the World: 1980*.[5] The *First World* consists of 24 industrial democracies located principally in Western Europe and North America. These nations account for slightly more than 16 percent of the world's estimated 1980 population and take up about 23.5 percent of its surface area. The Second World, the 16 Communist Party states located principally in Eastern Europe and Asia, accounts for slightly more than one third of the world's population (34.3 percent) and slightly more than one quarter of its land area (26.8 percent). About half the world's population (49.1 percent) and land area (48.9 percent) are found in the Third World, a category that includes 101 states by our count. Finally, we identify 26 states

---

[4]Gabriel A. Almond and G. Bingham Powell, *Comparative Politics: A Developmental Approach* (New York: Little, Brown, 1966), Chapter 8.

[5]Banks, op. cit.

TABLE I.1 CLASSIFICATION OF 167 STATES AS OF
JANUARY 1, 1980

| Name of State | Population (millions) | Area (thousands of square miles) |
|---|---|---|
| FIRST WORLD | | |
| 1. Australia | 14.6 | 2,966.1 |
| 2. Austria | 7.5 | 32.4 |
| 3. Belgium | 10.1 | 11.8 |
| 4. Canada | 24.3 | 3,851.8 |
| 5. Denmark | 5.1 | 16.6 |
| 6. Finland | 4.8 | 130.1 |
| 7. France | 53.8 | 211.2 |
| 8. Germany, Federal Republic of[a] | 61.3 | 95.9 |
| 9. Greece | 9.6 | 50.9 |
| 10. Iceland | 0.2 | 39.8 |
| 11. Ireland | 3.3 | 27.1 |
| 12. Israel | 3.9 | 7.8 |
| 13. Italy | 57.2 | 116.3 |
| 14. Japan | 116.8 | 143.7 |
| 15. Luxembourg | 0.4 | 0.9 |
| 16. Netherlands | 14.2 | 15.9 |
| 17. New Zealand | 3.4 | 103.7 |
| 18. Norway | 4.1 | 149.3 |
| 19. Portugal | 9.5 | 35.5 |
| 20. Spain | 37.5 | 194.9 |
| 21. Sweden | 8.4 | 173.7 |
| 22. Switzerland | 6.4 | 15.9 |
| 23. United Kingdom[b] | 56.0 | 94.2 |
| 24. United States | 221.9 | 3,615.1 |
| Total | 734.3 | 12,100.6 |
| SECOND WORLD | | |
| 1. Albania | 2.8 | 11.1 |
| 2. Bulgaria | 8.9 | 42.8 |
| 3. China, People's Republic of | 1,042.0 | 3,691.8 |
| 4. Cuba | 9.9 | 44.2 |
| 5. Czechoslovakia | 15.4 | 49.4 |
| 6. Germany, Democratic Republic of[c] | 16.7 | 41.8 |
| 7. Hungary | 10.8 | 35.9 |
| 8. Kampuchea | 7.7 | 69.9 |
| 9. Korea, Democratic People's Republic of[d] | 17.9 | 46.5 |
| 10. Laos | 3.7 | 91.4 |
| 11. Mongolia | 1.7 | 604.2 |
| 12. Poland | 35.7 | 120.7 |
| 13. Romania | 21.9 | 91.7 |
| 14. Union of Soviet Socialist Republics | 267.3 | 8,649.5 |
| 15. Vietnam | 45.9 | 128.4 |
| 16. Yugoslavia | 22.2 | 98.8 |
| Total | 1,530.5 | 13,818.1 |

**TABLE I.1    Continued**

| Name of State | Population (millions) | Area (thousands of square miles) |
|---|---|---|
| THIRD WORLD | | |
| 1.  Afghanistan* | 22.0 | 249.9 |
| 2.  Algeria | 19.9 | 919.6 |
| 3.  Angola | 6.5 | 481.4 |
| 4.  Argentina | 27.1 | 1,072.2 |
| 5.  Bahrain | 0.3 | 0.2 |
| 6.  Bangladesh* | 82.5 | 55.1 |
| 7.  Benin* | 3.6 | 43.5 |
| 8.  Bhutan* | 1.3 | 18.2 |
| 9.  Bolivia | 4.9 | 424.2 |
| 10.  Botswana* | 0.8 | 231.8 |
| 11.  Brazil | 121.9 | 3,286.5 |
| 12.  Brunei | 0.2 | 2.2 |
| 13.  Burma | 33.1 | 261.8 |
| 14.  Burundi* | 4.3 | 10.8 |
| 15.  Cameroon* | 8.6 | 183.6 |
| 16.  Central African Republic* | 1.8 | 240.5 |
| 17.  Chad* | 4.5 | 495.8 |
| 18.  Chile | 11.3 | 292.3 |
| 19.  Colombia | 27.0 | 439.7 |
| 20.  Congo | 1.6 | 132.0 |
| 21.  Costa Rica | 2.3 | 19.6 |
| 22.  Dominican Republic | 5.4 | 18.8 |
| 23.  Ecuador | 7.9 | 109.5 |
| 24.  Egypt | 45.7 | 386.7 |
| 25.  El Salvador* | 4.4 | 8.3 |
| 26.  Equatorial Guinea | 0.3 | 10.8 |
| 27.  Ethiopia* | 29.7 | 471.8 |
| 28.  Gabon | 0.5 | 103.4 |
| 29.  Gambia | 0.6 | 4.4 |
| 30.  Ghana* | 11.0 | 92.1 |
| 31.  Guatemala | 6.3 | 42.0 |
| 32.  Guinea* | 5.0 | 94.9 |
| 33.  Guinea-Bissau | 0.6 | 13.9 |
| 34.  Guyana* | 0.9 | 83.0 |
| 35.  Haiti* | 5.0 | 10.7 |
| 36.  Honduras* | 3.1 | 43.3 |
| 37.  India* | 671.9 | 1,222.5 |
| 38.  Indonesia | 159.0 | 741.0 |
| 39.  Iran | 37.1 | 636.3 |
| 40.  Iraq | 13.2 | 167.9 |
| 41.  Ivory Coast* | 7.6 | 124.5 |
| 42.  Jamaica | 2.3 | 4.2 |
| 43.  Jordan | 3.1 | 37.7 |
| 44.  Kenya* | 15.9 | 224.9 |
| 45.  Korea, Republic of[e] | 38.2 | 38.0 |
| 46.  Kuwait | 1.5 | 6.9 |
| 47.  Lebanon | 3.2 | 4.0 |

TABLE I.1  Continued

| Name of State | Population (millions) | Area (thousands of square miles) |
|---|---|---|
| 48. Lesotho* | 1.4 | 11.7 |
| 49. Liberia | 2.1 | 43.0 |
| 50. Libya | 2.9 | 679.4 |
| 51. Madagascar* | 9.3 | 226.7 |
| 52. Malawi* | 6.2 | 45.7 |
| 53. Malaysia | 13.5 | 127.3 |
| 54. Mali* | 6.7 | 478.8 |
| 55. Mauritania* | 1.7 | 397.9 |
| 56. Mauritius | 0.9 | 0.8 |
| 57. Mexico | 71.9 | 764.0 |
| 58. Morocco | 19.6 | 240.9 |
| 59. Mozambique | 10.4 | 302.3 |
| 60. Nepal* | 14.0 | 54.4 |
| 61. Nicaragua | 2.6 | 50.2 |
| 62. Niger* | 5.3 | 489.2 |
| 63. Nigeria | 72.6 | 356.7 |
| 64. Oman | 0.9 | 120.0 |
| 65. Pakistan* | 81.4 | 310.4 |
| 66. Panama | 1.9 | 29.2 |
| 67. Papua New Guinea | 3.1 | 178.3 |
| 68. Paraguay | 3.1 | 157.0 |
| 69. Peru | 17.9 | 496.2 |
| 70. Philippines | 49.1 | 115.8 |
| 71. Qatar | 0.1 | 4.2 |
| 72. Rwanda* | 4.9 | 10.2 |
| 73. São Tomé and Príncipe | 0.08 | 0.4 |
| 74. Saudi Arabia | 7.7 | 829.9 |
| 75. Senegal* | 5.8 | 75.8 |
| 76. Sierra Leone* | 3.1 | 27.7 |
| 77. Singapore | 2.4 | 0.2 |
| 78. Somalia* | 3.6 | 246.2 |
| 79. South Africa, Republic of | 28.7 | 471.4 |
| 80. Sri Lanka* | 14.5 | 25.3 |
| 81. Sudan* | 17.9 | 967.5 |
| 82. Suriname | 0.5 | 63.0 |
| 83. Swaziland | 0.5 | 6.7 |
| 84. Syria | 8.6 | 71.6 |
| 85. Taiwan | 17.7 | 13.6 |
| 86. Tanzania* | 17.6 | 364.9 |
| 87. Thailand | 47.8 | 198.5 |
| 88. Togo | 2.6 | 21.6 |
| 89. Trinidad and Tobago | 1.3 | 1.9 |
| 90. Tunisia | 6.8 | 63.2 |
| 91. Turkey | 48.6 | 301.4 |
| 92. Uganda* | 13.7 | 91.1 |
| 93. United Arab Emirates | 0.8 | 32.3 |
| 94. Upper Volta* | 6.1 | 105.9 |
| 95. Uruguay | 2.9 | 68.5 |
| 96. Venezuela | 13.8 | 352.1 |
| 97. Yemen Arab Republic* | 5.8 | 75.3 |
| 98. Yemen, People's Democratic Republic of* | 1.9 | 111.0 |

**TABLE I.1   Continued**

| Name of State | Population (millions) | Area (thousands of square miles) |
|---|---|---|
| 99.  Zaire | 28.8 | 905.6 |
| 100.  Zambia | 6.0 | 290.6 |
| 101.  Zimbabwe | 7.4 | 150.8 |
| Total | 2,191.4 | 25,186.4 |

### MIXED SYSTEMS, STATUS UNCERTAIN OR OTHERWISE UNCLASSIFIED

| Name of State | Population (millions) | Area (thousands of square miles) |
|---|---|---|
| 1.  Andorra | 0.04 | 0.175 |
| 2.  Bahamas | 0.25 | 5.4 |
| 3.  Barbados | 0.28 | 0.166 |
| 4.  Cape Verde Islands | 0.32 | 1.6 |
| 5.  Comoro Islands | 0.38 | 0.7 |
| 6.  Cyprus | 0.64 | 3.6 |
| 7.  Djibouti | 0.12 | 8.8 |
| 8.  Dominica | 0.08 | 0.29 |
| 9.  Fiji | 0.64 | 7.1 |
| 10.  Grenada | 0.1 | 0.133 |
| 11.  Kiribati | 0.06 | 0.335 |
| 12.  Liechtenstein | 0.02 | 0.06 |
| 13.  Maldives | 0.15 | 0.1 |
| 14.  Malta | 0.34 | 0.122 |
| 15.  Monaco | 0.03 | 0.0005 |
| 16.  Namibia | 1.05 | 318.3 |
| 17.  Nauru | 0.009 | 0.008 |
| 18.  St. Lucia | 0.12 | 0.238 |
| 19.  St. Vincent | 0.12 | 0.15 |
| 20.  San Marino | 0.02 | 0.024 |
| 21.  Seychelles | 0.06 | 0.107 |
| 22.  Solomon Islands | 0.22 | 11.0 |
| 23.  Tonga | 0.09 | 0.27 |
| 24.  Tuvalu | 0.008 | 0.01 |
| 25.  Vatican | 0.0008 | 0.00017 |
| 26.  Western Samoa | 0.15 | 1.1 |
| Total | 5.2 | 359.8 |
| Grand Total | 4,461.4 | 51,464.9 |

[a]West Germany.
[b]Great Britain.
[c]East Germany.
[d]North Korea.
[e]South Korea.

SOURCE: Arthur S. Banks, ed., *Political Handbook of the World, 1980* (New York: McGraw-Hill, 1980).

*Notes*: Third World nations marked with an asterisk (*) are identified as extremely poor or Fourth World nations by Helen C. Low and James W. Howe, "Focus on the Fourth World," in James W. Howe, ed., *The U.S. and World Development: Agenda for Action 1975* (New York: Praeger, 1975), Table 1, pp. 48–49.

whose status is uncertain, such as tiny European principalities (Andorra) or isolated Pacific islands (Western Samoa). These unclassified states account for about one tenth of a percent of the world's population and about seven tenths of a percent of its surface area.

This classification reflects rather closely the predominant tensions between and among competing models and ideologies in international politics (*e.g.*, east-west, north-south conflicts), and it is also tied explicitly to varying political approaches to the management of modernization and industrialization. Thus, the scheme is clearly political in nature rather than based on such criteria as economic status or geography—we classify states according to the way in which they have attempted to meet the challenges of industrial change and modernization. We will summarize below the most important details of each of the three approaches to these pressing challenges. However, we are giving only general descriptions of historical developments in several of the better known cases within each category, cases that typify the process that is broadly followed within each World. This scheme and its supporting assumptions cannot, and should not, be stretched to account for every detail in the developmental pattern of each country in the category.

In our framework, the First World countries in North America and Western Europe were on the whole successful at managing the tensions of modernization and industrialization while at the same time maintaining their respect for pluralist democracy. In many of these nations, industrialization began rather early, as early as 1750 in England and by the end of the nineteenth century in most of the remaining countries. There was little outside pressure on these nations as they industrialized because there were no comparable nations undergoing similar processes in other parts of the world although competition between and among First World nations progressed with the maturation of industrialization and eventually contributed to two world wars. Some of these countries also enjoyed the luxury of pursuing their goals at a relatively leisurely pace, frequently spreading the modernization process over

several generations. In Great Britain, the consolidation of a modernizing elite took place over a span of about 180 years; in the United States, it took about 90 years; and in some of the countries on the European continent, the average was about 70 to 75 years.

It would be a mistake to see the processes of industrialization and modernization spreading evenly and peacefully across all of the countries of the First World. The states that industrialized and modernized later, including Germany and the southern European fringe (Portugal, Spain, Italy, and Greece), faced much greater difficulty in dealing with these challenges, perhaps *because* of their relatively later start in the transformation. Whatever the cause, all these countries endured some form of dictatorship or authoritarian regime before they could achieve a stable industrial economy and a modern society. In the 1980s, the place of Germany and Italy in the First World of industrial democracies seems assured, but the transformation of such countries as Spain and Portugal rests on much less solid ground and will need more time to become consolidated. Even mature industrial democracies are shaken occasionally by challenges from groups that feel they have been left out of the process of change, such as the Celtic fringe (Ireland, Scotland, and Wales) of the British Isles, the American south or its Indian tribes on reservations, or French-speaking Quebec in Canada.

Nevertheless, although it seems that industrial growth and modernization were not free of conflict in the First World, these processes did go forward rather peacefully when compared with the stormy passage to modernity that confronted other states where these processes came later. In the First World, the impetus for modernization came from important leading segments of the economic and political communities within the nation rather than from outside the country, with the consequence that the policies of industrialization and modernization did not become mixed with the equally contentious issues of national self-determination and anticolonialism, as was the case elsewhere. Where the principal drive for change came from native modernizing élites as opposed to foreigners—a phenomenon we call *modernization from within* (following John Kautsky[6])—antimodern groups were more easily won over or absorbed into the modernizing élite itself. In some countries, like Canada and the United States, industrialization and modernization came with the culture of the British colonizers and, meeting with only primitive native tribes, proceeded to spread almost unopposed across the land. In England, traditional segments of the population, including villagers, peasants, and aristocrats, were pushed from their rural pursuits into an urban capitalist economy over the span of several generations. Even the relatively more violent French experience did not result in the destruction of the traditional forces, but rather eventually absorbed these forces into the modern society that emerged after the French Revolution. Generally, then, traditional guilds merged into modern labor unions, aristocratic landowners became capitalist farmers, and peasants moved to the cities to become wage earners in factories. There were high human costs in the process; the literature of the period is full of accounts of slums, pollution, child labor, sweatshops, and other abuses. But, in most cases, the forces that naturally opposed modernization—peasants, aristocrats, and small shopkeepers and artisans of the villages and towns—could be dealt with by absorption or transformation. It was not necessary to destroy them outright to advance the cause of modernization. As a consequence, politics in the First World tended to be much more pluralistic, in the sense that autonomous and competing centers of power were not only tolerated but also actually protected, and there was relatively less emphasis on the need to concentrate total power in the hands of a single individual, institution, or level of government.

In Communist Party states, what we call the Second World, matters were quite different. In such socialist countries as the Soviet Union and China, the processes of industrialization and modernization were delayed for decades before

revolution brought Communists to power. When they did begin the process of modernization, the new élites encountered severe obstacles in pursuing their goals; the entire process was much more shattering than it had been in the First World. For one thing, the impetus toward modernization in prerevolutionary times had tended to come from sources external to the nation, the phenomenon that John Kautsky calls modernization from without.[7] Prior to the change in power, external capital funded what little industrialization there was in these countries. The Marxists who came to power with the revolution were themselves bearers of ideas and techniques imported from abroad.

Within the country, traditional antimodern forces resisted Communist-directed change so strongly that the modernizing élites often had to engage them in violent struggle and destroy or expel them. In the countries that followed this path, landed aristocrats saw their land confiscated, peasants were regimented and often forced to collectivize their efforts, and urban laboring classes were mobilized into state-controlled unions. Thus, the process of industrialization followed a strategy that featured a centralized state apparatus much more authoritarian than its counterpart in the First World. Power was concentrated so that it might be used to advance revolutionary objectives in the face of stiff resistance.

Finally, in Communist Party countries, because the process of industrialization occurred at a time when major world powers had already industrialized, there was great external pressure on Second World states in the form of threats, economic boycott, intervention, and war. Accordingly, Communist governments frequently found themselves isolated, encircled, and under attack from those states of the First World that had industrialized earlier. All these characteristics taken together have produced in the Second World a modernizing state that has gathered into its hands enormous power to change its society in a short time and to introduce radical shifts in both the nation's political patterns and its eco-

[6]John Kautsky, *The Political Consequences of Modernization* (New York: Wiley, 1972).

[7]*Ibid.*

nomic order. Although most Second World governments emerged from violent beginnings, they fit into three different groups, depending on the exact circumstances surrounding their origins. The original Second World state, the Soviet Union, was born from internal revolution that came in the midst of large-scale suffering and destruction during World War I. A second group of socialist states, particularly those in Eastern Europe—including Czechoslovakia, Hungary, and Poland—were established after World War II out of the desire of the Soviet Union to foster a buffer of allied political systems on its western border. A third group grew out of a struggle for national liberation against foreign colonial domination—these states include China, Cuba, and Vietnam.

Another set of characteristics typifies the Third World states of Latin America, Africa, the Middle East, and Asia. These states were also late starters in the industrialization process, most of them beginning even later than most Second World countries. The majority of Third World states were not independent before World War II; those that were (including most of Latin America) did not embark on their industrialization drive before 1914. Apart from their relatively late start, however, the distinguishing characteristic of the Third World states is the inability of modernizing élites to resolve their struggle with the antimodern forces, either by absorbing and transforming them, as in the First World, or by destroying or expelling them, as in the Second World. In the Third World, the modernizing elites have tried to foster economic and political change without disturbing the complex power relationships that link together the wealthy and the poor in the traditional rural sectors of the country. This, in turn, has led in many instances to what A. F. K. Organski calls the syncratic state, a government based on a loose coalition of both modern and traditional élites who pursue modernization without changing the basically traditional nature of their society.[8]

The causes and effects of this phenomenon

[8]A. F. K. Organski, *The Stages of Political Development* (New York: Knopf, 1967).

are many. With few exceptions, political change in Third World countries has been halting, erratic, and violent and marked by radical swings in public policy as first one group and then another captured the state policy-making apparatus. The process is complicated because this struggle takes place within an international economic, political, and military arena in which powerful forces are seeking to perpetuate the global inequities of wealth and power that have existed since 1945. Although generalizations about such a large and disparate group of countries are hazardous, we argue that Third World states are having extreme difficulty in managing the tensions of industrial and political change.

Some observers of politics in developing countries occasionally refer to still another category of state, the Fourth World, where poverty is especially striking. The relative prosperity of a few oil-rich Third World countries has obscured the fact that a significant number of very poor countries, including densely populated states, like Bangladesh, India, and Pakistan, are simply not moving ahead in their progress toward industrial growth. According to some approaches, then, it makes sense to separate these states into a Fourth World; we have marked those countries with an asterisk in Table I.1. Despite this apparent split of the developing world into two camps, we choose to treat them as a single category. This book is about politics, political style, and public policy. Measured on that dimension, Brazil and Saudi Arabia have much more in common with their poorer neighbors, like Bolivia and India, than they do with industrialized countries. A relatively good performance on the scale of per capita gross national product (GNP) should not be allowed to obscure what we think is an important political phenomenon.

There are today also a growing number of states that could be placed in more than one category. Some Third World states, like Venezuela and Mexico, seem to have consolidated pluralist democracy and probably should be included with the First World before too much more time passes. Likewise, several Third World states, including Angola, Libya, and

Mozambique, have adopted a political order based on radical Marxist principles. If these experiments endure, they will have to be categorized with the Second World in future editions of this book. For the time being, however, we prefer to suspend judgment on these transitional cases and to treat them where many of their own leaders perceive their interests and identity to lie—with the Third World.

## HOW THE BOOK IS ORGANIZED

This book is divided into three main Parts, each of which is devoted to countries that exhibit one of the major political styles: the Western European democracies, the Communist Party states, and the developing countries. Within each Part, we compare countries with two questions in mind.

1. What similarities and differences exist among countries regarding the *goals* advanced by political élites for the allocation of values, the *actions* devised by political leaders to achieve these goals, and the degree of success attained in pursuing these goals, or the *outcomes*, of policy?

2. What important factors determine or shape the goals, actions, and outcomes of public policies of different countries? Are *political structures* and *institutions* crucial or is the social, economic, and cultural *environment* surrounding the political process more important? Some analysts treat these two factors as separate and distinct from the personality characteristics of the *individuals* who lead the political community, whereas, in other cases, the role of individual élite members blends imperceptibly into analysis of the structural and environmental factors.

In each Part, two chapters treat environmental characteristics of a social and economic nature that impinge directly on the political system. The first chapter shows the *historical* links among social, economic, and political factors that have been common to countries at similar stages of development and that also help to account for differences among countries that have many elements of similarity.

The environment of the political system is dealt with in a different way in the second chapter of each Part. Here we describe the *contemporary economic and social structures* of the countries under examination. Regardless of the level of development, contemporary political systems face a wide variety of recurring and severe economic problems, such as unemployment; inflation; scarcity of raw materials, energy sources, and food; poverty; cyclical fluctuations; and structural underdevelopment. Similarly, social conflict stemming from ethnic or religious cleavage is not confined to the Third World although it may be more of a problem in those countries.

The third chapter in each Part links the political system to its environment through its treatment of *political culture* and *political socialization*. Political culture may be seen as the pattern of attitudes and beliefs that people hold toward their political system; political socialization refers to the process by which new members of the system—the recent immigrant and the maturing young—are taught these attitudes and beliefs. One aspect of political culture, for example, has to do with the ideas an ordinary citizen has about his or her own ability to influence the political process. In some countries, like Great Britain, many citizens feel competent to make their influence felt on the political élites of the country; in many other countries, like Italy, China, and Mexico, the level of civic competence may be far less. These differences obviously have an impact on the willingness of citizens to participate actively in the politics of their nation.[9] In addition, within the study of political culture, we are able to consider the similarities and differences among political goals as they are articulated by the ideologies of various sets of political élites.

Political socialization is also dealt with in the third chapter. In many Third World countries, for instance, young people have traditionally been socialized into a localized system of beliefs and values through which they are taught that the community is the center of their life and

---

[9]Gabriel A. Almond and Sidney Verba, *The Civic Culture: Political Attitudes and Democracy in Five Nations* (Princeton, N.J.: Princeton University Press, 1963).

strangers are to be regarded with suspicion. These socialization practices reinforce age-old communal strife as well as breed an attitude of hostility against efforts by the central government to develop nationalist sentiment. In countries seeking to develop rapidly, such as China and Cuba, modernizing elites have found it necessary to disrupt conventional family structures to control the kinds of politically relevant lessons being taught to the children of the country. In many Third World countries, however, the government's failure to achieve this sort of breakthrough has meant the growth of ethnic, linguistic, and religious associations that aggravate communal strife and weaken the nation's ability to develop rapidly.

Three chapters deal directly with the political system itself. In two of these, the fourth and fifth chapters, we describe *political structures* and *the roles played by individuals* within them; the sixth chapter evaluates policy-making *styles and processes*. What we have in mind is the distinction between an essentially descriptive account of the similarities and differences among the institutions in different political systems (the fourth and fifth chapters) and an analysis (in the sixth chapter) of those structures and roles in terms of the allocation of values.

Each Part concludes with a seventh chapter that evaluates *political performance*. We attempt to assess the extent to which a political system's goals, actions, and outcomes contribute to enhancing human dignity. We make this rather abstract concept operational by comparing a political system's espoused goals with actual performance in the area of the four basic values.

Our evaluation of political performance also involves an explanatory feature. After appraising performance in terms of goals, actions, and outcomes, we want to isolate the factors that determine different performance levels. Here, our analytical distinction between environment and political system comes into play. Can a relatively high level of human dignity be attributed to qualities of the political system of a given country or must we emphasize its environmental advantages, such as its high level of economic development?

Finally, in the concluding chapter of the book, the evaluations summarized in this fashion are brought together and similarities and differences between the three worlds are analyzed.

## WHY STUDY COMPARATIVE POLITICS?

One is often jolted by students questioning, "What difference does all of this mean to me personally? How can I use this information in my life?" Although different scholars and teachers of comparative politics would answer these questions differently, we believe the study of politics in other countries is important to a student for three reasons.

**1.** The United States contains 5 percent of the world's population but consumes annually more than 30 percent of the world's energy and output of goods. These data tell you two things. First, the United States is in a distinct minority in the world; second, the other 95 percent of the earth's population is becoming increasingly important to the United States. Think back to the energy crises of the 1970s. It became obvious that oil-producing countries, like Saudi Arabia and Venezuela, possessed a good deal of influence over our government and our standard of living. In the 1980 presidential campaign between Ronald Reagan and Jimmy Carter, several major issues involved our relations with other nations, including our ability to defend ourselves against attack from the Soviet Union and our posture toward Third World governments that violate the human rights of their citizens. These issues (and many others) should make us want to know more about the 95 percent of the world's population whose fate is each day more closely intertwined with our own.

**2.** We must learn more about foreign countries to make sense out of our own government's efforts to influence those countries and to project U. S. power abroad. Since World War II, the United States has been involved in two major wars (producing nearly 100,000 dead Americans) and literally dozens of minor conflicts—ranging all around the globe, from Guatemala to Berlin to Iran. We have spent over $100 billion in foreign assistance since the Marshall Plan days of the late 1940s to improve (and influence) foreign economies; each year we also spend over $100 billion on weapons and other military items to defend our nation. Finally, since the early 1950s, we have created an intelligence network in the Central Intelligence Agency (CIA) and the Federal Bureau of Investigation (FBI) that has angered and shocked some American observers for what they feel are unwarranted intrusions into our private lives. Why have these things come about? What is it about the countries beyond our borders that makes some of them threats to us, others allies, and still others the cause of our great concern because of their very weakness? Could any of these expenditures be better made somewhere else? To know the answers to these questions, we must know more about the countries with which we share this planet.

**3.** Through our study of comparative politics, we can develop the skills of analysis and inquiry so necessary for knowledge of our own political world, locally as well as nationally. How many of you have ever felt bewildered by political events close to home that you could not understand? Most of us have had this experience. In this book, as you work toward a better understanding of foreign countries, you will also learn inquiry and analysis skills that can later be turned toward understanding better the local municipal or state government where you live. For example, we will help you ask and answer questions like these: Where does power *really* reside? What roles do mass publics play in policy making? How do some political leaders use the symbols of democracy to mask the reality of authoritarianism? How can the individual citizen make his or her influence felt at the point where it will count most? Our inquiry into politics in France or Yugoslavia or India will, of course, yield one kind of answer, but the questions are the same for understanding politics in St. Louis, Atlanta, or Washington, D. C.

# PART ONE
## Power and Policy in Western European Democracies

# CHAPTER ONE
## Historical Background

Since World War II, most of the countries of Western Europe have consistently been classified by their own standards as democracies. The extent to which the reality has approached the Western ideal of democracy has, however, varied. It is true that democracy is a goal toward which Western countries strive. However, it is questionable whether the term should be used descriptively, that is, as a category in which Western political systems, in fact, belong. The American political scientist, Robert A. Dahl,[1] has suggested that instead of the word democracy, we use the term polyarchy to characterize the type of political system that predominates in the First World countries of Western Europe and North America. Polyarchies are political systems in which the many rule, not just in the formal sense of universal or near-universal suffrage but in the sense that there is a meaningful degree of competition among groups contending for power. The many who choose among these contenders have meaningful choices to make and actually do rule in that they determine who will be making the decisions of government. The four countries on which we will focus—Great Britain, France, West Germany, and Italy—as well as most of those with which we will be comparing them are Western European polyarchies. The other major polyarchies in the First World,

which are located outside Western Europe, are the United States, Canada, Japan, and Australia. The First World polyarchies are listed in Table 1.1 together with their government structure, political party system, and other pertinent data.

It will be noted that most of these countries are rather advanced economically and socially. Indeed, they compete economically with one another and are also their own principal trading partners. It is characteristic of polyarchies that they rank high on the various indexes of socio-economic strength. Actually, most of the more advanced countries of the world are polyarchies, with the notable exceptions of the Soviet Union, East Germany, and Czechoslovakia, which are Communist (Second World) countries.

Another characteristic of most polyarchies is that they have parliamentary systems rather than presidential systems of government. Indeed, almost all of the Western European polyarchies currently have parliamentary systems or, as in the case of France, parliamentary traditions. Furthermore, more polyarchies have multiparty systems (that is, more than two major political parties) than have two-party systems as in the United States. Again, this is particularly true of Western Europe. Even Great Britain, traditionally regarded as a two-party country, has some of the characteristics of a multiparty system.

The four political systems we will be comparing are the four most populous polyarchies in Western Europe. All are advanced industrially

[1]Robert A. Dahl, *Polyarchy: Participation and Opposition* (New Haven and London: Yale University Press, 1971).

**TABLE 1.1**  First World Polyarchies

| Country | Type of Government | Party System | Population (in 1000s) | Population (per sq km) | GDP[a] per Capita (1976) |
|---|---|---|---|---|---|
| Australia | Parliamentary | Multiparty | 13,549 | 2 | $7,239 |
| Austria | Parliamentary | Multiparty | 7,456 | 90 | 5,401 |
| Belgium | Parliamentary | Multiparty | 9,651 | 322 | 6,916 |
| Canada | Parliamentary | Multiparty | 22,993 | 2 | 8,517 |
| Denmark | Parliamentary | Multiparty | 4,938 | 118 | 8,124 |
| Finland | Mixed presidential/ parliamentary) | Multiparty | 4,598 | 14 | 6,025 |
| *France* | Mixed (presidential/ parliamentary) | Multiparty | 52,656 | 97 | 6,599 |
| *Germany, Federal Republic of*[b] | Parliamentary | Multiparty | 60,651 | 247 | 7,267 |
| Greece | Parliamentary | Multiparty | 8,769 | 70 | 2,455 |
| Iceland | Parliamentary | Multiparty | 205 | 2 | 6,724 |
| Ireland | Parliamentary | Multiparty | 2,978 | 45 | 2,566 |
| Israel | Parliamentary | Multiparty | 3,148 | 167 | 3,885 |
| *Italy* | Parliamentary | Multiparty | 53,745 | 187 | 3,040 |
| Japan | Parliamentary | Multiparty | 111,940 | 306 | 5,002 |
| Luxembourg | Parliamentary | Multiparty | 340 | 148 | 6,717 |
| Netherlands | Parliamentary | Multiparty | 13,046 | 339 | 6,737 |
| New Zealand | Parliamentary | Two party | 3,129 | 12 | 4,251 |
| Norway | Parliamentary | Multiparty | 3,874 | 12 | 7,704 |
| Portugal | Mixed (presidential/ parliamentary) | Multiparty | 8,569 | 93 | 1,580 |
| Spain | Parliamentary | Multiparty | 33,956 | 73 | 2,909 |
| Sweden | Parliamentary | Multiparty | 8,209 | 18 | 9,010 |
| Switzerland | Parliamentary | Multiparty | 6,270 | 153 | 8,942 |
| *United Kingdom*[c] | Parliamentary | Multiparty | 55,506 | 229 | 3,949 |
| United States | Presidential | Two party | 203,235 | 23 | 7,878 |

[a]GDP = gross domestic product.

[b]West Germany.

[c]Great Britain.

SOURCE: The list of polyarchies is adapted and updated from Robert A. Dahl, *Polyarchy: Participation and Opposition* (New Haven and London: Yale University Press, 1971), pp. 84, 232. Data in the columns are taken from *United Nations Statistical Yearbook: 1978* (New York: United Nations, 1979), pp. 69–73, 749–750 and population figures are from the latest census data available in 1978.

(although the range is wide) and there is a considerable gap between the very strong West German economy and struggling Italy. All, except France, have parliamentary systems of government; France has a difficult-to-classify mixture of parliamentary and presidential elements. All, including Great Britain, have multiparty systems, however, the British and West German systems lean toward the two-party type.

In addition to the fact that these four countries are the largest polyarchies in Western Europe (where the largest number of the world's polyarchies are found), we can justify our choice of these countries because they represent four distinct combinations of important political and socioeconomic characteristics. Politically, two of them, Great Britain and West Germany, represent what we might call a centripetal type of polyarchy, one in which the major political parties vie with one another for middle-of-the-road voters with programs that overlap one another considerably in content—a characteristic not unlike that of the American parties. The other two, France and Italy, represent more of a centrifugal type. Here, the parties pull more strongly in opposite directions, trying to win the support of minorities of voters with distinct ideological persuasions. The political histories of France and Italy since World War II have both been characterized by greater instability than have the histories of Great Britain and West Germany.

Economically, the four countries can be fairly clearly ranked, almost regardless of the measure employed, from strongest to weakest: (1) West Germany, (2) France, (3) Great Britain, and (4) Italy. This ranking would have been rather startling 25 years ago, especially in the positions assigned to Great Britain and France. At the beginning of the postwar period, Great Britain almost certainly would have been at the top of the list. But the prosperity that all of the countries encountered in the 1950s and 1960s propelled West Germany, with its economic miracle, to the top and moved France and Italy (both of which started from weak positions) ahead more rapidly than Great Britain, which, since the mid-1950s has experienced relative economic stagnation.

If we now dichotomize our economic rankings as we have the political, the countries fall into four distinct categories:

### ECONOMIC STRENGTH

| | + | − |
|---|---|---|
| POLITICAL INTEGRATION + | West Germany | Great Britain |
| − | France | Italy |

Actually, this economic dichotomy may be somewhat arbitrary when one considers the distance between West Germany and France on most economic measures (see Tables 7.1–7.5, pages 156–159). But this diagram raises some interesting questions about the relationship between political and economic factors and why there have been changes in economic position during the past 25 years, placing West Germany at the top of the scale and inverting, at least for the moment, the positions of Great Britain and France. The uncertain positions of Great Britain and France invite speculation as to the directions in which both the economies and the political systems of these two countries may be moving at the present time. Of course, the declining economic fortunes of most countries in absolute terms, owing to the recent worldwide economic problems of the 1970s and 1980s, have important implications for the future of all polyarchies, including all four of the countries we are discussing.

In this chapter, we will discuss the history of the Western European polyarchies in an attempt to answer some of the questions raised above as well as such questions as: How have the political systems of these four countries (and those of other polyarchies) developed? What are the historical reasons for the similarities and differences among them? Why have they been able to develop economies that are generally more advanced than those of most other countries of the world? Are there historical reasons for the differences among them with respect to economic success? Although we cannot answer these questions fully in this introductory textbook, we can point to certain major developments in the history of Western European countries generally and in our four countries in particular that are partially responsible. We will also emphasize the development of Europe's social structure since the beginning of the Industrial Revolution in the eighteenth century. Our assumption is that the major political upheavals and economic changes during the past two centuries in Europe have been closely related to the conflicts among various social groups and the aspirations of these groups for larger shares of power, respect, well-being, and enlightenment.

The discussion will be divided into four parts, each taking a stage in the path of Western Europe toward modernity: (1) the *preindustrial* social, economic, and political structures of Western Europe as found in the early eighteenth century just before the Industrial Revolution, (2) the *early industrialization* period—an era of rapid change and great upheavals—that began about 1750 and lasted until around 1870 (although later in Italy and elsewhere in southern and eastern Europe), (3) the era of *mature industrialization*, beginning around 1870 and lasting until World War II, and (4) the post-World War II era in which Western Europe was developing the characteristics of *postindustrial society*.

## PREINDUSTRIAL WESTERN EUROPE

At the outset, it should be noted that what we are describing is the process of modernization as it took place in the countries of Western Europe. Modernization in those countries followed a different pattern from that which has taken, or is taking, place in most other countries of the world, especially in the Second World. For the most part, the industrialization of Western Europe was self-generated, whereas other countries have relied extensively on external stimulus for their industrialization. Western Europe already had certain factors that helped to facilitate self-generated industrialization.

## PREINDUSTRIAL ECONOMIES

Western Europe in the early eighteenth century was primarily agrarian, as are most of the Third World countries today. This means that the vast majority of the working population was engaged in agriculture. Many worked as agricultural laborers on large aristocratically owned estates, others divided their time between working for such landowners and working for themselves on their own small plots of land. Many people were independent small landowners able to subsist as such but probably finding it impossible to accumulate wealth because of the heavy state taxes or manorial dues owed to a local lord. Other impediments were the seasonal uncertainties and the rather primitive state of agricultural technology.

In the smaller towns, the economy was dependent on the nearby countryside. These were market towns where farmers sold their produce and where goods that the farmer might buy were manufactured and sold. Itinerant merchants supplied farmers and townspeople with other goods that were not produced locally; this was about the extent of the economic intercourse between the town and the outside world. Only in the larger cities were goods produced for wider distribution. Because such manufacturing and its marketing often required substantial amounts of capital, the cities became financial centers. At that time (before industrialization), manufacturing existed only on a small scale. The factory system had not yet been introduced. The main source of energy was still workers.

## SOCIAL STRUCTURE

The cities had grown sufficiently large by the eighteenth century so that there was a distinctive urban social class structure. It was based essentially on the ownership of property, which had not yet come into much conflict with the traditional social hierarchy of feudal times. At the top of the social scale was the aristocracy, whose economic and social position was based on the ownership of land and the possession of political power. The leading families of England and France as well as those of the smaller political units in Germany and Italy owned land but were also firmly established socially in the leading cities, especially London, Paris, and the other political capitals. Thus, they were found at the pinnacles of both the rural and the urban social hierarchies.

The urban middle class constituted a mixture of elements that was not yet too complex. Ownership of property conferred status within the middle class, and those with the most substantial fortunes were at the top of the social hierachy, just below the aristocracy. During the century or so before industrialization, upward mobility, at least within the middle class, was becoming increasingly possible. The conservative influence of the aristocracy and of established craftspersons in the towns was giving way to ambitious entrepreneurship. Markets were opening up in the New World and in the cities for goods, such as clothing and housewares, that could be produced inexpensively on a large scale by using rural laborers. Although such workers were less skilled than urban artisans, they could produce quantitatively by specializing in particular operations—a foreshadowing of the soon-to-emerge factory system.

This trend posed a serious threat to the position of the largest urban class, the artisans. These were craftspersons who worked with their hands, using tools that had not changed much over the centuries, to make a wide range of objects—mostly for the local market. The quality of the artisans' work remained their principal asset as they began to face the challenge of goods produced at lower cost. In the large cities, there was also another class of people, but fewer in number than the artisans. This class fluctuated in size, depending on economic conditions. These were the urban poor—the marginally employable and the unemployable. In the eighteenth century, the population growth and the migration of peasants to the cities increased the size of this class to almost dangerous proportions, but their preoccupation with bare subsistence dampened any real revolutionary threat.

Rural society was more hierarchical and had fewer class distinctions than urban society. Below the landed gentry on the rural social scale came the various gradations of peasants. The relative number of independent farmers and agricultural laborers varied widely from one part of Europe to another and from region to region within a given country. There were proportionately more independent farmers in northwestern Europe but more agricultural laborers toward the south and east.

## PREINDUSTRIAL POLITICAL SYSTEMS

The politics of the preindustrial period in Western Europe was dominated by the aristocracy or at least by those aristocrats who were concerned with national political matters. Attention focused on monarchs, whether their title was emperor or empress, king or queen, grand duke, or elector. Aristocratic factions would vie with one another for the monarch's ear, and one measure of the monarch's personal power was the ability to keep factions divided and to maintain alternative sources of support, such as the church or the urban middle classes. Some of the most powerful advisers of the most powerful centralizing monarchs were drawn from these alternative pools of talent. Nevertheless, the leading aristocratic families regarded political power and influence as their birthright, and they generally succeeded in maintaining it despite severe challenges, such as in seventeenth-century England or in France at the conclusion of each of the long Bourbon reigns.

The middle class and artisans were forces to be reckoned with within their own domains—the towns and cities. In Western Europe, including parts of western Germany and northern Italy, they generally controlled their own local affairs and resisted monarchical intrusion. The development of parliamentary bodies in such countries as England and the Netherlands represented the determined effort of the urban middle class to resist arbitrary monarchical taxes. In Germany and Italy, the cities were often independent of any kind of overlordship. In parts of Western Europe, urban-based property enjoyed substantial protection from arbitrary state taxes, a condition scarcely found anywhere else in the world at the time and a not insignificant factor to take into account in understanding why the Industrial Revolution began in Western Europe rather than somewhere else.

## EARLY INDUSTRIALIZATION

### INDUSTRIALIZATION DEFINED

The Industrial Revolution as a general European phenomenon began in the middle of the eighteenth century and ran its course in a little more than a century. As a localized phenomenon, however, it occurred at different times in different places and is still taking place today in

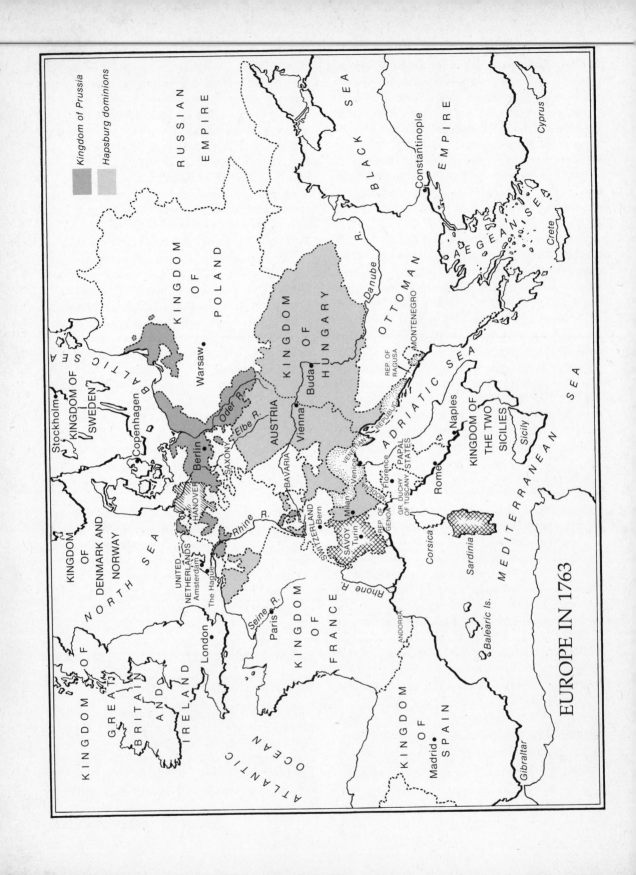

EUROPE IN 1763

Kingdom of Prussia    Hapsburg dominions

RUSSIAN EMPIRE

BLACK SEA

OTTOMAN EMPIRE

Constantinople

Cyprus

AEGEAN SEA

Crete

KINGDOM OF POLAND

Warsaw

KINGDOM OF HUNGARY

AUSTRIA

Buda

Vienna

Danube R.

ADRIATIC SEA

MONTENEGRO

REP. OF RAGUSA

KINGDOM OF SWEDEN

Stockholm

BALTIC SEA

Copenhagen

Berlin

Oder R.

Elbe R.

SAXONY

BAVARIA

VENETIAN REPUBLIC

Venice

MODENA

Florence

GR. DUCHY OF TUSCANY

PAPAL STATES

Rome

Naples

KINGDOM OF THE TWO SICILIES

Sicily

MEDITERRANEAN SEA

KINGDOM OF DENMARK AND NORWAY

NORTH SEA

HANOVER

UNITED NETHERLANDS

Amsterdam

The Hague

Rhine R.

SWITZERLAND

Bern

MILAN

Milan

REP. OF GENOA

Turin

SAVOY

Corsica

Sardinia

Balearic Is.

KINGDOM OF GREAT BRITAIN AND IRELAND

London

ATLANTIC OCEAN

Seine R.

Paris

KINGDOM OF FRANCE

Rhone R.

ANDORRA

KINGDOM OF SPAIN

Madrid

Gibraltar

many parts of the world. In Europe, it began in Great Britain and then spread to the northwestern part of the continent—to France, Belgium, and the Netherlands—by the late eighteenth century. Several decades later, it began to take hold in Germany and Sweden and still later in the Austro-Hungarian Empire; but it did not spread to Italy, elsewhere in southern Europe, or Russia until the end of the nineteenth century. By the early nineteenth century, industrialization was under way in North America, and it started in Japan toward the end of that century. In the earliest countries to industrialize, about 100 years were needed to complete what is often called the rapid industrialization stage. But early industrialization took longer in France because of a variety of factors that will be discussed. By contrast, in some of the later industrialized countries, notably Germany and Japan, the early phase of industrialization was telescoped to about half the usual length of time, undoubtedly in part owing to the fact that the groundwork had been laid in other countries, and, thus, the learning period could be greatly shortened.

We can define industrialization as the shift in the manufacturing industries from primary dependence on human energy to dependence on inanimate energy sources, thereby dramatically increasing productivity. This shift is accompanied by a reorganization of production so that larger numbers of workers are using machines driven by inanimate power to produce a substantially larger volume of goods for a much wider market than before industrialization. The factory system, an aspect of industrialization, means narrowing the tasks assigned each worker. Artisan production usually meant that each worker was responsible for the entire production process—from the raw material to the finished product. Now, each stage was assigned to a worker who specialized in only one or a few of the operations for producing the goods. The work hours were long and the work itself tended to be tedious and dehumanizing. Most scholars agree that the earliest decades of industrialization entailed the greatest human suffering. It was as if one generation were sacrificing itself so that

future generations could enjoy the fruits of its efforts.

## THE ORIGINS OF INDUSTRIALIZATION

Scholars disagree as to why the Industrial Revolution started when and where it did.[2] Before the dawn of industrialization, there was a class of fledgling industrial capitalists in Western Europe who were already experimenting with early forms of mass production, discovering far-flung markets, and accumulating great wealth. The ability of this class to break away from traditional patterns of production and marketing, especially in Great Britain, enabled them to experiment with still newer forms. As for the development of the requisite technology, it meant a pragmatic fitting of means to specific ends. According to the great German social scientist, Max Weber,[3] there emerged a certain spirit of capitalism, a spirit that blossomed more easily in Protestant, northwestern Europe than elsewhere. Protestant culture had freed itself from the inhibitions imposed on the individual by Roman Catholicism, thereby developing a greater sense of optimism, a faith in the human capacity to create and improve, and a belief in something like the modern concept of progress.

In the eighteenth century, certain factors characterized British society that made it virtually unique, even in northwestern Europe. At that time, the population in Great Britain was growing about twice as fast as that of France and approximating the growth rate of Prussia. This helped to create a domestic market for new industrial products. More important, the rigid social structure that prevailed in Europe was less pronounced in Great Britain. Workers' wages were higher, they ate better, and they spent a smaller portion of their income on food than did their counterparts on the continent. The percent-

[2]For an illuminating discussion of industrialization, see David Landes, *The Unbound Prometheus: Technological Change and Industrial Development in Western Europe from 1850 to the Present* (Cambridge, At the University Press, 1969).

[3]Max Weber, *The Protestant Ethic and the Spirit of Capitalism,* trans. Talcott Parsons (New York: Scribner's, 1958).

age of small businesspersons, artisans, and independent farmers in the active population was higher than in most other countries. Both in the cities and in rural areas, the gradations between the upper, middle, and lower classes were more gentle; upward mobility was easier; and social barriers were more relaxed. There was a strong tradition of entrepreneurial initiative that went back to the Middle Ages. Aggressive entrepreneurs could emerge from almost any social class or geographical area within the kingdom. The British were experimenters, tinkerers; they were less afraid to take risks than their continental counterparts; and they were less bound to traditional ways of doing things.

The earliest industrialization in Great Britain began in the clothing industry. The cottage system—men and women working on semifinished goods at home (usually in rural areas)— had already become widespread by the beginning of the eighteenth century. But the cottage system was unreliable. It could not be easily supervised, that is, controls over the rate and quality of output were inadequate. In terms of output per unit of manpower expended, it was superior to the older, artisan form of production, but, having abandoned traditional ways, entrepreneurs were psychologically freer to experiment with new modes of production in the hope of overcoming the disadvantages of the cottage system. Technological advances made it possible for some of the processes of converting raw wool or cotton to a finished product to be brought together in one place; thus, the factory system gradually emerged. However, not until later in the century, when steam power could be harnessed to still newer machines, could the real takeoff begin. But, even before the middle of the century, the production of cheap cotton goods had begun to revolutionize the entire clothing industry.

Major developments in other industries, such as metallurgy and eventually rail and sea transportation, had to wait until coal could be used as an energy source. This happened in the early nineteenth century, by which time Great Britain had established a half-century lead over her nearest rivals. France found that she could

not overcome this lead in the nineteenth century. Although France had been the most populous country of Europe in 1800, her population growth had been lagging and continued to decline during the next century. At that time, she was overtaken by Great Britain and eventually by the new Germany that emerged after the Franco-Prussian War in 1870. Industrialization began in France as early as anywhere on the continent, but its growth was sluggish and fitful throughout the nineteenth century even though the French Revolution removed many of the feudal restrictions and exactions that had previously hindered the budding capitalist class. For the most part, the French bourgeoisie preferred the safety of the small family firm with its assured but nonexpanding market and its handful of loyal workers; thus, they could be protected from economic hazards by the patronizing policies of their employers. During the nineteenth century, the French people shifted from rural to urban life much more gradually than the British. Whereas 50 percent of the British population was already urbanized by 1850, the same had not occurred in France even by 1900.

During the early nineteenth century, Germany and Italy were not yet unified nations. Both were still divided into a number of small and medium-sized political units that remained largely agrarian. By the 1840s, German entrepreneurs were beginning to exploit the vast mineral resources of the lower Rhineland. Encouraged by a change in state policy and able to take advantage of technological advances achieved elsewhere, German industry was soon expanding. By 1870, German technology had pulled alongside that of other leading countries in Europe. By 1900, she was playing a leading role in the rapidly developing chemical and electrical industries and was setting standards for precision in the production of industrial goods that were to make possible the technological explosion of the twentieth century. By this time, Great Britain's lead among the industrial countries of the world had all but disappeared.

As for Italy, her unification in 1860 did not facilitate immediate industrial development. Like other southern and eastern European countries, Italy lacked indigenous capital and would have to wait for the infusion of outside capital. Given Italy's relatively poor resource potential, relatively little capital was invested throughout the nineteenth century. On the other hand, her population growth was rapid, especially in the cities, which were overcrowded in the nineteenth century. Agricultural conditions were difficult in most regions of the country, yet, the population grew despite indadequate food because of the reduction of infant mortality—a phenomenon that accompanied improved health standards throughout Europe. More than the other three countries we are considering, Italy seemed to exemplify Thomas Malthus's dictum that population would outrun the economy's capacity to maintain it and lead to a vicious cycle of poverty and underproduction. Yet, Great Britain and Germany, among others, were proving that the dictum was not an iron law.

## EARLY INDUSTRIAL SOCIETIES

Another nineteenth-century political economist, Karl Marx, was more astute than Malthus in penetrating the dynamics of early industrialization although he was a better scientific observer than prophet. Observing British Society at mid-century, Marx came to the conclusion that industrialization was bringing about a simplification of the class structure, reducing the number of relevant social groups to essentially two: the capitalist class and the proletariat, that is, the owners of the dominant means of production and the workers whom they employed. Although the other classes were certainly not disappearing, it is true that these were the two most dynamic classes during early industrialization, both in terms of their growing numbers and of their growing importance to the smooth functioning of the economic order. Although these classes could be found before 1750, they really burst on the scene during the next 100 years, growing rapidly in numbers and transforming the social structure of every industrial country. Each took a place alongside the older classes, thereby

threatening their status, political power, and economic security. Politically as well as economically, these new classes were to be the instruments of change. More often than not, the older classes became the resistors of change, the reactionaries and conservatives.

The capitalist class is not as easy to distinguish from its neighbors in the upper echelons of society as is the proletariat in the lower reaches. Capitalists are distinguishable from other segments of the middle class more in terms of their psychological makeup and style of action, perhaps, than in terms of their economic activities. During the period of early industrialization, the true capitalist was probably in a minority among business owners. Peter N. Stearns makes a useful distinction between the middle class and what he calls the middling class.[4] The former was made up of adventuresome capitalists; the latter group was content simply to maintain their positions. Once a business had been established and had become sufficiently profitable so that a family could enjoy a somewhat more affluent lifestyle and greater security, the middling class businesspersons turned their attention from expansion to maintenance of what they had, and they expected their heirs to do the same. On the other hand, the middle class—the capitalists—were risk minded and expansion minded, awake to opportunities, and creative and innovative in management and marketing operations. There appears to have been proportionately more of these dynamic capitalists in Great Britain than in France (at least until the late nineteenth century) and more in Germany than in Italy. Another common term for the middling class is *petite bourgeoisie*, meaning, perhaps, small-time middle class. It has often been used as a term of contempt in the twentieth century, but only because capitalism as a value system has taken firmer root. Typical nineteenth-century French businesspersons could defend their conservatism in a way that most of their contemporaries would

[4]Peter N. Stearns, *European Society in Upheaval: Social History Since 1750,* 2nd ed. (New York: Macmillan, 1975), pp. 119–120.

understand. Making it up the slippery pole of success in a steeply graduated social order was difficult at best. French businesspersons felt that it was better to stabilize their position when there were clearly more behind them down the pole than ahead of them above.

At the lower levels of the social hierarchy, we see a common development everywhere with industrialization: the rapid increase in the size of the industrial proletariat—a class that scarcely existed before industrialization, indeed, whose very definition arises from industrialization. In part, the industrial working class was created through the *déclassement* of artisans in the manufacturing sectors that turned to the factory system. Small artisan shops could not compete with mass-production techniques, and many journeymen (and even some master artisans) found themselves with no alternative but to adapt to the machines and become what is termed skilled workers. But most of the new proletarian ranks were made up of uprooted peasants, those who had lost their means of making a living owing to the growing commercialization of agriculture. A family often made a transition from working on a farm to a cottage industry before finally moving to a city and securing factory employment. In the smaller industrial cities, almost all new workers might come from the surrounding rural areas, but the larger cities drew workers from much further afield. During early industrialization, a phenomenon began that later became increasingly common—people moving across borders from the less economically advanced countries to the industrial centers of Western Europe. One of the earliest migrations was of Irish workers to the new industrial cities of the English northwest.

Artisans were more acute at perceiving what was happening than were industrial workers. The latter were mainly preoccupied with getting through the long hours of work and making a barely sufficient income for their families. Artisans had more leisure time, were better educated, were often literate, and were more apt to join mutual improvement associations, thereby coming into contact with interpretations of the world around them. The sporadic bread riots in cities, such as London and Paris, as well as the periodic revolutions on the continent from 1789 to 1848 usually found the artisans in the forefront of battle. However, the middle classes generally reaped whatever benefits resulted. Much of the artisans' anger was directed against economic changes they could neither stem nor control, changes that were spreading from one manufacturing sector to another. Even though some artisans' jobs might be momentarily secure, they were plagued with the fear that their jobs would soon be threatened by some new technological development. Machine breaking was a common occurrence in artisan riots.

During early industrialization, commercialization was spreading in the agricultural sector. Independent peasants were assuming the status of modern farm owners in parts of France and Germany. By controlling the political system, the landed aristocracy was able to secure protective tariffs to shore up their domestic markets, which were also expanding because of the growth of the railroad. In Great Britain, however, earlier tariff legislation was repealed in 1846, representing a victory for industrial capital over agricultural interests and reflecting the degree to which Great Britain had already become an industrial nation. It was an acknowledgment that the country could not be self-sufficient in food production. Other European countries, lacking Great Britain's industrial advantage, did not follow suit, and their farmers remained protected. Although it can be said that industrialization led to the decline of the agricultural sector, this was not a common phenomenon in Europe during this time.

## POLITICAL DEVELOPMENTS

Early industrialization was the stage in which the political power of the capitalist class made the most rapid gains. However, these were not as striking as the economic gains. The aristocracy was edged a little to one side, but it certainly had not lost its grip on political power. Although the House of Lords lost ground to the House of Commons after the Reform Act of 1832, the British aristocracy took note of the fact and proceeded to dominate the House of Commons for the next few decades. British capitalism probably did not reach equal control with the aristocracy of the political system until about 1870. By then, Great Britain was a mature industrial nation.

The German aristocracy was even more successful in retaining its power; it continued to dominate politics after unification in 1871 as it had done before in the separate German states. The position of the monarchs and their aristocratic supporters was shaken momentarily by the Revolution of 1848, but, when the dust had settled, the monarchs were once again secure on their thrones and the newly introduced legislative bodies were firmly controlled by aristocrats. Some of the states of southwestern Germany had emerged from the period of constitution writing with relatively liberal regimes, giving the middle class an opportunity to share in political power; but, with unification, these states became subordinate to the imperial government where power was concentrated in the hands of the emperor, his hand-picked chancellor, and a coterie of aristocratic advisers and officials. The legislative body, the Reichstag, was a forum in which middle-class spokespersons could vent their political frustrations, but it was little more than that—at least in the early years of the empire. German capitalists remained content with their sizable economic rewards during the period of early industrialization; they usually went along with aristocratic initiatives in foreign and domestic policies.

Paradoxically, it was in France that the middle classes, which had been relatively sluggish economically, registered the most evident gains over the aristocracy in the nineteenth century. Formally, at least, the French political system had gone further in removing aristocratic privileges, beginning with the Revolution of 1789 and continuing with a series of political upheavals thereafter—in 1830, 1848, and the 1870s. The power of the Bourbon nobility was seriously undermined when the Revolution of 1789 abolished feudal privileges and when Napoleon Bonaparte created an administrative career service that was open to all, regardless of the accident of birth. After Napoleon's fall in 1815, there was an effort to restore the position of the old aristocracy but this ended with the Revolution of 1830. Universal manhood suffrage was adopted with the Revolution of 1848, and the principle of executive subordination to the legislature became established under the Third Republic in the 1870s. It should be noted that each revolutionary effort before the 1870s was aborted with the establishment of a new autocratic regime. The Revolution of 1789 paved the way for Napoleon's First Empire; that of 1830 led to the July Monarchy of Louis Philippe, head of the junior royal house; and the Revolution of 1848 was followed by the election of Louis Napoleon as president—nephew of the first Bonaparte, he subsequently declared himself Napoleon III, head of the Second Napoleonic Empire. Despite these disappointments, each revolution brought about further gains by members of the capitalist class, in that they shared increasingly in the distribution of high state offices.

It can be said that by 1850 capitalism was better established politically in France than in Great Britain, but its economic impact was uncertain. It was certainly more successful in utilizing the resources of the state for its own advancement. Although German capitalism relied on the state for its initial impetus, it could, and did, generate its own momentum after that; French capitalism, however, remained curiously dependent on the state. Although it is clear that the French aristocracy fought its last losing political battle in the 1870s and capitulated in the establishment of the middle-class Third Republic, it seems likely that French capitalism thereafter had to contend with a new political force, the *petite bourgeoisie*, a class that Marx believed was a dying element in the social firmament of capitalism. A somewhat similar phenomenon occurred in Italy after unification in 1860. The aristocracy essentially withdrew from the political field. Allied with the church in its disdain for the new regime, the aristocracy left the middle classes to vie with one another for control of the political system. Given the economic and social weakness of Italian capitalism, it is not surprising that the conservative values of the Italian middling class prevailed for the rest of the century.

Although the political star of the middle class was on the rise in early industrial Europe, that of the working class was just beginning to appear on the horizon. By the end of the early industrial period as artisans began to reconcile themselves to becoming skilled workers, they began to turn from unorganized, spontaneous expressions of anger and anxiety to better organized, focused industrial action. It was the artisans who sparked much of the development of organized trade unions around the middle of the nineteenth century. Artisans were coming to realize that industrial workers were their natural allies in their struggle against the common enemy, the capitalists. The earliest organized industrial action was taken by the more skilled occupations; the growing groups of unskilled workers, usually first-generation immigrants from more backward regions or countries, were not yet in a position to do so. Furthermore, the more highly skilled workers were anxious to emphasize their social and economic distinctiveness. Even so, the road upward was steep. Universal manhood suffrage, first extended in some countries in 1848, was maintained in France but withdrawn in Germany, to be restored on a limited basis with the establishment of the unified German Empire in 1871. In Great Britain, it was extended gradually to different groups of people but not fully established until 1918; however, skilled workers enjoyed the right to vote by the 1880s. Universal manhood suffrage was not established in Italy until the turn of the century.

Whenever the right to vote was extended to a new social group, there was usually a time lapse before the suffrage would manifest itself in new forms of political organization. In France, workers remained largely alienated from the political system until the Socialist movement began to turn its attention to action within the political system late in the century. Less alienated politically, British workers divided their votes between the aristocratic Conservative Party and the capitalist Liberal Party. The powerful Labour Party of the twentieth century only dates back to 1900. In Germany, the response was swifter. The Marxist Social Democratic Party was already entrenching itself within the German working class before 1871. Thereafter, it quickly became the most powerful Socialist Party in Europe although, owing to government repression and manipulation, it did not become a potent electoral force until after 1890. In general, one could say that during the later years of the early industrialization period, the groundwork was being laid for the working class to enter the political systems of Europe. They were arriving economically in terms of their significance to the new forms of production and in terms of their growing ability to organize for industrial action, but they had not yet arrived politically.

## INDUSTRIAL MATURITY

### THE ESCALATION OF CONFLICT

The next stage in industrialization is somewhat difficult to delineate sharply. Mature industrialization differs from early industrialization, not so much because of any overwhelming technological revolution, such as had occurred in England in the late eighteenth century, but because of a rapid acceleration of trends already started. During this period, Great Britain's industrial lead diminished and finally came to an end. Germany reached Great Britain's level and, then, fell back, although only momentarily, with her defeat in World War I. The United States emerged as the world's new industrial giant. France finally experienced an industrial upsurge at the turn of the century; Italy began her industrialization around 1900, reaching industrial maturity after World War II. But, despite great differences in the four countries' levels of economic development, there were certain similarities among them that permit developmental comparisons from about 1870 until World War II, the period we are labeling industrial maturity.

The most striking economic change during this period was the emergence of massive monopolistic corporations in most of the vital economic sectors, which replaced the smaller competitive firms of the preceding period. Anticombination laws were sometimes relaxed to permit this development; large corporations

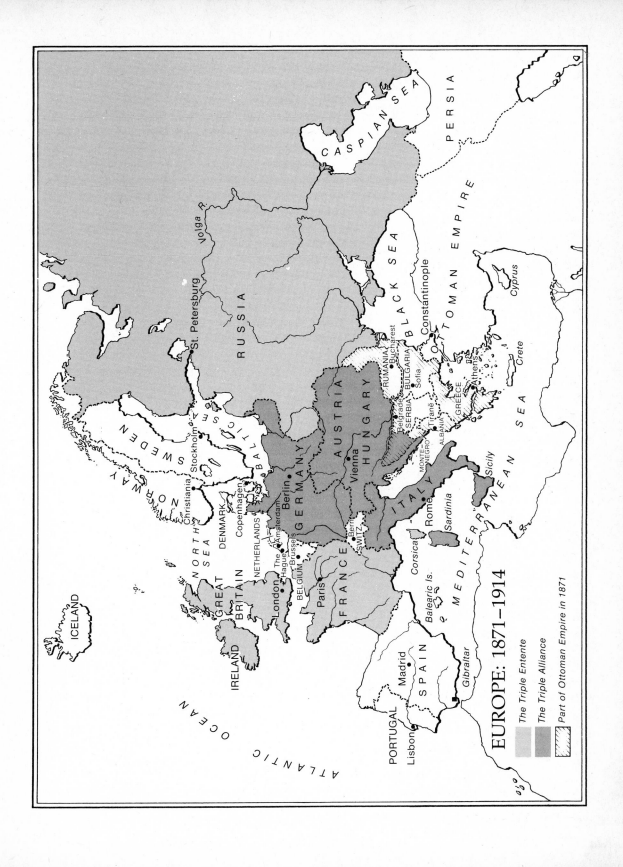

EUROPE: 1871–1914

ICELAND

ATLANTIC OCEAN

NORWAY

SWEDEN

St. Petersburg

RUSSIA

Volga R.

CASPIAN SEA

PERSIA

Stockholm
Christiania

NORTH SEA

BALTIC SEA

DENMARK

Copenhagen

GREAT BRITAIN

IRELAND

NETHERLANDS

Amsterdam
The Hague
Brussels
BELGIUM

London

GERMANY

Berlin

AUSTRIA

Vienna

HUNGARY

RUMANIA

Bucharest

BLACK SEA

Constantinople

OTTOMAN EMPIRE

Cyprus

Belgrade
SERBIA
BULGARIA
Sofia

MONTE-
NEGRO
Tiranë
ALBANIA

GREECE

Athens

Crete

Paris

FRANCE

Bern
SWITZ.

ITALY

Rome

Sardinia

Corsica

Sicily

MEDITERRANEAN SEA

Balearic Is.

PORTUGAL

Madrid

SPAIN

Lisbon

Gibraltar

The Triple Entente

The Triple Alliance

Part of Ottoman Empire in 1871

could acquire a much greater amount of capital and, thus, could promote the technological advances of the era. Joint stock corporations accumulated large amounts of capital as a result of the purchase of stock by a multitude of small investors. Businesses grew into giant bureaucracies, employing thousands of workers and generating an intermediate supervisory and clerical staff. The latter became the truly new social element of the period—the white-collar worker. Women entered the work force in large numbers as part of this new social category. The lives of most people were becoming more highly organized. Mass-production and assembly-line techniques accelerated, and the distance between employer and employee became much greater. In the larger corporations, the employer became virtually invisible, screened from blue-collar and white-collar personnel by layers of managerial staff.

The development of giant corporations stimulated trade unions to organize on a larger scale as independent craft unions joined together to form large federations. Late in the period, unskilled and semiskilled workers in mass-production fields, such as the automotive industry, were becoming organized as well. In response, the capitalists attempted to organize the industrial sectors. Where laws prohibited the formation of trusts or the combination of competing firms for purposes of market control, trade associations formed to exchange information across a sector. Furthermore, huge industrial cartels began to emerge, representing vertical (rather than horizontal) integration, so that industrialists could better control the supply and cost of needed raw materials and capital goods as well as the markets for their products within industry itself. By the 1920s, industrial concentration and trade union organization had reached the point where serious industrial conflict was a significant concern. Capitalists in the European countries enjoyed varying degrees of success in dealing with the trade union challenge, but, in all four of our countries before World War I and until after World War II, the state curbed the power of the working class on behalf of employers' interests. Although Socialist parties were achieving politi-

cal power in Scandinavia and although they secured a tantalizing share of power once or twice in Great Britain, Germany and France, capitalism was able to retain its hold in most of Europe between the wars. This was even reinforced by fascism in Italy and Germany.

Despite the sharpness of class conflict during this period, it is clear that the conditions of life for the vast majority of people were improving dramatically and that the social structure was experiencing profound changes. Wages were rising during the entire period, whereas prices continued to decline at least until about 1900. The resulting rise in purchasing power stimulated the perfection of mass-production techniques and the mass distribution of new commodities, such as bicycles and electrical appliances. This certainly helps to account for the increased willingness of Socialist parties to work within the system toward the end of the century. The parties of the working class were beginning to compete with the middle-class parties for votes and seats in parliament, hoping gradually to attain majority strength and to enact reforms rather than trying to achieve them through violent means.

Other trends were making it less likely that the transition to parliamentary socialism would be a smooth one. The four decades before World War I were marked by recurrent economic recessions that affected all countries more or less simultaneously. Each recession meant significant unemployment although price decreases helped to cushion the blow for the most vulnerable members of the working class. Financial sources would dry up mysteriously for awhile and, then, just as mysteriously begin to flow again. Whatever the state of the market, industrialists could not expand their operations without the needed capital. What was happening was that the pace of industrialization had increased so much that people were losing confidence in its ability to sustain itself. Despite the growth of the domestic market, increases in productivity were even greater, especially because new industrial nations had entered the field. Colonialism, which had once supplemented the domestic market as an outlet for goods, was no longer adequate because the most recently colonized areas, especially those in Africa, although valuable as sources of raw materials, were too primitive to be able to use the sophisticated products of Western Europe. Still, the imperialistic quest forged ahead. Finally, the secular trend of declining prices came to an end at the turn of the century and the twentieth-century nemesis of inflation began to increase the insecurity of both the working class and the middle class.

By the time of the Great Depression (the 1930s), capitalists and their political allies were beginning to recognize the advantages of turning to the state to ameliorate industrial conflict. After World War II, a much more enlightened capitalism was to see the advantages of trying to eradicate the sources of social unrest, poverty, and economic insecurity. Such insights were relatively few and far between among the pre-World War I ruling classes. Some of the social reforms that had been undertaken had been instigated by aristocratic conservatives who sought to outflank their liberal rivals and win working-class votes. Before World War I, it was often difficult to distinguish between liberals and conservatives on socioeconomic matters. Actually, in each country, there had emerged a ruling class made up of aristocrats and businessmen who controlled the instruments of state power and the powerful leverage points of the private sector, especially the banks. Political leaders, whether liberals or conservatives, radicals or moderates, left or right, were essentially extensions of the ruling class. The real political conflicts were between this combined ruling class on the inside and the Socialist parties and trade unions on the outside.

## WORLD WAR I AND ITS AFTERMATH

Historians will probably never resolve the question of whether World War I was inevitable or could have been avoided. On the one hand, it is possible to visualize Europe in 1914 as divided into two armed camps, both spoiling for war, both confident of victory, both simply waiting for the spark that would sooner or later set off the conflagration. On the other hand, one can review the history of diplomacy in the 15 years preceding the war and note how many times war was possible but was averted by the desire of the statesmen on both sides to preserve peace. From this perspective, the stakes in the various brink-of-war crises were never so great as to justify unleashing the holocaust. The major disputes before the war, such as those over Morocco and small slices of territory in the Balkans, seemed to be far removed from the central questions of the balance of power between Germany and France on the continent of Europe and between Great Britain and Germany on the high seas.

However, the armed-camps thesis is supported by the fact that by 1907 the European powers had maneuvered themselves into two opposing alliance systems that operated fairly coherently and were held together through a series of tests during the next half-dozen years. On the one side was the Triple Alliance of Germany, Austria-Hungary, and Italy; on the other side was the Triple Entente of Great Britain, France, and the Russian Empire. Except for Italy's refusal to enter World War I when it broke out in August 1914, the two alliances held firm as each partner honored its commitments by entering the war on the side of its allies.

Much of the blame for the events leading up to World War I can be placed on political leaders whose perspective on the world focused too narrowly on such balance-of-power factors as the number of armed divisions, battleships, and square miles of territory held. The desire for peace as a value in itself seems to have been virtually beyond their range of vision, perhaps because no one could yet foresee the devastation that mature industrial powers were capable of inflicting on one another. The loudest calls for peace were coming from those to whom the ruling circles had turned a deaf ear—the socialists.

The marriage of pacifism and socialism had, in fact, come rather late. Karl Marx had not been a pacifist, but the generation in command of Europe's Socialist parties at the turn of the century—such as Jean Jaurès in France and Karl Kausky in Germany—were committed internationalists as well as socialists. They saw socialism and, indeed, the working-class movement generally as an international phenomenon. The class conflict knew no national boundaries; the struggle between nations was simply an in-house fight among different branches of the capitalist class. Thus, it was certainly not in the interest of the proletariat to participate in it. National conscription was a way in which the capitalists of one country recruited the workers of that country to fight the workers of other countries on behalf of capitalist objectives. Therefore, true socialists should fight war and militarism just as they should fight capitalism. To these socialists, it was quite logical that a socialist should be a pacifist.

During the first dozen years of the twentieth century, the electoral gains of the Socialist parties in most European countries were impressive. Leading the way were the German Social Democrats who, in 1912, gained the largest number of seats of any party in the Reichstag. Projecting these trends forward, one could well imagine that, had the process not been interrupted by World War I, the pacifistic socialists would have reached power in most European countries within a matter of two or three decades at most. From this perspective, the days of militarism appeared to be numbered.

Nevertheless, the socialist tide began to recede somewhat in the last year or two before the war. As war became more and more likely, the European socialists found themselves forced to decide what approach they would adopt if it should come about. The conflict between revolutionaries and revisionists began to take on an unreal quality. Some revisionists, such as Jean Jaurès, held on to their pacifism; other, such as the main body of German Social Democrats, wrapped themselves in patriotic garb and supported the war. The revolutionary Marxists were also divided. Many followed the French Marxist, Jules Guesde, in supporting the war effort in their own countries, whereas others, like Vladimir Ilyich Lenin and Rosa Luxemburg, saw this as further evidence of opportunism and a sellout of the workers to capitalism. In short, the war had a devastating effect on European socialism. Because both the leaders and followers were already uncertain where socialism stood in the era of mature industrialization, their commitment to its fundamentals turned out to be rather superficial in the face of the much stronger pull of nationalism.

World War I brought about a profound transformation in the distribution of power, both in Europe and worldwide. Temporarily, at least, the defeat of the Central Powers left France as the most powerful nation on the continent, a position she sought to strengthen through punitive measures against Germany and support for the new states emerging in central and eastern Europe. Great Britain, more preoccupied with the international power balance, gave France only scant support in these pursuits, whereas the other major victorious power, the United States, after entering the war late and then participating vigorously in the peace negotiations, withdrew once more into a shell of isolationism, disdaining involvement in European affairs. On a worldwide scale, it appeared at first that the decline of Germany and Russia had removed the principal threats to the supremacy of the British Empire. But new rivals were emerging, in the Pacific at least. Both the United States and Japan had emerged from the war considerably strengthened as naval powers. Moreover, Great Britain was finding that her far-flung empire constitituted an enormous financial drain, leaving the mother country weakened in the face of postwar inflationary pressures and monetary crises.

In the 1920s, it became increasingly evident that the world was divided into two types of powers—the relatively contented and the relatively discontented. In the former category were the victors of World War I—Great Britain, France, and the United States. In the latter category were Germany, the principal loser; Russia, seriously weakened by revolution and civil war but, as the new Soviet Union, the possessor of enormous potential for development into a stronger power than the old Russian Empire; Italy, technically a victor as a result of her switch from the Triple Alliance to the Triple Entente but dissatisfied with her meager gains in the peace settlement; and Japan, gradually expanding her power base in the western Pacific and just reaching the status of a Great Power. There was a possibility that the division between the satisfied and the dissatisfied powers could constitute the basis for a new alliance system, foreshadowing a second, and even more devastating, worldwide conflagration.

## TOTALITARIAN DICTATORSHIP

In the meantime, developments within the discontented nations were leading toward a new kind of division—between the democracies and the totalitarian dictatorships. One by one the discontented powers as well as some of the smaller countries of Europe were abandoning the form or the substance of democracy for various types of autocratic rule designed to achieve a unity of purpose in the quest for a stronger position in the world. The first major country to move in this direction was Russia. In late 1917, the Bolsheviks had already converted a budding constitutional democracy into a one-party dictatorship. During the ensuing civil war and even during the period of relaxation that followed in the early 1920s, the power of the Communist Party bureaucracy and the state police was steadily expanding. Following Lenin's death in 1924, the Party Secretary, Joseph Stalin, drew the various instruments of power together and, after a series of successful clashes with his principal rivals, became the unchallenged supreme ruler by the late 1920s.

By this time, another dictator, Benito Mussolini, had consolidated his preeminent position in Italy. Invited by King Victor Emmanuel III, in 1922, to assume the premiership as a temporary solution to a political crisis, Mussolini manipulated the deputies in parliament and gained emergency powers. Then, he systematically eliminated his opposition, beginning with the extreme left and moving to the right. Eventually, he and his Fascist Party ruled as a one-man, one-party dictatorship, much as Stalin and the Communist Party did in the Soviet Union. While Stalin and Mussolini were establishing their leadership, the military leaders of Japan were in the process of undermining the unstable Japanese parliamentary regime. In 1931, they pushed the politicians aside and established a *de facto* military dictatorship. Although different in form, this was similar to the one-man, one-party dictatorships of Stalin and Mussolini, in that individual freedoms were curtailed and there was no viable opposition.

In all three of these cases, the emerging rulers justified their ruthless measures on the ground that it was necessary to combat a class enemy. Thus, Stalin spoke of a capitalist encirclement, implying that his domestic enemies were agents of the capitalist powers. Mussolini and the Japanese oligarchs justified themselves by claiming that there was a growing domestic threat of left-wing extremism, Communist subversion, and industrial disruption. These claims had been made credible by the split in the Socialist ranks in the early 1920s. In each parliamentary country, a militant Communist Party, taking its direction from Moscow, expressed irreconcilable opposition to the existing regime and vowed to come to power by revolutionary means. The fact that these Communist parties were numerically weak and isolated did not prevent the right-wing usurpers of power from claiming that they posed a real threat.

The extreme right in Europe was a curious mixture of elements. It drew most heavily on those strata of society that had been the least dynamic during the stage of early industrialization and that had found themselves displaced during mature industrialization. These especially included the members of the middling class discussed earlier. Their lack of dynamism and the fact that their business undertakings were on a small scale had rendered them incapable of competing or coping with the industrial and commercial giants of the twentieth century. The right-wing attacks on trade unionism and Communism probably focused more on the symptoms than on the causes of these people's fears and frustrations, but the attacks appealed to the members of this class, especially where, as in Italy and Germany, they could be associated with frustrated national aspirations. Because a minority of Jews in such countries as Germany and France had achieved conspicuous success in business or politics, the Jews as a people became special targets for vitriolic attacks, again appealing to the frustrations of downward-slipping social groups.

In the Weimar Republic of Germany, the extreme right posed a severe threat to the new regime on several occasions in the early 1920s. Here anti-Semitism combined with anti-Communism, providing a justification for a right-wing coup. The last of the early right-wing threats came in the fall of 1923 when a rebellious segment of the army took control of the government of Bavaria and called on the central government in Berlin to yield power to the right wing. When Berlin refused, an obscure right-wing leader, Adolph Hitler, with the help of the former head of the General Staff, General Erich Ludendorff, staged an unsuccesful bid to gain power in Munich. Hitler was arrested and given a short jail sentence. Thereafter, the Weimar Republic found temporary solutions for its economic problems and began a five-year period of political stability. Nevertheless, Hitler had gained the public notoriety he needed to enable him to expand his organizational base, the National Socialist (Nazi) Party, to the national level.

By the early 1930s, the Great Depression, which had started earlier and hit with greater force in Germany than in most other advanced countries, had undermined the fragile stability of the Weimar Republic. Hitler's National Socialists as well as the Communists on the far left registered a series of spectacular gains in the Reichstag elections of 1930 and 1932 and in the presidential election of 1932. By late 1932, the parties that were loyal to the Weimar Republic had virtually lost their majority in the Reichstag, and the country could be governed only by means of presidential emergency powers. Secret negotiations went on among conservative politicans and leading industrialists. This led to President Paul von Hindenburg's invitation to Hitler, in January 1933, to assume power as Chancellor. This scenario resembled that of Mussolini's rise to power. Once again, a popular demagogue was invited to assume power because of his reputed ability to hold the left in check and, again, by a ruling élite who believed that they could control his actions when in power. Even more rapidly than Mussolini, however, Hitler proceeded to eliminate all competing parties—those of the right, center, and left—and to construct a dictatorship in which the other power centers—the military, industrialists, and state bureaucracy— were subordinate to Hitler and his Nazi colleagues. The system of terror and domestic repression established by the Nazis was rivaled for its scope and ruthlessness only by that of Stalin at the height of the Great Purges in the late 1930s. By the eve of World War II, the Nazi and Soviet dictatorships stood as models of totalitarianism, a type of regime in which the individual is totally subordinate to the whims of the rulers of the state. By comparison, the fascist dictatorships of Italy, Spain, and certain smaller European countries, were inefficient and even humane.

Totalitarianism is a system of rule that is fostered by political leaders seeking to engage an entire population in far-reaching projects for social, economic, and cultural change. Both Stalin and Hitler were preoccupied with strengthening their nations in preparation for the world war that each saw coming in the near future, the war that Hitler would, in fact, instigate. To accomplish this, each opted for a herculean program of mass mobilization. In Hitler's Third Reich, the individual was to be subordinate to the interests of the *Volk* ("nation"). Loyal German citizens would enthusiastically dedicate themselves to the tasks prescribed by the Führer ("leader") and the Nazi Party, tasks designed to muster the maximum of human energy toward the goal of war preparedness. Even such previously private matters as the question of what career one might follow or whom one might marry were no longer left entirely up to individual choice but were required to fit within the regime's prescripts.

Totalitarianism attacks not only individual freedom of choice but also (at least in theory) the individual psyche, aiming to mobilize the thoughts and feelings of individuals as well as their actions. Two means are employed toward this end: terror and propaganda. Terror, the more negative device, is the instrument of a police state that creates diffuse uncertainty as to what is legal and what is illegal behavior. The individual must be constantly on guard lest a careless act or utterance lead to arrest, imprisonment, or death. The intense preoccupation that this uncertainty necessitates robs the individual of the freedom to think thoughts that do not fall within the bounds of what the regime officially permits. More positively the regime's propaganda bombards the citizen with its exclusive interpretation of situations and events inside and outside the country through a monopoly of the mass media and a forced screening out of contrary information emanating from whatever source.

The Nazi regime employed terror in essentially three domains: (1) as part of its racial purification program, designed to eradicate non-Aryan elements from the German population; (2) as part of Hitler's effort to eliminate political opposition, both inside and outside the Nazi movement; and (3) as a weapon against the German population at large, to enforce conformity to the regime's expectations and to weed out potential enemies and troublemakers. The instruments employed consisted of a confusing array of special police agencies, the most notorious of which were the Gestapo ("state police") and Hitler's élite corps of enforcers, the Schutzstaffel [(SS) Black Shirts]. It was the SS under Heinrich Himmler that maintained the concentration camps in Germany and eventually in German-ruled Eastern Europe. These were used systematically to snuff out the lives of countless millions of Jews. For the most part, the systematic elimination of those regarded by Hitler as political opponents occurred early in the Third Reich. In later years, the organizational complexity and confusion of the regime undoubtedly lessened its efficiency in identifying those who silently opposed it. But the confusion added to the uncertainty and arbitrariness of the system of repression and, therefore, must have enhanced the psychological insecurity of élites and ordinary citizens alike.

Nazi propaganda was assisted by the perpetration of a myth, repeated and repeated until most Germans had internalized it—or so, at least, was the intention. The fundamental premise on which the myth rested was the superiority of the German people as the purest strain of the Aryan racial type. High points in the history of Germany were emphasized in the schools, whereas the lows were ignored or excused on the basis of the treachery of racial enemies. Especially emphasized was the role played by Jewish business and political leaders in allegedly undermining the German war effort between 1914 and 1918. This, in turn, justified the Nazi demand for vengeance and the restoration of lost territory—if necessary, through military means. The myth of racial superiority was used to support Nazi claims to Eastern territory, the Lebensraum ("living space") rightfully owed to the German people although currently occupied by "inferior" Slavic and Jewish peoples. These peoples were marked for enslavement or, in the case of the Jews, extermination. The more extreme consequences of this doctrine may not have been spelled out to the German people, but the premises from which it might be inferred were systematically put forth in the schools, in the media, and in numerous speeches by Hitler and his propaganda chief, (Paul) Joseph Goebbels. Pervading all of these messages was the glorification of Hitler as the infallible leader, with the inference that those anointed by Hitler as his principal collaborators—Heinrich Himmler, Goebbels, Hermann Goering, and the Gauleiters (district party chiefs)—were to be obeyed without question as Hitler surrogates, chosen by the leader to implement his will and, in the event of his death, to carry on the work of the 1000-year Reich.

In the early days of the National Socialist Party, its official ideology had carried implications of a social revolution. After Hitler gained its leadership, the party continued to label itself a workers' party, but only a few of its leaders took the socialist component of its image seriously. After Hitler gained the support of German industrialists in his successful bid to come to power, he ceased to pay even lip service to the second half of the term National Socialism; the principal losers of the party purge of July 1934 were left-leaning colleagues, such as Gregor Strasser. In truth, the Nazi regime shored up German capitalism and enhanced the interests of employers, but it did away with independent trade unions and mobilized the industrial work force for war preparedness. This enhanced the profit-taking ability of German big business although at a price—the reinstitution of central planning that even in the mid-1930s reached a scale rivaling that of World War I. If there was a social revolution in Hitler's Germany, it took the form of the undermining of the aristocracy's superior social and political position, to the benefit of the middle classes. An eradication of the barriers between bourgeoisie and proletariat did not take place.

## WORLD WAR II

After the consolidation of Nazi rule in Germany, the world witnessed a series of daring expansionist thrusts by the have-not powers. Italy invaded Ethiopia in 1935; Germany reoccupied the demilitarized Rhineland in 1936; Germany and Italy intervened successfully in the Spanish Civil War (1936–1939) to ensure victory for the forces led by General Francisco Franco; Japan moved out from its base in Manchuria to invade China proper in 1937; and Germany and Austria formally joined together into a single German state ruled from Berlin in early 1938. Each of these steps was formally repudiated by the contented powers, but they did not lift a finger to stop the aggressors and violators of treaties. By mid-1938, when Hitler demanded the Sudetenland from Czechoslovakia, German military power had grown to the point where the combined forces of Great Britain and France could not be assured of victory. Rather than risk war, Great Britain and France chose appeasement at Munich, and Hitler's troops marched into the Sudetenland. This became their base of operations, from which, a few months later, they moved to occupy the whole of Czechoslovakia, again unchecked by Great Britain and France.

By early 1939, it had become clear that what was to become known as the Axis Powers—the coalition of Germany, Italy, and Japan—had in-formally divided the world into spheres of influence; they felt strong enough to impose their will on the French and the British, who were timidly shrinking from confrontation, and on the Americans, who were deeply ensconced in isolation. In fact, Hitler enjoyed a fair amount of sympathy in these countries, especially from right-of-center politicians who saw him as a bulwark against Communism. This perspective received a severe jolt when, in August 1939, Hitler concluded a mutual nonaggression pact with Stalin, thus, neutralizing the other have-not power in any potential world conflict. Shortly thereafter, Germany and Russia invaded Poland from different directions, tearing apart the buffer state. This was too much for the British and French, who had guaranteed Poland's security from just such an onslaught, and World War II began in September 1939. When Hitler turned his attention to the west, he quickly defeated and occupied France; Great Britain barely managed to escape a similar fate as the Royal Air Force (RAF) fought the Luftwaffe (German Air Force) to a standstill in the skies over the English Channel during the summer of 1940. For the next year and a half, Great Britain remained largely immobilized while Prime Minister Winston Churchill cast about for a means of bringing the United States into the war.

The alliance of the have-nots was relatively short lived. When Hitler invaded the Soviet Union in May 1941, he gave Great Britain an instant ally. The Allied coalition was completed when the Japanese attacked Pearl Harbor in December 1941 and when Germany declared war on the United States. What was left of the French forces outside occupied France gradually came together under General Charles de Gaulle, and they participated alongside the British and Americans beginning with the North African campaign. Gradually, after the reversal of the tide at the battle of Stalingrad, the Soviet forces began pushing the Germans and their allies westward while the British and Americans were winning battles in North Africa and, then, in southern Italy. With the establishment of the Western Front in France, in June 1944, it was only a matter of time until the ring closed. Hitler

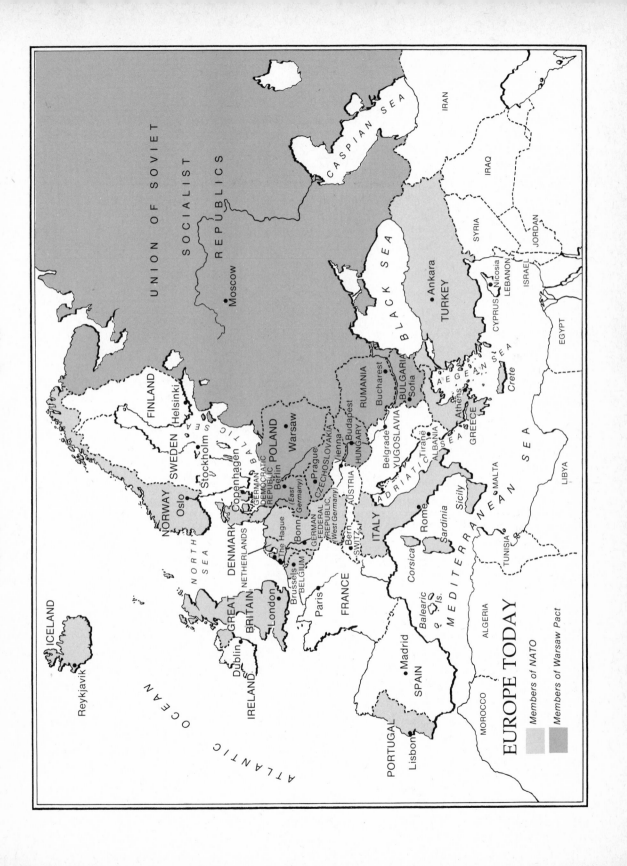

**EUROPE TODAY**

Members of NATO

Members of Warsaw Pact

UNION OF SOVIET SOCIALIST REPUBLICS

Moscow

CASPIAN SEA

BLACK SEA

IRAN

IRAQ

SYRIA

JORDAN

ISRAEL

LEBANON

CYPRUS

Nicosia

TURKEY

Ankara

EGYPT

AEGEAN SEA

GREECE

Athens

Crete

RUMANIA

Bucharest

BULGARIA

Sofia

FINLAND

Helsinki

SWEDEN

Stockholm

NORWAY

Oslo

BALTIC SEA

POLAND

Warsaw

GERMAN DEMOCRATIC REPUBLIC (East Germany)

Berlin

CZECHOSLOVAKIA

Prague

Vienna

AUSTRIA

HUNGARY

Budapest

YUGOSLAVIA

Belgrade

ALBANIA

Tiranë

ADRIATIC SEA

DENMARK

Copenhagen

NETHERLANDS

The Hague

GERMAN FEDERAL REPUBLIC (West Germany)

Bonn

BELGIUM

Brussels

SWITZ.

Bern

ITALY

Rome

Corsica

Sardinia

Sicily

MALTA

NORTH SEA

GREAT BRITAIN

London

IRELAND

Dublin

FRANCE

Paris

MEDITERRANEAN SEA

TUNISIA

Balearic Is.

SPAIN

Madrid

PORTUGAL

Lisbon

ALGERIA

MOROCCO

LIBYA

ICELAND

Reykjavik

ATLANTIC OCEAN

committed suicide on April 30, 1945, in a bunker underneath Berlin, while Soviet tanks were blasting their way into the heart of the city.

## POSTWAR POLITICS

At the end of the war, Europe lay devastated. Germany was in ruins, her territory occupied by Allied troops. In all of the belligerent countries, the economies needed rebuilding, with little or no capital available for the task. Great Britain and France still had commitments to their overseas empires, which promised to be more of a financial drain than an economic asset. The Soviet Union had extended its armed might far into Central Europe. Unless the United States was willing to retain its forces on the continent, Western Europe would be at the mercy of Stalin's expansionist ambitions. Germany was no longer a viable counterweight to Soviet power, and Soviet troops were occupying the smaller countries of Central and Eastern Europe, which had once been regarded as a buffer zone. At the end of the war, it was agreed that there would be four zones of occupation in Germany administered by the United States, Great Britain, France, and the Soviet Union. Berlin was also to be under four-power administration although it was located well within the Soviet zone of occupation. The Soviet Union, Poland, and Czechoslovakia all incorporated chunks of Germany into their own territory.

By 1947, it had become clear to the Western powers that the world was once again dividing itself into hostile blocs. In a series of initiatives taken between 1947 and 1949, the United States, Great Britain, and France moved to consolidate Western Europe politically and militarily. A bizonal Economic Council was established in the British and American zones of occupation to begin the process of restoring Germany's economy. Massive American economic assistance began flowing into Europe under the auspices of the Marshall Plan. Although West Germany was not a sovereign unit when the Marshall Plan began in 1947, she received a large share of the assistance. By this time, the other

defeated Axis Power in Western Europe, Italy, had been restored to full membership in the international community. Her government participated fully in the economic and political steps leading to Western Europe's recovery.

After economic rehabilitation, the Western powers moved to establish an effective military posture against the Soviet threat. In 1949, the North Atlantic Treaty Organization (NATO) was established. Then, in 1950, a beginning was made to unify Western Europe economically and politically through the announcement by the French Foreign Minister, Robert Schuman, of his plan to integrate French and West German coal and steel production. The first unit of today's European Community (EC), the Coal and Steel Community (ECSC), came into being in 1952. By this time, Western Europe had successfully completed its rebuilding program, thanks not only to American assistance and the lessons learned by the failures of prewar economic policy; but also to the division of Europe between East and West and the emerging Cold War.

In domestic politics, the left emerged from World War II considerably strengthened in most Western European countries. Socialists and Communists shared power in the early postwar governments of France and Italy as well as in several smaller countries.[5] But with the onset of the Cold War in 1947, the Communists voluntarily left or were forced out of governments and, with the exceptions of Iceland, Finland and, most recently, France they have not returned since then. Power, then, shifted to the right, with Socialist parties losing power or having to share it with center and center-right parties. Exceptions to these trends were the Scandinavian countries, which continued to be governed by coalitions dominated by the Socialists through the 1950s and into the 1960s and early 1970s, and Great

[5]The distinction between Socialist and Communist goes back to the Bolshevik Revolution in Russia and the establishment by Lenin of the Third International. Parties that remained a part of the Second International, or pre-1917 world organization of Socialist parties, are called Socialist. Those following Lenin's lead are called Communist. See Chapter Four for contemporary differences and also for a clarification of the terms, left, center, and right used in this section.

Britain, where the Labour Party emerged the victor in the election of 1945 and remained in power until 1951. During these early postwar years, the Labour government under Clement Attlee was able to put into effect an extraordinary program of economic and social reform, most of which the Conservatives were to leave intact during their long tenure in power from 1951 until 1964. When Labour returned to power in 1964, they refrained from instituting another sweeping era of reform, preferring to continue domestic policies essentially similar to those of their Conservative predecessors.

In West Germany and Italy, the threat of Communism immediately to the east helped propel voters in the direction of right-of-center parties after 1947. By the time the German Federal Republic (West Germany) came into being in 1949, the division of occupied Germany into two hardened semisovereign entities was an established, if not-yet accepted, fact. Because the eastern part of Germany (German Democratic Republic) was dominated by the Soviet-backed Communists, Communism in West Germany was shunned by the voters. Torn between revulsion to Communism and the suspicion that a too-Western-oriented foreign policy might postpone German reunification indefinitely, the Social Democrats were likewise disadvantaged at the polls although not to nearly the same degree as the Communists. This opened the field for the new Christian Democratic Union (CDU), a union of former Catholic and Protestant parties, led by former Cologne mayor, Konrad Adenauer. By the early 1950s, Adenauer's party had established its predominance over smaller center and right-wing parties. It was to govern West Germany alone or in coalition until 1969, at which time it gave way to a coalition headed by the Social Democrats who have governed West Germany since then.

In somewhat similar fashion, the strictly Catholic Italian Christian Democrats established their predominance over all rivals in the early postwar years. Left-oriented voters divided their support in the early years between Communists and Socialists. In the center and right regions of the political spectrum, however, the Christian Democrats easily outdistanced five smaller parties. With nearly a majority of seats in parliament, the Christian Democrats could reward and punish potential partners, maintaining a stranglehold on the principal instruments of power. In 1962, they moved somewhat to the left, dropping more conservative coalition partners and working out the opening-to-the-left agreement with the Socialists. During the 1960s and early 1970s, the Communists were steadily gaining strength in national and local elections, setting the stage for the near-equal confrontation of the giants (Communists versus Christian Democrats) that has been a principal characteristic of Italian politics in the past 10 years.

The withdrawal of the French Communist Party from government in 1947 had a significant impact on French politics. However, no party of the center-right was able to establish its supremacy in the ensuing years as happened in West Germany and Italy. Instead, loose and shifting coalitions of fairly evenly matched parties, ranging from the Socialists on the left to the Independent and Peasant Party on the right, shared power between 1947 and 1958. In the meantime, war hero General Charles de Gaulle, after resigning as head of the provisional government in early 1946, waged a protracted battle to discredit the new Fourth Republic. He attracted a loyal movement of Gaullist followers who formed a political party in 1946. The combined pressure of strong opposition from Communists on the left and Gaullists on the right helped destabilize the Fourth Republic, which staggered from one crisis to another until it finally collapsed in May 1958 in the wake of a civilian/military revolt in Algiers, which was staged to protest the way the government in Paris was running the Algerian War. The result was a return of de Gaulle to power and a radical shift of voter support to parties of the right. De Gaulle's loyal supporters forged an electorally potent political party, the Union for the New Republic (UNR), which became the functional equivalent of the West German and Italian Christian Democrats. Under de Gaulle and his successor, George Pompidou, the Gaullists drew smaller parties of the center and right into their orbit and successfully warded off the electoral challenges of the parties of the left throughout the 1960s and the early 1970s.

The 1960s saw a lessening of East-West tensions, especially in Europe. Tentative steps were taken by Soviet and American leaders to institute a dialogue regarding arms control and specific areas of tension, such as Berlin. Charles de Gaulle attempted to provide leadership within Western Europe, seeking relaxation of tension (*détente*) and greater understanding among the countries of Eastern and Western Europe, but Moscow and Washington lacked enthusiasm for his initiatives and his Western European economic partners were reluctant to follow his political lead. De Gaulle's quest was renewed in 1969 by Social Democrat, Willy Brandt, the leader of the new West German Government. Brandt's *Ostpolitik* (Eastern policy) sought normalization of relations between West Germany and East Germany as well as Soviet and East German guarantees for the permanent status of West Berlin as an internationally protected enclave within East Germany. To achieve these goals, Brandt recognized the validity of the territorial changes that had taken place in Central Europe after World War II, including the loss of German territory to the USSR, Poland, and Czechoslovakia and the division of what was left of Germany into two states. Brandt insisted, however, that Germany remained one nation, meaning that the possibility was not excluded that, sometime in the future, reunification of the nation might occur through the replacement of the two states by one state. Put in other words, this meant that two governments would rightfully govern the two geographical parts of what remained of the old Germany but that the German people residing in the two parts would remain one people. The success of Brandt's *Ostpolitik* accelerated the trends away from the Cold War and into an era of *détente* in relations between East and West, a period that may have come to an end with the Soviet invasion of Afghanistan at the very end of the 1970s.

## POSTWAR ECONOMIES

Participation by parties of the left in the earliest postwar governments resulted in important socioeconomic policy innovations in Great Britain, France, and Italy. Most striking of these were the extensive nationalizations of industrial sectors. In Great Britain and France, the postwar left-dominated parliaments converted the coal industry, railroads, major investment banks, and the electricity and gas supply utilities (among others) from private to public ownership. In Italy, nationalization was less of an innovation because the central government had already been buying into private industry during the Mussolini regime. Government financial participation through giant holding companies continued to spread in the postwar period, most notably in the energy sector.

In France, the governments of the latter 1940s began to make use of the leverage given them by government ownership to provide the leading wedge of a system of state economic planning, which was designed in the early years to modernize the war-damaged and seriously outdated French economy. Expansion of the public sector provided stimulus to the private sector by making energy, transportation, and raw materials more readily available at cheaper cost. The central planners assigned priorities to different industrial sectors and encouraged development of those with high priority through subsidies and tax incentives. As France emerged into the 1950s, this system of indicative planning, which was to be given part of the credit for the subsequent economic boom, was developed further, providing French manufacturers and distributors greater certainty regarding the size of future markets and the availability of unfinished and semifinished goods needed in the productive process.

By contrast, in West Germany, the more conservative Christian Democrats under Adenauer and Economics Minister, Ludwig Erhard, evolved an economic system that relied much less on the state sector and placed its faith in the play of the free market. The market was expected to generate its own incentives, with the state intervening primarily in the interest of stabilizing the value of the mark and maintaining a steady money supply. Depending on the orientation of the economist, either Erhard's social-market economy or the French system of indicative planning is cited as the model of effective economic policy. The fact is that both economies established remarkable records for economic growth and relative stability, especially in the late 1950s and early 1960s. On the other hand, Great Britain and Italy, both of which opted for more mixed economic policy strategies, were to experience less impressive economic records during the same timespan—Great Britain with a record of relatively low-growth rates and Italy with a record of economic instability, and geographically uneven growth, despite an overall growth rate that was very high.

In all four countries, the postwar period witnessed the expansion of the welfare state, featuring cradle-to-grave protection of those members of society unable, for whatever reason, to cope adequately with economic misfortunes. The upheavals of the 1920s and 1930s had left a lasting mark on Western Europe; leaders of both left and right in all countries converged on the Keynesian fiscal and monetary means of steering between the extremes of depression and runaway inflation. The end result was a much improved level of personal security for individuals and families after World War II than had existed before that time. Especially noteworthy were the provision of free medical care in Great Britain, through the National Health Service established in 1946, and the virtually equivalent result obtained in West Germany, through the extensive National Health Insurance scheme.

The combination of greater economic security and rapid economic growth meant that Western Europe underwent a remarkable transformation in the first two postwar decades. A poor second cousin to the United States in the 1940s, Western Europe became a fully modern competitive equal by the 1970s. Western Europe was catching up with the United States in affluence, and many of the European economies were recording higher growth rates as well as better records of economic stability. Even in those countries whose economies suffered chronic problems, such as Great Britain and Italy, the transformation for the ordinary citizen after World War II was dramatic.

As Western Europe turned into the 1970s, the economic picture began to change for the worse. In 1971, the Richard M. Nixon administration, in effect, devalued the dollar, thus, undercutting the trading advantage that European countries had enjoyed vis-à-vis the world's largest economy. More disastrously, the Arab-Israeli War of 1973 resulted in both a temporary curtailment of oil supplies to Europe and a longer term upward movement of unemployment and inflation rates, a trend that had appeared earlier, especially in Great Britain, and that seemed to violate the established laws of economics. These various developments not only lessened trans-Atlantic harmony but also created difficulties for the European Community, which had been both a principal stimulus and beneficiary of the economic success of the preceding decade.

In presenting the history of contemporary Western European polyarchies, we have shown the development of the elements of the political system, on the one hand, and the elements of the economic and social environment, on the other hand. In general, these countries have experienced many political and socioeconomic changes in the past 250 years. Economically, they have been transformed from preindustrial to highly sophisticated industrial systems. Their social structures have also been significantly altered. Elements of the agrarian and semifeudal societies of the early eighteenth century have largely disappeared in most of Western Europe. Moreover, the two dominant social classes of early industrialization—the bourgeoisie and the proletariat—have been further subdivided into a number of subgroups. In the political area, absolute monarchies have given way to parliamentary regimes that, in turn, have become progressively democratic. Today, power is much more widely distributed among various societal groups. In this century, government is influencing society substantially more as economic and social problems have led people to organize for the purpose of acquiring larger shares of well-being, enlightenment, and respect.

In studying the background of contemporary political systems, we are not considering simply the ways in which political systems and their environments emerged in the past; we are also concerned with the salient features of the received tradition of the present. In other words, memories of a country's past constitute part of the environment of political interactions among contemporary human actors. What we have learned of our past helps to shape the way we interpret the present, even though, as modern men and women, we are less burdened by the past than were our ancestors. However, when we are reading about countries with such rich received traditions as those of Western Europe, we must be alert to those developments of the past that help us to understand (1) how these countries differ today from newer nations elsewhere and (2) how Western European countries differ from one another.

# Suggestions for Further Reading

Bracher, Karl Dietrich, *The German Dictatorship: The Origins, Structure and Effects of National Socialism,* trans. Jean Steinberg (New York: Praeger, 1970).

Heilbroner, Robert L., *The Making of Economic Society* (Englewood Cliffs, N.J.: Prentice-Hall, 1962).

Kindleberger, Charles P., *Economic Growth in France and Britain: 1851–1950* (Cambridge: Harvard University Press, 1964).

Landes, David, *The Unbound Prometheus: Technological Change and Industrial Development in Western Europe from 1850 to the Present* (Cambridge: At the University Press, 1969).

Moore, Barrington, Jr., *Social Origins of Dictatorship and Democracy: Lord and Peasant in the Making of the Modern World* (Boston: Beacon, 1967).

Morazé, Charles, *The Triumph of the Middle Classes* (Garden City, N.Y.: Doubleday, 1968).

Pachter, Henry M., *The Fall and Rise of Europe: A Political, Social and Cultural History of the Twentieth Century* (New York: Praeger, 1975).

Rostow, W. W., *Politics and the Stages of Growth* (Cambridge: At the University Press, 1971).

Stearns, Peter N., *European Society in Upheaval: Social History Since 1750,* 2nd ed. (New York: Macmillan, 1975).

Thompson, E. P., *The Making of the English Working Class* (New York: Random House 1963).

Tilly, Charles, ed., *The Formation of National States in Western Europe* (Princeton, N.J.: Princeton University Press, 1975).

Tuchman, Barbara W., *A Distant Mirror: The Calamitous 14th Century* (New York: Knopf, 1978).

Urwin, Derek W., *From Ploughshare to Ballotbox: The Politics of Agrarian Defense in Europe* (Oslo: Universitetsforlaget, 1980).

Wallerstein, Immanuel, *The Modern World System: Capitalist Agriculture and the Origins of the European World-Economy in the Sixteenth Century* (New York and London: Academic Press, 1974).

# CHAPTER TWO
## Postindustrial Economy and Society

## POSTINDUSTRIAL ECONOMY

The economic and social environment of the Western European political systems has experienced substantial changes since World War II, and knowledgeable scholars differ sharply as to their significance. Some have gone so far as to suggest that quantitative changes, such as dramatic increases in the gross national product (GNP) and a marked alteration in the proportions of the various occupational groups in the work force, have resulted in a qualitative leap, that a corner has been turned, or that we are now experiencing postindustrial society.[1] Others are more cautious, suggesting that quantitative changes are simply that and no more and that the First World countries of the 1970s are simply more mature industrially than they were 30 years ago.[2] Because the same data can be used to reach different conclusions, the argument is more a matter of interpretation than one that can be

resolved scientifically. For purposes of comparative analysis, the concept of postindustrialism helps to emphasize environmental elements that differentiate one country from another. For that reason, we will use that concept here.

## THE SERVICE ECONOMY

Although the origin of the term, postindustrial society, is somewhat obscure, it is clear why it is being increasingly used. Industrial society differed from preindustrial society because of the declining role of agriculture in the economy and the lower percentage of persons employed in the agricultural sector, especially when compared with the growing ranks of the industrial proletariat. By the same token, postindustrial society differs from industrial society because of the increasing importance of the service sector in relation to both agriculture and industry and the growing ranks of persons employed in the service sector as compared with both agriculture and industry. What is the service sector? According to Daniel Bell, it includes the following areas, where *services* rather than *goods* are produced: transportation, utilities, trade, finance, insurance, real estate, health, education, research, recreation and, finally—a catchall category—government. In the United States, the first coun-

[1] Among many works that discuss postindustrial society, see Daniel Bell, *The Coming of Post-Industrial Society* (New York: Basic Books, 1973); Leon N. Lindberg, ed., *Politics and the Future of Industrial Society* (New York: David McKay, 1976); Alain Touraine, *The Post-Industrial Society*, trans. Leonard F. X. Mayhew (New York: Random House, 1971).

[2] Lawrence C. Mayer, *Politics in Industrial Society: A Comparative Perspective* (New York: Wiley, 1977).

try to achieve postindustrial status, employment in the goods-producing sectors of the economy increased from 25.6 million in 1940 to 29 million in 1968. In the service-producing sectors, employment increased from 24.3 million to 51.8 million during the same period.[3] Between 1968 and 1976, the number employed in the goods-producing sectors remained static, whereas the number in the service sector increased by another 7 million.[4] Among the service sectors, employment increased most rapidly in government, especially at the state and local levels.

Whether or not Western European countries have reached postindustrial status is a matter of definition. In 1976, 51 percent of the French work force was in the service sector, as against 11 percent in agriculture and 38 percent in industrial production. In Italy, on the other hand, only 41 percent of the work force was employed in the service sector. There were 43.5 percent in industrial production and 15.5 percent in agriculture.[5] One could, perhaps, say that France had crossed the threshold to postindustrialism, whereas Italy had not; but this judgment would not be universally accepted. Italy also lags behind the other major Western European countries in another measure of economic development: GNP per capita. The United States was well ahead of even the most productive Western European economies in the 1960s, but the gap closed in the 1970s. Several other economies have now reached or surpassed the U.S. level (see Tables 1.1, p. 24, and 7.1, p. 168). France and West Germany have a GNP per capita that puts them among the more productive European economies, whereas Great Britain and Italy lag behind in what might be regarded as an intermediate range. Perhaps it would be best to view France and West Germany as having just crossed the threshold of postindustrialism, with Great Britain not far behind. Italy should be viewed as having a mature industrial economy, but, considering only the northern part of the country, Italy's economic indicators would come fairly close to those of other countries.

In Western Europe as in the United States, the service sector of the economy has become increasingly important in recent decades. This has meant that certain kinds of occupations have become more prominent than they were before. In general, nonmanual employment has increased more rapidly than manual employment. It was pointed out in Chapter One that, with the achievement of mature industrialization, a new social class—white-collar workers—appeared on the scene. This component of the work force continues to grow in postindustrial society, but especially in the professional and technical category rather than in such white-collar occupations as secretaries and office clerks. In the United States between 1958 and 1974, the number of white-collar workers increased by 55.5 percent, whereas blue-collar workers rose by only 27.5 percent. Within the white-collar category, those in professional and technical occupations increased by 77.5 percent, the largest increase in any single category.[6] This category includes those with the highest educational requirements, such as doctors, lawyers, engineers, teachers, scientists, and computer specialists, among others.

As society becomes more complex, there is a growing demand for skills that involve the application of *knowledge* to large-scale problems. If Western Europe has been slower than the United States to achieve postindustrial society, it may not be due simply to inferior material resources and the disadvantages of working on a smaller national scale. Possibly the social structure of twentieth-century Europe still retains enough of its preindustrial and early industrial features to impede the rapid development of a new class of professional and technical masterminds. Thus, European educational systems have been slow to change, whereas the American educational system has been decades ahead in the development of mass education and in the transition from the nineteenth century classical curriculum

[3]Bell, *op. cit.*, pp. 129–142.

[4]Statistical Office of the European Communities, *Basic Statistics of the Community*, 16th ed. (Luxembourg; The European Communities, 1978), p. 18.

[5]*Ibid.*, p. 19.

[6]Bell, *op. cit.*, p. 135.

to the more practical curriculums of the twentieth century. The pool of talent available to meet the demanding standards of a postindustrial occupational structure is more restricted in Europe. But the trends in most Western European countries are such that it is only a matter of time before they will catch up to where the United States is now in the matter of education. In any event, even if we are talking about Western Europe's future as well as its present, it is surely the immediate future—and it is coming more into focus with each passing year.

## STAGFLATION

Americans are familiar with the fact that postindustrial society is not utopia. The most productive economies in the world's history are producing the largest amounts of waste materials and transforming the natural environment in ways that make it less livable. The raw material and energy requirements of these economies are staggering, yet, their supply is limited. It takes little foresight to realize that our present standard of living may have to be scaled down. Production costs have skyrocketed since the 1960s owing to raw material and energy scarcities as well as the ability of producers (employers and employees) to obtain higher compensation for their contributions. Chronically high rates of inflation seem to be endemic to postindustrial economies. As in the past, higher prices restrict consumer demand for goods and services. However, in previous times, restricted demand eventually resulted in lower prices, thus, righting the balance. Today, the inexorable rise in costs means that producers have no choice but to pass these costs on to the consumer in the form of higher prices even if it means a further slowing down of economic activity and a rise in unemployment. To prevent such a downward spiral, governments attempt to add an ounce of economic stimulus here or a pint of economic depressant there, but each remedy only seems to produce a new set of ills. Thus, a tax cut to stimulate the economy often increases the inflationary pressures; a tight money policy designed to reduce inflation may actually exacerbate unemployment.

Tables 2.1 and 2.2 show unemployment rates and rates of inflation (as measured by consumer price increases) from the early 1960s until 1979 for nine of the larger First World countries. The energy crisis, which began in late 1973, obviously had a severe impact on the rates of inflation, which were much higher in the 1970s than before. The rising levels of unemployment are not as striking, but, with the exception of Sweden, they went up in all countries after 1973. In general, unemployment has been lower in Western Europe (except for Italy) than in North America. Nevertheless, the high levels of unemployment in the 1970s proved troublesome for the parties in power in Western Europe because voters were more likely to measure present performance against the past in their own country rather than to compare that country's record with the contemporary records of other countries.

The rise in consumer prices was much swifter in the 1970s than previously in both Western Europe and North America. Table 2.2 shows that, in relation to the major European countries, the United States and Canada fall in the middle with respect to inflation. West Germany shows a particularly favorable picture on a comparative basis, whereas inflation rates for France, Italy,

**TABLE 2.1** Adjusted Unemployment Rates in Selected Countries (Percent of Total Labor Force Seasonally Adjusted)

|  | Average 1964–1973 | Average 1974–1979 |
|---|---|---|
| United States | 4.4 | 6.6 |
| Japan | 1.2 | 1.9 |
| West Germany | 0.7 | 3.2 |
| France | 2.2 | 4.5 |
| United Kingdom[a] | 3.1 | 5.1 |
| Italy | 5.5 | 6.6 |
| Canada | 4.9 | 7.2 |
| Spain | 1.8 | 5.6 |
| Sweden | 2.0 | 1.9 |

[a]Great Britain.

SOURCE: Organization for Economic Cooperation and Development, *Economic Outlook*, 27 (1980), p. 21.

**TABLE 2.2** Consumer Prices (Percentage Change from Previous Period, Not Seasonally Adjusted)

|  | Average 1961–1970 | Average 1971–1976 | 1979 |
|---|---|---|---|
| United States | 2.8 | 6.6 | 11.3 |
| Japan | 5.8 | 11.1 | 3.6 |
| West Germany | 2.7 | 5.9 | 4.1 |
| France | 4.0 | 9.0 | 10.8 |
| United Kingdom[a] | 4.1 | 13.6 | 13.4 |
| Italy | 3.9 | 12.2 | 14.8 |
| Canada | 2.7 | 7.4 | 9.1 |
| Spain | 6.0 | 13.0 | 15.7 |
| Sweden | 4.0 | 8.3 | 7.2 |

[a]Great Britain.

SOURCE: Organization for Economic Cooperation and Development, *Economic Outlook*, 27 (1980), p. 44.

West German children riding their bicycles alongside a Ruhr factory near Duisburg.

and Great Britain are more serious. In these countries, the problem was neither unemployment nor inflation *alone*; it was *both* together, the dilemma known as stagflation.

**Unemployment.** To the economist, unemployment is part of a larger phenomenon, underemployment of the nation's productive forces. As stocks of goods accumulate unsold in warehouses and retail outlets, factories shut down and employees are laid off, temporarily or permanently. Some businesses weather the storm by cutting back production, others are swept away forever. Workers without jobs are forced to seek new employment. They often find that the only options are the unacceptable ones—moving to another part of the country (or to another country) to find work or going through the arduous process of retraining for a skill that is in greater demand. The impact of a recession on the individual and his or her family is often tragic, representing the loss of hope for a better future. To a country, recession means missed opportunity owing to unused productive capacity. Markets at home and abroad may be permanently lost to competition from companies in other countries because businesses have folded or have temporarily cut back production. Recession also means that national income falls short of its full potential; the standard of living of the nation fails to improve. Indeed, the standard of living for certain categories of the population actually declines as certain disadvantaged groups feel the brunt of unemployment.

After the buoyant decades of the 1950s and 1960s when all groups of society were seeing the economic pie expand, the experience of the 1970s and early 1980s has come as a severe shock with potentially serious consequences for political systems.

The causes of recession and unemployment are varied. When economies of countries are compared with one another, it becomes clear that some countries suffer more severely than others during a worldwide recession. The relative losers lose to the relative winners because their producers cannot compete on an equal basis in the world market. If world demand is shrinking, it will be shrinking more rapidly for the less competitive and may not even be shrinking at all for those whose productivity and cost structures put them in a position to take over the markets of the losers. But why does a worldwide recession come about? The simple answer is that there is a worldwide shrinkage of consumer demand, a factor that itself may result from a variety of causes. Among these is government economic policy, especially the policies of the governments responsible for the largest economies, such as the governments in Washington, Tokyo, and Bonn. It is only now being fully realized, as the First World comes to grips with the phenomenon of stagflation, that government policies designed to curtail inflationary forces have a direct and almost immediate impact on the level of productive activity. The productive forces of an economy slow down whenever government attempts to use deflationary measures to combat inflation. If the measures (such as action to raise interest rates or fiscal policies designed to reduce consumer spending power) are too strong or are carried out for too long, the more dramatic consequence may be a downturn in economic activity, leading to a recession rather than to the desired result of bringing rates of inflation down to acceptable levels.

Left-of-center politicians, whether American Democrats or European Socialists and Communists, often appear to be saying that one must choose between protecting the value of money (avoiding inflation) and maintaining full employment (avoiding recession) and that the choice to be made is clear. They hold that, when the values that make up human dignity are considered, one must protect the underprivileged and disadvantaged. This means taking whatever action is necessary to maintain workers in their jobs, even if this runs the risk of adding to inflationary pressures. Those on the left are all the more inclined to approach the economic dilemma in this fashion because there are equally strong voices on the right who agree with the premise that one must choose between monetary stability and full employment and who opt for the former. They argue that human dignity is best enhanced if we protect the purchasing power of the dollar, the pound, or the franc.

**Inflation.** Although siding with neither left nor right in this debate, we are constrained to point out that inflation has its costs as does unemployment. This must be acknowledged whether or not we conclude that the costs of inflation are as great as those of unemployment. Inflation affects the lives of millions of people adversely, just as unemployment does; the difference is that the incidence of inflation (i.e., who will be affected) is less predictable. If the inflation is severe enough, it will have a distortive effect so that some groups will lose ground while others are gaining ground. Not all groups will see their shares of the pie expanding; some will enjoy disproportionate gains. Among those who may gain are real property owners, big and small; corporate executives whose incomes are supplemented with bonuses for high rates of profit; government employees, if higher revenue yields permit salary increases that exceed the cost of living; and employees in the private sector who are protected by effective unions. Probable losers are generally those who rent rather than own the places where they live; pensioners not adequately protected by cost-of-living increases; employees of debt-saddled local units of government; and nonunionized or inadequately unionized employees. The losers to inflation are not precisely the same groups as the losers to unemployment, but there is overlap. For example, the nonunionized are often the most vulnerable to an abrupt loss of purchasing power, either through sudden loss of a job or through steep rises in the cost of living. In any event, excessive inflation has a redistributive effect that is clearly not the same as that which social reformers seek to bring about. In other words, it does not distribute well-being more evenly. Indeed, its net effect is probably to increase inequality in the scales of well-being, enlightenment, respect, and power although not so neatly and dramatically as does recession and unemployment.

Inflation entails costs for a nation's economy as well as for individuals and families within it. Those responsible for guiding the economy as a whole (the government) and those making decisions for the economic sectors (the managers of giant corporations) find that inflation reduces their capacity to predict economic trends beyond the short run. Thus, they are forced to focus their attention on finding solutions to immediate problems. The result is a stop-go mentality, which was first noticed in Great Britain in the early 1960s. For over 20 years, British governments have tinkered with the economy, continually attempting to shore up the purchasing power of the pound by periodic deflationary measures, which were taken every few months. The British economy has spluttered along with the lowest rate of growth in the First World and Great Britain has fallen from near the top of the league standings of positive economic indicators to the lower third. Today, it leads only the countries of Mediterranean Europe, which started from a vastly weaker economic base at the end of World War II. The parallel result has been that British industry, lacking certainty and confidence in the future, has not invested as heavily in modernization anywhere near to the extent that its rivals in Western Europe and elsewhere in the world have done. With lagging productivity and high production costs, the share of the world market that British industry is capable of capturing has steadily declined over the past 30 years. But it may be argued that the costs of *not* coping with inflation would have been equally as high. Inflation means higher prices for the goods and services a country produces and offers to the world. A country that experiences higher rates of inflation than do others is pricing its goods and services out of the world market, the end result of which would again be a loss of jobs.

Theories explaining what causes inflation abound. The most familiar debate is probably that between the Keynesians and the monetarists. They are not far apart in assessing the causes of inflation but they differ in their proposed solutions. Both schools of economic thinking accept the orthodox position that prices rise because demand for goods and services exceeds supply. Both agree that this is because consumer purchasing power has risen too fast while increases in productivity have lagged behind. The two schools part company when they begin to look for remedies. Keynesians tend to look to short- or middle-range government fiscal and monetary adjustments designed to reduce purchasing power to ease the inflationary pressure. The fiscal remedies they propose consist of increasing government revenue, thus, taking purchasing power out of the hands of the consumer, or reducing government expenditures, thus, lessening the amount of money available to both the consumer and the investor. The monetary adjustments they suggest involve a number of methods, for example, forcing interest rates up, thus, the government restrains the expansion of the money supply and prevents the inflationary condition in which too much money chases too few goods.

Monetarists prefer a longer term solution to inflation, arguing that the Keynesian approach dooms the economy to continuous oscillation between recession and inflation. They focus on ways of controlling money supply. They argue in favor of a stable supply of money or a gradual growth in the money supply at a stable rate of growth, and they insist on the necessity of keeping government revenue and spending in balance so as not to undo the effects of the desired monetary policy. Keynesians, on the other hand, believe that the government should gain a surplus of revenue over spending in inflationary times and incur a deficit when the economy is heading toward a recession. This practice of fine-tuning is self-defeating according to the monetarists, who argue that both economic growth and monetary stability can be achieved through a steady, consistent application of monetary measures.

The demand-pull explanation for inflation is shared by the Keynesians and the monetarists, constituting two competing versions of the same orthodoxy. Opposed to both versions are a variety of cost-push theories that start from the premise that rising prices are the result of the acts of producers and suppliers passing on their costs to the consumer. According to these theories, prices would rise in response to increasing costs regardless of the levels of demand for, and supply of, goods and services. A very simplified version of such a theory is the one that assigns responsibility for rising prices to increased energy costs resulting from arbitrary decisions by the Organization of Petroleum Exporting Countries (OPEC) to raise the price of oil sold on the world market. Because petroleum serves as the principal energy source for First World industry, these massive oil price increases must be reflected ultimately in precipitous elevations of the consumer price index (CPI). This theory is especially popular in the United States, where energy costs and the price of gas at the pump have been kept much lower than in Western Europe owing to government price controls. Although the real effect has been no greater in the United States, the oil price increases of the 1970s and early 1980s have come as a greater shock to Americans than to Europeans. This can be better understood when it is realized that, unlike the United States, before the 1970s, Western Europe was not energy self-sufficient. Thus, Europeans were more aware of their vulnerability to energy suppliers.

A cost-push explanation for inflation that is more popular in Western Europe, especially in inflation-prone Great Britain, is the wage-push subtype. This theory suggests that inflation reaches high levels because of the power of trade unions and their ability to force wage increases that exceed price increases and do not reflect corresponding increases in productivity. If the wage increases were geared to rises in output per man-hour, the unit cost of producing a particular good would not increase. But the ability of trade unions to pull their membership off the job if wage demands are not satisfied impels employers to give in to wage demands that are far in excess of productivity gains because they realize that they will be able to pass on the cost increase to the consumer. The employers lose nothing because they are able to recoup their profits by matching cost increases with price increases. If the consumers are also wage earners whose trade unions have succeeded in keeping their wages ahead of inflation, they will not suffer. But, if they belong to no union or to a weak union, they are victims of inflation.

Political parties and groups of the left will not buy the wage-push argument however. They advance still another cost-push theory of inflation. This theory centers on the power of monopolistic and oligopolistic corporations, especially multinational corporations, to administer prices. They raise prices at will because there is a lack of competition that would otherwise force prices to respond to the true relationship of supply and demand. Thus, not only can giant producers charge the consumer excessive prices for the goods they sell directly on the market but they can also increase the cost of producing other goods if they are supplying the energy, raw materials, or semi-finished goods that go into the production of consumer goods. Even though producers of these consumer goods may be in a competitive situation, the fact that all of them are charged the same high prices by their suppliers means that there is an absolute floor below which the price passed on to the consumer will not fall. Even if the demand for goods sold under monopolistic conditions falls, it is unlikely that the price will fall because the manufacturer can continue to realize a profit by cutting back production while maintaining the higher price; or the manufacturer can turn to production of alternative goods for which there is a market. The result is loss of jobs in certain economic sectors and for certain categories of employees while prices remain at high levels, that is, stagflation.

It can be seen from the foregoing that one's explanation for stagflation and its dilemmas depends on what one chooses to pay attention to, and the same may be said of proposed solutions. In turning to questions of public policy in Chapters Six and Seven, we will address ourselves to the question of why some First World countries have found stagflation more manageable than have others. Returning to Tables 2.1 and 2.2, it will be recalled that West Germany has had relatively low levels of *both* unemployment and inflation until very recently, levels that Americans, Britons, and Italians can only envy. Perhaps the comparison of First World countries with one another can give us insight into why stagflation varies in intensity and what remedies have had a better track record than others.

## POSTINDUSTRIAL SOCIAL CLASS STRUCTURE

It was emphasized in Chapter One that a prominent feature of mature industrialism in Europe was intensified conflict between social classes. Is this still the case as European societies reach postindustrialism? Let us review the postindustrial social class structure; this will enable us to assess the impact of social structure on the politics of postindustrial societies in later chapters. We will focus on the hierarchy of social groupings that is based essentially on occupation and the prestige assigned by the society to each occupational category. In other words, we will look at the varying shares that different social classes have of the four values of power, respect, well-being, and enlightenment. Do postindustrial societies distribute these values differently than in earlier periods?

### THE COMPLEXITIES OF CONTEMPORARY SOCIAL STRUCTURE

One factor that complicates the analysis of class structure for all Western European countries is that, even if one focuses on occupation for assigning individuals or families to positions on the scale, there is no single, unambiguous scale. Instead, one must deal with the concurrent existence of old and new occupations that require different criteria for placing them somewhere in a hierarchical order. The Italian sociologist, Luciano Gallino, has suggested that the social structure in Italy today can be understood only if one realizes that there exist simultaneously a *traditional*, a *modern*, and a *contemporary* class structure.[7] The continuation of an agrarian economy in southern Italy, with its dominant land-

[7]Luciano Gallino, "Italy," in Margaret Scotford Archer and Salvador Giner, eds., *Contemporary Europe: Class, Status and Power* (London: Weidenfeld and Nicolson, 1973), pp. 110–115.

Contrasts in postindustrial societies: a pastoral scene in rural Scotland, and an urban street scene in industrialized England.

owning class and numerically large peasantry, is a carryover of traditional society into the late twentieth century. In our terms, southern Italian society is still largely preindustrial or early industrial although important changes are taking place. In different parts of northern and central Italy, what Gallino calls modern and contemporary social structures can be found. Gallino's modern class system corresponds roughly to what we described as mature industrial society, whereas his contemporary class system would be that which is found in postindustrial society. In the former, the capitalist is preeminent; in the latter, it is the new class of managers and technocrats who provide leadership. The industrial working class is numerically the largest in modern society, whereas those in the service sector predominate in contemporary society.

In the case of the artisans, whose plight was depicted in Chapter One, their position is strongest in Gallino's traditional society. It is already becoming eroded in modern society as artisans are becoming indistinguishable from skilled industrial workers. By the time we reach contemporary, or postindustrial society, artisans have all but disappeared. Thus, as a class, the occupational category first slipped downward on the social scale and then became essentially a noncategory. If Gallino is right, we would expect to find artisans still an important component of the social structure in southern Italy. Elsewhere in Western Europe, they will be fading from the scene. In the case of independent farmers, their position will be strongest where the modern class structure prevails, for example, in Bavaria or in parts of western and central France today. Industrialization is taking place in these areas, leading farmers to profit from the increased use of labor-saving farm machinery and from the growth of urban markets for farm products. However, as the economy advances further toward postindustrialism, the medium-sized farm will be squeezed out by large agribusinesses and the independent farmer may have to give up farming altogether. In parts of northern France, particularly in the breadbasket for the Paris region, this has been taking place.

In fact, even in southern Italy, it can no longer be said that the social-stratification system is clearly of one type more than any other. Since 1950, the Italian state has invested heavily in the modernization of the *Mezzogiorno* ("southern region"). Heavy industry has been fostered and the development of commercial agriculture encouraged. Much of the effort of industrialization has been undertaken by the public sector through large state holding companies, notably in the petrochemical industry. However, the impact on the occupational structure has been selective. Relatively little of the investment has gone into the development of labor-intensive industry. Thus, although the south has registered substantial economic growth since 1950, nevertheless, employment has actually declined. Unemployment levels have remained well above national averages and large numbers of workers have left to find employment in northern Italy or in other European countries. There remain many small manufacturing firms and marginal farms, and considerable numbers of southern Italians, both in the larger cities and in the small towns and villages, exist at, or below, the poverty level. Incomes and living standards of others have risen, but this has also meant higher southern rates of consumption of goods produced in the north with accompanying trade deficits for southern Italy in relation to the north.

In some ways, southern Italy resembles the semi-industrial nations of parts of the Third World that exist economically in a symbiotic, but essentially dependent, relationship with the core nations of the First World. Investment capital comes from the north, but return on investment returns to the north. Migrant workers move from south to north, learning skills in northern industry and sending money to families back home. But many remain where the higher paid jobs are and never return with their skills to their home region. Much of the technically sophisticated, highly paid supervisory personnel in the new industries of the south are northerners sent by their firms or agencies for tours of duty in the south; but their career objectives lie northward. Nor do bright young southerners display counterbalancing tendencies. Moreover, state investment funds often have to be routed through a maze of offices that siphon off overhead to maintain overinflated staffs. Despite the considerable expenditure of state funds earmarked for the development of the southern region, the relative per capita income of the region remains where it was before 1950—at approximately one-half that of the rest of the country.

Elsewhere in Western Europe (including northern Italy), the features of postindustrial society are taking shape in the sense that the occupational structure is increasingly oriented to large-scale public and private units that are coming to dominate the primary, secondary, and tertiary (service) sectors of the economy. Small-scale producers and distributors have not ceased to exist, but they now find themselves dependent on large-scale suppliers and often on large-scale purchasers of their goods or services. They are also the most vulnerable to economic uncertainties, such as precipitous increases in energy costs or interest rates. The trend has been for small family farms and businesses to merge with one another into larger units, to be bought out by agribusinesses or chains, or to be liquidated by creditors. This has, of course, accompanied the movement of population from farms and small towns to larger population centers. It has also meant that many of the offspring of self-employed parents have become employees of the government or of large corporations, with little intergenerational movement in the opposite direction. The result of all this has been a complex social structure that reflects the superimposition of a new postindustrial pattern on a still existent industrial/early industrial pattern. There is also the fact that the new structure is itself quite complex because large-scale organization is complex.

## POSTINDUSTRIAL SOCIAL CLASSES

At the top of today's stratification system in Western Europe, the old aristocracy has been largely displaced by the owners and top executives of private corporations as well as by professionals of various kinds (doctors, lawyers, government officials) who are in a favorable market position concerning the supply of, and demand for, their services. For example, in Great Britain, the richest 5 percent of income earners earn approximately 15 percent of all personal income.[8] In France, whereas only 4 percent of income earners in 1970 earned more than 60,000 francs (about $15,000 at 1970 values), 45 percent earned less than 15,000 francs (about $3750).[9]

In the middle range of the postindustrial stratification system, occupational categories are the most diverse. One finds both the declining ranks of small businesspersons and independent farmers and the growing numbers of scientific and technical professionals, middle-management personnel, white-collar workers, and skilled workers. The first two categories are the better paid, sharing with the upper-income earners a better education and a more favorable market position. Younger men and women in these categories may aspire to considerably higher incomes later in their careers as they move up the corporate ladder or shuttle back and forth between the public and private sectors. What distinguishes these various types of professionals from those below them in the middle-income ranks is their possession of *knowledge* that enables them to manipulate postindustrial technology and economic factors. They have invested time early in their careers to acquire this knowledge. The investment has more often than not been the result of early socialization in middle-class families, where acquisition of knowledge and investment for future gain are values in which high priority is placed. It is also likely to reflect a superior education at the primary and secondary levels, more readily available to middle-class than to working-class children in the stratified Western European educational systems. Although these higher occupational categories of the middle-income range represent at most (perhaps) 15 percent of the total employed in Western European countries, they are the most rapidly growing categories.

The two remaining middle-income categor-

[8]John Westergaard and Henrietta Resler, *Class in a Capitalist Society: A Study of Contemporary Britain* (New York: Basic Books, 1975), p. 40.

[9]Jane Marceau, *Class and Status in France: Economic Change and Social Immobility 1945-1975* (Oxford: Clarendon, 1977), p. 48.

ies, white-collar workers and skilled manual workers, differ in many respects from the above categories and from one another. It has been the tradition in European sociology to place the first category in the middle class and the second in the working class. This reflects attitudes and life-styles of an earlier era as well as the heavy influence of Karl Marx on European sociology. Today, one can question whether the earlier classifications of industrial Europe are still relevant, whether, for example, the social and economic distance between skilled and unskilled workers has not become greater than that between white-collar workers and skilled workers. Indeed, it might be argued that by function and training skilled workers are more akin to the engineers and technicians discussed above than are the white-collar workers. By length of education and by income levels, secretaries, file clerks, and keypunch operators may, indeed, have become the new proletariat of postindustrial society. However, two arguments can be made to support the counterposition that nonmanual workers, including white-collar workers, still enjoy advantages over even the highest paid manual workers.

In the first place, it is questionable whether, strictly in economic terms, the reputed overlapping has actually taken place. The tendency to focus on wages and salaries has probably been encouraged by the fact that European trade unions have made these their principal indicators of success. Wage increases are the most tangible evidence of a trade union's ability to promote worker interests. What has tended to go unnoticed has been the relative disadvantage of manual workers as compared with nonmanual workers in other respects. Manual workers are paid weekly, biweekly, or monthly wages, whereas nonmanual workers have annual salaries. Often, the manual workers must add overtime work to their usual number of hours per week to reach the income level of the white-collar worker in the same firm at the same level of seniority. Nonmanual workers enjoy greater security of tenure; cutbacks usually affect the manual before the nonmanual employees.

There is also an impressive array of fringe benefits that are more likely to be enjoyed by nonmanual than by manual workers. In a 1968 survey of British corporations, it was found that 90 percent of the firms had formal pension schemes for clerical workers, whereas only 67 percent had them for manual workers. In 74 percent of the firms, clerical workers enjoyed holidays of 15 days or more, whereas the same was true for manual workers in only 38 percent of the firms. Clerical workers in 84 percent of the firms could take time off with pay for personal reasons; manual workers could do so in only 29 percent of the firms. For lateness, 90 percent of the firms deducted from the pay of manual workers, whereas only 8 percent did so for clerical workers![10] Some observers have pointed to the rise of white-collar unionism in Europe as a sign that white-collar workers perceive that the distance between them and blue-collar workers is diminishing. This may be so, but the effect of white-collar unionism is likely to be the maintenance of the distance already enjoyed.

A second argument emphasizes the psychological differences that prevail between industrial workers and members of the middle class. The future prospects of young persons entering the ranks of construction workers and those of junior clerks sitting behind a desk are not at all similar. The former will see their earnings increase gradually over the years, but their chances for status advancement within their occupational category are dim. Clerks, on the other hand, can anticipate a career that promises periodic advancement up a status hierarchy with accompanying salary increases as well. Although junior clerks may be earning less than 40-year-old construction workers, the chances are that they will be earning noticeably more than construction workers by the time they reach 40—and substantially more by the time they reach retirement.

What this suggests is that office clerks and their families can plan a rational program of investment in the future, a future that holds great potential for improvement in economic position

[10]Dorothy Wedderburn and Christine Craig, "Relative Deprivation in Work," in Dorothy Wedderburn, ed., *Poverty, Inequality and Class Structure* (London: Cambridge University Press, 1974), pp. 141–164.

and in social status. For construction workers, the prospects for the future seem only marginally better than the present. Their tendency is to focus on the here and now. If, since the 1950s, European manual workers have begun to acquire the material prerequisites of middle-class status —washing machines, televisions, and automobiles—it has simply been part of a well-established working-class tendency to spend now the money they have rather than invest it in the future. Installment buying has become the fashion among European working-class families, whereas middle-class families are more apt to save for the future.

Similar differences can be seen in attitudes toward education. Unlike the American educational system, most European countries make a fairly rigid distinction at the secondary level between schools that prepare the student for university education and the professions and schools that prepare the student for various manual and nonmanual occupations, which can be entered on finishing school at 17 or 18. The grammar school in Great Britain, the *lycée* in France, and the *gymnasium* in Germany are means by which the cream of the crop are separated at around the age of 12 from the majority of their age group and prepared for those roles in life that will mean higher income and status. Despite the fact that these schools are maintained by the state and are free and open to anyone who is qualified, children from middle-class families have a much better chance of meeting the entrance requirements than do children from working-class families. Still greater is the disparity between the classes in the likelihood of one's advancement to higher education. In all Western European countries, there has been a massive expansion of the state-supported university system since about 1960, but the net result has been to improve the chances of middle-class children for higher education without significantly increasing the chances of working-class offspring.

What accounts for these disparities? One explanation is similar to one often cited in the United States to account for the poor educational record of blacks and other deprived ethnic minorities. The schools are middle-class institutions. The language taught, the intellectual tools employed, the standards of evaluation used, and the teachers who apply them are all middle class. Even if the teacher is from a working-class background, he or she has become socialized into the middle class through advanced education. Teaching is, after all, a middle-class occupation.

A related explanation emphasizes the resistance of working-class families to the education of their children beyond the level required to assure them of manual jobs. Again, we see the disinclination of the working-class family to invest in the future. Without the incentives usually supplied by middle-class families to encourage their children to achieve in school, working-class children are likely to be satisfied with a mediocre performance, and their life prospects are, thus, fore-doomed to be mediocre. However, there have been indications that, at least, the higher paid elite of the European working class have begun to adopt certain aspects of the middle-class lifestyle: more time spent by the father at home with his family, the adoption of middle-class norms and values through the mass media, and a widening of one's geographical horizons by having an automobile. Perhaps an increasing percentage of working-class families are also encouraging their children to achieve in school. Since the 1960s, the British Labour Party has been making a concerted effort to replace the élite grammar schools with comprehensive schools that are organized somewhat like American high schools. This effort has been emulated by left-of-center parties in other European countries as well. It may help to lessen the educational disadvantage of the working-class child.

## WOMEN AND IMMIGRANTS IN THE WORK FORCE

The above arguments ignore a crucial factor of increasing political significance in Western Europe as well as the United States: the fact that large percentages of white-collar workers are women and that overwhelmingly the largest percentages of women are found in the lowest paid white-collar jobs. In Western Europe, as in the United States, efforts are being made by governments and by private employers to place more women in higher paid positions of greater responsibility. Yet, the chief beneficiaries thus far have been women with advantageous social and educational backgrounds. Young women from middle-class families are entering universities in greater numbers and coming out with qualifications that enable them to compete with men on a more equal basis in the liberal professions and for junior management positions. As yet they have not invaded postindustrial fields, such as the natural sciences and engineering, in great numbers. But young women from working-class families are even less likely than their male counterparts to go on to higher education; nor are they anywhere near as likely to go on to technical schools or the apprenticeships that will lead to their becoming skilled workers. Accordingly, on leaving school at around age 16, perhaps having learned to type and take shorthand, they seek jobs as store clerks, secretarial assistants, or as members of typing pools.

Prospects for advancement are limited for women in the lowest paid white-collar jobs. The expectation of their employers is that they will soon get married and raise families, thus, becoming dependent on their husbands for their future economic and social positions. After the child-raising years, they may return to similar jobs at about the same rank as before but now with even less chance for future promotion to higher paying jobs because they have less future ahead of them. What this adds up to is the fact that, if we can say that the white-collar worker has better long-term job prospects than the skilled worker, it is clearly the *man* white-collar worker that we have in mind. In terms of both the tangible and intangible rewards of their work, women in the lower paid clerical jobs should probably be classified with the semiskilled and unskilled workers at the bottom of the occupational scale.

An industrial proletariat still exists in Western Europe. It consists of manual workers who now perform the tasks that technological advances have not yet rendered unnecessary—and probably never will. These include a wide variety of jobs, from watching over and occasionally adjusting the automated machines to serving as waiters in restaurants, to collecting trash, to sweeping public buildings. If women occupy the lowest paid levels of the nonmanual occupational categories, migrant workers, both men and women, are their counterparts in the manual categories. Like women white-collar workers, migrant workers occupy the jobs that are the worst paid and the least likely to enjoy union protection. As individuals, they are marginal to the employment structures of the countries where they work. As a class of workers, however, they are indispensable. They perform tasks that must be performed by someone if the factories are to be kept running and the streets are not to become blocked by mountains of garbage. Workers (especially men) indigenous to the more highly industrialized regions and countries of Western Europe will no longer engage in such work. If necessary, they prefer unemployment compensation while waiting for more desirable jobs to reopen. Hence, governments and employers in northern Europe have encouraged the immigration of hundreds of thousands of unskilled workers from countries along the shores of the Mediterranean and, in the case of Great Britain, Commonwealth citizens from West Indian, Asian, and African countries that were formerly part of the British Empire.

During the 1960s, large numbers of young men from Portugal, southern Italy, and Spain, from Greece, Turkey, and Yugoslavia; and from Algeria, Morocco, and Tunisia arrived in northern Europe and became important percentages of the working populations of Belgium, France, Great Britain, Switzerland, and West Germany, among others. In France, by 1968, their numbers had reached 6.3 percent of the labor force, including 8.7 percent of skilled workers, 10.6 percent of semiskilled workers, and 21.6 percent of unskilled workers. Moreover, they concentrated in the larger cities. Immigrants in the West German cities of Frankfurt, Munich, and Stuttgart constituted 17 percent of the population of those cities by the early 1970s. Approximately one third of the immigrants in Great Britain and France lived in the London and Paris areas. This meant around 500,000 residents in each city. Paid the poorest wages and discriminated against

"Instant slums" outside Paris. These are called Bidonvilles (shanty-towns, or literally "tin-can towns"). Such slums in France and in other Western European countries house North African and other foreign workers who perform low-paid service labor.

by landlords, they occupied the lowest standard housing, often crowded several to a room.[11]

When economic conditions took a turn for the worse in the 1970s, the governments of the host countries sought to restrict the flow of immigrants, and, indeed, the number of workers entering these countries declined. But, because indigenous workers could not be found to take over jobs that were still available in the recession, many of the immigrants who had originally entered on a temporary basis stayed. Much of the influx of the 1970s came in the persons of wives and children who had earlier been left behind. Second generation southerners were now entering the schools and the job market in increasing numbers. What had been regarded as a temporary expedient, to assist the economy in a boom period, now was becoming a chronic social condition. Homogeneous societies, like West

Germany and France, were becoming multiethnic, and neither governments, private corporations, nor trade unions were geared to deal with the resulting problems. There has been increasing militancy on the part of migrant workers. They have formed their own organizations and have engaged in wildcat strikes, sit-ins, and demonstrations, sometimes touching off backlash violence by native workers who feel economically and socially threatened. In France, the Communist Party has called for the ending of legal as well as illegal immigration, thus, echoing the demands of rightwingers in Great Britain. Postindustrial society may have lessened the social distance between the relatively highly paid and skilled indigenous men workers (manual and nonmanual), but it seems to have created the roots of a new class struggle, which may be all the harder to resolve because occupational and economic bases of distinction are overlaid by racial, linguistic, and even sex distinctions.

At the bottom of the scale of material well-being are those members of society in the First

[11]Thierry Baudouin, et al., "Women and Immigrants: Marginal Workers?" in Colin Cronch and Alessandro Pizzorno, eds., The Resurgence of Class Conflict in Western Europe Since 1968, vol. 2 (New York: Holmes & Meier, 1978), p. 74.

World who, for a variety of reasons, are unable to meet the requirements of the postindustrial occupational structure. These include the elderly, the handicapped and disabled, single mothers and orphans, among others. The state welfare system provides the minimum necessary to ensure that these unfortunate minorities will be able to subsist at a low standard of living. When recession hits, their numbers are swollen by the addition of the temporarily unemployed. Along with women and immigrants at the margins of the occupational structure, these are the people who are most vulnerable to upward and downward economic spirals. Indeed, the numbers of the chronically poor who are women and who are members of minority ethnic groups are disproportionately large. In prosperous times, although their numbers are smaller, the poor are apt to suffer the disadvantage of being relatively invisible while the majority of society assumes their nonexistence. Most First World countries, despite their material abundance, are far from having eradicated poverty.

## INTERCOUNTRY DIFFERENCES IN CLASS STRUCTURE

Let us now see what elements in the class structure of each of our four principal countries diverge from the general model of postindustrial social structure and stand out most sharply. France and Italy will each be treated separately because these two countries have not experienced postindustrial conditions as universally as have Great Britain and West Germany. We will begin by comparing the social structures of the latter two countries, pointing out certain differences that may not appear on the surface. Then we will turn individually to the two Latin countries, where past, present, and future seem to be mixed together in equal proportions.

### GREAT BRITAIN AND WEST GERMANY

One should not assume that either Great Britain or West Germany is uniformly industrialized and urbanized. Parts of southwestern England, northern Wales, and northern Scotland are still rural although certainly far removed from the nineteenth century. Preoccupation with the industrial sophistication of the Ruhr area should not blind one to the fact that much of the land area of West Germany is devoted to agriculture, such as in Bavaria and the Rhineland-Palatinate. Nevertheless, there is little left in either society to remind one of preindustrial times; little remains of the localized, precommercial farming of the early industrial period. In Western Europe, only small countries, like Belgium or the Netherlands, have gone further toward full-scale postindustrialism, that transcends regional diversities. The social characteristics that are relatively unique to Great Britain and to West Germany, respectively, are to be found, not in the agricultural sector, but in how the postindustrial social structure differs from the norm set forth earlier. To put it simply and without implying stark contrasts, British society exhibits greater distance between its social classes, whereas West German society shows a greater degree of interclass amalgamation.

Since World War II, social change in West Germany has been more evident than it has in Great Britain. On the other hand, it must be acknowledged that Germany had further to go to achieve a relatively egalitarian society, especially if one compared the two countries' class structures at the turn of the century. Nor has West Germany ceased to be a class-conscious society; elements still remain of the preindustrial hierarchy. We are simply suggesting that class consciousness has eroded to a greater degree than in Great Britain. There are two principal ways in which class consciousness has been perpetuated in Great Britain. First, there is still a relatively high correlation between high rankings on the scales of power, well-being, respect, and enlightenment. Second, the British working class continues to see itself as separate and distinct from the middle class and to behave accordingly; the middle class does likewise. In West Germany, perceptions of interclass differences are diminishing as working-class and middle-class lifestyles become less distinguishable from one another.

The association of the bourgeoisie with the aristocracy to form a new ruling class occurred earlier and with less friction in Great Britain than in the other major European countries. This permitted the new ruling class to establish itself firmly during the nineteenth century and to maintain its hold on the economy and political system in this century. In the nineteenth century, the exclusive public schools (what Americans would call private secondary schools) became the training ground for the sons of the emerging ruling class. The boys of both aristocratic and capitalist families came together in the commons rooms and on the playing fields of Eton, Rugby, and Winchester, and, then, went on together to Oxford and Cambridge. Later, they entered careers in politics, government service, banking, and industry. To a remarkable extent, the public schools and Oxbridge are still the socializers and recruitment channel for the British Establishment.

Oxbridge graduates predominate in the House of Commons (in both major parties), the higher civil service, and the executive ranks of the private sector. However, the state grammar schools are preparing larger percentages of students for Oxford and Cambridge, and the newer universities have begun to infiltrate the seats of power with their graduates. The Labour Party has made a concerted effort, despite Conservative resistance, to expand the comprehensive school at the expense of the grammar school in the state educational sector; but it has done very little to threaten the position of the prestigious public school. Although the numbers of those educated by the latter are small, their significance in the larger world is great.

The journalist, Anthony Sampson, has documented the large number of interconnections that can be found between the top leadership of government, the trade unions, banks, and insurance companies, industry, the press, the universities, and other seats of power and influence in Great Britain.[12] He does not go so far as to suggest that this complex constitutes a power élite in the sense of a conspiracy of the few to monopolize power in what is a democracy in name only, but some British writers do.[13] Indeed, Sampson argues that there are conflicts of interest among these various élites so that the structure fits a pluralist rather than an élitist model of power. This is undoubtedly true (see Chapter Six). Nevertheless, it must also be acknowledged that similar backgrounds and socialization experiences have made it possible for most of these wielders of British institutional power to communicate easily with one another because they share the same assumptions as to how things should be done and what the outcomes should be.

Much attention has been paid to the role of the monarchy, the House of Lords, the Established Church, and other dignified institutions in sustaining the image of British society as hierarchical and foreordained. The Queen today is far less of a political leader than she is a social leader who sets the standards of social propriety. It is unlikely that the titled nobility, both old and new, could survive if the monarchy were to be abolished. If titles in general were to be abolished, however, the British upper classes would probably find new ways to distinguish themselves from those below them on a social scale. Harold Wilson, the son of a skilled worker in Yorkshire, accepted knighthood on retiring as Prime Minister. Winston Churchill, grandson of the Duke of Marlborough, declined an earldom. The contrast suggests the continuing aura of upper-class symbolism for those of lower social origins and the confidence of the aristocracy in its position on the social scale regardless of the badges of status.

Perhaps it is the smooth evolutionary pattern of social change that occurred in Great Britain during industrialization that helps explain the tenacity of this interlacing of wealth, social status, and power. Here, the contrast between Great Britain and Germany is sharpest. Germany's *Junker* class was as firmly entrenched in the seats of power as any aristocracy in Europe in 1914. But two world wars, severe economic

---

[12]Anthony Sampson, *Anatomy of Britain Today* (New York: Harper & Row, 1965).

[13]See Ralph Miliband, *The State in Capitalist Society: An Analysis of the Western System of Power* (London: Quartet Books, 1973).

crises, and the coming of new men to power with the rise of Adolph Hitler all helped to disband the various sectors of Germany's ruling class. The defeat in World War I began the process of seriously undermining the class's political position. Although retaining its foothold in the army and the state bureaucracy, the ruling class lost its possession of the leading political roles to representatives of the middle class and even the working class during the Weimar Republic. Inflation and severe agricultural depression in the 1920s dealt a death blow to the economic position of the *Junkers*, while creating vast new wealth in the industrial sector. In the early 1930s, the *Junkers* and industrialists formed a coalition, which, after exploring several unsuccessful alternatives, finally gave Hitler the financial and political support necessary to bring him to power.

But Hitler had ideas of his own. The rapid military buildup of the 1930s was distinctly advantageous to German industry, as was the Nazi policy of holding down wage demands and enforcing industrial discipline. This assured the new regime of continued support from German industry. The aristocracy fared less well, however, as German agriculture was given relatively low priority and the Nazis systematically undermined the position of the aristocracy in the state bureaucracy and the judiciary by placing the party faithful, drawn from all sectors of society, at their level in parallel hierarchies and by continuously overriding their authority. The last stronghold of the *Junkers* was the military, but Hitler treated the warnings of his General Staff lightly in forcing the pace of diplomatic deterioration that led to World War II. His early successes virtually brought the military opposition to an end, including the strong reservations about his later disastrous invasion of the Soviet Union. As the tide of war began to turn against Hitler, the military became the one center of power that could topple him. In June 1944, the German aristocracy failed in its last political act as a class—the attempted assassination of Hitler.

Military defeat and occupation by the victorious powers ensured that the newly emerging postwar political systems in East Germany and West Germany would be led by representatives of new social groups. In the Federal Republic of Germany today, it can safely be said that there is no longer a self-perpetuating ruling class or even a British-style establishment. The aristocracy has all but disappeared as a cohesive social class. The capitalist class has managed, despite denazification efforts during and after the occupation, to hold on to its economic base of power. Thus, the Krupp family has retained its massive empire in the Ruhr, despite the open complicity of the head of the family with the Nazi regime in the 1930s and 1940s. But one can find a greater degree of functional specialization among the German élites today than exists in Great Britain or than existed before the war in Germany. Industrialists contribute to the campaign chests of the Christian Democratic Union (CDU) and the Free Democratic Party (FDP). But when either of these parties is in power, the leading positions in government are filled by professional politicians drawn from a wide variety of social ranks.

In the economic sector, although the older families retained a share of their former assets, the directive power of the economy passed, as elsewhere, into the hands of new men—corporate executives, financial experts, and economists—who also came from a wider variety of social origins than is the case of their counterparts in Great Britain. If enlightenment is the primary key to the acquisition of other values in postindustrial society, then, it is likely that West Germany has gone further than most other Western European societies. Postwar knowledge and expertise have been substituted for prewar power, well-being, and respect as resources commanding access to the higher positions in the system.

Now let us look at the British and German working classes. Here the differences are less clear. Since the 1950s, the working classes in both countries have enjoyed unprecedented affluence. Families that were lucky enough to be able to afford a bicycle or a radio in 1950 now have medium-priced automobiles and color television sets. Yet, since the mid-1960s, industrial unrest has become increasingly prevalent in Great Britain, whereas West Germany still appears to enjoy one of the easiest relationships between employers and employees to be found anywhere in the capitalist world. It is not by accident that the British economy has experienced a slower rate of growth since 1960 than it had before. British workers have improved their position economically through strident demands and strikes, often expressed in the form of wildcat strikes initiated by union militants against the wishes of the union leadership. These have produced a number of economy-shaking confrontations with employers and the government. Although British workers tend to reinforce their solidarity as a class against other classes in the face of economic challenges, German workers generally tend to reinforce their solidarity with other classes against the common economic problems facing the nation.

What might account for this difference? Impressionistic comparisons of the two working classes suggest that class consciousness is greater among British than among German workers. German workers are more likely than their British counterparts to aspire not only to the material prerequisites but also to the actual status of the middle class—both for themselves and their offspring. Wherever possible, they will emulate middle-class styles of dress (even at work), and they have a greater tendency to accumulate future-oriented capital than do British workers. To at least the older British worker, the desire to distance oneself from one's working-class origins would be seen as a betrayal of those origins. But recent studies have shown a decline in British class consciousness and of the class basis for voting for political parties, which nonetheless remains greater than in most Western European countries.

Part of the reason for the workers' orientation to upward mobility may be found in the German educational system. Although Germany has the same division at the secondary level between the university-oriented school for the talented minority and the more generalized schools for the majority, she also has more alternative technical schools available. Particularly important are the widespread opportunities for further education beyond the point when one leaves school. This means that if children are placed in the lower stream at the secondary level (in West Germany, the *hauptschule* or *realschule* rather than the upper-stream *gymnasium*), they are not cut off from opportunities for later upward mobility. The opportunity to improve one's skills and even to move from blue-collar to white-collar status does not merely exist in West Germany, it is required. Young workers must continue their education on a part-time basis after leaving the ordinary school (if they have not completed 12 years), and employers must provide facilities or release time from work for that purpose.

Probably the most decisive factor in reducing the sense of interclass barriers in West Germany has been the rapid economic growth experienced until the mid-1970s. Increasing affluence seems to have played a greater role in the *embourgeoisement* of the West German worker than has been true in the other Western European countries. As a consequence, the response of the Social Democratic Party (SDP) to the economic crisis of the mid-1970s was to move to the right, toward the center of the political spectrum in its social and economic policies. In so doing, it has moved against the leftward current that can be found in other European Socialist parties—for example, the British Labour Party and the Swedish Social Democrats whose leadership has moved sharply to the left since 1970 as well as the French and Italian Socialists who sought closer ties with the Communists during the mid-1970s. Under the leadership of their moderate Chancellor, Helmut Schmidt, the German Social Democrats have, in effect, repudiated their left wing and worked closely with the middle-class FDP. This reflects not only an effort to attract middle-class support but also a realization that the party's working-class base prefers the *status quo*. Working-class and middle-class voters in West Germany are attracted by essentially the same middle-of-the-road programs.

FRANCE

Slower to industrialize than Great Britain or Germany, France had long had both a rural-urban dimension in its social structure, which dated back to preindustrial times, and the more recently developed bourgeois/proletariat dichotomy of industrialism. In 1950, 28 percent of the French work force was engaged in agriculture as against 22 percent in West Germany and 6 percent in Great Britain. By 1976, the French figure was down to 11 percent and that of West Germany and Great Britain was down to 7 percent and 3 percent respectively.[14] Before this decline began, most French agricultural production was carried out in small, relatively uneconomical farm units with landholdings often divided up into bits and pieces that were not adjacent to one another. In the 1950s and 1960s, substantial consolidation took place, often by enterprising young farmers who managed to combine their holdings and buy up surrounding land while increasing the land's productivity through mechanization. Other young people left the farms and were absorbed in white-collar and blue-collar occupations in a period of rapid economic growth. As a result, the much smaller agricultural population is more affluent and less distinguishable in attitudes and lifestyle from the middle class in France's many medium-sized cities and small towns. French farmers are better organized today and are more influential in the making of agricultural policy—as seen by the substantial benefits the French Government was able to win for French agriculture in bargaining over the Common Agricultural Policy (CAP) of the European Community (EC). The rural-urban cleavage, so prominent in earlier French politics, has now become (as in Great Britain and Germany) largely a thing of the past.

The same cannot be said of the other longstanding social cleavage in France—between the urban middle class and the industrial workers—which is symbolized by the rigid division of the Paris population into the middle-class neighborhoods, found in the center of the city and the western suburbs, and the working-class suburbs, found immediately north, east, and south of the central city. Although the revolutionary tradition in France means that all social classes support the principle of full equality in civic and political rights, the social barriers have always been high and virtually insurmountable. This remains the case today. Only an insignificant percentage of the students in French universities are of working-class origin. The universities are regarded as a middle-class preserve, which neither working-class parents nor their children would seriously consider invading. This remains true even for the more affluent workers at a time when economic benefits are more widespread. The workers in the highest paying industries, such as automobile manufacture and metallurgy, are organized in the most militant trade union affiliates of the militant General Confederation of Labor (CGT)—Communist-dominated—and the French Democratic Confederation of Labor (CFDT)—non-Communist, but aggressively assertive. Members of the working class prefer to live in homogeneous working-class areas and to associate with similar others.

On the other hand, it is true that younger workers have recently been choosing a different lifestyle from that of their elders. Instead of attending trade union meetings and spending their Sunday mornings selling copies of the Communist weekly newspaper, l'Humanité, they may be taking their families for drives in the country or staying home to watch television—tendencies noted in Great Britain and West Germany as well. A not insignificant number of workers have been leaving the CGT in favor of the CFDT and have been showing their preference for the rejuvenated Socialist Party over the time-worn Communist Party; nevertheless, these are still left-of-center choices. If anything, working-class solidarity behind the parties of the left has been greater in recent years than it was during the 1950s and 1960s, especially when General Charles de Gaulle was cutting into Communist and Socialist working-class support.

Despite some disaffection among younger members of the working class, the CGT and the Communists have been holding their own, largely through the recruitment of workers who have

[14]Stanley Rothman *et al.*, *European Society and Politics: Britain, France and Germany* (St. Paul, Minn.: West, 1976), p. 57; Statistical Office of the European Communities, *op. cit.*, p. 19.

just arrived from the countryside. The rural exodus has included former peasants who see greater opportunities in the cities than on the farms. They enter the industrial work force, however, on the lowest rung, usually in the worst-paying industries where they must work for a number of years to gain the skills that will enable them to move up to higher paying jobs. The more militant trade unions have found that these dissatisfied workers are ripe for organizing. In the midst of rapid economic growth, these workers feel that they are getting the smallest slice of the pie. Thus, they are most susceptible to the argument that the system is rigged for someone else's benefit. The left wing clearly uses different tactics with different groups of workers. With the relatively affluent, they point to concrete benefits that could be gained through the unions' efforts; with underprivileged newcomers, they exploit discontent through time-honored ideological appeals. Thus, the trade unions and parties of the left, especially the Communists, help to reinforce the barriers between the classes, which otherwise might be in the process of coming down because of economic changes.

What seems to emerge, then, is the idea that the French working class retains a sort of psychological image of itself as socially distinct from the middle class. This translates itself into organizational and political behavior that reflects a greater cross-class hostility as well as a hostility to a political system that the French working class believes is dominated by the middle class. This would appear difficult to understand if we looked only at economic indicators, such as the GDP per capita (see Table 1.1, p. 12), according to which France ranks as one of the most affluent countries in Western Europe. Some observers have attempted to explain this anomaly by emphasizing that much of French industry is still divided into small units of production, wherein the daily contact between employer and employee reinforces feelings of class resentment. But this is changing in France, as elsewhere. Consolidation has been taking place rapidly in industry as well as in agriculture, and industry is being directed more by salaried managers rather than by the

owner-families who profit more directly from the labor of their wage-earning employees.

It is still possible that, despite growing affluence, the shares of the expanding pie have been inequitably distributed and that the French worker may be right to perceive the social order as unjust. A study sponsored by the Organization for Economic Cooperation and Development (OECD), published in 1976, lent some support to this possibility. The author of the study, Malcolm Sawyer, measured income distributions in 12 selected Western polyarchies. He measured both pretax and posttax income, employing a variety of standard measures that gave somewhat different, but not radically different, results. In measures of pretax income, France and the United States consistently showed the greatest inequality, and France consistently showed the most unequal distribution of income *after taxes* in Western Europe. Figure 2.1 shows the shares of posttax income of the two lowest deciles of the population in each of the 12 countries. Thus, it can be seen that the poorest 20 percent in France had 4.3 percent of the posttax income, whereas the comparable group in West Germany had 6.5 percent, in Italy 5.1 percent, and in Great Britain 6.3 percent. On the other hand, the richest 20 percent in France had 46.9 percent of the posttax income. The comparable percentages were 46.1, 46.5, and 38.7 for West Germany, Italy, and Great Britain respectively.[15] However, lest one assume too readily that French workers are viewing things objectively and that their hostility to the middle class simply reflects an accurate assessment of their own relative deprivation, it should be noted that the same study found a steady improvement in the economic circumstances of the poorest groups in France in relation to the circumstances of the richest. This has been a slow process, and it is not surprising

[15]Malcolm Sawyer, "Income Distribution in OECD Countries," Organization for Economic Cooperation and Development, *Occasional Studies* (July, 1976), pp. 3–36. Estimates in the study are carefully made from a variety of sources, including government statistics and surveys of households. Narrow differences among countries should be interpreted cautiously; wider differences should be quite reliable however.

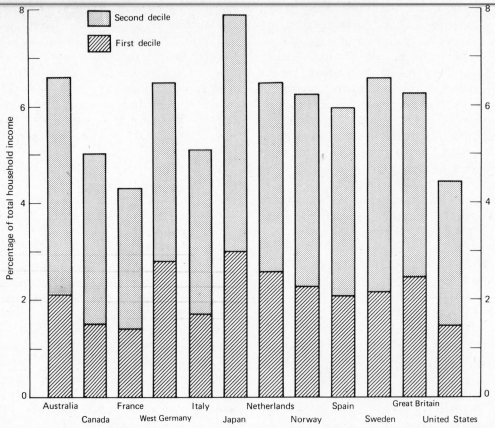

Figure 2.1 Shares of lowest two deciles in posttax household income distribution. [Malcolm Sawyer, "Income Distribution in OECD Countries," Organization for Economic Cooperation and Development, *Occasional Studies* (1976), p. 15.]

that it has not yet affected the perception of the French working class.

## ITALY

Despite what has been said about the differences among Great Britain, West Germany, and France, it should be kept in mind that these are all industrial societies and that the similarities among them outweigh the differences when viewed on a world scale. When we turn to Italy, however, we find in the south what might be called an early industrial subsociety, one that has certain elements in common with some of the more advanced Third World countries and, thus, should be described in terms that differ from those used for most of the rest of Western Europe

and, indeed, for northern Italy as well. For centuries before unification in 1860, southern Italy had been under the rule of absentee monarchs who had had little interest in the development of the area. On the other hand, northern and some of central Italy had been divided into numerous city-states, which were dependencies of Austria-Hungary, and independent kingdoms, many of which had experienced periods of prosperity and had been at one time or another among the most advanced political units in Europe. A measure of this disparity can be seen in the fact that, in 1871, the illiteracy rate of southern Italy (including the islands of Sicily and Sardinia) was nearly 85 percent, whereas that of northwestern Italy was 45 percent. Illiteracy declined rapidly throughout the country in the late nineteenth and early twentieth century, but the disparity between the north and the south remained. In 1971, the illiteracy rate for the south was above 10 percent, whereas in the north it was below 2 percent.[16]

During the years of rapid Italian industrial growth in the 1950s and early 1960s, the industrial work force was growing at the expense of the agricultural and service sectors. Most of this growth was occurring in the north and central parts of Italy. In the south, the service sector has always comprised an unusually large segment of the work force, a phenomenon familiar to many Third World countries. This sector held its own during the period of rapid industrialization; but the agricultural sector in the south declined, whereas the industrial sector was growing. The southern birthrate has always been higher than the northern, but, during this period, the population of the north was growing more rapidly because young southern Italians were moving to the industrial cities of the north as well as to the industrially more advanced countries of Western Europe. The net out-migration from the south between 1951 and 1961 was 1.8 million; in the next decade it rose to 2.3 million. From 1951 to 1961 the net in-migration to the north was 616,000; during the next decade it was 956,000.[17] Beginning in the early 1960s, the government made a concerted effort to stimulate economic development in southern Italy, and the results have been substantial, but emigration has not ceased. Although industrial expansion in northern Italy has meant that an increasing proportion of the out-migrating southerners remain in Italy rather than going to other European countries, the southern Italians are playing the same role in northern Italian cities as the Algerians are in France or the Spanish and Yugoslavians are in West Germany. They are essentially aliens in an unfamiliar territory, and they take the lower paid, less attractive jobs that are shunned by local workers.

In fact, the characteristics of the indigenous northern Italian working class are in many ways similar to those of industrial workers in the other societies we have described. They have been enjoying increasing affluence and have been becoming more of an integral part of the economy and society. As in France, workers in the most advanced industries tend to be the best organized and often the most militant. Italy has more workdays lost because of strikes than any of our other three countries. But the focus of the trade unions, as in Great Britain, is on economic gains—improvement of the material status of the working class. Rapid economic growth has been a heady experience for the Italian working class, giving it the illusion that rising living standards would wipe out existing social barriers. Actually, the industrial explosion of the 1950s brought increased opportunities to exchange working-class for middle-class status. In northern Italy, there was a blossoming of small manufacturing and service-oriented firms, often started by workers who saved some of their wages and invested with the help of friends and relatives. The inhibitions that seem to confine members of the French working class to their own social status do not seem to be so compelling for Italians; the barriers between the classes do not seem to be restrictive. Often an industrial worker will have relatives who have made it across the dividing line and who provide the incentive for their more clever kinfolk to follow in their footsteps. Thus a kind of *embourgeoisement* seems to be taking place at least among the elite of the northern Italian working class.

In southern Italy, where certain preindustrial features (such as the large estates of absentee landlords and the cottage industry system) have persisted into the late twentieth century, there is less adventurousness and willingness to take risk. The ambitious children of peasants, artisans, or agricultural workers are more apt to call on relatives to help them find positions in the central bureaucracy—in Rome or in the provincial bureaucracy in Naples or other overcrowded southern Italian cities—than to seek employment in a factory with the intention of saving up enough money to start a business. The public and semi-public bureaucracies are filled with relatives of

[16]S. S. Acquaviva and M. Santuccio, *Social Structure in Italy: Crisis of a System,* trans. Colin Hamer (London: Martin Robertson, 1976), p. 13.

[17]*Ibid.,* p. 33.

Homeless southern Italians with all of their possessions after the 1980 earthquake that left thousands dead and hundreds of thousands homeless. Many such destitute families were already living at the poverty level before this disaster hit them.

officials who are able to create low-paying, but secure, jobs. Thus, the middle classes in southern Italy are structurally different from those in the north and center. They tend to be more conservative and self-protective, somewhat like the nineteenth-century middling class described in Chapter One than like the aggressive middle class that has been flourishing in the rapidly industrializing northern Italy.

Despite the out-migration of large numbers of workers from southern Italy, there is still a substantial proletariat in the vicinity of the larger cities of the region. Many of these have returned from the north or elsewhere in Europe and are providing the skilled and semiskilled work force for the new industries that are arising in the south with government assistance. But there is also a strikingly large number of what might be called marginal workers who divide their time between farm labor and seasonal work (e.g., in the construction industry). Similar classes can be found on the fringes of other cities in Europe, but they are for the most part foreigners—temporary

workers who are earning hard currency to send home to their families in southern Europe and other Mediterranean countries. The difference is that in Italy these workers are native to the area, but they lack the means to raise themselves and their families above subsistence level. As noted earlier, in all postindustrial countries, there is a class that hovers on the brink of poverty. But, in most countries, this class is made up primarily of the aged and others who cannot secure gainful employment. In southern Italy, it includes a large number of able-bodied workers.

The Italian Communist Party (PCI), has found this marginal element to be a fertile recruiting ground, but these workers are quite different in character from the disciplined, well-organized ranks of the Communist-dominated trade unions in northern and central Italy. They serve as a reminder that Italy is still, in part, an underdeveloped, indeed, a Third World country. In the Third World, when Communist parties are allowed to recruit support, they are generally more militant and revolutionary in objectives than Communist parties in more advanced countries. The Communists in northern Italy have been making moderate appeals and seeking to accomplish their objectives by working within the system. In the south, their clientele is in a much more desperate economic situation. There, the Communists rely on their traditional appeals to a millennial future that will come about as a result of a great proletarian uprising. In this, as in other respects, when one speaks of southern Italy, one must use categories and generalizations that are often used for the Third World today or that were used for Western Europe in the nineteenth century.

## OTHER SOCIAL DIVISIONS

Although social class is the most important social structural factor in the environment of Western European political systems, brief mention should also be made of two other factors that affect social class in different ways in different countries—religion and ethnicity.

## RELIGION

Historically, religion has played a very important role in the politics of all Western European countries. The Protestant Reformation had an immense impact on the countries of northern Europe as did the backlash reaction of the Roman Catholic Church in southern Europe. Religious political parties have, at different times and different places, been central to the politics of almost all continental Western European countries. Our four countries can be readily characterized as follows: Great Britain is a Protestant country, France and Italy are Catholic countries, and West Germany is approximately half Protestant and half Catholic. The situation is actually much more complex than that.

In the first place, in the late twentieth century, despite signs of a renaissance here and there, organized religion is not such an important factor in the average European's life as it was a half-century ago. Many people, especially in urban areas, are atheists, agnostics, or nominal church members who never attend services. Church membership figures in Western European countries usually far exceed that portion of the membership that could be regarded as "religious." This is particularly true in Great Britain where 61 percent of the population identify themselves with the established Church of England but where actual Church of England attendance is only a small fraction of the potential.[18] Generally, the same holds true for the Scottish Presbyterians (the established Church of Scotland). Although British Catholics (8 percent) and nonconformist Protestants (8 percent) show higher attendance rates, those Britons who take religion seriously are decidedly a minority of the overall population.[19]

Religion is more important to more people in the other three countries, and it has greater political significance elsewhere than it has in Great Britain. The Anglicans tend to vote Conservative and the other religions lean to Labour, but social class is much more important in Great Britain in accounting for the two-party vote than is religion. In West Germany, 50 percent of the population is Protestant and 46 percent Catholic. A majority of Catholics support the CDU, the successor of the old Catholic Center Party of the Weimar Republic. But the Christian Democrats have renounced a strictly confessional orientation. They have sought Protestant support and have obtained about one third of the Protestant vote. Indeed, they have captured about 50 percent of the vote of self-employed, middle-class Protestants, which accounts for the inability of their rival, the Social Democrats, to gain more than 45 percent of the Protestant vote. Still, social class is a more important determinant of voting than is the Protestant/Catholic division.[20]

Although France and Italy are both Catholic countries, Roman Catholicism is much more solidly entrenched in the latter. In France, there has always been a very strong strain of anticlericalism. This is not the same as a personal philosophical position about the existence of God. The anticlerical French need not be atheists or agnostic, although many are. What distinguishes the anticlerics is their opposition to any church influence in political matters. What is sought is a complete separation of church and state, which means, for example, the abolition of state subsidies to religious schools.

Although anticlerics are difficult to distinguish from other French men and women, at least for purposes of census taking, voting studies show that there is a strong relationship between anticlericalism and left-wing voting. This can be seen from electoral maps of France that show what regions of the country have the strongest left-wing voting. Anticlericalism flourishes in the south and southwest, the regions that have consistently provided the greatest support for the left for more than a century. It has also been found that strong adherents to the Catholic faith in France tend to vote right of center. For

---

[18]Richard Rose, "Britain: Simple Abstractions and Complex Realities," in Richard Rose, ed., *Electoral Behavior: A Comparative Handbook* (New York: Free Press, 1974), p. 517.

[19]*Ibid.*, pp. 517–518.

[20]Derek W. Urwin, "Germany: Continuity and Change in Electoral Politics," in Rose, ed., *op. cit.*, pp. 133, 148.

example, in a 1967 survey, the Communist Party was chosen by only 1 percent of churchgoing Catholics, whereas it was chosen by 32 percent of the nonreligious and nonchurchgoing Catholics. By contrast, the Gaullists, the leading party of the right, were supported by 32 percent of the former group and only 9 percent of the latter.[21]

This distinction between church attendance and nonchurch attendance is also important in Italy and West Germany. Parallel studies[22] in the two countries showed that, in both cases, church attendance was the most important variable explaining left-wing versus right-wing voting; it was more important than social class, trade union membership, or, in the case of West Germany, Catholicism versus Protestantism. Thus, religion in its usual sense—that is, one religion versus another or religion versus nonreligion—as an environmental factor affecting politics in postindustrial societies may no longer be so important as it once was. But, in some Western European countries, the intensity of religious participation still plays an important role in politics. This is particularly true in countries with substantial Catholic populations; other examples include Austria, Belgium, and the Netherlands.

### ETHNICITY

In two of the smaller Western European countries, Belgium and Switzerland, there is another important factor—the concentration of people who speak different languages in separate regions of the country. In Belgium, the division is between French-speaking Belgians (Walloons) in the south and Dutch-speaking Belgians (Flemish) in the north. In Switzerland, there are four separate regionally based linguistic groups, of which the most important are the French-speaking Swiss in the west and the German-speaking Swiss in the north and east. Political party support in both countries has been profoundly affected by these linguistic divisions, but, in Switzerland, they have not disrupted the overall political harmony. The opposite has been true in Belgium. There, the numerically superior Flemish have claimed that the Walloons enjoy a privileged political and social status, and the Walloons resent the economic decline of their region relative to prosperous Flanders. Disruptions of the Belgian political system have sometimes approached the scale of that in Canada. There a similar division can be found between French-speaking and English-speaking Canadians.

In each of our four countries, the principal language group far exceeds the minorities in terms of its share of the population. West Germany has no significant geographically based minority. In Italy and France, the linguistic minorities are found in border areas that adjoin other countries: the Alsatians on the French side of the Franco-German border speak a dialect that is similar to German; the Basques in the southwestern corner of France that adjoins the Basque region of Spain have their own language; the French-speaking Italians are found in the Alpine region adjacent to France; and the peoples of the South Tyrolean Alps speak German but live on the Italian side of the Austro-Italian border. In all areas, except Alsace, there are movements seeking reattachment to the appropriate ethnogeographic entity, but the problems thus far have been of little more than nuisance value, except for the French Basque region. Basques on the French side of the Franco-Spanish border have given refuge to fugitive Basque separatists from the Spanish side. This has been a source of strain in relations between Paris and Madrid in recent years.

There is a different kind of problem for certain minorities in regions of France and Great Britain where there are no international boundary lines dividing linguistic groups who speak the same language. In these cases, a combined cultural and economic deprivation is felt by the minorities in relation to the dominant populations. In France, this is the case of the Bretons in Brittany, the westernmost region of the country,

[21]Philippe Braud, *Le comportement electoral en France* (Paris: Presses universitaires de France, 1973).

[22]Derek W. Urwin, "Germany: Continuity and Change in Electoral Politics," and Samuel H. Barnes, "Italy: Religion and Class in Electoral Behavior," in Rose, ed., *op. cit.*, pp. 109–170, 171–225 respectively.

and of the Corsicans on the Mediterranean island of Corsica, which is legally and administratively an integral party of France. In Great Britain, it is true of the Welsh and the Scots. In all of these cases, the political system has been affected: by outbursts of violence in Brittany and Corsica and by the electoral success of Welsh and Scottish nationalist parties. The responses in all cases have been halting attempts by the central government to provide greater material resources to the aggrieved regions and to experiment with means of giving more power to regional levels of government to stave off the demand for full-scale independence. Regionally based ethnicity bears watching as an old source of a new strain in postindustrial societies, especially if social class and religious divisions become less important politically than they once were and if economic disparities between regions within a country continue.

## CLASS VERSUS OTHER LINES OF CLEAVAGE

Social divisions can be found in all four of our countries, and they have political significance in all. Of the four, France seems to have the greatest distances among the major groups and West Germany the least; Italy falls closer to France on the scale and Great Britain closer to West Germany. In summarizing this chapter, let us briefly compare France with Italy, and West Germany with Great Britain.

Regional disparities are greater in Italy than in France with respect to socioeconomic matters. Nevertheless, a sort of north/south division still exists in France—the north is more highly developed, the south is less developed—and the two areas tend to support different combinations of parties. In Italy, the sharp disparity between north and south with respect to socioeconomic matters does not seem to bring about sharp political conflict along regional lines. The two leading political parties, the Christian Democrats and the Communists, have substantial areas of strength in both north and south although each party must vary its strategies and appeals in the different regions.

Social class divisions are at the root of in-tense conflict in both countries. As noted earlier, the distance between the middle class and the working class is greater in France than in Italy. This is shown by the fact that the French Communist Party (PCF) is more isolated from the mainstream of political life than is the PCI. Class divisions are intensified in France by the continued division along religious lines—between devout Catholics and those who are opposed to the Church's role in political affairs—a division that reinforces the class-based wedge between left and right. Although anticlericalism can be found in Italy, this view is held by a smaller proportion of the population. Those who have a strong attachment to the Church provide significant support for the Christian Democratic Party (DC). But this support cuts across social class lines, just as the DC appeals to a wide ideological spectrum from left to right. Thus, class-based sociopolitical cleavage is reinforced by religion in France, whereas religion bridges the social class chasm in Italy.

Religion performs a similar bridging function in West Germany, assuring the right-of-center CDU substantial Caltholic working-class support and the Social Democrats an important share of Protestant middle-class support. Religion plays a much less important role in predominantly Protestant Great Britain. Party voting is very much along social class lines. Moreover, as noted above, the distance between the social classes appears to be greater in Great Britain than in West Germany, which shows the most consistent signs of having become a postindustrial society. Still, the distance between the classes in Great Britain does not produce as much interclass hostility as in France. Similarly, the conflict between the Labour and Conservative parties has not been as sharp as that between the left and the right in France. It should, however, be noted that strains have begun to appear in the ethnic structure of Great Britain. Rather than helping to bridge the class gap, as they have in the past, the ancient divisions between the English, Welsh, and Scots may lead to strong Welsh and Scottish separatist movements with unpredictable consequences for political stability in Great Britain.

In summary, it would seem clear that environmental factors are important in influencing politics. The level of a country's economic development and the degree of equality in the distribution of well-being among its social groups will help determine the shape of its political system. But these economic factors will undoubtedly be affected by the social cleavages, some of which have existed over the long historical period that preceded a country's industrial development.

# Suggestions for Further Reading

**Acquaviva, S. S.,** and **M. Santuccio,** *Social Structure in Italy: Crisis of a System,* trans. Colin Hamer (London: Martin Robertson, 1976).

**Bell, Daniel,** *The Coming of Post-Industrial Society* (New York: Basic Books, 1973).

**Crozier, Michel,** *The Stalled Society* (New York: Viking, 1973).

**Dahrendorf, Ralf,** *Society and Democracy in Germany* (Garden City, N.Y.: Doubleday, 1967).

**Halsey, A. H.,** ed., *Trends in British Society Since 1900* (London: Macmillan, 1972).

**Hirsch, Fred,** and **John H. Goldthorpe,** eds., *The Political Economy of Inflation* (Cambridge: Harvard University Press, 1978).

**Kramer, Jane,** *Unsettling Europe* (New York: Random House, 1980).

**Krejci, Jaroslav,** *Social Structure in Divided Germany* (New York: St. Martin's, 1976).

**Marceau, Jane,** *Class and Status in France: Economic Change and Social Immobility 1945–1975* (Oxford: Clarendon, 1977).

**Means, Gardner C.,** *et. al., The Roots of Inflation: The International Crisis* (New York: Burt Franklin, 1975).

**Parkin, Frank,** *Class Inequality and Political Order: Social Stratification in Capitalist and Communist Societies* (New York: Praeger, 1971).

**Ryder, Judith,** and **Harold Silver,** *Modern English Society: History and Structure: 1850–1970* London: Methuen, 1970).

**Seers, Dudley,** *et al.,* eds., *Underdeveloped Europe: Studies in Core-Periphery Relations* (Atlantic Highlands, N.J.: Humanities Press, 1979).

**Wedderburn, Dorothy,** ed., *Poverty, Inequality and Class Structure* (London: Cambridge University Press, 1974).

**Westergaard, John,** and **Henrietta Resler,** *Class in a Capitalist Society: A Study of Contemporary Britain* (New York: Basic Books, 1975).

# CHAPTER THREE
## Political Culture

It should be clear from the preceding chapter that Western European economies have been struggling in the past decade and that the accompanying social strains have been growing in severity. In subsequent chapters, we will see how the political systems of these countries have adjusted to these strains. In some cases, as in Great Britain, France, and Italy, important changes have taken place in voting patterns, partisan alignments, and public policy goals. Overall, the West German political system, which earlier underwent the greatest transformation from pre-World War II patterns, has been the most resistant to the recent winds of change, probably because, as we have seen, the West German economy and social order have been the least subject to strain during the past decade. Thus, we can see a relationship between the stability of the socioeconomic order and political stability. Disequilibrium in one realm is likely to produce discontinuity in the other.

Social and economic strains do not simply translate into political events without first having some impact on the people who make the political events. In First World polyarchies, the political stage is a crowded one. Political actors include not only the élites who make the principal policy decisions that affect society but also ordinary citizens, citizens acting as voters and in other ways participating in the political process. The importance of voters for political outcomes should be obvious to anyone who has witnessed

the changes at the top that occurred in three major First World polyarchies—Great Britain, the United States, and France—between May 1979 and May 1981. But political participation of other kinds—participation in strikes, public meetings, and demonstrations, even acts of violence—have an impact on the political system although often a less calculable impact than that of dramatic changes in voter behavior. As shown in the previous chapter, ordinary citizens feel the impact of recession and inflation in their paychecks and at the grocery store.

How do ordinary citizens respond politically to the traumas of daily life? The answer depends on how citizens view politics. Do they see it as a very distant realm inhabited by a few knowledgeable persons or as an arena affording opportunities for personal involvement and potential relief from social, economic, and even psychological ailments? In other words, what are the political beliefs of ordinary citizens? How do they perceive the values of power, well-being, enlightenment, and respect to be distributed within their society and what responsibility do they assign to government for these distributions? What role do they see for themselves in reinforcing or bringing about changes in these distributions? Do the citizens of different countries have different political beliefs? In what ways do different segments of the population of the same country differ in their political beliefs? The study of political culture is the study of such belief systems. It enables us better to explain and make predictions about the ways traumatic events affect the political behavior of citizens in different societies.

## DEFINITIONS

The term political culture was coined two decades ago by the political scientist, Gabriel A. Almond.[1] Its meaning has changed somewhat since then as perspectives borrowed from social psychology have come to have greater influence in the fashioning of the concept. According to Almond and G. Bingham Powell:

> Political culture is the pattern of individual attitudes and orientations toward politics among the members of a political system. It is the subjective realm which underlies and gives meaning to political actions. Such individual orientations involve several components, including (a) cognitive orientations, knowledge, accurate or otherwise, of political objects and beliefs; (b) affective orientations, feelings of attachment, involvement, rejection and the like, about political objects; and (c) evaluative orientations, judgments and opinions about political objects, which usually involve applying value standards to political objects and events.[2]

Essentially, Almond and Powell are saying that political culture is a pattern of individual attitudes and orientations toward political objects. The key words are (1) *pattern*, (2) *attitudes* and *orientations*, and (3) *political objects*.

Let us begin with the second of these elements. Attitudes and orientations, especially when the word, individual, is placed first, should lead us into the realm of individual psychology. How do people think and feel about themselves and about the world around them? How they think or feel, of course, is not necessarily an indication of how they will act. At best, it simply gives us some insight into the potential for ac-

tion. One must also take into account the situational opportunities and constraints that surround any such potential action. I might have a very strong feeling that the mayor of my city is corrupt and has been robbing the city blind for years. Yet, I might hesitate to take action unless I know that others feel the same way and unless I believe that something could be done to get the mayor out of office. Still, if many people feel the same way I do (impotent), that is one significant reason why the mayor has been able to get away with it for so long. If such people could know who shared their view and realize that the discontent was widespread, perhaps the mayor could soon be ousted from office. The potential is there; the problem is to convert the potential into action.

This brings us to the first element—the pattern of attitudes and orientations. Suppose that only a tiny minority of relatively well-educated citizens opposed the mayor, whereas the vast majority of people were either apathetic or believed he or she was doing a good job. The mayor would have less to be concerned about in this situation than if the city were polarized, that is, fairly evenly divided between strong supporters and strong opponents. Here, we see the difference between two attitudinal patterns: a consensual and a polarized pattern; these patterns can be depicted graphically as distribution curves (see Figure 3.1). The J-shaped and normal curves represent consensual patterns, whereas the U-shaped curve indicates polarization. In the case of the J-shaped pattern, there is what one might call a one-sided consensus because there is a minority that is far removed from the majority in this case. The normal curve reflects something of a middle-of-the-road consensus. Here, it would be easier to work out a compromise be-

[1]Gabriel A. Almond, "Comparative Political Systems," *Journal of Politics*, *18* (3) (1956), 391–409.

[2]Gabriel A. Almond and G. Bingham Powell, *Comparative Politics: A Developmental Approach* (Boston: Little, Brown, 1966), p. 50.

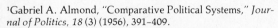
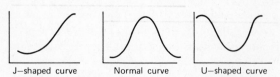

J-shaped curve    Normal curve    U-shaped curve

**Figure 3.1**    Three types of attitudinal distribution.

tween the competing opinions than in the first situation.

The final element of our definition is the political object toward which the attitudes and orientations are directed. In the case at hand, the incumbent mayor is the political object. But political culture encompasses a much wider array of political objects; it may include a number of questions of public policy, how government should allocate scarce resources among competing needs. It also includes attitudes and orientations toward the structures of politics and government and how power is distributed between citizens and their government and between government offices. In other words, the political culture of a country is the pattern of attitudes and orientations of its citizens toward power, well-being, respect, and enlightenment, and how they are distributed.

In studying political culture, we may want to know whether certain political attitudes and orientations are distributed among the entire population of a country or only among a portion of its citizenry. We have already used the political culture of a single city as an example. Any national political culture can be subdivided into a variety of political subcultures if certain groups that can clearly be differentiated on the basis of certain attributes also have distinct political orientations. For example, the youth of a country, who are distinguishable on the basis of age, may also share certain distinct political beliefs and feelings. Perhaps women or the elderly or Catholics share sufficiently distinctive political orientations to warrant being treated as subcultures in certain countries. In Chapter Four, we will consider the political élites of our four countries—those public officials and influential private citizens with the greatest share of political power—and ask whether there are distinct subcultures among political élites, that is, the different ideologies that divide political parties, such as socialists and conservatives, from one another. In some countries, such as the United States, the ideological differences between political parties are probably not fundamental enough to warrant the judgment that even their more active members belong to different subcultures. In other countries, however, the ideological walls are steeper and thicker, and such a judgment would be quite appropriate.

We should not be surprised to learn that French Communist ideology constitutes a separate political subculture. But the active Communists, after all, constitute only a small minority of the population, almost professionally separate from the rest—like doctors, lawyers, or engineers. What about the masses of people? In postindustrial society, do typical French people differ so much from typical Britons or Germans to make it worth while to examine differences in political culture? If you have ever traveled in these countries, perhaps you can answer this question. People *do* differ in how they feel about things, and their reactions may seem unpredictable to anyone who is unfamiliar with their culture. Try presenting a French ticket seller with a handful of pennies ("*centimes*") and see if he or she will give you a ticket without first registering displeasure in no uncertain terms. A British ticket seller will cheerfully accept pennies and might even wish you a "good day."

People in different countries have different attitudes toward politics. By and large, Britons were able to empathize with the trauma that Watergate represented to Americans, but they could also better sympathize with the plight of a disgraced president than could most Americans. Germans, on the other hand, could understand neither. They could not relate to the agony most Americans were experiencing. Obviously, Richard M. Nixon had done wrong; obviously, he should be removed from office. What was all the fuss about? The French displayed still a third reaction—cynicism. To them, politicians are all corrupt and what Nixon did was no better or worse than what most politicians do. But if Americans wanted to clean up their political system, they should have started much earlier; in any event, it probably would not have done much good.[3]

[3]These generalizations are based on direct observations by the author in Western Europe during 1974.

How can people living in such close proximity to one another have such different responses? Part of the answer lies in the fact that people are brought up differently in these countries. Here we come to the subject of political socialization. Each country has typical ways in which children are brought up and typical ways in which adults are politically influenced that continue to reshape the orientations they learned in childhood and adolescence. In these social learning experiences, one acquires a set of "correct" attitudes that enables one to get along with one's fellow human beings with a minimum of friction. This training and conditioning process is only partly at the conscious level. Parents have certain ideas about how to bring up their children, but most of them are not trained child psychologists. Children growing up in France during the presidency of Charles de Gaulle may have gotten a clear impression from their parents that the General was greatly admired and respected, even though their parents may never have said anything explicit to this effect. Later on, this same respect and admiration may be transferred to the office of the president itself, with de Gaulle's successors benefiting from the halo effect. Whatever orientations children gain from parents will not be easily changed later in life.

Certain kinds of political orientations are also learned in school. In Western European polyarchies, children are not so likely to learn partisan affiliations as to learn of their position in the larger world. No longer screened from this world by the warmth of the family circle, children begin to experience the various authority patterns with which they will have to live later on, and they also begin to get an idea of their position in the hierarchy of respect within the general society. The relatively élitist educational systems of Western Europe help to transmit a stronger sense of class difference than is true of the schools in the United States. European children going through the privileged upper stream are likely to have greater confidence in their ability to influence political events than are children in the lower stream who are learning that they will have lesser shares of well-being, respect, and enlightenment.

Political socialization takes place elsewhere as well. Peer influences can be quite important in shaping attitudes both in school and later on in various occupations and organizations. Such influences may reinforce or conflict with those learned in the family and the school. In postindustrial society, many individuals are exposed to influences that lead them to become quite different from their fathers and mothers. The acceleration of change has been so great in recent decades that could a time machine transport average Italian adults from the 1940s to the 1980s, their efforts to adjust to the new Italy might bring about a severe trauma requiring confinement to a mental institution. Older Italians have gone through precisely this process but at a slower pace, which has enabled them to build up their psychological defenses. But how well can an Italian of 20 communicate with an Italian of 60? Change the word Italian to American and see what your answer is.

Television and the other mass media have also helped to break down the attitude structures acquired in early life. The process of challenge probably begins in late childhood, accelerates in adolescence, and comes to full bloom in adulthood. The degree to which the media are deliberately purveying certain messages varies from country to country. The matter of government control over French broadcasting is one of the most important issues in France and has been ever since the Gaullist leadership began shaping media messages more than 20 years ago. Opponents of the Gaullists argued that they used radio and television to condition attitudes in ways that helped them remain in power. But the potential influence of the media goes far beyond partisan advantage and disadvantage. The crises of American cities, the tragic struggle of Northern Ireland, student protests in all Western countries, wildcat strikes in vital industries, the grim economic statistics of the last decade—all reach the living rooms of people in Western polyarchies. No matter how objectively these traumatic events are portrayed by media newsstaffs, they are bound to affect people's confidence in the efficacy of their political system and in the dependability of their own future.

## POLITICAL ALLEGIANCE

### ALLEGIANT AND ALIENATED POLITICAL CULTURES

When political scientists compare the political cultures of different countries, their attention is focused primarily on what we have called the value of *power*. They are concerned with the values of well-being, enlightenment, and respect insofar as they bear on the way people in a society value the political power structure and the élites who hold power. Political scientists have asked two very general sorts of questions about attitudes toward the distribution of power. The first relates to the way people view the structure of political élite roles within the political system; the second concerns people's view of themselves and of people like themselves as nonélite political actors. The political élite is a body larger than that set of individuals who hold important public offices at any given time. In Western European countries (as we will see in Chapters Four and Five), the political élite includes the leaders of the opposition party or parties who hold seats in the legislative body (parliament) and who stand ready to replace the leaders of the majority party or parties who presently hold power.

The first aspect of political culture is the study of how nonélites perceive the political élites of their country. When we ask how people view political élites, we are not asking simply how well they like the incumbents. Such questions are frequently found in public opinion polls: people are asked how well they think President Ronald Reagan or Prime Minister Margaret Thatcher is doing, for example. In studying political culture, we ask a more fundamental question: <u>how well people believe the country is being run by *whoever* is in power.</u> This question has a longer term quality to it. We are interested in how well the ordinary citizen

feels his or her country has been run in recent experience, including periods of time during which more than one president or prime minister, or, for that matter, political party, has been in power. In essence, we are asking both (1) how well the system of political institutions is structured to insure that the most appropriate team of political élites will be in a position to make public policy and (2) how reliable the *entire pool* of political élites is.

Individual citizens who have positive attitudes toward their political institutions and political élites can be termed allegiant. They are so in more than the sense that they have a strong national identification, meaning a sense of patriotism. They also believe that their system of government is one that works, at least most of the time, and that the people who specialize in the work of government are capable of making it work. Alienated citizens, on the other hand, are those who lack confidence in their governmental system and in their political élites. They may not trust those in power; they may be disenchanted with all politicians; and they may very well be searching for substantial changes in the structures of the system that will make it work better. It is possible to go from the level of the individual to the citizenry as an aggregate and say that the political culture of a country is allegiant or alienated if a strong majority of the citizenry shares attitudes of one type or the other. These two types of political culture are depicted in Figure 3.2.

It is easier to define aspects of political culture, such as political allegiance, than it is to measure them. Ideally, one would like to be able to determine how every citizen of a particular

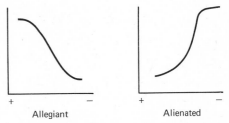

**Figure 3.2** Two types of political culture.

country felt at a given time about the political élites. Although this is impossible, the next best thing—the public opinion poll or attitude survey—is in principle available and reliable. Prohibitive costs, however, have limited its use on a cross-national basis so that although we have many good surveys of the political attitudes of people in individual countries, they can seldom be combined with similar studies of other countries to enable comparative analysis. One of the pioneering studies in this field—the five-nation survey conducted by Gabriel A. Almond and Sidney Verba in 1959–1960[4]—is still a landmark, but its findings are now quite out of date. Therefore, we will supplement some of those findings with more recent studies made either cross-nationally or within single countries.

Almond and Verba asked their respondents in the United States, Great Britain, West Germany, Italy, and Mexico the following question: "Speaking generally, what are the things about this country you are most proud of?"[5] The respondents came up with their own answers rather than being compelled to answer in categories supplied by the interviewer. The responses were then coded into a discrete number of categories (see Table 3.1).

The Americans and British most often cited aspects of their governmental or political institutions, including social legislation. Nearly twice as many Americans as British said they felt most proud about aspects of their political system, but more British cited this category than any other aspect of their country or its people. Only negligible percentages of the Germans and Italians mentioned this category at all. The largest percentage of German respondents mentioned characteristics of the people, such as industriousness and efficiency, and the success of the West German economy. As for the Italians, the largest single category was "nothing or don't know." The physical attributes of the country came ahead of any category dealing with the qualities or achievements of the Italian people.

## RECENT DEVELOPMENTS

In the past 20 years, changes have taken place in mass attitudes in the countries Almond and Verba studied.[6] Particularly striking has been the increased allegiance among citizens of West Germany. In 1978, a sample of West Germans was asked to specify of what things about their country they were proudest, and the results were noticeably different from those in 1959–1960. The percentages who volunteered some aspect of governmental or political institutions had risen from 7 percent to 31 percent, the second highest category after the economic system, which had risen to the 40-percent level.[7] Although West Germans were still proud, indeed, even prouder, of their economic record in 1978, they now were registering allegiance to the political system in much higher frequencies than 20 years before. It can be imagined that the sustained superiority in economic performance of West Germany had built up a stock of specific support among its citizenry. This is allegiance to the existing regime that is based on a positive evaluation of its performance but that is not necessarily indicative of a deeper sense of allegiance to the political institutions. The latter has been termed diffuse support by political scientists.[8] It may be developing in West Germany, but one wonders whether the high levels of allegiance shown in recent surveys would be sustained in the face of a significant reversal in the performance of the West German economy. However, it seems safer today than 20 years ago to predict that democracy as a general system of government would continue to receive

[4]Gabriel A. Almond and Sidney Verba, *The Civic Culture: Political Attitudes and Democracy in Five Nations* (Princeton, N.J.: Princeton University Press, 1963).

[5]*Ibid.*, p. 102.

[6]See the collection of essays in Gabriel A. Almond and Sidney Verba, eds., *The Civic Culture Revisited* (Boston and Toronto: Little, Brown, 1980). These essays evaluate the Almond-Verba study in the light of findings of more recent studies. The Almond-Verba study itself has never been updated through replication of the original survey.

[7]David P. Conradt, "Changing German Political Culture," in Almond and Verba, eds., *op. cit.*, p. 230.

[8]David Easton, *A Framework for Political Analysis* (Englewood Cliffs, N.J.: Prenctice-Hall, 1965), pp. 124–126.

**TABLE 3.1**   Aspects of a Nation in which Respondents Report Pride (by Nation)

| Percentage Who Said They Were Proud of: | U.S. | U.K.[a] | West Germany | Italy |
|---|---|---|---|---|
| Governmental, political institutions | 85% | 46% | 7% | 3% |
| Social legislation | 13 | 18 | 6 | 1 |
| Position in international affairs | 5 | 11 | 5 | 2 |
| Economic system | 23 | 10 | 33 | 3 |
| Characteristics of people | 7 | 18 | 36 | 11 |
| Spiritual virtues and religion | 3 | 1 | 3 | 6 |
| Contributions to the arts | 1 | 6 | 11 | 16 |
| Contributions to science | 3 | 7 | 12 | 3 |
| Physical attributes of country | 5 | 10 | 17 | 25 |
| Nothing or don't know | 4 | 10 | 15 | 27 |
| Other | 9 | 11 | 3 | 21 |
| Total percent of responses[b] | 158 | 148 | 148 | 118 |
| Total percent of respondents | 100 | 100 | 100 | 100 |
| Total number of cases | 970 | 963 | 955 | 995 |

[a]Great Britain.

[b]Percentages exceed 100 because of multiple responses.

SOURCE: Gabriel A. Almond and Sidney Verba, *The Civic Culture: Political Attitudes and Democracy in Five Nations* (Princeton, N.J.: Princeton University Press, 1963), p. 102.

support. This has been shown in survey after survey taken over the past two decades in which West Germans in overwhelming percentages consistently expressed positive feelings toward democracy and rejected authoritarian forms of government.

The positive movement of West Germans along the allegiance/alienation dimension is all the more striking because, if anything, the movement of American and British citizens has been in the opposite direction in the past 20 years. The evidence for Americans is quite clear. Periodically, Americans have been asked about their levels of confidence in various political and social institutions. Comparisons of results for 1966 and 1972 show a remarkable decline in confidence for all institutions, including organized religion, the medical profession, major companies, organized labor, and the various branches of national government. Among the latter, the Supreme Court declined from a 51 percent expression of public confidence to 28 percent in the six-year

period. The Senate and House of Representatives were supported by only half as many respondents in 1972: 21 percent for both houses of Congress versus 42 percent in 1966. Support for the executive branch declined from 41 percent to 27 percent. This declining confidence appears to have been accompanied by a growing cynicism among Americans. The percentage of those who agreed with the statement that government is "run by a few big interests" increased from 29 percent in 1964 to 65 percent in 1974.[9] The latter figure can be compared with that of only 27 percent in West Germany who agreed with the same statement the same year. Also, in 1974, 47 percent of British respondents agreed with the same cynical proposition, a figure approximately midway between those for West Germany and the United States.[10]

[9]Alan I. Abramowitz, "The United States: Political Culture Under Stress," in Almond and Verba, eds., *op. cit.*, pp. 189–190.

[10]Conradt, *op. cit.*, p. 235.

Although West Germans are gaining in allegiance and Americans seem to be moving in the direction of disaffection, if not alienation, the evidence for Great Britain is less clear. Cynicism appears to have reached only a moderate level in the evidence cited above, but it is noteworthy that the strong support for the British two-party system, registered in election after election in the 1950s and 1960s, dropped off significantly in the 1970s, both in terms of votes for the two major parties in elections and in terms of the levels of party identification. As in the United States, increasing numbers of voters, especially young voters, are showing a lack of attachment to the two political parties that have dominated British politics since World War II. However, it should be pointed out that the identification of Britons with the social classes of the industrial era has also declined in postindustrial Great Britain. Loss of party identification can be partially explained by the fact that the two political parties, Labour and Conservative, are strongly associated in the public mind with the manual and nonmanual classes of the industrial social order.

It is possible that the British have recently withdrawn specific support from their political élites, at least to an extent; it is not so certain that the same can be said of the diffuse support that had accumulated in Great Britain over centuries of gradual political development. Surveys have shown that the British still support the institution of the monarchy in overwhelming numbers, something that cannot be said of any of the American political institutions, including the presidency and the Supreme Court. However, British respondents also acknowledge that the monarch has little power, so that the appropriate American analogue might be a purely symbolic feature of the American political system, such as the flag or the Washington Monument.

More to the point, perhaps, is the continued support in Great Britain for the system of law and for the obligation of the citizen to obey the law. Higher percentages of British respondents, in a recent survey, were willing to give approval to police using force against illegal demonstrations than was true of American or West German respondents.[11] Once again, however, a qualifier is in order. Police in Great Britain are less likely than their American counterparts to use violent means in dealing with strikes and demonstrations; thus, this support for the maintenance of law and order in Great Britain is less likely to carry with it support for police action in violation of the basic civic and political rights of the citizenry. To repeat, it appears that specific support has declined in recent years but that the stock of diffuse support, built up over a long period of time, has scarcely been depleted, despite the waning of British power in the world and her dismal economic record of recent decades.

Almond and Verba found a substantial degree of alienation and cynicism among their Italian respondents in 1959. This fit the stereotypes that most observers shared in viewing the Italian political culture of the time. During the 1960s, with the Italian economy booming, attitude surveys revealed more positive assessments, especially in policy-related areas, such as jobs, housing, and income. The political system seemed to be gaining its share of popular credit for improving well-being in Italy. But the 1970s have brought a reversal in this trend. In 1971, only 17.5 percent of an Italian national sample agreed with the statement that "there is something basically wrong with the social and political system." By 1974, the percentage had risen to 34.6. In 1975, over 77 percent of respondents assigned to government great responsibility for solving problems in the fields of jobs, crime prevention, and inflation. Less than 18 percent evaluated government performance positively in any of these areas. It is unlikely that evaluations have improved in the years since 1975.[12] These survey results indicate that in the case of Italy, where neither diffuse nor specific support for the political system was apparent at

[11]Samuel H. Barnes, et al., Political Action: Mass Participation in Five Western Democracies, (Beverly Hills and London: Saga, 1979), p. 88.

[12]Giacomo Sani, "The Political Culture of Italy: Continuity and Change," in Almond and Verba, eds., op. cit., pp. 308–310.

the time of the Almond-Verba study, the political culture has remained an alienated one.

In the light of the evidence from the United States, Great Britain, and Italy, the West German case seems all the more striking. It is difficult to escape the impression that economic success can engender and help sustain political support, whereas poor or mediocre economic performance can have the opposite effect. Especially when one considers the disastrous earlier German experiment with democracy, the Weimar Republic, does the West German case seem significant. Generalizations about the German national character have long stressed the tendency of the German people to accept authority unquestioningly as a civic obligation. The early attitude surveys taken after the establishment of the Federal Republic of Germany indicated that acceptance of the authority of the state, its laws, and the actions of its official state agents—bureaucrats and the police—did not necessarily mean a strong attachment to the existing political leadership found in the governing and opposition parties. More recent studies have found that not only are the government institutions of the Federal Republic accepted today, but the phenomenon of competing political parties, always viewed with ambiguity at best, have now become an accepted feature of the institutional framework. Still, there remains a residue of distrust for politicians, especially among older Germans, and there is little tolerance for the occasional examples of corruption or incompetence that occur in high office. Civil servants continue to be viewed with greater respect than are their political superiors.

## FRANCE: ALLEGIANCE OR ALIENATION?

In the case of France, the fact that Almond and Verba did not include that country in their study deprives us of a similar baseline for comparing today's political culture with that of 20 years ago. Nor have French scholars been preoccupied with asking the same kinds of questions about political culture as have students of American, British, and West German political cultures. The survey results that are relevant are those that bear on attitudes toward the two most recent political regimes that have prevailed in France, the Fourth and Fifth republics. As in West Germany and, briefly during the 1960s in Italy, evaluations of the new French regime improved swiftly during the economic boom years of the 1960s.[13] Although there has been a leveling off of the upward curve of support in the 1970s, French citizens continue to assess the Fifth Republic instituted by General de Gaulle more positively than they do its predecessor, but the disparity is in no way as striking as that between West German evaluations of the Weimar and Bonn republics.

Students of French political culture have focused a great deal of their attention on French attitudes toward authority, viewed in the abstract and studied in a variety of settings, such as in offices of large bureaucratic organizations and in the classroom at various educational levels.[14] The prevailing view is that most of the French are ambivalent toward authority, whether it be found in their more immediate small-group experiences or as they view the authority of their political leaders and the state. There is a strong distaste for manifestations of authority that are experienced at too-close range. The French reputedly have an abhorrence of face-to-face contact with those who hold authority over them. They prefer that authority remain impersonal and distant and that they be expected to adhere to formal rules that apply equally to all in the same situation as well as that allow them a maximum of freedom to assert their own individuality within the framework established by these rules. If authority becomes too immediate and oppressive, the French may well rebel against rules that they consider arbitrary or unjust. The rebellion may be covert, taking the form of surreptitious noncompliance with the rules—as in the case of tax fraud or of students

---

[13]Henry W. Ehrmann, *Politics in France*, 3rd ed. (Boston and Toronto: Little, Brown, 1976), p. 131.

[14]See the discussions in Ehrmann, *op. cit.*, Chap. 3; and John S. Ambler, *The Government and Politics of France* (Boston: Houghton Mifflin, 1971), Chap. 3.

ridiculing teachers behind their backs—or it may take a more overt and collective form—as, in 1968, when tens of thousands of French men and women discovered, almost spontaneously, a common resentment against the authority of the French state and went on a collective strike that eventually evaporated as suddenly as it had formed, once the pent-up resentment had been sufficiently vented.

The other side of this ambivalence is a need for order and a fear of chaos that will be reasserted when rebellion against authority threatens to get out of hand. General de Gaulle is said to have fit the French expectation of authority especially well (Valery Giscard d'Estaing appeared to be striving unsuccessfully for an approximation of this during his presidency), in that he was an aloof, aristocratic figure, preferring Delphic generalities to specific commands. It was reassuring that de Gaulle was *there*, as living proof that the capacity of the state to maintain law and order was intact; and it was especially comforting, in that de Gaulle did not appear to be making excessive demands on his people to achieve goals of *his* choosing, goals that they as individuals had not chosen for themselves. His grand designs tended to be directed outward toward the leaders of other countries, especially the superpowers and his European neighbors. His people could watch his maneuvers, as they would watch a spectator sport or the performance of a great theatrical actor, without feeling any obligation being thrust on them, other than the obligation to admire. Contrast this style of leadership with that of John F. Kennedy, which was better attuned to the American culture. Kennedy said, "Ask not what your country can do for you; ask what you can do for your country." At the same time in history, de Gaulle was saying, in effect: ask not what you can do for France; observe and see what France (that is de Gaulle) does for France.

French ambivalence toward authority is also related to a tendency, as in Germany, to disassociate the state from the current political regime. In the French case, the concepts of state and nation are intermingled. Throughout the many successive poltical regimes that France has experienced since the French Revolution of 1789, the state has remained relatively intact, meaning that the bureaucracy, the courts, the army, and the diplomatic corps have not experienced great upheaval, whatever has happened at the political level. The state, with its permanent bureaucratized institutions housed in their elegant old buildings, is the living proof of the nation's permanence. By contrast, state and nation for West Germans cannot be so readily equated. Whatever its historic meaning as a geographic and cultural expression, Germany did not exist until 1871; its boundaries were subject to radical fluctuation between 1918 and 1945; and, today, what is left of its former territory is divided into two separate states fashioned on rival political and social philosophies. Although the West German continues to feel a strong sense of civic obligation to obey the commands of the state and does not feel the same sense of ambivalence toward the state's authority as do the French, there is not the same confidence in the state's permanence. Should support be withdrawn from the Bonn Republic (the political regime), one cannot predict with confidence that there would not be a convulsion affecting the structure and authority of the West German state and threatening the viability of West Germany as a political entity. Should support for the French Fifth Republic be withdrawn, on the other hand, the institutions of the state would likely survive without difficulty even if a *Sixth* Republic came into being.

## ATTITUDES TOWARD POLITICAL PARTICIPATION

### EARLIER FINDINGS

The second aspect of political culture that concerns us is the question: How do people feel about themselves, ordinary citizens, as political actors? Much of the Almond and Verba study was directed toward answering the question: Do people believe that they—as ordinary citizens—can influence the decisions made by those in power? This question taps people's perceptions of the way political power is, in fact, distributed. Such perceptions may not actually be correct.

**TABLE 3.2**  Percentage of Respondents Who Said They Could Do Something About an Unjust Local or National Regulation (by Nation)

| Country | Can Do Something About Local Regulation | Can Do Something About National Regulation |
|---|---|---|
| United States | 77% | 75% |
| Great Britain | 78 | 62 |
| West Germany | 62 | 38 |
| Italy | 51 | 28 |
| Mexico | 52 | 38 |

SOURCE: Gabriel A. Almond and Sidney Verba, *The Civic Culture: Political Attitudes and Democracy in Five Nations* (Princeton, N.J.: Princeton University Press, 1963), p. 185.

People may naïvely feel that they have a greater share of power than they, in fact, have or they may be overly cynical, believing that power is concentrated in fewer hands than it really is. But, whether their perceptions are correct or not, they are of interest because they can help predict the way people will act. It is likely that citizens who believe they have access to the political system will be more apt to try to do something about a political situation they regard as unfavorable. On the other hand, citizens who cynically detach themselves from a political system they believe is rigged against them would be more likely to ignore opportunities that may actually be available to them.

To answer this Almond and Verba asked their respondents questions designed to discover levels of what they called civic competence. The citizen who feels competent is one who believes he or she actually has the capacity to influence government decisions. Almond and Verba asked whether the individual, if confronted with an unjust national regulation, felt he or she could do something about it.[15] Table 3.2 presents the percentages who responded affirmatively to this question about both a nationally and a locally imposed regulation. Intercountry differences are not particularly great on the question of local decisions, but the differences are striking at the national level. Clearly, more Americans and Britons felt they were competent to influence na-

tional decisions than did West Germans or Italians.

Almond and Verba made certain judgments on the basis of the response patterns to their whole array of questions.[16] They found that the Italians are highly distrustful of one another, are preoccupied with self-protection, and are dubious that the government can be enlisted to help them.[17] They believe that government is run by the few in the interest of the few; democracy is an illusion. Therefore, why not accept the fact and live with it? Italians find they can get along most comfortably in life if they let the politicians worry about politics while they worry about the welfare of their family. In this way, Italians avoid disappointment; therefore, their cynicism may be of positive value for them psychologically.

Almond and Verba made a more complex judgment of West German political culture. They observed what they called political detachment and subject competence among the West Germans.[18] Voter turnout is high in West Germany, and Almond and Verba found that the West Germans are more knowledgeable about politics than their respondents in the other countries. But they also found that the Germans were more pre-

[15]Almond and Verba, *op. cit.*, p. 184.

[16]*Ibid.*, pp. 402–414.

[17]*Ibid.*, pp. 135–136, 267. See also Edward C. Banfield, *The Moral Basis of a Backward Society* (New York: Free Press, 1958).

[18]Almond and Verba, *op. cit.*, pp. 428–439.

Chancellor Helmut Schmidt addressing a gathering in Delmenhorst as a candidate of the Social Democratic Party in the campaign for Bundestag elections, August 1976.

The poster in the image reads:

**Der bessere Mann muß Kanzler bleiben:**

**Helmut Schmidt. Deshalb SPD.**

occupied with economic than with political matters. Voting is seen as a civic obligation, and keeping informed about political matters is only prudent for people in a country that has undergone such drastic political upheavals in this century. But Almond and Verba's study shows that a majority of West Germans in 1960 did not feel particularly competent to influence political events, and there was no majority who even felt one ought to try. The conclusion is that, although the West Germans were not necessarily antidemocratic, they had not yet internalized truly democratic norms and values. On the other hand, it appeared that they felt themselves competent as subjects, that is, as consumers of the goods and services provided by government. Relatively large percentages of West Germans trusted government administrators and the police to treat them fairly. Apparently, the professional traditions of these officials could be relied on as a protective device against arbitrary official behavior, despite the inclination of the German people not to exercise effective popular control.

To characterize Great Britain and the United States, Almond and Verba coined the term, civic culture.[19] A civic culture is a political culture in which citizens value popular participation in political affairs and an equal distribution of political power, but they are sufficiently content with the political system so that they have no motivation to participate very actively in politics. Most of the time, they prefer to leave politics to their leaders, the specialists. Almond and Verba found that the British were more passive than the Americans but the differences were not great; therefore, they labeled the former a deferential civic culture and the latter a participant civic culture. In both cases, the commitment to democracy was strong enough to ensure that the political system would operate essentially as a democracy; but the commitment was not so strong that large numbers of people would be constantly intervening in the decision-making process, overloading the normal channels and threatening to destabilize the system. Almond

[19]*Ibid.*, pp. 440–469.

and Verba felt that the civic culture is a solid underpinning for stable democracy.[20] The future of democracy seemed more certain in Great Britain and the United States than it did in West Germany and Italy.

What about France, which was not included in the five-nation study? Students of French political culture are generally agreed that the French tend to be cynical (like the Italians) about the extent to which France is indeed a democracy.[21] In 1969, a survey was made in France that asked a number of questions that were similar to those in the Almond-Verba study. Among these, the respondents were asked if they agreed with the following statement: "The people decide how the country shall be run through the vote." The percentage of the French who responded positively (58 percent) was lower than that for any of the five Almond-Verba countries, in which the percentages ranged from 83 percent (Great Britain) to 62 percent (Italy).[22]

## THE BARNES-KAASE STUDY[23]

Once again, we must ask whether attitudes in the various countries have changed in the years since the Almond-Verba study. Three of the countries that Almond and Verba examined, the United States, Great Britain, and West Germany, were included in a more recent five-nation study in which the focus of attention was on popular attitudes toward political participation. The international team of researchers who conducted the study in the mid-1970s was headed by an American, Samuel Barnes, and a West German, Max Kaase. The Barnes-Kaase team conducted surveys in the Netherlands and Austria as well as in the United States, Great Britain, and West Germany. An important feature of this study was to answer those criticisms of Almond and Verba that stated they had paid insufficient at-

tention to modes of political participation often considered unconventional. Activities, like demonstrations, unofficial strikes, boycotts, and sit-ins, had not been prevalent in the late 1950s, and, in failing to inquire into popular attitudes toward these less common modes of behavior, Almond and Verba rapidly became outdated as the instances of unconventional participation multiplied during the 1960s and 1970s.

Many of the questions Barnes and Kaase asked differed from those that Almond and Verba had posed, but, in some cases, comparison of the two time periods is possible. Regarding conventional modes of participation, Barnes and Kaase asked what types of activities respondents actually had engaged in, activities such as attending public meetings, contacting public officials, and trying to convince friends to vote in particular ways. If we leave aside those respondents who had done no more than read about politics in newspapers or discuss politics with friends in a neutral fashion, we find the percentages for the more active respondents listed in Table 3.3.

In 1974, when the Barnes-Kaase survey was administered, Americans still rated at the top of the scale in political participation, at least of the conventional type. But the British no longer ranked higher than the West Germans, quite the contrary. As in the case of the allegiance/alienation dimension, democratically relevant attitudes have increased in West Germany. Table 3.3 also suggests that today the West Germans rank high among Western Europeans in their propensity to employ conventional modes of participation. At least in northwestern Europe, the British political

[20]Ibid., pp. 473–505.

[21]A classic analysis is Laurence Wylie, *Village in the Vaucluse*, 3rd ed. (Cambridge: Harvard University Press, 1974), pp. 206–239.

[22]Ambler, *op. cit.*, p. 54.

[23]The material in this section is drawn from Barnes *et al., op. cit.*, pp. 57–94.

**TABLE 3.3**  Conventional Political Participants

| Country | Percent |
| --- | --- |
| United States | 42% |
| West Germany | 28 |
| Austria | 21 |
| The Netherlands | 20 |
| Great Britain | 16 |

SOURCE: Samuel H. Barnes *et al., Political Action: Mass Participation in Five Western Democracies* (Beverly Hills and London: Sage, 1979), p. 85.

**TABLE 3.4** Percentage of Respondents Who Say They Can Do Something About an Unjust or Harmful Local Regulation or National Law, 1959–1960 and 1974

| Country | Local Regulation | | National Law | |
|---|---|---|---|---|
| | 1959–60 | 1974 | 1959–60 | 1974 |
| The Netherlands | —% | 62% | —% | 43% |
| Great Britain | 78 | 64 | 62 | 57 |
| United States | 77 | 71 | 75 | 78 |
| West Germany | 62 | 67 | 38 | 56 |
| Austria | — | 43 | — | 33 |

SOURCE: Samuel H. Barnes *et al., Political Action: Mass Participation in Five Western Democracies* (Beverly Hills and London: Sage, 1979), p. 141.

culture now appears to rank among the least participant.

A similar impression is gained if we look at the Barnes-Kaase findings on civic competence. The Almond-Verba study found the United States, Great Britain, and West Germany to rank first, second, and third, respectively, in both local and national civic competence. Table 3.4 displays percentages for both 1959–1960 and 1974 for these three countries as well as percentages for 1974 for the Netherlands and Austria. The rankings for local competence have changed, West Germany replaces Great Britain in second place; the rankings for national competence remain the same. But it is noteworthy that the gap between West Germany and the Anglo-Saxon countries has narrowed markedly. Civic competence has increased among West Germans at the local level and especially at the national level, whereas it has declined among the British at both levels and among Americans at the local level, but not at the national level.

When Barnes and Kaase asked their respondents about unconventional modes of political participation, they shifted the focus from activities in which respondents *had* engaged to those in which they *would* engage given proper stimulus. The principal dividing line was between legal activities considered unconventional, such as legal demonstrations and boycotts, to activities that were illegal as well as unorthodox, such as rent strikes, sit-ins, blockades, and unofficial work strikes. In terms of the percentages of

those who said they would engage in the illegal type of activity, the ranking of the United States, West Germany, and Great Britain remained the same (in that order); the only change was the rise of the Netherlands from fourth to first place (tied with the United States), with 46 percent of the respondents willing to engage in at least one of the illegal activities (as compared with 31 percent in West Germany and 30 percent in Britain).[24]

## ITALY AND FRANCE

In the past (as noted earlier), the Italian and French political cultures have not seemed to have as heavy an incidence of participant orientations as has been the case with the other countries we are examining. Earlier studies focused primarily on conventional modes of participation. It is clear that France and Italy have been among those European countries in which the rise of unconventional, including illegal and even violent, political activity has been most striking since the late 1960s. However, speculation that Italians rate high in propensity for unconventional activity is belied by a survey taken in 1975 in which Italians were asked whether they would engage in various forms of activity. Violent forms were overwhelmingly repudiated, and, at most, only about 20 to 25 percent of respondents indicated a willingness, in theory, to engage in any illegal activities.[24A] This can be compared with the figure of

[24]*Ibid,* p. 81.

[24A] Sani, op.cit. page 306.

30 percent that Barnes and Kaase found for Great Britain and West Germany. It must be remembered that Italy is a Catholic country. Despite strong support for the Italian Communist Party (PCI), a great many Italians are taught by the Church and at home to respect the authority of the established government and the police who enforce its laws. This is especially true because the established government is in the hands of the Christian Democratic Party and, therefore, enjoys the Church's blessing. It is even likely that many Communist voters would disdain illegal activity. The PCI has become an established part of the structure of political institutions in Italy, and Communist leaders have little desire to see those institutions rocked by widespread acts of defiance of the state's authority, as they have demonstrated in condemning terrorist acts and in seeking to discourage unauthorized strikes in industrial disputes.

What we might call the theory of French political culture suggests that the typical Frenchman or woman, ambivalent about established authority, will avoid conventional modes of participation approved by those in authority and potentially involving face-to-face contact. They will avoid such contact with the authorities themselves and with other like-minded citizens in any organized context in which the legitimacy of the authorities is mutually acknowledged.

Although France is officially a Catholic country, nonbelievers and lukewarm Catholics are found with greater frequency there than in Italy. Thus, the restraining hand of the Church and Catholic family are less likely to inhibit attitudes toward unconventional participation in France. The other side of the coin is that the French would not be expected to engage in sustained, organized protest. Their ambivalence toward authority would mean oscillation between periods of intense antagonism and periods in which the desire for order and predictability would return. The tendency of French leftist groups toward endless internal bickering and splintering into innumerable offshoots would be an expression of the reputed French disdain for long-term stability in relations with peers as well as with those in authority. However, the success

French President Francois Mitterrand. With his Socialist Party, he won the presidential and legislative elections of May–June 1981, thus bringing the left to power in France for the first time in 25 years.

of the French Socialist Party (PS) in channeling youthful energies into the successful campaigns of the 1981 presidential and legislative elections challenges these speculations. More of the French may today be gaining respect for, and confidence in, conventional modes of political action.

## FACTORS UNDERLYING POLITICAL PARTICIPATION

The differences among our Western European countries with respect to the dimensions of conventional and unconventional participation do not stand out as clearly as do those on the allegiance/alienation dimension. A possible explanation may be that there are underlying factors that account for attitudes toward participation essentially in the same ways in all of our countries. For example, Almond and Verba found that civic competence increased in all countries with the level of education. Citizens with university-level educations, for example, would be more likely than those who had not completed secondary education to display civic competence, regardless of whether they were American, German, or Italian.

## DEMOGRAPHIC FACTORS

In point of fact, the relationship between level of education and political participation is one of the most consistent findings in the research on political culture.[25] Studies have also found that it is a stronger predictor of political participation than are indicators of social class, such as occupation and family income. The consistent finding that level of education is the strongest predictor of political participation can be explained in terms of the heightened awareness and understanding of politics that the student gains at the higher levels of education.

Other possible predictors of political participation are sex, age, and religion. Of the three, Barnes and Kaase found that sex was the most strongly related to conventional political participation. Age and religion bore little, or no, relationship to conventional participation although there was a tendency for participation to increase with age, only to level off in the oldest age brackets. In all five countries, men were more likely to participate through normal channels than were women, but the difference was greatest in West Germany, least in the United States. This suggests that one aspect of the greater liberation of women in the United States is their greater involvement in politics, whereas the gap between West German men and women remains relatively wide.

With respect to unconventional participation, age assumes an importance at least equal to that of education. In fact, in the United States, Great Britain, and West Germany, age was a somewhat better predictor of attitudes toward unconventional participation than was education. The relationship is a negative one in the case of age, that is, the older the individual, the less likely he or she is to favor unconventional participation. The relationship between education and unconventional participation is a positive one, that is, the higher the educational level, the greater the inclination toward unconventional participation. Sex and religion

[25]The discussion in this section is drawn from material in Barnes et al., op. cit., pp. 97–135.

showed some relationship to unconventional participation, but the correlations are weaker than in the cases of age and education. Men are slightly more likely than women to favor protest activity. Those who have no religious belief or little intensity of belief (whatever their religion) are somewhat more likely than the more intensely religious to favor unconventional participation.

## POLITICAL SOCIALIZATION

The strong relationship between level of education and conventional political participation is a standard finding that we should expect to find on the basis of common sense. But that the social category most likely to engage in unconventional activities is that of younger people with higher levels of education would not have been so self-evident before the era of the campus protests of the 1960s and 1970s. Those with higher levels of education would have been expected to display a greater appreciation for the beneficial qualities of the democratic political system because they were the very people who had benefited most from the educational opportunities provided by that system and could also command the other values that education can bring. Because youth were typically less likely than their elders to participate in conventional ways, it might also have been expected that they would not show a penchant for unconventional participation either. Nor did many students in either the United States or Western Europe spend much time protesting perceived political injustices before the mid-1960s.

When the student rebellions began, the older generation was hard pressed to understand the new phenomenon. These young people certainly were not behaving in ways taught them by their parents. Young people participating in demonstrations and university sit-ins, on the other hand, could not comprehend the lack of comprehension on the part of their parents. Observers of this new dimension of political conflict in the First World—parents versus children—began to speak of a generation gap.

Concern about a generation gap came at about the same time that political scientists were exploring an area of research that was new to them and that they conceived to be closely related to the study of political culture. The study of political socialization is the study of the ways in which political orientations are transmitted from generation to generation through the mediation of institutions in which older people communicate with younger people. Especially noteworthy among these institutions are the family, the school, and the media of communications. Something seemed to be happening in Western society that was interfering with traditional lines of communication between the generations. The same sort of break in continuity was being observed in studies of political socialization in Third World countries, but it was to be expected there, given the fact that such countries were undergoing rapid modernization. What students of political socialization in the First World in the 1950s and early 1960s failed to recognize was that rapid change was occurring in the First World as well and that it was affecting the perceptions the younger generation held of their elders and of the institutions in which the authority of the older generation had always prevailed. The family, the school, and the political system were becoming arenas of conflict that centered around the question of the right of the older generation to command the obedience of the younger generation. It was a conflict between the power asserted by older people as their right and the respect demanded by younger people as their right. What has been happening to the process of political socialization in Western Europe during this era of institutional change?

If we begin with the traditional role played by the primary socializer—the family—we are struck immediately with the more authoritarian nature of the family in our three continental European countries than in Great Britain or the United States. Almond and Verba found a higher percentage of Britons and Americans than of West Germans or Italians who (1) remembered having had an influence in family decisions as children, (2) remembered being free to protest

family decisions, and (3) remembered that they had actually protested family decisions on occasion.[26] In the past, the typical European (non-British) family was dominated by the father, whereas the father and mother played (and continue to play) more equal roles in family decision making in the United States. The latter is also true among British middle-class families. However, in the British working class, the father was an authoritarian figure although he was traditionally absent when it came to bringing up the children. Thus, the mother played a greater role by default. The resulting authority pattern was probably more ambiguous than that found in a working-class family on the continent.

Traditionally, authority patterns learned in the family served as models as the child grew up. If he or she had experienced the father having the final decision-making responsibility and had been used to obeying these decisions without question, the child would assume this pattern to be normal and, thus, expect to find it in later life situations. In this connection, European (including British) school systems were more authoritarian than the American, as the Almond-Verba study documented.[27] The authority of the teacher was absolute. In French schools, the child learned certain principles by rote and was then expected to reproduce them to the teacher's satisfaction. If the child failed the teacher might call on the ridicule of the other children as a means of reinforcing the expectation.[28] In Italy and in parts of France and West Germany, religious instruction in the public shools or instruction in church schools added the absolute authority structure of the Catholic Church to an already authoritarian pedagogical system.

Once again, it should be pointed out that the Almond-Verba surveys were conducted more than 20 years ago. In the meantime, important changes have taken place in Western Europe, some of which were discussed in Chapter Two. A decrease in family size has made it more likely

[26] Almond and Verba, *op. cit.*, p. 331.

[27] *Ibid.*, pp. 332–333.

[28] Wylie, *op. cit.*, pp. 84–87.

that the wife will work at least part of the time to supplement the family income. This increases her status within the family and gives her a stronger voice in the family decision-making process. With a more pluralistic family power structure, the children are not so overwhelmed that they cannot exert influence, especially as they grow older. The schools have been doing a certain amount of experimentation in curriculum development and teaching methods, often along American lines. West Germany has gone especially far in this direction. Ever since the Allied Occupation, a concerted effort has been made to democratize the educational system with respect to both the authority patterns within the schools and the explicit content of the teaching.[29] German children are given a much more extensive civics education than are British, French, or Italian children, and the content is often of a superior quality to what can typically be found in American schools.

It is possible that the real generation gap in Western Europe today is between children and grandparents, with the generation of the parents being caught somewhere in between. The parents experienced a more rigid authority pattern in their families as they were growing up, but the changes going on around them in society made it impossible, and probably undesirable, to maintain the same patterns in dealing with their offspring. In viewing the protest behavior of their children, they find echoes in their own earlier attitudes toward their elders; yet, they are also anxious that their children do not turn their backs on the opportunities provided by the rapid improvements in life conditions, which they have witnessed in their own lifetime. They fear that the young people may be upsetting an applecart that only needs to be pushed along gently. Barnes and Kaase included a considerable number of pairs of parents and their teen-aged offspring in their sample. Differences between parents and their children were found on a number of attitudinal dimensions, especially

those relating to the legitimacy of protest, but there was also considerable agreement. Good examples of the latter were on questions of policy dissatisfaction and policy trust, suggesting that the generation gap has had more of an impact on styles of political participation than it has had on political allegiance.[30] If positive views of the political system are learned by children early in life, negative views held by the parents may be too.

## THE VALUE GAP

What has brought about the generation gap? Why has it manifested itself in an expanded repertory of political participation modes? An answer to these questions was implicit in the preceding section. In making it more explicit, we will draw on the work of American political scientist, Ronald Inglehart, who has examined the changing structure of values in First World countries.[31]

Inglehart has been interested in whether the affluence and relative security of postindustrial society has shifted people's value preferences from a preoccupation with getting on in daily life to more abstract, less mundane values. In our terms, this would mean a shift from the value of well-being to those of power, enlightenment, and respect. He hypothesized that older citizens, having experienced the Great Depression and World War II, would be more concerned with maintaining a healthy economy as well as domestic and international order. Younger citizens would see less value in such things because they had experienced them all their lives. Instead, they would be concerned with expanding the scope of individual expression, both politically and in their personal lives. Table 3.5 indicates that Inglehart's expectations were essentially borne out by the findings. In all five of the countries included in the table, the percentage of respondents exhibiting (what he called) materialistic values

[29]See Sidney Verba, "Germany: The Remaking of Political Culture," in Lucien W. Pye and Sidney Verba, eds., *Political Culture and Political Development* (Princeton, N.J.: Princeton University Press, 1965), pp. 130–170.

[30]Barnes *et al., op. cit.*, Chap. 15.

[31]Ronald Inglehart, "The Nature of Value Change in Postindustrial Society," in Leon N. Lindberg, ed., *Politics and the Future of Industrial Society* (New York: David McKay, 1976), pp. 57–99.

**TABLE 3.5**  Value Type by Age Cohort in Five Countries, 1972–1973 (Percent of Each Country's Respondents in Each Age Cohort)

| Ages | West Germany | | France | | Italy | | U.S. | | Great Britain | |
|------|------|------|------|------|------|------|------|------|------|------|
| | Mat.[a] | P-M[b] | Mat. | P-M | Mat. | P-M | Mat. | P-M | Mat. | P-M |
| 19–28 | 24%[c] | 19% | 22% | 20% | 26% | 16% | 24% | 17% | 27% | 11% |
| 29–38 | 39 | 8 | 28 | 17 | 41 | 8 | 27 | 13 | 33 | 7 |
| 39–48 | 46 | 5 | 39 | 9 | 42 | 7 | 34 | 13 | 29 | 6 |
| 49–58 | 50 | 5 | 39 | 8 | 48 | 6 | 32 | 10 | 30 | 7 |
| 59–68 | 52 | 7 | 50 | 3 | 49 | 4 | 37 | 6 | 36 | 5 |
| 69+ | 62 | 1 | 55 | 2 | 57 | 5 | 40 | 7 | 37 | 4 |
| Total point spread across cohorts | 38+18 =56 | | 33+18 =51 | | 31+11 =42 | | 16+10 =26 | | 10+7 =17 | |

[a]Mat. = Materialistic value system.

[b]P-M = Post materialistic value system.

[c]Percentages do not total 100 for each country because of respondents in intermediate categories.

SOURCE: Ronald Inglehart, "The Nature of Value Change in Postindustrial Society," in Leon N. Lindberg, ed., *Politics and the Future of Industrial Society* (New York: David McKay, 1976), pp. 70–71.

increases as one moves to successively older age categories (cohorts), whereas the percentage of his respondents exhibiting postmaterialist values declines.[32] The same was true of the five smaller countries included in his study—Belgium, the Netherlands, Luxembourg, Denmark, and Ireland.

Table 3.5 also reveals several differences among the larger countries. For one thing, the range of percentages from younger to older respondents is greater for three of the countries—West Germany, France, and Italy—than it is for the other two—the United States and Great Britain. Inglehart explained this by citing events that caused a greater generation gap in continental Europe than in the Anglo-Saxon countries. World War II was experienced much more directly and probably left a much greater and more lasting impression on the generations who experienced it in Germany, France, and Italy than on generations in the United States and Great Britain; for another, postwar economic growth has been more rapid in the former countries than

in the latter, suggesting that younger people in the former countries have become as accustomed as younger people in the latter countries to expecting progressive improvement of material conditions.

In addition to his independent research, Inglehart participated in the Barnes-Kaase five-nation study and measured the relationship between his materialism/postmaterialism dimension and the Barnes-Kaase measures of conventional and unconventional political participation. He found a strong association between materialism/postmaterialism and conventional/unconventional participation, postmaterialists being more favorably disposed than materialists to protest activity. Extending Inglehart's theory, therefore, we can suggest that the reason younger people are more inclined to protest what they perceive to be wrong in their societies is not that they have a greater sense of material deprivation than do their elders; rather, they are likely to have a different ordering of value priorities. Among those values that they are likely to rank in high position are (1) the value of power, which they believe should be distributed more widely in their societies instead of being concentrated in the hands of the few, especially when the few are

[32]Postmaterialists, in our terms, express a preference for the less tangible values of power, respect, and enlightenment over the value of well-being. Materialists express the opposite preference.

apt to be older persons and (2) the value of respect, which they feel is denied to them to the extent that there are limits placed on their ability to communicate their political beliefs. Material values (well-being) are of lesser concern to them but this does not mean that they are, for that reason, quiescent. This may have been the case of their parents when they were the younger generation in the 1940s and 1950s. For them, the experience of enhanced material well-being was going on in their formative years. The solidification of these gains was a principal preoccupation. Moreover, in Western Europe, at least, few of them were afforded the opportunity for higher education, something that their sons and daughters have had available to them in much greater numbers. These young persons do not experience material deprivation, but it is possible that the value deprivation they *do* feel is of a greater magnitude than that of their parents.

Inglehart's principal study was undertaken in the early 1970s, before the economic difficulties associated with the 1970s had yet been perceived as a chronic condition of postindustrial society. It has often been observed in more recent years that young people have turned their backs on the idealism of the previous decade and are showing greater tendencies toward conformity with their elders' expectations because they are concerned with their futures in terms of economic security. In fact, follow-up studies that Inglehart undertook later in the 1970s contained some evidence that postmaterialism had receded among the very youngest age cohort, making them more materialistic than their immediate elders, the sixties generation.[33] But the differences are slight, and, at any rate, the youngest cohort is less materialistic than are the cohorts of the parents and grandparents of today's teenagers. As we have seen, younger people appear to be less allegiant (except in West Germany) and more inclined (in all countries) toward protest activity than are their elders. Perhaps, if materialism reemerges in an extended period of economic crisis at the same time as the numbers of young persons willing to engage in unconventional political activity continue to grow, the 1980s could be an era of industrial unrest in which material deprivation enhanced by frustrated expectations moves people to take direct action against the established authorities in the economic sphere—the state and the private corporations. The scenario may resemble the decades before World War II, before the coming of the postindustrial era. The next decade may see a repetition of the stormy politics of the mature industrial era rather than what the optimistic models of postindustrial society anticipate.

# Suggestions for Further Reading

Almond, Gabriel A., and Sidney Verba, *The Civic Culture: Political Attitudes and Democracy in Five Nations* (Princeton, N.J.: Princeton University Press, 1963).

_____, eds., *The Civic Culture Revisited* (Boston and Toronto: Little, Brown, 1980).

Barnes, Samuel H., *et al., Political Action: Mass Participation in Five Western Democracies* (Beverly Hills and London: Sage, 1979).

Barzini, Luigi, *The Italians* (New York: Bantam, 1965).

Dawson, Richard E., *et al., Political Socialization*, 2nd ed. (Boston and Toronto: Little, Brown, 1977).

[33]Ronald Inglehart, "Political Dissatisfaction and Mass Support for Social Change in Advanced Industrial Society," *Comparative Political Studies, 10* (3) (1977), pp. 452–472.

**Edinger, Lewis J.,** *Politics in West Germany,* 2nd ed. (Boston and Toronto: Little, Brown, 1977).

**Ehrmann, Henry W.,** *Politics in France,* 3rd ed. (Boston and Toronto: Little, Brown, 1976).

**Goldthorpe, J. H.,** *et al., The Affluent Worker: Political Attitudes and Behavior* (Cambridge: At the University Press, 1968).

**Inglehart, Ronald,** *The Silent Revolution: Changing Values and Political Styles Among Western Publics* (Princeton, N.J.: Princeton University Press, 1977).

**McClelland, David C.,** *The Achieving Society* (New York: Free Press, 1961).

**Pye, Lucien W.,** and **Sidney Verba,** eds., *Political Culture and Political Development* (Princeton, N.J.: Princeton University Press, 1965).

**Rose, Richard,** *Politics in England,* 3rd ed. (Boston and Toronto: Little, Brown, 1980).

**Schonfeld, William R.,** *Obedience and Revolt: French Behavior Toward Authority* (Beverly Hills and London: Sage, 1976).

**Tapper, Ted,** *Political Education and Stability: Elite Responses to Political Conflict* (London: Wiley, 1976).

**Wylie, Laurence,** *Village in the Vaucluse,* 3rd ed. (Cambridge: Harvard University Press, 1974).

# CHAPTER FOUR
## Political Parties

### THE IDEOLOGICAL SPECTRUM

In Chapter Three our focus was on the political beliefs of ordinary citizens. Political culture is a diffuse set of attitudes that are generally shared by large numbers of citizens. The individual citizen may or may not be able to relate his or her political attitudes to an integrated set of political beliefs that we would dignify with the label, ideology. Only a minority of citizens have this capability. Usually, they are those who are more highly educated, who follow politics regularly, and who at least discuss politics on a regular basis with friends and associates. Political ideologies are more highly developed than political culture. They can usually be traced to the writings of influential political philosphers who fit into established philosophical traditions, and they can be assigned recognizable labels, such as Liberalism, Conservatism, or Socialism. In this chapter, we will consider the political parties in Western Europe that are readily identifiable in terms of political ideologies and that compete with one another for power, contesting elections and seeking government office on the basis of their stated, ideologically based, programs.

Ideology plays a more important role for European political parties than for their American counterparts. Americans, who are used to thinking of themselves as Democrats or Republicans so long as they more or less consistently

vote for the candidates of one or the other party, have difficulty understanding that political parties in Europe have a corporate identity that separates them clearly and distinctly from the body of voters to whom they appeal for votes. The parties, in effect, are groups of men and women who fill party offices and actively participate in party functions. They constitute a small minority of the population. Thus, if French political parties are sharply at odds with one another on ideological grounds, that does not necessarily mean that the average French man or woman cares much about these interprofessional battles.[1] If French voters divide their votes among a relatively large number of parties, it could be because the French political élites give them a relatively large number of choices. The separate ideological families in France are subsets of political activists—the minority of the French who devote their time and energy to such matters. Thus, to speak of the ideologies that divide political parties from one another in Europe is to speak of several different political subcultures— essentially élite subcultures.

Let us briefly survey the range of these sub-

---

[1]For supporting evidence, see Philip E. Converse and Georges Dupeux, "Politicization of the Electorate in France and the United States," in Angus Campbell *et al.*, eds., *Elections and the Political Order* (New York: Wiley, 1966), pp. 269–291.

| Radical Left | Communism | New Left | Democratic Socialism | Liberalism | Christian Democracy | Conservatism | Reactionary Right |
|---|---|---|---|---|---|---|---|

**Figure 4.1**   The left-right ideological spectrum.

cultures as they are typically found in Western Europe. We will use the traditional left-right spectrum because most subcultures can be fairly easily placed along it (see Figure 4.1). Two of the eight subcultures, Liberalism and Conservatism, have their origins in the nineteenth century; one, Democratic Socialism, was a turn-of-the-century creation; the remainder are distinctly twentieth-century phenomena—all, however, have their nineteenth-century antecedents.

Nineteenth-century Liberalism and Conservatism differed from one another primarily in terms of the struggle to democratize European political systems. Liberals favored a measured, steady reform that would expand the electorate and reduce the power of the entrenched aristocracy, whose privileges and prerogatives Conservatives sought to protect. In Europe today, there is little to distinguish Liberalism from Conservatism; both accept political, economic, and social institutions essentially as they are. Although Conservatives resist efforts to redistribute well-being, respect, and enlightenment through government action, Liberals are amenable to moderate reform but are not likely to be in the vanguard advocating it. Liberalism and Conservatism have both adapted to modern capitalism. Indeed, it is not clear to what extent they can any longer be regarded as separate subcultures although most Western European countries have separate Liberal and Conservative political parties.

Socialism as an ideology and as a subculture goes back nearly as far as Liberalism and Conservatism. In the nineteenth century, there were both utopian and scientific versions of Socialism existing side by side; the former was more prevalent in France, whereas the latter was more prevalent in Germany, the home of Karl Marx. By the end of the century, Marxist Socialism was the predominant variety, but there was emerging within Marxism a doctrinal conflict over the appropriate means for achieving the agreed-on ends. The revisionist wing of the movement

became stronger after the turn of the century as its prescription to work within the parliamentary democratic system began to pay dividends. What we now call Democratic Socialism is the product of early twentieth-century revisionism. The Democratic Socialists advocate a substantial redistribution of the values of well-being, respect, and enlightenment in favor of those social classes that have relatively small shares of them. However, they do not believe that a major redistribution of power is also necessary because parliamentary democracy enables classes that are weak in other resources to use their superior numbers to gain the necessary power to make redistributive decisions.

Western European Communism, on the

Italian Communist leader, Enrico Berlinguer, in April 1977.

other hand, is a direct descendant of that branch of Socialism that remained faithful to the Marxist revolutionary blueprint. Until recently, at least, Communists denied that a fundamental redistribution of well-being, respect, and enlightenment could take place unless the political system were radically changed. Thus, if the Communists were to come to power in Western European parliamentary democracies, they would use their newly acquired political resources to destroy the power base of the capitalist class, thus, removing resistance to Socialist redistribution and achieving dictatorship of the proletariat. Recently, however, Communism has become more ambivalent about how to achieve Socialist goals. The leading Communists in Italy and France, the two countries in Western Europe where Communism is strongest, have argued (much as Democratic Socialists have argued all along) that it would not be necessary to change the rules of parliamentary democracy. Although this would mean living with capitalism longer than the Communists in the Soviet Union, Poland, or East Germany were willing to do, contemporary Western European Communism seems content to let the existing distribution of power remain intact while working on the redistribution of other values. Thus, differences between Communism and Democratic Socialism have been considerably lessened.

In the mid-1970s, the term Eurocommunist was applied to most of the Western European Communist parties, implying that they have evolved in a direction different from that of the Soviet Communist Party (CPSU) and its fraternal parties in Eastern Europe. The term was first assumed by the Spanish Communist Party (PCE), which even went so far as to deny that it is any longer a Marxist-Leninist party, preferring to be regarded as simply a Marxist party, thus, implicitly denying any necessity to follow the guidance of the CPSU, the party of Lenin. Both the Italian and French parties have permitted themselves to be labeled Eurocommunist, but recent evidence suggests that there are important differences between the two parties, including differences of an ideological nature. The Italian Communist Party (PCI) has gone a considerable

distance in pragmatically adapting their program to the expectations of the ruling Christian Democrats with whom they have sought a partnership. This search for an historic compromise has led the PCI into close working relationships with both private capitalists in those cities where the PCI holds power as well as with the Christian Democrats in the Parliament where the PCI has frequently played a cooperative role in the fashioning of legislative compromises. The French Communist Party (PCF), on the other hand, had persisted in a determined opposition to the parties in power until the victory of the Socialist Party in the 1981 legislative elections. Many observers who take at face value the claim of the PCI that they have abandoned the objective of a dictatorship of the proletariat are more skeptical of the same claim when it is made by the PCF. One indicator of the difference between the two parties is the fact that the Soviet invasion of Afghanistan was denounced by the PCI, whereas the PCF defended it.

Into the vacuum left by the Communist drift away from the extreme left since the mid-1960s, younger Socialists have moved. Calling themselves Marxists, Leninists, Trotskyites, Maoists, or Anarchists, they have rejected Moscow-oriented Communism as essentially defensive of the *status quo*. But their position on the distribution of basic values in Western capitalist systems is essentially the same as that of the revolutionary Socialists at the turn of the century or even of the Communists of the 1950s. They feel that only a thoroughgoing destruction of the capitalist base of power will make it possible to achieve a radical redistribution of other values. This radical left differs from the earlier brand of Communism by dividing its criticism equally between Western capitalism and the Socialist regimes of Eastern Europe. Because inequalities persist in the latter regimes, the radical left in Western Europe argues that this is a form of state capitalism that does not differ in principle from the private capitalism of the West. But their wholesale rejection of the Western institutional structure places them on the far left of the ideological spectrum.

Although there would be general agreement

among political scientists regarding most of the placements along the ideological spectrum in Figure 4.1, there are a number of so-called fringe political parties in Western Europe that defy placement, often because the issues with which they are preoccupied are not the class-based conflicts over shares of material well-being that have traditionally indicated where political parties belong on the spectrum. They are parties that have highlighted new issues or resuscitated old issues that appeared or reappeared on the agenda of First World politics only rather late in the twentieth century. Frequently, they have placed more emphasis on the value of respect, insisting on greater recognition of the rights and status of groups, such as youth, ethnic minorities, or women, that is, those who feel deprived of respect by the power holders of the political system. Usually, however, demands for greater material well-being are interlaced with demands for greater respect, and, so, these parties are probably appropriately placed somewhere on the left.

In a number of Western European countries, new left parties have emerged of late, attracting the support especially of the educated youth, whose preoccupation is with the expansion of political rights, including the right to engage in forms of political action labeled in Chapter Three as unconventional. The most successful of such parties has been the Radical Party in Italy, which came from almost nowhere in the 1979 national election to capture 3.4 percent of the popular vote and 18 seats in the Chamber of Deputies. Sometimes encompassed within new left parties and sometimes constituting separate parties on their own are the Environmentalists (or Greens). The Green parties in France and West Germany have appeared strong enough in recent elections to threaten to take crucial segments of votes away from the larger parties. Another type of fringe party found in many Western European countries is the regional or ethnic separatist party—exemplified by the Scottish Nationalist Party in Great Britain and the South Tyrolean People's Party in Italy—which, at the minimum, seek greater autonomy for the region in which their ethnic minority is concentrated. In some cases, as for some Scottish Nationalists, actual independence from the larger nation is sought.

Another primarily twentieth-century development in some Western European countries was the emergence of Christian Democracy, which came about as an effort to reconcile Europe's Catholics with parliamentary democracy and with economic and social reform. Before World War II, there had been strong Catholic elements who rejected democracy and sought to preserve the existing distribution of values in society. These groups were especially strong in the Mediterranean Catholic countries—Italy, Portugal, and Spain—but they constituted at least a minority among the politically active Catholics in France and Germany. In all of these countries, some leading Catholics embraced Fascism. Yet, Catholics also played an important role in resisting Mussolini's Fascist rule in Italy and the German occupation of France during World War II. In France and Italy, Christian Democracy, which stemmed from smaller parties of earlier decades, earned its democratic credentials during the resistance and emerged from the war with a large mass following. In Germany, Christian Democracy was made up of the leaders of the old Catholic Center Party of the Weimar Republic who had gone into deep retirement during the Nazi years and emerged after the war untainted if also rather unheroic. But Christian Democracy in West Germany has taken a somewhat different turn from that in Italy and France because half of the West German population is Protestant. In West Germany, Christian Democracy has been able to appeal to Liberal and Conservative middle-class Protestants as well as to Catholics of all social classes.

What is Christian Democracy today? It remains the ideological basis of two strong political parties—in Italy and West Germany—whereas its political expression in France has become weaker and weaker, until, today, it is not clear that there is still a Christian Democratic party. The party's survival in Italy and West Germany has depended on the capacity of Christian Democratic leaders to broaden their appeal, adopting in their party platforms elements of Conservatism, Liberalism, and even Democratic

Socialism. In the early years after World War II, Christian Democracy in all three countries had a strong reformist strain, a commitment to a truly democratic political system and to moderate redistribution of well-being, respect, and enlightenment. After the onset of the Cold War in the late 1940s, these reformist aspects became increasingly muted in favor of a strong anti-Communism. In the 1950s, it was customary to classify Christian Democracy with Conservatism. But, since the early 1960s, the willingness of Christian Democratic political leaders to cooperate with the Democratic Socialists in programs of moderate reform has made it much harder to place them very far to the right on the ideological spectrum. Christian Democracy today is a mixture of many ideological elements with considerable pragmatism and even opportunism. It is probably safest to locate Christian Democracy in the center right of our ideological spectrum.

As for the far right, it is not so easy to find *bona fide* right-wing extremists in Western Europe as it was a few decades ago. With respect to political movements, there is nothing even faintly resembling the virulent Nazis in Germany or Mussolini's Fascists in Italy. Short-lived right-wing movements have appeared from time to time, such as the Poujadists in France in the mid-1950s, which was a movement of small businesspersons who were protesting the dislocations that affected them as France moved toward a postindustrial society. The strongest right-wing party today, the neo-Fascists in Italy, are a somewhat similar phenomenon, likewise appealing to threatened social groups and gaining their principal strength in the less advanced southern portion of Italy, just as the Poujadists were strongest in the rural areas of central and southwestern France. It is not easy to characterize what today's reactionary right represents ideologically. In some ways, it resembles the radical left in its aversion to big capitalism and big government. But prewar Nazism and Fascism showed that bringing the reactionary right to power will only lead to bigger capitalism and bigger government without effecting any real redistribution of well-being, respect, and enlightenment whatever the upheavals in the structure of power. The racism of the Nazis finds only faint echoes today, as in the National Front, a right-wing party in Great Britain. But, given the spectacular rise of the Nazis from humble origins, profiting from economic catastrophe, it would be foolish to ignore even its faint echoes today.

Perhaps a more reliable distinguishing feature of the reactionary right is its strong nationalistic strain. The far right in Western European countries has been hostile to European integration because they feel it threatens national sovereignty. In this, there is only a shade of difference between the reactionary right and certain Conservative political leaders, such as the Gaullist, Michel Debré, or Franz Josef Strauss, leader of the Bavarian Christian Social Union (CSU) in West Germany. These leaders are strongly nationalistic, but they can by no stretch of the imagination be called racists.

Table 4.1 matches ideologies with the more important political parties in our four countries. Some parties defy classification, such as the French Gaullists (RPR) whom we have placed in the conservative category. They actually comprise a broad coalition of elements much like the Christian Democrats in Italy and West Germany. Some Gaullists are Liberals, others are clearly Conservatives, and still others, in their strong nationalism at least, resemble adherents of the reactionary right. Indeed, it was customary to classify the forerunner of the contemporary Gaullist Party, the Rally of the French People (RPF) of the late 1940s and early 1950s, as a party of the far right. Still, in terms of the behavior of the Gaullist leadership since the party came to power in 1958, it seems appropriate to classify the party as Conservative, but it is a very practical, flexible kind of Conservatism (on domestic matters, at least)—more like that of the British Conservative Party than, for example, that of the Italian Liberal (!) Party.

Table 4.2 attempts to specify the attitude of each of the subcultures regarding the redistribution of power, well-being, respect, and enlightenment. Clearly, the zeal for redistribution diminishes as one moves from left to right although we

**TABLE 4.1**  Location of Political Parties on the Ideological Spectrum

| Country | Radical and New Left | Communism | Democratic Socialism | Liberalism | Christian Democracy | Conservatism | Reactionary Right |
|---|---|---|---|---|---|---|---|
| *Great Britain* | | | Labour Party | Liberal Party | | Conservative Party | |
| *France* | Unified Socialist Party (PSU) | French Communist Party (PCF) | Socialist Party (PS) | Union for French Democracy (UDF) | | Gaullists (RPR) | |
| *West Germany* | | German Communist Party (DKP) | Social Democratic Party (SPD) | Free Democratic Party (FDP) | Christian Democratic Union (CDU) | Christian Social Union (CSU) | National Democratic Party (NPD) |
| *Italy* | Proletarian Democracy (DP) Radicals | Italian Communist Party (PCI) | Italian Socialist Party (PSI) Social Democratic Party (PSDI) | Republican Party (PRI) | Christian Democratic Party (DC) | Liberal Party (PLI) | Italian Social Movement (MSI) |

note that the reactionary right would probably attempt a redistribution of power, as the Nazis and Italian Fascists did when the opportunity arose. The choices indicated here with respect to particular ideologies and particular values are rather arbitrary and would not command universal agreement. Do the Christian Democrats seek a redistribution of well-being and respect? If we look at the left wing of the Italian Christian Democratic Party, the answer would be yes. However, if we look at the right-wing of the party, the answer would be an unqualified no. One could argue that the left-wing Christian Democrats are really Democratic Socialists, whereas the right-wing component is really conservative. Here, the best compromise seemed to be to label Christian Democracy ambivalent on these issues.

## POLITICAL PARTY SYSTEMS

We have noted that political parties in Western Europe have more readily identifiable ideologies than those in the United States. When we turn from the United States to Western Europe, we also find that the political process is generally more highly structured, with fewer pressure points available where ordinary citizens might

**TABLE 4.2**  Attitudes of Subcultures Toward the Redistribution of Basic Values

| Subculture | Power | Well-being | Respect | Enlightenment |
|---|---|---|---|---|
| Radical and new left | R | R | R | R |
| Communism | A | R | R | R |
| Democratic Socialism | N | R | R | R |
| Liberalism | S | A | N | R |
| Christian Democracy | S | A | A | A |
| Conservatism | S | S | S | S |
| Reactionary right | R | S | S | N |

Note: R = redistributive tendency (favor more equal distribution).
  S = *status quo* orientation (oppose more equal distribution).
  A = ambivalence
  N = neutral.

hope to affect political outcomes. This is partly due to the nature of political party organization in Western Europe. In the United States, those who vote regularly for the Republican Party's candidates are likely to think of themselves as members of that party. In Western Europe, the larger parties have an official definition of what a party member is; there is usually a dues-paying requirement and perhaps a certain minimal expectation of participation in party activities. The membership will, therefore, be easily identifiable and stable; it will not fluctuate widely from year to year, and the party itself will function on a continuous basis. Party meetings will be held, locally as well as nationally, with regularity,

British Prime Minister, Margaret Thatcher. As leader of the Conservative Party, winner of the May 1979 elections, she became the first woman to be British Prime Minister.

whether it is an election year or not. Party activity will naturally increase at election time, just as it does in the United States; but the point is that the ground troops are already in place, ready for action. They do not have to be recruited on the eve of the campaign.

What this suggests is that the political party in Western Europe, as a channel for popular participation, offers opportunities, but one must first establish his or her credentials as a party regular before having any hope of playing a weighty role either in the electoral or in the public policy-making process. The rules of the game of popular participation are, thus, more firmly established in Western European countries. Because the two major parties are looser and more fluid in the United States, the participant may be in a position to help redefine the rules as well as to influence the outcome. Nevertheless, the existence of a number of political parties in most Western European countries means that the individual has a variety of choices. This may be a reason why voter turnout rates are higher in Western Europe than in the United States.

On both sides of the Atlantic, the electoral process is the principal means by which most people participate in politics. The political parties are the instruments through which the electorate expresses its preferences at election time as follows: (1) those citizens who are active in the political parties may have a role in selecting candidates for elective office and (2) the choices that are offered on the ballot are usually distinguishable to the average voter according to the differences between the parties they represent. The first point is truer of the United States than of Western European countries, which do not have primary elections for choosing candidates. The second point is truer of Western Europe, where the voters may not be clearly aware of who the candidates for legislative office are, but they feel competent to choose anyway because of the candidates' party affiliations.

In each of the Western European political systems, two or more political parties interact with one another in what we call a party system. The central focus of this interaction is the contest among political parties for the power to govern the country—a contest that takes place at two levels: (1) in elections, where the voters determine the respective share each party will have of the seats in parliament and (2) within parliament, where the distribution of seats among the parties and the coalitions worked out among them will ultimately determine what party or parties will constitute the government. In characterizing the different types of party systems and understanding the consequences of different party arrangements in the countries we are studying, three questions should be asked: (1) How many parties of any consequence are there? (2) What are their relative strengths? (3) What, if any, coalition patterns can be found among the parties? Our four countries differ considerably with respect to these questions, but all four may be tending in a common direction.

## NUMBER OF PARTIES

Political scientists usually distinguish between two-party and multi-party systems, the American and British party systems being the prototypes of the former, the French and Italian of the latter. But do the United States and Great Britain really have two-party systems? Are there not important differences between three-party systems and say, eight-party systems? In other words, the dividing line between two and three parties is a rather arbitrary one and may not capture a significant distinction. Look at the British party system today. In the general election held in October 1974, the two leading parties, Labour and the Conservatives, together gained 75 percent of the popular vote. The third largest party, the Liberals, captured 18 percent, whereas other parties, including Scottish Nationalists, Welsh Nationalists, Ulster Unionists, Communists, the right-wing National Front, and various independents, totaled nearly 7 percent. Clearly the two largest parties far outdistance the others, but can we really omit the Liberals from consideration? Is the British party system not at least a three-party system?

One reason political scientists have clung to the two-party label for Great Britain is that the British electoral system seriously discriminates against all but the two largest parties. As in the case of the American House of Representatives, Great Britain is divided into geographical units, each returning one member to the 635-member House of Commons. When a general election is held, all, or almost all, 635 seats are contested. Some of these are safe Labour seats, returning the Labour candidate in election after election; some are safe Conservative seats. Few if any can be taken for granted by the Liberals. In fact, Liberal strength is quite evenly distributed around the country, unlike that of the Scottish, Welsh, and Ulster parties, which, of course, is concentrated in their respective geographic regions. Because only one candidate can win the seat in a given constituency and because the winner is whoever gains a plurality—not necessarily a majority (more than 50 percent) of the votes—the Liberals often find themselves running a strong second to one or the other of the two major parties, but seldom taking the first spot. Thus, in May 1979, although the Liberals won more than 13 percent of the popular vote, they captured only 11 of the 635 seats. With 81 percent of the popular vote, the two largest parties obtained 96 percent of the seats—and this was one of their less impressive combined showings. So, is the British party system a two-party system or a three-party system, or even an eight-party system?

Before trying to answer that question, let us look at the situation in West Germany, whose party system bears some resemblance to that of the British. There, too, the three leading parties are a large party on the left, the Social Democrats, (SPD), a large party on the right, the Christian Democrats (CDU), and a smaller party in the center, the Free Democrats (FDP). In October 1980, the two larger parties (the Christian Democrats are federated with the Bavarian CSU) gained 87 percent of the popular vote, and the FDP obtained 10.6 percent. If this result had occurred in Great Britain in 1979, the Liberals would have been fortunate to have gotten their 11 seats. Yet, the FDP captured 53 seats out of 497, or the same 10.6 percent as their share of the popular vote. This enabled them to hold the balance of power between the two major parties, neither of which had secured a majority of seats in the Bundestag (the lower house of the West German Parliament). Obviously, we must regard the West German party system as at least a three-party system. If so, then, why does not Great Britain have a three-party system? Can not Great Britain's third party capture a larger share of the vote than can the West German third party?

What accounts for the more advantageous position of the FDP? It is the electoral system. West Germany has a complex combination of proportional representation and the single-member plurality system; however, the proportional representation principle predominates. This means that seats are distributed among parties in proportion to their percentages of the popular vote. Half of the 496 Bundestag seats are based on single-member constituencies, as in Great Britain. The other half are distributed on a proportional basis among party lists drawn up at the state (land) level. The distribution among land lists corrects for any disproportion that arises in the single-member district results so that the total distribution of seats among the parties will be proportional to their percentages of the national popular vote.

Proponents of the proportional representation system argue that it is only simple justice to allow a party the parliamentary representation it has earned. Otherwise, the votes of those who support a party like the British Liberals are often discounted. The counterargument stresses the fact that proportional representation tends to encourage the proliferation of parties. The horrible example often cited is the Weimar Republic of Germany (1919–1933), where a pure system of proportional representation encouraged literally dozens of parties to vie for Reichstag seats and actually rewarded many of them. Building and maintaining governing coalitions under such circumstances is extremely difficult. The framers of the Bonn electoral law had the Weimar experience in mind when they sought to modify the extreme proliferating effect of proportional representation. They accomplished this by denying representation in the Bundestag to any party that could not gain at least 5 percent of the national-list vote. This rule has kept the Communist Party out of the Bundestag since the earliest years of the Federal Republic, and it has worked to the disadvantage of right-wing parties and various regional splinter parties. Among the smaller parties, only the FDP has been able to remain above this minimum level. The advantage that the FDP gains by means of proportional representation is somewhat offset by its uncertain future. In any event, we will use this 5-percent standard as the criterion for whether a party should be counted when we decide how many parties a given party system has. By this standard, the British party system is a three-party system as is that of West Germany.

Table 4.3 shows the parties that count in each of our four countries, including their percentages of the popular vote and the number of seats they obtained in three recent legislative elections. Using our 5-percent criterion, we can say that France now has a four-party system. The non-Communist Left is dominated by the Socialists. The Union for French Democracy (UDF) comprises mainly the Democratic Center, Valéry Giscard d'Estaing's Republicans, and the part of the old Radical Party that did not ally with the Socialists. Because the Radicals, the Democratic Center, and the Giscardians each commanded more than 5 percent of the vote not too long ago, it can be suggested that the French party system has shrunk from six to four parties. Italy seems to be doing something rather similar although it is still perhaps too early to say. Before the 1970s, at least six parties usually passed the 5-percent mark; in 1976 and 1979, only four were able to do so. One of the two principal casualties, the Liberals, captured less than 2 percent in the last two elections. The other, the Social Democrats, were united with the Socialists in 1968 when the combined parties were able to obtain 14.5 percent of the vote. Separated again in 1972, the Social Democrats just barely exceeded 5 percent, but they have fallen to 3.8 percent in the past two elections. All four systems might be converging on approximately the same number—four. West Germany would reach that number if the Bavarian CSU were considered separately;[2] the British will have four parties if the Scottish Nationalists should resume their growth in strength or if the Social Democratic Party, a breakaway from the Labour Party, should prove viable.

## PARTY STRENGTH

Even if the convergence discussed takes place, the four systems will still differ with respect to the relative strengths of their parties. We have noted that the British and West German party systems are similar, in that there are two giants, one on the left and one on the right, with a smaller centrist party in between. Superficially, one might say the same of Italy. There, the Communists and Christian Democrats together captured 69 percent of the popular vote in June 1979. The next largest party, the Socialists (10 percent), has a position on the spectrum in between the two giants. But there is also a party on the far right—the Italian Social Movement (MSI)—that exceeds the 5-percent standard; however, the positioning of the three largest parties on the spectrum is skewed to the left as compared with the spectrum in Great Britain or West Germany. This has implications for the coalition possibilities that are available in Italy, as we will see in a moment.

The four parties in France are of more nearly equal size although their voting support varies from election to election. The Gaullist Party (now RPR) enjoyed the greatest strength during most of the Fifth Republic, but the Socialists far outdistanced all of their rivals in 1981. Not only did the Socialists establish their superiority over the other party of the left, the Communist Party (PCF), but the two parties of the left together gained more votes than did the combined parties of the right, the first time the left had gained such a clear victory since 1936. But the election left the future of the PCF uncertain. Whereas the Social-

British Opposition leader Michael Foot, the leader of the Labour Party, at the special party confernce held in Wembley, England, in January 1981. At his conference the mode of electing Labour party leaders was changed to give a greater role to trade unions and to left-leaning party activists.

ists and their allies (the small Left Radical Party) increased their percentage of the vote from 25 percent to 37.5 percent—an increase of 50 percent over 1978—the Communists were suffering a 25 percent loss. Whether these changes represent long-term trends or are the result of the momentary popularity of the Socialist leader, François Mitterrand, who had just been elected President of the Republic, remains to be seen. Fluctuations in the support of the two right-of-center parties, the RPR and the UDF, which were nearly even in strength in 1981, have followed closely the popularity of their respective leaders, Paris mayor, Jacques Chirac, and former President Valery Giscard d'Estaing.

## COALITION PATTERNS

It should be clear by now that none of the four party systems can be labeled two-party without serious qualifications. On the other hand, three of them—the British, West German, and Italian —have at least the potential of behaving very

[2]Following the October 1976 Bundestag elections, Franz Josef Strauss, leader of the CSU, actually severed the CDU-CSU connection. But the rift was patched up by the CDU leader, Helmut Kohl, a month later.

much like two-party systems because each system has two strong parties that can serve as poles of attraction for the coalescence of the smaller parties. In fact, this is clearly what happens in Great Britain and West Germany. If one of the characteristics of a viable two-party system is that the two major parties alternate with one another in power, such has been the case in these two countries. In the 10 elections for the House of Commons since World War II, power has changed hands between the Conservatives and Labour six times, most recently in May 1979. Since the Bundestag was first established in 1949, there have been 8 elections in West Germany. Power has really only changed hands there once —in 1969—when the Social Democrats came to power in a coalition with the Free Democrats. If the West German electoral system were as sensitive to shifts in support for the two major parties as is the British, there would probably have been two (or possibly three) changes in power-holders since 1949—most recently in October 1976, when the Christian Democrats recaptured the lead in popular vote but were outdistanced by the coalition of the Social Democrats and Free Democrats, a result that was reproduced four years later.

Because of its strategic position, the FDP holds the key to whether or not power will change hands frequently in West Germany. Most of the time from 1949 to 1966, the FDP was in coalition with the CDU; then, in 1969, they joined a coalition government with the SPD. Today, some CDU leaders are seeking to woo the FDP away from their left-center alliance and into a right-center alliance; and some FDP leaders are attracted by the prospect. But, for the moment, the SPD-FDP coalition prevails and power remains anchored to the left of center. Thus, in West Germany there is a two-tendency rather than a two-party system. There are two alternative coalitions; this means that the potential exists for a fairly frequent alternation in power, but it has not been realized because of rigidities in the coalition pattern.

In Italy, it is not clear whether there is even the potential for alternation between the two leading parties. The Christian Democrats have governed either alone or in coalition since 1946. The Communists have not had a share of power since 1947, and, until the mid-1970s, there was little likelihood that they would regain it. Until 1962, the Christian Democrats relied on the support of smaller parties in the center and on the right to maintain their majority. Then, the coalition pattern shifted to the left, with the Socialists replacing the Liberals as the principal coalition partner. Unable to gain a majority in their own right and unwilling to turn either to the Communists on the far left or to the neo-Fascist MSI on the far right, the Christian Democrats and Socialists became virtual prisoners of one another although the former were clearly the senior partners. Both parties were divided internally over whether to keep the coalition alive.

Finally, in 1975, the Socialists abandoned their partners and joined the Communists in opposition. This left the Christian Democrats with-

**TABLE 4.3** Distributions of Seats and Votes in Three Recent Legislative Elections

| | United Kingdom | | | | | |
| --- | --- | --- | --- | --- | --- | --- |
| | February 1974 | | October 1974 | | 1979 | |
| Party | Votes | Seats | Votes | Seats | Votes | Seats |
| Labour | 37.2% | 301 | 39.3% | 319 | 36.9% | 268 |
| Liberal | 19.3 | 14 | 18.3 | 13 | 13.8 | 11 |
| Conservative | 38.2 | 297 | 35.8 | 277 | 43.9 | 339 |
| Others | 5.3 | 23 | 6.5 | 26 | 5.4 | 16 |

## France

| Party | 1973 Votes | 1973 Seats | 1978 Votes | 1978 Seats | 1981 Votes | 1981 Seats |
|---|---|---|---|---|---|---|
| Communists | 21.4% | 73 | 20.6% | 86 | 16.2% | 44 |
| Socialists and Left Radicals | 20.6 | 102 | 25.0 | 112 | 37.5 | 283 |
| Centrists and Giscardians (UDF) | 19.6 | 86 | 20.4 | 119 | 19.2 | 61 |
| Gaullists | 30.9 | 201 | 22.4 | 145 | 20.8 | 83 |
| Others | 7.8 | 11 | 11.6 | 12 | 6.3 | 17 |

## West Germany

| Party | 1972 Votes | 1972 Seats | 1976 Votes | 1976 Seats | 1980 Votes | 1980 Seats |
|---|---|---|---|---|---|---|
| SPD | 45.9% | 230 | 42.6% | 213 | 42.9% | 218 |
| FDP | 8.4 | 41 | 7.9 | 39 | 10.6 | 53 |
| CDU/CSU | 44.8 | 225 | 48.6 | 244 | 44.5 | 226 |
| Others | 0.9 | 0 | 0.9 | 0 | 2.0 | 0 |

## Italy

| Party | 1972 Votes | 1972 Seats | 1976 Votes | 1976 Seats | 1979 Votes | 1979 Seats |
|---|---|---|---|---|---|---|
| Communists | 27.2% | 179 | 34.4% | 228 | 30.4% | 201 |
| Radicals | — | — | 0.8 | 0 | 3.4 | 18 |
| Socialists | 9.6 | 61 | 9.6 | 57 | 9.8 | 62 |
| Social Democrats | 5.1 | 29 | 3.4 | 15 | 3.8 | 20 |
| Republicans | 2.9 | 14 | 3.1 | 14 | 3.0 | 16 |
| Christian Democrats | 38.8 | 267 | 38.7 | 262 | 38.3 | 262 |
| Liberals | 3.9 | 21 | 1.3 | 5 | 1.9 | 9 |
| Italian Social Movement | 8.7 | 56 | 6.1 | 35 | 5.3 | 30 |
| Others | 3.8 | 3 | 3.6 | 14 | 4.1 | 12 |

SOURCE: For Britain: Howard R. Penniman, ed., *Britain at the Polls: The Parliamentary Elections of 1974* (Washington, D.C.: American Enterprise Institute, 1975), pp. 243–244; *Keesing's Contemporary Archives*, June 8, 1979, p. 29645. For France: Howard R. Penniman, ed., *The French National Assembly Elections of 1978* (Washington, D.C.: American Enterprise Institute, 1980), pp. 16–18; *Le Monde, Sélection Hebdomadaire*, June 11–17, p. 1 and June 18–24, 1981, p. 5. For West Germany: Stanley Rothman *et al.*, *European Society and Politics: Britain, France and Germany* (St. Paul: West, 1976), pp. 204, 207; *New York Times*, October 4, 1976, p. 1; *Keesing's Contemporary Archives*, December 5, 1980, p. 30597; For Italy: P.A. Allum, *Italy: Republic Without Government* (New York: Norton, 1973), p. 65; *Keesing's Contemporary Archives*, September 10, 1976, p. 27926; *New York Times*, June 6, 1979, p. 3.

out a majority. They continued on for several months as a minority government but were finally forced to call new elections for June 1976. As Table 4.3 shows, both of the major parties gained or maintained strength, whereas some of the smaller parties lost ground. But the parliamentary situation remained basically unchanged. A new Christian Democratic government was formed with the tacit willingness of the Communists to allow it some breathing space in exchange for a more progressive program. Following the June 1979 election in which the PCI lost 27 Chamber of Deputy seats, a Christian Democratic-Socialist coalition again became possible. This is what has been governing Italy in the early 1980s, the Communists having returned to the role of constructive opposition. Although the present system works, even if just barely, the Italian party system remains fraught with uncertainty for the future. It is not really a two-tendency system of the type found in Great Britain and West Germany. There may be two political parties that are numerically superior, but no mechanism has yet been worked out by which there can be an orderly transfer of power as there was in West Germany in the late 1960s.

Curiously, although France does not have two dominant parties (as the other three countries do), something like a two-tendency system has been developing, with a fairly stable alliance on the right facing a fairly stable alliance on the left. Part of the reason for the two-tendency system lies in a two-ballot-type election for both president and legislative representatives that encourages electoral alliances. As will be discussed at some length in Chapter Five, France's system of government differs from the parliamentary regimes of the other three countries. There is both an elected president and an elected legislative body. Because they share power, both elections are important. The balance of power established at the last legislative election can be upset by the next presidential election and *vice versa*. For the legislative election, France is divided into single-member constituencies as is Great Britain. But a candidate must win a majority of the vote on the first ballot to be elected. Otherwise, there will be a second ballot the following week, dur-

ing which any candidate who obtained at least 12.5 percent of the vote on the first ballot can remain in the race or withdraw. The second ballot operates the same way the single ballot does in Great Britain: whoever receives a plurality of the vote will be elected for that constituency. The arrangement for the presidential election is similar, except that (1) France is one entire constituency and (2) the second ballot is automatically a runoff between the two candidates who receive the most votes on the first ballot.

Because no French party is ordinarily strong enough to win a majority in its own right in more than a handful of constituencies in legislative elections, the parties need to have allies who will agree with them in advance that there will be only one candidate representing the two parties against a common enemy on the second ballot. Traditionally, the left has been better able than the right to work out such arrangements. During the Third Republic (1870–1940), the Socialists and Radicals were quite successful in maintaining discipline between the two ballots. The expectation was that, in any given constituency, whichever candidate, Socialist or Radical, did better on the first ballot, the other would step aside and urge his supporters to vote for the first candidate on the second ballot. In the Fifth Republic, the Socialists and Communists have had a similar arrangement. In response, the right has had to work out its own arrangement. In 1967, 1968, and 1973, there was only one candidate of the majority coalition (primarily the Gaullists and the Giscardians) in each constituency on the first ballot. With the formation of the UDF before the March 1978 election, separate Gaullist and Giscardians candidates fought each other on the first ballot, but unity was restored on the second ballot. In June 1981, following their loss of the presidency to François Mitterrand, the parties of the right again agreed to run only one candidate in each constituency on the first ballot, a stratagem that did not help them prevent the Socialist victory.

For the presidential election, such prior agreements are not necessary because all except the two top candidates are automatically eliminated after the first ballot. But there is a special need for unity on both the left and the right. If the parties on one side cannot agree on a common candidate before the first ballot, whereas those on the other side can, the common candidate will far outdistance his rivals on the first ballot so that the parties on the divided side will really have to scramble to try to secure support for the surviving candidate during the two weeks between the first and second ballots. An excellent example was the 1969 presidential election. Georges Pompidou, the only candidate of the right, was facing three rivals of the left and center. Pompidou won nearly twice as many votes as his nearest rival on the first ballot and, then, went on to win the runoff easily, partly because one of the losing parties on the first ballot, the Communists, refused to support his second-ballot opponent. In 1981, neither the left nor the right presented a single candidate on the first ballot. The failure to do so was more costly to the surviving right-of-center candidate on the second ballot, incumbent President Giscard d'Estaing. His defeated rival, Jacques Chirac, gave him only lukewarm support, whereas the Communists strongly endorsed François Mitterrand, the eventual victor. Thus, the presidential election as well as the legislative puts a premium on solidarity between the parties on each side.

One must not put too much stress on the importance of the electoral systems in France. The country has had electoral alliances of a fairly stable nature in the past. However, what was truly remarkable in the first 23 years of the French Fifth Republic was a stable governing coalition, consisting of Gaullists, Giscardians, and minor partners on the center right. At least three factors have been responsible for this: (1) the strong leadership exercised by General de Gaulle in the early years of the Fifth Republic; (2) the superior electoral position of the Gaullists, which enabled them to play the role of senior partner, rewarding their allies for loyalty; and (3) the fact that the office of President of the Republic is the preeminent prize to be won and the fact that, because important decision-making powers are concentrated in the President's hands, the coalition partners must mute their dissent. With the capture in 1981 of the presidency and a

majority of the National Assembly, the Socialists under François Mitterrand are in a position similar to that enjoyed earlier by the Gaullists.

## CONCLUSION

Despite the various dissimilarities among our four political party systems, they do appear to share one common characteristic at the present moment. In all four cases, there is sharp, clear-cut competition between left and right, whether it is a party on the left facing a party on the right or a coalition of parties facing one party or another coalition. Figure 4.2 depicts the four ways in which such competition is expressed in our four countries. Actually, the existence of such left-right competition is remarkable when we consider the history of three of these four party systems—the French, the German, and the Italian. If we go back to the 1920s in Germany and as recently as the 1950s in France and Italy, we see a different sort of party system, one in which power is anchored in the center of the spectrum and opposition comes from the left and right extremes. In the Weimar Republic of Germany, the center parties were committed to the existing democratic regime. But, during much of the Republic's life, these parties were scarcely able to maintain majorities in the Reichstag because of the antidemocratic parties on the left and right. A similar situation prevailed in France and Italy in the 1950s.

Under these circumstances, anchoring power in the center of the political spectrum in a coalition of beleaguered parties that are committed to the preservation of the existing regime means that there is no possibility of alternating power from left to right. Power remains where it is, or the regime falls. From the voters' standpoint, either they support the coalition in power or they face unknown upheavals. This is really not a choice for many voters who may feel disenchanted with the performance of the governing coalition. Some will abstain; others will vote for one of the parties opposing the governing regime under the assumption that it could not come to power anyway; others will decide it is time for a sweeping change and will throw caution to the

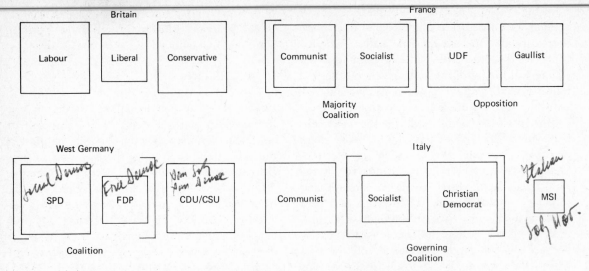

**Figure 4.2** Party systems: Number and sizes of parties and coalition patterns.

winds; still others will resign themselves to the continuation of the present regime and will vote accordingly although not out of any great conviction. Under the circumstances, the disgruntled voter will feel disenfranchised.

On the other hand, today, it is not just the voters in traditionally two-party Great Britain who have a real choice between alternatives. Those in the other three countries do as well although there are greater reservations about this in Italy than in France and West Germany. The voters in Italy have yet to give the left a majority. Nevertheless, all four party systems have become vehicles for meaningful political participation. Election campaigns in all four countries have been intensely fought in recent years, and there have been high voter turnout rates in the three countries without a two-party tradition.

In other words, the voters are being given choices between alternative priority rankings of values. The left in all four countries is redistributive in its orientation toward well-being, enlightenment, and respect. The right is basically oriented toward the *status quo*. The left places greater emphasis on raising real wages, reducing unemployment, and eliminating poverty. The right shows greater concern for the probable inflationary impact of policies implementing such objectives. In all four countries, the left encounters resistance from the right in its attempts to alter the structure of secondary education. In all four countries, the left shows greater sympathy for the principle of dissent, whereas the right is more interested in maintaining domestic stability. Nevertheless, in all four countries, the left and right are essentially agreed as to the mechanics of how power should be distributed in the political system.

# Suggestions for Further Reading

**Barnes, Samuel H.,** *Representation in Italy: Institutionalized Tradition and Electoral Choice* (Chicago and London: University of Chicago Press, 1977).

Butler, David, and Donald Stokes, *Political Change in Britain,* 2nd college ed. (New York: St. Martin's, 1976).

Cerny, Karl H., ed., *Germany at the Polls: The Bundestag Election of 1976* (Washington, D.C.: American Enterprise Institute, 1978).

Dahl, Robert A., ed., *Political Oppositions in Western Democracies* (New Haven, Conn.: Yale University Press, 1966).

Duverger, Maurice, *Political Parties: Their Organization and Activity in the Modern State,* trans. Barbara and Robert North (New York: Wiley, 1954).

Frears, J. R., *Political Parties and Elections in the French Fifth Republic* (New York: St. Martin's, 1977).

Galli, Giorgio, and Alfonso Prandi, *Patterns of Political Participation in Italy* (New Haven, Conn.: Yale University Press, 1970).

Henig, Stanley, ed., *Political Parties in the European Community* (London: Allen & Unwin, 1979).

Kriegel, Annie, *The French Communists: Profile of a People,* trans. Elaine P. Halperin (Chicago: University of Chicago Press, 1972).

LaPalombara, Joseph, and Myron Weiner, eds., *Political Parties and Political Development* (Princeton, N.J.: Princeton University Press, 1966).

Penniman, Howard R., ed., *Britain at the Polls, 1979: A Study of the General Election* (Washington and London: American Enterprise Institute, 1981).

_____, ed., *The French National Assembly Elections of 1978* (Washington: American Enterprise Institute, 1980).

Rose, Richard, *Do Parties Make a Difference?* (Chatham, N.J.: Chatham House, 1980).

_____, ed., *Electoral Behavior: A Comparative Handbook* (New York: Free Press, 1974).

Sartori, Giovanni, *Parties and Party Systems: A Framework for Analysis* (Cambridge: At the University Press, 1976).

Tökès, Rudolf L., ed., *Eurocommunism and Détente* (New York: New York University Press, 1978).

# CHAPTER FIVE

## The Distribution of Government Power

In this chapter we will be considering most directly the question of how power is distributed in Western polyarchies. Chapter Six will discuss how power is used to affect the distribution of well-being; Chapter Seven will assess the outcomes of these uses of power. In this chapter, for the most part, we will examine the formal power relationships among units of government. Wherever informal forces, especially the system of political parties, come into play and affect the working of the formal mechanisms, this will be taken into account. Our focus is on those institutions and roles that are, legally speaking, supposed to have the power to make decisions for society as a whole. In Western polyarchies, the distinction between formal and informal power structures is somewhat easier to make than in the case of political systems in the Second and Third worlds. Western polyarchies are characterized by an adherence to the form of their constitution and organic laws to a greater extent than is true elsewhere. A description of the forms does provide some understanding of the way a political system works in the First World although it is certainly not the entire story.

In analyzing the formal distribution of power in a country, it is convenient to make a distinction between what might be called the horizontal and vertical distributions. Vertically, power is distributed among the various levels of government—national, regional, and local. We are concerned with the vertical distribution of power in the United States whenever we talk about the system of federalism—the distribution of power between the federal government and the states—or when we discuss the problem of the cities attempting to gain financial assistance from the federal or the state governments. The horizontal distribution of power, on the other hand, exists among units of government that are all located at the same level. Power, as we know, is distributed at the federal level in the United States among the three branches of government—legislative, executive, and judicial. Further, each of these branches has subunits so that power of the branch itself is further distributed. For example, the federal executive is divided into a multitude of agencies that vary widely in the amount of power they exercise and in their relationship to the White House. Let us begin our discussion of the formal distribution of power by seeing how our four European political systems divide power horizontally at the national level of government.

# HORIZONTAL POWER DISTRIBUTION

## PARLIAMENTARY SYSTEMS

**Britain and Italy.** In the first place, it is important to understand that most Western European political systems differ from the American political system, in that power is distributed horizontally according to the principle of parliamentarism. Parliamentarism exists in a relatively uncomplicated form in Great Britain and Italy. It is qualified in certain respects in West Germany, and it has been partially displaced in favor of the competing system of presidentialism in France. France, however, is an exception among Western European countries, whereas the other three—all essentially parliamentary systems—adhere to the norm. Figure 5.1 depicts the basic formal differences among British parliamentarism, American presidentialism, and the mixed French system.

In a parliamentary system of government, unlike the presidential type of system, the voters do not directly elect the executive head of government. They elect only the members of the legislative body, called Parliament. The head of government, usually called the Prime Minister (Chancellor in West Germany), is, then, chosen on the basis of the distribution of political party strength in the newly elected Parliament. The Prime Minister must be someone who is able to hold together a majority of members of the Parliament. Usually he or she will be the leader of the party with the most seats in Parliament or perhaps the leader of a smaller party capable of forming a coalition with other parties large enough to ensure majority support for the Prime Minister. The Prime Minister will, then, form a cabinet, consisting of heads of government departments (ministries) and drawn usually from among leading members of the party or the coalition of parties that the Prime Minister leads in Parliament. The Prime Minister and cabinet may continue in office as long as they retain the support (confidence) of a majority of the Parliament. If they do not lose majority support, they may stay in office until the end of the Parliament's term (four or five years). Should the majority be lost on a vote of confidence or a vote of nonconfidence, the Prime Minister will resign or ask the head of state to dissolve Parliament, meaning that new elections will be held before the end of the Parliament's term.[1]

The characteristics of parliamentarism as seen in Great Britain and Italy are such that, in a formal sense, these two systems operate in a somewhat similar fashion, but there are certain informal differences that make their actual functioning different in important respects. In both Great Britain and Italy, there is an organic relationship between the composition of the legislative body and the composition of the leading executive body, the cabinet. In both countries, if a single political party wins a majority of the seats in Parliament at the general election, it has the right to form a cabinet on its own without seeking coalition partners. In fact, this happens regularly in Great Britain. It has happened only once since World War II in Italy—in 1948—when the Christian Democratic Party won a slim majority in both houses of Parliament, the Chamber of Deputies (the lower house), and the Senate (the upper house). Since that high point, the Christian Democrats have declined in strength. Although still the largest party in Parliament, they must find coalition partners to have the majority necessary to form and sustain a government.

In both countries, if a single party has won a majority, there will be a single-party cabinet. If a coalition of parties wins the majority, the cabinet will be either a coalition cabinet, made up of leaders of the parties in the coalition, or it will be a minority cabinet, like the Labour Government in Great Britain from 1976 to 1979. The Labour Party held office by itself but required the support of other parties to remain in power. A sim-

---

[1]A vote of confidence is a vote in Parliament on a motion introduced by supporters of the Prime Minister; a vote of nonconfidence is a vote on a motion introduced by the opposition. Dissolution of Parliament is an act that prematurely terminates the life of the present Parliament and means that new parliamentary elections will be held.

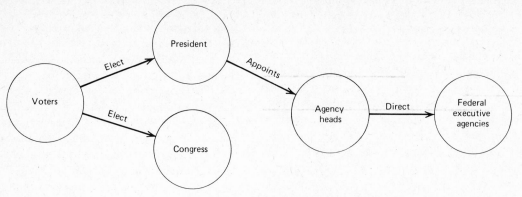

The American presidential system

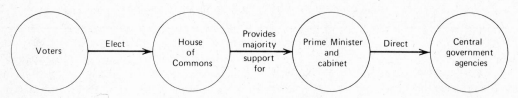

The British parliamentary system

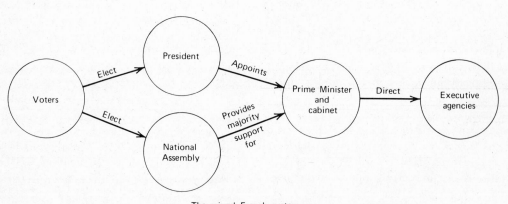

The mixed French system

**Figure 5.1**  Essential elements of three systems of government.

ilar situation has existed in Italy at various times in recent years.

Both the British and Italian parliaments have five-year terms, at the end of which elections must be held. If, however, a cabinet loses its majority in Parliament, it has the option of calling new elections, as Harold Wilson, then Great Britain's Prime Minister, did in September 1974; or it may resign and allow a new cabinet to be formed, as has happened frequently in Italy.[2]

[2]This presents the alternatives a bit too sharply. It is sometimes possible for governments to soldier on for a few months without a majority if a negative majority cannot (or will not) vote it out of power on a confidence motion.

Thus, elections may be held before the end of the five-year term, depending on the political situation and the judgment of the leaders of the existing cabinet.

Suppose that the result of an election is not a clear-cut one. Neither the February 1974 British election nor the June 1976 Italian election produced an automatic majority. What then? Who decides what cabinet should be chosen? In both countries, the place to look is the internal deliberating processes of the leading political parties, the Labour and Conservative parties in Great Britain, the Christian Democrats and the Communists and Socialists in Italy. Formally, there is a sort of referee, although it would be misleading to emphasize the importance of this role. In both countries, there is a head of state who performs essentially ceremonial and non-discretionary functions. In Great Britain, this is the monarch, currently Queen Elizabeth II. In Italy the head of state role is played by the President of the Republic. Both are to be distinguished from the political leader of the country—the head of government. This individual is called the Prime Minister in both countries. British monarchs, of course, inherit their throne. Because the monarchical principle is so far removed from twentieth-century democratic norms, it is unthinkable for the sovereign to exercise real political discretion. In a murky situation, such as existed in February 1974, the Queen waited for the political leaders to make their decisions. Once the choice became obvious, she called on one of them to become Prime Minister.

Unlike the British monarch, the President of the Italian Republic is usually a politician of some prominence who has been elected to his office by members of the two houses of Parliament voting jointly. It is expected that he will defer in his judgments to the leaders of the party (or parties) in power. During the life of the Italian Republic, this principle has been followed although with some notable exceptions. However, the political situation in Italy has become sufficiently troubled since the mid-1970s that a latent role of the President of the Republic might come to life—that of a safety valve, a national asset held in reserve in case of total stalemate. Should

the party leaders be incapable of steering Italy out of her present political and economic crises, it might become necessary for the President of the Republic to take a more active part. The precedents are ominous however. It was the head of state in an earlier era, King Victor Emmanuel III, who handed power to Mussolini. These memories undoubtedly have played a part in convincing the leaders of the DC to keep the reins of power firmly in their hands.

One additional formal difference between the two systems should be noted. Although both the British and the Italian parliaments are bicameral, that is, divided into two houses, the upper houses differ considerably in power. The House of Lords in Great Britain is a body of residual importance whose principal function may be to enable leading politicians, government servants, businesspersons, and trade union leaders to be honored for service to their country. Such an honor is likely to be given rather late in life, at a time when the individual is handing over responsibilities to younger colleagues. Elevation from the House of Commons to the House of Lords is actually a sort of political demotion when viewed in these terms. The Lords

Westminster Palace, London, which houses the mother of Parliaments, the famous Big Ben clock and tower.

will debate and amend bills coming from Commons; but they will seldom refuse them passage, and the amendments will stay in effect only if Commons (which usually means the cabinet) accepts them graciously. The Lords will usually avoid direct confrontations with the majority in Commons. The upper chamber suffered two reductions in its power in this century (1911 and 1949) because the cabinet of the left felt it was necessary to overcome the real or potential opposition by the Conservative-dominated Lords to its legislative program. The clue to the weakness of the Lords is that, because of the hereditary principle, it has a permanent Conservative majority. This has been tempered somewhat since the 1950's by the creation of life peers, new members of the House of Lords whose titles will not pass on to their heirs. Although many of these are Labourites, Liberals, or political independents, the Conservative majority remains. Thus, the composition of the House of Lords does not reflect changes in popular support for the parties. Therefore, its wishes are not taken into account when a new cabinet is being formed or when it is being decided whether the present one should stay in power.

By contrast, the Italian Senate is a coequal of the lower chamber, the Chamber of Deputies. Legislation must pass both houses; the Senate can just as easily be a stumbling block as the Chamber. The cabinet must retain the support of the Senate as well as the Chamber to stay in power. Nevertheless, having two chambers in Italy is actually rather arbitrary and of limited significance for two reasons. First the electoral systems for the two chambers are similar; they are both based essentially on proportional representation (see Chapter Four). Whenever one house is dissolved, the other is as well; therefore, elections are held at the same time, and the results are usually quite close. Distributions of party strength vary little in the two houses. Thus, it is possible to form a cabinet on the basis of the distribution in either chamber without doing injustice to the distribution in the other. Secondly, major decisions about the disposition of legislative matters are made at party headquarters among leaders representing factions of the party

in both chambers. A decision made for the party, whether Christian Democrats, Communists, or Socialists, will generally be binding on members of the party in both chambers, and the voting on legislation cannot be expected to differ significantly in either house. This is not to suggest that there is never disagreement between the two; it is still important to recognize the formal coequal status of the Italian Senate in comparing its power with that of the House of Lords.

When one turns fully to the informal aspects of the horizontal distribution of power, especially when one asks about the role of party systems, there is a sharp contrast between Great Britain's near two-party system and the Italian multiparty system. In one respect, though—party discipline in Parliament—the two are similar. Members of parliamentary parties in both countries vote as blocs most of the time. If the control exercised by party headquarters over Italian legislators shocks American students, they should remember from the last chapter that party discipline in legislative bodies is generally greater in Western Europe than it is in the United States. Great Britain is certainly no exception. As in Italy, the many in both major parties are directed by the few who are party leaders. The difference lies in the greater role the British Members of Parliament (MPs) actually play in choosing their leaders and in their capacity to withhold their approval, forcing the leaders to bend to their will. But this rank-and-file control is not exercised very often. On a day-to-day basis, the leadership

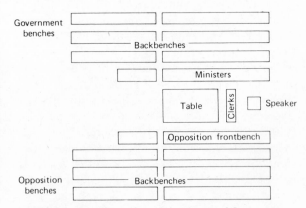

**Figure 5.2** Floor plan of the House of Commons.

formulates policy, communicates it to the rank and file, and expects to see them filing into the appropriate division lobbies when a vote is called.

Mention should be made of the method of voting on important questions in the House of Commons. Figure 5.2 shows the physical layout of the House. Unlike the houses of Congress in the United States and also unlike the parliamentary bodies in France, West Germany, and Italy, MPs do not sit in rows facing a common podium. Instead, they sit in rows of benches facing each other. On the one side are the governing party's benches, on the other are the opposition's; third- and fourth-party MPs ordinarily sit on the opposition's side. Debate flows back and forth between the two sides. Much of it is informal and impromptu, a characteristic that is facilitated by the small size of the chamber because there are fewer seats than there are MPs.

On either side of the chamber there are rooms known as division lobbies. MPs vote by filing into the appropriate lobby whenever the division bell rings. The bell can be heard throughout Westminster Palace and out on the street as well so that any MP in the vicinity is alerted and can down his pint at the local pub before hurrying back to vote. Actually, the party whips will have informed MPs when to expect the division. It is their job to see that the troops are marshaled whenever a vote is important. If the balance between the two parties is very close, then, MPs on both sides will remain away only at the risk of their leaders' severe displeasure. But, even if there is a comfortable majority, both sides will want to make a good showing. Too many absentees will indicate weakness in the current leadership's support on the backbenches. The convenient aspect of the division lobbies from the leadership's point of view is that the whips can station themselves at the heads of the lobbies and make sure that their backbenchers are whipped in. To file into the opposite lobby takes an act of overt defiance, which most MPs would rather avoid most of the time.

Too much should not be made of these physi-cal aspects however. Most observers find two other explanations for party cohesion in the House of Commons more persuasive.[3] In the first place, Labour and Conservative MPs are team players. The results of the divisions are like cricket scores. It looks better for the party in power to win a division by, say, 330 to 261, than by 305 to 296. The latter score would be at least a moral victory for the other side if the normal spread between the two parties is wider. Of course, if the party balance in Commons is very close, a poor result could actually mean the government's defeat (this happened to the James Callaghan government in the spring of 1979.) Such a result on a motion of confidence would force the government either to resign or to call new elections. Although the latter is the more likely choice in Great Britain, it could still mean the loss of power if the electorate so decides (as also happened in 1979). Taking all these factors into consideration, the team player usually goes along with his mates.

A second consideration is the practical consequence for the MP of violating party discipline. If an MP should lose the backing of his or her political party, the MP would be in the political wilderness. Candidates without the backing of one of the major parties stand little chance in a general election in Great Britain. Although it does not happen very often that a party in Parliament will expel an MP from its ranks, it is possible that an MP who votes with the opposition on a crucial division will be dropped by the local constituency association of his or her party in favor of another candidate.[4] Moreover, within the parliamentary party, potential dissidents who are ambitious for higher office may find their path blocked by the leadership whom they have defied and who control access to government office. However, despite all of the above, party cohesion in the House of Commons declined in the 1970s. Backbench dissent, or voting in the opposite lobby, occurred within the majority party on a number of important issues, causing difficulties for both Labour and Conser-

[3]See Robert J. Jackson, *Rebels and Whips* (London: Macmillan, 1968).

[4]As a result of recent changes in party rules, this may become a fairly frequent occurrence in the Labour Party.

vative governments. Party cohesion has generally held on motions of confidence and nonconfidence, but the dissent registered on important policy questions probably reflects a greater spirit of independence among backbench MPs and, in the case of the Labour Party, serious within-party conflict over domestic and foreign policy.

The Italian deputies and senators are likewise known for the high level of party cohesion they display in Parliament. However, in the Italian Parliament, votes are taken only after elaborate negotiations among factional leaders have been undertaken and common party positions worked out.[5] The result is a much more cumbersome *intra*party decision-making process than is found in the House of Commons. This is to say nothing of the *inter*party deliberations that must go on among coalition partners before a majority can be built behind a single position. The individual deputy or senator may be able to influence this process as can the MP in Great Britain with respect to particular policy areas where the interests he or she represents are at stake. But, for the most part, the legislator is dependent on his or her factional and party leaders to get results. Whether or not the leaders can get results depends on the stands of other leaders and on the overall distribution of party strength in Parliament. When a British party leadership comes to power after gaining a solid electoral victory, it can proceed to put its program into effect. However, this certainty is not possible in a party system where no single party can hope to gain a majority. Even in a country, like the Netherlands, where the differences between the parties on substantive issues are not so great as in Italy, it usually takes several weeks or even months of negotiation before a governing coalition can be formed with an agreed-on program. But, in Italy, the members of a new coalition cabinet have come to power with only the vaguest idea of a common program. Policy tends to emerge on an *ad hoc* basis in response to

urgent necessities when decisions can no longer be postponed. Under similar circumstances in France in the 1950s, the political system was characterized as immobile; this term accurately describes the situation in Italy today.

**West German Parliamentarism.** Immobility of this type had plagued the earlier German attempt to construct a polyarchy—the Weimar Republic (1919–1933). Just as in the Italian Republic today, a multiplicity of political parties had immobilized policy making. As was shown in Chapter Four, the West German party system has come a long way from the extreme multipartism of the Weimar period. As of 1949, however, when the Basic Law (Constitution) of the new Federal Republic was being formulated, it was not at all clear whether or not there would be the same multiplicity of parties as in the past. Accordingly, the framers of the Basic Law added certain complications to the model of a parliamentary system to prevent the potential destabilizing effects of a multiparty system. Because of the subsequent consolidation in the party system, these complications have not been as significant in the Bonn Republic as they might have been otherwise.

The two most important additions to the normal rules of a parliamentary system are the so-called constructive vote of nonconfidence and the important role played by the upper chamber of Parliament, the Bundesrat (Federal Council). In most parliamentary systems, when the cabinet decides that a vote in Parliament will be a motion of confidence, it must resign or call for new elections if defeated. Under the West German Basic Law, resignation is forced on the Federal Chancellor (the West German counterpart of a Prime Minister) only if the vote of no confidence has been on an opposition motion that names a new Chancellor and passes by a majority vote. If this does not occur, the Chancellor may remain in office even if he has lost his majority on the vote of confidence or he may call for new elections. This was the situation facing Chancellor Willy Brandt in 1972. He had lost his majority in the Bundestag (the lower house), but no alternative Chancellor could have secured a majority.

[5]It should be noted, however, that the enactment of many bills in the Italian Parliament is done by smaller committees where party control may not be as strong as it is in the entire Chamber or Senate, thus, providing the individual legislator somewhat wider scope.

West German Foreign Minister, Hans-Dietrich Genscher, addressing his Bundestag colleagues in the very modern West German Parliament building in October 1975.

Therefore, Brandt called for new elections, which his coalition (SPD-FDP) won comfortably; this changed the balance in the Bundestag in his favor and gave him a reliable majority.

The closest thing to an actual constructive vote of nonconfidence happened at the end of 1966 when the FDP withdrew its support from the Ludwig Erhard cabinet and a new cabinet was formed. The ruling CDU simply changed coalition partners, abandoning the smaller CDU-FDP coalition for the Grand Coalition of the CDU and SPD. This was accomplished through interparty negotiations behind the scenes. There was no actual vote of nonconfidence, and the eventual Bundestag vote installing the Kiesinger cabinet came only after the CDU and the SPD had reached a full understanding. Thus, although there was not, strictly speaking, a constructive vote of nonconfidence, the party system had enough flexibility and self-discipline to achieve the same result.

Both the 1966 and 1972 cases show the importance of having few political parties in West Germany. The calculations necessary to avoid a loss of confidence in the first place or, once it is lost, to find a new majority, are much easier to make when there are only three political parties operating at the national level. The number of potential defectors from a governing coalition are far fewer than in the Weimar Republic, and there are fewer alternatives to any given coalition. Had the extreme multiparty system prevailed after 1949, it is conceivable that the provisions of the Basic Law on motions of confidence would have been used more often. This might have increased the importance of the President of the Republic, who plays a neutral role in the political process as does the Italian President.

The role of the upper chamber, the Bundesrat, is a unique feature of the Basic Law. Its composition is based neither on the hereditary principle that prevails in the House of Lords nor on direct popular election found in the Italian Senate. It reflects the fact, as will be outlined later, that West Germany is a federal republic and, therefore, gives an important place in its system to its regional units of government, the *Länder*. Members of the Bundesrat are actually members of the *Land* cabinets who are sent to Bonn to represent the interests of their governments in the upper house of Parliament. The Bundesrat enjoys an absolute veto over the acts of the Bundestag whenever they directly affect *Land* interests. This is true for at least half the bills adopted by the lower house because much federal legislative policy is actually administered by the *Länder*. On other legislative measures, the Bundesrat has a suspensory veto, meaning that bills must be repassed by the Bundestag by a majority if they are to become law without the Bundesrat's consent.

These powers actually put the Bundesrat in a strong position, not only with respect to the Bundestag itself but also with respect to the Federal Chancellor and his cabinet, who reflect the wishes of a majority in the Bundestag. When the party balance in the Bundesrat differs from that in the Bundestag, as it has during the past decade, the opposition party or coalition is in a position to stymie the actions desired by the party or coalition in power. The present situation is one in which the SPD-FDP coalition with a majority in the Bundestag faces a majority of CDU/CSU votes in the Bundesrat. This is all the more likely to occur because, unlike the case of Italy, members of the upper house are not chosen at the same time as those of the lower house. *Land* elections, which determine the composition of *Land* governments, are staggered out at different times during the period between federal elections. This partial veto power held by the upper chamber in West Germany (potentially at least) interferes with the responsibility of a cabinet to its majority in the lower house. A cabinet could bend to the wishes of the majority in the upper house and find itself losing the confidence of the majority in the lower house. When this danger exists, the party or coalition in power has no choice but to give the opposition a role in its policy-making deliberations.

Thus, the Basic Law has some built-in features that could, under certain circumstances, produce instability or immobility. On the other hand, a cabinet can keep going despite the loss of its Bundestag majority so long as it has the support of the Federal President and the Bundesrat. But what the framers of the Basic Law may have gained in flexibility they seem to have lost in terms of the parliamentary theory of democracy. Neither the President nor the Bundesrat is directly elected by the people. Still, because the party system has permitted stable government, power has been concentrated in the Chancellor and his cabinet at least as much as in the case of the British cabinet. Once again, a high degree of party discipline works to the advantage of party leaders. Because they have the support of a majority in the popular house of Parliament and because this majority has been chosen from essentially only two alternatives by the voters, the democratic link is there.

## THE MIXED FRENCH SYSTEM

From the establishment of the Third Republic in the 1870s until the fall of the Fourth Republic in 1958 (except for the brief interlude of German occupation, 1940–1944), France, too, had a parliamentary system of government. However, because of the fragmented party system, cabinet coalitions were unstable and government was weak throughout the Third and Fourth republics. The Fifth Republic, instituted under the leadership of Charles de Gaulle in 1958, represents a departure from French parliamentary traditions in a number of important respects. As the Fifth Republic has matured, it has developed features that are more typical of a presidential system—as in the United States. The result has been a combination of constitutional elements.

Several features of the constitution of the Fifth Republic were designed to reduce the hold of Parliament over the process of policy making and turn it decisively over to the executive. In the Third and Fourth Republics, Parliament's ability to withdraw majority support from cabinets on short notice deprived the latter of the capacity to make strong, coherent policy—at least in areas where Parliament was sharply divided (for example, on colonial policy during the Fourth Republic). Among the new procedural means, several enable the Prime Minister and the cabinet virtually to ignore or circumvent the legislative process. For example, the lower house of Parliament, the National Assembly, has been deprived of the power to lay down more than the basic principles of legislation in many areas; in others, relegated to the administrative sphere, it cannot legislate at all. Furthermore, in those areas where the Assembly can still legislate, the Prime Minister is authorized to deny it an actual vote! Whenever the Prime Minister declares that a bill is a matter of confidence, the bill will pass without a vote, *unless* the opposition puts down a motion of censure. In that case, the motion must pass by an absolute majority (that is, 50 percent + 1 of all members of the Assembly— not just a majority of those voting). During the life of the Fifth Republic, some Prime Ministers have been more heavy handed than others in using these and other provisions in short-circuiting Parliament. But the stability of governing coalitions has consistently made sure that the power of Parliament in the Fifth Republic to assert its will against the Prime Minister and cabinet has not been as great as that of its predecessors.

The Constitution of 1958 departed further from the parliamentary principle by creating a potentially powerful President of the Republic without incorporating a system of checks and balances, such as that which is found in the American Constitution. The President is elected for a seven-year term. The President's more important powers include: (1) the power to decide when to dissolve the Assembly, something the President could do before only on the advice of the Prime Minister; (2) the power to put a question to the voters in the form of a popular referendum (on the advice of the Prime Minister); (3) the power to choose the Prime Minister without having to secure approval for this choice by a parliamentary vote; and (4) the power to declare a state of emergency, thus, suspending Parliament's power to legislate. The last of these was a cause of grave concern to many French observers, but it was deemed a necessary evil because of the Algerian War, which was raging at the time the Constitution came into effect and because of the near-military coup that had brought down the Fourth Republic.

Charles de Gaulle was elected the first President of the Fifth Republic in December 1958. Of the various powers available to him, the emergency power—potentially the most extensive—was the one he exercised with moderation and essentially within constitutional limits. He declared a state of emergency only once, in April 1961, in the face of an imminent *coup d'etat* by army generals in Algeria. The powers he assumed at this time were phased out gradually with only minor breaches of what experts regarded as legality. There was no doubt in anyone's mind that a real emergency existed and that strong measures were needed to save the Republic. By contrast, in another civil crisis seven years later, the May-June revolt of 1968, de Gaulle refrained from invoking the emergency clause, Article 16. Nor has it been used by any of his successors.

In other areas, de Gaulle seemed to be fashioning the role of the President into something beyond that of a mere referee among competing political forces. He appointed his own Prime Minister, Michel Debré, who had been a loyal follower of the General from the beginning; he also decided who the members of Debré's cabinet should be—a practice he continued with subsequent cabinets. Furthermore, he intervened on a daily basis in policy decisions, essentially devising his own national security strategy and often interjecting his views among those of his ministers in the area of domestic policy.

In short, de Gaulle acted much more like the very partisan and powerful President of the United States than like the neutral and largely powerless heads of state of Great Britain, Italy, and West Germany. His Prime Minister was not expected to be a political leader in his own right, but rather a policy coordinator and manager of the majority in the National Assembly; however, the long tenure of Georges Pompidou (1962–1968) in that post enabled him to transcend the limits of the role and ultimately to rival de Gaulle himself. Yet, Pompidou as President and his successor, Valéry Giscard d'Estaing, largely continued to exercise the functions of the presidential office along the lines established by de Gaulle. The President of the Republic is by far the most powerful figure in the French political system.

Probably the most controversial use de Gaulle made of the Presidency was his attempt on two occasions to use the popular referendum to amend the Constitution. Although Article 89 of the Constitution of 1958 provides several means for amending the Constitution, all of them require the participation of both parliamentary chambers, the National Assembly and the Senate. Yet, in October 1962 and April 1969, de Gaulle submitted constitutional amendments to the voters without first consulting the two chambers. The first, which changed the method for selecting the President to direct popular vote,[6] was adopted by the voters with a wide margin. The second, designed to change the composition and powers of the Senate and to give certain powers of the central government to new regional units of government, was rejected—which brought about de Gaulle's retirement from politics. Both referendums were heavily criticized by non-Gaullists. Part of the criticism was directed at the unconstitutional method of amendment, a criticism that probably carried more weight with political élites than with the general public.

In fact, the referendum of October 1962 profoundly changed the spirit of the Constitution of 1958. It introduced something foreign to French political traditons. The idea of a popularly elected President had been anathema to died-in-the-wool republicans ever since the middle of the nineteenth century when the only previous popular presidential election had resulted in the victory of Napoleon Bonaparte's nephew and the consequent transformation of the Second Republic into the Second Empire. By making the President of the Republic a popularly elected official, the 1962 amendment went a long way toward changing the French system of government from a modified parliamentary system to a near-presidential system. Because the longest standing and most-copied presidential model is the American one, it may be worthwhile to compare the present Fifth Republic with the American political system (see Figure 5.1). In both systems, whatever the orginal intentions, the President is the central figure in the structure of power. Both

presidents name whomever they choose to their cabinets. Both are in charge of foreign and defense policies. Both are popularly elected, with major attention in the election being given to the personalities of the competing candidates. Both carry a great deal of authority with the public, the press, the legislature, and their subordinates in the executive branch of government.

Nevertheless, the President of the French Fifth Republic has a greater share of the horizontal power within his own political system than does the President of the United States. The French President is elected for a seven-year, rather than a four-year term and, unlike the case of the American President, there are no constitutional limits on the number of times a French President can be reelected. The American President cannot do three things that are permitted to his French counterpart under the Constitution of 1958.

1. He cannot dissolve Congress and call new elections. The terms of members of Congress are fixed, and the dates of the elections are determined by the Constitution. The only restriction of the French President in this respect is that he cannot dissolve the National Assembly twice during a one-year period.

2. The American President cannot submit a proposition to the voters in the form of a referendum. De Gaulle made effective use of this device in mobilizing support for his objectives in the Algerian War. Presidents Lyndon B. Johnson and Richard M. Nixon might have found a similar device useful in handling the war in Vietnam.

3. The American President cannot declare a state of emergency, thus, suspending the legislative powers of Congress. American presidents sometimes assume extraordinary powers during a crisis, but their actions can be revoked by Congress or declared invalid by the Supreme Court. The French Parliament is powerless to act if Article 16 is invoked, and no judicial body in France is anywhere near as powerful as the U.S. Supreme Court.

On the other hand, there is a counterweight in the French system that is not found in the American system—the capacity of the National

[6]Under the Constitution of 1958, the President was to be elected by a sort of electoral college that is made up of more than 80,000 members, consisting mainly of small-town mayors and councillors. This was the mode by which de Gaulle was first elected in December 1958.

Assembly to censure the President's handpicked Prime Minister, either forcing him to resign or the President to dissolve the Assembly. But this is not a means for removing the President himself. If the U.S. Congress had this power, it could remove members of the President's cabinet from office. There is a procedure in the French Constitution that resembles impeachment and removal from office of the American President. The French President can be indicted by an absolute majority of both chambers in an open ballot and, then, be tried by a High Court of Justice made up of members of Parliament elected by their colleagues in the two chambers. However, according to Article 68, "The President of the Republic shall not be held accountable for actions performed in the exercise of his office except in the case of high treason." This would seem to constitute a greater limitation on the capacity of the French Parliament to remove a President from office than is true in the case of Congress, which has twice instituted impeachment proceedings against a President thought to be guilty of "high crimes and misdemeanors." Thus, rather paradoxically, the French President himself seems to be more immune to removal by the legislature than is the American President, but the latter's cabinet cannot be brought down on a motion of censure.

In fact, what the French Constitution seems to guarantee is that, in normal times, the President will have enough power to fashion policy, to gain its acceptance by Parliament, and to coordinate its implementation, relatively free of the kind of roadblocks and detours that often confront American presidents. The French President enjoys the position normally held by British and West German cabinets that are assured of stable majorities in their respective parliaments. Even an American President whose party has majorities in both houses of Congress cannot count on the passage of his entire legislative program because cross-party coalitions can block passage of certain bills. The threat of dissolution might make quite a difference here, but it would also disrupt the balance in the American system that has developed during two centuries of trial and error. On the other hand, the French President enjoys at least as much immunity against removal from office as does the American President. This puts him in a position superior to the British Prime Minister and the West German Chancellor, who serve only so long as they can retain the support of majorities in Parliament. What this means is that the French President has the best of both the parliamentary and the presidential worlds. If we are speaking of the normal situation, it seems that this is the single most powerful government office in the countries we have been examining.

But will the normal situation always be the case? In May 1981, Socialist François Mitterrand was elected the fourth President of the Fifth Republic. Momentarily, France had a President of the left facing a parliamentary majority of the right. To correct this situation, Mitterrand dissolved the National Assembly and called for new legislative elections in June 1981. The result was a decisive victory for Mitterrand's Socialists that ensured the President a friendly majority for the first five years of his seven-year term. But suppose his victory had not been so decisive and he had been faced by a National Assembly majority less friendly to his programs. Under the Constitution, Mitterrand could not have dissolved the Assembly for a year. A condition of stalemate might have prevailed in the meantime. More serious, what would happen in the next legislative elections—scheduled for 1986 at the latest—if the voters should repudiate Mitterrand's party and elect a National Assembly majority of the right? Would the President resign with two years remaining in his term or would he struggle along and try to make the best of a difficult situation? The Constitution of 1958, because it mixes together elements of the presidential and the parliamentary systems of government, has the potential for deadlock between executive and the legislature even more severe than that which often beset the Third and Fourth republics. Thus far the French voters have managed to avoid such deadlock-producing choices.

There are some very delicate balances in the French system, which hovers between parliamentarism and presidentialism. Perhaps it is not possible to combine the two principles in one system without running the risk of deadlock. The flexibility may be there to enable the political élites to work out their difficulties, but the heat of partisan battle in recent years would suggest otherwise. Still, we have seen problems in the other countries. In Great Britain it has become harder for either of the major parties to maintain a reliable majority in Parliament, which traditionally has enabled cabinets to play the dominant role. In Italy, there is the virtual impossibility of finding a stable majority as long as the Communists are not invited to share power. In West Germany, the problem is the powerful role of the Bundesrat and the danger of stalemate whenever it is controlled by the opposition. In all four countries, the least workable situation seems most likely to materialize whenever the balance between left and right is closest, because the ability of executive leaders to command the support of legislative majorities is most uncertain at such times. That is precisely the situation that prevailed in all four party systems during the 1970s. Under such conditions, the usual predominance of the executive and passive role of the Parliament can be undermined by the potential veto capacity held by the latter.

## ADMINISTRATIVE ÉLITES

On the right-hand side of Figure 5.1 are the administrative agencies that implement the policies formulated by presidents, prime ministers, and cabinets and enacted into law by legislative bodies. In Western Europe, administrative authority is largely in the hands of permanent civil servants, especially those in the higher ranks, the administrative élites.

For our purposes, the term, adminstrative élite, will be reserved for civilian administrative officials. In Western Europe, the line between the political heads of government agencies and neutral civil servants who are their subordinates is drawn at a higher level of the administrative hierarchy than it is in the United States. At the top levels of executive branch agencies in the United States, the patronage system remains, to the extent that at least the top two or three layers are staffed with fellow partisans of the President

who have been rewarded for their service to the party and to the President himself. In most Western European countries, on the other hand, only the top-line position in each department is held by a leader of the party or parties in power. Below that level are high-ranking civil servants, who are chosen, in large part, for their demonstrated merit according to criteria established for the civil service of that country. These civil servants are highly educated experts in the art of governing. They are expected to maintain neutrality between the contending political parties. When compared with the United States, the principal of neutrality of high-ranking government officers in at least three of our countries holds up, but, when compared with each other, it appears that the British and West German civil services maintain a higher level of political neutrality than do the French and Italian, especially the latter. Together with a lower level of political neutrality, the administrative élites in France and Italy also have greater independent power than do those of the other two countries. This is especially the case of the French adminsitrative élite.

**The Socialization of the Administrative Élite.** Part of the explanation for these differences can be found in the administrative traditions of the four countries, traditions that have been handed down from generation to generation through the process of socialization.[7] In part, this process takes place in the family. A fair percentage of recruits to the administrative élite in all four countries come from families headed by civil servants. But, in general, in all four countries, a very high percentage of the administrative élite is recruited from the upper strata of society, is educated in the most prestigious schools and universities, and enters the ranks of the civil service at a level commensurate with their education but high enough to guarantee that they will end their service careers in positions of considerable responsibility. Family and school socialization patterns for Europe's upper classes

[7]In the preparation of this section, John A. Armstrong, *The European Administrative Elite* (Princeton, N.J.: Princeton University Press, 1973), has been very useful.

do not vary greatly from country to country. What is different is the type of professional training recruits to the upper administrative ranks have received, both in their formal education and in the years of their apprenticeship as higher civil servants. Three essential patterns may be distinguished for our four countries: the classical-generalist (Great Britain), the legalistic (West Germany and Italy), and the technocratic (France).

In Great Britain, the administrative élite is a well-defined minority within the civil service, known until recently as the adminstrative class. It consists of only a few hundred officials in the top nonpolitical ranks of agencies headed by ministers. Below this class is a much larger executive class, consisting of subordinate officials who follow the orders of their administrative class superiors. However, they may in turn be responsible for supervising the activities of large numbers of employees. Administrative-class civil servants have university degrees, whereas those in the executive class usually do not although they may have spent some time at a university before taking the executive-class examination. The latter is geared for those who have completed no more than the secondary level of education. The administrative-class examination is partly an academic-style written examination and partly a test of the candidate's capacity to respond to situations designed to simulate actual administrative experiences. Because the curriculum in the élite university-preparatory secondary schools is classical in its orientation— emphasizing history, literature, languages, and philosophy—and because the administrative-class examination allows university graduates with a humanistic education to specialize in their subjects, well-rounded generalists are not at a disadvantage and may even have an advantage over their more technically specialized peers. Economics and public administration, disciplines in which American students frequently major if they want to enter the federal civil service, do not convey any particular advantage to British aspirants for the higher civil service.

The British education system produces liberally educated generalists. Therefore, the administrative class of British civil service is filled with generalists, whose forte is the ability to master the general terms of a particular problem and to offer a solution that takes a maximum number of considerations into account. The solution may not, however, be a clean, economical way of optimizing any given objective. To achieve that end, the technical specialist—the economist, the natural scientist, the accountant, the engineer—may be better equipped. But the British way has been to keep the expert "on tap, not on top." Administrative agencies in Whitehall consign the highly trained specialist to staff positions, which are subordinate in the hierarchy to generalists, who occupy the principal decision-making posts. This practice has been heavily criticized since the 1960s by academic specialists in public administration, and, most significantly, by the influential Fulton Commission, which made a number of sweeping recommendations for changing the civil service. Although the Fulton Report appeared in the late 1960s, the most important recommendations—to phase out the administrative class and to place specialists on an equal footing with generalists—have been implemented very slowly. Although the administrative class has now ceased to exist as such, its spirit is likely to pervade the British administrative élite for a number of years to come.

The counterpart of the British generalist in the West German and Italian administrative services is the higher civil servant with a generalized legal education. In both countries, officials trained in law are more likely than those with other academic specialties to be found at the topmost levels of the administrative hierarchy although, in West Germany, economics has been gaining in favor in recent years as a preferred academic background second only to law. Civil servants in these two countries are expected to pay strict attention to the procedural and substantive legalities of their work. This helps to assure a relatively impartial bureaucracy, in West Germany at least, but it may also lead to overly cautious and even obstructive implementation of the state's business—a characteristic that numerous critics of the Italian bureaucracy have noticed.

The route to administrative élite positions in West Germany normally leads from the *gymnasium* through the university to a first state examination in law. The requisite qualifications are determined by the state, and the universities are expected to gear their curriculum in law to fit these expectations. This is unlike the situation in Great Britain where university standards have been used since the late nineteenth century to determine the content of the examinations. Success in the first state examination will enable the German aspirant to begin a training period of about 2½ years in one of the administrative agencies at the federal, land, or local level or in the administrative service of a court at one of these levels. Here, the prospective civil servant will build on this background in the study of law and prepare to take a second state examination, which will determine whether he or she is qualified to become a higher level civil servant ("Beamter"). The criteria for admission to this élite are precise and objective, unlike those in Great Britain where a fair amount of emphasis continues to be given to the intangibles of style.

If anything, training in the law is even more exclusively the mode of entry into the Italian administrative élite than it is in West Germany. However, the recruitment process is not as carefully regulated in Italy as it is in West Germany. In the Federal Republic of Germany, one seeks to enter the civil service of the federal government or of one of the *länder* just as in Great Britain, one is recruited into the civil service of the central government. In both countries, generalized criteria apply, regardless of the government agency in which the recruit will ultimately be employed. In Italy, one seeks employment in a given ministry, not (in general) in the service of the Italian central government. And, to be assured of employment in that ministry, one ought to have family or political connections in addition to a law degree. Without such connections, the waiting period may last several years, no matter how well the recruit does in the entrance examination. Here, the power of the Christian Democratic Party (DC) can be clearly perceived. Certain ministries have been headed by leaders of the DC for years. Different factions of the party regard particular ministries as their exclusive fiefdoms. This is especially true of those factions whose power base is located in the area south of Rome. Ambitious young people from southern Italy are more likely to be attracted to a relatively secure position in the central government than to a riskier, if potentially more rewarding, job in the private sector.

In all three of these countries, civil servants who have been trained in such academic disciplines as economics, mathematics, engineering, and the natural sciences—disciplines that are most apt to put them in touch with the most decisive changes taking place in postindustrial society—are more likely to have subordinate and advisory positions to the more traditionally educated civil servants, who hold the real decision-making power in the administrative élite. This is not the case in France, which has a long-standing tradition of relying on the state to take a dynamic part in driving and shaping the economy. The élite corps of highway and mining engineers were already playing a major role in laying the basis for French industrialization early in the nineteenth century. After World War II, France established a model for training an administrative élite by creating the *École Nationale d'Administration* (ENA) where recruits to the higher civil service undergo a three-year training program before entering the service of one of the central ministries. The academic side of the program contains a heavy dose of economics—not the classical *laissez faire* economics that prevailed in France and elsewhere in Western Europe before the War—but rather the Keynesian, growth-oriented economics that caught on in government circles more rapidly in France than elsewhere in Western Europe, including John Maynard Keynes's native Great Britain. Graduates of ENA have come to occupy top-ranking positions in the central agencies that direct and regulate the French economy, including the Ministry of Finance and the important Planning Commissariat. Aside from ENA, there is the *École Polytechnique*, which provides the finishing academic touches for future mining engineers and highway engineers, some of whom will spend their entire careers in the Ministry of Industrial Production or the Ministry of Transport. These various kinds of technocrats can anticipate careers in which they will eventually reach high-level positions with important decision-making responsibilities. The expert, whether economist, legal specialist, or engineer, can eventually hope to get to the top rather than to remain on tap in the French bureaucracy.

**The Role of the Administrative Élite in Policymaking.** What are the consequences of these differing socialization patterns for the positions that administrative elites occupy in the horizontal power structures of our four countries? These élites differ with respect to the self-perceptions that they carry with them in fulfilling their role specifications; these self-perceptions, in turn, affect their actual performances. Generally speaking, it can be said that the British and West German administrative élites are relatively self-restrained in their approach to the exercise of administrative discretion, whereas the French are relatively free of self-restraint. The Italian administrative élite falls somewhere in between these two other types.

Administrative neutrality is a well-established tradition in both Great Britain and Germany. However, it has been severely strained in the latter country at certain times in the past. In Great Britain, the role of the neutral civil servant prepared to serve whichever party comes to power goes back to the middle of the last century. If it were ever in doubt, it met the supreme test after World War II when the Labour Party came to power and put into effect its sweeping program of economic and social reform. Although the program contained many items that must have been fundamentally at odds with the personal views of many senior civil servants, the Labour ministers later said that the administrative élite carried out the directives of the Labour government as loyally as they had those of earlier Conservative governments. The higher civil service is a career whose professional standards require a high degree of intelligence

employed in the mastery of detail and in the assessment of the implications of alternative courses of action. It is the duty of civil servants to advise their political superiors about these implications; however, even if civil servants privately disagree with the latter's judgment they will implement the chosen action with skill and dispatch. That, at least, is the self-image of the British administrative elite; it corresponds with the facts to a considerable extent, especially when the British higher civil service is placed in comparative perspective.

There is, however, the other side of the coin. Although the senior civil servants have been trained as generalists, they have spent their career in government service. If they have been successful, they have gained the reputation of being a quick study, which means that they can master the essential details of whatever problem might arise. They are very likely, therefore, to be more of an expert and less of a generalist than their political superior, the minister. As a result, it would be foolish to suggest that such civil servants do not have a great deal of influence on the policy-making process, especially where complicated adjustments to the needs of particular interest groups are concerned. They have information, something which their minister, who may be new to the job, desperately needs. In this respect, British civil servants may even have an edge over their counterparts in Italy where the turnover in particular ministerial positions occurs less often than it does in Great Britain.

The lawyers who occupy important positions in the West German administrative structure are probably not so deferential to their political superiors as are their British counterparts. After all, they regard themselves as experts. They view the politicians as generalists against whose intervention they (the specialists) must safeguard their professional standards. In the past, this insistence has escaped the boundaries of administrative neutrality. For example, the Socialist Ministers in the early Weimar Republic (about 1920) did not benefit from the civil servants' willingness to carry out their wishes as did the Labour Party Ministers in Great

Britain during the late 1940s. When Adolph Hitler came to power, he made certain that he would not encounter the same obstructiveness and so he abolished the security of tenure that the German administrative élite had traditionally enjoyed. This was restored after World War II for the reconstituted West German administrative élite; and, since that time, the civil service has rediscovered the principle of neutrality. This time, when the Social Democrats replaced the Christian Democrats in power, they could count on the loyal implementation of their programs.

However, when it is said that there is a tradition of neutrality in the German civil service, it means something different from the British case. The self-restraint of the German administrative élite is based on its long established adherence to the rule of law as understood in German jurisprudence. Whereas in Great Britain, the rule of law is a set of principles that define the limits beyond which the state may not go vis-à-vis the individual, in the German legal tradition it has meant a set of rights that the state has precisely defined in written law, as well as precise limitations on the state's power. The rights and obligations of the state's servants are, therefore, clearly defined, and their legalistic training equips them to know exactly what these are. In this respect, their expertise puts them in a position above that of their political superiors. They will insist that the latter observe the letter of the law; but the certainty with which they will make their point results from the almost automatic nature of their response. They are not really exercising discretion in policy matters; rather, they are expressing what the law is on a given matter at a given time, and their political superiors may well be in a position to change that law, thus, removing the basis of their objections. So long as the directives received from above are in accordance with the letter of the law, the West German civil servant will carry it out faithfully and with considerable competence. These characteristics constitute their self-perception; this self-perception also corresponds fairly closely to reality.

The case of the French administrative élite is decidedly different. High-ranking French civil servants expect to have an important voice in the policy-making process and they do. Their demanding, relatively highly specialized academic training, capped with a final period of socialization at one of the *grands écoles*, gives them a sense of their own self-importance. The self-assurance exhibited by the French diplomatic corps in international negotiations, often to France's advantage, can be observed among the higher civil servants who are responsible for administering domestic policy as well.

The high degree of formal concentration of power in the hands of the executive of the French central government enhances the position of the administrative élite in the horizontal power structure. Deputies in the National Assembly cannot hope to influence the course of policy making through their own legislation. Often, what they want to accomplish can be achieved only through administrative action or, if legislation is necessary, only if the government will draft it and present it to Parliament. Either way, it will be necessary to work with civil servants who will be sure to incorporate their own views into whatever decision is made by the appropriate ministry. The political heads of these executive units are frequently former civil servants who have moved to the political level either directly or indirectly from the permanent civil service. Even when ministers have not had administrative experience, they will include in their inner cabinet rising young members of the Conseil d'État or (perhaps) the Finance Inspectorate—men and women on loan from their respective agencies. Their role will be frankly a political one, to aid the minister in making decisions that will enhance his or her career. Such rising young stars are likely to move back and forth between administrative and political positions in their careers. The newer breed of French administrators who have come out of ENA since World War II are pragmatic men and women of action.

Whatever advantages there may be when the state is expected to play a dynamic, innovating role, stimulating other social institutions to change in keeping with the changing times, this aggressive type of role presents a problem from the standpoint of democratic theory. Administrative self-restraint is a guarantee that the ultimate rulers will be the representatives of the people. Professional civil servants who have the security of tenure are responsible, first and foremost, to their own professional standards. If those standards permit a forceful, imaginative policy-making role, then, considerations of what the public really wants are likely to take second place to the civil servants' beliefs as to what is best for the public. This brings us back to a principal uncertainty regarding the French Fifth Republic, the fact that until 1981 power did not leave the hands of the center-right parties. Uncertainty as to the loyalty of the administrative élite may have been one reason why administrative reform is a high-priority item for the new Socialist-led government.

Somewhat similiar questions could be raised about the Italian administrative élite, not so much because of their self-image but because of the political situation in which one party has monopolized, or nearly monopolized, power for 30 years. Socialization in legal norms makes Italian civil servants protective of legal niceties in the same way it does their West German counterparts. But it is not an element of Italian culture to hold fast to legalities to the exclusion of all other considerations. This is especially true if it is a question of adhering to a legal principle as opposed to the interests of one's political friends. If these friends have been responsible for one's getting a job in the bureaucracy in the first place, for example, as a favor to a member of one's family, the civil servant will find an excuse to ignore the legal principle. In the eyes of an Italian, this is not necessarily corruption. It may even be regarded as highly moral behavior—loyalty to one's family and friends, displaying reliability (in their eyes), and even demonstrating a sense of one's responsibilities. Such personal responsibilities come before the abstract responsibilities associated with the role of public servant. A jealous guarding of one's status also leads to a conservative stance regarding ideas for reform. Italian civil servants are not the dynamic force for innovation that their French counterparts are, and they also lack the firm commitment to

neutrality found in Great Britain and West Germany. Accordingly, the Italian civil service is a force to be contended with in the policy-making process. Unlike the French administrative élite, however, it is not a force for change. Quite the contrary, it is inclined to protect the *status quo* against the winds of change, whether they come from within the DC or from the left. If the Communists should gain a share of power in the near future, they will probably face a hostile permanent officialdom in the ministries whose political leadership they assume. A good many personnel changes are likely to take place.

## THE VERTICAL DISTRIBUTION OF GOVERNMENT POWER

When we speak of the vertical distribution of power in a political system, we mean the relationship among various levels of government rather than among different units at the same level. In any system of government, there will be at least a national (or central) level of government and a local unit that corresponds to the city, town, or village in which people reside and interact with one another. Usually, there is also one or more intermediate levels between the center and the localities. There may be some sort of district that is larger than the locality, which includes several nearby localities and the adjoining countryside—a district that resembles the county in the United States. In some countries, there will be a larger intermediate level, which might be called a regional level—an area that comprises more than one city and a significant proportion of the country's population. The states in the United States would fit this definition, as would various kinds of regional units in the countries we are studying. Western polyarchies differ substantially from one another with respect to their intermediate and local units and the distribution of power among national, intermediate, and local units.

The first, and most basic, distinguishing question is: What, if any, regional level of government is there? There are two types of answer to this question among the Western polyarchies. Either there is a regional level with powers that are clearly defined by a constitution and protected from the encroachment by the central government or there is not. If there is such a regional level, then the system can be called federalism; if there is no regional level or if it is weak and dependent on the center, the system should be termed a unitary one. The United States is generally regarded as having a federal system of government because the regional units—the states—have powers granted to them by a constitution, and these powers are protected by a court system that is pledged to uphold the constitutional balance. Great Britain, on the other hand, has a unitary system because there is virtually no regional level, and the local level of government is dependent on Parliament for whatever powers it has. The courts in Great Britain will defer to acts of Parliament. There is no constitutional distribution of powers to which Parliament must refer when it defines what local government units may and may not do. Of our four political systems, only West Germany can properly be called a federal system; the other three are unitary systems.

## UNITARY SYSTEMS

In our three unitary systems, cities, towns, and villages generally constitute what is often called the first tier of local government. In France and Italy, this first tier is made up of communes, irrespective of their size; in Great Britain, the terms for the units vary depending on their size. In all three countries, there is a second tier comparable to the American county: it is called the *county* in Great Britain, the *département* in France, and the *province* in Italy. Both tiers of government in all three countries exercise powers that have been granted to them by laws enacted through the normal law-making processes of the central government. They are not, however, simply administrative arms of the central government any more than, say, the city of Detroit is just an administrative branch of the state of Michigan. They have their own elected councils, which make policy for the local area, subject to certain restrictions imposed from above.

As in the United States, local units of government do not monopolize the administration of government policies within their boundaries. In Detroit, there are offices of both the federal and the Michigan governments, with administrative responsibilities and jurisdiction within the city of Detroit. Similarly, there are central government field offices in Birmingham, England; Bordeaux, France; and Bologna, Italy—the post offices in these cities, for example. But the city governments are responsible for such things as maintaining law and order, fighting fires, and collecting refuse. In Great Britain, the two levels of government, central and local, exist side by side and cooperate with one another when it is deemed necessary, but they do not intermingle in one another's jobs. Each has its own responsibilities and is responsible ultimately to its own electorate. A British political scientist, Gordon Smith, has called such a unitary system, a dual-type system.[8] Each level of government has the power to make policy in its own policy areas and to administer that policy with its own administrative services directed by its own responsible government officials.

France and Italy, on the other hand, have what Smith calls a fused type of unitary system.[9] Here, the administration of both central government and local government policy is coordinated by a single central government official. Whereas, in Great Britain, local governments may administer policies that have been made by their elective councils (provided that these policies fit within the general guidelines established by Parliament), the decisions of local councils in France and Italy are subject to review by a central government official, an agent of the Ministry of the Interior at the second-tier level, who is called a *prefect*. The prefect can withhold authorization for the implementation of these policies and can often withhold funds. As a result, there is (potentially at least) a more efficient coordination of administration in each local area in France and Italy—especially in France—

[8]Gordon Smith, *Politics in Western Europe: A Comparative Analysis* (New York: Holmes & Meier, 1973), pp. 257–258.
[9]*Ibid.*

than there is in Great Britain; but local government in Great Britain is closer to the electorate to whom it is supposedly responsible.

## WEST GERMAN FEDERALISM

The distinction between dual and fused systems can also be applied to various kinds of federal systems. Federalism in the United States constitutes a dualism. The federal government and the states each have their own spheres of power. Under the Constitution, the federal executive implements policy that has been enacted in the form of legislation by Congress. Spheres of power that have not been explicitly granted to the federal government in the Constitution are, according to the 10th Amendment, reserved to the states. We know, of course, that the meaning of the Constitution has been stretched considerably as the powers of the federal government have expanded. But the states continue to exercise primary responsibility in the many areas that are of direct importance to people's lives—providing for public education; maintaining public order; caring for the indigent, the elderly, and the mentally infirm. The federal government plays an important auxiliary role in these areas, but the discrepancies in the quality of the service and in the amount of money per capita spent by individual states attests to the fact that state prerogatives are jealously guarded against extensive federal encroachment.

In West Germany, there are fewer obvious regional disparities in the quality of public services than in the case in the United States. Part of the reason for this is that the Basic Law of the Federal Republic encourages greater standardization among the *Länder*. It must also be acknowledged, however, that West Germany is a much smaller country than the United States and one would, therefore, expect less diversity. Moreover, except for Bavaria and the two city-states of Hamburg and Bremen, the *Länder* are artificial creations of the Allied Occupation after World War II and would, thus, be less likely to try to preserve local particularisms than would, say, a Mississippi or a New Hampshire. Still,

regional differences have always been important in German life, and it must be remembered that Germany as a national political unit has existed for only a little more than 100 years. Parts of what is now West Germany, such as Bavaria, Baden, and Württemberg, were sovereign states before 1871.

Under the Basic Law, both the federal government and the *Länder* possess explicitly delineated spheres of power. The most important powers held exclusively by the federal government are, as for any sovereign state, those pertaining to national security. For the *Länder*, education, religion, and cultural affairs are among the more important areas that are exclusively within their jurisdiction. There is a further area of concurrent powers—for example, transport, nuclear energy, and criminal law—where both may legislate but with the stipulation that federal law supersedes *Land* law. Where the fusion occurs in West Germany is in areas in which the federal government may enact broad framework laws but where implementation is left up to the governments of the *Länder*. The federal government plays more of a supervisory role than a direct administrative one. This means that, in relation to the other countries with which we are dealing, the Federal Republic of Germany maintains a relatively small central bureaucracy. Public employment is, relatively speaking, dispersed in West Germany.

On the other hand, the federal government holds the upper hand with respect to taxation. The taxes with the highest total yield, including the income tax, go into the federal treasury. These are then distributed to the *Länder* so that they can implement federal policy. This has much more of a redistributive effect than does the grant-in-aid system or even the newer revenue-sharing system in the United States. Taxes collected in the richer *Länder*, like Hamburg and Baden-Württemberg, are used to help bring public services in the poorer *Länder*, such as Lower Saxony or the Saarland, up to a common national standard. This financial power gives the federal government considerable leverage to make sure that the states are carrying out federal policy as intended by those in power in Bonn, regardless of the balance of party strength in the various *Länder* or of differences among local political subcultures.

Two counterweights protect the *Länder* against excessive federal control. The Federal Constitutional Court plays a role resembling that of the U.S. Supreme Court in refereeing the system. By American standards, this is an activist court that seeks to accommodate the Basic Law to existing social realities. Important constitutional decisions have sometimes gone against the *Länder* and sometimes against the federal government. The second counterweight is an organ discussed earlier—the Bundesrat. Through this body, the state governments are able to play a direct role in the federal legislative process. Although the federal government has powerful means for guiding and controlling the management of *Land* affairs, the *Länder* can help shape the ways in which this guidance and control will be exercised.

## REGIONAL DEVOLUTION IN UNITARY SYSTEMS

Some German critics of the West German system of government feel that the decentralization of administration is not advantageous for effective coordination and, therefore, for governmental efficiency.[10] The inability of the federal government to get the *Länder* to devise a coordinated education system is sometimes cited in support of this judgment.[11] It may be tempting to attribute such an evaluation to some sort of German passion for order and consistency. When we look at the unitary systems of government in Great Britain, France, and Italy, we find that the weight of critical opinion runs in quite the opposite direction. There, it is felt that power is too highly centralized, that local units of government are too

dependent on the center, which pays too little attention to regional diversity and to the need to stimulate economic activity in the more depressed areas of the country. If these critics are right, then, it would seem that too much government centralization can be as inefficient as too much decentralization. In all three of our unitary systems, efforts have been made since the 1960s to find some sort of happy medium without destroying the efficacy of government at the center. The solution toward which all three systems seem to be working is the establishment of a viable regional level of government, intermediate between the central and local levels. Such a level exists in West Germany in the form of the *Länder*. But developments in Great Britain, France, and Italy do not seem to be leading toward federalism. Central governments are jealously guarding their powers. At the present time, at any rate, attention is being given to the creation of regional consultative bodies—with very limited powers of their own but able to serve as a vehicle through which regionally based politicians and interest groups can have some influence on the implementation of central government policy in their areas.

Regionalism in Great Britain is a case in point. Change is in the wind, spearheaded by the demands from Scotland and Wales for a greater devolution of central government power to their regions. Until now, there have been no elective bodies in Scotland and Wales similar to the now-suspended Parliament in Northern Ireland. Instead, Scotland and Wales elect representatives to the Parliament in London just as throughout England. Once there, they form part of the majority or opposition. Whichever party is in power has members from Scotland and Wales in the cabinet; one member serves as Secretary of State for Scottish Affairs and another does the same for Welsh Affairs. In Scotland, there are administrative offices with headquarters in Edinburgh under the Secretary of State. These administer legislation that has been enacted by Parliament, especially as they relate to Scotland in such fields as education, health, and social welfare. Administrative devolution has not even

[10]See Renate Mayntz and Fritz W. Scharf, *Policy-making in the German Federal Bureaucracy* (Amsterdam: Elsevier, 1975), pp. 17–20.

[11]See Günther Kloss, *West Germany: An Introduction* (London: Macmillan, 1976), pp. 111–112.

proceeded this far in the case of Wales. Scottish and Welsh nationalists have called for separate parliaments in Edinburgh and Cardiff as well as for separate Scottish and Welsh governments, which would be responsible to these regional legislative bodies. In Scotland, there are even cries for total independence from the United Kingdom.

After the strong showing of the nationalist parties in the 1974 parliamentary elections, both major political parties were forced to come to grips with the question of devolution. The Labour government of 1974–1979 committed itself to the establishment of legislative assemblies for Scotland and Wales, to which some portion of the power held by the Parliament in London would be devolved. The actual devolution bills, which the government presented to the House of Commons, constituted a compromise that did not go far enough to suit the Scottish and Welsh nationalists but that went too far in the opinion of the Conservative opposition. The assemblies were to be given legislative powers in a restricted sphere, subject to revocation if the government in London should deem that a regional assembly had exceeded its powers. In Scotland, there was also to be an executive committee elected by the assembly, but it was not to be given actual administrative power. The devolution bills passed the House of Commons in 1978 and were submitted to the voters in a referendum in March 1979. However, the opposition to devolution, including most of the Conservatives and a minority of the Labour MPs, succeeded in adopting an amendment that required that at least 40 percent of the registered voters in Scotland and Wales must vote for devolution for the referendum vote to be regarded as positive. As it turned out, the issue was badly defeated in Wales while, in Scotland, although a bare majority of the voters supported devolution, the 40-percent requirement was not met. Devolution was, thus, regarded as having been repudiated by the voters in both regions. Following this setback, the Labour government of James Callaghan lost a vote of confidence in the House of Commons owing to the withdrawal of support by the Scottish Nationalists. In the ensuing election, the Conservatives were returned to power. Because the Conservatives had opposed devolution, at least in the form that Labour had proposed, the issue was placed on the back burner for the time being. The system of vertical power distribution in Great Britain remains essentially what it had been before the devolution battle began.

In summary, it seems clear that the greatest concentration of power in the countries we have examined is found in France. This is true on both the horizontal and vertical dimensions. If we take as the standard for horizontal concentration the amount of executive predominance over Parliament, the French President has more power than the cabinets of the strictly parliamentary countries. His power is reinforced by the strong role played by French civil servants. But the West German Chancellor ordinarily enjoys a strong hand as well. Athough Great Britain has a more collective form of leadership so long as one party has a solid majority in Parliament, power is held securely by the cabinet. In Italy, on the other hand, the existence of a minority or weak coalition government and the inefficiency of the bureaucracy makes it difficult for the cabinet to do more than conduct a holding operation. Thus, power is more dispersed in the horizontal sense in Italy. On the vertical scale, France again has the highest concentration of power—in the central government. The fused nature of France's unitary system, coupled with the strong position of the administrative élite, gives the central government almost overwhelming power over the periphery.[12] West Germany, on the other hand, goes the furthest toward decentralization with her federal system although she probably has a much higher degree of actual centralization than is found in the United States. Italy and Great Britain fall somewhere in between. Both seem to be moving haltingly toward a greater degree of decentralization.

[12]The Socialist government of President François Mitterrand made decentralization one of its first priorities in mid-1981.

# SUGGESTIONS FOR FURTHER READING

Allen, Kevin, and M. C. MacLennan, *Regional Problems and Policies in Italy and France* (Beverly Hills: Sage, 1970).

Armstrong, John A., *The European Administrative Elite* (Princeton, N.J.: Princeton University Press, 1973).

Conradt, David P., *The German Polity* (New York and London: Longman, 1978).

DiPalma, Giuseppe, *Surviving Without Governing: The Italian Parties in Parliament* (Berkeley: University of California Press, 1977).

Dogan, Mattei, ed., *The Mandarins of Western Europe: The Political Role of Top Civil Servants* (New York: Wiley, 1975).

Heidenheimer, Arnold J., and Donald P. Kommers, *The Governments of Germany*, 4th ed. (New York: Crowell, 1975).

Jackson, Robert J., *Rebels and Whips* (London: Macmillan, 1968).

Kommers, Donald P., *Judicial Politics in West Germany: A Study of the Federal Constitutional Court* (Beverly Hills: Sage, 1976).

Loewenberg, Gerhard, and Samuel C. Patterson, *Comparing Legislatures* (Boston and Toronto: Little, Brown, 1979).

Peters, B. Guy, *The Politics of Bureaucracy: A Comparative Perspective* (New York and London: Longman, 1978).

Rose, Richard, and Ezra Suleiman, eds., *Presidents and Prime Ministers* (Washington: American Enterprise Institute, 1980).

Safran, William, *The French Polity* (New York: David McKay, 1977).

Smith, Gordon, *Politics in Western Europe: A Comparative Analysis* (New York: Holmes & Meier, 1973).

Suleiman, Ezra N., *Elites in French Society: The Politics of Survival* (Princeton, N.J.: Princeton University Press, 1978).

Zariski, Raphael, *Italy: The Politics of Uneven Development* (Hinsdale, Ill.: Dryden, 1972).

# CHAPTER SIX

## Socio-Economic Policy Making:
## The Case of Industrial Relations

### INTRODUCTION

The formal institutions and roles of government are an important indicator of where power is located in Western polyarchies. Presidents, prime ministers, cabinets, civil servants, and parliaments make decisions that have a major impact on the ways in which well-being, respect, and enlightenment are distributed among the populations of polyarchies. The power to make significant decisions is not confined to leaders and agents of government however. Private citizens and institutions also hold power in countries where a private sector exists together with the public one and where the state does not attempt to control all facets of social life. Two important institutions that hold potential power are private business enterprise, especially the giant corporations, and trade unions, representing workers' interests. The former, through their capacity to determine levels of prices, wages, and investment for an economy, can collectively have a greater impact than can the economic policy decisions of government. The power of private corporations can, of course, be effectively checked by the countervailing power of large, well-organized trade unions, but only in certain areas, such as the determination of wages. Big business and big labor may even combine their forces to nullify any government efforts to counter inflation through successive wage and price increases.

### PLURALISM

The policy-making process in all First World polyarchies features the interaction of major economic interest groups with one another and with government in a continuous process involving both conflict and cooperation. When contrasted with the policy-making processes of Second and Third World countries, policy making in the First World roughly corresponds to the pluralist model, according to which the conflict between major actors takes place within an agreed-on set of rules of the game. Over the long run, gains by one side are balanced by those of the other, the government playing a mediating role. Public policy can be understood as the outcomes of contests between the competing groups in which both sides have agreed in advance to comply with these outcomes or to seek to change them through normalized processes. Whether public policy sides with one of the contenders or another, it will be a reflection of the momentary balance of power between the contenders, a balance that the temporarily weaker is free to seek to rectify.

Pluralism is the image of the policy-making process that most interest groups and political parties in First World countries present in seeking to justify their actions. They will say that they have acted according to established procedures and within normal channels or that they have acted to keep such channels open—or, in extreme cases, to reopen them—when others have sought to close them. They will insist that they respect the rights of their opponents and are merely acting to ensure that their own rights will be respected. On the other hand, they may accuse their opponents of seeking to circumvent legality and to deny legitimate rights. Trade unions may accuse employers of constituting a privileged class interested only in preserving their unjustly large share of wealth; employers' groups may accuse the unions of trying to divide society into warring classes, thus, weakening the nation in the face of economic and international dangers. In all such efforts, the pluralist image is put forth as both normal and desirable. Others are seeking to subvert a system that would work to the advantage of everyone if all would approach it with good will.

The problem in understanding policy making in the First World is that, although most interest groups and political parties pay public lip service to the pluralist model most of the time, they often act as if they harbored a different model. Intellectuals who do not share the consensual assumptions are ready at hand to supply elaborate justifications for alternative models, and some of the contending actors are fairly forthright in advancing them publicly. The two alternative models we will look at are corporatism and neo-Marxism. Each purports to show that there is a better model than pluralism to explain how the system normally works and that group actions are justifiable on the basis of this alternative model.

## CORPORATISM[1]

Corporatists share the belief that the adverse economic conditions of recent years are attributable to the selfish actions of groups in society that have placed their own particular interests ahead of the interests of all. This can be seen in the inflationary spiral, wherein producer groups seek to pass the burden of price increases on to the consumer, that is, to the economically weak who are not in a favorable position to protect their purchasing power. To combat this tendency, government must intervene to curb the power of the acquisitive. But government is often in too weak a position to do so because its leaders are dependent on the same groups for their power. Elections are seen as a bidding process in which promises of tax cuts, wage indexing, increases in social security benefits, and job-creating spending programs vie with one another for available votes.

The largest share of blame for these problems is usually reserved for the working class, who are said to undermine economic stability through their excessive demands. The central aim of corporatism has always been to bring wage demands and class conflict under control, subordinating them to what is perceived to be in the general interest. What this means, first and foremost, is the interest of the employer in maintaining profit levels and of the government in maintaining economic stability. Instruments that are used to bring about wage restraint range from coercive strike-breaking actions by government to incentive schemes designed to induce voluntary compliance on the part of wage earners and their organizations. In practice, these can be grouped into two sets, the instruments of

[1]Philippe C. Schmitter, "Modes of Interest Intermediation and Models of Societal Change in Western Europe," *Comparative Political Studies* 10 (1) (1977), pp. 7–38; Roger Benjamin, *The Limits of Politics: Collective Goods and Political Change in Postindustrial Society* (Chicago and London: University of Chicago Press, 1980), Chap. 7.

what we might call negative and positive corporatism.[2]

At the extreme, negative corporatism would take the form employed by Fascist Italy and Nazi Germany before World War II, a form in which independent trade unions were dissolved and state-dominated workers' organizations were created in their place. This resulted from a bargain between employers and government, one in which state controls over production were accepted by employers in return for the state's guarantee of a compliant labor force. Forced to accept lower wages than a free labor market would otherwise have brought them, the workers could take some consolation, in Germany at least, from the fact that jobs were once again relatively plentiful after the early dark days of the Great Depression. The justification for this exploitative system was the assumption that society was a corporate entity, the functioning parts of which were intimately interdependent. Action taken on behalf of the employers' interests would be to the benefit of all groups, and action on behalf of the selfish interests of one group would be detrimental to the interests of all. Thus, cooperation in the common effort was both normal and desirable. Conflict was seen as abnormal and counterproductive.

Since World War II, the more negative variety of corporatism has been dressed in a less coercive garb by European conservatives who continue to espouse it. However, it still proceeds from the assumption that it is the working class that, pursuing its selfish interests of any other group, threatens the good of the collectivity and that it is natural for government and the employer to ally in an effort to bring about worker compliance. Although workers' organizations are permitted an independent existence, a legal structure is advocated that stacks the cards in favor of the employer in industrial disputes and interferes both with the ability of trade unions to gain members and with their use of the strike as a legitimate means of pursuing their objectives. A

further characteristic is a posture on the part of both the employers and the government that only *approved* representatives of the workers should have a right to bargain on their behalf, with the employers and the government determining who is approved and who is not.

The more positive version of corporatism, and the version that is more prevalent in Western Europe today, has been promoted most consistently by left-of-center Christian Democrats. It maintains the same assumptions—that society is an interdependent corporate entity and that cooperation is a more normal mode of behavior than conflict. But it also harbors a more optimistic view of the likelihood that workers and their organizations will voluntarily moderate their claims on society so that all in society will enjoy the benefits of cooperative effort. In this version, workers should be induced to cooperate with employers and with the state through efforts to maintain stable prices. Some would go further and grant workers a legitimate share in the profits and even the management of the firms in which they work as a means of socializing them to the large stake they have in the health of the economy and of each of its functioning units. That this is a more benign version of corporatism from the workers' point of view is evidenced in the fact that some Democratic Socialists and leaders of workers' organizations, at least some of the time in recent years, have adhered to some of its features.

## NEO-MARXISM

If corporatists reject the pluralistic belief that conflict can have positive benefits, neo-Marxists reject the pluralist (and positive corporatist) belief that playing by the rules of the game will yield positive results for all. True to the thought of Karl Marx, the neo-Marxist divides society into social classes and sees the conflicts of interests between them as ineradicable so long as capitalism persists. Efforts by agents of the government to gain workers' cooperation are seen as efforts on behalf of the class of capitalist employers to gain worker compliance with what

---

[2]This distinction corresponds to Schmitter's categories of state corporatism and societal corporatism, *op. cit.*

is basically an exploitative system. Pluralist and positive corporatist theories are so much window dressing for a system that differs from that of Nazi Germany only in that it is better disguised, less self-declamatory. Conflict between classes is the normal state of affairs in capitalist society. To the extent that it has been sublimated through token material inducements, it is the task of Marxist political parties, workers' organizations, and intellectuals to unmask the hypocrisy and mobilize the workers for the inevitable struggle ahead.

The influence of neo-Marxism has waxed and waned in Western Europe since World War II but, in those periods when its adherents have had access to the leadership of Democratic Socialist parties and the trade union movement, the potential for industrial conflict has risen. At such times, there have been real tests of strength that have, in certain cases, altered the prevailing atmosphere as well as the balance of power among actors. Later in this chapter, we will examine the circumstances surrounding the making of industrial relations policy in each of our four countries to assess the effect of different combinations of these factors on the outcomes. First, we take a look at the principal economic groups that seek to influence socioeconomic policymaking.

## ECONOMIC SECTOR INTEREST GROUPS

### FARMERS' AND BUSINESS GROUPS

In the private economic sphere, as distinct from the state administrative and political circles, three types of interest groups play an important part in influencing economic policy in all Western European countries: farmers' associations, businesspersons' associations, and workers' organizations. All three are regularly consulted by their governments in the making of economic policy and in the determination of each country's position on economic matters within the European Community (EC), of which all four of our Western European countries are members. In postindustrial societies, economic policy making has become a central preoccupation of political

elites in general. The leaders of the major economic interest groups are, therefore, an essential element in the power structure of each country. Their advice is solicited when major economic decisions are to be made, and they can often precipitate events that will compel government decision makers to come to grips with unpleasant situations.

Farmers' associations carry considerable weight in the economic policy-making process of all Western European countries, despite the decreasing size of the farm population. In all four of our countries, independent farmers tend to support the parties in the center and on the right. In France and Italy, the parties on the left have a large share of the votes of sharecroppers and agricultural workers in regions where they are numerous, but the leading farm associations in these countries represent independent farmers who produce for the larger market, at least on a regional basis. Thus, the farm associations are not in the best position to bargain between parties on the left and right. In Great Britain, they are tied closely to the Conservative Party; in Italy and West Germany to the Christian Democrats. Only in France, where they can shift their votes back and forth between parties of the center and right, can they exert some leverage through the ballot.

Nevertheless, in all four countries the economic role of the farmers is crucial. Whether the country is relatively self-sufficient in farm products, as is France, or heavily dependent on imports, as are Great Britain and West Germany, the agricultural sector has an important impact on the balance of payments. France and Italy earn a substantial part of their foreign currencies through agricultural exports, especially to their Common Market partners. The EC's Common Agricultural Policy (CAP) has been worked out and is continually being adjusted, with the interests of the key farm-produce sectors of each member country in mind. Farmers' interest groups do a lot of lobbying both in their own national capitals and in Brussels, the headquarters of the EC.

There are three types of organized business

interests in Western Europe as in the United States: large private corporations, trade associations (of firms in the various productive and distributive sectors), and peak employers' confederations. The employers' confederations are the principal spokespersons for employers in national-level conflicts with organized labor, such as wage disputes, disagreement over working conditions, government policy issues (such as wage and price controls), and questions of the participation of workers in the management of the firm. In each of our four countries, there is a leading peak confederation: the Confederation of British Industries (CBI), the National Confederation of French Employers (CNPF), the Federation of German Employers (BDA), and the General Confederation of Italian Industry (Confindustria). With the exception of Confindustria, these tend to be dominated by the larger firms, which maintain specialists in employer-employee relations and related matters. Contacts among employers' spokespersons, leading politicians, and high-ranking civil servants tend to be very close, especially in France where the parties of the center right held on to power for a long time and where traditions of administrative neutrality are weaker than in Great Britain and West Germany.

Sector-specific trade associations play an important part in the overall economic planning for growth and modernization and in the development of trade policy nationally and internationally. Trade associations work closely with government experts and officials of the EC in developing these policies. Their ability to commit an entire industrial or commercial sector makes their cooperation indispensable. The major opponent of a trade association (for example, the West German chemical industry) is the corresponding trade association in a competing country (for example, the British chemical industry). But in negotiations at the EC level, cooperation may be more important than competition since promotion and protection of the industry in Western Europe against outside competitors will be emphasized. The interlocking relationships among trade association officials, national political leaders, high-ranking civil ser-

vants, and the growing army of Eurocrats based in Brussels are making it increasingly impossible to view national economic policy making in isolation.

To further complicate the picture, the major industrial giants—private corporations like British Petroleum, Fiat, or Siemens—have an impact on both national and European-level economic policy making, over and beyond that of the trade and employers' associations to which they belong. Political contributions by corporations and their leading officers, private friendships between the latter and leading political figures, and the movement of corporate managers back and forth between employment in the private and public sectors all lead to the conclusion that the corporate directorate in all four countries constitutes an important, if unmeasurable, part of the power élite.

Furthermore, many of the leading private firms in Western Europe are subsidiaries of the gigantic multinational corporations, many of which have headquarters elsewhere, especially in the United States. This has led to a substantial body of critical literature in Europe, asserting that the multinationals are Trojan horses that enable American interests to influence substantially not only the economics but also the political systems in Western Europe.[3] Much of the discussion in Western Europe has emotional overtones, reflecting resentment over the preeminent economic, political, and military position of the United States since World War II. However, the discussion may be losing some of its urgency as the U.S. position declines. It is difficult to assess to what extent parent corporations are able to control the actions of their affiliates abroad. But it cannot be denied that the multinationals make it difficult for Western European governments to regulate these businesses because too harsh a regulatory policy could drive a certain firm out of a country, resulting in considerable hardship

[3]For example, Jean-Jacques Servan-Schreiber, *The American Challenge*, trans. Ronald Steel (New York: Atheneum, 1968); Christopher Tugendhat, *The Multinationals* (New York: Random House, 1972).

for the local economy. We do not yet know enough about the political influence of multinational corporations to be able to make any confident generalizations.

## TRADE UNIONS

Can organized labor rival organized business as a political force in Western Europe? That Western European business interests have a secure position within the power structure of each country (although varying from country to country) would be difficult to refute. Like the United States, Western European countries, despite a generally larger public sector, are, in the final analysis, capitalistic. Although governments as well as the EC can regulate and induce certain behavior on the part of the private sector, their economies are still at the mercy of decisions made by a relatively small number of corporation heads. On the employees' side, there is a potentially similar power in that trade unions can bring economic activity to a standstill through use of the strike weapon. Nevertheless, there is considerable variation among our four countries with respect to which trade unions are actually equipped to use this weapon to their advantage.

Industrial relations in Western Europe have been in a state of flux since the 1960s.[4] Except for Great Britain, collective bargaining has not been as well established as it is in the United States. Efforts to institutionalize it more firmly have led to more-or-less formal arrangements at the national level between employers' and employees' organizations. For example, minimum wages may be agreed on by representatives of the two sides in industry at meetings presided over by members of the government and high-ranking civil servants. But the actual level of wages above these minimums will vary from industry to industry and from plant to plant within an industry, depending on the relative bargaining power of the workers and employers at these lower levels.

Often the unions are left out of this process altogether because agreements are worked out in committees that represent management and employees; for this purpose, the employees elect their representatives directly with or without union participation in the election.

In all four of our countries, wildcat strikes may break out, and the national employees' federations cannot control them. Local workers, whether members of unions or not, can present their national leadership with *faits accomplis*. Although the latter may oppose such strikes at the outset, they are often obliged to support them to maintain some semblance of union solidarity. Because the national leadership of the unions often has little control over local activity, employers and government may both be at the mercy of worker demands for higher wages. When concessions are made in one industry or even by one firm, it becomes harder to resist parallel demands elsewhere, and, so, the inflationary spiral continues. In fact, governments may find themselves having to combat not only the trade unions but also the employers as well whenever they attempt to pass on a higher wage bill to the consumer in the form of higher prices.

Nevertheless, there is a fairly wide variation in the strength of organized labor as it faces both the employers and the government in our four countries. Relatively speaking, workers have been in the weakest position in France, in the strongest in Great Britain, and in between in Italy and West Germany—for different reasons. Three factors account for these judgments: (1) the unity of the trade union movement nationally, (2) the strength of the unions at the plant level, and (3) the strength of the central government as a potential adversary seeking to frustrate union objectives.

In France, all three factors have worked against the emergence of a strong trade union movement. There are three major national confederations of trade unions in France, each with a different ideological orientation. The Communist-dominated *Confédération Générale du Travail* (CGT) is the oldest and largest, but the long-standing exclusion of the Communist Party from government kept the CGT in an isolated posi-

[4]For a useful recent overview of industrial relations in the First World, see Klaus von Beyme, *Challenge to Power: Trade Unions and Industrial Relations in Capitalist Countries*, trans. Eileen Martin (London and Beverly Hills: Sage Publications, 1980).

tion, not only in its relations with the government but also, until recently, in its relations with other workers' confederations. Of the two major non-Communist confederations, the largest is the *Confédération Française et Democratique du Travail* (CFDT), an offshoot from a Christian Democratic confederation. The smaller one, *Force Ouvrière* (FO), is Démocratic Socialist in its leanings and is also more anti-Communist than the CFDT, which has recently found that cooperation with the CGT is advantageous. The division of French organized labor extends from the national level to the various industrial sectors and even to the plant level where the competing unions put up competing candidates for election to local workers' committees. Wherever more than one union confronts the employer, the latter will be in a position to divide and conquer.

At the national level, the French trade unions face not only a united employers' movement but also a highly centralized and technically expert government. Trade unions send representatives to the various committees that participate in formulating the five-year plans, but they are usually outclassed by the highly proficient representatives of the trade associations and the appropriate ministries. Moreover, because the right was in power continuously from 1958 until 1981, trade unionists have felt that they were dealing with a monolith when it comes to national-level decisions on wages, prices, and other issues that are vital to workers' well-being. Business interests were well represented politically in the economic ministries in the guise of Gaullist and Giscardist ministers. The higher civil servants have often had a tour of political duty in the service of the leaders of these political parties, and they may have aspirations of ending their careers in management positions in private corporations. Now that the left has returned to power in France, the trade unions will no longer be on the outside looking in with respect to economic policy making.

The Italian labor movement is also divided between Communist-leaning and non- or anti-Communist confederations. The largest, the

An Italian union official addressing a workers' rally in Milan during a four-hour general strike called to protest government economic policy, March 1976.

General Confederation of Italian Labor (CGIL), is made up of workers who are members of, or tend to support, either the Communist Party or the Socialist Party. The Communists are in the principal leadership positions within the CGIL however; and, unlike the case of the CGT in France, they are less isolated politically and can have a greater voice in industrial disputes both nationally and locally. The Christian Democratic trade union confederation, moreover, is allied with the left wing of the DC and favors Communist participation in government. Thus, the trade unions in Italy speak with a more united voice both nationally and locally. Trade union strength is further enhanced by the weakness and internal division of the Italian government. Lacking a majority in Parliament the Christian Democratic governments have had to woo the Socialists and even the Communists for support. Such support has been gained only by making concessions that benefit the Italian labor movement in part. Still, employers' interests are well represented in the DC's leadership, which means that the concessions are often passed on to the consumer as can be attested by the high rate of inflation in Italy.

A mixed image likewise emerges from examining the West German labor movement. Here the movement is not divided. The German Trade Union Federation (DBG) has the overwhelming majority of organized industrial workers affiliated with it. Until recently, however, union members have not been organized at the plant level because the national federations have preferred to negotiate nationally with employers and the government. Although the DGB leadership is heavily Social Democratic, Catholic trade unionists are also affiliated with this federation, and an effort has been made to maintain harmonious relations with both CDU and SPD governments. A great deal of give and take has occurred in negotiations at these levels, and the unions have tended to forgo resorting to strikes in return for assurances by the government that the standard of living of the German working class will continue to rise. When these assurances failed to materialize during the recession of the mid-1960s, West German workers began to grow restive and their leaders faced insubordination at the local level.

In response to a wave of wildcat strikes in the late 1960s, the national leadership has begun to extend union organization to the plant level. At the same time, the SPD-FDP coalition government has extended the principle of worker-management codetermination throughout West German industry. Workers' representatives sit on the directing boards of private corporations. Although their ability to influence crucial corporate decisions, such as the distribution of profits and the price of products, is very limited, these representatives have been exerting greater weight on such issues as workplace conditions and the deployment of pension funds, which are actually of greater immediate concern to the workers. As the unions have been establishing a firmer presence at the plant level, they are taking a more important part in selecting workers' representatives. The strength of the West German trade unions, already secure at the national level, has, thus, been increasing at the local level as well.

As in West Germany, organized labor in Great Britain is united under one federation—the Trades Union Congress (TUC). The political links of British trade unions are tighter than is the case in the other three countries. National federations are affiliated directly with the Labour Party, and a portion of the dues that trade union members pay to their federations is automatically turned over to the party, unless members contract out by signing a statement of refusal to have their union dues so used. Because only a small percentage of trade unionists contract out, the majority of British trade union members are indirect members of the Labour Party. Or, to put it another way, approximately five-sixths of the membership of the Labour Party is indirect membership. The same ratio of votes is cast by the trade unions at the annual party conference as a result of this arrangement, which means that, whenever the unions speak with a united voice, they dominate the party. When this voice is at odds with that of the party's parliamentary leadership, the latter finds itself isolated from its rank and file—a vulnerable position.[5] But such direct conflict between the parliamentary leaders and the trade unions seldom arises. In recent years, the trade union movement and the Labour Party have both been divided internally, with the parliamentary leadership of the party serving as mediator on divisive issues.

Such close ties between the trade unions and one political party can be disadvantageous whenever the party is out of power and economic policy is being made by the opposite party. On the other hand the unions cannot expect a Labour government simply to translate their wishes into public policy without significant alterations. Since the period of acute industrial unrest in the late 1960s and early 1970s, the Labour Party has been at pains to convince the voters that trade union self-restraint is more likely to be exercised at the urging of a Labour than of a Conservative government. The claim was sufficiently credible that, after narrowly gaining power in February 1974, Labour was able to strengthen its hold in a second election eight months later. But the claim was no longer credible to British voters five years later. After a series of strikes in early 1979, which the Labour government had been unable to prevent, Labour was voted out of power.

What makes British trade unions more powerful than those in France, West Germany, or Italy? It is certainly not because they speak with a single voice when addressing the government or the employers. In fact, the TUC can only exhort powerful unions, such as the Transport and General Workers' Union and the Amalgamated Engineering Union—both of which have hundreds of thousands of members and both of which sometimes have militant leftists among their leaders. Such giants are free to steer their own course even if these conflict directly with the policy of the Labour Party and the TUC. Paradoxically, the power of the trade unions since the

1960s has stemmed in considerable part from their disunity or, more specifically, from the inability of national union leaders to control the actions of their rank and file at the local level. A moderate national leadership, attempting to cooperate with the government in a policy of wage restraint, may find that the local branches are electing militant leftists, even Communists, to the key positions of representation at the plant level.[6] Some of these same conditions have developed recently in continental European countries, but the fact that their unions are weaker at the local level means that the grass roots of organized labor cannot impose awkward situations on national policy makers as well as they can in Great Britain. The general points made in this section will now be elaborated on in case studies of industrial relations policies in our four countries.

## FOUR CASE STUDIES IN THE POLITICS OF INDUSTRIAL RELATIONS[7]

During much of the 1950s and 1960s, industrial conflict in Western Europe was relatively muted. Strikes occurred in certain industries at certain times when, for one reason or another, negotiations for wage increases broke down. But this was a time in most European countries of rapid economic growth and relatively full employment and low inflation. Wages were rising faster than prices; thus, purchasing power and lifestyles were improving. In 1966–1967, a recession occurred, affecting Western European industrial nations generally; after that, the periods of rapid economic growth and relatively full employment

[5]In a January 1981 party conference, it was decided to give the trade unions a 40 percent share in the election of the party's parliamentary leader. This election up to that time had been the exclusive province of Labour MPs.

[6]For a useful treatment of these various factors, see Leo Panitch, *Social Democracy and Industrial Militancy: The Labour Party, the Trade Unions and Incomes Policy, 1945–1974* (Cambridge: At the University Press, 1976).

[7]These case studies draw on, among others, Colin Crouch and Alessandro Pizzorno, eds., *The Resurgence of Class Conflict in Western Europe Since 1968*, vol. 1 (New York: Holmes & Meier, 1978); Anthony Carew, *Democracy and Government in European Trade Unions* (London: Allen & Unwin, 1976); Geoffrey K. Ingham, *Strikes and Industrial Conflict: Britain and Scandinavia* (London: Macmillan, 1974); and E. C. M. Cullingford, *Trade Unions in West Germany* (Boulder, Colo.: Westview, 1977).

began to alternate with periods of relative stagnation. Worker militancy began to rise in the first upsurge period after 1966–1967 when governments were turning to deflationary policies and efforts to impose wage restraints as means of countering the inflationary tendencies of a hyperactive period. Workers' demands began to take a more radical turn. Although demands for wage increases still were the most prevalent, demands began to be heard for a greater say in the determination of such things as piece rates, productivity bonuses, and wage differentials, in other words, demands for a greater share of power at the shop-floor level. Often, these demands went beyond what national union leaderships were seeking and reflected a groundswell of dissatisfaction not only with government and the employer (often one and the same) but also with national trade union leadership, which often seemed remote from the concerns of factory workers. In later periods of recession, with higher rates of unemployment, militancy receded and demands deescalated, enabling national workers' organizations to regain control of the base of the movement. But the upsurge in militancy of the late 1960s and early 1970s resulted in a greater self-confidence on the part of the unions, especially in countries where the corporatist mentality of leaders of government and employers' organizations had sanctioned an arms-length attitude toward the national representatives of the industrial workers. But antecedents, intensity of conflict, and outcomes varied considerably from country to country.

## WEST GERMANY

Both the reality and the rhetoric of industrial relations have come closer to the model of positive corporatism in West Germany than in the other large Western European countries. The evolution of West German industrial relations has gone through several distinct phases since 1945. In the early years, while the economy was recovering, unemployment levels were relatively high and the bargaining position of the workers relatively weak, but it cannot be said that employers took full advantage of their bargain-

ing superiority during this early period. Both employers' organizations and trade unions modified their claims for wage and price increases in the interest of containing inflationary pressures, and both workers and employers shared in the growing prosperity although profits increased at a more rapid rate than did wages.

In the late 1950s, the relative positions of employers and employees began to change as continued economic growth achieved full employment, and German employers were seeking to supplement the work force with immigrant labor for the jobs native workers were no longer interested in filling. Until the recession of 1966–1967, the positions of profits and wages were reversed, the latter now increasing more rapidly than the former. Nevertheless, relative to neighboring countries, the West German inflation rate remained low as growth rates began to slacken while near-full employment was maintained. This reflected the continued willingness of both industrial parties to moderate demands for income gains to preserve economic stability.

Throughout the postwar years, the offical industrial relations policy stance of the West German Government accorded with its overall commitment to a social market economy. This set of economic strategies and tactics was most closely identified with Christian Democratic Economics Minister, Ludwig Erhard, who eventually succeeded Konrad Adenauer as Chancellor. The strategy of the social market was to permit economic forces as much autonomy as possible to pursue their own interests, a policy guided by the *laissez faire* assumption that state interference in the economy would impede natural productive forces, stifling the incentives to innovate and take risks. It also expressed the strong German aversion to inflation, stemming back to the disastrous experiences of the early 1920s. The most interventionism the Erhard policy would permit was orthodox monetary control over the supply of money. The policy did not extend to efforts to control incomes through imposed restraints on wages and profits. Erhard placed his faith in a stable growth in money supply to moderate demand and limit price increases during full-scale economic expansion. Given the seemingly voluntary moderation on the part of employers and employees, the policy attained substantial success, to the mutual satisfaction of the government, the employers' organizations and private corporations, and the trade union leadership.

Officially the philosophy espoused by the Adenauer-Erhard government followed pluralist lines. Independent economic actors were free to pursue their own objectives. Conflict between them was natural but not harmful so long as it could be moderated through a sense of common interest in economic well-being for the good of all participants. Because the economy was doing very well and the economic interest groups were cooperating, the pluralist assumptions were never put to a test. Whatever the philosophy prevailing in Bonn, it appears that both employers' and employees' groups were operating under the positive version of corporatism, rather than pluralism, especially during the early to middle 1960s when industrial conflict was at a low ebb. The unions accepted a large measure of wage restraint in return for employers' restraint in pricing decisions. This aided the government's drive for a competitive edge for German products on the world market, the success of which helped maintain full employment at home and insulated West Germany from the importation of other countries' inflation.

So long as the Erhard strategy and tactics were working, there was no reason to call into question the basic *laissez faire* and pluralist assumptions. Yet, when West German industrial relations are compared with those of its neighbors, one central fact stands out: the existence of rather elaborate and stringent legal constraints in the employer-employee bargaining process. Unlike the situation in Great Britain, for example, unofficial strikes are illegal in West Germany, meaning that national union leaders, challenged by insurrection on the shop floor, can cloak themselves in a wrap of legality and refuse to support unofficial strikes and their objectives. This serves to reinforce the determination of national union leaders to cooperate with employers

in following a policy of wage restraint. It also belies the pluralist rhetoric of the Erhard philosophy. In fact, whatever the role of the government, West German law and the enforcement structure maintained to insure compliance with the law had a more corporatist flavor to it, and, compared with other West European countries, it gave an advantage to the employers.

That corporatism was the underlying economic outlook of a large share of the West German élite became evident as the recession of 1966–1967 took hold. Its almost immediate political impact was to discredit Chancellor Erhard and force him out of office. In December 1966, a new government was formed, the Grand Coalition of Christian Democrats and Social Democrats led by Kurt Georg Kiesinger, the CDU Chancellor, and SPD leader, Willy Brandt, as Vice Chancellor and Foreign Minister. Seeking a way out of the recession, the leaders of both partners of the coalition were willing to renounce those aspects of the Erhard policies that restrained the state from intervening in the economy. The commitment to export-based economic growth remained paramount. The new Economics Minister, Keynesian economist, Kurt Schiller of the SPD, developed a new West German economic policy: the policy of concerted action. It meant that the state would now take a more active role in controlling economic fluctuations through fiscal as well as monetary policy, a commitment that had been reached in Great Britain and France over a decade earlier. On its face, this represented a more interventionist stance for the government in a still essentially pluralist environment. But the Grand Coalition went a step further and announced an incomes policy that would involve the state in putting forth wage and price guidelines for acceptance by both employers and employees. Banking on the willingness of the trade unions to cooperate with an SPD Minister during a time when the SPD was attempting to establish its credentials as a governing party, Schiller asked the trade unions to go along with severe limitations on wage increases while profits would be allowed to rise at a modest rate to stimulate investment and get the economy back on a growth pattern. Desirous of ending the recession as well as giving the Grand Coalition a successful start, the trade unions exercised wage restraint. In 1967, the recession indeed came to an end and economic growth resumed.

The bargain was short lived however. Although the unions attempted to hold up their end, in 1968 they were overcome by a wave of wildcat strikes, which they first opposed but eventually had to support as the frequency of industrial strikes reached all-time post-World War II highs for West Germany. Employers and government leaders as well became preoccupied with bringing the industrial unrest to an end in order not to threaten the competitive edge West Germany held over its economic rivals. As a result, wage settlements reached much higher levels than Schiller's guidelines would have permitted. The SPD commitment to incomes policy, insofar as it contained enforceable teeth, had been proven untenable. Under the Brandt SPD-FDP coalition government that followed the Grand Coalition in 1969, wage and price restraint was made voluntary again.

Nevertheless, the Schiller experiment indicated that there was substantial support among West German élites for some version of positive corporatism involving government leadership. Although 1968 demonstrated that such policies could not be imposed on the workers, the Brandt government continued to seek employer and trade union cooperation in limiting wage and price increases and in containing industrial unrest. The effort was assisted by the success gained by the national trade unions in establishing their presence at the plant level. Whereas localized disputes had previously been negotiated with the firm by works councils elected by employees with little or no trade union participation, in the early 1970s, trade union representatives began actively to seek election to the councils and came to control them in numerous instances. On the other hand, 1968 by no means constituted the high-water mark for shop-floor militancy. In the 1970s, left-wing rebels continued agitating their companions to solidify their stand behind demands that now went beyond the traditional preoccupation with wages and hours of work. They began to attack not only the employers and management of the firms they worked for but also the trade unions, which had traditionally been dominated by the skilled, more highly paid workers. Now, demands were put forth for greater wage equalization through increases designed to narrow the gap between the higher and lower paid workers, in absolute as well as percentage terms. Immigrant and women workers were for the first time prominent among the more militant workers because they stood to gain, as subclasses, from the demands for equalization. The national unions found themselves having to yield ground to these demands to maintain some control over the shop-floor situation.

In this contest between the neo-Marxist conflict model and the government's positive corporatism, the Brandt and subsequent Helmut Schmidt coalition governments have had the large majority of workers supporting their political and economic objectives. National trade union leadership has been supportive most of the time, having to withdraw some distance from the government whenever plant-level militancy is at its height. This has tended to vary with the fortunes of the West German economy, which was subject to greater fluctuation in the 1970s than in earlier periods, but not, it should be emphasized, when compared with other postindustrial economies in the 1970s.

In general, worker restlessness had been greatest in periods when the economy was on an upswing after a period of relative inactivity. Trade union efforts to cooperate with government and employers during the preceding downswing had resulted in a momentary decline in real wages, all the more easy to impose on the workers because of the threat of unemployment. In the succeeding upswing, however, expectations for restoration of purchasing power outstripped the willingness of the bargaining élites to grant it, and the unions found themselves forced to deal with a groundswell of demands and work stoppages. The level of industrial conflict grew and the ability of élites to achieve wage restraint correspondingly declined. Then, a sudden increase in world oil prices brought on recession in First World economies, which, despite the best efforts of the West German government to withstand it, was visited on the export-dependent West German economy as well. Industrial militancy thereafter declined and wage restraint policy became viable once again.

During the 1970s, the SPD under Brandt and Schmidt sought to secure greater worker support for its policies by advancing the objective of worker participation in management, *Mitbestimmung*. The idea was to elevate the institution of the works council from the plant level to the level of the business firm's corporate headquarters and to give workers representation on the governing boards. To achieve this objective, the SPD leadership was forced to negotiate with the coalition partner, the Free Democrats, a party with considerable financial dependence on business interests. The compromise has meant the limitation of codetermination to larger firms and to those corporate policies that directly concern the interests of the work force, not to decisions of major economic importance, such as pricing policy or industrial mergers. The failure to extend codetermination further has undoubtedly limited its effect as a means of gaining worker acceptance of the corporatist framework. Another indication of the FDP influence has been the Schmidt government's strong stance against the neo-Marxist-inspired agitation in the industrial setting and in society at large.

What distinguishes the West German pattern from that in the other three countries is a pair of important characteristics: (1) industrial conflict has consistently been lowest in West Germany, even in periods where it is intense by West German standards; (2) agreement among West German élites (including trade union leaders) on the efficacy of positive corporatism is not found in Great Britain, Italy, and France where élites typically diverge in their outlooks on industrial relations (as we will see). The West German pattern of relative industrial peace and élite consensus is found in some of the smaller West European countries, notably the Scandinavian countries, the Netherlands, and Switzerland. Industrial conflict and intraélite discord is often regarded as a Mediterranean pattern that France and Italy share with Spain, Portugal, and Greece, whereas Great Britain and Belgium fall somewhere in between the two types.

Regarding West Germany, it should be noted that the northern pattern has been especially characteristic of the period of coalition government when the SPD has been the senior partner, a condition reinforced by electoral victories for the coalition in 1972, 1976, and 1980. Were the CDU/CSU to return to power—by itself or in a new center-right coalition with the FDP—or were the SPD to win a majority in its own right, the pattern might change in a more conflictive direction. A return of the right to power would severely tax the ability and willingness of trade union leaders to withstand the pressures of the militant left within their ranks; and an outright SPD majority would remove the restraint of having to satisfy the coalition partner by resisting pressures from the left wing of the party. Moderate trade union leadership would likewise find it difficult to resist its militant left. In short, a balanced industrial relations policy may well be dependent on the continued well-being of the West German economy and its moderating effect on the electorate.

## GREAT BRITAIN

Committed from the end of World War II to a policy of maintaining full employment, British governments have employed a Keynesian approach, using both fiscal and monetary instruments to control both inflation and unemployment. Completing the postwar rebuilding period earlier than did West Germany, Great Britain saw its period of rapid economic growth come to an end in the middle 1950s. Thereafter, not only did the British growth rate fall behind that of its principal rivals but also the competitiveness of its industries sagged and severe trade imbalances began to be felt. Efforts to pump up the economy were invariably short lived and soon gave way to deflationary measures which further deterred economic growth and took the economy further from full-employment levels. Nor could inflation be controlled with any consistency. The so-called stop-go policies of the late 1950s and early 1960s only seemed to intensify the paradoxical coupling of unemployment and inflation. The British were early pioneers in the virgin territory of postindustrial *stagflation*.

Throughout the 1950s, the consequences for the working class of Great Britain's worsening economic picture were obscured by rising real incomes, a fact that enabled Harold Macmillan's Conservative Party to win reelection in 1959 with the "you've never had it so good" slogan. But a resurgence of unemployment in the early 1960s forced the Macmillan government to come to grips with the failure of Great Britain to keep up economically with her neighbors across the Channel. In addition to the decision to seek entry into the European Common Market, Macmillan turned to a milder version of the economic planning that had seemingly been so successful for the French economy. Prior to this time, the Conservative commitment had been to Keynesian economics minus the heavy array of controls the Labour government of 1945–1951 had carried over from World War II. Great Britain had evolved too far in the direction of state intervention for a complete return to free market economics, something that the Conservatives had never been enthusiastic about anyway. But the basic underlying philosophy applied to industrial relations was essentially pluralist. That is, government intervention in the economy should not extend to employer-employee relations. Rather, the outcome of such contests (it was held) should reflect the relative strengths of the contestants.

Rising purchasing power and living standards reduced the perception of interclass hostility among British workers. In the later 1950s, impressed by the Conservatives' repeated electoral victories, the Labour Party modified its basically neo-Marxist position and came to accept the pluralist outlook of the Conservatives as offering greater electoral advantage. This meant effective abandonment of the wholistic commitment to a socialist Great Britain. On the one hand, the existing mixed economy and welfare state could be improved, on the other hand, perpetuation of a private industrial sector and of unequal shares of the nation's wealth held by different social classes could now be tolerated.

The interventionist pluralism of the Labour Party contained a corporatist potential, which could be stimulated by adverse economic conditions. When the party returned to power in 1964 under Harold Wilson's leadership, it inherited a desperately adverse balance of payments situation, which had been fostered by the Conservatives' efforts to restimulate the economy in time for the election. Under pressure from the international banking system (what Wilson labeled, "the gnomes of Zurich"), the new government was forced to abandon its hopes for a government-led technological revolution in Great Britain and to opt for deflationary measures. In addition to the typical Keynesian countercyclical measures, Wilson chose an incomes policy of wage and price restraint, banking on the support of the trade unions for a Labour government. But given the perception on the part of union leadership that their bargaining position with the employers was a strong one, union compliance with wage restraint was halfhearted at best, especially as grassroots pressure was intensifying and the incidence of wildcat strikes sharply increasing. In 1968–1969, the volume of strike activity reached new postwar highs for periods with the Labour party in power.

But the corporatist tendencies within the Wilson government had not yet run their course. Unlike the West German legal system, British law contained no means by which unofficial strikes could be legally contained. Nor were there regulations allowing for periods of cooling off or for compulsory resort to state-appointed mediators or arbitrators. By the time the Wilson government had concluded that wage restraint was not going to work, a considerable amount of pressure had built up from the Conservatives and from employers' associations for legislation restricting strike activity and (implicitly) restraining employees' bargaining position relative to that of employers. The Wilson government introduced legislation to the House of Commons designed to limit the right to strike by imposing fines on workers engaging in unofficial strikes and on trade unions resorting to strikes before exploring government-induced opportunities to negotiate. Although the legislation also provided for expansion of union rights in grey areas not previously covered by legislation, the unions mounted a campaign against it, and, with support from Labour backbenchers, forced the Wilson government to withdraw it and abandon its experiments with corporatist policy instruments.

After the reversal of the Labour policy initiative, it was the Conservatives' turn. Following the Conservative victory in the June 1970 elections, the government of Edward Heath introduced legislation similar to that of the Wilson government although providing a wider array of countermeasures and antistrike penalties. It was enacted into law as the Industrial Relations Act of 1971. Although gaining some support from white-collar workers' unions, the act became a dead letter once it became clear that the industrial workers' unions would not comply with its provisions that required unions to register under the act to gain official status. By that time, unofficial strikes had given way to official, union-sponsored ones. The Labour Party, then, returned to a hands-off policy and strongly opposed both passage and enforcement of the act and promised to repeal it, which, in fact, they did when they returned to power in 1974.

Meanwhile, the Heath government had turned to another instrument that was designed to curb the power of organized labor to push successfully for inflationary wage claims. In 1972, Heath reversed his government's opposition to wage and price controls and, after failing to gain union support for voluntary wage restraint, instituted a statutory incomes policy. This imposed rigidly enforced limits on wage and price increases, thus, abruptly reducing the power of labor in its bargaining relations with management. Although the policy met with relative success in its first year, it fell apart in the wake of the Arab oil embargo that followed the October 1973 Arab-Israeli War. With their bargaining power suddenly enhanced by the nation's energy shortage, the National Union of Mineworkers called a strike in the coal mines. Heath countered by declaring a state of emergency, which a

number of other unions defied by striking in sympathy with the miners. The winter of 1973–1974 was made particularly severe through reduction of industrial activity to a three-day week and through numerous work stoppages and shortages of supplies. Finally, Heath called an election for February 1974. He fought the election on the issue of whether the government or the unions were running the country. Although no party won a majority in the election, Labour returned to power as a minority government, having a plurality of seats in the House of Commons. Harold Wilson, then, proceeded to negotiate a settlement of the miners' strike that was favorable to the miners' demands and touched off an inflationary wave of wage settlements.

Thereafter, the Labour governments of Harold Wilson and his successor, James Callaghan, followed an incomes policy that sought voluntary cooperation from the unions as part of a social contract, a counterpart element of which was legislation, enacted in 1976, that strengthened the legal position of the unions, especially restricting the ability of employers to interfere with the unions' right to organize and represent employees. Through the middle 1970s, the unions were able to gain rank-and-file acceptance of these policies as the British economy struggled through a period of recession coupled with an inflation rate that at times reached higher than 20 percent. But, as unemployment and inflation figures began to descend to more normal ranges, the disincentive against unofficial strikes lessened and industrial unrest resumed. A series of interconnected strikes in the state sector in early 1979 further undermined a weak Callaghan government, and the Labour Party, after an adverse vote of confidence in the House of Commons, suffered defeat at the hands of Margaret Thatcher and the Conservatives in the general election of May 1979.

Margaret Thatcher had gained the leadership of the Conservative Party when Edward Heath had failed to gain a vote of confidence from Conservative Members of Parliament in early 1975. In addition to two consecutive electoral defeats, Heath had been blamed for the rigidity of his economic policies during his

1970–1974 government. The *laissez-faire* wing of the Conservative Party, which had felt abandoned by Heath when he turned to an incomes policy in 1972, now reasserted itself and elected a leader with whom they felt an ideological affinity. Thatcher surrounded herself between 1975 and 1979 with economic conservatives on the opposition front bench. When she came to power, she appointed a monetarist, Sir Geoffrey Howe, as Chancellor of the Exchequer, and her government committed itself to a policy of allowing market forces a maximum of independence to pursue their own interests free of government controls. Like the Labour Party, the Conservatives moved from pluralism to corporatism and back to a sort of mixed position in which (verbally at least) commitment to pluralism appears to take precedence. Their supporters in the ranks of employers seem to have taken this circuitous route along with them. Policy hesitations in the first years of the Thatcher government have not met with an increase in industrial unrest, probably in large part because unemployment has had its usual inhibiting effect on worker militancy.[8]

Having returned again to opposition, the Labour Party has turned inward in a power struggle between its left (neo-Marxist) and moderate wings. Late in 1980, following the resignation of James Callaghan as party leader, the Labour MPs elected a lifelong leftist, Michael Foot, as their new leader—and, therefore, candidate for Prime Minister in the next elections. Although Foot had been brought hesitantly into the party center during Callaghan's consensus-building leadership, his victory over moderate Dennis Healey signalled a notable shift in the party's center of gravity toward the left. This was further reinforced by the decision of an extraordinary party conference in January 1981 to take away the exclusive right of MPs to elect the party leader and to give the party outside of Parliament, including rank-and-file activists and the affiliated trade unions, a say in the leadership selection. This makes it more likely that the left, which is stronger among activists and some of the trade unions, would be able to name a leader of its choice in the near future, perhaps irreconcilable leftist, Anthony Benn, who led the effort to change the party rules. What this means is the existence of a fierce struggle for supremacy within the Labour Party between the proponents of pluralism and neo-Marxism. The recent victories of the neo-Marxists on the left have moved a number of moderate leaders, including Roy Jenkins, Shirley Williams, and Dr. David Owen, to leave the Labour Party and form the new Social Democratic Party. The new party offers itself as the true proponent of pluralism in Great Britain, renouncing what they perceive as the neo-Marxism of the leftward-tending Labour Party and the unreconstructed corporatism of the rightward-drifting Conservatives. Whether British voters will see things quite the same way remains problematical.

Nevertheless, it can be said that pluralism is a more genuine commitment on the part of British élites than it is of élites on the continent. The fluctuating role of the trade union movement fits into this perspective. Although it has its neo-Marxist components, their strength ebbs and flows and is offset by a typical British pragmatism that recognizes that conflict for its own sake will in time be counterproductive. Throughout most of postwar British economic history, the predominant theme of the British labor movement has been cooperation. Conflict takes precedence only in certain periods when the party is out of power, not always even at such junctures, as the moderation of the late 1950s and early 1960s attests. That period suggests that, when the movement becomes sufficiently hungry for a return to power, its pragmatic pluralist side will reassert itself. Above all, there is a broad commitment to the institutional framework of the British policy-making process, with legitimacy accorded to the roles of both majority government and responsible opposition and to the rights of economic actors to pursue their interests with relatively little restraint emanating from the government.

[8]Urban rioting in Great Britain during the summer of 1981 can, however, be traced to unemployment, among other causes.

## ITALY

The early postwar Italian system of industrial relations was strongly influenced by the two decades of Fascist rule the country had experienced. Benito Mussolini's state had explicitly opted for a system of negative Corporatism in which state-controlled trade unions assisted the government and the employers in enforcing labor discipline. Although the Constitution and statutory law of the new Italian Republic repudiated the Fascist system and removed legal restrictions on both employers and employees, Italian employers did not easily give up the corporatist model to which they had grown accustomed during the Fascist years. The weakness of the trade unions during the 1940s and 1950s allowed them to impose a corporatist reality on a pluralist legal framework, despite the fact that workers' organizations and political parties espoused an intransigent Marxism.

Economic circumstances worked against the success of trade union militancy. Rapid modernization and economic growth occurred in the 1950s in Italy as it did elsewhere in Western Europe, but the early period of underemployment lasted somewhat longer because industrialization was less far advanced and there was an overabundance of semiskilled and unskilled workers, especially in southern Italy. Organizationally, the trade unions in Italy were very nearly the weakest in Western Europe. Their memberships tended to be confined to the minority of skilled workers, and they were notably weak in the semiindustrialized southern regions.

Most important, at the national level, the unions did not speak with one voice. The largest, the General Confederation of Italian Labor (CGIL), had strong links with the opposition Communist and Socialist parties. The Catholic union, the Italian Confederation of Workers' Syndicates (CISL) was linked with the left wing of the ruling Christian Democratic party. The tactic of divide and conquer worked well for employers throughout most of the 1950s.

Confindustria, the employers' organization, enjoyed easy access to the Christian Democratic governments and especially to the ministries that administered industrial relations policy. Such access was totally lacking to the CGIL. Thus, Confindustria was able to gain tacit state approval for its negative corporatism. Often, this meant state abstention from intervening in situations in which the employer had the upper hand. Although the system did not operate in as blatant a fashion as it had in Fascist times, the philosophy shared by Italian élites had not evolved very far. But, as the 1950s progressed, the Christian Democrats began to lose support among lower income earners in the industrial and agricultural sectors. The loss in voting support for the Christian Democrats between 1948 and 1958 was exactly matched by a gain in the combined vote of the opposition Communist and Socialist parties.

By the late 1950s, Italian industrialization was in full expansion. The demand for both semiskilled and unskilled labor was growing not only in Italy but also in northern Europe where industries were attracting immigrant workers from the south. These twin pulls reduced Italian unemployment and improved the bargaining position of the trade unions. The incidence of strikes began to increase. The employers who felt the impact most severely were often the most modern and competitive, those whose market was global. The strikes put them in a disadvantageous position relative to firms in countries where industrial unrest was minimal. In many

Italian workers striking in protest against government anti-inflation measures. Red flags of the Italian Communist Party are on their shoulders.

such cases, the employer was the state. The state sector had been expanding substantially during the growth period in areas where the expansion had been greatest, petrochemicals for example. But those firms most affected by the strikes included American-based multinational corporations as well as large private Italian corporations, notably Fiat and Olivetti. An additional reason why these public, semipublic, and private giants were the most affected was that the unions were best organized in precisely these same firms.

This meant, first, that the state itself was becoming an interested party in industrial disputes; and, second, that among the private employers' ranks a minority was arising with interests distinctly different from those that continued to predominate in Confindustria. Established in 1956, Intersind, an organization of large-scale employers, began to gain strength in the early 1960s, whereas Confindustria, increasingly the voice of medium-sized and smaller firms, lost influence. In 1962, to reflect this changing balance in industrial relations, the Christian Democratic party reoriented its coalition strategy and gained the support of the Socialist Party—the so-called opening to the left. A year later, after further electoral gains by the left, the Socialists gained a share of government posts, leaving the Communist Party alone in opposition on the left.

What the opening to the left reflected was a simultaneous shift in perception in the direction of positive corporatism by a majority of both the Christian Democratic and Socialist party élites, the more progressive elements of the state bureaucracy and the employers' movement, and trade unions of Catholic and Socialist orientation. Remaining outside this consensus were (1) the Communists and the left-wing Socialists and allied trade unionists still attached to neo-Marxist perspectives and (2) the majority of employers with their allies on the right side of the political spectrum and in the less dynamic regions of the state bureaucracy—for them, the negative version of corporatism did not die easily. The decisive political change was the convergence in the center of those élites in a position to implement their philosophy through a more aggressive government role in industrial relations. The result was a very tangible advance in real wages for Italian employees throughout the 1960s. It was far from the case, however, that all sectors of Italian society benefited equally—as the positive-sum assumption of positive corporatism would have it. Although the real wages of all sectors of the working class rose in this period, those of the skilled—and more thoroughly unionized—workers climbed the most rapidly; and although, under Socialist prodding, state-inspired investment in the south was greatly expanded and modernization proceeded there as it had earlier in the north, the northern share of the overall national income grew during the 1960s, whereas that of the south declined.

The influx of southern Italian workers into northern cities provided the Communist Party with an opportunity to increase its base of support. During the 1960s, the Italian Communist Party and the Communist-linked trade unions made a concerted effort to reach the growing number of semiskilled and unskilled workers occupying the lowest paid jobs, often in smaller firms where union organization was the weakest. The disoriented and estranged workers from the south were a uniquely available target. For them, the Communist Party and the trade union offered a sort of home away from home. The Communists provided assistance in finding housing and recreational facilities. In return, the newly recruited were socialized to accept the Communist world view. At the same time, however, that world view was changing. The growing prosperity, the more positive attitude of the government and of many of the northern employers, and the rising electoral support for the PCI were factors that mitigated the neo-Marxist tendency to see the world exclusively in terms of class conflict.

For the moment, however, in the late 1960s, the consequence of the growing strength of the PCI and the CGIL was an increase in industrial militancy that coincided, as in other countries, with an upturn of the economy. The particular forms that the Italian version of the revolt of rising expectations took were essentially intensifications of minor themes to be found during the late

1960s and early 1970s in labor unrest elsewhere in Western Europe. Demands for wage equalization played a greater role in Italy than elsewhere because unskilled and semiskilled labor constituted a relatively large component of the industrial labor force in relatively underindustrialized Italy, because the immigrant workers filling these unskilled and semiskilled occupations were native Italians from another part of Italy, and because the leading working-class party and leading trade union confederation were making a concerted effort to organize and advance the claims of these workers. The forms that industrial action took often showed a greater tendency to depart from the conventional mode. Wage equalization was put forth by the entire movement as a leading strike demand rather than as a minor theme by immigrant and women workers. The unconventional strike methods included extensive use of the technique of rolling strikes, which were coordinated staggered work stoppages, especially effective when used by semiskilled assembly-line workers. One worker on the line would fail to perform his or her function for 15 minutes while the assembly line continued to move; then, another would lay his or her tools down for another 15 minutes, and so on. The finished products would emerge slightly flawed, but different items would contain different flaws, the detection of which would be difficult, especially if inspectors participated in the strike as well.

Industrial unrest in Italy between 1968 and 1973 resulted in a number of gains for workers and for the trade union movement. Most important was the achievement of legislation in 1970 that established the right of trade unions to organize workers at the shop level, a right that many employers had successfully denied the unions in the past. From this point, the unions pushed for the establishment of workers' councils with which management would have to negotiate concerning wages and conditions of work, councils that the unions themselves could expect to dominate. Although no national legislation was achieved in this regard, many employers succumbed to this demand in the face of strikes or the threat of strikes. The strikes also secured substantial increases in real income for the workers, bolstered by indexing arrangements that promised automatic increases in the future to keep workers' incomes ahead of price inflation, thus, serving to exacerbate inflationary tendencies. The PCI played an active role in supporting these demands and in neutralizing the government as a recourse for beleaguered employers. The rising strength of the PCI was verified by substantial gains in the municipal elections of 1975 and the parliamentary elections of 1976. Finally, the 1970s saw the tentative beginnings of a move to merge the CGIL and the CSIL into a single trade union confederation. Greater progress was made in this direction at the local level than nationally however.

The announcement of the Communist offer of an historic compromise with the Christian Democrats that would enable the PCI to participate in government reflected the enhanced position of the Communists and also the fact that the industrial balance of power had shifted favorably for the trade unions. What the Communists were proposing was a bargain in which they would trade parliamentary support and the unions would trade wage restraint for Christian Democratic and employers' willingness to concede the legitimacy of the trade unions and of their demands on behalf of the workers.

In fact, Italian industrial relations had evolved into a two-tiered system in which a pluralist contest of relative equals prevailed in the modern, more competitive sectors and firms; employers in the less advanced sectors and firms, in which production and distribution were oriented to a more localized market and in which underemployment of labor was the norm, sought (often successfully) to sustain the negative corporatist pattern of industrial relations. The Communists were seeking to gain state support for an equalization of relations in the sectors where the trade unions were weakest in return for Communist and trade union support for government economic policies designed to protect Italy's position in the world economy.

The Communists gained only a partial measure of their objectives. Politically, after their electoral gains in the mid-1970s, they began giving the Christian Democrats support on legislative matters, gradually moving to the position of consistent members of the parliamentary majority. However, they failed to gain the objective of membership in a governing coalition, the Christian Democrats preferring to retain unstable minority governments during the period. The Communists were consulted on policy matters, but Communist and trade union acquiescence in wage restraint was not reciprocated; the government argued that social and economic reforms would be out of the question so long as double-digit inflation prevailed and the lira remained vulnerable.

By 1978, in part because of the success attained in wage restraint, Italian levels of inflation were coming down and investor confidence in the Italian economy was growing. At the same time, the PCI was under strong attack from its own left wing and from radical elements of the student and working-class movement who argued that the PCI had sold out to the enemy. Left-inspired terrorism had become an almost daily phenomenon in Italy, as some of the disaffected were moved to desperate action to express their belief that no one was any longer listening. The Communists found themselves supporting a hardening of government antiterrorist methods. Fearing the loss of electoral support, the PCI finally withdrew its support from the government, precipitating another cabinet crisis and eventually premature elections in June 1979. The result was a PCI loss of 3 percent of the national vote, whereas the Socialists and the Christian Democrats held their ground.

The Communist moves can be explained in terms of their jockeying for position in an effort to gain a share of power; but it is also true that, for whatever motive, their tactics have shifted with changes in the fortunes of the Italian economy. Willingness to cooperate with the government has been greater in periods of economic crisis, whereas efforts to reestablish links with a more militant base have been resumed when the economy provided more leeway. Strike activity has followed its saw-toothed pattern according to a parallel rhythm. It appears that the Communist perception of industrial relations and, more generally, of economic policy continues to rest on the assumption that conflict is the norm, but, with the abandonment of orthodox Marxism, this has been supplemented with the belief that, under unfavorable circumstances, cooperation can at least help preserve the gains the working class has previously achieved. The Communists appear to have made a pragmatic decision that conditions now permit them to carry their defense of working-class interests into what has become a more evenly balanced pluralist arena of contest. More flexible use of the workers' weapons of industrial combat as well as a more nuanced role for the party itself in expressing parliamentary opposition have met with some response from the other side. But how to deal with the Communists and with organized labor is an issue that continues to divide Christian Democracy and the employers' movement in Italy.

### FRANCE

The French pattern of industrial relations has traditionally exhibited characteristics similar to what prevailed in Italy prior to the 1960s. A divided and restricted trade union movement faced employers (the *patronat*) who believed in maintaining their authority over their employees even at the expense of peaceful industrial relations. They relied, when possible, on economic conditions to give them a superior bargaining position. The French Communist Party (PCF) has always played a role similar to that of the PCI in the 1950s. It maintained strong links with the largest trade union (the CGT) and operated from a Marxist perspective, avoiding cooperation with the employers and with the state except when able to operate from a position of strength—which was seldom the case in France before the late 1960s. Employers were frequently able to deal with non-Communist trade unions, arriving at settlements to which the state gave its accord.

What differentiated the French situation from the Italian was the more important role of the state in industrial relations and especially in the planning of economic policy and the coordination of economic-policy instruments. The state intervened in industrial relations to the extent that it offered its services as mediator in disputes, but it did not go so far as to attempt to impose solutions. Nevertheless, the state planning network established after World War II was actively engaged in setting targets for production in key industrial sectors. A growth-oriented policy motivated the state to intervene in such a way as to avoid the escalation of industrial conflict that would disrupt the productive process. During the Fourth Republic, the policies of the divided governments tended to be *ad hoc* and inconsistent. Although governments were not completely successful in keeping the level of industrial conflict down, the French economy did enjoy remarkable growth in the middle and late 1950s, and workers shared in the benefits. But tax incentives and state subsidies ensured that the employers would benefit to a greater extent. Wage increases might have been greater had the political left and the trade union movement not been deeply divided. It is noteworthy that French workers on the average put in the longest hours of work in Western Europe without this being reflected in appreciably higher income gains owing to overtime compensation.

With the return of General Charles de Gaulle to power, certain changes took place that brought this picture into sharp focus. Through strengthening the executive constitutionally and through his own personal authority, de Gaulle was able to strengthen the hand of the government relative to competing interest groups. Greater administrative coordination was achieved through the lessened role of the National Assembly as a conduit for group influences toward the bureaucracy and by reason of the fact that loyal Gaullists commanded the ministries relevant to economic policy. These ministries had hitherto been divided among leaders of different political parties. Because the party in power was a party of the right, more favorably disposed to the propertied classes, and because the political left, including the non-Communist left, was relegated to a protracted period of opposition, policies made by the Fifth Republic governments could be expected to have a certain bias, and they did.

In the Gaullist perception of economics, the interest of the government in maintaining a productive and stable economy came first. This proceeded from the commitment of de Gaulle to a strong French posture in international affairs, including his insistence that France be equipped with an effective, credible nuclear deterrent. Considerable state resources were channeled into scientific research and technological development. At the same time, his government sought to cope with growing needs and demands in society for such services as education and health delivery systems. At a time when defense spending as a share of the gross national product was declining for all advanced industrial countries (even the Soviet Union), de Gaulle was seeking, not altogether successfully, to swim against the current.

As the Gaullists saw the situation, the combined demands being put on the state were fraught with inflationary potential, a potential that could threaten the willingness of investors to gamble on French economic potential. Investment capital came second only to the state in the Gaullist system of priorities. Therefore, the government economic policy turned from emphasis on economic growth for its own sake to emphasis on improving productivity through technological development and through joining employers in pressing for greater worker productivity as a prerequisite to satisfaction of wage demands. Deflationary policies in the middle 1960s further weakened the workers' position by building a certain "tolerable" level of unemployment into the economy. Despite levels of days lost to strikes (high for the time in Western Europe), the lack of unity in the French trade union movement meant that long-term strikes could not be sustained. Thus, bolstered by the moral support of the Gaullist state, employers could usually hold out against wage demands. Moreover, until 1967 at least, de Gaulle's position was unassailable from the left. Enchanted by his anti-Americanism and his withdrawal of

France from the unified North Atlantic Treaty Organization (NATO) command structure in 1966, the Communists tended to direct their attack at the Gaullists, but to refrain from training their heaviest guns at de Gaulle himself.

Nevertheless, the strong showing of the *ad hoc* coalition of Communists and Socialists in the 1967 legislative elections was a sign that working-class disenchantment was beginning to improve the chances of a solid opposition to Gaullist policy. The response of de Gaulle's government was to draw its ranks together and to use emergency powers to continue implementing unpopular policies. As the French economy turned upward after the 1966–67 slump, the volume of unsatisfied demands began to rise. The result was the explosion of May 1968 in which student protests against the overcrowded and alienating conditions in the system of higher education led to confrontations with the police and, ultimately, to work stoppages in factories. The latter began as sympathy strikes directed against government antistudent actions, but they soon developed into a general strike of workers all over France who demanded higher wages and changes in industrial organization. The demands and the tactics of the French workers were not different from those arising at about the same time in other countries. What distinguished the French explosion was its dimensions. The general strike was of sufficient scope and intensity to threaten the existence of the Fifth Republic. In retrospect, it is clear that it forced de Gaulle to reorder his domestic and foreign policy priorities and, ultimately, to leave office after unsuccessfully testing his popularity in a referendum he could easily have won a few years earlier.

The explosion also had an effect on the trade unions and the political left that was virtually unique to France. The spontaneity of the first wave of strikes took the Communist Party and the CGT by surprise. Their first reaction was to oppose the strikes, denouncing Trotskyite and Maoist elements involved in them. But the smaller trade union confederation, the CFDT, more flexible than the CGT ideologically, was quicker to respond favorably to the strikes and to endorse the strikers' demands. Although the

French police demonstrating in January 1979 in front of the Notre Dame cathedral in Paris. They are on their way to a meeting with the prefect, the head of city administration, to call his attention to "the deplorable conditions" under which the police work.

Communists and the CGT eventually gained control of the situation and helped to win for the workers a substantially favorable—and inflationary—wage settlement, they had momentarily appeared to be a conservative, even establishment-oriented element in the scenario. Thereafter, the Leninist party of the working class had to strive mightily to regain its standing as the intransigent enemy of the capitalist class, whereas the CGT had to take up the more excessive demands of the rank and file in order not to lose militants to the CFDT. Whereas the principal development on the left in Italy in the 1970s was the movement of the leftist parties and trade unions toward the center of the spectrum, the movement in France has been that of the more moderate elements of the left toward the position of a Communist Party and a Communist-led trade union movement that refuse to budge from their accustomed ground. The events of 1968 radicalized younger members of both the working and the middle class who 10 years earlier would have stayed out of politics or joined the more moderate organizations. As the 1970s wore on, their youthful counterparts in other countries either rejoined the system or, in the case of a small minority, opted for still more radical and dangerous action. In France, the *enragés* of 1968, were now approaching the magic age of 30 themselves and were coming into positions of leadership in the Socialist party and the CFDT, both organizations oriented toward active pursuit of the objective of restructuring French society in a neo-Marxist image. Although de Gaulle's policies had helped draw a clearer distinction between left and right, the events of 1968 achieved a polarization that reached its peak around 1976, only to diminish as fissures on both right and left began to encourage moderates on both sides to reassert themselves.

But despite the ebbs and flows of party politics in France, the fact that power remained anchored on the right meant that the essentially corporatist nature of industrial relations fixed by the policies of Charles de Gaulle continued to be reflected in the policies of his successors. Despite the promises of a more socially conscious state in the early years of the Georges Pompidou presidency and of a more liberal state under Valéry Giscard d'Estaing, the strong interest of the state in maintaining French commercial competitiveness led to repeated state interventions directed toward advantaging French private firms and state enterprises. Worker demands invariably threatened these advantages and the state intervened in industrial disputes. Often the effort was to reduce employer intransigence in bargaining, but the concessions urged to worker demands fell short of those having inflationary consequences. Thus, the employers retained the upper hand. The strong verbal commitment of Giscard d'Estaing's second Prime Minister, Raymond Barre, to a reduction of state controls and incentives did not prevent his government from

turning to wage and price controls when inflationary pressures mounted in the late 1970s. This is a further indication that the reflexes of the French bureaucracy and the technocratic political leaders who commanded it tended always to be in the direction of imposing the hand of the state when (as usual) private actors were unable to produce solutions to economic problems when left to their own devices. Before 1958, the lack of a coordinated political will often restrained the hand of the state in industrial relations. The Fifth Republic superimposed a corporatist intellectual model on a pluralist pattern, but, unlike the case in West Germany, working-class cooperation was minimal. Thus, industrial conflict remained at a high level in France, with the state relying on the weakness of the opposition as the best means of insuring that the more severe economic consequences of industrial conflict would usually be avoided.[9]

## CONCLUSION

A feature common to all four of the above cases is that there is a certain *rhythm* to industrial relations policy in First World countries, a rhythm that may extend to economic policy in general. The rhythm is associated with the phenomenon of business cycles, which have not been eliminated by the advent of postindustrial society, only elevated in intensity in the phenomenon of stagflation. When the economy is at the productive end of its pendulum swing, workers are in an advantageous position relative to their employers because labor is then a scarce commodity, much in demand. But at times when the pendulum has swung to the opposite extreme and unemployment is high, the advantage shifts to the employer. When workers perceive conditions to be favorable to their demands, they can afford

[9]The government of the left that came to power under President François Mitterrand in May 1981 portends a radical reversal in the relative positions of employers' and workers' organizations in the policy-making process. The government came to office with a list of seven major private corporations to be brought under government ownership along with investment banks and the steel and armaments industries. The corporatist framework of French economic policy making will undoubtably give way to elements of neo-Marxism while Mitterrand and the Socialists are in power.

to take risks, and the rank and file become more amenable to the militancy of their neo-Marxist left. When employers feel the labor market conjuncture to be in their favor, their corporatist instincts come to the fore. By and large, government policy tends to fluctuate depending both on the economic circumstances and on what political party or coalition of parties happens to be in power at the time. Needless to say, the economic circumstances can have an effect on the latter variable, but there is apt to be a certain time lag because elections are held only once every four or five years.

In addition to this general characteristic, which is common to all four of our countries, each country exhibits some unique characteristics as we compare their industrial relations policies with one another. In the first place, West Germany is the only country that displays substantial élite consensus regarding the goals of economic policy in general and the instruments of industrial relations policy in particular. Leaders of all three political parties share a commitment to export-led economic growth and stability and would choose means of regulating industrial relations that would accord with that goal. Although the means would vary somewhat depending on whether the government were led by the Social Democrats or the Christian Democrats, it is safe to say that the means would involve some mix of pluralist and positive corporatist techniques in any case.

In France, Italy, and Great Britain, élite consensus is much less in evidence although the recent tendency in Italy has been toward a convergence in the center, whereas movement in both France and Great Britain has been toward opposite left and right poles. On the left, in all three countries, the choice today appears to be between the neo-Marxism espoused by the far left and the pluralism advanced by moderate Socialists. The voices of the former have grown fainter in Italy, those of the latter are currently diminished in volume in Great Britain and France. On the right, in all three countries, there seems to be greater convergence on a single model: positive corporatism. Nevertheless, advocates of a more negative type of corporatism, heavily weighted in favor of the interests of smaller scale industry, can be heard, especially in Italy. In France, there is relatively little overlap at present in the conceptions of élites of the left and élites of the right. The possibility of accommodation between left and right continues to exist in Italy and Great Britain: in the persisting possibilities for compromise between Communists and Christian Democrats in Italy and in the efforts by the more moderate Labour and Conservative leaders, now in minority positions in their respective parties, to restore the broad elite consensus that had existed in Great Britain on economic policy before the disastrous 1970s. Industrial relations in Western Europe have evolved toward a more cooperative, less conflictive mode in the postindustrial era than was the case earlier in this century; but conflict remains intense, at least some of the time, in some countries. As we have seen, postindustrial economies are not as conducive to placid relations among social classes as had been imagined by the early harbingers of the Age of Affluence.

# Suggestions for Further Reading

**Beer, Samuel H.,** *British Politics in the Collective Age* (New York: Random House, Vintage Books, 1969).

**Benjamin, Roger,** *The Limits of Politics: Collec-* *tive Goods and Political Change in Postindustrial Society* (Chicago and London: University of Chicago Press, 1980).

**Beyme, Klaus von,** *Challenge to Power: Trade*

*Unions and Industrial Relations in Capitalist Countries*, trans. Eileen Martin (London and Beverly Hills: Sage, 1980).

**Cerny, Phillip G.,** and **Martin A. Schain,** eds., *French Politics and Public Policy* (London and New York: Methuen, 1980).

**Crouch, Colin,** and **Alessandro Pizzorno,** eds., *The Resurgence of Class Conflict in Western Europe Since 1968* (2 vols.) (New York: Holmes & Meier, 1978).

**Cullingford, E. C. M.,** *Trade Unions in West Germany* (Boulder, Colo.: Westview, 1977).

**Heisler, Martin O.,** ed., *Politics in Europe: Structures and Processes in Some Postindustrial Democracies* (New York: David McKay, 1974).

**Ingham, Geoffrey K.,** *Strikes and Industrial Conflict: Britain and Scandinavia* (London: Macmillan, 1974).

**La Palombara, Joseph,** *Interest Groups in Italian Politics* (Princeton, N.J.: Princeton University Press, 1964).

**Mayntz, Renate,** and **Fritz W. Scharf,** *Policy-Making in the German Federal Bureaucracy* (Amsterdam: Elsevier, 1975).

**Panitch, Leo,** *Social Democracy and Industrial Militancy: The Labour Party, the Trade Unions and Incomes Policy, 1945–1974* (Cambridge: At the University Press, 1976).

**Rose, Richard,** ed., *Challenge to Governance: Studies in Overloaded Polities* (Beverly Hills and London: Sage, 1980).

**Shonfield, Andrew,** *Modern Capitalism: The Changing Balance of Public and Private Power* (New York: Oxford University Press, 1965).

**Sturmthal, Adolph,** *Comparative Labor Movements: Ideological Roots and Institutional Development* (Belmont, Calif.: Wadsworth, 1972).

# CHAPTER SEVEN
## The Performance of
## Political Systems

We come now to an overall evaluation of Western European polyarchies as promoters of human dignity. How should we assess the performances of these political systems with respect to our four dimensions: power, well-being, enlightenment, and respect? In the preceding chapters, we have made a number of evaluative statements, but an overall assessment remains for this concluding chapter. We will devote principal attention to the value of well-being. Although this means an imbalance in our treatment of the four values, we consider that the overwhelming predominance of material issues on the agendas of First World political systems in the late twentieth century justifies giving them predominant consideration. First, we will undertake brief assessments of the performances of the four political systems regarding the other three values.

## POWER

In analyzing Western European polyarchies, we have been mainly concerned with how power is distributed within the political system rather than with how much power the political system has been able to mobilize as it faces the outside world. Historically, the larger countries have found it necessary to have a relatively high con-

centration of power internally in order to be prepared for whatever threat might arise externally. The frequent wars on the continent of Europe have testified to this necessity. Today, the Western European polyarchies no longer threaten one another militarily. Whatever threat exists—whether of Soviet military power or of economic and political domination by the United States—comes from outside the region. Such dangers have seemed real enough (in the recent past, at least) so that certain Western Europeans have wanted a closer association with one another through a regional political organization. Later, we will take note of the progress that has been made in that direction.

The political systems in Western Europe have retained enough power in the central organs of government so that they have been able to speak with one voice in international affairs. This has not meant such a high degree of concentration that ordinary citizens have no access channels to the policy-making process or that the pluralistic nature of highly industrialized and urbanized societies has not been able to express itself through representative political institutions. The Second World countries, even those that are now relatively advanced industrially, have found it necessary to concentrate power. The Third World countries have often sought to limit free access to policy-making circles although their leaders sometimes find that their resources are limited.

In comparison with the United States, it appears that power is more highly concentrated both horizontally and vertically in Western Europe. Among the First World countries, power is more dispersed in the United States than elsewhere, both because of the constitutional dispersion on both the vertical and horizontal scales and because of the strong political culture bias against allowing power to be too highly concentrated in a few hands. The reaction against an imperial presidency, aroused by the sometimes high-handed tactics of the Lyndon B. Johnson and Richard M. Nixon administrations, was, from a European perspective, a reassertion of intrinsic American values and a renewal of American determination to have these values prevail. In Western Europe more reliance is placed on the political leaders' commitment to relatively explicit value systems and on senior government officials' commitment to their professional standards. These political and administrative professionals can be held to their standards by their equally professional colleagues. There may be considerable cynicism in France and Italy as to how much those in power are really acting on behalf of the best interests of the citizenry at large, but people also believe that the system will operate in such a way as to prevent the worst excesses. In Great Britain and West Germany, there is a strong belief that political leaders and public officials will adhere to well-established legal norms and that the opposition will see that they do so in fact. The latter belief is thoroughly entrenched in Great Britain; the relatively orderly course of political events in the Bonn Republic has gradually implanted it in the West German political culture as well.

This suggests that political culture acts to restrain the concentration of power less in the Western European polyarchies than in the United States. In actual performance, it can be said that élites have exercised a considerable amount of self-restraint in ensuring that power will not be concentrated beyond certain well-recognized limits. The notable exception is France. Power

has always been rather highly concentrated on the vertical scale in France. Steps toward regional decentralization have been taken haltingly and with obvious reluctance on the part of central power holders. Horizontally, the concentration of power has varied considerably from regime to regime. In devising the political institutions of the Fifth Republic, General Charles de Gaulle and his advisers were acutely aware of the debilitating effect that power dispersion at the center had had upon the capacity of the Fourth Republic to respond to external challenges. Today, one might suggest that they had overcompensated.

The Fifth Republic established an imperial presidency that was the envy of Richard M. Nixon. Without de Gaulle's imperious personality, the authority of the French President has diminished somewhat, but the President remains the supreme policy maker in the French political system with no need to answer to Parliament. Even though power is, in principle, more highly concentrated in a parliamentary than in a presidential system, the combination of the presidential and parliamentary features in the Fifth Republic gives the French President the best of both worlds, as explained in Chapter Five. To be sure, power is concentrated in the cabinet in Great Britain, West Germany, and Italy, and the British Prime Minister and West German Chancellor are in superior positions vis-à-vis their respective colleagues. But prime ministers and chancellors must retain the support of their fellow partisans in parliaments. The political demise of such figures as Anthony Eden and Harold Macmillan in Great Britain, of Konrad Adenauer and Ludwig Erhard in West Germany, and of numerous short-term prime ministers in Italy attests to the uncertain base of personal political support that these parliamentary leaders need. By contrast, the French President is assured of holding office for seven years.

It should be recalled that we are talking about political systems in which, whatever may be the concentration of formal (or government) power, informal (nongovernment) power is generally dispersed. There are a number of political parties that are not quasi-government organs, as in Second World and some Third World systems; and each country has strong parties in the opposition. There are also a number of interest groups that contend with one another for scarce resources and counteract the power of one another and of the government itself. Where parties alternate in power, as in Great Britain and West Germany, the advantage one group (such as organized labor) might have is offset by the disadvantage of being too closely tied to the fortunes of one party or coalition. Where one party or coalition has enjoyed power for many years, as in Italy, the advantage that one group (such as organized business) might have is threatened by the danger that the opposition might come to power and turn that advantage into a disadvantage. What this suggests is that there are built-in adjustive mechanisms in Western polyarchies that assure a kind of rough balance between contending political forces over the long run at least, if not in the short run.

## ENLIGHTENMENT

The goal of providing an adequate education for everyone through the secondary level and of making a college education widely available has long been backed by the U.S. Government. In the early 1970s, 6 percent of the American gross domestic product (GDP) was being spent by all levels of government on education, as compared with 5.6 percent for Great Britain, 3.1 percent for France, 4.2 percent for West Germany, and 4 percent for Italy.[1] Moreover, only West Germany's expenditure had gone up at a more rapid rate than that of the United States in the preceeding 10 years. It should be pointed out, however, that some First World countries had higher rates of public expenditure on education than did the United States. Canada and the Netherlands were the highest—at 7.7 percent and 7.6 percent of their GDP respectively—and the Scandinavian countries were at, or slightly above, the American level. On the other hand,

the United States leads the First World in expenditure on higher education.[2]

Quantitatively, at least, the outcome matches the goals and actions. In the early 1970s, full-time and part-time students from the early primary grades up to the highest levels of higher education made up 28.5 percent of the total American population as compared with 18.8 percent of the British, 20.5 percent of the French, 17.4 percent of the West German, and 16.3 percent of the Italian populations.[3] These figures include students in what might be called the private educational sector, including privately endowed schools and church-supported schools. At the highest level of education, the United States again led the field, with more than 30 percent of the appropriate age groups enrolled in institutions of higher education, a much higher figure than that of any of the larger Western European countries. For example, in 1975–1976, France and West Germany had 16.8 percent and 11.4 percent, respectively, enrolled in institutions of higher education.[4]

It is difficult to make an assessment of outcomes in a qualitative sense. In earlier chapters, we emphasized the role of the secondary school in Western Europe in sorting out children destined to go on to the university from those who will finish school at the secondary level and go into blue-collar and nonprofessional white-collar occupations. This goes a long way to explain the much larger proportion of American young people who attend colleges and universities because, for the most part, American secondary education is not similarly segregated. The possibility of being able to go on to institutions of higher education is not decided once and for all at age 11 or 12 for the majority of American students as it has been for European students. On the other hand, the quality of secondary education available to the favored European minority is undoubtedly

[1]Organization for Economic Cooperation and Development, *Public Expenditure on Education* (2) (1976), p. 12.

[2]*Ibid.,* p. 21.

[3]*Ibid.,* p. 10.

[4]Arnold J. Heidenheimer *et al., Comparative Public Policy: The Politics of Social Choice in Europe and America* (New York: St. Martin's, 1975), p. 46.

higher than it is for the average American high school student who plans to go on to college. The first two years of college often serve the same function as the last years of secondary school do in Europe in giving the American student the intellectual tools necessary to specialize at higher levels, something the European student begins to do immediately after entering the university. But the European student is generally a year or two older than the American when he or she enters the university. West German students frequently are 20 years of age or more. Thus, it can still be said that the American outcome is better quantitatively and not necessarily inferior qualitatively.

If many Europeans would argue that the qualitative gap is greater than what has been suggested here, many others are demonstrating their belief in the superiority of something like the American approach by pushing for a reform of secondary-level education in the direction of the comprehensive school, which brings together students of all intellectual levels and does not prematurely foreclose the possibility of some youngsters going on to the university. Steps have been taken under the impetus of Democratic Socialist parties in all four of our countries to reform their educational systems, but progress has been slow. It has been considerably faster in Sweden, where the comprehensive principle is firmly established. Not coincidentally, the percentage of the appropriate age groups enrolled in higher education in Sweden is far ahead of the figures for the larger Western European countries.[5] But, aside from the Scandinavian countries, Western Europe appears to have placed enlightenment at a lower level on its priority scale than has the United States.

## RESPECT

Almost by definition, the First World has countries in which (at least most of the time) governments are bound by legal norms that restrain them from acting in ways that would violate local concepts of human rights. In a survey of political systems in all parts of the world, it was found that 22 countries had high scores for maintaining civil liberties and political rights relatively free of government interference.[6] Of these, 13 were in Western Europe (including Iceland and the British Isles). Great Britain, France, West Germany, and Italy were all among the 13. At least four general reasons can be cited for this favorable record:

1. Most First World countries have longstanding legal traditions in which the rights of individuals are clearly defined. In the case of the United States and Great Britain, the *common law* traditions handed down from medieval England consist of a body of precedents found in earlier court decisions with a number of legal norms applying to the relationship between the individual and the state. These have been supplemented by acts of the national legislatures in both countries as well as by state legislatures in the United States; such acts are, then, subject to court interpretation. In a very real sense, judges make law in common law countries because they are continually reinterpreting old precedents in the light of modern circumstances. In continental European countries, including France, West Germany, and Italy, systems of *code law* prevail. These derive from the Roman law tradition. In such legal systems, laws originally enacted by Parliament or promulgated by the sovereign have been codified into complex bodies of categories and subcategories that contain the legal norms that apply in various kinds of cases. The role of the courts is more limited in such countries than it is in Great Britain and the United States because the codes are sufficiently specific and, thus, the courts have limited discretion in handling particular cases. It is up to the legislative bodies in these countries to determine what new laws will apply to new situations not envisaged in the codes. Still, in both systems, bodies of law exist that clearly define rights and

[5]*Ibid.*

[6]Richard P. Claude, ed., *Comparative Human Rights* (Baltimore: Johns Hopkins University Press, 1976), p. 67.

obligations, at least in settled areas of the law; institutions exist to ensure that these laws are observed—by itself, this is a greater safeguard for the individual than where the law is uncertain and at the mercy of the whims of those in power.

2. In addition to their ordinary role of interpreting and applying the law, courts in First World countries perform the function of restraining the Executive, or law-enforcement, arm of government. Government actions that go beyond delegated powers or that violate established norms may be revoked by court actions. In common law countries, the courts may declare executive actions *ultra vires,* that is beyond the scope of power granted by the legislature and, therefore, unenforceable. In code law countries, there is a network of administrative tribunals that hear cases brought by individuals against state officials. Although technically part of the bureaucracy, they are noted for standards of impartiality and consistent adherence to precedent. Moreover, in both types of legal system, there are appellate courts at the top of the ordinary court system that can reverse the decisions of the lower courts on the ground that norms protecting individual rights have been violated in the administration of justice.

Finally, there is the power of *judicial review,* that is, the power to declare legislative actions unconstitutional—in some cases on the ground that they violate rights listed in a country's Constitution. In the United States, the U.S. Supreme Court possesses such power, which is emulated by *constitutional courts* in West Germany and Italy, both of which have been active in insisting that constitutional provisions for human rights be respected. Although no such body exists in Great Britain (where, indeed, there is no written constitution) and although the Constitutional Council established by the Constitution of the French Fifth Republic has much more limited powers, it is doubtful whether the absence of such courts makes any difference with respect to human rights. It could be argued that Parliament itself exercises as much self-restraint as a constitutional court would in Great Britain. As for France, it would appear that the highest administrative tribunal, the Conseil d'État, is effective in protecting individual rights against unconstitutional executive action in a country where, in any event, the executive has been given the upper hand over the legislature in the law-making process.

3. Because of the First World's pluralist political systems, the role played by the political opposition, and the ready availability of channels of public communication, it is unlikely that gross violations of human rights will go unprotested. These phenomena interact with and reinforce one another. Thus, the greater the level of individual freedom, the more confidence individuals will have in group action, including political opposition and the collective voicing of dissent publicly. Many political systems in the world attest to the fact that the opposite characteristics form a syndrome as well: repression of voluntary groups, of political opposition, and of public dissent as well as disdain for the many safeguards for the individual that are taken for granted in Western polyarchies.

4. Postindustrial societies are witnessing the emergence of a new *agenda* of public policy problems. Here, we should include a heightened concern for human rights. Critics of the alleged violations of human rights in the Soviet Union and other Second World countries, many Third World countries, and in the Republic of South Africa have shown an increased unwillingness to allow long-standing abuses to continue simply at the discretion of those countries' leaders. Many of the same critics have also directed attention to the continuing denials of respect in their own countries. Progress has been made in such areas as equal rights for minority groups and women. The former has especially been a problem in the United States and Great Britain with their significant populations of racial minorities as well as in Northern Ireland with its large Catholic minority. Progress has probably been swifter in the United States (although only after many decades of neglect), where there has been a greater willingness on the part of the dominant racial group to look at the problem and attempt to find solutions to it—a willingness, no doubt, stimulated by the militancy of the minority groups themselves. This has not been the case in Northern

Ireland, where British troops had to take civil power away from the Ulster Parliament because of blatant discrimination by Protestants against Catholics. Although France, West Germany, and Italy do not have similar minority groups whose rights are so seriously in jeopardy, these countries have been slower than the United States and Great Britain to promote equal rights for women in such areas as employment opportunities and divorce law. But, in all the cases mentioned, there seems to be a growing awareness of the problem as one of human respect.

When compared with their own traditions and established standards, First World countries have not gotten universally high marks in recent years. Thus, student and working-class unrest have been met in some Western European countries, notably France, West Germany, and Italy, with violent police action or repressive legislation removing legal safeguards for certain groups of citizens. Such actions have been defended as required because of the threat of terrorist attacks, such as assaults on embassies, airliner hi-jackings, or the kidnapping and assassination of prominent public figures.

The dilemma is quite clear, especially for countries with uncertain traditions of political stability. Is it worse to deprive acknowledged enemies of the public order of their individual rights or to allow them relative freedom to deprive innocent citizens of their freedom and sometimes their lives? This is not an easy question for anyone, but especially not for people with recent memories of political warfare between strong-armed groups of the left and right.

Even in Great Britain, where the instinct to protect the individual from arbitrary action is probably as strong as it is anywhere in the world and where leadership has been taken in certain human rights areas (such as the rights of homosexuals), traditional rights, such as *habeas corpus* and the right to a speedy trial, have been suspended in Northern Ireland because of the civil strife going on there. Significant lapses in all four countries in the matter of human rights make it difficult to give highest marks to them

Northern Ireland is a battleground between Catholics and Protestants. The ultimate question is whether it will continue to belong to largely Protestant Great Britain or become a part of Catholic Ireland. Here, Catholic youth are throwing stones at armed security forces in Londonderry.

**TABLE 7.1**  Economic Growth in Six Countries

|  | France | West Germany | Italy | Japan | U.K.[a] | U.S. |
|---|---|---|---|---|---|---|
| GDP per capita (1978) | 8,827 | 10,426 | 4,180 | 8,533 | 5,514 | 9,602 |
| Percent annual growth (1966–1976) | 3.9 | 3.1 | 3.4 | 6.7 | 1.9 | 1.8 |
| Percent annual growth (1973–1978) | 2.9 | 1.9 | 2.1 | 3.7 | 0.9 | 2.4 |
| Capital formation, annual growth (1972–1977) | 1.5 | –1.1 | –0.2 | 4.4 | –0.6 | 0.3 |

[a]Great Britain.

SOURCE: Organization for Economic Cooperation and Development, *OECD Economic Surveys: Germany*, May, 1980, p. 78; for percent of annual growth (1966–1976) figures, Statistical Office of the European Communities, *Basic Statistics of the Community* (Luxembourg: The European Communities, 1978), p. 28.

for the value of respect, especially if we recognize that the basic concern for the value of the individual has grown out of the Western tradition.

## WELL-BEING

### THE RECORD

The economic difficulties experienced by First World countries in the 1970s and early 1980s have raised considerable speculation as to the future of postindustrial society. The problem of stagflation was treated in general terms in Chapter Two. However, when we look at the economic record on a country-by-country basis, we are more impressed by the differences in this record among countries than we are by the similar fates of postindustrial countries. Among our four examples, West Germany has had by far the most successful economic record in recent years, Great Britain and Italy have vied with one another for the worst, and France generally falls somewhere in between the two extremes. However, the West German record is more impressive in some respects than in others, and France, Great Britain, and Italy can each point selectively to certain economic indicators wherein their respective economic performances have been more commendable. Let us look at the recent

record. In so doing, we will compare our four countries with the largest economies in the First World, the United States and Japan.

Table 7.1 provides us with an overview of the productive capacities of the six economies and of their growth patterns from 1966 through 1978. Although the American economy is by far the most productive in terms of total output, it has lost ground in recent years on a per capita basis. West Germany surpassed the United States very recently in GDP per capita, and Japan and France are now close behind. Great Britain and Italy have lower levels of GDP per capita. This brings into question whether, in economic terms, they rate the label postindustrial. But an examination of growth rates in the 1960s and 1970s shows that Italy's economy has grown at a much more rapid pace than has Great Britain's. Similarly, West Germany and France have shown considerably faster rates of growth than has the United States, whereas the 6.7 percent annual growth rate of Japan between 1966 and 1976 was truly phenomenal.

If we look at only the last five years represented in Table 7.1, we see that all growth rates have lowered, except that of the United States, which experienced a modest upsurge between 1973 and 1978. Although the differences among countries in these rates were condensed,

Japan retained the highest growth rate and Great Britain the lowest. The West German decline is particularly noticeable. A reason can be found in the data in Table 7.1 (last row), where the annual percent of fixed capital formation is also presented. Comparing West Germany and Japan, it can be seen that investment in West Germany is sluggish, whereas Japan continues to invest at rates that will assure superior economic growth. It would appear that the Japanese economy is likely to overtake both the United States and West Germany in GDP per capita in the near future. Although less growth oriented than the Japanese, the French continue to invest in growth at a rate that is respectable by Western European standards.

Highly productive economies are economies that must consume vast quantities of energy, but the first row in Table 7.2 shows that it is not necessarily the most productive economy in per capita terms that consumes the greatest amount of energy per capita. Western European complaints that American industry and American consumers are profligate in their energy use are certainly given support by the fact that the American economy consumes nearly twice as much energy per capita as does the more productive West German economy and more than twice as much as do the Japanese and French economies. By Western European standards, the

British seem wasteful of energy, but they are frugal compared to the Americans. Given the high price of imported oil, why should Americans be so seemingly cavalier in their use? Certainly, an important answer can be found in the second row in Table 7.2 where it is clear that domestic production of energy is more adequate for American needs than is the case of the other major First World countries. France, Italy, and Japan fall particularly short of their needs and are, thus, more dependent on foreign energy sources. West Germany is less dependent because of its coal production, which is, however, diminishing. Great Britain is currently favored with North Sea oil as well as coal, but her relative independence of foreign energy sources will not last for long because her North Sea oil reserves will be short lived. However, these comparisons should not be used by Americans to excuse their relatively wasteful consumption of energy. The problem is to find ways of reducing that consumption without drastically lowering the American standard of living.

The data in Table 7.3 suggest that although the average American enjoys greater material well-being than the average European, the gap is not as great as the differences in energy consumption might suggest.

Americans are by far the leading consumers of automobiles and television sets, but the

**TABLE 7.2**  Energy Self-sufficiency in Six Countries

|  | France | West Germany | Italy | Japan | U.K.[a] | U.S. |
|---|---|---|---|---|---|---|
| Energy consumption, tons of energy per capita (1976) | 3290 | 4240 | 2400 | 3090 | 3670 | 8100 |
| Kilotons primary energy production (1976) | 36.9 | 118.7 | 24.8 | 45.3 | 131.6 | 1474.1 |
| Percent foreign dependence | 76.7 | 57.7 | 82.4 | 87 | 24.3 | 14 |

[a]Great Britain.

SOURCE: Data for U.S. and Japanese energy dependence are for 1972. They are drawn from Joel Darmstadter, et al., *How Industrial Societies Use Energy: A Comparative Analysis* (Baltimore and London: Johns Hopkins University Press, 1977), p. 200; other data (1977) are from Statistical Office of the European Communities, *Basic Statistics of the Community* (Luxembourg: The European Communities, 1978), pp. 69, 74, 170.

**TABLE 7.3** Indicators of Living Standards in Six Countries

| | France | West Germany | Italy | Japan | U.K.[a] | U.S. |
|---|---|---|---|---|---|---|
| Private consumption per capita in $US (1977) | $4450 | $4690 | $2220 | $3510 | $2580 | $5600 |
| Passenger cars per 1000 population (1976) | 300 | 308 | 283 | 163 | 255 | 505 |
| TV sets per 1000 population (1977) | 268 | 308 | 224 | 235 | 324 | 571[b] |
| Doctors per 1000 population (1976) | 1.5[c] | 2.0 | 2.2 | 1.2[c] | 1.3 | 1.6 |
| Infant mortality (1977) | 11.4 | 15.5 | 17.7 | 8.9 | 14.1 | 15.2[d] |
| Percent full-time school enrollment, ages 15–19 (1977) | 54.6 | 41.5 | 40. 8[c] | 70. 9 | 44.6[c] | 70.0[c] |

[a]Great Britain.

[b]1974 figure. [c]1975 figure.

[d]1976 figure.

SOURCE: Organization for Economic Cooperation and Development, *OECD Economic Surveys: West Germany*, May 1980, p. 78.

French, German, and British figures are not as far behind the American as might be expected when energy consumption is remembered. When we move from private consumer items to collective goods, the United States no longer leads the league. The United States is well below West Germany and Italy in the number of doctors per 1000 population. Here, the Japanese have the least impressive record. On the other hand, it should be pointed out that Japan has the lowest infant mortality rate of the six countries. Japan has also reached the level of the United States in the measure of education. Full-time school enrollment is at the level of 70.9 percent for the 15-to-19-year-old age group in Japan. As noted earlier in this chapter, the record of the Western Europeans, especially the Germans and the Italians, is a relatively poor one.

The Western European countries are more dependent on world trade than is either the United States or Japan, at least if total trade figures are examined. In Table 7.4, combined 1978 exports and imports are listed as percentages of total GDP. Of the four major Western European countries, France is relatively self-sufficient, being able to meet most of its food consumption needs with domestic production. This is not the case of West Germany, Italy, or Great Britain. But some of the smaller Western European countries are even more dependent on foreign trade. Import and export totals approach 100 percent of GDP for Belgium; Irish imports reached 66 percent of GDP in 1978. But, large or small, Western European countries usually show a negative balance of trade, importing a higher percentage of GDP than they export. The exception is West Germany, which has consistently shown a healthy positive balance in the 1970s. Japan, Canada, and Australia have also shown positive balances, but not as substantial as those of West Germany. The favorable West German trade record has been a source of complaint for her partners in the European Community (EC) because their own negative balances are in part attributable to West Germany's success—often as their principal trade partner. A further consequence has been that West Germany has accumulated considerable amounts of gold and reserve currency (third row), somewhat more than has Japan and considerably more than have the countries with trade deficits.

The positive German and Japanese trade

**TABLE 7.4**  Foreign Trade in Six Countries

| | France | West Germany | Italy | Japan | U.K.[a] | U.S. |
|---|---|---|---|---|---|---|
| Exports and imports combined as percent of GDP (1978) | 33.7 | 41.1 | 47.4 | 18.0 | 48.8 | 15.1 |
| Balance of trade, EUA[b] (in millions) (1976) | −7,732 | +12,243 | −5,807 | +2,128 | −8,744 | −6,078 |
| Reserves as percent of imported goods (1978) | 17.1 | 44.7 | 26.3 | 42.2 | 21.7 | 11.3 |

[a]Great Britain.

[b]EUA = European Units of Account.

SOURCE: Organization for Economic Cooperation and Development, *OECD Economic Surveys: West Germany*, May 1980, p. 78; for balance of trade, EUA figures, Statistical Office of the European Communities, *Basic Statistics of the Community* (Luxembourg: The European Communities, 1978), pp. 120–121.

balances are both a consequence and a cause of the fact that both have enjoyed relative economic stability in a period when most countries have experienced high levels of unemployment and inflation. The West German record has been more consistent than the Japanese. As displayed in Table 7.5, West Germany has been less successful than Japan in holding down unemployment; but, with respect to price increases, West Germany has held inflation to modest levels, whereas prices in other economies have soared. The Japanese experience in the 1970s was erratic

**TABLE 7.5**  Economic Stability in Six Countries

| | France | West Germany | Italy | Japan | U.K.[a] | U.S. |
|---|---|---|---|---|---|---|
| Percent unemployment (average 1973–1977) | 3.4 | 3.1 | 5.8 | 1.8 | 4.0 | 6.6 |
| Percent unemployment (estimated 1979) | 6.0 | 3.8 | 7.7 | 2.1 | 5.3 | 5.8 |
| Consumer prices, average percentage increase (1973–1978) | 10.7 | 4.8 | 17.0 | 11.3 | 16.1 | 8.0 |
| Percent consumer price increase (1979) | 11.8 | 4.1 | 14.8 | 3.6 | 18.7 | 11.3 |

[a]Great Britain.

SOURCE: For percent unemployment (average 1973–1977) figures, Statistical Office of the Economic Communities, *Basic Statistics of the Community* (Luxembourg: The European Communities, 1978), p. 20; for consumer prices, average percentage increase (1973–1978) figures, Organization for Economic Cooperation and Development, *OECD Economic Surveys: West Germany*, May 1980, p. 78. For percent unemployment (estimated 1979) and for percent consumer price increase (1979) figures, *OECD Economic Surveys: France*, May 1980, pp. 7, 14; . . . : *West Germany*, May 1980, pp. 74–75; . . . : *Italy*, March 1980, pp. 68–69; . . . : *Japan*, July 1980, p. 17, 19; . . . : *United Kingdom*, February 1980, pp. 11, 14; . . . : *United States*, August 1980, pp. 86–87.

regarding inflation. Japan has double-digit infla-tion rates similar to those in France during most of the crisis period of the middle and late 1970s; but they were able to bring price increases under control at the end of the decade, whereas French, British, and American rates continued their up-ward movement.

When one considers unemployment and in-flation on a comparative basis, as we are doing here, the relatively good and relatively bad rates stand out and virtually become absolutes. West Germany appears to get very high marks for maintaining economic stability, but in the mid-1970s (at least), the West Germans were not so impressed with their own performance, and the coalition government led by Helmut Schmidt had a lot of explaining to do in the election cam-paign of 1976. The coalition lost ground to the Christian Democratic opposition that year. By the 1980 elections, however, with West German unemployment and inflation figures remaining approximately where they had been four years before, the coalition regained most of its lost ground. Although the West Germans were still not overjoyed with the performance of their economy, they could no longer ignore the fact that, relative to their neighbors, they were well off. In the meantime, a British Government had been voted out of office and Italian governments had struggled through a period in which there had been a real possibility that the Communists would gain a share of power. During the same election years in which the West German coali-tion twice survived challenges, two incumbent American presidents were defeated at the polls. Seven months after the second Schmidt victory, the French President was repudiated by a majori-ty of French voters amid rising unemployment figures and continued double-digit inflation. In Japan, on the other hand, the turning around of the inflation rate preceded a surprising recovery in the 1980 election for the governing party, which had experienced several years marked by scandals, internal dissidence, and seeming voter disaffection. It would be difficult to refute the proposition that electoral success for incumbents in postindustrial political systems is closely tied to the recent economic record and especially to the indicators of economic stability.

## POLICY CHOICES

The foregoing begs a question: Whatever the voters may think, can we really say that govern-ments are *responsible* for the records of their economies? Can the government legitimately take credit for good economic news? Should the public blame the government for poor indica-tors? Political scientists have struggled with the problem of how to measure government per-formance and government responsibility for economic outcomes. The very term, outcome, seems to imply continuity between the goals that governments set for the economy, the policy in-struments they employ in the attempt to bring these goals about, and what subsequently hap-pens to the economy. But it is undeniable that unforeseen factors and factors beyond a govern-ment's control intervene to aid or impede their efforts. It may be that governments with suc-cessful economic records are just plain lucky and that things turn out well *in spite of* their actions rather than because of them; or, perhaps, the leaders are simply lucky in having come to power in the country when they did because of already existing economic advantages. Their skill may have consisted in failing to ruin a good thing. Perhaps West German leaders would have had to work overtime to bring about bad eco-nomic results. Perhaps the Italian leaders should be given credit for not making matters any worse for the Italian economy. That such speculation is not entirely absurd suggests that we are not go-ing to be able to answer the question of govern-ment responsibility with any precision. The best we can do is to look at the stated intentions of policy makers, examine the actions they have taken in pursuit of those intentions, and see if they match up with the results.

Undoubtably the leaders of all First World countries would like to accomplish all six of the following goals:

1. High levels of economic growth.
2. Energy self-sufficiency.

3. The highest possible standard of living for their country's citizens.
4. A favorable balance between exports and imports.
5. Full employment.
6. Stable prices.

Some leaders (those on the left) would also like to bring about greater equality in income and wealth; others (those on the right) seek monetary stability, that is, a strong currency in world money markets; still others (not so readily located on the left-right spectrum) stress the overriding priority of environmental protection. If we take the first six goals—about which we might imagine that (in the abstract) all reasonable men and women would agree—we might ask: Why do not all governments pursue all of these goals with equal vigor?

The answer, of course, is that these economic goals have a tendency to get in each other's way. Or, to put it in more technical terms, there are *trade-offs* among them or *costs* with respect to other goals that will be incurred in single-mindedly pursuit of the *benefits* of any given goal. If, for example, we push full steam ahead for economic growth, we run into at least three consequences we would like to avoid:

1. The economy is going to use larger amounts of energy, which is in short supply, thus increasing our dependence on foreign energy suppliers and taking us further away from our goal of energy self-sufficiency.
2. Increasing production will require a greater supply of the factors that go into production. These include (in addition to energy sources) raw materials and capital goods, such as machines and transportation equipment. Some of these productive factors will have to be purchased from abroad, meaning an increase in imports without any necessary increase in exports. Stimulating the economy risks creating or exacerbating negative trade balances.
3. Industrial expansion will require investment capital. Whether this is supplied by government lending agencies or by private lenders, it will entail an increase in the money supply.

Although a positive consequence will be an increase in jobs, it will also mean more money in people's pockets enabling them to demand more goods, thus, risking higher rates of inflation.

Because of this trade-off between economic growth on the one hand and energy dependence, the balance of trade, and inflation on the other hand, we can also predict that an effort to reach goals on one of the latter three dimensions will necessitate slowing down economic growth. For example, to curtail inflation we must curtail expansion of the money supply, which will have a depressant effect on economic activity.

In general, we can identify two sets of three goals each among the six. Economic growth, high living standards, and full employment are goals that are roughly compatible, at least over the short run. Politicians of the center in Europe and the United States have tended to be more enthusiastic about this set of goals than they have about the other set, which comprise energy self-sufficiency, favorable trade balances, and stable prices. The latter set is that which the politicians of the right prefer, arguing that the key to the set is the maintenance of monetary stability. The right is committed to monetary stability because, without it, investment profitability is threatened and the risk level on which the capitalist economy is theoretically based becomes unacceptably high. Monetary stability and price stability are two sides of the same coin. Both are made more secure by energy self-sufficiency and favorable trade balances, but both are also seen as essential preconditions to maintaining a positive balance of exports over imports. The right insists that economic growth must not be purchased at the cost of monetary instability.

Politicians of the left have been critical of the centrist set of goals in that it ignores the goal of achieving greater social equality, whereas environmentalists insist that the consequences of greater economic growth for the biological and physical environment are unacceptable. The conflict between the center and the left over the issue of social equality tends to be expressed in terms of shares of the pie. Centrists argue that economic growth produces a larger pie in which all can share, thus making actual equality of material conditions unnecessary. The left argues that the focus on economic growth is a way of diverting the attention of the poor from the injustice of their disadvantages and that, in any event, the high rates of economic growth that capitalist countries experienced earlier will not be repeated. The pie will not again expand; therefore, it is necessary to turn to the postponed agenda item of finding ways to cut it into more equal shares.

As for the dispute between environmentalists and productionists, it appears to be a case in which each has focused on an absolute goal to which all other goals must be subordinated. For the environmentalist, economic growth is an expendable value. For the productionist (in the consensual center of the spectrum), if the technological developments needed for industrial expansion must entail a little pollution, so be it. It should be made clear that, if we have given the environmentalist perspective scant attention, it is because it has not as yet come to enjoy high priority in the goal-setting of policy makers (or even their leading opponents) in our four countries.

The choices among goals that have been made by political leaders in two of our countries have been more clear-cut than have those in the other two. Not coincidentally, the two countries with clearer choices have been the two with relatively better economic records: West Germany and France. However, the choices made by German and French political leaders have not been the same. In the case of West Germany, the one consistent thread that has been woven through the entire life of the Federal Republic has been the commitment to *exports* as the key—not only to the achievement of a favorable trade balance but also to the realization of all other economic goals. This was a feature common to both the economic policy of the Christian Democratic governments pursuing Ludwig Erhard's social market policy in the 1950s and 1960s and to the Social Democratic-Free Democratic coalition led by Willy Brandt and Helmut Schmidt in the 1970s and 1980s. The difference was that, throughout most of the Erhard years, high levels

of export-led growth were maintained, whereas in the Brandt-Schmidt era it has been necessary to choose between economic growth and continued favorable trade balances. Pursuit of exports is not incompatible with economic growth when the world market is expanding. With markets growing abroad in the late 1950s and early 1960s, West Germany found it possible to expand production to meet the growing demand without, at the same time, creating an excessive domestic demand for foreign goods. Both exports and imports expanded rapidly during the period, but export expansion remained safely ahead of import expansion.

Once the period of rapid growth in world trade came to an end in the early 1970s—resulting first from the rapid decline of the dollar (the principal reserve currency) and, then, from the precipitous rise in oil prices—West German political leaders could no longer equate economic growth with export expansion. To maintain favorable trade balances, West German industry had to be able to meet the low-price competition of Japanese and other relatively low-cost producers. This has meant a strong effort to curtail inflationary pressures, including demands for higher wages. The cooperative relationship among government, the private sector, and the trade unions was spelled out in Chapter Six. Equal emphasis has been placed by Bonn on the demand-pull side of inflation (see Chapter Two); the Social-Democratic governments of the past 10 years have pursued counterinflationary fiscal and monetary policies. The consequence has been a consciously accepted one: slower rates of economic growth and even a negative rate of gross capital formation (see Table 7.1). The tradeoff among economic goals has dictated that something would have to give. Yet, the centrist goals have not all been abandoned by the centrist coalition. Unemployment levels remain relatively low in West Germany, attesting to the fact that healthy export industries can alleviate the potentially most serious consequence of slow growth rates. By the early 1980s, however, it began to appear that the underemphasis on investment was catching up with West German policy makers. Unemployment was rising, and the coalition faced the likelihood that inflation would rise in response to any effort to restimulate the economy.

The clear-cut choice that French policy makers have made is one that goes back to before Charles de Gaulle's return to power in 1958. But the Fifth Republic has been more consistent in its pursuit than was its predecessor. In their economic policy (as in de Gaulle's foreign policy), the Gaullist leaders of the Fifth Republic, before 1974 at least, demonstrated that they could not easily be given a rightist label. Perceiving a productive economy as an element of national strength, they put their primary emphasis on economic growth, at times to the neglect of monetary stability—in spite of their concurrent belief that a strong franc was indicative of a strong French nation.

When de Gaulle returned to power, one of his government's first actions was to devalue the franc, thus putting it on a more realistic footing in face of the competition that would inevitably arise in the newly formed Common Market. In the next few years, the expansive years of the early 1960s, France enjoyed the same luxury—as did West Germany—of not having to choose between growth and stability. But the emphasis on growth for growth's sake finally caught up with the Fifth Republic in 1968 when riots and strikes inundated the government owing to the unplanned nature of the growth—an irony, in that the French system of indicative planning was at the time being studied by British economists as an example of how to run an economy. Urban sprawl, an overgrown, understaffed educational system, and wide disparities in income between employees in different economic sectors were among the characteristics that seemed to be felt more acutely in France than in other Western European countries.

Following de Gaulle's retirement in 1969 and especially after the accession of Valéry Giscard d'Estaing to the presidency in 1974, French policy makers sought a better balance between growth and stability. The government of Giscard d'Estaing's Prime Minister, Raymond Barre, sought to curtail inflationary tendencies through an austerity program that slowed down the growth

rate and brought French unemployment levels up to near the top of the list. Nor was the Barre government notably successful in curbing inflation, unless 10 to 12 percent annual inflation rates are now considered acceptable. The Gaullist leader, Jacques Chirac, rivaled the left opposition in criticizing Giscard d'Estaing and Barre for these indicators, highlighting the sloweddown growth rates and high unemployment. This became a principal theme in the April 1981 presidential election, just as it was in the elections in Great Britain, Italy, and the United States in the two preceding years. But the stagflation tradeoff suggests that any French Government must steer a middle course between growth and monetary stability, else it will ground the economy on the sandbar of Irish-level unemployment (10 percent) or send it over the rocky rapids of British-Italian level inflation.

The two countries, Great Britain and Italy, that have experienced particularly severe economic woes in the 1970s and 1980s share a characteristic that is true of neither West Germany nor France. In the cases of both, their political leaders have sought to reconcile *both* economic growth and stability with a greater amount of social justice, something that neither the Federal Republic nor the Fifth Republic were willing to elevate to top-priority level before 1981. In Great Britain, the commitment to social justice was made early in the postwar era by the Labour government of Clement Attlee. Statistics on income and wealth distribution in Great Britain show that a substantial redistribution occurred between 1938 and 1950 as a result of the imposition of steeply graduated income taxes and the establishment of a full-scale welfare state.[7] The Attlee government was also committed to rebuilding the war-torn British economy to maintain full employment. But, by the late 1940s, it had become evident that—given the effort to maintain British presence overseas and the status of the pound as a world reserve currency alongside the dollar *in addition to* the commitment to the welfare state and an economy func-

[7]John Westergaard and Henrietta Resler, *Class in a Capitalist Society*, (New York: Basic Books, 1975), pp. 39-40.

Unemployed workers in France reading the employment ads. In France, as elsewhere, when unemployment rises, many immigrant workers are among the first to lose their jobs.

tioning at full employment level—the British economy was overextended. British inflation rates were high, trade balances were unfavorable, and the government found itself having to undertake austerity measures to keep from the distasteful necessity of devaluing the pound, an option to which the government finally had to turn in desperation anyway.

When the Conservatives returned to power in 1951, they reordered priorities, placing primary emphasis on the goal of monetary stability. However, they only slightly dismantled the welfare state, and their period in power during the 1950s saw considerably more rapid rates of economic growth than Great Britain has enjoyed since that time. Still, the rates were lower than those of other Western European economies in the same decade, reflecting the continued commitment of British governments to shoring up the pound as a reserve currency. Before any other consideration could be taken, both the Conservatives, under Harold Macmillan, and the subse-

quent Labour government, under Harold Wilson, sought clearance from the Bank of England officials who were the guardians of the pound's value. In order not to take the seemingly obvious, but politically dangerous, step of devaluing the pound, both Macmillan and Wilson pursued the stop-go pattern—a pinch of stimulus here, a dash of depressant there—as British growth rates fell out of sight, well below those of even the more sluggish First World countries.

When Wilson finally devalued the pound in 1967, the British Government in essence abandoned its attempt to maintain a strong pound artificially. Since then, however, there has not been a clear-cut commitment to anything else. When Labour has been in power, it has been torn between the growth/full-employment orientation of the party center right and the income-equalization thrust of the party left. In fact, inflation levels were so high during the mid-1970s that the Wilson-Callaghan government was forced to put economic growth aside for the time being, while concentrating on attaining price stability. Margaret Thatcher's Conservative government has, since 1979, sought to follow a monetarist policy pattern, which is inspired by the economic right, with which Thatcher herself identifies. Nevertheless, spending ministers and their civil servants have been able to keep the social needs accompanying Great Britain's high level of urbanization from descending in priority too drastically. Although the British inflation levels and trade imbalances have not been less severe with the Conservatives in power than they were during the last years of the Labour government, unemployment levels were pushing over the 10 percent mark by 1981.

As for Italy, the quest for social justice has been a fairly recent input into the policy-making process. Under the center-right governments of the 1950s and early 1960s, a growth orientation prevailed that was nevertheless tempered by the desire to keep inflation under control. The latter was achieved principally through downward pressure on wage levels, which the importation of cheap southern Italian labor into industrializing northern Italy permitted. As a result, in spite of growth rates that were among the highest in the world at the time, Italian inflation rates were, at most, only slightly higher than the relatively low rates then prevailing in Western Europe.

Beginning in the mid-1960s, especially after the opening of the governing coalition to the Socialist Party, social justice through income equalization came to be at least the minor theme in Italian economic policy making, displacing the goal of monetary stability. This displacement became particularly clear with indexing agreements made with the trade unions in the wake of the damaging strikes of the late 1960s. By these agreements, Italian workers (at least those working full time) were guaranteed automatic wage increases in accord with every increase in the price index, a policy that also guaranteed a perpetuation of the wage-price spiral. In the 1970s, the necessity to accommodate both the Socialists and the Communists (although each at a different time) moved the Christian Democratic leaders to open the central government coffers to subsidize projects in Communist-run municipali-

ties, to finance lavish wage increases in the public sector, and to buy into failing industries in the private sector. Periodic austerity cures imposed by Italy's creditors in the International Monetary Fund and the European Community only served to depress the growth rate and keep unemployment at high levels while doing no more to inflation than preventing it from reaching South American levels.

What seems to emerge from the foregoing analysis is the observation that West German economic success has at least in part been due to the willingness of policy makers, of whatever political coloration, unflinchingly to accord higher priority to the same set of compatible goals. The relegation of the competing set of goals to secondary status has not meant their nonrealizability, only that the goals of economic growth, higher living standards, and full employment can not be realized at the expense of the favored set. In fact, with the exception of economic growth, the recent record of West Germany with respect to its secondary goals has been quite respectable by First World standards.

## HUMAN DIGNITY AND THE EUROPEAN COMMUNITY

We cannot conclude our discussion of the performance of Western European polyarchies without mentioning an effort that some of them have made *collectively* to enhance human dignity on at least certain dimensions. The European Community as it has developed over the years, has probably performed best on the dimension of well-being because the principal steps taken toward European integration have been economic ones. The members of the European 10 are currently: France, West Germany, Italy, Belgium, the Netherlands, and Luxembourg (the original six) as well as Great Britain, Denmark, Greece, and Ireland (the four that have entered the EC since 1973). Clearly, the outstanding accomplishment of the EC has been the establishment of a common market among the 10 countries for industrial and agricultural products, which has meant the removal of trade barriers among them and the establishment of joint restrictions on the importation of products from nonmember countries.

For the six original countries, at any rate, the common market served as an additional stimulus to economic growth during the 1960s. For the later entrants, this has not been so obvious. Their entry has coincided with the energy crisis and with the concomitant reversal in the general economic fortunes of the Western polyarchies. The EC could not prevent the member countries from responding separately to the energy crisis. Disgruntlement over the fact that some countries have had more serious economic problems than others has made cooperation (especially economic) more difficult than it had generally been before the EC expanded. Nevertheless, it should be noted that achievements of the EC in the economic sphere have been remarkable if measured against original expectations. Given the history of protectionism and economic warfare before World War II (and even stretching back into the nineteenth century), such developments as the pooling of coal and steel production in the 1950s and agreement on a Common Agricultural Policy (CAP) in the 1960s are truly remarkable.

It is possible to view the EC from a standpoint that is not idealistic, but eminently practical. For the countries that first formed the Common Market, at least, the new organization became an *instrument* of their economic policies —an extension of other instruments employed at the domestic level. Each member government, from this standpoint, saw the EC as meeting a particular need in its own efforts to deal with economic problems. For the French, the CAP has been, among other things, a means by which a large, inefficient, agricultural sector could be assured of sheltered markets in the partner countries while time was bought for a policy of encouraging consolidation and mechanization of French farms. This has been accomplished (to a considerable extent) through the EC policy of imposing levies on farm commodities imported into the EC from non-EC countries. The levies are collected by member governments and the proceeds are distributed to farmers in the member countries. This involves the payment of large sums by the governments of food-importing countries, especially Great Britain and West Germany, to the governments of food-exporting countries which, in turn, disburse the funds to their farmers. Because the French farm sector is by far the largest of the 10 countries, it has been the main beneficiary of the policy along with the French state, which has had its burden of farm subsidization greatly eased.

There have been considerable advantages for the other original member countries as well. West Germany and the Benelux countries are heavily dependent on foreign trade and the Common Market represents an assurance of a high volume of such trade. In fact, trade among the member countries increased rapidly after 1958, adding substantially to the factors promoting rapid economic growth in these countries. More specifically, it meant for West German manufacturers the opening up of the large French market that had been previously guarded behind relatively high tariff barriers. For Italy, the advantages have included the availability of additional sources of development funds for the southern region and sympathetic partners when credits are needed to keep the weak lira viable. Industry in the modern north of Italy has also benefited from the expanded market, just as has industry in the other original member countries. In addition, the more efficient Italian farmers share in the benefits of the CAP.

The CAP has also been an attraction for Danish, Irish, and Greek farmers as well as for their governments. In the case of Great Britain, whose farm sector is a very small portion of its economy, but whose farmers are highly efficient and, therefore, not in need of subsidization either from their own government or from Brussels, the CAP is viewed as a negative feature of the EC, involving high British contributions to the EC budget through the levy system, most of which goes to farmers across the Channel. Nor do many Britons perceive great advantages to the industrial and commercial sectors of their economy resulting from EC membership. By the time Great Britain entered the EC in 1973, her economy was lagging far behind those of her new partners, who had enjoyed the full benefits of the earlier boom period. But the boom was over, and membership in the EC no longer could provide the stimulus to British manufacturers to modernize and become more competitive, as it had done for French and Italian manufacturers 15 years earlier. In 1980, the opposition Labour Party went officially on record as seeking Great Britain's exit from the EC. Although Prime Minister Thatcher and her Conservative government wish Great Britain to remain within the fold, they are in a position to apply conditions through a reform of the CAP, conditions that will make the EC less burdensome to British consumers/taxpayers.

On the other hand, the EC has accomplished very little in getting the member countries to coordinate their policies in other sectors. Thus, it has had little effect on redistributive policies, on educational policies, or on upholding human rights.[8] These are areas in which the performance of the member countries is uneven and often falls short of their own aspirations.

As for the value of power, it might be expected that experience in dealing with common problems within a common decision-making framework would encourage national political élites to transfer certain elements of national sovereignty to EC executive and legislative bodies and that some sort of European parliamentary system would emerge, gradually taking on a shape somewhat like that which prevails in most of the member countries. In fact, the institutions that could assume such roles already exist. There is a Community executive in the form of the European Commission, which consists of 14 commissioners who are appointed by the member governments. If this body were to become truly responsible to the rudimentary legislative body, the European Parliament, the dominant role of the national governments, as currently exercised in another body, the Council of Ministers, might diminish over time.

The European Parliament consists of members directly elected by the voters in their coun-

tries. The first direct elections to the Parliament took place in June 1979. It is the hope of committed Europeans that a popular base will enable the European Parliament to be more assertive in EC affairs, even to the extent of encouraging the European Commission to form an alliance with it and promote policies that may be unacceptable to some of the member governments, thus defying the Council of Ministers. This would be a reversal for the European Commission, which has adopted a very cautious stance toward the Council ever since its knuckles were rapped by General de Gaulle in the mid-1960s. It would also seem to be contrary to government policies of the three most powerful member states—West Germany, France, and Great Britain—which seem to view the EC as a useful vehicle for intergovernmental cooperation and the occasional coordination of their foreign policies toward the rest of the world, especially the Untied States and the Soviet Union. These governments are themselves responsible to their own parliaments or, as in the case of the French President, directly to the electorate. Opponents of greater European integration can argue that abandoning national sovereignty would actually be giving up well-established national systems of democratic control for a yet-to-be-tested system at the EC level.

Clearly, arguments can be made on either side from the standpoint of our set of value commitments. In principle, the EC could be an admirable vehicle for the integration of national policies that would enhance well-being, enlightenment, and respect for the peoples of Western Europe. Democratization of the EC would mean effective popular control over what is potentially a formidable concentration of power to produce good or evil. But a very real question is whether such democratization could actually be made to work and whether officials of the EC with the power to make decisions affecting human lives would not be so remote from those people as to render the latter powerless. As we have seen, many valid questions can be raised along these lines when we look at the way contemporary postindustrial societies are governed within the existing national units. In many ways, the theory of postindustrial society points to decision-mak-

---

[8]It is likely that the EC's influence on the new polyarchies in Portugal, Greece, and Spain with respect to human rights has had some positive effect. Greece joined the EC in 1981 and Portugal and Spain may do so in the near future.

ing units on the scale of the EC as the wave of the future. But does this future bode well or ill for the dignity of humankind?

## CONCLUSION

In the more prosperous and expectant years of the late 1960s, impatient youth in the United States and Western Europe demanded greater respect for itself as a social category and sought a wider distribution of power and enlightenment within society. Progress has been registered on these dimensions, especially that of enlightenment, but, in the meantime, the trend away from concern for material security has been reversed. Western economies have registered disappointing results on a whole array of indicators, and there is little optimism to be found today about the possibility of returning to what, in retrospect, were the benign years of the 1960s. Today, economics has become an all-consuming preoccupation of governments, political parties, and voting publics in most First World countries. In the United States, with its global commitments and responsibilities, economics shares the spotlight with international affairs. Events, such as the hostage crisis of 1979-1981 continually intrude on the consciousness of American élites and nonélites alike. But, after the hostages were released by Iran in January 1981, it is noteworthy how swiftly and with what insistence the Ronald Reagan administration directed the attention of Americans back to the compelling issues of economic policy.

For Western European countries, the preoccupation with foreign affairs is more an intellectual matter, the province of the politically involved and alert minority. The average citizen is more concerned with the immediate health of the domestic economy, in part because the outside world is seen as a constant source of problems that are beyond the capacity of one's own government to resolve anyway. The Italian government can hardly be blamed for the overthrow of the Shah of Iran, nor can the French President shoulder much of the blame for events in Central America. Crises closer to home, such as that in Poland, reach the consciousness of almost every

Western European, but few imagine that their governments can have much impact on decisions that are made in Warsaw and Moscow. Americans tend to expect more of their government in the realm of foreign policy than do the British, the French, the Germans, or the Italians. But citizens of all Western countries, at least the larger ones, are prepared to judge their governments on the performance of the economy. We have seen evidence of this fact in earlier chapters: in the declining allegiance of Americans as contrasted to West Germans; in the tendency of voters to oscillate between parties of the left and parties of the right, seemingly unwilling to give either side decisive parliamentary majorities; and in the fall of parties and presidents from power in the wake of voter unrest over high levels of unemployment and inflation.

An economist, William D. Nordhaus, and a political scientist, Edward D. Tufte,[9] have each found evidence of a tendency of voters to reward incumbents if times are prosperous and unemployment is low and a corresponding tendency of governments to gear economic policy deliberately to the election timetable so that prosperity will, in fact, coincide with elections. The evidence has been drawn largely from the good old days in which declining unemployment could be purchased at the price of only modest levels of inflation. The advent of stagflation has upset the calculus. It is now possible that policies designed to restimulate the economy prior to an election will only make the voters angrier because of price increases reaching truly unacceptable rates. Such may have been the fate of President Jimmy Carter in 1980. Something similar may also have happened to James Callaghan's Labour government in 1979. On the other hand, Giscard d'Estaing may have lost the 1981 Presidential election precisely because he worried more about containing inflation than about holding down unemployment. Inflation affects everyone to some extent; when it is at a high level, it may affect more

[9]William D. Nordhaus, "The Political Business Cycle," *Review of Economic Studies*, 42 (130) (1974), pp. 169–190; Edward D. Tufte, *Political Control of the Economy* (Princeton, N.J.: Princeton University Press, 1978).

votes than does unemployment. The evidence on this point is mixed; but what is important is that governments increasingly seem to be *acting* as if they believed this to be the case. Economic growth was the chief standard for evaluating government performance in the 1960s; dealing with the energy crisis may well have been the acid test of the 1970s; how the government handles inflation seems to be what is getting the media attention and, therefore, the attention of the public officials in the 1980s.

Yet, studies have also shown that changes in the parties in power *do* have an impact on economic performance. The left concentrates on reducing unemployment, the right on fighting inflation.[10] If the two alternate in power, then, both problems will get fairly evenhanded attention over time. What is disturbing about a preoccupation with a single problem that may come to transcend left-right differences is that it (1) may take other important problems off the agenda and (2) could make some of the costs of some of the instruments chosen for the high-priority problem to appear less risky than heretofore. In the purely economic realm, preoccupation with unemployment has declined and willingness to tolerate higher levels of unemployment has grown apace. This may or may not cost incumbent governments elections, but it costs individuals and their families a higher standard of living. Moreover, although there is no evidence that inequality of material well-being has declined in the West since the early postwar years, governments that concentrate on fighting inflation promote austerity measures, such as cutting government programs and raising interest rates. The economically weak are more vulnerable to the adverse consequences of these measures than are the economically strong. Counterinflationary policies are more conducive to greater inequality than is inflation itself, the distributive impact of which is mixed.

To be regretted, too, is the fact that the newly emerging agenda items of the late 1960s have been shoved aside. If the primary preoccupation today is a material one, it should be added that it is dominated by very short-range perceptions. The value of environmental protection continues to be accorded lowest priority by most élites. Counterinflationary policy, by slowing down economic growth, may reduce the contamination of the physical and biological environment that would otherwise take place; but that is not its programmed intent. The fact that thinking about the economy is fixed on the short run, means that the positive and imaginative steps that might be taken to make postindustrialism safe for future generations are not being taken. This is as evident in Western European countries as it is in the United States.

# Suggestions for Further Reading

**Andrain, Charles F.,** *Politics and Economic Policy in Western Democracies* (North Scituate, Mass.: Duxbury, 1980).

**Andrews, William G.,** and **Stanley Hoffmann,** eds., *The Impact of the Fifth Republic on France* (Albany: State University of New York Press, 1981).

**Caves, Richard E.,** and **Lawrence B. Krouse,** eds., *Britain's Economic Performance* (Washington, D.C.: Brookings Institution, 1980).

**Claude, Richard P.,** ed., *Comparative Human Rights* (Baltimore: Johns Hopkins University Press, 1976).

[10]Douglas A. Hibbs, "Political Parties and Macroeconomic Policy," *American Political Science Review,* 71 (4) (1977), pp. 1967, 1987; Andrew Martin, *The Politics of Economic Policy in The United States: A Tentative View from a Comparative Perspective* (Beverly Hills and London: Sage, 1973). [Sage Professional Paper, Comparative Politics Series, 4 (01–040)].

Coombes, David, *Politics and Bureaucracy in the European Community* (Beverly Hills, Calif.: Sage, 1970).

Darmstadter, Joel et al., *How Industrial Societies Use Energy: A Comparative Analysis* (Baltimore and London: Johns Hopkins University Press, 1977).

Enloe, Cynthia H., *The Politics of Pollution in a Comparative Perspective* (New York: David McKay, 1975).

Halls, W. D., *Education, Culture and Politics in Modern France* (Oxford: Pergamon, 1976).

Heidenheimer, Arnold J. et al., *Comparative Public Policy: The Politics of Social Choice in Europe and America* (New York: St. Martin's, 1975).

MacLennan, Malcolm et al., *Economic Planning and Policies in Britain, France and Germany* (New York: Praeger, 1968).

Mendershausen, Horst, *Coping with the Oil Crisis: French and German Experiences* (Baltimore and London: Johns Hopkins University Press, 1976).

Rose, Richard, and Guy Peters, *Can Government Go Bankrupt?* (New York: Basic Books, 1978).

Siegel, Richard L., and Leonard B. Weinberg, *Comparing Public Policies: United States, Soviet Union and Europe* (Homewood, Ill.: Dorsey, 1977).

Tufte, Edward D., *Political Control of the Economy* (Princeton, N.J.: Princeton University Press, 1978).

Wallace, Helen et al., eds., *Policy-Making in the European Communities* (New York: Wiley, 1977).

# PART TWO

## Power and Policy in Communist Systems

# CHAPTER ONE
## Historical Setting

Where do the millions of people around the world thought of as Communists come from? The contemporary Communist Party states they call home represent a heterogeneous collection of different nations, cultures, traditions, and socio-political systems.[1] Although there is a tendency to think of Communist Party states and their peoples as being essentially alike, a trip to Moscow, Beijing, and Belgrade will quickly cure that misconception. The present-day diversity found in the Communist world is linked to the past; therefore, to better understand the past, the present and the future, let us briefly examine the historical development of Communism. Who originated the ideas of Communism and how did different states come to practice them?

### KARL MARX AND THE NINETEENTH CENTURY

Contemporary Communism cannot be understood without studying the man one American journalist called the least funny of the Marx brothers. The philosophy of Karl Marx has had a greater impact on twentieth-century life than any other philosophy or creed. The son of a Jewish lawyer who later became a Christian, Karl Marx was born in Germany in 1818. During his educa-

tion at the universities of Bonn and Berlin, he became attracted to the philosophies of Georg Hegel and Ludwig Feuerbach. After graduation, Marx became a political writer and joined the staff of the liberal newspaper *Rheinische Zeitung*. After he was named editor, he became involved in various revolutionary causes and, in protest against the Prussian Government, moved to Paris in 1843. In France, Marx undertook the serious study of what he called scientific socialism and met many prominent socialist thinkers. One not so prominent at that particular time, but who later became one of the era's great radical philosophers, was another German, Friedrich Engels, with whom Marx formed a lifelong friendship and collaboration.

Engels, the son of a wealthy German manufacturer, had been sent abroad by his father to oversee the family's business interests. While earning his livelihood from the system he so vigorously condemned, Engels came to France where be became involved in socialist thinking and writing. When he met Marx, they formed a deep bond that lasted through Marx's lifetime.

In 1848 Marx and Engels wrote one of the most important political documents of modern history. This document was a short but stirring call to arms for the working class and became the creed of the Communist Party. Known as the *Communist Manifesto*, it contains the immortal words: *"Workers of the world unite! The proletarians have nothing to lose but their chains."* In

---

[1] The adjectives Communist, Marxist-Leninist, and Second World are used interchangeably to refer to the Communist Party states in the chapters that follow. Although none of these adjectives are totally satisfactory, they are the most useful terms available.

Karl Marx (1818–1883), seen here with his eldest daughter, Jenny, was described by some as a warmly affectionate family man. Because of his radical political views, Marx was forced to leave his native Germany. After meeting his collaborator Friedrich Engels (1820–1895), Marx settled in England where he prepared his major works.

In contrast to the *Communist Manifesto*, which is a rousing declaration, *Das Kapital* is a mammoth, plodding, scientific study of capitalism that describes its origins and its predicted demise. Because his writings and theories were based on observed facts, Marx wanted to distinguish himself from the utopian socialists. He believed he had developed a scientific theory of socialism. The utopians hoped for socialism; his theory predicted that it was inevitable.[2]

Marx's lifelong endeavor was to discover the laws of human and social development and to provide evidence of their scientific validity. Believing that the world was governed by predictable forces, he spent most of his life trying to understand them. He had a voracious appetite for reading and his typical day in the British Museum began early and ended late. During this exhaustive research he reached several important conclusions.

According to Marx, all traditional societies—for example, feudal or capitalist—were divided into two main classes. Because the interests of these two classes were constantly at odds, they were involved in class struggle. The *Manifesto* notes:

> The history of all hitherto existing society is the history of class struggles. Freeman and slave, patrician and plebeian, lord and serf, guildmaster and journeyman, in a word, oppressor and oppressed, stood in constant competition to one another.[3]

concise, ringing language, the *Communist Manifesto* sets forth the basic tenets of Marxist philosophy. Telling of the bourgeoisie's (the owners') exploitation of the proletariat (the workers), Marx predicted a proletarian uprising and an end to capitalism and exploitation.

Marx returned to Prussia for a short time following publication of the *Manifesto* but was tried for sedition and expelled from the country in 1849. He then went to England where he remained for the rest of his life. During his years in Great Britain, Marx worked long hours in the reading room of the British Museum on his chief endeavor, *Das Kapital*. Although the first volume appeared in 1867, the second and third volumes did not appear until after his death in 1883.

In nineteenth-century Europe, the class struggle between the bourgeoisie (those in control of the means of production) and proletariat (the working class) was generated by the Industrial Revolution. Capitalism had developed in Europe and, although economic development soared, great human costs were incurred. Those in control of the means of production were exploiting the working class in the production process. According to Marx, the proletariat had no means of production and were forced to sell their labor to live. Marx predicted that the ex-

[2]For a useful collection of the basic writings of Marx and Engels, see Robert C. Tucker, *The Marx-Engels Reader*, 2nd ed. (New York: Norton, 1978).

[3]*Ibid.*, pp. 335–336.

ploited working class would develop a political consciousness and throw off the ruling bourgeoisie. This revolution would result in a new form of society—a form called socialist—in which the working class would rule. Because classes would be dissolved, exploitation and class struggle would disappear. This societal form would finally evolve into Communism, a utopian state free of classes, exploitation, material scarcity, and government supervision.

Marx was a man of his times. He lived in nineteenth-century Europe and observed some of the worst features of industrialization. Attracted from the countryside to the cities, the new working class was subjected to treatment incomprehensible by today's standards. Because labor unions and collective bargaining had not developed, the proletarian class had no voice against the powerful bourgeoisie, was paid subsistence wages, and lived in deprivation and poverty.

As a humanitarian and social scientist, Marx was forced to rebel against the injustices he saw. Not a man of the sword, he utilized the written word to call attention to the degraded state of mankind. Marx wanted the quality of life to be improved for the impoverished masses and he wished to develop a theory that demonstrated improvement was not only possible but inevitable and scientifically predictable.

Before his death in London in 1883, Marx experienced constant hardship and frustration. He and his family lived near the poverty level and suffered from poor housing, lack of nutrition, and inadequate medical care. His two sons and a daughter died as a result of these conditions. He was often without any means of subsistence and had to rely on the financial support of his friend and collaborator, Engels.[4]

But, to Marx, the physical suffering was minor compared with his broken dream of proletarian revolution. Marx hoped and predicted that workers' uprisings would occur in nineteenth-century Europe. By his death, however, there had been no major proletarian revolution

[4]Isaiah Berlin has written a splendid book about Marx's life: *Karl Marx: His Life and Environment*, 3rd ed. (London: Oxford University Press, 1963); also see David McLellan, *Karl Marx: His Life and Thought* (New York: Harper & Row, 1974).

and no founding of a Marxist state. Although we must acknowledge Marx's contribution to the beginning of modern social science analysis, we must also recognize that he was a product of the period in which he lived and limited by it. It is obvious that he did not predict many of the developmental nuances of the twentieth century.

By the end of the nineteenth century, socialism and revolution were discussed by students, workers, revolutionaries, and other interested observers across the continent. Throughout the coffee houses of Europe, revolutionaries of different viewpoints and motives plotted to end the injustices they perceived around them. Many were without direction, lacking either political theory or power; others found inspiration and guidance in the writings of Marx and had firm ideas on how power could be obtained. One such individual was the Russian, Vladimir Ilyich Ulyanov, later to become known by the pseudo-

Vladimir Ilyich Lenin (1870–1924) and his wife, Nadezhda Konstantinovna Krupskaya. In organizing a "party of a new type" to engineer the Bolshevik uprising and bring about the Russian Revolution in 1917, Lenin began a tradition of centralized Communist Party rule.

nym, Lenin.[5] ~~Born in Simbirsk (renamed Ulya~~novsk), Russia, in 1870, Lenin was the son of a school and civil service officer. Although the Ulyanov family was of a conservative and religious background, the children were radical and became involved in a plot to overthrow the tsarist autocracy. Lenin's sister, Anna, and brother, Alexander, were arrested on charges of belonging to a revolutionary organization conspiring to kill the tsar. Alexander was hanged in 1887 along with four fellow conspirators for his complicity in the abortive plot.

One year later, in 1888, Lenin was introduced to Marxism and before long began writing revolutionary materials that plotted the overthrow of the tsarist government. Traveling between St. Petersburg, the capital of tsarist Russia, and the nations of Europe, Lenin established his credentials as a Marxist and a revolutionary. On his return to Russia in 1897, he was arrested and sent to Siberia where he was incarcerated until 1900.

By the spring of 1900, Lenin was a free man in the city of St. Petersburg, renamed Leningrad in 1924. Dedicated to the overthrow of the autocracy that had imprisoned him and had executed his brother, Lenin plotted with other Russian Marxists. When he returned to exile in Switzerland and Germany, he published the article, "What Is to Be Done," in the party journal, *Iskra* (The Spark). In that article, he argued for a small, centralized, revolutionary organization and against a broad-based, mass movement. The plan was accepted by a faction of the Russian Marxists, who adopted the name, Bolsheviks, and Marxism was soon put to the test.

## THE BOLSHEVIK INSURRECTION

At the beginning of the twentieth century, the autocracy of Russia under Tsar Nicholas II was in serious trouble. Europe was industrializing and generally prospering, but Russia, always comparatively backward, was falling further and

~~further behind. Economic difficulties, including a~~ scarcity of food and consumer goods, declining services, and poor wages, were worsened by ill-advised military ventures. The Russo-Japanese War of 1904–1905 proved an embarrassing defeat to Imperialist Russia and a great drain on her available resources. Then, Russia became involved in World War I at enormous cost, and the human and physical resources of the state were further depleted.[6]

During the 1907–1917 period, Russian Marxists were a disorganized, faction-ridden organization, unprepared to assume political power or even to apply pressure to the failing tsarist regime. Many were in exile (Lenin) or imprisoned (Stalin); most of the remainder were involved in ideological disputes and intraparty fighting. One major conflict among the Marxists was between the Bolsheviks (the majority) and the Mensheviks (the minority). While the Mensheviks favored a broad-based movement and a more evolutionary path to power, the Bolsheviks were inclined toward a small, conspiratorial movement that could assume power quickly and decisively. Led by Lenin, the Bolsheviks prevailed over all other revolutionary and opposition movements and brought about the Communist takeover.

The stage was set for a Bolshevik victory with the abdication of Tsar Nicholas II in February 1917 and the political vacuum that followed. Power was initially assumed by the non-Communist, but democratic-liberal and Socialist Provisional Government of March to November 1917, under Alexander Kerensky's leadership; but it, too, was incapable of quickly resolving Russia's difficulties. Returning from Switzerland to St. Petersburg in April 1917, Lenin organized the insurrection. Under his leadership, the Bolsheviks prepared for their takeover by appealing to the masses with such slogans as "Bread, Peace, Land" and by organizing a conspiratorial military organization. Care-

[5]David Shub, *Lenin, A Biography* (New York: Penguin, 1976); Rolf Theen, *Lenin: Genesis and Development of a Revolutionary* (Princeton, N.J.: Princeton University Press, 1980).

[6]Several books analyze the decline of tsarist Russia. Among the best are Hugh Seton-Watson, *The Decline of Imperial Russia, 1855–1914* (New York: Praeger, 1952); and M. T. Florinsky, *The End of the Russian Empire* (New Haven: Yale University Press, 1931).

ful planning, utilization of a new organizational weapon (the Communist Party), the use of armed force and propaganda, the revolutionary leadership—all aided in their successful seizure of the Winter Palace, the symbol of Russian authority, on the night of November 7, 1917. The Bolshevik victory was incredibly easy; the provisional government had few answers and little support; the Russian army had been so consumed by World War I that it had no energy or inclination to try to keep power from the revolutionaries; other opposition and revolutionary groups were largely ineffective. Suddenly in power, Lenin was confronted with almost insurmountable economic and social problems as he began the construction of the first Marxist state.

It may appear surprising that the tsarist regime and the traditional political structure could be toppled by such a small band of untested revolutionaries. But the victory was neither as difficult nor as easy as it may seem. Imperial Russia was a sick and dying state; even if it had been able to cope with the challenges of modernization, its entanglement in World War I proved costly. This situation left the Bolsheviks with an incredibly vulnerable opponent, and when the political vacuum developed in 1917, the organized, determined, and politically astute Communists grasped power. The major difficulties for the Bolsheviks came after they had seized power, not so much from the tsarist autocracy, but rather from other groups (Mensheviks, Socialist Revolutionaries, many anti-Communist groups) that challenged the Marxist leaders. Although the Bolsheviks had grasped power, a struggle for the rule of Russia would continue for many years.

To the Bolsheviks' dismay, the writings of Marx were of little help in the ensuing years. Although Marx went to great lengths to explain the impending fall of capitalism and the victory of socialism, he wrote little *about the nature and construction of socialism*, and therefore, was of minimal help to the new Russian leaders as they began their difficult task. As a result, Lenin and the Communist leaders had to set out largely on their own. Their problem was worsened because Russia was not "prepared" for the socialist victory, in the sense that it had not gone through, although it definitely had begun, the capitalist stage of industrialization and development. According to Marx, socialism would triumph after capitalism had outlived its usefulness. But the Bolsheviks' seizure of power came before Russia had completed that important stage of development. As a result, Lenin and his fellow leaders had to complete Russia's industrialization before they could devote their attention to the construction of Communism.

Other pressing problems also confronted the Bolsheviks in the immediate postrevolutionary period. World War I continued to drain Russian resources. In addition, Bolshevik rule was not readily accepted throughout the Russian state and a bloody civil war broke out (1918–1921) that saw Western intervention (including the United States) on the side of the anti-Communist forces. Subsequently, international hostility and suspicion of the Bolsheviks and Communism precluded the possibility of assistance from abroad. So, although the Bolshevik victory of 1917 placed the Marxists in power, it in no way guaranteed the future success of Communism.

Lenin's first objective was to get Russia out of World War I. On March 3, 1918, Russia signed the Treaty of Brest-Litovsk, obtaining peace with the Central Powers in return for yielding valuable land and resources. The Communist leaders then began consolidating the homeland. During the Civil War, opposition movements, such as the White Russians, Tsarists, and Cossacks, were eliminated as the Communist Party moved to assert dictatorial control. Then, to facilitate economic recovery, the leaders adopted the New Economic Policy (NEP) (1921–1928) that permitted a partial return to private enterprise and eventually got the economy back on its feet.

During the postrevolutionary construction years, the Communist leaders were concerned with survival, both of the state and of their regime. The Communist Party became a leading organizational tool for consolidating power and organizing political rule. In these building years, the ideals of proletarian rule and democracy were lost among the pressing needs for survival.

According to most Western observers, the ideal of a dictatorship of the proletariat in which the workers were supposed to rule became in reality a dictatorship of the Party.[7]

After the death of Lenin in 1924, this dictatorship invested increasing power in the hands of one man, Joseph Stalin. Although a dying Lenin warned the Party against Stalin's ascendancy to the reins of power, a power struggle ensued and Stalin soon achieved dominance. During his rule (1926–1953), Stalin revised Marxism in many ways. Differences in degree grew into differences of kind. The combination of environmental forces (for example, the need to industrialize) and Stalin's pathological character resulted in a highly centralized, totalitarian state. Most observers agree that Stalin's imprint on Marxism during these formative years of development took Communism far afield of the more humanitarian theories of Marx, and this Stalinist brand of Communism was exported to Eastern Europe and China at the end of World War II.[8]

At the time of the Bolshevik victory, the Russian leaders expected victorious revolutions elsewhere in Europe.[9] During the early 1920s, optimism about this possibility began to fade. The recognition that these victories would not occur was made official by Stalin in 1924 when he formulated his famous "socialism in one country" doctrine. According to this doctrine, attempts to promote world revolution would be abandoned.[10] Because capitalism had temporarily stabilized itself, it was better to turn inward and

Joseph Stalin (1879–1953) delivers an order to his Foreign Minister Vyachuslav M. Molotov at Yalta in 1945. Stalin placed the USSR on the road to becoming an industrial and military power, but his oppressive rule cost greatly in terms of social welfare, democracy, and human rights, and took Soviet ideology far afield from classical Marxism.

concentrate efforts on building Russia into a bastion of socialism.

Closely tied to the Bolshevik victory was the establishment in 1921 of the second Communist Party state, Mongolia. Dominated through history by both Imperial Russia and Imperial China because of its unfortunate location between the two more powerful countries, Mongolia finally gained statehood in 1911. Shortly thereafter, the Russian Civil War brought Red Army troops to Mongolian soil. Using Mongolia as a base of operations, renegade White Russian bands were tracked down and destroyed by the Red Army and the partisan Mongols. In 1921, the victors established the Provisional Revolutionary Mongol People's Republic. Since that time, the Soviet and Mongolian states have had close ties and relations.

Although Marxist states were established in Russia and Mongolia early in the century, no other revolutions were successfully carried out until after World War II. But the absence of new Marxist states did not mean the absence of Communist revolutionary activity. The most violent, intense, and significant activity occurred behind the Great Wall of China.

[7]Solzhenitsyn argues that the roots of the dictatorship of the Party are to be found in the nature of the ideology itself.

[8]Two excellent accounts of Stalin and his rule are Robert C. Tucker, *Stalin As a Revolutionary, 1879–1929* (New York: Norton, 1973); and Adam B. Ulam, *Stalin: The Man and His Era* (New York: Viking, 1973).

[9]At the Third International Party Congress held in 1919, Lenin told the delegates that conflict between the capitalist and socialist world was inevitable and that socialism would soon result from proletarian uprisings throughout Europe.

[10]Stalin's policy conflicted with Leon Trotsky's theory of permanent revolution (formulated in 1905). The fiery Trotsky was expelled from the country in 1929 for his views and was assassinated by a Stalinist agent in Mexico in 1940. Trotsky's book, *The Revolution Betrayed* (New York: Pathfinder Press, 1972), provides an interesting personal account of this and related issues.

# REVOLUTION IN CHINA

A powerful determinant of present-day diversity in Communist states is the past. Examining this point, one scholar argues that the remarkable differences in Chinese and Russian revolutionary outcomes can be attributed in large part to the influence of distinct prerevolutionary sociopolitical structures and patterns of economic development. According to Professor Theda Skocpol, old regime structures helped to shape specific variations in the revolutionary outcomes not merely by surviving but also by influencing the consolidation and use of state power.[11] China's prerevolutionary experience was certainly of great importance.

China's ancient ruling tradition was one of upper-class government; the city ruled over the countryside and the few ruled over the many. To the peasant, the central government seemed remote and unconcerned with the problems of the masses. A Chinese folk poem expresses what must have been the feelings of the masses.

> We work when the sun rises,
> We rest when the sun sets.
> We dig wells for drink,
> We plow the land for food.
> What has the Emperor to do with us?

The institutions of family, gentry, and government perpetuated ancient Confucian traditions and provided the mortar that gave China its long, stable history.[12] But the events of the nineteenth century drastically changed the course of Chinese history. Conceived of by its leaders and the masses as the Central Kingdom, China was now battered by Western imperialism, resulting in intense national humiliation. This intensified in the latter part of the century

[11]Theda Skocpol, "Old Regime Legacies and Communist Revolutions in Russia and China," *Social Forces*, 55 (2) (1976), pp. 284–315.

[12]The ancient traditions are deeply embedded in China and represent conservative forces even today. For an excellent analysis of the past, see Mark Elvin, *The Pattern of the Chinese Past* (London: Eyre Methuen, 1973); for a contrast of the past with the present, see Lucian W. Pye, *China* (Boston: Little, Brown, 1972); also see John K. Fairbanks, *The United States and China*, 4th ed. (Cambridge: Harvard University Press, 1979).

by unequal treaties imposed on China by the European powers and by her defeat to Japan in the Sino-Japanese War (1894–1895). During this period, parts of China became Western colonies, such as Hong Kong and Shanghai, where the local populace was subject to foreign law. Evidence of this is the now famous photograph of a sign in a city park of Shanghai: NO CHINESE OR DOGS ALLOWED!

The twentieth century presented not only the dawn of a new Chinese culture but, more importantly, the birth of Chinese nationalism. The spirit of this movement was Dr. Sun Yat-sen, a radical but compassionate politician, educated in the Chinese classics and Western medicine. In 1911, Sun's political followers toppled the Manchu dynasty and established a Chinese republic based on democracy, socialism, and nationalism. The revolutionary's accomplishment brought about the end to more than 2000 years of dynastic rule in China, but even he was unable to cope with the political, social, and economic problems that contributed to the fall of the Manchus. One major problem was posed by the warlords. From 1916 to 1926, China was torn by strife between provincial dictators, who pitted Chinese against Chinese in their greed for increased power and wealth. Combined with the humiliation at the hands of the imperialist European powers, this internal conflict made it difficult for Sun and his supporters to unite the Chinese and promote social and political development.

By the second decade of the twentieth century, China found a more interested and active sector of the Chinese population committed to speak out against foreign and domestic exploitation. In the spring of 1919, large groups took to the streets to protest foreign domination and imperialism. Known as the May Fourth Movement, a wave of patriotism touched off street demonstrations and political harangues that motivated the Chinese delegation to refuse to sign the Treaty of Versailles at the 1919 Paris Peace Conference, an agreement that would have legitimated and prolonged foreign imperialism in China.

In the early part of the century, several Chinese scholars became acquainted with Marxism and other varieties of socialism and interest grew when the antiquated Russian autocracy was overthrown in 1917. Many Chinese intellectuals followed the events in Russia closely and began to study the Russian experiment with Marxism; one was Li Dazhao[13] (1888–1927), a history professor and chief librarian at Beijing University. While studying Marxism, Li met with students in his office, which became known as the Red Chamber. One of the young intellectuals attending these meetings was Mao Zedong, a man soon to take a leading role in the growing Chinese drama.

A major reason for the growing appeal of Marxism-Leninism in China resulted from the Soviet's position on imperialism. To many Chinese intellectuals, Marxism-Leninism represented the key to Chinese development. It told them

how to be scientific and "modern" in dealing with the problems of development and how to be uncompromisingly anti-imperialist and nationalist in being Chinese. Soon Russian agents from the Communist International (Comintern) arrived in China to aid Chinese Marxist-Leninists in promoting Communism. In July 1921, the Chinese Communist Party (CCP) was established and a new actor joined the revolutionary cast.

The Russian Comintern agents advised the Chinese Communists to form a united front with the Nationalists [Kuomintang (KMT)], which was under the leadership of Dr. Sun Yat-sen. Although the native Communists found this a bitter pill to swallow because they preferred to organize for revolution on their own, it was sweetened somewhat by the fact that the Nationalists were also committed anti-imperialists. The alliance, although often shaky, lasted through Sun's death in 1925 and the rise of his successor, Chiang Kai-shek. However, in April 1927,

[13]Chinese names are transliterated in the Pinyin system now standard in China. Traditional names, like Confucius, Kuomintang, Chiang Kai-shek, and Sun Yat-sen are not rendered in Pinyin but follow the Wade-Giles system used in the past.

Mao Zedong (1893–1976) on the reviewing stand at a mass political rally in Beijing. After establishing Communism in China in 1949 by ousting Chiang Kai-shek and the Nationalists, Mao developed a more radical brand of Communism, and split with the Soviets in the early 1960's.

Chiang turned on the Communists in Shanghai, slaughtered them by the thousands, and established himself as the head of the new Chinese Government. Stalin, then, ordered the Chinese Communists to seize power, but this only resulted in the killing of more Communists. After Stalin's disastrous plans led to the eviction of all Soviet advisors and a new annihilation of the Chinese Communists, the CCP grew more estranged from the Russian Communists. Stalin turned to his "socialism in one country" doctrine and Mao became more concerned with organizing the peasants.

It was during this period that Mao advanced to power. With a brilliant understanding of the use of organizations, Mao groomed the CCP into a political force that would re-direct the course of Chinese history. In 1934, Nationalist military pressure forced the CCP troops to take an epic trek—the Long March—across 6000 miles of difficult terrain—100,000 forces began the march; only 20,000 survived. The conclusion of the Long March in the northern city of Yanan in the province of Shaanxi, began an important stage of CCP development, commonly called the Yanan period. During these years, Mao consolidated his power within the party and formulated the ideological and military plans that would carry the Communists to victory. Building on the power of human will, Mao engaged the CCP in a "proletarian revolution" in a society without a proletariat, a peasant society. Mao and the CCP called on the power of the Chinese peasantry to accomplish the seemingly impossible: the founding of a Marxist state in China.

Chinese involvement in World War II aided the Communists' ascendancy to power. When China entered World War II against Japan in 1937, Chiang Kai-shek was faced with an important decision—whether to concentrate his forces and efforts against the Japanese, which he referred to as a disease of the skin and body, or against Mao and the Communists, which he considered a disease of the heart and spirit. Considering the latter the more pressing evil, Chiang set out once again to destroy the CCP forces. While the Nationalist and Communist forces were engaged in a civil war, Japan launched a relentless attack on the Chinese mainland that destroyed Chinese industrial capabilities and caused widespread suffering. Under such conditions, the Nationalist government had limited capabilities, few answers, and even less success at resolving the pressing social and economic difficulties facing the Chinese people. The government and KMT Party under Chiang were marked by corruption and were out of touch with the Chinese masses. At the same time, the war gave Mao and the CCP time to consolidate their forces, to appeal to the Chinese masses, and, ultimately, to challenge and defeat the Nationalists. Just as World War I encouraged the downfall of tsarist Russia, World War II did the same to Nationalist China.

With the Japanese surrender in 1945, the Communists and the Nationalists tried to negotiate an agreement to end their conflict. Although the United States attempted to mediate the dispute, it was in a compromising position because of its past and continuing financial and military support of the Nationalists. By 1946, the negotiations had failed and the two factions reverted to a state of civil war. Although the Nationalists had superior equipment and support, the Communists were able to draw on the vast Chinese populace to defeat Chiang's forces. The Nationalists retreated to the island of Taiwan (Formosa) and in 1949 the Communists controlled the entire Chinese mainland. It was at this time that the People's Republic of China (PRC) was formed.

The Russian and Chinese revolutionary experiences were quite different. Whereas the Bolshevik takeover occurred quickly and the real test of the new leaders came after the revolution, the Chinese takeover took several decades.[14] This meant that when Mao and his comrades finally took office in 1949, they had been tested under fire. They were a united, cohesive, militarized group. Because they had won power on their own, they were loath to have someone else dictate to them concerning their postrevolutionary development. As we will see, who wins

[14]For an analysis of the Chinese approach, see Chalmers Johnson, *Peasant Nationalism and Communist Power* (Stanford, Calif.: Stanford University Press, 1962).

power is of considerable importance in determining who gives orders after power is won.

Following World War II, China's neighbor, Korea, also became Communist. Similar to the division and occupation of Germany after World War II, Korea was divided at the 38th parallel into northern and southern zones with the USSR and the United States serving as occupational powers. During the three-year Soviet occupation of the North (1945–1948), the Red Army installed Communist-oriented leaders to manage the affairs of the occupied zone. The head of the Communist government was Kim Il Sung, a military figure who had fought along with the USSR in World War II. The Soviets initially set up a coalition government—the North Korean Provisional People's Committee—before establishing a more monolithic Communist regime. Although the Korean Communists were not initially in a particularly strong position, Soviet assistance and the fusion of the socialists and Communists into the Workers' Party provided the necessary power base to ensure a Communist government in North Korea. In 1950, the Communist regime of North Korea launched a fratricidal war to take over South Korea and brought about U. S. military involvement on the side of South Korea and Chinese involvement on the side of North Korea. When the Korean armistice was signed on July 27, 1953, the division of Korea into a Communist North and non-Communist South was perpetuated.

## COMMUNISTS COME TO POWER IN EASTERN EUROPE

Perhaps more so than in Asia, World War II markedly altered the political setting of Eastern Europe. Before the war, none of the eastern states were Communist; within a few years after the war's conclusion, all eight countries were governed by Communist regimes.[15] What had happened in this short span to prepare the way for Communism? We can identify two distinct patterns: (1) Communist parties winning power

[15]For an excellent account, see: Hugh Seton-Watson, *The East European Revolution*, 3rd ed. (New York: Praeger, 1956).

during World War II, principally through their own internal efforts (Yugoslavia and Albania), and (2) parties obtaining power through the occupation, pressure, and assistance of the Soviet Union (Czechoslovakia, Poland, Romania, East Germany, Bulgaria, and Hungary).

## COMMUNIST VICTORY FROM WITHIN

Yugoslavia is a state of recent political origin. Prior to World War I, the South Slavic peoples—who comprise contemporary Yugoslavia—were subjects of larger European empires or lived in independent states. Most of the southern part of the land area was under the administration of the Ottoman Empire, whereas the north was part of the Austro-Hungarian Empire. From the ashes of World War I came a new state, The Kingdom of Serbs, Croats, and Slovenes, later, in 1929, to be called Yugoslavia.

The South Slavic ethnic groups of this new state represented different cultures, languages, religions, and traditions. The northern part of the country used the Latin alphabet, was Catholic, and mostly Western in culture and tradition; the southern part was inhabited by nationalities who used the Cyrillic alphabet, was Orthodox or Moslem in religious faith, and held more to Eastern cultures and traditions. This complex mix of nationalities and ethnic groups generated intense conflict in Yugoslavia between the two world wars. To quell such conflict, unite the country, and move the state toward its goals, autocratic King Alexander established a dictatorship in 1929. This centralized form of government only exacerbated the existing problems and undermined still further the regime's fading support.

Through the 1920s and 1930s, a small group of Yugoslavs were attracted to Marxist philosophy and what it might do for Yugoslavia. One such individual was Josip Broz, later known as Tito, a young man who had been wounded fighting for the Austrians in World War I and had been taken to Russia as a prisoner of war. On his release in Russia, he became interested in the Bolshevik cause and later returned to Yugoslavia to promote the ideals of socialism and Communism. Although King Alexander outlawed the Communist Party, Tito and the Yugoslav Communists were able to organize a secret party that relied on Moscow for guidance and direction.

On March 25, 1941, the government under Prince Paul, who replaced the King after his assassination in Marseilles, signed the Tripartite Pact guaranteeing collaboration with the Nazis. In the national uproar that followed, the army revolted, deposed the government, and repudiated the pact. Yugoslavia virtually was without a government until the end of the war. In its place, various resistance movements acted on behalf of the people, including the Chetnik movement representing the Serbs and the Ustashi, which was pro-Nazi and primarily Croatian. But the most successful was the Communist movement led by Josip Broz Tito.[16]

Tito and the Communist partisans, gaining considerable support from all of the South Slavic groups of Yugoslavia, waged a courageous battle against the Nazis as well as against such other anti-Communist Yugoslav forces as the Chetniks. Because Tito and the Communists were perceived by the West as the most effective force against the Nazis, they ultimately won the backing of the Allied Powers. After years of guerilla warfare in the mountains of central Yugoslavia, the victorious partisans recaptured the capital of Belgrade from the Nazis and quickly established a Communist Party state. This was all accomplished with little aid or advice from the hard-pressed Soviets, a fact significantly affecting the Yugoslav experience as a socialist state.

The Communist's advent to power in Albania was closely tied to the Yugoslav movement. During World War II, Albania was occupied by Italy and later Germany. As in Yugoslavia, various resistance groups arose, one Communist inspired. This movement received both aid and advice from Yugoslav emissaries and, under the leadership of Enver Hoxha, seized power in 1941 and has held it to the present day. The fraternal ties that originally characterized Albanian and

Joseph Broz Tito (1892–1980) led Yugoslavia during its national liberation struggle in World War II, guided the country through over 30 years of postwar development, and brought about a distinctive Yugoslav brand of Communism during his years of leadership. He is shown here at the 10th Congress of the Yugoslav League of Communists in 1974.

Yugoslavian relations, however, soon deteriorated into fear and suspicion. Today, Albania is an isolated, xenophobic enclave on the southern boundary of Yugoslavia.

## COMMUNIST VICTORY FROM WITHOUT

During and following World War II, the Soviet Union was instrumental in uniting anti-Fascist opponents and, subsequently, for eliminating non-Communist alternatives and placing Communist Party regimes in power in the remaining six East European states. In view of Soviet military predominance in the area at the end of the war, the USSR was in a strong position to determine the character of the postwar governments in these liberated states. The Teheran Conference of 1943 and the Yalta and Potsdam conferences of 1945 gave the Soviet Union great freedom in determining the political character of

[16]For an interesting account of the life of Josip Broz Tito, see, Milovan Djilas, *Tito: The Story from the Inside*, trans. Vasilije Kojbic and Richard Hayes (London: Weidenfeld and Nicolson, 1981).

postwar Eastern Europe. Some contend that it could have gone so far as to incorporate the liberated areas into the USSR.[17]

The Soviets chose not to adopt the more radical policy of incorporating these European states into the Soviet Union; instead, they opted for the more moderate and gradual policy of national fronts. This meant that the governments in the liberated states were to be reconstituted into coalition governments with the Communists sharing power; at the proper moment, the Communists were to seize complete control. Although there are certain similarities in all cases, there are sufficient differences to warrant brief discussion of each.

The Communists' advent to power in Czechoslovakia occurred under unique circumstances. In the prewar Czechoslovak state, the Communists were an influential and respected political party. Liquidated by Adolph Hitler in 1939, the Czechoslovak government under the non-Communist President, Eduard Beneš, went into exile in London for the duration of the war. But back at home, the Czech and particularly the Slovak Communists formed underground resistance movements to fight against the Nazis. While in London, the Czechoslovak Government maintained good relations with both the Soviet and the home Communists and, with the liberation of the country, President Beneš returned home to preside over a coalition government with strong Communist representation. Although the coalition appeared to be working well, the Communists staged a coup in 1948—strong Soviet involvement was suspected—and occupied broadcasting stations, government buildings, and other key power organs. Quickly and decisively, the coalition was transformed into a solid Communist Party regime under the leadership of Klement Gottwald.

Like Czechoslovakia, the prewar Polish government went into exile in London during World War II. Although the non-Communist government initially maintained reasonably good relations with the Soviet Union, a series of disputes ensued, resulting in full Soviet support of the Polish Communists. In 1942, a group of Polish Communists traveled from Moscow to occupied Poland to join the native Communists who had stayed at home. One of these who came from Moscow was Wladyslaw Gomulka, who was to become the head of the postwar Soviet-oriented regime. As the Nazis were driven from the country, a predominantly Communist Committee of National Liberation was formed to administer the liberated areas. Following the full liberation of the country, the Committee acted as a provisional government and assumed control of the Polish state. Although the Western powers intervened at the 1945 Yalta Conference and succeeded in having representatives of the London government included, the Communists retained predominant influence. With the help of the Soviet Union, local Communists were eventually successful in eliminating political opposition and in placing Gomulka and his associates in full control.

As in the Polish case, the takeover in Romania was a relatively protracted process occurring at the end of World War II. The takeover began with the Soviet Red Army's "liberation" of the country from Nazi occupation and Soviet diplomatic pressures based on the national front policy. This included disarming the Romanian army, prohibiting non-Communist political parties, and severely restricting political suffrage. Western pressure in 1945 again added non-Communists to the coalition government but dominant power remained in the hands of the Communists under the leadership of Peter Groza. Elections held in an atmosphere of Communist intimidation, the arrest of opposition leaders, and the abdication of King Michael placed Communists in a position of power under the secretary-general of their party, Gheorghe Gheorghiu-Dej.

In East Germany, the Soviet Red Army was the sole occupying power following the war and automatically was placed in a position of exclusive control. Walter Ulbricht, a German who had returned from Moscow to Berlin with the Red Army, assumed the key ruling position in the new government. Although political parties

[17]In fact, it did so in the case of the Baltic States and the eastern sections of Czechoslovakia, Romania, Poland, and Germany.

continued to exist and performed certain political and administrative functions, the occupying Soviet officials and German Communists assumed total control. In October 1949, the German Democratic Republic (East Germany) was formed and the dedicated Communist, Ulbricht, and his monolithic Socialist Unity Party were firmly in command.

The Red Army entered Bulgaria on September 8, 1944 and departed late in 1947. During that three-year period, domestic anti-Communist opposition was crushed and dominant political control of the Bulgarian Communist Party was assured. The day after the Red Army's intervention in 1944, a Soviet-backed coup brought power to a Socialist movement called the Fatherland Front. Under the leadership of General Kimon Georgiev, a government was formed that placed Communists in key leadership positions. After a series of political purges and pressure tactics, the Communist-dominated Fatherland Front won 78 percent of the vote in the 1946 elections. This new Bulgarian Government was headed by a former general-secretary of the Comintern, a long-time Communist and friend of the Soviets, named Georgi Dimitrov.

As in Bulgaria, Soviet intervention in Hungary placed native Communists on the inside track to power. Because Hungary had taken an active part in military operations against the Soviet Union, the Red Army took an aggressive position concerning postwar political developments. The occupying Soviet Army purged non-Communist leaders, accused many of collaboration with the Nazis, and, by 1947, had moved Hungarian Marxists into power, including the leader of the Hungarian Communists, Mátyás Rákosi. Having spent 16 years in Hungarian prisons for being a Communist, Rákosi was now intent on achieving absolute power in the postwar Hungarian state. Although non-Communist parties initially had considerable influence—in the open election of 1945 the Smallholders Party's victory led to the formation of a non-Communist coalition—Rákosi and the Soviets soon achieved a dominant position through the controlled 1947 elections.

Suddenly and somewhat unexpectedly, the political character of Eastern Europe was radically transformed. The proud young states of pre-World War II Europe were now cast behind what became known as the Iron Curtain. The Soviet's strategy had succeeded remarkably well in establishing Communist regimes in its neighboring states of Europe. It had established a buffer zone, which helped calm Soviet fears of German invasion and American aid to a resurgent Europe; little blood was shed; and minimal adverse international opinion was incurred. Caught up in their own concerns of postwar reconstruction, the Western powers were slow to react. Soviet involvement in and control of Eastern Europe was so complete and so successful that by the time the West fully recognized what had been done, diplomatic action was hopeless. A military response from the Western powers would have undoubtedly brought another violent military conflict. In its place, the Cold War developed—a period of extreme ideological hostility and enmity between the West and the Communist Party states of Europe.[18]

## THE SPECIAL CASES OF CUBA AND SOUTHEAST ASIA

Given its proximity to the United States and the continuing acrimony in United States-Cuban relations, the establishment of a Communist government in Cuba takes on special interest and meaning. Closely tied to, and highly dependent on, the United States, pre-Castro Cuba was run by an unpopular and inefficient dictator named Fulgencio Batista. Fidel Castro, a gifted revolutionary who had apparently not yet become a Marxist or Communist in the 1950s plotted and then fought against the dictatorship in an effort to promote representative democracy. As a result of growing Cuban sympathy and the support of other groups and sectors in Latin America, and even in the United States, Castro was able to stage a successful revolution against Batista's corrupt and inefficient army.

[18]Soviet military intervention in Afganistan in the early 1980s shows certain similarities with some of the East European cases. It will be interesting to note if the outcome will also be similar.

Castro and his miniscule force of less than 100 persons, subsequently reduced to around a tenth of that, began their takeover with an invasion from Mexico in 1956. Basing their guerilla warfare in the Cuban mountainous region of the Sierra Maestra, Castro and his forces attacked depots, cities, bases, and other key targets throughout the country. With growing popular support and revolutionary power, Castro forced the Batista regime to surrender in January 1959 and took over the reins of government. Unlike so many of the other countries discussed, the Cuban countryside was not in a state of total revolution and disorder. Rather, Castro was able to take over a country with a flourishing economy and a relatively healthy populace.

Contrary to considerable opinion, available evidence suggests that the Cuban revolution was not initially directed by a Communist Party or by any political or ideological organization other than Castro's nationalistic, revolutionary band. Apparently, at that time, Castro did not consider himself a Marxist-Leninist.[19] Although there was a Cuban Communist group, known as the Popular Socialist Party, the first contact between it and Castro's forces did not take place until 1958. The Communists were extremely skeptical of Castro's movement and placed their faith in a popular front strategy that would unite all anti-Batista forces.

At what point Castro, or Castro's Cuba, became Communist is still debatable. Castro was and is a radical with a deep desire for the social transformation of Cuba; but he is not a disciplined Communist in the sense of being a strict adherent to Marxism-Leninism or the Soviet Union. Although Communist ideology played a minor role in the revolution and initial period of Cuban transformation, that soon changed. It seems clear in retrospect that Castro felt Cuban socialism was threatened by the United States in such challenges as the Bay of Pigs, which prompted him gradually and apparently reluc-

[19]For an account of Castro's ideological philosophy prior to, and during, the Cuban revolution, see Hugh Thomas's monumental work, *Cuba: The Pursuit of Freedom* (New York: Harper & Row, 1971).

tantly to turn to Soviet patronage and, thus, eventually to Soviet-style Communism.

The territory today known as Vietnam had been under French control since the late nineteenth century. During World War II, the rather larger area of Southeast Asia was the scene of warfare between national troops under Ho Chi Minh and the Japanese occupational forces. With the defeat of the Japanese and the withdrawal of the Chinese Nationalist troops from the northern part of the Indochinese peninsula, Ho established the Democratic Republic of Vietnam (North Vietnam). At first, the French accorded them provisional recognition; then, negotiations broke down and the Ho regime initiated military action against French forces and the South Vietnamese (September 2, 1945). Carrying on a people's war, Ho and the Vietnamese Communists were involved in almost constant struggle for the next quarter of a century, first against France (1946–1954) and later against the United States. The United States had come to the aid of the South Vietnamese in the 1960s. On April 30, 1975, the American forces were withdrawn from Southeast Asia. Under the party leadership of First Secretary Le Duan (Ho Chi Minh had died in 1969), the North Vietnamese entered Saigon, and brought an end to the partition of Vietnam.

Refused an enclave on Cambodian soil by the royalist government under Prince Norodom Sihanouk, Ho Chi Minh's Cambodian Communist allies spent most of their time exiled in North Vietnam. With Lon Nol's successful right-wing coup against Sihanouk in 1970, the Cambodian Communists returned home to wage war against the new republic under Nol. The bloody war that had been raging in Vietnam during the 1960s and had spread to Laos now engulfed Cambodia as well. Old and new revolutionaries known as the Khmer Rouge resistance movement waged a relentless guerrilla war against the new and weak Cambodian Republic supported by the United States. The revolutionaries won the conflict and ousted Lon Nol in 1975 and adopted a new constitution the next year that established an independent state called Democratic Kampuchea. In December 1978, the Vietnamese invaded Kampuchea and installed a puppet regime headed by President Heng Samrin.

During the Vietnamese conflict, the Laotian Communist movement, known as the Pathet Lao, controlled the northeastern section of Laos bordering on North Vietnam. Advised and supplied by the North Vietnamese, the Pathet Lao exploited the ineptitude and weakness of the royalist government and spread its control over an expanding portion of the country. Finally, in December 1975, the Lao People's Revolutionary Party emerged from the coalition government to abolish the monarchy and establish the Lao People's Democratic Republic.

It should be apparent by now that the establishment of Communist regimes in Vietnam, Cambodia (Kampuchea), and Laos did not bring immediate peace and prosperity to the area of Southeast Asia. Conflict continues to rage at staggering costs to the human dignity of the people of that troubled region.

## A COMPARATIVE OVERVIEW

It is clear that Communism came to many different countries, under a variety of circumstances, and for many different reasons. We will now try to identify the most significant similarities and differences by considering the following questions. Generally speaking, *how* did Communist movements come to power? *When* and *where* did they come to power? *Who* led these successful movements? And, perhaps the most interesting and important question, *why* did they come to power? As students of comparative politics, our guiding purpose is to establish some general patterns that explain the advent of Communism throughout the world.[20]

### HOW DID COMMUNIST MOVEMENTS COME TO POWER?

Most observers of Communist Party states agree that the way in which a party comes to power is

[20]The advent of Communism in Communist Party states is analyzed in Thomas T. Hammond, ed., *The Anatomy of Communist Takeovers* (New Haven: Yale University Press, 1975). Also see Hugh Seton-Watson, *From Lenin to Khrushchev: The History of World Communism* (New York: Praeger, 1960).

important in determining how it uses power and makes policy in subsequent years. Communist parties that come to power through independent revolutionary movements—for example, the USSR, China, Yugoslavia, and Cuba—are likely to assume much more autonomy and latitude in planning and carrying out policy than states—for example, Mongolia, Bulgaria, and East Germany—in which the party came to power through the outside influence of others.

Communist parties have either come to power as a result of independent internal movements, through the imposition of a Communist Party regime by an outside force, or as a result of some combination of the two. The first column in Table 1.1 summarizes the experiences of each country. The two major powers within the Communist world—the Soviet Union and China—came to power primarily as a result of internal movements. In addition, two countries in Eastern Europe—Albania and Yugoslavia—as well as Cuba and Vietnam had independent movements and became Communist largely as a result of their own actions.

In the remaining countries of Eastern Europe, the Soviet Occupation at the end of World War II led to the imposition of Communist-dominated regimes. Although the conditions, timing, and exact strategies varied somewhat from case to case, the idea of a national front served as the guiding policy. Coalition-type governments were initially installed but were soon transformed into Communist-controlled governments. Although it occurred in a different part of the world, the Communist ascendancy to power in North Korea was initially similar to the East European experience, particularly to that of East Germany and Poland. North Korea escaped Soviet domination after 1950, however, when China's influence increased and growing Sino-Soviet competition in North Korea allowed the Koreans to follow a more independent road.

The Vietnamese and Cuban revolutions are quite different from the East European examples where the Soviet Union played a dominant role. Ho Chi Minh and Fidel Castro were both nationalists and revolutionaries intent on ending ex-

**TABLE 1.1** Chronological Listing of Successful Communist Movements

| State | How | When | Where | Who |
|-------|-----|------|-------|-----|
| | | *Attributes for Comparison* | | |
| *Soviet Union* | Independent movement | 1917 | Europe | Vladimir Ilyich Lenin |
| Mongolia | Armed occupation (USSR) | 1921 | Asia | Sukhe-Bator and Khorloin Choibalsan |
| Albania | Independent movement | 1944 | Europe | Enver Hoxha |
| *Yugoslavia* | Independent movement | 1945 | Europe | Josip Broz Tito |
| Vietnam | Independent movement (unification) | 1945 (1975) | Asia | Ho Chi Minh (Le Duan) |
| North Korea | Armed occupation (USSR) | 1945 | Asia | Kim Il Sung |
| Romania | Armed occupation (USSR) | 1945 | Europe | Gheorghiu-Dej |
| Bulgaria | Independent and outside (USSR) | 1946 | Europe | Georgi Dimitrov |
| Hungary | Independent and outside (USSR) | 1947 | Europe | Mátyás Rákosi |
| Poland | Armed occupation (USSR) | 1947 | Europe | Wladyslaw Gomulka |
| Czechoslovakia | Independent and outside (USSR) | 1948 | Europe | Klement Gottwald |
| East Germany | Armed occupation (USSR) | 1949 | Europe | Walter Ulbricht |
| *China* | Independent movement | 1949 | Asia | Mao Zedong |
| Cuba | Independent movement | 1959 | Latin America | Fidel Castro |
| Laos | Independent and outside (Vietnam) | 1975 | Asia | Kaysone Phomvihan |
| Cambodia | Independent and outside (Vietnam) | 1975 | Asia | Pol Pot |

*Note:* The Soviet Union, China, and Yugoslavia are in italics in all figures and tables to emphasize their use as comparative cases.

ploitation and imperialism and bringing democratic socialism to their governments. Unlike the East European cases, they were successful in doing so without major assistance from or the occupation of an outside power. With few exceptions, those regimes that established Communism on their own exhibit greater independence and autonomy in the international arena today. On the other hand, with the notable exceptions of Romania and North Korea, those coming to power as result of an outside occupation show less independence of action, particularly in relation to the USSR. In addition, those leaders coming to power by means of the independent route (e.g., Mao, Tito, Castro) enjoyed relatively cohesive, stable reigns. Although there are exceptions, such as North Korea, those placed in power by outsiders tended to be less popular among their own people and more susceptible to Soviet interference, power struggles, or other developments resulting in abbreviated tenure.

In summary, Communist movements can be, and have been, generated by internal and external forces. The greatest fear of anti-Communists throughout the world has tended to be the threat of espionage, infiltration, and sabotage; yet, history indicates that half of all contemporary Communist Party states came to power through their own means and primarily as a result of internal forces in the country. At the same time, Soviet intervention in post-World War II Europe resulted in the establishment of a number of Communist Party regimes in the Eastern European states. Thus, we can conclude that both domestic and international factors determine the manner in which Communism develops in various nations.[21]

## WHEN AND WHERE HAVE SUCCESSFUL COMMUNIST MOVEMENTS OCCURRED?

The chronological listing in Table 1.1 shows that most successful movements occurred at the end

[21]It should be noted that Marxist rule was brought to Chile in 1970 through the ballot box. Although duly elected, the Communist-oriented government of Salvador Allende Gossens was subsequently overthrown by military leaders in 1973.

of World War II. With the exceptions of the Russian (1917) and Mongolian (1921) takeovers at the end of World War I and the relatively recent Cuban and Southeast Asia experiences, most successful movements followed the serious disorders of World War II. Wars and other major destabilizing forces establish the conditions for revolutionary change. In one way or another, Communist victories tended to come in the wake of international or civil war.

Geographically speaking, Communist movements have been victorious in both East and West. Although most contemporary Communist Party states are concentrated in Eastern Europe, movements in Asia and Latin America illustrate that Communism is not bound to any one part of the world. Recent developments in the Third World, particularly in some countries in Africa, and the strong showing of the Eurocommunists in Italy, France, and Spain suggest that Communism may have a future in other regions as well.

Communism also shows no particular bounds in terms of culture. When Communism first took hold in Russia, some experts attributed its success to the nature of Russian culture. Their Slavic culture, "soul," and general spiritual characteristics (according to these theorists) made them well suited for an ideology emphasizing collectivism and socialism. Because of these spiritual and cultural requisites, scholars noted, Communism was unlikely to catch on in other parts of the world. Subsequent movements and the spread of Communism to the different cultures in Asia and Latin America seem to invalidate the idea of cultural requirements.

Communism has also developed in countries at different levels of economic development. Most have been agricultural societies at the early stages of economic growth. Some, such as Czechoslovakia and East Germany, have had rather advanced economic systems, others have been at intermediate stages of development; still others, in Asia, have had very primitive economic systems. Overall, it is fair to say that Communist movements can achieve success under many different geographical, cultural, and socioeconomic conditions.

## WHO LED THESE VICTORIOUS MOVEMENTS?

Were Lenin, Mao, Tito, Ho Chi Minh, Castro, and others indispensable elements in the revolutionary process or could victory have been achieved without them? Perhaps more important: Which came first—the revolution or the revolutionary? To evaluate an individual's impact on a process as complex as revolution is risky. What can be said is that most had extremely capable leaders, men who understood their countries well and the military and organizational dynamics of the revolutionary process. Leaders like Mao and Tito were able to seize on international forces (e.g., World War II) and to combine them with domestic needs to build successful resistance and revolutionary forces. Although they were "great" leaders in many respects, we can probably observe that the social and economic forces were larger than the men. If a Tito, Mao, Lenin, or Castro had not existed, it is likely that some other individual would have come to the fore and directed the revolutionary movement. "Great" men cannot necessarily make history, but they can influence it. At the very least, the individuals listed in Table 1.1 were the right men in the right place with the foresight and ideas to bring revolutionary visions to fruition.

## WHY WERE THE COMMUNIST MOVEMENTS SUCCESSFUL?

Table 1.1 contains no entry with the heading, why. Although the why of successful movements is far too complex to summarize in a brief word or two, we can make some broad generalizations about the trends leading to the demise of the old state systems and to the success of Communism.

All the regimes that preceded the establishment of Communism suffered from a number of severe shortcomings. Most had lost the confidence of the broader society and their leaders were unable to inspire and gain the support of the mass populace. Often there was government corruption and inefficiency that resulted in disillusionment and disappointment with the old autocracy. The difficulties of the times were further exacerbated by forces of international and civil war, conflicts in which the armies were either unable or unwilling to protect incumbent regimes. In every case, either internal or international wars (and often both) contributed to the final collapse of the old regime. What followed was disorder, economic stagnation, and a political vacuum.

But why were the successor states Communist rather than some other political doctrine or creed? One reason for the success of Communist movements concerns the use of a new organizational weapon, the Communist Party. Centralized, conspiratorial, and militant, the party became the organizational agent for affecting revolutionary change. Operating in a period of political disorganization and general social disorder, the organized parties of the revolutionaries capitalized on the unstable setting to grasp the reins of power. It is in this respect that the leaders often showed the attributes of the greatmen syndrome. Understanding the use of organizations and the domestic and international contexts in which they were operating, the leaders assumed and consolidated political power.

The revolutionary leaders and the parties they represented also understood the meaning and role of military power. "Power grows out of the barrel of a gun," proclaimed Mao Zedong. Use of the party as a military as well as a political organization was a major factor in most takeovers. In some states, armed force meant the intervention of the Soviet Army and a period of military occupation. This factor represented a key element in the Communists' ability to assume and retain political power, especially in those states often referred to as being in the Soviet bloc.

Although comparison is difficult because of the many differences among the Communist movements, we can identify some general patterns concerning the advent to power. Authoritarianism, misrule, mass discontent, and alienation when combined with international warfare and foreign imperialism are the factors that have led to a toppling of old state systems. Then, organized resistance and revolutionary movements, led by astute leaders operating within centralized Communist Party organizations,

often with the armed assistance of the USSR, helped establish new Communist systems. Because there are obviously other states that have experienced such conditions and have not gone Communist, we should not consider these patterns universal laws. At the same time, there are enough similar conditions and forces to point up general patterns that involve the establishment of Communist rule.

## COMMUNIST PARTY STATE RELATIONS

The national forces and ethnocentrism that have caused problems within Communist Party states have been just as pronounced in affecting the relations among them. Although the Soviet leaders anticipated fraternal relations among the new Communist Party states following World War II, the experience has often been marked by considerable conflict and antagonism. The Soviet leaders, first under Joseph Stalin, later under Nikita S. Khrushchev, and then, under Leonid I. Brezhnev, have attempted to unite the international socialist movement under the leadership of the Soviet banner. History indicates, however, that they have experienced a number of challenges.

The first major crack in the facade of Communist internationalism came with the dispute between Stalin and Tito and Yugoslavia's expulsion from the Cominform in 1948. When Stalin sensed that Tito was failing to toe the Soviet line fully, he promptly excommunicated the Yugoslavs from the Communist camp. Yugoslavia's subsequent independent course suggested that the building of socialism was possible (and in the eyes of some, even preferable) outside the Soviet fold. This and other feelings concerning sovereignty resulted in a series of national uprisings in several of the other East European states against the dominant Soviet role and in favor of more autonomous interstate relations within the socialist bloc. The most notable of these uprisings occurred in Hungary in 1956 as the Hungarian leadership and people sought to gain more sovereignty over the building of socialism in their country. After the Yugoslav experience, the Soviet leadership was unwilling to see their

The government delegations of the USSR and China meet on October 17, 1979, in Moscow to discuss the Sino-Soviet conflict. Leading their respective groups are Soviet Deputy Foreign Minister Leonid F. Il'ichev (third from the left) and Chinese Deputy Foreign Minister Wang Yuping (third from the right).

hopes of Soviet-directed internationalism suffer another setback; accordingly, they crushed the Hungarian movement in the fall of 1956.

The next great setback to a united movement of socialist states came with the growing disaffection between the Chinese and the Soviets in the late 1950s. Resulting in an open split in 1960, the Sino-Soviet dispute buried all illusions concerning the possibility of socialist harmony.[22] Chinese and Soviet animosities reached the level of open warfare in the late 1960s as both sides prepared for war. The Sino-Soviet border became the site of numerous military skirmishes and the encampments of huge armies prepared for war. Although recent years have seen a partial lull in hostilities between the two powers, ideological conflict continues to rage.

With the Chinese split, the position of Soviet leadership in the socialist world was further challenged. Albania also broke away from the

Soviet bloc, transferred its allegiance to the Chinese Communists and became China's beachhead in Europe.[23] Disagreeing with China's new domestic and foreign policies in the post-Mao era, Albania cut its relations with China and now is isolated from both Communist Party and non-Communist states. Romania, too, was affected by the Sino-Soviet dispute and, although it remained in the Warsaw Pact, the Romanians challenged the role of Soviet leadership and began to walk a tightrope between China and the Soviet Union. We will not outline all the points of conflict and contrast among the states, but it should be clear that the view of the Communist world as being a monolithic union of like-minded states is a gross misconception.

The USSR is obviously the one great superpower in the Communist world. According to most informed observers, the Soviet Union is very near the United States in overall power. Ac-

[22]See Donald Zagoria, *The Sino-Soviet Conflict, 1956–61* (New York: Atheneum, 1964).

[23]Harry Hamm, *Albania—China's Beachhead in Europe* (New York: Praeger, 1963).

| | Country Rank[a] | Total Power Capability[b] | Critical Mass[c] | Economic Capability | Military Capability— Strategic | Military Capability— Conventional | National Strategic Purpose[d] | Will to Pursue National Strategy[d] |
|---|---|---|---|---|---|---|---|---|
| Albania | 73 | 1 | – | 1 | – | – | – | – |
| Bulgaria | 67 | 3 | – | 1 | – | 2 | – | – |
| Cambodia | – | – | – | – | – | – | – | – |
| *China* | 3 | 171 | 100 | 29 | 10 | 32 | 0.5 | 0.2 |
| Cuba | 69 | 2 | – | – | – | 2 | 0.7 | 0.6 |
| Czechoslovakia | 60 | 10 | – | 6 | – | 4 | – | – |
| East Germany | 49 | 22 | 10 | 7 | – | 5 | 0.8 | 0.2 |
| Hungary | 64 | 5 | – | 4 | – | 1 | – | – |
| Laos | – | – | – | – | – | – | – | – |
| Mongolia | 40 | 30 | 30 | – | – | – | 0.5 | 0.3 |
| North Korea | 51 | 22 | 10 | – | – | 12 | 0.8 | 0.6 |
| Poland | 25 | 48 | 35 | 9 | – | 4 | 0.5 | 0.2 |
| Romania | 46 | 24 | 20 | 3 | – | 1 | 0.5 | 0.5 |
| *Soviet Union* | 2 | 402 | 100 | 105 | 100 | 97 | 0.8 | 0.5 |
| Vietnam | 26 | 48 | 40 | – | – | 8 | 0.8 | 0.4 |
| *Yugoslavia* | 36 | 36 | 30 | 3 | – | 3 | 0.5 | 0.2 |
| USA[e] | 1 | 468 | 100 | 174 | 100 | 94 | 0.4 | 0.5 |

[a]Rank out of 76 countries ranked. United States ranked 1 with total power capability of 468; the Soviet Union ranked 2, with total power capability of 402.

[b]Total Power Capability is calculated by adding Critical Mass and Economic and Military Capabilities. Strategic Purpose and Will are important factors, but are not added to the capability index.

[c]Critical Mass is population plus territory.

[d]The higher the coefficient, the higher the level of national strategic purpose and the will to pursue national strategy.

[e]USA is included for comparative purposes.

SOURCE: Adapted from George Thomas Kurian, *The Book of World Rankings* (New York: Facts on File, 1979), pp. 69–70.

cording to Ray Cline's world power assessment, a country's power is a product of a variety of different forces (Cline's are listed in Table 1.2). According to Cline's assessment, the Soviet Union is far more powerful than China and almost as powerful as the United States. The other states listed in Table 1.2 reflect different levels of national power, but none approach the level of great power status. Of course, the East European countries (with the exception of Albania and Yugoslavia) join the USSR in the Warsaw Treaty Organization (WTO). This Soviet sponsored counterpart to the North Atlantic Treaty Organization (NATO) represents a formidable defense alliance. What is one of the most interesting facts about Communist power in the contemporary world is that it is not a united force as Marx and others might have expected. In fact, much of the power in the Communist world is divided and diverted to perceived threats from one another. A great deal of Soviet and Chinese military resources are devoted to their continuing conflict. One quarter to one third of Soviet troops are stationed on the Sino-Soviet border.

Yugoslavia's main concern is not with the military threat of the capitalist states of the West but with the possibility of Soviet intervention. So, although Communist Party states are formidable forces in the world, their global power is diminished as a result of the deep divisions among them.

In the following chapters, we concentrate on three different types of Communist political systems. Using the comparative approach, we consider all 16 Communist Party states discussed but concentrate our attention on the USSR, China, and Yugoslavia. As the succeeding chapters will illustrate, these three states represent contrasting and competing models of socialism.[24]

Established in 1917 as the first Marxist-Leninist state, the USSR became the leader of the international Communist movement. Conceived by its leaders as the beacon and guardian of orthodox Marxism-Leninism, Soviet leaders subse-

quently attempted to get other socialist states to follow their approach to Communist construction and to emulate their system of government. The first leaders to balk at the dominating Soviet role were the Yugoslavs who, as a result of their actions, were expelled from the international Communist movement in 1948. In the following years, Yugoslavia remained a Communist Party state but set out on its own to develop a more democratic and humanistic, self-managing form of socialism.

The next defection came in the late 1950s as the Chinese began to chafe under the dominating influence of the Soviet Union. As a result of this feeling and the ensuing Sino-Soviet conflict, China also set out on its own and began to follow a more radical road to Communism. Following Mao Zedong's death in 1976, the post-Mao leadership has revised this approach and now emphasizes a more developmental-oriented model. We will not attempt to define or explain them here, but these orthodox, self-managing, and developmental models of Soviet, Yugoslav, and Chinese socialism have been selected for more intensive comparison later on.

---

[24]For a book that explores the different historical, environmental, and political characteristics of these models, see Gary K. Bertsch and Thomas W. Ganschow, eds., *Comparative Communism: The Soviet, Chinese, and Yugoslav Models* (San Francisco: W. H. Freeman, 1976).

# Suggestions for Further Reading

Brzezinski, Zbigniew K., *The Soviet Bloc: Unity and Conflict*, rev. ed. (New York: Praeger, 1961).

Burks, R. V., *The Dynamics of Communism in Eastern Europe* (Princeton, N.J.: Princeton University Press, 1961).

Drachkovitch, Milorad M., ed., *Marxism in the Modern World* (Stanford, Calif.: Stanford University Press, 1965).

Fejto, Francois, *A History of the People's Democracies (New York: Praeger, 1971).*

Gasster, Michael, *China's Struggle to Modernize* (New York: Knopf, 1972).

Goodrich, L. Carrington, *A Short History of the*

Chinese People, 3rd ed. (New York: Harper & Row, 1959).

Hammond, Thomas T., ed., *The Anatomy of Communist Takeovers* (New Haven, Conn.: Yale University Press, 1975).

Hunt, R. N. Carew, *The Theory and Practice of Communism*, 5th ed. (Baltimore: Penguin, 1963).

Johnson, Chalmers, *Peasant Nationalism and Communist Power* (Stanford, Calif.: Stanford University Press, 1962).

Lichtheim, George, *Marxism: An Historical and Critical Study*, 2nd ed. (New York: Praeger, 1965).

Meisner, Maurice, *Mao's China: A History of*

the People's Republic (New York: Free Press, 1977).

Pares, Bernard, *A History of Russia*, 5th ed. (New York: Knopf, 1949).

Schapiro, Leonard, *The Origins of Communist Autocracy* (Cambridge: Harvard University Press, 1955).

Seton-Watson, Hugh, *From Lenin to Khrushchev: The History of World Communism* (New York: Praeger, 1960).

————. *The East European Revolution* 3rd ed. (New York: Praeger, 1956).

Singleton, Fred, *Twentieth Century Yugoslavia* (New York: Columbia University Press, 1976).

Snow, Edgar, *Red Star over China* (New York: Random House, 1938).

Trotsky, Leon, *A History of the Russian Revolution*, trans. Max Eastman (3 vols.) (New York: Simon & Schuster, 1932).

# CHAPTER TWO
## The Contemporary Setting

People often think of the Communist world as a monolithic bloc of grey, nondescript, undifferentiated states. This stereotype is a gross misconception and has led to an unfortunate amount of naiveté and misunderstanding about the countries we call Communist. If we examine them closely, we will find extreme diversity in their social, economic, and political features. In 1977, the USSR had a gross national product (GNP) of $861 billion, whereas Cuba and Vietnam's GNPs were approximately 1 percent of that figure. East Germany's per capita GNP (a measure of personal income) was $5094 in 1977, whereas Laos's was under a $100.[1] When considering ethnic and cultural characteristics, we learn that North Korea is ethnically homogeneous—almost totally Korean—whereas the USSR is made up of over 100 diverse ethnic and national groupings. Understanding the nature of politics in Communist Party states requires careful study of this rich variety of national characteristics.

This chapter will examine the different economic, social, and demographic characteristics and the role they play in determining the setting in which politics takes place.

[1]For an extensive listing of political and social indicators, see Charles Lewis Taylor and Michael C. Hudson, *World Handbook of Political and Social Indicators*, 2nd ed. (New Haven: Yale University Press, 1972); and Arthur S. Banks, ed., *Political Handbook of the World: 1980* (New York: McGraw Hill 1980).

## THE ECONOMIC SETTING

Economics is at the heart of Marxist ideology. Marx predicted that the socialist revolution would occur in capitalist countries that had undergone the Industrial Revolution. In point of fact, Communism arose in agriculture-based societies where the proletarian sector was a very small percentage (generally 5 to 25 percent) of the working population (see Table 2.1). The countries of Asia—China, Cambodia (Kampuchea), Laos, and Vietnam—were even more agriculturally oriented than their European counterparts. The United Nations estimates that nearly 80 percent of China's present-day labor force still works in agriculture. Therefore, although Marx predicted that economic abundance and equality would come with the victory of socialism, the social and economic conditions of most aspiring Marxist states were not conducive to the realization of Communist ideals.

### THE SOVIET UNION

The initial challenge facing Lenin and the Communist leaders after the Bolshevik victory was Russia's reconstruction. After extricating the country from World War I, the Bolsheviks went about the task of consolidating power and building socialism within their country. In 1918, Lenin's decree nationalized heavy industries,

**TABLE 2.1** Working Population Before Socialism, by Sector of Economy

|  | Czechoslovakia (1934) | Hungary (1930) | Poland (1931) | Romania (1930) | Bulgaria (1935) | Yugoslavia (1936) |
|---|---|---|---|---|---|---|
| Industry | 38.3 | 24.1 | 19.4 | 7.7 | 8.0 | 9.9 |
| Agriculture | 25.6 | 53.0 | 60.6 | 76.9 | 80.0 | 76.3 |
| Trade | 9.2 | 5.9 | 6.1 | 3.3 | 2.4 | 4.2 |
| Other | 26.9 | 17.0 | 13.9 | 12.1 | 9.6 | 9.3 |
| Total | 100.0 | 100.0 | 100.0 | 100.0 | 100.0 | 99.7 |

SOURCE: Walter D. Connor, *Socialism, Politics, and Equality: Hierarchy and Change in Eastern Europe and the USSR* (New York: Columbia University Press, 1979), p. 31.

land, and the means of production; private ownership of land and industry was strictly forbidden. During the ensuing period of civil war and foreign intervention (1918–1921), however, little could be done to set up a rational system of economic administration. It was during this period of "war Communism" that economic output fell to 20 percent of what it had been before the outbreak of World War I.

To get the economy going again, the Russian leaders adopted the New Economic Policy (NEP) in 1921. Although large industries remained nationalized, this new policy called for a mixed economic strategy that denationalized small industries and agriculture. Representing a temporary return to capitalism, the NEP saved the Bolshevik government from bankruptcy and got the Russian economy back on its feet again. By 1926, economic output had reached its prewar levels.

With Lenin's death in 1924 and Stalin's assumption of power, Russia's leadership embraced the monumental task of rapid industrialization. With the first Five-Year Plan of 1928–1933 (a centralized plan coordinating economic goals and policies for the entire country), the Stalinist strategy of economic development began to materialize. Because there was no real possibility of bringing foreign capital into the country—the socialist leaders did not want to become dependent on the capitalist West and the West was suspicious of, and unwilling to support, Russian development—Soviet economic policy had to devise a method of generating capital internally. By adopting a policy that exacted high costs from the peasantry and that fun-

neled nearly all economic surpluses back into the industrial sector, the Soviets attempted to accumulate funds on their own. To achieve the Party's economic goals, Stalin established a centralized administrative structure and re-adopted the policies of nationalization and collectivization. Designed to mobilize the population to attain what many people felt to be unreasonably high economic goals, this developmental policy incurred great human costs. Individuals or groups who disagreed with nationalization or the collectivization of agriculture were sent off to Siberia or annihilated.[2] The human costs surrounding Stalin's programs were high, but the economic benefits were substantial. Even in view of the devastation and economic setbacks caused by World War II, the Soviet economic strategy propelled the USSR to the stature of a world power by the end of the Stalinist era in 1953. Utilizing a command-type economic system based on government control of the means of production, central planning, and a high rate of capital investment, production in the Soviet Union drew close to, and even surpassed, that of some of the Western powers.

Between 1950 and 1980, the Soviet Union's economy grew even further. In 1950, the Soviet GNP was estimated at less that one third that of the United States. By 1965, Soviet GNP had grown to approximately half that of the United States and three times that of Great Britain; by

[2]Stalin's collectivization drive of 1920–1936 was a radical program to transfer the private ownership of land to collective farms under state administration. The drive ended with the abolition of 90 percent of private farming and the deportation of over 1 million peasant households.

**TABLE 2.2**  Socioeconomic Indicators, 1977

| Country | GNP (million US $) | GNP per capita (US $) | Global Economic-Social Standing[a] |
|---|---|---|---|
| Albania | $  1,672 | $  665 | 55 |
| Bulgaria | 25,000 | 2,840 | 26 |
| Cambodia | na[b] | na[b] | 116 |
| China | 372,800 | 378 | 82 |
| Cuba | 7,216 | 752 | 42 |
| Czechoslovakia | 63,640 | 4,234 | 20 |
| East Germany | 85,400 | 5,094 | 14 |
| Hungary | 32,940 | 3,094 | 29 |
| Laos | 290 | 86 | 132 |
| Mongolia | 1,333 | 870 | 52 |
| North Korea | 11,379 | 648 | 82 |
| Poland | 114,280 | 3,303 | 27 |
| Romania | 60,200 | 2,780 | 31 |
| Soviet Union | 861,300 | 3,326 | 24 |
| Vietnam | 8,350 | 167 | 93 |
| Yugoslavia | 45,586 | 2,094 | 40 |
| USA[c] | 1,896,100 | 8,743 | 5 |

[a]Represents average rankings based on 140 countries for GNP per capita and education and health indicators.

[b]Not available.

[c]The USA is included for comparative purposes.

SOURCE: Adapted from Ruth Leger Sivard, *World Military and Social Expenditures, 1980* (Leesburg, Va.: World Priorities, 1980), pp. 21–29.

1977, the Soviet economy continued to grow (see Table 2.2). The general economic goal through the first 60 years of Soviet development had been that of basic capital investment. Stated simply, the Soviets opted for the development of heavy industry—hydroelectric plants, steel mills, and so forth—at the expense of the consumer sector.[3]

## CHINA

Assuming power in 1949, Mao Zedong and the Chinese Communists faced an even less developed economy, more devasted country, and a more chaotic economic system than the Bolsheviks confronted. The economy was in such a deteriorated state that it did not even have the ca-

[3]For an excellent economic history of the Soviet Union, see Alex Nove, *An Economic History of the USSR* (London: Allen Lane, 1969).

pability to manufacture the primary vehicle for Chinese transportation, the bicycle. Unlike the Bolsheviks, Mao and his compatriots did not rush to nationalize industry and collectivize agriculture. To stimulate economic recovery, they attempted to use capitalist industry and redistribute agricultural land among the peasants; nationalization and collectivization would occur gradually over the span of several years. This policy of gradual transformation was carefully followed during the 1949–1952 period and resulted in political consolidation, economic recovery and growth, and improved internal and international prestige. Slowly, the leadership began to transform privately owned enterprises into a cooperative form of state/private management. At the outset of the first Five-Year Plan in 1953, these joint enterprises accounted for approximately half of China's economic output; by 1956, practically all private enterprises had been changed to the cooperative private/state operation. The first Five-Year Plan (1953–1957)—based on a general conception of Stalin's model although benefiting from the hindsight of Soviet mistakes—resulted in substantial material growth and economic progress. Utilizing aid and advice from the USSR and East European states, China appeared well on the way to economic recovery.

Soon after the second Five-Year Plan was proclaimed (1958–1962), however, the recovery encountered a number of serious setbacks, the first of which was the Great Leap Forward campaign beginning in 1958. Based on the general line of "going all out and aiming high to achieve greater, quicker, better, and more economical results in building socialism," this radical program was intended to make China a world economic power in a matter of decades. With expectations of surpassing Great Britain in industrial output in 15 years, the strategy called on both modern and traditional (what the Chinese refer to as "walking on two legs") methods of development. Sacrificing quality for quantity and suffering from poor planning and execution, the Great Leap Forward resulted in a "small step backward." Planning became difficult, product quality declined, economic imbalances were experienced, and the idealistic but misguided campaign ended in disgrace.

The period of 1959–1961 also brought a series of natural calamities, such as droughts and floods, that further reduced Chinese economic capabilities, diminished agricultural production, and hindered development. In their midst came the Soviet Union's withdrawal of material aid and technical assistance in the summer of 1960. Precipitated by a growing ideological dispute, the Soviet Union's withdrawal interrupted many developmental programs that relied on foreign assistance.[4] At this point in Chinese reconstruction, the future looked bleak indeed.

In the early 1960s, the Chinese brought an end to the Great Leap Forward program and began to reevaluate their economic policies. This period ushered in an emphasis on greater self-reliance and a search for policies uniquely suited to Chinese needs and capabilities. The reappraisal changed the general strategy from one emphasizing heavy industry (the Soviet Union's approach) to one emphasizing agriculture. The new order of priorities became agriculture first, light industry second, and heavy industry third. As recovery proceeded and the third Five-Year Plan entered its second year in 1967, however, the economic system encountered another destabilizing campaign. Intended to "take firm hold of the revolution and stimulate production," the Great Proletarian Cultural Revolution (GPCR) of 1966–1969 once again set the economic system into a state of disarray. Young revolutionaries, the Red Guards, were dispatched to the factories and all other social and economic organizations to stimulate production through revolutionary and ideological means; their intrusion had certain political benefits but also great economic costs. Although intending to rejuvenate the revolutionary spirit of the populace, the GPCR exacted a considerable price before it ended in 1969.

## YUGOSLAVIA, EASTERN EUROPE, AND CUBA

Always less developed than Western Europe, the Balkan countries were further devastated by two world wars. During their evacuation of Yugoslavia at the end of World War II, the Nazis destroyed much of the country's transportation system and industrial facilities. The Yugoslavs began the task of reconstruction by nationalizing and collectivizing private holdings according to the Stalinist mode of development. However, growing friction between Joseph Stalin and the Yugoslav leaders culminated in a decision that shocked the world. Unexpectedly, in 1948, Stalin expelled Josip Broz Tito and the Yugoslavs from the international Communist organization, Cominform, and initiated a sudden freeze in Soviet-Yugoslav relations.[5]

A few years after the expulsion, Tito and his associates began considering alternatives to the Soviet command-type economic system. Slowly experimenting with and implementing a number of reforms, the Yugoslavs moved to a decentralized form of market socialism that based production more on the laws of supply and demand, less on the expectations of a central economic plan. Movement to a market-based economy was in part motivated and certainly swiftened by the Soviet's economic blockade of Yugoslavia that followed their expulsion from the Cominform and the socialist camp. Weathering this blockade and severe natural catastrophes with economic assistance from the United States, the Yugoslavs began a steady period of economic growth. Through the 1950s and 1960s, the Yugoslav economic growth rates were among the highest in the world.

Although some countries fared worse than others, World War II also unleashed destructive forces on the economies of the other East European states as well. The extent of these damages and the amount of reparation required by the region's victor, the Soviet Union, largely deter-

[4]These and other events resulted in the so-called Sino-Soviet conflict, a dispute characterized by hostile interstate relations through the 1960s and 1970s and continuing into the present.

[5]The Communist Information Bureau (Cominform) was established in 1947 to bind the East European socialist states more closely to the USSR. In a letter of March 27, 1948, addressed to Tito and the Yugoslav Communists, Stalin and the Soviet Central Committee castigated the Yugoslav leaders and excommunicated them from the socialist camp. Because they considered themselves loyal to the Soviet Union, this was initially a bitter blow to the Yugoslav Communists. For a firsthand account of their reactions and subsequent search for alternative economic and social policies, see Vladimir Dedijer, *The Battle Stalin Lost* (New York: Universal Library, 1972).

mined the initial pace and extent of postwar recovery.[6] In many cases, the Soviets stripped factories of machinery or dismantled entire plants for shipment to the USSR to help pay for war damages. By the early 1950s, however, all the states were back to their prewar levels of production. East Germany was the last to reach this level because of the unusually high extent of war damage and equally high reparations to the USSR.

Following similar policies of Soviet-oriented socialist construction, the economies of the East European states were virtually all nationalized by 1950. Emulating the Soviet economic model and working within the supranational Council for Mutual Economic Assistance (CMEA or COMECON) established in 1949, the different states adopted rather similar economic policies and procedures.[7] Attempting to expand the industrial base (particularly mining, machine building, ironworks, and steelworks) while simultaneously retarding consumption, the states hoped to increase the margin for capital investment. The resultant economic systems were generally inefficient. Economic recovery from the ravages of war was achieved at unnecessarily high costs in terms of poor working conditions, low salaries, and a scarcity of basic consumer goods.

Unlike the war-torn countries of Europe and Asia, Cuba had a relatively stable and productive economy to greet Fidel Castro on his assumption of power. In a series of moves to punish the followers of the ousted dictator Fulgencio Batista, Castro expropriated properties, including factories, shops, hotels, and so forth; reduced rents; lowered property values; raised wages; and prohibited the export of cap-

ital. Soon after, he nationalized the oil industry and expropriated all foreign companies. All these policies helped to undercut the former capitalist system and, by 1960, Cuba was well on the road to socialism.

## SOCIALIST ECONOMIC FORMS

The ideal of Communism described by Karl Marx envisioned an economic system based on the principle "from each according to his abilities, to each according to his needs." This principle presupposes an economic system in which there are no shortages and where the members of society do not have to pay for food, goods, or services. Individuals work and produce according to their abilities and consume only what they need. A cursory review of economic relations in contemporary Communist Party states indicates that this level of development is still an ideal and rather far removed from reality.

To move toward the utopian ideals of Communism, all Communist Party states have established some sort of socialist economic system. Under socialism, workers produce according to their ability and are paid according to their contribution. In this economic system, theoretically speaking, the factors of production are owned collectively and controlled by the public. Marx believed that this system was a lower stage than Communism but, although it was an unjust system because more important work would be more highly rewarded than less important work, it would accomplish certain necessary benefits. Basically, socialism would result in a system of abundance culminating in a period when an "oppressive government of men" would be replaced by the "administration of things." According to Marx, government would "wither away" and the utopian socioeconomic condition of Communism would appear.

The Communist Party states of today display a variety of socialist institutional arrangements and policy preferences, each officially designed to facilitate the evolution from socialism to Communism. The Soviet Union's economic system has often been referred to, especially by

[6]For a discussion of Soviet demands for reparation payments from the new Communist Party regimes to cover war damages inflicted by the Axis Powers as well as other forms of Soviet involvement in the postwar economic setting of Eastern Europe, see Nicholas Spulber, *The Economies of Communist Eastern Europe* (Cambridge: MIT Press, 1957).

[7]COMECON was established as a response to the Western Marshall Plan and was intended to coordinate reconstruction, planning, production, and foreign trade within Eastern Europe. It originally included Bulgaria, Czechoslovakia, Hungary, Poland, Romania, and the USSR. Subsequently, it was broadened to include Albania (since withdrawn), Cuba, East Germany, and Mongolia.

its Marxist detractors, as one of state socialism.[8] In this system, state ministries and government bodies at different levels manage the factors of production. Because industries and enterprises receive their directives from central planning agencies, the term, command-type system, is also used to describe the Soviet economic system. Although the market and the idea of supply and demand have some effect on production, the planning agencies assume primary power and responsibility for determining the type and level of economic output. Profits and losses accrue to the state, not to the enterprise or to the workers.[9]

The centralized economy under the model of state socialism allows the central government to control key policy decisions, but there are still some economic interests and enterprises that remain outside direct government control. Some agricultural and industrial cooperatives, usually quite small, administer their own economic affairs. There are also private artisans (jewelers, tailors) and professionals (doctors and dentists) in some Communist Party countries who, although required to be registered, function very much on a private basis. At the same time, ownership of the majority of the means of production resides in the hands of the state and is under the control of government authorities. In theory, at least, this system is to serve the collective interest and avoid the type of "man over man" exploitation that Marxists contend characterizes private ownership in the capitalist system.

Although a basic purpose and desired benefit of the centralized, administered system of state socialism is that of economic efficiency, many economists have called attention to considerable waste and inefficiency in the Soviet and East European systems. The administered system is useful in tackling high priority tasks, like the development of heavy industry or the decision to promote intensive capital investment. However,

vesting ownership in the state and control in the goverment ministries has ruled out certain economic dynamics that promote efficiency and development. A key example involves the attitude and commitment of the average worker. Marx contended that under capitalism workers had become estranged from their work, but that under socialism they were to regain control of their work because the work enterprise was to be publicly owned. But under a centralized system of state socialism, as in the Soviet Union, workers have once again been separated from their work. In the eyes of many observers, the state has merely replaced the bourgeoisie and, thus, the role and attitude of the worker has not changed significantly.

There have been a number of reactions to this development in the form of experimentation with alternative forms of socialism. Perhaps the most far-reaching and interesting is the Yugoslav experiment with their self-managing form of socialism. Referred to by a variety of terms, including decentralized socialism, *laissez-faire* socialism, or a mixed free enterprise/public ownership system, the Yugoslav experiment represents an attempt to resolve some of the problems of state socialism. Hoping to eliminate excessive bureaucracy, low productivity and efficiency, and a relative absence of motivation and initiative, they have developed a hybrid economic system that combines elements of both socialism and capitalism.[10]

Beginning in the early 1950s, Yugoslavia began to abandon many features of the Soviet command-type system. In a series of reforms, Yugoslav leaders de-emphasized centralized planning, provided economic enterprises with more decision-making autonomy, and made competition and profit a central motivating feature of the economy. All of these and additional policies came under the movement toward self-managing, market-oriented socialism.

[8]Because the state rather than the public owns the factors of production, the term, state socialism, is widely used to describe the Soviet economic system.

[9]For a review of the organization and functioning of the Soviet economy, see Robert W. Campbell, *Soviet Economic Power: Its Organization, Growth and Challenge* (London: Macmillan, 1967).

[10]For a useful review of Yugoslav economic policy, see Rudolf Bicanic, *Economic Policy in Socialist Yugoslavia* (New York: Cambridge University Press, 1973); for a general introduction, see Joel B. Dirlam and James L. Plummer, *An Introduction to the Yugloslav Economy* (Columbus, Ohio: Merrill, 1973).

Although accounts of the motivating forces behind self-management vary, most include Yugoslavia's desire to put power in the hands of the worker, where, according to Marx, it rightly belongs. The first major move in the early 1950s involved the establishment of workers' councils in economic enterprises. These councils of elected workers were to assume major responsibility for running the affairs of the firm. Under this system, central government planning was de-emphasized while the autonomy of the enterprise was increased. That is, considerable authority was transferred from central planning ministries to the enterprises themselves, and the enterprises began to base their decisions on the market. This change had a drastic effect on the economic system and the broader society. Rather than produce what the central plan required, enterprises began to produce what would sell on the market. This action upgraded the quality of Yugoslav goods and made them more competitive both domestically and internationally. It also moved the economy in a more consumer-oriented direction because the enterprises were motivated to produce goods that the consumer would be willing to buy. This has made the Yugoslav system one of the most consumer-oriented economies of the Communist Party states we are studying.

As one might expect, the Yugoslav form of socialism came under hostile attack from both the Chinese and Soviet leaders. A pamphlet published in Beijing in 1964 noted:

> Although the Tito clique still displays the banner of "socialism," a bureaucrat bourgeoisie opposed to the Yugoslav people has gradually come into being since the Tito clique took the road of revisionism, transforming the Yugoslav state from a dictatorship of the proletariat into a dictatorship of the bureaucrat bourgeoisie and its socialist public economy into state capitalism.[11]

The Soviet leaders also looked with disdain on the economic revisionism being followed in Yugoslavia and warned their fellow leaders in the other European socialist states to stay clear of this heresy.

Taking the advice of the Soviet leaders, the East European states have adopted a much more orthodox (Soviet-oriented) path to economic development. In these states, an initial mixed-economy period after World War II was followed by the adoption of a command system emulating the Soviet model. Launching Five-Year Plans that emphasized industrial development, nationalizing trade and industry, and subordinating labor unions to the Communist Party, the economic models of the other East European states looked like miniature copies of the Soviet system.

From the late 1950s to 1980, however, many of the East European states began to experiment with reforms. Some observed with keen interest the successes of economic experimentation in Yugoslavia. Many felt that the planned economies established in their countries with Soviet assistance after World War II were impeding optimal development. In some cases, having experienced prewar histories of rather successful economic growth and possessing definite economic potential, economic planners in some of these states blamed their present difficulties on the Soviet-style administered system. Although the responses differed from country to country, many were eager to experiment with new economic forms. Significant policy changes based on economic liberalization were initiated at different times in a number of the countries, particularly Czechoslovakia, Hungary, and Poland. However, because the USSR perceived these policies as endangering the preservation of the command system, the Soviets often intervened and forced these countries back into more orthodox positions. Witness, for example, the Czechoslovak experience in the late 1960s when they attempted to undertake far-reaching social and economic reforms. One dimension of this experiment was economic liberalization designed to take some of the planning and policy-making functions away from the party and central ministries. Although significant economic progress was being made and other social and political reforms were gathering momentum during the spring of 1968, Soviet reservations about the ad-

[11]*On Khrushchev's Phoney Communism and Its Historical Lessons to the World* (Beijing: Foreign Languages Press, 1964), p. 47.

visability of these reforms resulted in military intervention that brought an end to Czechoslovak economic and political liberalization.[12] Organizing a joint intervention by the Warsaw Treaty Organization (WTO) states, troops and tanks from Bulgaria, East Germany, Poland, and the Soviet Union marched on to Czechoslovakian soil on August 20, 1968, and brought an end to the Prague spring.[13] Most Czechoslovak leaders, including the Communist Party leader, Alexander Dubcek, were ousted as the country returned to the more orthodox position that characterizes the economic systems of the other WTO and COMECON states.

The Chinese and Cuban economic systems, also referred to by a number of different terms, including mobilization and leftist systems, have both significant similarities to, and differences from, the Soviet and East European forms. Involved in a cyclical, or zigzag, course over the years, the Chinese sytem has moved back and forth, emphasizing more radical and more moderate economic forms. At some periods, particularly during the Great Leap Forward (1958–1960) and at the height of the GPCR (1966–1969), the Chinese approach to economic development was based primarily on mass ideological mobilization of the populace. The hope was to attain higher output and greater growth through the human efforts and ideological commitment of the Chinese people. During these periods, revolutionary values and attitudinal changes were emphasized at the expense of technological expertise. The motto of the workplace, "higher profits through greater study," meant study of the *Quo-*

tations from Chairman Mao, China's ideological primer. Since Mao's death in 1976, more moderate and less ideological methods have prevailed. At all times, however, the Chinese economy has emphasized both capital accumulation over consumption and state ownership of the means of production. Unlike the more centralized Soviet system, however, the Chinese have promoted a rather significant level of decentralized planning and local administration.

In the early 1960s, the Cuban economic system assumed several of the features of the Soviet model and blended them with a variety of mobilization campaigns. Like Mao, Castro relied heavily on ideological exhortations to motivate the populace. One campaign of particular significance was the Revolutionary Offensive of 1968 that had a close resemblance to the GPCR in China. But unlike China, centralization, state planning, and central budgetary control have been constant features of the Cuban economy.

After nearly two thirds of a century of socialism in the Soviet Union and one third of a century in other Communist Party states, the utopian socioeconomic state of Communism still remains an ideal. During the current stages of socialism, the leaders continue to experiment with different economic strategies and formulas. Let us now see where they stand.

## COMTEMPORARY ECONOMIC CAPABILITIES

The Marxist-Leninist states of the Second World vary markedly in their levels of production, total wealth, and resources. The most frequently employed index to measure these economic capabilities, GNP, shows that one of these states (the Soviet Union) has the second highest capabilities in the world, whereas another (its neighbor, Mongolia) ranks around 100 out of 150 countries. The East European countries tend to rank behind the highly developed Western countries of the First World but ahead of the less developed nations of the Third World. Laos and Cambodia (Kampuchea) rank among the lowest in the world.

Table 2.2 shows some of the diversity in economic capabilities among the states. The

[12]The Soviet leaders were worried by factors other than economic liberalization. There were fears, for example, concerning Western influence and involvement in Czechoslovakia and the possibility that the reforms would result in withdrawal from the Warsaw Treaty Organization (WTO) and COMECON pacts.

[13]The Warsaw Treaty was signed in 1955 by Albania, Bulgaria, the German Democratic Republic [GDR (East Germany)], Hungary, Poland, Romania, and the USSR as a response to the establishment of the North Atlantic Treaty Organization (NATO). Like NATO the treaty pledged mutual military assistance in the event of an attack on one of the signatories. The so-called Brezhnev Doctrine that grew out of the 1968 intervention in Czechoslovakia appeared to broaden the assistance to include perceived domestic threats to socialism.

Soviet Union has a GNP nearly three times that of its nearest competitor, China. This is particularly noteworthy when we realize that the USSR has a population less than one third that of the Chinese. The East European countries reflect two definite subgroups, one subgroup representing the northern states (Czechoslovakia, East Germany, and Poland) and the other subgroup representing the southern states (Bulgaria, Hungary, Romania, and Yugoslavia). Albania is far less developed than the rest of the states of southeastern Europe and assumes a position even below some Asian states.

Although economic capabilities vary broadly, it is reasonable to say that the postwar reconstruction efforts in most of the more established states have been generally successful. Torn and devastated by either the ravages of their revolutionary struggles or World War II, economic output had fallen sharply in many Eastern states; yet, most countries managed to stabilize their economies and undertake policies of economic recovery.[14]

Most evidence suggests, for example, that the Second World states have done quite well even when compared with their First World counterparts. When we compare the growth rates of the East European states with those from the West during the critical years of postwar development, we find generally higher growth rates in the East.[15] In fact, some of the GNPs (those of Romania and Yugoslavia) have been among the highest in the world. We should note that the impressive GNPs and growth rates can be attributed in large part to the decision to emphasize industrial instead of consumer-oriented development. This policy means the building of hydroelectric plants, steel mills, and heavy industries while de-emphasizing the light industry and manufacturing related to expansion of the consumer sector. Such an investment policy leads to major advancements in the overall output of goods and services and is clearly reflected in the GNP figures of the socialist states.

Other indicators point to advancements in the realm of industrial development. Historical experience indicates, for example, that industrialization and general socioeconomic development are typically accompanied by decreases in the agricultural work force. The rural-urban figures are now changing rapidly in socialist countries as peasants move from the countryside to assume jobs in the cities where they are likely to find employment in the growing number of factories. Overall, the changes since World War II have been most dramatic in Eastern Europe—whereas approximately 75 percent of the work force was involved in agriculture before the war (see Table 2.1), less than 50 percent now hold such occupations.

The growth in industrial capacities is also marked by an increase in energy consumption. On a per capita basis, Czechoslovakia and East Germany are among the top five energy consumers in the world. As Western experience has shown, energy sources will be increasingly valuable resources in the future. Some Communist countries are (comparatively speaking) quite wealthy in energy resources. Untapped oil and gas reserves in the USSR, Mongolia and China represent vast storehouses for the future although they may require Western technology to unlock them. Other countries, especially those of Eastern Europe, rely heavily on foreign sources of energy and have begun to feel the serious consequences of energy dependence.

Another key to future economic development involves scientific and technological capabilities. The socialist states have emphasized—with the exceptions of Maoist China and the Asian countries—the role of education and scientific progress in the development process, yet, they still lag behind the First World in these areas. Considerable investments have been made over the postwar years in scientific research institutes, institutions of higher education, and advanced technical schools. This emphasis has been particularly strong in the Soviet Union and the Eastern European states where great investments have been made in scientific education as well as in the importation of science and technology from abroad.

[14]The war-torn countries of Southeast Asia—Vietnam, Laos, and particularly Cambodia (Kampuchea)—are still facing severe economic problems.

[15]Taylor and Hudson, *op. cit.*, p. 306–311.

China's emphasis on scientific and technological development, on the other hand, has been less clear and somewhat cyclical. During Mao's rule and the GPCR, for example, many universities and schools were closed and study became synonymous with a careful reading of the ideological exhortations of the late Chairman Mao. While visiting a Chinese medical hospital during the GPCR, a Western observer asked some advanced medical students what books they used in preparing for the medical profession. All held out Chairman Mao's *Little Red Book* of ideological quotations. As the students' professor began to name some more conventional sources, he was quickly silenced by the students and told to refrain from questioning the advisability of mixing medicine and Maoism.

The Maoist emphasis on ideology did great damage to Chinese modernization and economic development. Members of the intelligentsia were sent to rural communes for physical labor and ideological study. The importance of science and technology to development was denied. Interestingly, Mao's successors appear to recognize the costs of the previous ideological campaigns and upheavals. During the current post-Mao period (which began in 1976), Chinese leaders are giving considerably more emphasis to the important role that science and technology can play in promoting national development. Stressing the four-modernizations—agriculture, industry, national defense, and science and technology—the leaders are encouraging the indigenous development and importation of scientific and technological expertise.

In the 1970s, most all countries of the Second World turned to the West for increased technological and scientific expertise. Permitted under the policy of détente, which relaxed tensions between the Communist and non-Communist world, the flow of technology into the socialist states grew significantly during the 1970s. The motives of the socialist states were clear. Party leaders hoped that the infusion of Western technology would obviate the need to undertake massive economic reforms required to salvage their sagging economic fortunes, and they hoped to avoid the decentralization of economic control that would challenge their monopoly of power. They also hoped that the importation of Western technology would promote industrial development and result in a saving of time and resources that the indigenous development of these capabilities would require. Although it is still too early to judge the long-term consequences of this policy, it appears to have boosted socialist capabilities in science and technology in several areas. For example, Western technology has made significant contributions to the Soviet automotive industry. In the 1970s, a number of Western nations, including the United States helped the Soviets build the largest truck factory in the world. The Italian automobile company, Fiat, also helped the Soviets build a massive passenger car factory. By 1980, the Chinese were entering into various forms of economic cooperation with the West to promote the four modernizations.

Even with the economic progress that most Second World states have experienced over the past few decades, the socialist economies confront a variety of pressing challenges. There are problems concerning the output and efficiency of collective farms, which remain less productive than private farms. The quality of industrial output is often substandard and consumer demands still go unmet. There are also problems of poor planning, waste, and inefficiency in all sectors of the economies. These and other problems have resulted in significant slowdowns in the economic growth of the socialist countries. Finally, there are the growing concerns with energy resources and how shrinking reserves and future shortages will affect economic growth. As we will see, these economic issues are important environmental forces that help determine the availability of certain values and their distribution in socialist societies.

## THE SOCIAL SETTING

Gross National Product per capita is sometimes used as one indicator of the social well-being of a population. In 1977, the GNP per capita (GNP divided by population) in the United States was $8743, whereas in China, it was only $378. Obviously, at least by this measure, the well-being of the average American citizen is considerably higher than that of the average Chinese.

One must be careful in interpreting GNP per capita figures, however, for a number of reasons. First the proportion of the GNP invested in the social and consumer realm may vary markedly from one country to another; second, the distribution of wealth from one individual to another or from one social group to another may differ considerably. In the Communist Party states considered here, however, these two factors are not of great importance because the amount of GNP expended in the social and consumer realms is relatively constant from one country to another, as is the level of income inequalities between individuals and groups within each country. For these reasons, the GNP per capita figures presented in Table 2.2 provide fairly useful comparative measures of at least one indicator of social welfare in the 16 states.

Impressions gained while traveling in these countries tend to reinforce the GNP per capita indicators. The traffic jams in Moscow, Prague, East Berlin, and Belgrade contrast markedly with the bicycle traffic in Hanoi and Beijing. It seems that almost everyone has a car in Yugoslavia, most are expecting to get one in Czechoslovakia and East Germany, and everyone hopes someday to get one in the USSR.

In addition to per capita contrasts, differences in consumer-oriented investment can result in considerable and obvious contrasts in the levels of consumption among the various socialist states. Although it has a GNP per capita below that of Bulgaria and Romania, for example, Yugoslavia exhibits higher consumption levels among its population. That is, athough living in a relatively less developed socialist state, Yugoslavs enjoy an unusually high level of consumerism. Cars, boats, vacation homes, and other items considered bourgeois luxuries in most socialist states have become commonplace within this particular country.[16] The Yugoslavs relatively high level of consumption is a result of their market-oriented economy and illustrates the impact that economic policies can have on the populace. The national Soviet basketball team was seen touring the shops of a Yugoslav city during their free time away from the European Championship Tournament. Their expressions of amazement at the variety and quality of

[16]In the early 1970s, however, Tito declared war on Yugoslav "millionaires" who had acquired seaside villas, large savings accounts abroad, and other material excesses accumulated under the liberal Yugoslav economic system.

East German cars cover this storage lot in Hungary. Although cars are the most desired consumer item in Eastern Europe and are theoretically available to everyone, high prices and long waiting lists discourage many buyers.

consumer items available was an accurate indicator of Yugoslavia's unique consumerism among the socialist states.

Compared to his Asian counterpart, particularly those in Southeast Asia, the average family in the Soviet Union leads a relatively comfortable life although there are few signs of luxury. One expert notes:

> Some people do have two or more dwellings, a large boat, or an invaluable collection of 18th century porcelain. But spectacular American-style consumption and accumulation patterns are virtually unknown.[17]

Visits to Soviet apartments found comfortable although small living quarters; relatively balanced diets, with meat often in short supply; and few collections of eighteenth-century porcelain. "We get by," workers will say, "but we can't imagine living with the excessive luxury you have in America." It is hard for the Soviet teenager to conceive of an American counterpart having his or her own car or a young married couple having their private home.[18]

Televisions, refrigerators, and automobiles are by now common features of many households in the European Communist Party states, but they are still seldom seen luxuries in their Asian counterparts. One observes television antennas throughout the East European countryside, including even in the most remote villages, but they are seldom found in China. In economic terms, the Asian socialist states and, perhaps, Cuba and Albania might more appropriately be classified with the Third World states. As one might suspect, the leaders of these states have been the most outspoken critics of the individualism and excessive materialism associated with Western and particularly American conceptions

[17]Mervyn Matthews, "Top Incomes in the USSR," in *Economic Aspects of Life in the USSR* (Brussels: NATO Information Service, 1975), p. 133.

[18]For vivid portrayals of the social and cultural setting in the Soviet Union, see Robert G. Kaiser, *Russia: The People and Power* (New York: Atheneum, 1976); and Hedrick Smith, *The Russians*, (New York: Ballantine, 1976).

For the Soviet Union, despite advances in the consumer realm, long lines to purchase the basic staples of daily life are not uncommon. Here, women in Moscow wait to buy bread in the GUM department store on Red Square across from the Kremlin.

of well-being. Although we tend to emphasize private accumulation of goods and services, these Communist Party states consider well-being a public good entitled by all. As we note later, there is considerable difference of opinion on this question among the Communist Party states—say, between China and Yugoslavia—differences clearly reflected in the social milieus of the countries.

Although consumerism is much higher in many other parts of the world and particularly in Western Europe and North America, social services such as health care and education are impressive features of the social setting in Marxist-Leninist states. When examining overall socio-economic standing based on GNP per capita, education, and health indicators, most Communist Party states rank reasonably well compared with the rest of the world (see Table 2.2). The East Germans rank 14, the Soviets 24, and the Chinese 82 out of 140 nations. The abysmal rankings of the Cambodians (Kampucheans), Laotians, and Vietnamese call attention to the perilous socioeconomic conditions in Southeast Asia. Now, let us examine how certain ideological principles influence the distribution of wealth in Marxist-Leninist systems.

## SOCIALISM AND EQUALITY

In the *Communist Manifesto*, Karl Marx and Friedrich Engels wrote: "The history of all hitherto existing society is the history of class struggles." According to their theory, modern industrial society had given birth to the proletariat and bourgeoisie, the two antagonistic classes of the capitalist stage of development. With the establishment of Communism, a new historical epoch was to occur. This socio-economic system was to be free of classes and exploitation and based on the principles of social equality.

The avenue leading to Communism, said Marx and Engels, leads through the socioeconomic stage of socialism in which property is made public and private ownership abolished. According to Marxist theory, private property is the force that divides people during the capitalist stage of development. If you forbid private prop-

erty, you dissolve the basis for class antagonism.

In the Marxist-Leninist states, the ruling Communist parties moved, sometimes quickly and at other times more gradually, to nationalize private property and place power, at least theoretically, in the hands of a proletarian dictatorship. Although the dissolution of private property was more gradual in some states, such as in China where Mao wanted to use the capitalists and avoid class warfare, or incomplete, as in some East European societies where small private farms and businesses still exist, large holdings of private property were outlawed and transferred to collective social or state ownership. Under socialism the proletarian dictatorship was to be a temporary arrangement preceding Communism, the idealized classless society. The basic question concerning this theory and the hypothesized developments involves their validity. Would socialism necessarily lead to equality? Would class boundaries and distinctions dissolve under Communist Party rule? Would this lead to the development of the classless community of peoples envisioned under Communism?

The experience of the Communist Party states suggests that, although inequalities have been radically reduced, development of a classless society under socialism is not, at least in the short run, a certainty. There are a number of forces making the transition difficult, if not impossible, and these involve some central features of an industrializing society. Most social theorists maintain that a division of labor is a necessary prerequisite to or at least a component of industrialization. Division of labor refers to the structure of jobs and the specialization of occupational skills most likely to achieve optimal industrial development. For example, an industrializing society requires engineers, planners, and workers; these occupations vary in terms of training and skills. Because some occupations are more necessary than others, additional rewards may have to be attached to them to attract people into training for them. As we have noted, the guiding principle of socialism is "from each according to his abilities to each according to his contribution"; therefore, those occupations that contribute more important skills receive greater rewards. All the countries we are studying have adopted this philosophy of a differentiated reward system during their present socialist phases of development. The Communist ideal of "from each according to his abilities, to each according to his needs" still remains remote.

Although Vladimir Ilyich Lenin and the Bolsheviks initially instituted a policy of wage leveling, they soon opted for a system providing incentives in the form of rather sizable wage differentials. Through the 1930s and 1940s, Stalin was quite willing to rationalize inequality in wages as a necessary incentive to attract workers into desired occupations. Soviet industrialization during this phase of development required skilled workers, planners, and engineers as well as clerical and administrative personnel. These and other occupations provided crucial functions required of an industrializing society; they represented the division of labor that characterize all modernizing societies. Although Nikita S. Khrushchev launched a campaign in the 1950s to reduce these wage differentials, they were never eliminated and remain in the USSR today.[19] Table 2.3 indicates the differentials between some selected occupations in the USSR and four East European countries. Using worker salaries as a base unit (100), the data indicate that although pay generally became more egalitarian between 1960 and 1973, particularly in the USSR, significant differences according to occupation still remained.

It is easy to see why a growing specialization and division of labor has made the establishment of a classless society difficult. When you have a relationship between skills and occupations as well as considerable differences between the highest and lowest paid workers, you encounter strong forces encouraging the formation of classes. Spokespersons of the socialist states would refute this argument by noting that al-

TABLE 2.3   Average Pay by Occupational Category[a]

|  | 1960 | 1973 |
| --- | --- | --- |
| *Bulgaria* | | |
| Intelligentsia | 142.1 | 132.1 |
| Routine nonmanual | 93.8 | 95.5 |
| Worker | 100.0 | 100.0 |
| Peasant | 92.1 | 91.5 |
| *Czechoslovakia* | | |
| Intelligentsia | 116.8 | 120.4 |
| Routine nonmanual | 77.0 | 81.3 |
| Worker | 100.0 | 100.0 |
| Peasant | 79.2 | 98.1 |
| *Hungary* | | |
| Intelligentsia | 157.2 | 142.4 |
| Routine nonmanual | 94.8 | 92.4 |
| Worker | 100.0 | 100.0 |
| Peasant | na[b] | 94.1 |
| *Poland* | | |
| Intelligentsia | 156.7 | 144.3 |
| Routine nonmanual | 105.1 | 100.1 |
| Worker | 100.0 | 100.0 |
| Peasant | na[b] | 77.5 |
| *USSR* | | |
| Intelligentsia | 150.9 | 134.1 |
| Routine nonmanual | 82.1 | 84.5 |
| Worker | 100.0 | 100.0 |
| Peasant | 57.7 | 76.5 |

[a]Intelligentsia, routine nonmanuals, and workers (all in state industry) and peasants (workers in state/socialist agriculture).

[b]Not available.

SOURCE: Adapted from Walter D. Connor, *Socialism, Politics, and Equality: Hierarchy and Change in Eastern Europe and the USSR* (New York: Columbia University Press, 1979), p. 231.

though their societies do exhibit occupational and wage differences between individuals and groups, they do not represent the traditional classes of earlier forms of society. In a capitalist society, they would argue, the *bourgeoisie* control and exploit the working class. In earlier societies, the nature of class differences led to an inevitable class struggle—"the history of all hitherto existing society." Therefore, Marxists contend that although wage and status differences may exist in their societies and may lead to a system of social stratification, they will not result in the social classes and resultant conflict

[19]Wage differentials remain a characteristic of all socialist societies, even within the most allegedly egalitarian, the Chinese. For a study of the use of wages to motivate the industrial work force in China, see Carl Riskin, "Workers Incentives in Chinese Industry," in U.S. Congress, Joint Economic Committee, *China: A Reassessment of the Economy* (Washington, D. C.: U.S. Government Printing Office, 1975).

of old. Although the question is debatable, we can at least conclude that social divisions are present in Communist societies and that they do have some of the characteristics of social classes under capitalism.[20]

Another factor that works to deter the development of a classless society is the old value structures that are holdovers from the pre-socialist societies in each country. Throughout history, attitudes and values associated with certain occupations and pursuits tended to divide people. Income, education, and occupation, among other factors, placed some individuals in more privileged groups than others. The landed gentry in China and the old aristocracy and land-holding classes in Europe represented privileged groups that became part of the new Communist Party societies. The societal values that supported and rationalized these traditional divisions were deeply imbedded in the value structure of the people. The mere event of a proletarian revolution did little to wipe away the status and class consciousness of the past. Values concerning privileges and perquisites are displayed constantly in contemporary Soviet society. The common bureaucrats are concerned with proper dress and social grace; they would never want to be mistaken for peasants from the village. Marriages among different groups—for example, the daughter of an intellectual with the son of an industrial worker—are uncommon. It is often beneath the dignity of one of a more privileged tradition to associate with those of a working-class background. Although the egalitarianism of the current ideology is intended to combat such pre-socialist values, particularistic value systems still pervade the societies of the Communist Party states.

Before we can develop a better understanding of the ways in which these social distinctions affect the political process, we should get a fuller picture of their presence and meaning in the Communist Party states of the contemporary world.

## SOCIAL STRATIFICATION

The division of society into a hierarchy of strata partly results from the political process: Who gets what, when, and how? In most societies, different strata, or classes, are distinguished by unequal shares of the values received by individuals and groups. The landed gentry of traditional China, for example, enjoyed greater respect, well-being, enlightenment, and power than did the peasantry; the bourgeoisie in tsarist Russia had a disproportionate share of these values when compared with the proletariat. Although the ideology of Communism is based on the principle of equality, contemporary socialist societies also have strata possessing a disproportionate share of the values their citizens deem important. Most of the states have undergone campaigns where concerted efforts were made to abolish differences of this sort. In the immediate postrevolutionary years in Russia, for example, the Bolsheviks abolished all official ranks and titles as well as such preferential treatment as different class accommodations in rail coaches and public facilities. Although now changed, before Mao's death all ranks in the People's Libertion Army (PLA) were abolished, thus, precluding any outward distinction between the lowest ranking foot soldier and the highest ranking officer. Castro has gone into the sugarcane fields to labor among the workers. But, whereas serious efforts have been made to promote equality, various forces continue to create inequality and stratification in these societies.

Occupational and income differences are among the primary attributes associated with social stratification in contemporary socialist societies. A top ranking engineer or a dean in a university are much more likely to have a disproportionate share of respect, well-being, enlightenment, and power than a blue-collar worker. The official ideology maintains that all occupational roles contribute equally to the building of socialism, but some are considerably more valued than others. A nuclear physicist at Moscow

[20]For a revealing review of the issue of classes in post-Mao China, see "On Class and Class Struggle," *Beijing Review, 23* (20, 22, 25) (1980), pp. 24–26, 24–26, 13–16 respectively. With the change to the Pinyin system in 1979, *Peking Review* became *Beijing Review*. Libraries catalog the periodical under the former title for issues before 1979 and under the latter for issues after that year.

State University, an engineer in Poland, and the director of a thriving economic enterprise in Yugoslavia command a higher income and more respect than rank-and-file workers. In addition, their opportunities for attaining the values associated with enlightenment are greater, as are their opportunities for achieving a preferred state of well-being and political power.

Although it is rather dated now, a classic and still accurate study based on written questionnaires from 2146 former Soviet citizens shows how occupations are related to such values in Soviet society.[21] The study ranks 13 occupational groups on the basis of the respondents' evaluations of the occupations in terms of five characteristics (general desirability, material position, personal satisfaction, safety, and popular support). Surprisingly, the study shows an occupational hierarchy in the Soviet Union that corresponds very closely with that of Western societies, including the United States. Doctors rank first in terms of general desirability and popular respect, for example, and workers rank last. In fact, all professional occupations, such as engineers and accountants, rank considerably higher than agricultural or rank-and-file workers. This interesting finding, taken along with similar research conducted in other countries as well, points to a general pattern of stratification in industrializing Communist societies.[22] Although the proletarian revolution was intended to establish a workers' state, blue-collar occupations under socialism still command considerably less respect than professional and white-collar positions.

As a result of such value systems, families encourage their children to go to the universities and prepare for careers that will bring greater respect, material wealth, and personal satisfaction. Although the official ideology and propaganda attempt to emphasize the importance of working-class occupations in building socialism, a certain stigma is still attached to them. As in

the West, an upwardly mobile, achievement-oriented citizen does not aspire to a career on the collective farm or in the factory. Like his or her Western counterpart, the citizen tends to dream of a career in law, medicine, science, or some other professional line of work. Students in the Soviet Union and Eastern Europe seem every bit as achievement oriented as students in the United States. They value university study and strive to excel because a diploma is often a necessary condition for a desirable occupation.

Joining the Communist Party is also a key to advancement in these societies. Nonconformists sitting in university coffee houses can be heard ridiculing classmates who are particularly achievement oriented and who joined the party in order to climb the ladder of social and economic success. Being a party member and becoming part of the establishment usually means opening doors for future employment and advancement that are often closed to the equally qualified, but less conforming citizens.

Although those of us in the West sometimes equate socialism with welfarism, Communist Party states have tended to abide by the principle: "He who does not work, neither shall he eat." In most states, health and social services are provided through the workplace. For one to eat and enjoy medical care and other social services, one must be gainfully employed. This means that all employed persons are guaranteed a minimal level of health and social welfare. This system is not followed for reasons of control or coercion but rather for administrative convenience. For those who are retired or unable to work, the state provides at least a subsistence standard of living. At the same time, if one has the financial resources, irrespective of whether or not one is employed, he or she can privately buy higher quality care. Paying an extra fee for a choice of medical doctors or simply buying private medical care from a moonlighting physician are common practices in most all socialist states.

The type of employment is of considerable importance in determining the size of one's personal income. General Secretary Leonid I. Brezhnev is rumored to make approximately 900 rubles a month, whereas an average agricultural

---

[21]Peter H. Rossi and Alex Inkeles, "Multidimensional Ratings of Occupations," *Sociometry*, 20 (3) (1957), p. 247.

[22]Walter D. Connor, *Socialism, Politics, and Equality: Hierarchy and Change in Eastern Europe and the USSR* (New York: Columbia University Press, 1979).

worker makes near 100 rubles. A director of a research institute will make between 500 to 700 rubles, whereas an industrial worker will take home around 150 rubles a month (1 ruble equals approximately $1.50).[23] Of course, we must remember that party leaders and other officials enjoy important perquisites in addition to their incomes. Shopping in exclusive stores set aside for party leaders only, superior medical care and attention, personal attendants, chauffeurs, and so forth, are examples of the special privileges they enjoy. Yet, evidence suggests that retiring leaders have seldom accumulated vast private holdings and resources while in power. Most leaders retire to a comfortable apartment or *dacha* ("country villa") on a healthy pension, but only a few (e.g., Josip Broz Tito) enjoy luxury or opulent income.[24]

The gap between the highest and lowest paid occupations tends to be smaller in Communist Party than in non-Communist states, and it is unusual for anyone to accumulate great wealth, yet, the hierarchy is still there. In the Soviet Union and East European states, the difference between a factory director and a skilled worker may average around 5 to 1. In China, Cuba, and the Asian states the range tends to be somewhat less.

The distinguished American sociologist, Gerhard Lenski, notes that the range of salaries and incomes seems generally to have been reduced in Marxist societies to levels well below those in most comparable non-Marxist societies.[25] His research indicates a ratio of 50 to 1 between top salaries and the minimum wage in the USSR in the 1970s, 40 to 1 in China prior to Mao's death, and 7.3 to 1 in Cuba. By contrast, the corresponding ratio in the United States in re-

cent years has been approximately 300 to 1. As Lenski cautions, these figures should not be taken at face value because they do not provide a direct measure of differentials in living standards. However, Lenski concludes that the Marxist experiments have, in fact, resulted in the reduction of inequalities in income and living standards in Communist societies. At the same time, he calls attention to a number of Marxist failures, including (1) the persistence of very high levels of political inequality, (2) the persistence of worker alienation, (3) the persistence of sex inequalities, (4) the persistence of rural-urban inequalities, and (5) the failure of these Marxist societies to give birth to the new socialist man.[26]

Urban and rural distinctions contribute to a stratified society. The differences between the modern pulsating life in Moscow, Warsaw, or Belgrade compared with the backward peasant life of the villages is extreme. Urbanization has been a major agent of social change and, in some respects, has had a leveling effect on a whole host of social differences. The common experiences of city life have softened some occupational and cultural differences, whereas life in the agricultural areas remains parochial and provincial. The social differences between the typical college student in New York City and Moscow are considerable but tend to be no greater than those between the Russian student in that city and his same-age counterpart in a remote Siberian village.

Communists stood and fought for the emancipation of sexes as well as workers. In some respects, however, sex also tends to stratify societies within the Communist world because women predominate in many of the unskilled "physical" professions (see Table 2.4) Unlike many First and Third World societies, women in socialist states represent an extremely large and important sector of the total workforce. And while women predominate in many of the unskilled, "physical" occupations, they also represent an important sector of the work force in many professional occupations. Table 2.5 shows that women predominate in such "mental" oc-

[23]See Mathews, *op. cit.*, pp. 135–139.

[24]There are some exceptions to this general rule. President Tito of Yugoslavia, for example, was known to possess and enjoy the excessive luxuries of many villas, a private island retreat in the Adriatic Sea, numerous cars, boats, and so forth. Former President Richard M. Nixon's reminiscences of General Secretary Brezhnev also draw attention to Brezhnev's appreciation for material goods, notably expensive automobiles.

[25]Gerhard Lenski, "Marxist Experiments in Destratification: An Appraisal," *Social Forces, 57* (2) (1978), pp. 370–371.

[26]*Ibid.*, pp. 371–376.

**TABLE 2.4** "Physical" Occupations with Unexpectedly High Numbers and Percentages of Women in the USSR

| Occupations | Number of Women | Percentage of Women |
|---|---|---|
| Construction: painters and plasterers | 953,000 | 70% |
| Chemical workers | 392,000 | 68 |
| Printing workers | 149,000 | 72 |
| Machine building: forge and press operators | 120,000 | 66 |
| Machine building: reelers and winders | 80,000 | 77 |
| Leather workers | 80,000 | 68 |
| Paper and boxboard workers | 57,000 | 65 |
| Machine building: galvinizers | 50,000 | 68 |
| Machine building: insulator and cable workers | 38,000 | 70 |
| Streetcar, trollybus, and bus drivers | 38,000 | 54 |

SOURCE: Adapted from *Itogi vsesoyuznoi perepisi naseleniya 1970 goda, tom 6,* (Moscow: 1973), pp. 165–169.

cupations as economic planners, doctors, and dentists.

The greatest sex discrimination in the Soviet Union, and in most other socialist states as well, is in the area of politics. One expert notes that although there is a relatively high proportion of women in ceremonial political roles, there is a very small percentage in significant positions of real power in either the party or government.[27] Underrepresentation of women is also evident for some nonpolitical directing posts, such as in hospitals, factories, and in the field of higher education. Another interesting and more subtle form of discrimination seems to take place in the home. After putting in a full day as a machine builder, bus driver, or economic planner, women typically return home to assume all the household responsibilities. Perhaps to a greater extent than in the West, Soviet and East European men do little to share in the burdens of housework. Social discrimination against women, deeply imbedded in the traditional value structures of the

cultures, will have to be further eradicated before a genuine equality of sexes can be achieved.[28]

One of the features that strikes Westerners most as they travel to socialist states concerns the contrasts in the material standards of the people. Some are dressed in the finest tailored suits and are motored around the cities in sleek Mercedes; others wear drab work clothes as they walk or peddle by bicycle to their workplace in the factory. Some eat regularly at posh cosmopolitan restaurants, whereas still others are unable to purchase the basic cuts of meat at the neighborhood market. The leaders of these states are certainly aware of such inequalities, but they tend to view them as necessary evils at their country's particular stages of socioeconomic development. They hope that development will blur the distinctions between job types and reduce differences in financial rewards, leading to greater equality in life styles. Some states are indeed marked by more extreme inequalities than others. Chinese society exhibits much greater social equality than the East European states. At the same time, substantial income differentials persist in all of them.

We should now be aware that standards of living and the systems of social stratification with which they are associated vary considerably among the socialist states comprising the Second World. Although some of these differences can be attributed to political choices, the most important determinants appear to be environmental. The country's level of socioeconomic development is perhaps the primary factor determining who gets what in the socialist states. Nobody gets very much in China simply because there is not very much to pass around. The average citizen gets a little more in the Soviet Union, primarily because the state is at a somewhat more advanced economic level. Then, the average citizen in Leningrad or Moscow enjoys a higher standard of living than his or her counterpart in the less developed republic of Kazakhstan largely owing to the fact that the socioeconomic

[27]Norton Dodge, "The Role of Women in the Soviet Economy," in *Economic Aspects of Life in the USSR, op. cit.,* pp. 186–188.

[28]See Barbara Wolfe Jancar, *Women Under Communism* (Baltimore: Johns Hopkins University Press, 1978); and Gail Warshofsky Lapidus, *Women in Soviet Society* (Berkeley: University of California Press, 1978).

**TABLE 2.5** "Mental" Occupations with Unusually High Numbers and Percentages of Women in USSR

| Occupations | Number of Women | Percentages of Women |
|---|---|---|
| Planning and record-keeping personnel: | | |
|     Economists, planners | 565,000 | 82% |
|     Inspectors, controllers, checkers | 385,000 | 68 |
| Medical personnel: | | |
|     Physicians | 417,000 | 74 |
|     Dentists | 48,000 | 77 |
|     Chief physicians and other heads of public health institutions | 32,000 | 53 |
| Scientific personnel, teachers, and training personnel: | | |
|     Heads of scientific research institutes and organizations, scientific personnel (except teachers in higher educational institutions) | 182,000 | 40 |
|     Teachers in higher education | 130,000 | 43 |

SOURCE: Adapted from *Itogi vsesoyuznoi perepisi naseleniya 1970 goda, tom 6,* (Moscow: 1973), pp. 165–169.

capabilities of the Russian Soviet Federated Socialist Republic (RSFSR) are higher than those in Kazakhstan.

Yet, there are political choices that account for some of the differences in the values people enjoy. The Soviet leaders could give all of the people more if they decided to lower their investments in the industrial sector or in defense and increase them in the consumer sector. Also, the Soviet Government could see that the citizens of Kazakhstan got the same as their counterparts in the Russian Republic if it decided to subsidize more heavily the former republic with income from the more highly developed republics. In addition, Soviet decision makers could see that a street sweeper would earn the same income as a

Chinese women participate actively in the building of China. They administer hospital and scientific institutes, shoot rifles in the People's Militia, and harvest grain on a people's commune as shown above.

nuclear physicist if they decided to level all income inequalities in the Soviet state. These are the perplexing questions and choices of politics. Therefore, the social environment in which the citizen resides largely determines the level of welfare and human dignity; the political choices of the decision maker also have an effect in determining the total picture. Some of the differences outlined above are the products of these choices, a topic to which we return in much greater detail in Chapters Six and Seven.

## SOCIAL MOBILITY

It is common knowledge that inequalities in social characteristics, such as status and income do exist in the Communist Party states, yet, equality (or inequality) of opportunity is another question. That is, although some theorists say that perfect social equality is both impossible and undesirable in modern society, equality of opportunity is usually considered a desired feature of the just political system. Little is generally said about this notion in socialist states because general equality is still considered theoretically synonymous with socialism.

As in other parts of the world, this intention is easier said than done. General social laws deeply ingrained in society place those on top—that is, those with higher levels of status, income, and education—in privileged positions vis-à-vis those at the bottom of the social hierarchy. The son or daughter of a Soviet engineer or high Communist Party official may have certain opportunities that result from their social circumstances and that are not available to the children of workers and peasants. The individual in a more privileged position may have connections that promise easier entrance into the university, the opportunity to travel and study abroad, a highly desired job, or other privileges that are not open to the rank-and-file citizen. These facts result from social conditions or laws that tend to transcend ideology and government action and that seem to be at work in all states throughout the world. To counteract the special opportunities that are open to more privileged

sectors of socialist society, special government actions are necessary.

All Communist Party states have acted to establish equality of opportunity in their societies. These actions have taken a number of different forms and are discussed in considerable detail in subsequent sections of this book. We will see that most of them involve the provision of equal educational and employment opportunities. Table 2.6 shows, relatively, the high level of educational advancement in the European Communist states. Enrollment in education is generally high, as are levels of literacy. The relatively low levels of educational development in the Asian states result from their less developed socioeconomic positions and, in the case of Vietnam, Cambodia (Kampuchea), and Laos, the political conflict and warfare that has plagued Southeast Asia for decades. If these countries stabilize, they are likely to improve their performance in the educational sector as well.

Soviet leaders are particularly proud of and call attention to their general success in opening up what, during the tsarist years, was a relatively closed social hierarchy. Observers traveling with Khrushchev during one of his trips to the United States tell how he and a Hollywood movie millionaire traded rags-to-riches stories. As the Hollywood magnate boasted of his Horatio Alger story and extolled the virtues of the "land of opportunity" in America, Khrushchev was not about to be outdone. Where else but in the USSR, he countered, could a miner of peasant origins become the leader of one of the strongest nations on the face of the earth.[29]

Although it varies somewhat by country, a careful review of the backgrounds of Communist Party officials, dentists, doctors, lawyers, and other professionals will show many to be of humble social and economic backgrounds. This phenomenon is particularly true regarding party officials because those of humble socioeconomic origin are naturally more attracted to the

[29]For an interesting comparison of John F. Kennedy and Khrushchev's backgrounds and ascents to power, see Zbigniew K. Brzezinski and Samuel P. Huntington, *Political Power: USA/USSR* (New York: Viking, 1963), pp. 129–190, 235–268.

**TABLE 2.6**   Demographic Indicators in Contemporary Communist Party States

| Country | Population | | | Area | | Education | |
|---|---|---|---|---|---|---|---|
| | In 1000s | Percent Urban | Growth Rate[a] | 1000²km | Density per 1000²km | Literacy | Percent of School-age Children in School |
| Albania | 2,513 | 34% | 266 | 29 | 87 | 75% | 64% |
| Bulgaria | 8,804 | 60 | 47 | 111 | 79 | 95 | 57 |
| Cambodia | 7,748 | 12 | 289 | 181 | 43 | 48 | na[b] |
| China | 987,406 | 26 | 163 | 9,597 | 103 | 70 | 65 |
| Cuba | 9,597 | 64 | 135 | 115 | 83 | 94 | 75 |
| Czechoslovakia | 15,031 | 67 | 78 | 128 | 117 | 99 | 60 |
| East Germany | 16,765 | 76 | −111 | 108 | 155 | 99 | 66 |
| Hungary | 10,648 | 52 | 65 | 93 | 114 | 98 | 55 |
| Laos | 3,365 | 15 | 189 | 237 | 14 | 28 | 35 |
| Mongolia | 1,533 | 47 | 295 | 1,565 | 1 | 95 | 56 |
| North Korea | 17,571 | 33 | 258 | 121 | 145 | 85 | 61 |
| Poland | 34,595 | 57 | 98 | 313 | 111 | 98 | 54 |
| Romania | 21,658 | 48 | 97 | 238 | 91 | 98 | 64 |
| Soviet Union | 258,932 | 62 | 90 | 22,402 | 12 | 99 | 58 |
| Vietnam | 49,922 | 19 | 22 | 330 | 151 | 75 | 62 |
| Yugoslavia | 21,775 | 39 | 95 | 256 | 85 | 85 | 60 |
| USA[c] | 216,880 | 74 | 75 | 9,363 | 23 | 99 | 85 |

[a]Per 10,000 population. These growth-rate figures are from Arthur S. Banks, ed., *Political Handbook of the World: 1980* (New York: McGraw-Hill, 1980), pp. 612–614.

[b]Not available.

[c]The USA is included for comparative purposes.

SOURCE: Adapted from Ruth Leger Sivard, *World Military and Social Expenditures, 1980* (Leesburg, Va.: World Priorities, 1980), pp. 21–29.

ideology of Communism. Communist doctrine attracts such individuals because it explains the perceived injustices in their backgrounds and how they can be improved under socialism.

The two forces that have done the most to enhance the opportunities for social mobility in the Second World Communist-run states are ideology and rapid socioeconomic change. The ideology of socialism has a strong egalitarian base and, although perfect equality is impossible, socialist elites have felt some responsibility in protecting equal opportunity. Gaps have often existed between the ideal and the reality, yet, the principle of equality has motivated all governments to promote the ideal of equality and the opportunities for upward mobility.

The rapid pace of socioeconomic change that has characterized the Second World states is the second force that has also promoted social mobility and the value of equal opportunity. During phases of rapid industrialization and growth and the increasing need for the new training and skills they bring, great opportunities are open to the populace. The Soviet need for construction engineers in the 1930s and 1940s and their need for nuclear physicists in the 1970s provided great opportunities for personal advancement, regardless of one's social background. Educational opportunities combined with new occupational opportunities open many doors to an upwardly mobile society.

In summary, the social consequences of modernization and industrialization, including social stratification, inequalities, and mobility, are of great importance to the building of Communism. If stratification and inequalities are unavoidable outcomes of socialist modernization and industrialization, then, it may be impossible to attain the Communist ideal of genuine equality. Like the economic forces described earlier, these social forces are part of the environment impacting on the policy process in socialist states.

## DEMOGRAPHIC CHARACTERISTICS

Close to one third of the world's population lives in the 16 Communist-ruled states. Roughly a quarter of the world's population (close to 1 billion) lives in China, making it by a large margin the world's most populous state. Ranking behind China and India, the Soviet Union is the world's third most populous state. The remainder of the Communist Party states are of average population size, with three—Albania, Laos, and Mongolia—ranking among the world's smallest populations (see Table 2.6).

Despite certain benefits, a large population also presents definite hardships. The problems of food and living space present particular difficulties for China where over 90 percent of the population is concentrated on one-sixth of the land and less than 20 percent of the land is agriculturally productive. Its cultivated land is only 70 percent that of the United States, which has about one fourth of China's population. Feeding the immense population in China has been a difficult task through the centuries and still represents a problem not fully resolved. The Soviet Union also has difficulty in feeding its large population and has had to rely on foreign countries to survive. American shipments of grain in the 1970s helped the Soviet people avoid severe shortages in basic foodstuffs. Despite government efforts and exhortations, Soviet and Chinese agriculture has not been productive when compared to the West and has suffered from a shortage of arable land and inefficient production methods.

The area of a country and the resources on which its economic might is based have important effects on political behavior. The Soviet Union is the world's largest state with a land area of approximately 22.4 million square kilometers. The USSR has approximately the same area as the United States and the 14 states of the NATO Alliance put together. Slightly larger than the

United States is China, the world's third largest state (Canada is second). The next largest, Communist state, Mongolia, has the smallest population of all socialist states and the lowest population density of any state in the entire world. With 1 person per square kilometer in Mongolia, compared to 155 in East Germany, the Mongolian steppes provide plenty of space for future expansion.[30]

Land area and population size are important attributes in the world of international politics. If a country has a labor shortage (such as East Germany) or a surplus (such as Yugoslavia) or food shortages (such as China and the Soviet Union) or energy shortages (such as much of Eastern Europe), it is forced to enter into dependency relationships with other countries. Although small states are sometimes able to defy larger states, as Albania and Yugoslavia have defied the Soviet Union, political power and international relations are closely associated with the population and physical size of states. Smaller, weaker states without abundant resources are naturally dependent on states who can ensure their security and meet their resource needs.

The contemporary settings in Communist Party societies are also very much affected by the sociocultural features of nationality and ethnicity. In the *Communist Manifesto*, Marx and Engels predicted that nationality was a dying force in the contemporary world. They believed that with the increasing freedom of commerce in the international market and in the growing uniformity of production and conditions of life, national differences would dissolve; furthermore, as exploitation and antagonism between classes under socialism began to cease, so, too, would hostility among nations. As national differences began to disappear, (according to Marx and Engels), we would witness the development of internationalism within the socialist world. In this phase of historical development, workers of

---

[30]With its small land area, sizable population, and high level of industrialization, East Germany is quickly depleting its natural resources. The contrasting conditions in Mongolia provide many opportunities for future growth and development. The Mongolian birthrate, among the highest in the world, will provide an expanding work force for this process of socioeconomic expansion.

the world would be united by the bonds of socialist or proletarian internationalism and the forces of nationalism and ethnocentrism would cease to exist.

As we witness international politics in the contemporary world, we can see that Marx and Engels underestimated the power of nationalism. Nationality, or nationhood, is a strong and enduring sociocultural force that grows out of the history, geography, language, and culture of groups of people. As we enter the last few decades of the twentieth century, we seem to be witnessing a growth rather than a decline in nationalism, which has a definite effect on world politics. The continuing Sino-Soviet conflict, the tension among nations in the Soviet bloc,[31] and the animosity that at times surfaces among national and ethnic groups within socialist states point to the importance of the idea of ethnicity and nationhood in the international arena today.

Although we usually refer to the "nations" of the Communist world, strictly speaking, this is misleading. Some of the socialist states are composed of many distinct nationalities, each with its own language, customs, and sense of the past. Yugoslavia, for example, is a multinational state comprised of five South Slavic nationalities —Croats, Macedonians, Montenegrins, Serbs, and Slovenes—as well as other national and ethnic groups. Tending to be concentrated in rather homogeneous regions and constitutionally guaranteed a high level of autonomy within the federated Yugoslav system, these groups maintain a strong sense of individual identity.[32]

The Soviet Union is also a multinational state and includes such nationalities as Russians, Ukrainians, Armenians, Georgians, Latvians, Tatars, a variety of Asian nationalities, and many, many others. There are over a 100 different national and ethnic groups in the Soviet Union. Although Russian, the official language of the state, tends to be spoken by most members of all groups, Soviet street corners and buses are still the sight of a rich mix of languages which represent many distant points in Europe and Asia.

The largest Soviet nationality by far is Russian, which, according to the 1971 census, comprised just over half of the total population. The bulk of these Russians reside in the RSFSR, which stretches from Moscow and Leningrad eastward to the Pacific (see the map of the USSR). This one republic in the Soviet Union has almost twice the area of the United States. The Russian Republic contains 16 autonomous republics, 5 autonomous regions, 10 national areas, and represents a heterogeneous multinational mosaic of groups. The next largest Soviet nationalities are the Ukrainians, who reside primarily in the Ukrainian Soviet Socialist Republic, and the Uzbeks, who inhabit the Uzbek Soviet Socialist Republic. The fourth largest are the Byelorussians, or White Russians, and they, too, have a republic within which members of their nationality predominate.

Administratively, the Soviet leaders designed a federal political arrangement to reflect the extreme diversity in the society. This federal structure divides the Soviet state into 15 union republics, which in some cases contain autonomous republics, autonomous regions, and autonomous areas. The 15 union republics and the autonomous republics are indicated on the map. The units coincide with the complex array of national and ethnic groups in the state and vary in status according to the size and strength of the groups. The powers of the various units are described in detail in the Soviet Constitution.[33]

Demographic changes in the USSR are of considerable political importance. The Muslim Turkic nationalities of Central Asia, Kazakhstan, and the Azerbaidzhan Republic are growing at a much faster rate than such western nationalities as the Russians and Ukrainians. The

[31]The term, Soviet bloc is often used to refer to the member nations of the WTO. Over the years, there have been a number of national conflicts among these nations, the major ones being Hungary in 1956, Czechoslovakia in 1968, and Poland in 1981.

[32]For a superb analysis of the role of nationality in Yugoslav politics, see Paul Shoup, *Communism and the Yugoslav National Question* (New York: Columbia University Press, 1968).

[33]For a description of the ethnonational setting in the USSR and Soviet nationality policy, see Edward Allworth, ed., *Soviet Nationality Problems* (New York: Columbia University Press, 1971).

# EASTERN EUROPE

*The Eight Communist States*

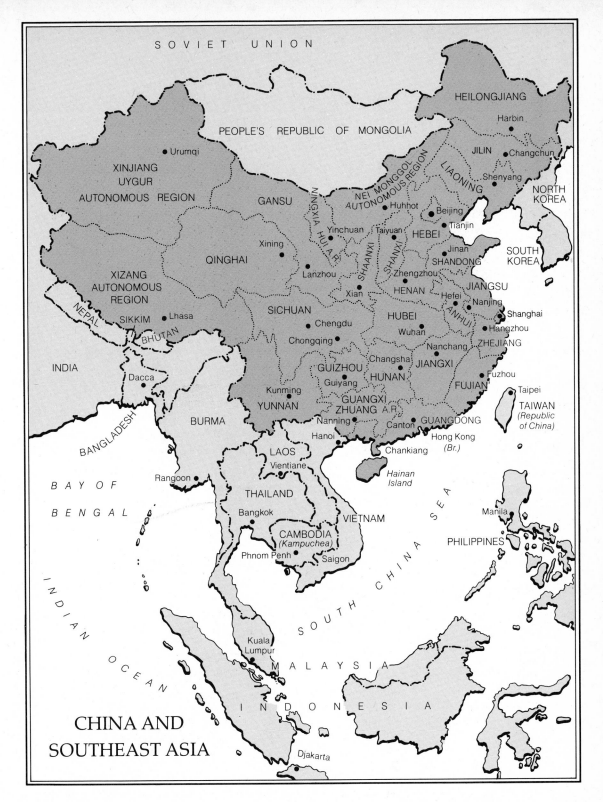

SOVIET UNION

HEILONGJIANG

Harbin

PEOPLE'S REPUBLIC OF MONGOLIA

JILIN

Changchun

• Urumqi

XINJIANG
UYGUR
AUTONOMOUS REGION

GANSU

NINGXIA HUI A.R.

NEI MONGGOL
AUTONOMOUS REGION

LIAONING

Shenyang

NORTH
KOREA

Huhhot

Beijing

Tianjin

Yinchuan

Taiyuan

HEBEI

Xining

SHAANXI

SHANXI

Jinan

SHANDONG

SOUTH
KOREA

QINGHAI

Lanzhou

Zhengzhou

JIANGSU

HENAN

Hefei

Nanjing

XIZANG
AUTONOMOUS
REGION

Xian

ANHUI

Shanghai

SICHUAN

HUBEI

Hangzhou

NEPAL

SIKKIM

Lhasa

Chengdu

Wuhan

ZHEJIANG

BHUTAN

Chongqing

Nanchang

INDIA

Changsha

JIANGXI

GUIZHOU

HUNAN

Dacca

Guiyang

FUJIAN

Fuzhou

Kunming

GUANGXI
ZHUANG A.R.

Taipei

YUNNAN

Canton

GUANGDONG

TAIWAN
(Republic
of China)

BANGLADESH

BURMA

Nanning

Hanoi

Hong Kong
(Br.)

Chankiang

BAY OF
BENGAL

LAOS

Vientiane

Hainan
Island

Rangoon

THAILAND

VIETNAM

SOUTH CHINA SEA

PHILIPPINES

Bangkok

Manila

CAMBODIA
(Kampuchea)

Phnom Penh

Saigon

INDIAN OCEAN

Kuala
Lumpur

MALAYSIA

INDONESIA

CHINA AND
SOUTHEAST ASIA

Djakarta

Soviet Union already has the fifth largest Muslim population in the world, exceeded only by Indonesia, Pakistan, Bangladesh, and India. Important political choices confront the Soviet leaders. How should they respond to the possibility of Islamic movements that may spill over from other southwest Asian countries such as Iran, Afghanistan, and Pakistan? Because there is a severe labor shortage in the industrial, western part of the USSR, what should be done to encourage the Central Asians (who have been reluctant to migrate) to move and fulfill this labor shortage? What can be done to raise the level of development of the Central Asian areas? Zbigniew K. Brzezinski has observed that nationalities in the USSR could become a political issue of greater importance than race has been in the United States.[34]

China also is a heterogeneous multiethnic state. Although 94 percent of the population are of basic Chinese stock (the Han people), they are divided into groups characterized by many social, cultural, and linguistic differences. The spoken word of one Chinese group, such as the Cantonese, may be completely unintelligible to another group. In addition to the Han people, China has over 50 million members of minority groups, more than double the total population of Yugoslavia. Of these, over 50 groups have been designated as minorities and have been given 98 autonomous areas at the provincial, intermediate, and county levels. These autonomous areas, usually named after the group (or groups) who predominate, provide the minorities greater freedom and government rights; although as Henry G. Schwartz cautions, all of these rights are subordinate to national programs, laws, regulations, and organizations.[35] The map of China outlines the 21 provinces and 5 autonomous regions. Autonomous regions are areas heavily populated by non-Chinese minorities.

The environmental factors surveyed in this chapter provide the setting for our political analysis that follows. The economic setting tells us something about what contemporary leaders have to allocate. The social setting provides us with some idea of the status and stratification of various groups. The demographic setting gives us a clearer picture of the importance of political choices in molding a unified political community from heterogeneous, ethnically divided societies. Politics is the art of the possible and these environmental forces set the boundaries for political action and performance.

[34]Zbigniew K. Brzezinski, ed., *Dilemmas of Change in Soviet Politics* (New York: Columbia University Press, 1969), p. 161.

[35]Henry G. Schwarz, "The Treatment of Minorities," in Michel Oksenberg, ed., *China's Developmental Experience* (New York: Academy of Political Science, 1973), p. 200.

# Suggestions for Further Reading

**Bergson, Abram,** *Soviet Post-War Economic Development* (Stockholm: Almqvist & Wiksell, 1975).

**Connor, Walter D.,** *Socialism, Politics, and Equality: Hierarchy and Change in Eastern Europe and the USSR* (New York: Columbia University Press, 1979).

_____, *Deviance in Soviet Society* (New York: Columbia University Press, 1972).

**Dubey, Vinod,** *Yugoslavia: Development with Decentralization* (Baltimore: Johns Hopkins University Press, 1975).

**Eckstein, Alexander,** *China's Economic Revolution* (Cambridge: At the University Press, 1977).

**Gati, Charles,** ed., *The Politics of Modernization in Eastern Europe* (New York: Praeger, 1974).

**Hinton, Harold C.,** ed., *The Peoples Republic of China: A Handbook* (Boulder, Colo.: Westview, 1978).

**Hoffman, George W.,** *Regional Development*

*Strategy in Southeast Europe* (New York: Praeger, 1972).

**Hohmann, H. H., M. Kaser,** and **K. C. Thalheim,** eds., *New Economic Systems of Eastern Europe* (London: Hurst, 1975).

**Jancar, Barbara Wolfe,** *Women Under Communism* (Baltimore: Johns Hopkins University Press, 1978).

**Lane, David,** *Politics and Society in the USSR* (New York: Random House, 1971).

**Lewis, Robert A.,** *et al., Nationality and Population Change in Russia and the USSR* (New York: Praeger, 1976).

**Matejko, Alexander,** *Social Change and Stratification in Eastern Europe* (New York: Praeger, 1974).

**Matthews, Mervyn,** *Privilege in the Soviet Union* (London: Allen & Unwin, 1978).

**Mickiewicz, Ellen P.,** ed., *Handbook of Soviet Social Science Data* (New York: Free Press, 1972).

**Mihailovic, Kosta,** *Regional Development Experiences and Prospects in Eastern Europe* (The Hague: Mouton, 1972).

**Perkins, Dwight H.,** ed., *China's Modern Economy in Historical Perspective* (Stanford, Calif.: Stanford University Press, 1975).

**Prybyla, Jan S.,** *The Chinese Economy: Problems and Policies*, 2nd ed. (Columbia: University of South Carolina Press, 1981).

**U.S. Congress, Joint Economic Committee,** *Soviet Economy in a Time of Change*, vol. 1–2 (Washington, D.C.: U.S. Government Printing Office, 1979).

———, *Chinese Economy Post-Mao*, vol. 1–2 (Washington, D.C.: U.S. Government Printing Office, 1978).

———, *East European Economies: Post-Helsinki* (Washington, D.C.: U.S. Government Printing Office, 1977).

# CHAPTER THREE

## Political Culture and Political Socialization

What do we know about the political ideas of the millions upon millions of ordinary citizens who live in Communist-run societies? Do they support their leaders? Would they revolt if they had the chance? Are there signs of psychological and attitudinal change in these societies? These important questions take us to the topics of political culture and political socialization.

Because of Communist leaders' strong public commitment to build Communism, and because of the important human dimension of the building process, the concepts of political culture and political socialization are of special significance in our study. Gabriel Almond, a distinguished American political scientist, has noted: "Every political system is embedded in a particular pattern of orientations of political action."[1] This pattern of attitudes and beliefs that people hold toward their system is referred to as political culture; it represents the orientations that define the setting in which politics takes place. The political culture of the Soviet Union is the total composite of that society's ideas about political life. Orientations about justice and democracy, welfare and equality, and other political issues all represent dimensions of the larger Soviet political culture. As in all other states,

these orientations have an influence on power and policy in Communist political systems.

Although we refer to a Chinese political culture, a Soviet political culture, and so forth, we should realize that it is a simplification to speak of the total set of attitudes and values of the populace and to consider it a homogeneous whole. Obviously, like other societies, the Communist societies of the Second World are heterogeneous in their beliefs and values, just as they are in social and economic characteristics. But, when we discuss and compare societies, it is useful to have a general concept to refer to the general attitudinal and psychological setting within political systems. Political culture is the term for such a concept.

How can one study something as abstract as political culture? What does one try to observe? Some researchers have conducted massive opinion surveys of large samples of national populations. For example, in their book, *The Civic Culture*, Almond and Verba surveyed attitudes and values of over 5000 citizens from the United States, Great Britain, West Germany, Italy, and Mexico to better understand the political cultures of these states.[2] There is also a large study of

[1] Gabriel A. Almond, "Comparative Political Systems," *The Journal of Politics, 18* (3) (1956), p.395.

[2] Gabriel A. Almond and Sidney Verba, *The Civic Culture: Political Attitudes and Democracy in Five Nations* (Princeton, N. J.: Princeton University Press, 1963).

May Day Ceremony in Moscow's Red Square draws the country's leaders who adorn the reviewing stand atop Lenin's mausoleum, as rank-and-file Soviet citizens crowd the adjoining streets. State celebrations illustrate the patriotism and nationalism that is deeply embedded in Soviet political culture.

political culture in Yugoslavia that analyzes the political orientations of over 1000 Yugoslav citizens.[3] Bertsch and Zaninovich in that study were able to determine more accurately the political cultures of the various Yugoslav nationalities —Croats, Macedonians, Montenegrins, Serbs, and Slovenes. In these and other studies, researchers went into the countries and gathered massive amounts of opinion data that allowed detailed, systematic studies of the people's political orientations. With the partial exception of Yugoslavia and a few other cases, this quantitative approach to the study of political culture is generally not possible in Communist Party

states because their governments are usually unwilling to allow Western scholars to study such sensitive issues. In this book, we take an inductive approach and base our study on a large body of research conducted by native and foreign scholars. Although this research is not always based on scientific surveys, it draws on the personal contacts and research of scholars who know these countries well.

Political culture has certain things in common with—but is quite distinct from—a state's ideology. Although the term has been conceptualized in many ways, ideology commonly refers to the set of arguments and beliefs used to justify an existing or desired social order. Although there is bound to be considerable overlap, the ideologies of the Second World states deviate in certain important respects from their political

[3]Gary K. Bertsch and M. George Zaninovich, "A Factor Analytic Method of Identifying Different Political Cultures: The Multi-National Yugoslav Case," *Comparative Politics*, 6 (2) (1974), pp. 219–244.

cultures. Though Marxist-Leninist ideology represents the official arguments and beliefs set forth by the Communist parties to explain and justify their social order, the political cultures of these countries represent the personal values of the broader society. In some respects, these two sets of beliefs differ. Although a Communist Party official would be able to enumerate (and sincerely believe) the basic ideological tenets of the state, his son or daughter might hold political attitudes that conflict with the prevailing ideology. Currently, there is considerable concern in many Communist Party states that the political culture of the youth is not sufficiently supportive of official ideology and that efforts must be made to bring young people more in line with the official doctrines.

This issue and attempts to mold political culture introduce us to the concept of political socialization. Most political scientists conceive of political socialization as the process by which official or prevailing attitudes and beliefs are transmitted to a society and particularly to newcomers, such as children or immigrants. Because Communist Party states adopted the revolutionary ideology of Marxism-Leninism rather recently in their political histories, in a sense all of their citizens are newcomers and great efforts have been made to inculcate political orientations conducive to the building of socialism. Because the prerevolutionary societies in these countries have had distinctive traditions and political cultures of their own, the transmission of new political orientations to the populace has not been easy. The leaders of the new states have realized that if their political and economic policies are to be carried out successfully, traditional political beliefs must be replaced. In their place, the leaders hope to develop a new set of attitudes and values, orientations that correspond with and support their interpretations of Marxist-Leninist doctrine and their drives for modernization and rapid industrialization. It is this task that makes the topics of political culture and political socialization so interesting and important in the study of contemporary Communism.

At a sports event, 10,000 students with placards form the backdrop for the marching People's Liberation Army (PLA) and People's Militia during a parade in Beijing's Workers' Stadium. Such events were typically combined with political and military presentations during the highly politicized Maoist period.

## CHANGING THE TRADITIONAL POLITICAL CULTURES

When Vladimir Ilyich Lenin, Mao Zedong, Josip Broz Tito, and others assumed power in their states, the traditional political cultures were not conducive to, and (in many respects) were even hostile about, changes the leaderships felt were necessary for building socialism. The political orientations of the people in these countries had been molded over hundreds, perhaps even thousands, of years. Centuries of tsarist rule in Russia, imperial rule in China, and foreign domination and dictatorial rule in Yugoslavia taken together with peasant societies and backward socioeconomic traditions resulted in undemocratic, élitist political cultures. We must remember that all three societies and most others that went Communist were composed primarily of peasants, with the bulk of the population working on the land. These tillers of the soil generally accepted the prevailing social hierarchy: the strong ruled, the weak were ruled. In all three countries, the traditional belief was that the select few who governed the masses had been chosen by divine mandate. The coronations and the ritualistic ceremonies, such as those accorded the Russian tsars, Chinese emperors, and East European kings and ruling families, made the rulers and masses acutely aware of the divine significance of the rulers' power. The masses were expected to remain passively in the background sowing the crops, working in factories, or laboring in whatever jobs they could find. The thought of popular politics and the ideas of democracy were as remote as distant North America. When the peasants heard news of democratic rule in the West, they neither understood its meaning nor comprehended its significance to their backward lot. As the age of democracy grew in other parts of the globe, the masses of these three countries remained largely isolated and, for the time being, unaffected by the winds of change.

When the Yugoslav Communist Party seized power in 1945, for example, the existing political culture was based on authoritarian, élitist, and nonparticipant norms. Centuries of foreign domination by the Ottoman and Austro-Hungarian empires as well as the more recent periods of nineteenth-and twentieth-century rule under indigenous authoritarian regimes served to mold a resigned, apathetic, and conformist society. The authoritarian Stalinist approach to political life, initially followed by Tito and the Yugoslav Communists at the end of World War II, corresponded with the nonparticipant political culture of the populace. The masses had never been widely consulted and involved in the affairs of politics before and did not really expect to be included after the war.

In China, the traditional political culture was steeped in the ideal of harmony with nature and a strict, hierarchical set of social and political relations. Power was entrusted to the emperor or empress, his or her supporting officials, and those who had worked their way up the hierarchy through intellectual attainment. To the masses, political power was the right of the emperor; the hierarchy was viewed as natural and the government tended to be remote. On those few occasions when the common peasant or laborer had contact with the government, the authorities appeared unjust and harsh. Because of this experience, the large bulk of the society was resigned to a life of political passivity and acquiescence. In a large peasant society, the common man and woman had little interest in, and few orientations about, politics; an early Chinese Communist leader commented on this matter in 1922:

> The peasants take no interest in politics. This is common throughout the whole world, but is particularly true in China. . . . All they care about is having a true Son of Heaven (emperor) to rule them, and a peaceful bumper year.[4]

Mass values about democracy and power in China, Russia, and Yugoslavia were shaped by centuries of authoritarian rule. Although the leaders of these countries—the rulers, ministers, counselors, representatives, magistrates, and others who served the empires—possessed a set of political orientations that represented an authoritarian political culture, the masses were

[4]Chang Kuo-tao, cited in Jerome Chen, *Mao and the Chinese Revolution* (London: Oxford University Press, 1965), p. 193.

characterized by a general absence of political sentiment.[5] They held few political feelings and were uninvolved in politics because of their isolation from political affairs. To transform this massive parochial, nonparticipant sector of society into one that would support and advance the ideas of Communist rule was a major task facing the new leaders in the postrevolutionary periods.

The leaders of the Communist political systems recognized that the building of Communism would be difficult, if not impossible, because of the political cultures (and subcultures) inherited from the pre-socialist states. Accordingly, they adopted heavy-handed strategies of political socialization to mold the orientations required for their ideal societies.

Perhaps it should be pointed out that all countries, including the United States, attempt to foster attitudes and beliefs in their people that are supportive of their systems of government. For example, in our country children at an early age are taught the Pledge of Allegiance, the Star-Spangled Banner, and the stories of our founding fathers; we may call it civics or citizenship training, but it is political socialization aimed at instructing the newest generation about the functioning of our political system. The key question in regard to this topic is not whether it exists, for it exists in all societies; we must instead examine who determines what ought to be taught, how it is accomplished, and how far governments go in changing the belief structures of their people. Do they stamp out all differences or are they tolerant of diverse beliefs and opinions? Our exploration of this issue in Communist Party states will point to the fact that a higher premium may be placed on ideological purity in these states than in our own country—as is the case in most of those countries found in the First and Third worlds.

A variety of different tactics have been used in Communist Party countries to reform the minds of the citizenry and to develop a new "enlightened" community of Communist citizens.

After the revolution in China, emphasis was placed on thought reform, self-criticism, and rectification programs. Those with bourgeois mentalities were given the opportunity to reform themselves and become productive members of Chinese society.[6] In some countries, more coercive methods, such as deportation, imprisonment, terror, and even death and genocide, were used to force transformations in political culture. Stalin was notorious for brutal tactics as he ruthlessly sought to transform Soviet society to suit his purposes. Still others used less violent and more effective methods. One of Castro's strategies for dealing with Cubans with hostile or nonconforming political orientations has been to deport them. Thousands of Cubans came to the United States during the 1960s and again in 1980 because, among other reasons, they were unable or unwilling to change their beliefs and opinions concerning socialism in Cuba.[7] Perhaps the most significant element in changing political culture is simply time itself. After over a half century in the USSR and a quarter century in most other Communist Party states, attitudes appear to conform more and more with the leader's expectations. This observation must be qualified to some extent, however, in view of the events in Poland in the early 1980s. Once again, Polish citizens spoke out and voiced their dissatisfaction with government policy and leadership. What was particularly noteworthy about the most recent demonstration was the coalescence of worker, intellectual, and other sources of opinion in opposition to Communist Party rule. The Polish events of the early 1980s may go down as one of the most significant chapters in Communist history since the Bolshevik takeover. At the very least, Polish demonstrations of popular opinion on a number of occasions in the 1970s and early 1980s should suggest to all that citizens in Communist Party states will not, necessarily, remain docile and apathetic.

[6]Robert J. Lifton, *Thought Reform and the Psychology of Totalism: A Study of "Brainwashing" in China* (New York: Norton, 1961).

[7]See Richard R. Fagen, *The Transformation of Political Culture in Cuba* (Stanford, Calif.: Stanford University Press, 1969).

[5]An authoritarian political culture represents a set of beliefs and attitudes supporting or, at least, tolerating nondemocratic (autocratic) political rule.

In the Chinese classrooms, which have been traditionally more ideologically charged than their Soviet counterparts, revolutionary posters and slogans accompany daily lessons. Although political consciousness is considered a necessary ingredient of the new socialist person and Chinese political culture, more emphasis is now placed on scientific training and expertise.

The leaders in Communist Party states have used a number of important agents of political socialization, that is, institutions or instruments by which orientations are transformed. If we examine the processes of political socialization in these countries over the years, we will find that the family has played an important role. After reviewing the results of Soviet research on the topic, one scholar concludes that "most children seem to learn their values from the social environment of their families."[8] Soviet leaders and scholars alike recognize this fact, and although there is little they can do to force families to promote desired attitudes and values, they do make it clear on occasion that the regime has high expectations about the personal examples set by mothers and fathers in the home.[9]

One agent of socialization that has continued to plague the socialization intentions of the leaders is the church. Particularly in the East European states where the Catholic and Ortho-

dox religions are deeply imbedded in the cultures of the people, the church is a troublesome institution with which the party must contend. At some points in Communist history, the parties undertook aggressive and oppressive campaigns to eradicate religion from their countries. At other points, when they needed to mobilize support for the government and promote unity within the country, they eased their politics of persecution.[10] At all times, however, the leaders have correctly assessed the contradiction between Communism and religion and viewed the latter as an obstruction that impedes the optimal development of Communism. Some regimes, like the one in Poland where Catholicism is very strong, have perceived religion as a necessary evil with which they have to live. Others, like China and Albania, consider religion an evil they can ill afford and have undertaken coercive policies to eradicate fully its presence and influence from their societies.

The agent of political socialization that Communists take the most interest in and (unlike family life and religion) over which they find it easiest to exert considerable influence, is the school. The educational system in all Communist Party states is closely controlled by the Communist Party. Through the coordinating arm of a central ministry for education, the Communist parties have great influence in designing curriculums, selecting texts, and setting instructional policies within the schools. Although the party leaders do not usually become directly involved in these activities, they recommend certain policies, which are implemented through the ministries and by the local organs. The content of courses, textbooks, and the general educational philosophy, however, vary markedly among the different states.

Perhaps the most politicized and ideologically infused education system in Communist history was the Chinese during the Maoist period. Throughout the Great Proletarian Cultural

[8]William K. Medlin, "Education," in Allen Kassof, *Prospects for Soviet Society* (New York: Praeger, 1968), p. 257.

[9]Editorials in *Pravda* and elsewhere exhort parents to set examples that are in the best interests of building Communism.

[10]Stalin's persecution of religion was abandoned in 1941 in an effort to foster greater support and national unity to address the Nazi threat. Nikita S. Khrushchev resumed the more oppressive policies and initiated a campaign (1960–1964) to eliminate religious life completely from the Soviet Union.

Science and ideology coexist in Soviet education as shown by the artifacts in this classroom in Moscow. Major Soviet advances in science and technology attest to the success of its educational system. The effects in the area of political socialization are less clear.

Revolution (GPCR) (1966–1969), Maoist doctrine accompanied almost every lesson. In the subject of elementary school mathematics, for example, the exploiting capitalist and the downtrodden peasants were typically found in the daily exercises:

> PROBLEM: If a peasant works 4 plots of land and the capitalist takes the products of 3, what does that leave the peasant?

The writings of Chairman Mao played a major role in the educational process. Pictures from China showed the ever-present *Little Red Book* held proudly by the Chinese grade schooler. Bulletin boards and texts were adorned with the pictures of leaders and the slogans they extolled to mobilize the masses. Even at the more advanced levels of Chinese education, including the univer-

sities, ideology represented a significant element in the course content. One did not even approach the topics of medicine or physics without recognizing the relevance of Maoist ideology to them. Western observers witnessed college seminars dedicated solely to the reading of Chairman Mao's sacred thought.

To what extent these Maoist methods brought about enduring changes in Chinese political culture is open to question. What is clear is the changing emphasis in Chinese education in the post-Mao period. Less stress is now placed on ideology and much more is placed on the scientific understanding needed to promote the Four-Modernizations Program. In 1980, the new Premier of China, Zhao Ziyang, noted:

> There is an urgent need for training talented people for the modernization program. For this reason, we are attaching importance to teaching work and to the study of cultural and scientific knowledge. It is our duty to arm the minds of youngsters with the cultural legacy of mankind and with scientific and technological knowledge; we must train our generation into people with genuine talent.[11]

Although Soviet and East European schools are also important, highly regimented agents of socialization, they, too, take a much less politicized and ideological approach than Maoist China. Politics and ideology are, of course, important parts of their lessons, and textbooks are infused with the themes of patriotism, socialist morality, and internationalism. However, the Maoist parroting of ideological slogans and the long and intensive periods of political training are generally not found. Specific courses on ideology, such as the typical high school course, "The Bases of Our Ideology," are common. These courses are infused with Marxism-Leninism and take a value-laden approach to the interpretation of national and world events.

The Yugoslav approach is even less ideologically inclined than the typical Soviet or East European approach. There is a strong dose of politically oriented study on self-managing socialism and Marxism-Leninism "Yugoslav style,"

[11]Zhao Ziyang, "Educating the Younger Generation is a Great Task," *Beijing Review*, 23 (24) (1980), pp. 14–16.

but the content of their educational process is not much different from that found in Western, First World states. Teachers are expected to provide the proper ideological interpretation of events and issues when the occasion arises, but the emphasis is much more on general education and considerably less on political indoctrination.

Another influential agent of socialization carried out through the schools is the youth organizations. These youth groups range from the elementary grade Young Pioneers through the high school and college-age youth leagues. Although all Communist Party states have rather similar groups, they vary widely in functions and behavior. The Chinese Communist Youth League in the 1970s, for example, constituted the primary training ground for revolutionary successors. It had a militant philosophy and was infused with the Chinese revolutionary spirit. During this period, Young Pioneers in China were even instructed in the arts of making revolution. Whether marching in parades, chanting Maoist slogans, or operating rifles with live ammunition on the firing range, these elementary grade schoolers were taught the finer points of Maoist strategy for revolutionary warfare. Youth organizations in the post-Mao period have assumed a less revolutionary, pro-modernization orientation. Party official, Zhao Ziyang, comments,

> By organizing various levels and absorbing activities involving astronomy, geology, zoology, botany, chemistry, biology, culture and art, the Young Pioneers play a special irreplaceable role in discovering and training young personnel.[12]

New members of the Young Pioneers in the USSR pledge to "warmly love my Soviet motherland" and to "live, to study, and to struggle as Lenin willed and as the Communist Party teaches." The new member also promises to observe the following rules[13]:

[12]Ibid., p. 16.

[13]Allen Kassof, *The Soviet Youth Program* (Cambridge: Harvard University Press, 1965), p. 79.

During Mao's reign art and culture in China were expected to communicate the goals and values of the revolution. "The Red Detachment of Women", a folktale made into a revolutionary ballet, exemplifies adoration of Mao and his *Little Red Book*. Today, the Chinese leaders take a more relaxed attitude concerning political socialization.

The Pioneer loves his motherland and the Communist Party of the Soviet Union. He prepares himself for membership in the Komsomol.

The Pioneer reveres the memory of those who have given their lives in the struggle for the freedom and the well-being of the Soviet motherland.

The Pioneer is friendly with the children of all the countries of the world.

The Pioneer studies diligently and is disciplined and courteous.

The Pioneer loves to work and to conserve the national wealth.

The Pioneer is a good comrade, who is solicitous of younger children and who helps older people.

The Pioneer grows up to be bold and does not fear difficulties.

The Pioneer tells the truth and guards the honor of his detachment.

The Pioneer strengthens himself and does physical exercises every day.

The Pioneer loves nature; he is a defender of planted areas, of useful birds and animals.

The Pioneer is an example for all children.

Like members of Western organizations, Young Pioneers do not always take these promises seriously.

To some extent, it is instructive to compare Young Pioneers in the USSR and Eastern Europe with Boy and Girl Scouts in the West. Although the Communist Party administers centralized control and guidance, and, therefore, more emphasis is placed on ideological and political themes, children in Communist Party countries enjoy the Young Pioneers just as children in the United States enjoy scouting. The children in Communist Party states view the Young Pioneers as a fun group where they can meet playmates, go on field trips, and spend a week or two at summer camp. Social service projects are a main activity of the organization, but children participate primarily because they enjoy the recreational activities.

Social service and political education are more important functions of the Communist Youth League. These groups represent the primary training ground for future generations of socialist society. Leonid I. Brezhnev has referred

to their mission as that of "bringing up youth in the spirit of Communist commitment" and to carry on the "cause of their fathers, the cause of the great Lenin." Many teenagers in Eastern Europe and the Soviet Union seem bored by the group activities; they often complain that they are ineffective organizations for social work and that the activities do not interest them. One expert concludes that, "Social activity, as currently implemented through youth organizations in the school, may no longer be the best means for the upbringing of Soviet youth."[14]

The mass media—television, radio, newspapers, books, and the like—also represent important agents of political socialization. All television networks schedule a heavy dosage of ideological and political programming. These propaganda programs assume a variety of formats but always present the party, government, and the countries' leaders in a complimentary light. Propaganda does not have the pejorative meaning in Communist Party states that it holds in the West. Lenin felt that all party members should act as theoreticians, propagandists, agitators, and organizers. Propaganda means advertising the party's work in an attempt to win new adherents to the cause. Even those programs that are expressly intended for entertainment will typically have a political message; the vast majority of novels, short stories, and magazine articles will include the same. This concern with ideology has had a sobering effect on the written word in all socialist countries. The loading of ideology into everything from newspaper reports to romance novels has severely reduced the quality of writing. Writers unwilling to yield to ideological themes—often some of the very best writers—are forced to pick other professions to survive.

Some of the East European countries— Hungary, Poland, and Yugoslavia are the most notable—have experimented with less censorship and more freedom of expression in the mass

[14]Charles D. Cary, "Political Socialization of Soviet Youth and the Building of Communism," in Gary K. Bertsch and Thomas W. Ganschow, eds., Comparative Communism: The Soviet, Chinese and Yugoslav Models (San Francisco: W. H. Freeman, 1976), p. 298.

Even in Yugoslavia, which is considerably more open to a diversity of ideas than most Communist Party states, much of its art deals with heroic themes and symbols. Here a Yugoslav monument pays tribute to soldiers lost in World War II.

media and particularly in film, theater, and the demonstrative arts. These less ideological (and sometimes nonideological) expressions have met with wide approval among the masses and illustrate the great interest in apolitical or nonideological culture and arts among East Europeans.

Yugoslavia is again a deviant case when it comes to ideology in the mass media and arts. The vast majority of movies shown in Yugoslavia come from the West, most from the United States. Many television programs on the Yugoslav networks are American reruns; Western literature dots bookshelves and newsstands. Yugoslavia is the only country in the Second World where you can walk up to a newsstand and buy a copy of the Paris edition of the *Herald Tribune,* or *Newsweek,* or *Playboy.* The ap-

parent philosophy in Yugoslavia is to let Communism compete with other ideologies and values in a freer market place of ideas. This is only to a relative degree, however, because the Yugoslav Communists have made it clear that they will not allow the present system of socialism to be overturned.

Although the emphasis is definitely on youth in the socialization process, adults are certainly not ignored. The Communist parties and trade unions have vast networks concerned with ideological training and propaganda. Often the training is tied to one's job—classes and programs are offered to heighten workers' political consciousness and to call attention to the continuing class struggle. Although many adults ignore such activities, the social pressures are great enough to generate a significant level of participation.

The primary agent of political socialization in Communist Party states is of course the Communist Party itself. As will be noted in more detail in Chapter Four, the Communist Party controls public information in the Second World states and, in so doing, plays a powerful, nearly omnipresent role in determining what people see, hear, and learn. Because of its organization and socializing strategy, the Communist parties are able to oppose the agents of socialization that may run counter to the desired political culture (e.g., church, family) and use those agents (mass media, schools, youth organizations) that are under their direction. For example, organizations are present in factories, collective farms, and other places of work. Members of these party organizations are expected to be exemplary citizens and to set good examples for their peers. In addition, the mere presence of party members and party organizations in the workplace and throughout the society has a powerful socializing impact of its own. Now we will take a look at the type of political cultures the Communist leaders desire.

## DESIRED POLITICAL CULTURES

One way of viewing the political cultures Communists desire and consider most conducive to their political goals and the building of Communism is to examine what they expect of the ideal citizen. The Soviet leaders would like their citizens to live by what they have identified as the "Moral Code of the Builder of Communism"[15]:

> Devotion to the pursuit of Communism, love for the socialist homeland, for the countries of socialism;
>
> Conscientious labor for the good of society; whoever does not work does not eat;
>
> The concern of everyone for the conservation and increase of social property;
>
> A high consciousness of social obligation, an intolerance toward infringements of social interests;
>
> Collectivism and comradely mutual aid; one for all and all for one;
>
> A humane relationship and mutual respect among people; one person to another person—friend, comrade, and brother;
>
> Integrity and truthfulness, moral purity, simplicity, and humility in social and personal life;
>
> Mutual respect in family life, concern for the upbringing of children;
>
> Implacable opposition to injustice, parasitism, dishonesty, careerism, greed;
>
> The friendship and brotherhood of all the peoples of the USSR; intolerance toward nationalist and racist hostility;
>
> Implacable opposition toward the enemies of Communism, the pursuit of peace, and the freedom of nations;

Soviet leaders would like their people to be devoted and patriotic, conscientious and industrious, comradely, respectful, truthful, pure, and humble. In other words, they want good socialist citizens who will listen to, and support, the leaders and do a full-day's work without expecting unreasonable rewards in return. One gets the distinct impression that the Soviets view their citizens as authoritarian parents view their children, that is, they are to be seen but not heard. The leaders want their people to participate in politics but not challenge the party line, to be industrious and generate resources but not question where these resources will be spent. These are the decisions to be reserved for the party élite. If all Soviet citizens were to hold these traits, it would of course make the leaders' tasks in governing much easier. A political system characterized by an environment of committed, yet like-minded citizens, is much easier to govern than one that is actively outspoken and divided by deep political cleavages.

Mao also recognized the importance of political socialization and the desirability of a new political culture. Over 40 years ago, Mao noted,[16]

> It is necessary to train a great many people as vanguards of the revolution. People who are politically far-sighted. People imbued with the spirit of struggle and self-sacrifice. People with largeness of mind who are loyal, active and upright. People who never pursue selfish interests, but are wholeheartedly for liberation of the nation and society. People who fear no difficulties, but remain steadfast and advance courageously in the face of difficulties. People who are neither high or mighty nor seekers after the limelight, but are conscientious and full of practical sense. If China has a host of such vanguard elements, the tasks of the Chinese revolution will be successfully fulfilled.

Like the Soviet leaders, Mao also wanted an ideologically committed and active political culture. In fact, Mao placed more emphasis on political participation and, during certain periods of his rule, mobilized what may have been the highest level of mass political activity in modern history. Yet, Mao and the Chinese leaders also placed severe limits on the nature of participation. The people were expected to work within the system, and this meant parroting Maoist slogans and supporting the official party doctrine. There was to be no dissent, but rather a united, mobilized populace led by the Great Helmsman, Mao Zedong.

Mao's successors also recognized the importance of political culture to Chinese development

[15]Donald D. Barry and Carol Barner-Barry, *Contemporary Soviet Politics* (Englewood Cliffs, N.J.: Prentice-Hall, 1978) p. 360.

[16]Mao cited in "Transform Schools into Instruments of Proletarian Dictatorship," *Peking Review, 19* (11) (1976), p. 7.

and have attempted to outline its ideal features. In 1980, one high party official emphasized the following points[17]:

1. loving the socialist motherland;
2. utilizing western things useful to the four modernizations and rejecting things unhealthy and against the national spirit;
3. making the ideal of communism a guide to action; and
4. cultivating and strengthening communist ethics.

The political culture desired by the post-Mao leaders is both "Red" and "expert." Red means that the culture is thoroughly Communist; it should recognize the importance and validity of Communism and abide by a code of Communist morality. Expert means that the culture should also be based on knowledge, skills, and scientific knowhow. The political culture desired in contemporary China is, therefore, based on many of the ideological principles of the Maoist period (although emphasizing that they should not be carried to extremes) but it adds a new dimension—knowledge—which is required by the new emphasis on modernization. In addition, there has been a greater opportunity for discussion, different points of view, and even some dissent in post-Mao China. The leaders have experimented with something known as Democracy Wall—a place where citizens can place posters and express values and opinions that often conflict with party policy. Although the new leaders have experimented with the development of a more modern political culture (*i.e.*, less ideology, more skills and knowledge), they have been explicit in setting certain boundaries and reminding the people that the Chinese Communist Party (CCP) is still in charge.

The Yugoslav leaders place even less emphasis on ideology and more on knowledge in the political culture they desire. Giving special attention to the needs of self-management, Yugoslav political culture is one in which individuals

Become familiar with the essence of socio-economic relations, political structure, and the rights

and duties of citizens in the self-managed socialist society; in addition, they should be prepared for direct decision-making on the conditions and results of their work, and for progressive changes in social relations; finally, they must master democratic methods in the realization of personal rights and freedoms and develop a sense of solidarity in work and in communal life.[18]

The ideal political culture to the post-Tito leaders is one that reflects the attitudes and skills required by the developing, self-managing Yugoslav system. In addition, it should be tolerant of the national differences within the country and support the idea of a united Yugoslav state. Finally, it should support the Yugoslav foreign policy on nonalignment and the independent Yugoslav road to socialism.

There are common elements in the political cultures desired by the leaders of all three countries. They all prefer patriotic, devoted, and industrious citizens, and they want them skilled and knowledgeable and willing to live according to certain Communist ethics. That is, of course, the ideal. The important and interesting differences among these countries concern two basic features: first, the balance between ideology and knowledge; second, what the leaders are willing to do to see the culture they desire implanted in the minds and behavior of the people.

Mao's regime went the farthest in emphasizing ideological themes in the Chinese political culture. More recently, however, the post-Mao leaders have attempted to balance ideology and knowledge. Yet, they still appear to emphasize more ideology than do the leaders of the USSR. The Yugoslavs have gone the longest way in deemphasizing ideology and encouraging the knowledge and skills required in a modern industrial state.

The Communist parties of the Soviet Union and China have gone to greater lengths and utilized more extreme tactics to implant the desired political cultures in their people than have most of the East European states, Yugoslavia included. In the latter states, the people

[17]Wang Renzhong "Striving for the Future of Socialist China," *Beijing Review, 23* (24) (1980), pp. 16–19.

[18]*Resolution on the Development of Education on the Basis of Self-Management* (Belgrade: Contemporary Administration, 1971), p. 9.

Pope John Paul II, the former Archbishop Karol Wojtyla of Crakow, walks among a crowd of fellow Poles after celebrating a mass in Warsaw's Victory Square on June 2, 1979. To the right is the late Stefan Cardinal Wyszynski, the former Primate of Poland. The Catholic Church represents a powerful agent of political socialization with which the Communist leaders have to contend.

and the social and religious organizations to which they often belong have often resisted the parties' forcing certain value patterns on them. For example, the predominantly Catholic population of Poland has made it difficult for the Polish leaders to take an antichurch stand in their socialization strategies. As a consequence, there is a tacit, but precarious truce between the Catholic Church and the Communist leaders on the nature of Polish political culture. The desired political culture, then, has to be based on certain social, political, and cultural realities, even in Communist states.

## THE DOMINANT POLITICAL CULTURE

Dominant political culture is a term we use to describe the prevailing beliefs and opinions that define political life in the Communist Party states today. This does not mean that every citizen subscribes to an all-encompassing set of beliefs and opinions, but rather that we can identify a modal set of values that fairly accurately describes the political cultures of these countries. Later we note that the dominant political culture is not accepted by all and that a full understanding of the topic requires an examination of certain subcultures within the various countries.

Because we want to examine those orientations that most significantly affect politics, we will address those related to the four values outlined in the introduction of this book: power, respect, well-being, and enlightenment. For a political system to allocate these values in an authoritative and peaceful manner, the citizens of a particular state should ideally have uniform expectations concerning their proper distribution. If 50 percent of the population feels that political power ought to be confined totally to a small number of leaders within the Communist Party, whereas the other 50 percent strongly feel it should be shared broadly among the entire society, then, it will be difficult for policy makers effectively to satisfy both sectors in their decisions. On the other hand, if the society widely shares one distribution or the other or if they are largely apathetic, the policy makers may have an easier time accomplishing their objectives. A useful way of viewing the dominant cultures, then, will be to examine mass orientations and behavior relating to the four values defined earlier.

## POWER

The first value and dimension of political culture concerns the role of the individual citizen in the policy-making process. Should the average Soviet, Chinese, Yugoslav, or East European citizen be involved or should he or she leave political affairs in the hands of a small number of Communist Party officials? Based on the goal of worker control and mass participation, one of the basic reasons for the socialist revolutions was to destroy what was perceived to be a dictatorial state that prohibited mass involvement in political affairs and replace it with a more democratic set of social and political relationships. Accordingly, such institutions as legislatures, public courts, and mass organizations have been established in all socialist states to facilitate the goals of worker and mass participation. But, although ideologies have emphasized democratic participation and mass involvement in political life, the political cultures of the different states deviate considerably from the ideal.

One leading scholar of Soviet political culture uses the term subject-participatory, to describe this aspect of the dominant political culture in the USSR.[19] Barghoorn notes: "Sub-

ject-participatory denotes the relationship among Soviet citizens of subordination to superiors in one or more bureaucratic chains of command and the obligation of all citizens to do their best to assure the performance of the collective."[20] Barghoorn contends that although mass participation definitely occurs in the Soviet Union, it does so "within a framework of values, directives, and controls emanating from a ramified national bureaucracy subject to the commands of the Moscow Politburo."[21] Other observers of the Soviet Union feel that participation is much less controlled than Barghoorn describes it, but the prevailing opinion seems to correspond with his position.[22]

Over the 70 years of Soviet development, political orientations reflecting the subject-participatory culture have been ingrained rather effectively throughout all sectors of the society. The average Soviet citizen, whether inhabiting the far eastern reaches of the Russian Republic or the political center in Moscow, possesses a set of beliefs and attitudes defining his or her subject role in the political system. Even those persons whose attitudes and beliefs deviate from official Communist Party doctrine tend overwhelmingly to accept their roles as passive participants without protest. Most citizens in and out of the Communist Party endorse the norms of partisanship ("partiinost"), the collective ("kollektiv"), and a sense of responsibility ("otvetstvennost") corresponding with the official ideology.

The idea of partisanship represents a strong belief in the validity of the Marxist-Leninist way. Tolerance of other points of view is seldom dem-

---

[19]The term, subject-participatory, comes from Almond and Powell's three basic varieties of political culture: a "parochial" political culture where individuals manifest little or no awareness of the national political system; a "subject" culture where individuals are oriented to the political system and the impact it has on their lives but are not oriented to participation; and a "participant" political culture of individuals

oriented to engage actively in the political process. Gabriel A. Almond and G. Bingham Powell, Jr., *Comparative Politics: A Developmental Approach* (Boston: Little, Brown, 1966).

[20]Frederick C. Barghoorn, *Politics in the USSR*, 2nd ed. (Boston: Little, Brown, 1972), p. 23.

[21]*Ibid.*, p. 25. The Politburo is the highest decision-making authority within the Communist Party.

[22]Professor Jerry F. Hough has written a number of pieces arguing that Western evaluations of participation and power in the USSR have not been altogether unbiased. For a statement of his argument, with supporting data, see Jerry F. Hough, "Political Participation in the USSR," *Soviet Studies*, 28 (1) (1976), pp. 3–20; and "The Soviet Experience and the Measurement of Power," *Journal of Politics*, 37 (3) (1975), pp. 685–710.

onstrated, nor is a willingness to change one's own viewpoint. The average Soviet citizen is quick to provide an ideological response to almost any sociopolitical event in the world. Accordingly, if you ask a Soviet worker about labor strikes in Detroit or the general situation of American laborers or if you ask a Soviet official about race relations in the United States or Africa, be prepared for a response grounded in Marxist-Leninist doctrine.

The ideal of the collective is also supposed to hold an important place in the Soviet citizen's orientation concerning political power. All citizens are expected to be politically involved, yet, they should not do so to serve their personal self-interests or those of a particular group or organization, rather, it is the interests of the collective that must be promoted. Whether the collective is a factory, the community, or the entire Soviet population, the common citizen is expected to develop a public spirit and to participate to serve the common or collective good. Yet, after over 60 years of socialism, the typical Soviet citizen still puts self-interests ahead of those of the collective.

A majority of the Soviet people tend to feel some responsibility for participating in public life, but far fewer participate with any real commitment and enthusiasm. Although the ideology justifies the special role of the party leaders in making policy, the citizens are told of their personal responsibility in participating in the affairs of the state. From kindergarten age through their adult years, the Soviet citizen is reminded that building socialism and achieving Communism is not a task to be assumed by leaders alone. All citizens, young and old, white- and blue-collar, must share a common responsibility by participating in the social and political order. Soviet citizens have trouble resolving this contradiction. The party tells them to participate, yet places firm constraints and limits on the nature of their participation.

When we explore the policy-making structures and processes of the USSR in later chapters, we will notice that there is a clear distinction between leaders and followers in Soviet society. Some of the leaders hold élitist values protecting and justifying their dominant roles in the policy-making process. Many workers, peasants, and white-collar personnel, on the other hand, could not care less about participation. They prefer the role of followers and will remain apathetic regardless of the ideological exhortations of the party leaders. Others, however, hold orientations contending that Communism can best be achieved through the active participation of all. They feel that political power is both a right and a responsibility. And, although it is carefully coordinated within an oppressive party bureaucracy, those who desire the role of political activists have the opportunity to involve themselves in political affairs. The opportunity to participate means working within the system however, and unorthodox forms of political involvement (e.g., demonstrations) are seldom tolerated.

Obviously, Communist Party leaders and officials hold the preponderance of power in the USSR. How the people view these leaders and whether they consider them legitimate are important issues. Soviet people do, for the most part, respect their leaders and believe that their government is basically a just and honorable one. As we saw when we explored the topic of political socialization, the government has gone to considerable lengths to ensure that the masses gain a complimentary picture in this regard. To do so, the leaders take great care to see that government misdeeds go unreported. There would never have been a Watergate exposé in the Soviet Union. Soviet leaders would have covered their tracks more effectively than had the Richard M. Nixon administration; and, if they had not, they would simply have prohibited by fiat any reporting or investigation of the misdeeds.[23]

Occasionally, Soviet leaders do report certain indiscretions that call into question the honor and goodness of their comrades. In 1972, the First Secretary of Georgia's (a Republic along the Turkish border) Communist Party was dropped from his position. It was discovered that his wife was in partnership with an individual who was sentenced to 15 years in prison for

[23]In fact, because of the close and friendly relations between Nixon and Brezhnev during the period, Soviet newspapers generally refrained from reporting on Watergate. When they finally did, they described it as a plot by those Democrats opposing detente who wanted to evict Nixon from office.

embezzling about 1 million rubles in state funds, for establishing a vast network of underground retail outlets, and for commiting a variety of other crimes. Although the First Secretary was not personally indicted, his successor had numerous officials and party functionaries arrested in an effort to restore respect in the Georgian Government.

A far more significant reporting of government misdeeds was First Secretary Khrushchev's so-called secret speech at the 20th Party Congress in 1956. Apparently against the advice of his closest associates and other Soviet leaders, Khrushchev denounced the deceased Stalin and his excesses at this important forum of the Communist Party of the Soviet Union (CPSU).[24] By calling into question the infallibility of Soviet leadership (at least Stalin), Khrushchev set the USSR on the course of de-Stalinization. Although this episode might have temporarily lowered the Soviet peoples' respect and trust in the CPSU and the government, they developed increased respect for Khrushchev's openness and the proposed new course.[25]

Because of the close historical connection between the political systems of the USSR and the six Warsaw Treaty Organization (WTO) states, (Poland, East Germany, Czechoslovakia, Hungary, Romania, and Bulgaria), the political cultures of these states are in many respects similar to that of the Soviet Union. There are important differences, such as stronger democratic and participatory values within certain nations (*e.g.*, Czechoslovakia), which grow out of a more democratic political heritage. The adoption of the Soviet political model, on the other hand, has tended to dilute the national differences and the idea of a subject-participatory culture tends to hold for these states as well. In some of these na-

tions, there appears to be considerable tension resulting from the contradictions between democratic rhetoric and the authoritarian realities involving contemporary political life.[26] The dramatic events in Poland in the early 1980s called attention to this fundamental problem. The people began to speak out. They wanted to be more than subject-participants.

But to what extent can people generally speak out about politics in these countries? Most citizens reflect deeply ingrained orientations concerning the limits of dissent and the accepted rules for working within the system. At the same time, the Western stereotype of mute citizens' councils and oppressive party demagogues serving out orders in commissar fashion is overdrawn. People participating on local committees and in community councils do speak out and frequently argue in support of their personal and collective interests. At the same time, however, they realize that there are certain institutions (e.g., the CPSU) that are not challenged and certain individuals who are not criticized (e.g., the party leaders). Individual dissenters, such as Andrei Sakharov, Aleksandr Solzhenitsyn, and Andrei Amalrick, overstepped these bounds and were either imprisoned, exiled, or harrassed.[27] Many others like them in the USSR and other Communist Party states have been brutally suppressed. It is clear that citizens in these countries are not at liberty to challenge or criticize the basic tenets of the system.

We should also ask to what extent individuals feel they should become involved in committees and councils and participate in local and national policy making? Although it is difficult to get a full and objective picture without greater opportunities for field research and opinion studies, most observers agree that there are large

---

[24]In his memoirs, Khrushchev notes: "We exposed Stalin for his excesses, for his arbitrary punishment of millions of honest people, and for his one-man rule, which violated the principle of collective leadership." *Khrushchev Remembers*, trans. and ed. Strobe Talbot (Boston, Mass.: Little, Brown, 1974), p. 250

[25]Khrushchev's speech was not universally acclaimed. Many party leaders and sections of the country were openly critical—Stalin's homeland, the republic of Georgia, for example, was rocked with widespread anti-Khrushchev demonstrations a few weeks after the speech—and considered the speech a typical harebrained Khrushchevian mistake.

[26]Ernst Kux, "Growing Tensions in Eastern Europe," *Problems of Communism*, 29 (2) (1980), pp. 21–37.

[27]The Soviet writer and historian, Andrei Amalrick, predicted a set of cataclysmic events leading to the disintegration of the Soviet state in his book *Will the Soviet Union Survive Until 1984?* (New York: Harper & Row, 1971). Amalrick was jailed by the Committee for State Security (KGB) in 1970 and finally forced to emigrate in 1976. Solzhenitsyn was forced to emigrate in 1975. Sakharov, a leading spokesman for human rights, was banished to Gorki in 1979, a Russian city off-limits to Westerners.

cadres (elected or appointed officials performing professional, political functions) and nonprofessional participants who are willing to involve themselves, sometimes at considerable personal sacrifice, in politics. And most of those who are not active participants tend to view the government as legitimate and are quite willing to accept political outcomes as the authoritative allocation of values.[28]

In contrast to the USSR, Mao's China was a system of mass involvement, what some scholars refer to as a mobilization system in which all individuals—leaders and peasants alike—were expected to become involved actively in the struggle for socialist construction.[29] Although we referred to the dominant Soviet political culture as subject participatory, the designation of mobilized seems to be more accurate for the Chinese. The average Soviet citizen tends to be a more passive participant in the political realm, but the Chinese is impelled to be actively involved. During the early years of Chinese Communism right through to his death in 1976, Chairman Mao was the primary mobilizer and undertook a variety of campaigns and programs to encourage active and voluntary political participation. Following the ideal of populism, the leaders expected all citizens to participate in communal affairs and to serve the people. Although there was a distinction between national and local political cadres and the masses, subordination and privilege were to be removed from all other social relations; political involvement was to be unobstructed and encouraged. Although it is difficult to judge accurately to what extent the traditional élitist culture has been replaced by the Maoist brand of populism, there is reason to believe that the common Chinese citizen has come to assume more participatory values and a more active, yet constrained political role. Although it

is risky to generalize, given the differences between city dweller and peasant, worker and intellectual, it does seem fair to conclude that the role of the individual in political affairs is more meaningful than at any other time in modern Chinese history.

With Yugoslavia's break with Stalin and expulsion from the Communist Information Bureau (Cominform) in 1948 and the subsequent growth of self-management and industrial democracy, the traditional authoritarian political culture became outmoded. The basic task then confronting the leaders was to involve the broader society in political activity even though the general population tended to view the political realm with some fear and suspicion and were neither fully prepared not equipped to participate in day-to-day social, economic, and political affairs. Through the 1950s and 1960s, the leaders attempted to transform these features of the traditional culture and expand the self-management concept to many areas of Yugoslav life. To do so, they passed laws and established constitutional guarantees providing (and requiring) the participation and involvement of all working people.

Although there is considerable evidence that Yugoslavia has succeeded in flattening the conventional power hierarchy, what has happened to the traditional political culture? Is it still authoritarian, élitist, and nonparticipant or has it conformed more to self-management ideology?[30] Great strides have been taken in developing a "new citizen" and a participant political culture yet, remnants of the old value systems still persist. And, although middle-level political, social, and economic leaders tend to support the principles of self-managing socialism, they are still reluctant to place full policy-making power and responsibility in the hands of the people and relinquish their positions of primary control. They share and support the ideals of democracy and associate these ideals with a more just, more Communist society, but they remain skeptical of the efficiency, effectiveness, and overall feasibili-

[28]A study of Soviet attitudes based on questionnaires and interviews with 3000 Soviet refugees in the 1950s concluded that even during the years of Stalinism, the Soviet system enjoyed the support of popular consensus. Alex Inkeles and Raymond A. Bauer, *The Soviet Citizen* (Cambridge: Harvard University Press, 1959).

[29]See Franz Schurmann, *Ideology and Organization in Communist China* (Berkeley: University of California Press, 1966). Mobilization systems utilize government control to activate the people in the quest for high-priority goals.

[30]For an interesting account, see Sharon Zukin, *Beyond Marx and Tito: Theory and Practice of Yugoslav Socialism* (London: Cambridge University Press, 1975).

ty of mass democracy. The mass populace, on the other hand, tends to distrust the sincerity of the leaders and also has certain doubts about the desirability of mass democracy. Is it the most efficient and productive system? Do the masses have the knowledge, training, and general wherewithall to assume such integral responsibilities in political life? These and other questions suggest that Yugoslavia has a diverse political culture, one that has undergone great change over the past 25 years, but still has a long way to go before becoming a democratic, participant culture.

A comparative summary of the power dimension of the dominant political cultures in the Soviet Union, China, and Yugoslavia reveals not only certain similarities but also some important differences. The subject-participatory culture of the USSR closely reflects the prevailing power relationships in Soviet society. In the broadest terms, there are those who rule (the élites) and those who follow (the masses); the followers recognize the privileged position of the party élites and seldom challenge it. The rank-and-file masses are typically content with their roles as subject-participants. They can and do participate in some constrained and narrowly defined political activities, but they are always cognizant that the leaders hold ultimate power and have the final say.

The dominant culture concerning power in China differs from the Soviet model in many ways. The Chinese people exhibit even greater deference to authority than the Soviets and do not have high expectations about their personal influence in the national policy-making process. Yet, they are more widely involved at the local level than the Soviet people and feel a real obligation to participate in the modernization program. This deep sense of responsibility for the collective good and the destiny of modern China is reflected in high rates and intense forms of involvement; this dominant culture is best described as a mobilized-participant one.

The Yugoslavs have made the greatest strides toward a more democratic political culture. The party leadership obviously controls almost exclusive power at the national level, yet, the typical citizen rightly perceives considerable opportunities for influence at the local level and particularly in his or her workplace. Rates of participation are high within communities, factories, and schools; the term, participant political culture, seems to be an increasingly accurate description of contemporary beliefs and opinions in Yugoslav society, at least in comparison with other Second World political cultures.

## RESPECT

In his opening remarks at the 24th Congress of the Communist Party of the Soviet Union in 1971, Brezhnev spoke of the need for action "whereby trust in and respect for people is combined with principled exactingness toward them" to create a "businesslike comradely atmosphere."

In praising the performance of General Secretary Brezhnev during the 25th Party Congress in 1976, a number of Soviet speakers drew attention to the value of respect. It was said, for example, that Brezhnev had "an ability to establish an atmosphere of trust, respect, and dedication to standards among people." Although the accolades of Communist Party congresses exaggerate (as do those of U.S. presidential conventions), what do trust and respect really mean in the Soviet context and why are they important in the building of Communism? The qualities of which Brezhnev's comrades spoke are a vital element in Communist construction because they pertain to the subjective feelings governing interpersonal and intergroup relations. Citizens in Communist Party states are expected to be comrades, which means that they are to have a common outlook and common interests. To promote comradeliness means to encourage a common class perspective. Because all Soviet citizens are conceived of as workers, they are expected to possess similar attitudes and opinions and to relate to one another in a respectful, trusting way.

Communists from the Soviet Union, for example, believe that the problems of crime and racism in the United States are insoluble because Americans are unable to relate and work together humanely and on the basis of mutual respect. Divided by the class struggle and cleavages endemic in capitalist, bourgeois society, they claim that fear, suspicion, and violence are natural outgrowths of our social and economic system. Although some of these undesirable remnants of traditional relations are obviously present in Soviet society, Communists expect them to dissolve with the further construction of Communism.

As we observe the religious, ethnic, and class strife that pervades so many of the nations on the globe today, we can appreciate the great importance of a cohesive community of people who can work together and relate to one another on the basis of trust and respect. The diverse peoples of the Soviet Union are still unable to do this. One hears rude and ethnocentric comments and sees forms of discrimination throughout the USSR. The more advanced nationalities of the industralized West (the Russians and the Ukrainians) sometimes see the less advanced Central Asians as primitive and backward. Although it is fair to say, then, that there is a certain sense of comradeliness, trust, and respect among the Soviet people that surpasses that found in some other First, Second, and Third World societies, it is unrealistic to assume that there is no suspicion, dishonesty, prejudice, or distrust in contemporary Soviet society. Indeed, there is! Even if one disregards the general rudeness Soviet people accord one another—pushing and shoving in queues and harsh and gruff service in stores and restaurants and the like—as a cultural trait that does not represent their true feelings about one another, there is still ample evidence to call into question the CPSU's complimentary assessments of Soviet culture. For example, there is a general distrust, cynicism, and suspicion of the "system," that is, of local officials, common bureaucrats, and so on. Everyone knows that petty officials who control such things as apartments, travel abroad, and the like are open to graft and that to get things done often requires the payment of small bribes to the "right" people. This is a widespread illness of Soviet society and one that appears to present a serious obstruction to the desired ideals of brotherhood and equality.

How are the Chinese doing in developing respectful and comradely relations among their people? In a revealing article, Ezra F. Vogel outlined Maoist objectives in this regard as well as the important changes that took place during the early period of Communist rule.[31] Vogel described a major movement away from what we know as friendship (a personal, private relationship between close companions) and the concept of comradeship. Comradeship in the Chinese context is based on a universal ethic in which individuals treat all other individuals as equal members of a political community. With the emphasis on collective rather than private relationships, comrades are obligated to mutually reinforcing roles within their society. The emphasis on the collective and helping was reflected in the common slogan and required reading: "Serve the People."[32] In attempting to establish comradely relations of this sort in China, the Western concept of private trust is lost. Under the system of comradeship, you would not tell a comrade a secret, something you wanted withheld from others. If a comrade knew for instance, that you fudged on your income tax or that you took more than your allotment of rice from the storehouse, he or she would be expected to report you to the peoples' court. If you were found guilty of these transgressions, you would engage in self-criticism and admit to your crime against the people. In establishing a public surveillance system where few indiscretions avoid the public eye, China has been able to build a society extraordinarily free of corruption, crime, and graft. Although the personal costs might remind some of the ferocious efficiency of Orwell's "big brother," the benefits have also been of great merit in the Chinese context.

Overall, the comradeship movement in Mao's China did have an impact. Personal relationships were changed; the role of the family was modified; the idea of personal friendships was altered. Although Mao did not fully succeed in "wiping out the old," as he so often exhorted the people to do, he and his contemporaries did have a major impact on the attitudes and values

[31]Ezra F. Vogel, "From Friendship to Comradeship: The Change in Personal Relations in Communist China," The China Quarterly, (21) (1965), pp. 46–60.

[32]"Serve the People" was one of the three political writings that was required by the Chinese government for all citizens.

guiding interpersonal relationships in Chinese society. Whether these changes will last in the present period of modernization and more moderate rule is open to question.

In Yugoslavia, the qualities of comradeliness, trust, and respect are particularly important in a setting where ethnic and religious enmity has characterized intergroup and interpersonal relations for centuries. With so many religious, ethnic, and lingual groups concentrated in this compact Balkan region, the propensity for intergroup conflict is dangerously high. Today, after over three decades of Communist rule, mass attitudes are still marked by strong doses of prejudice and discrimination, for example, intermarriage between different ethnic groups is infrequent, as is population movement between the different ethnic regions. The Yugoslav leaders acknowledge that their national problem has *not* been solved—the Soviet leaders claim the problem *has* been solved in their country—and have had their observations verified by nationalist movements and demonstrations (*e.g.*, Croatian and Albanian) in some of the Yugoslav regions recently. The question of comradeship also tells us something important about the political culture of Yugoslavs. It is clear that friendship has not been replaced by the comradeship that Vogel describes in China. To the contrary, interpersonal relations tend to be a carbon copy of those in most Western states. Greetings between people are made on a first name or a more formal Mr./Mrs./Miss basis; the designation of someone as comrade is seldom used except in official party or government activities.

The Yugoslav leadership's greatest accomplishment concerning this dimension of political culture is in their ability to win the support and trust of the Yugoslav people. Although average Yugoslav citizens express occasional cynicism and criticism toward the government or their leaders, as most of us do on occasion, they will defend the country when the chips are down. The Yugoslav people have a good sense of world politics and they understand and appreciate their privileged position in the Communist world. No other Communist-run society has the degree of personal freedom found in Yugoslavia—the right to travel or emigrate abroad, freedom of expression, and the like. But the Yugoslav people are well aware that if the government loses their support and is overturned, it could very easily be replaced by a more repressive, pro-Soviet regime.

To summarize, all the Marxist governments of the Second World have attempted to eradicate the class-based feelings of their pre-socialist periods and replace them with more respectful and fraternal orientations based on the concepts of brotherhood, equality, and unity. A close examination of behavior and belief systems in these countries shows definite gaps in these desired orientations, but it is fair to say that considerable changes have taken place. The more authoritarian system of government in the Communist Party states has something to do with the relative calm within their societies. A relaxation of government authority and an increase in civil rights might be followed by a dangerous upswing in intergroup animosity and violence.

Although the people may have at least some minimal level of trust and respect for others within their own state, distrust and animosity often reflects feelings and relations among Communist Party states and their peoples. The continuing conflict in the war-torn states of Southeast Asia is a good example. The advent of Communism to Laos, Cambodia (Kampuchea), and all of Vietnam in the 1970s obviously did not bring respect, peace, and prosperity. And, respect and trust certainly do not exist among the Soviets and the Chinese or between the East Europeans and the Soviets. There appears to be a notable absence of respect for the Soviet Union throughout the Communist world, both at élite and mass levels. Although Communism was to bring fraternal feelings among all worker states, one encounters considerable anti-Soviet sentiment in China, Yugoslavia, and in most of the countries of Eastern Europe.

## WELL-BEING

What do the average people expect in the way of health care, social services, and consumer goods in Communist-run societies? What are their attitudes concerning a fair and proper distribution of these values? At the 24th Party Congress, Secretary Brezhnev announced: "The growth of the people's well-being is the supreme goal of the party's economic policy." At the 25th Party Congress, five years later in 1976, he noted that the most important goal remained "a further increase in the people's well-being." Brezhnev went on to say that this meant improvement in working and living conditions, progress in public health, culture, and education, and everything that facilitates "improvement of the socialist way of life." Similar pledges were given at the 26th Party Congress in 1981. But do the people believe them?

First, we ought to be aware that the Soviet Union is a welfare state. It spends the equivalent of billions of dollars on education, health care, social security, and, at even greater cost, on the massive bureaucracy that coordinates these programs. However, in contrast to the leaders' hopes and perhaps good-willed intentions of upgrading the material and social well-being of the Soviet populace, the contemporary scene shows considerable shortcomings. There are critical shortages in housing and basic foodstuffs as well as poor service in many of those programs (e.g., medical and dental care) in which the regime prides itself most.

At the same time, when traveling through socialist countries one hears "We're living well"; "We can't complain," "We've never had it better." To the average citizen, life appears to be getting better, and it certainly is when one compares present-day living standards with those of the past. On the other hand, those citizens who compare Soviet life with that in the West are often critical and frustrated; but they are a minority of the broader society.

The dominant orientations of the Soviet populace also reflect the contradiction between the Communist ideal, where material goods are to be allocated on the basis of need, and the Soviet reality of reward on the basis of work. For the most part, the more poorly paid seem reconciled to their less privileged position on the income hierarchy, whereas the better paid tend to believe that a differential system of rewards is the only fair and reasonable way to handle income.

The American visitor views the living standard as one of general deprivation. To us, the most striking feature of this aspect of Soviet political culture is the passivity of the population in accepting the status quo. There are always some people intent (and sometimes successful) in ripping off the system and becoming millionaires in a proletarian state; still other people show a total lack of initiative and would prefer not to work if they are able to find some means of subsistence. But these two groups are almost invisible minorities in the enormous Soviet populace. The great majority on the other hand, are hard-working people who report daily to their jobs and seldom show signs of frustration or discontent. With a strong sense of history, they remember the difficult times of the past and generally agree that "We've never had it so good."

Some Western observers dispute this general picture of content and call attention to the unusually high level of alcoholism that continues to plague Soviet society. Party authorities have tried their best to alleviate this problem, including the encouragement of such soft drinks as Pepsi-Cola as preferred substitutes for vodka and wine, yet alcoholism continues to exist. The high percentage of personal income spent on liquor substantially reduces the general social and material well-being of the average Soviet family. Vladimir Treml, an American economist, estimates that the average Soviet family spends two months' salary a year on drink. However, the problem of vodka in Russia is far older than the Soviet state. Although we cannot conclude that Communism has caused alcoholism, we can conclude that its Soviet proponents have done little to alleviate this historical problem.

An important component of this dimension of political culture concerns a society's expectations for the future. Soviet policy regarding material well-being has been very sensitive, almost paranoid, on the question of rising expectations. One of the reasons for the party leadership's reluctance to loosen foreign travel is tied, no doubt, to their fear of increasing mass expectations, which the government will be unable to meet. Rising and unmet expectations have been more prevalent and, as a result, more of a problem among certain East European populations, such as Poland and Yugoslavia, where contact with the West is greater. In addition, the populations of these countries are less docile than the Soviet populace and frequently make their feelings known. Just before Christmas in 1970, for example, the Polish leaders instituted a major price increase in a variety of foodstuffs. Perceiving a substantial reduction in their level of material well-being, the Polish populace protested the government's policy, rioted in some coastal cities, stopped work, and burned down the party headquarters in one major city. This action led to the removal of the party leader, Wladyslaw Gomulka, and abolition of the price increases.[33] The next party leader, Edward Gierek, attempted a new set of price increases in 1976 and also encountered mass dissatisfaction. The government was forced once again to rescind the increases. Gierek was ousted in 1980 during the workers' strikes when he, too, proved incapable of meeting the aspirations and demands of the Polish people. This calls attention to the power of a society's expectations and the importance that orientations concerning the fair and proper allocation of well-being can have on political life. As the awareness and sophistication of the Soviet populace increases with the normal and inevitable process of modernization, we can expect them to develop more discriminating attitudes and become involved in this important question of social and political affairs.

With the Maoist emphasis on equality and the collectivity, the Chinese people have come to de-emphasize, at least when compared with the West, private material interests and to work in the interests of society as a whole. To solve the problems of mass starvation and the general deprivation that characterized much of Chinese society at the time of the Communist assumption of power in 1949, a massive program of redistribution was adopted. Because egalitarianism was not then a dominant part of Chinese political culture, redistribution toward increased material equality did not meet with universal approval. Over the years, however, attitudes have changed concerning the proper distribution of values. Most Chinese people accept the principle of greater equality within the guidelines of "from each according to his abilities, to each according to his contribution."

The Chinese compare their well-being with what was experienced in the past: almost without exception, they find it much improved and getting better. They have jobs and shelter, no one is starving, and they receive adequate medical and health care. These alone are enough to command the support of the Chinese people. Televisions, private cars, and vacation homes are distant fairy tales. As China opens to the West and as Chinese people see more of the well-being and consumerism enjoyed in other societies, their aspirations are bound to change.[34]

In contrast to the more centralized control over the distribution of well-being prevalent in the Soviet and Chinese systems, Yugoslavia allows individuals more freedom and opportunity to maximize their personal well-being. To be sure, Yugoslavia is a welfare state that provides a public system of social services, as do the Chinese and Soviets. In contrast, however, more decentralized Yugoslav economic and political systems provide greater opportunities and incentives for increased personal welfare and consumption. In the late 1960s and early 1970s, many Yugoslavs proudly and openly displayed their material possessions, such as a car or a private vacation home on the Dalmatian Coast. The system was loose enough to allow the accumulation of a considerable amount of personal possessions. Many people were moonlighting, thousands were working abroad in Western

[33]For a description of Poland at that time and in the recent aftermath, see Adam Bromke, "Beyond the Gomulka Era," *Foreign Affairs*, 49 (3) (1971), pp. 480–492.

[34]For excellent treatments of a broad variety of issues relating to cultural change in post-Mao China, see Godwin C. Chu and Francis L. K. Hsu, eds., *Moving a Mountain: Cultural Change in China* (Honolulu: The University Press of Hawaii, 1979).

Europe and were sending home large amounts of hard currency,[35] and some were simply corrupt and absconded with public funds. Whatever methods were used, many Yugoslavs were becoming rich even by Western standards, and the distance between the upper and lower income levels was growing excessively pronounced. After being generally tolerant of this feature of economic growth through the 1960s, Tito and the party leaders aggressively attacked bourgeois materialism and corruption in the early 1970s and initiated policies that prevented the excessive accumulation of personal wealth. The action was only a partial success, however, and simply drove many of the striving Yugoslav entrepreneurs underground, forcing them to be a little more discrete in bragging about their material success. Although the government's hard-nosed policy lowered the level of prideful boasting, it had little influence on the deep-seated Yugoslav values of materialism and consumerism.

Such orientations in Yugoslavia represent a more individual-centered and consumption-oriented political culture than exists in either China or the Soviet Union. When a young party member, dressed in the latest Italian fashion and excessively desirous of Western material possessions, was asked how the Marxist ideal of "to each according to his needs" would ever become a reality in view of the materialism so evident in her society, she said, "We are the babies of socialism. It may be 100 or even 200 years before we can free ourselves from the materialist values of our former society." Although this bit of honesty is a refreshing characteristic of the Yugoslavs, one wonders if Karl Marx would be so self-assured and flippant.

Overall, one gets the impression that self-interest still is the dominant feature of this aspect of political culture in Communist societies. Although there are differences among countries, people tend to place their personal interests before those of the collectivity. If the leaders of these states were suddenly to adopt the principle, "from each according to his abilities, *to each according to his needs*," people would probably react according to how this new policy would affect them. If they expected to raise their level of well-being, they would tend to support the new policy. If they were an engineer or a party official and already making and enjoying more than they really needed, they would be likely to oppose it. In other words, attitudes and values in most Communist societies concerning well-being may not be all that different from those in the West. As the young Yugoslav said, it may take 100 or even 200 years!

## ENLIGHTENMENT

The final dimension of political culture to be examined concerns the value, enlightenment. How "enlightened" are people living in Communist Party states? What are the values and characteristics of the "enlightened" citizen?

After the takeovers, Communist leaders knew they would have to develop a new set of values, new ideas, new skills, and new behaviors—in other words, a new socialist person—before they could succeed in building Communism. One way of examining the enlightenment dimension of political culture, then, is to examine the people in terms of a set of standards describing this new person. Using the following characteristics outlined by T. H. Chen, we can draw attention to both similarities and differences in the political cultures found in the Second World states.[36]

1. *Absolute selflessness.* The model Maoist citizen, according to Chen, held no ambitions beyond serving the cause of the revolution and China. This characteristic, ingrained to some degree in the Chinese populace during the Maoist period is in conflict with Western concepts of individualism and liberty. More closely tied to this Western concept are the Soviet and Yugoslav people who have not yet reached the level of selflessness so fervently desired in Maoist China. Soviet and Yugoslav citizens are, of course, pa-

[35]According to the 1971 Yugoslav census, there were 671,909 Yugoslavs temporarily living or working abroad; this amounted to 15.2 percent of the total registered nonagricultural work force. Miloje Nikolic, "Some Basic Features of Yugoslav External Migrants," *Yugoslav Survey, 13* (1) (1972), p. 4.

[36]Theodore Hsi-en Chen, "The New Socialist Man," in C. T. Hu, ed., *Aspects of Chinese Education* (New York: Columbia University Press, 1969), pp. 88–95.

triots and will often sacrifice their individual interests for what they perceive to be in the best interests of their country.[37] But in everyday life, one gets the impression that they think first of themselves, then of their families and friends, and then perhaps remotely of their country.

The political cultures of the East Europeans and Cubans also seem to approximate Western standards. The mass exodus of refugees from Cuba in 1980 suggests that these people placed personal interests over those of the Cuban revolution. Although it is hard to characterize the Cubans who chose to stay or were unable to emigrate, one must conclude that at least a sizeable minority have not assumed the characteristics of a selfless, model citizen.

2. *Obedience to the Communist Party.* Commitment to the leaders and to the party is also to be a dominant feature of Communist political culture. Chen quotes the words of the song, "East is Red," that the Chinese children were taught to express their worship of the now deceased Mao:

> The East is red,
> The sun rises.
> China has brought forth a Mao Zedong.
> He works for the people's happiness.
> He is the people's great savior.
>
> Chairman Mao loves the people,
> He is our guide.
> He leads us onward
> To build the new China.
>
> The Communist party is like the sun,
> Wherever it shines, there is light.
> Where there's the Communist party,
> There the people will win liberation.

Although adoration and respect for the Communist parties and leadership are desired features of Soviet and Yugoslav political culture, they do not appear deeply ingrained. The party

[37]A good indicator of selflessness is the willingness with which people come to the aid of their country. During World War II (renamed the "Great Patriotic War" by Soviet authorities), the Soviet people fought valiantly and selflessly against the Nazis. In 1968, the Yugoslav people rushed to the support of their government and were willing to take up arms against the USSR when it was rumored that the Soviets were going to follow their intervention into Czechoslovakia with an invasion of Yugoslavia.

leaders do command a certain amount of respect, and the party is considered by some to be acting in the best interest of the people. However, there is a certain amount of cynicism and lack of respect displayed in the jokes that circulate in these countries, particularly in the East European countries, concerning the incompetence of the leaders and party organizations. This cynicism is less widespread in the USSR and Yugoslavia, where the people are more likely to consider the party leaders those of their own peoples' choosing, than it is in many of the East European countries, such as Czechoslovakia and Hungary, where the leadership is perceived to have been picked by the Soviet Union. In these countries, the party and leaders—especially the Soviet CPSU and its leaders—are the objects of some of the most caustic jokes ever told. These stories represent a good indicator of the legitimacy of the party as well as the obedience the population will accord it.

3. *Class consciousness.* The model Communist citizen should always be on guard against remnants of the class struggle, such as bourgeois ideas at home and abroad, the global threat of capitalist imperialism, and the like. For example, because of intense indoctrination by the schools, the arts, and the media during the Maoist period, the Chinese are immersed in the class struggle and have assumed a political consciousness as part of their belief systems.[38]

Although there are some differences of opinion among the post-Mao leaders concerning exploiting classes in their society, some caution that the class struggle is still around. Because of earlier Maoist indoctrination and continuing attention during the more recent period, some Chinese people still appear sensitive to the so-called remnants of capitalism and the old elements of the exploiting classes. Yet, one gets the impression that few really believe deeply in the significance of the class struggle.

Again, there is evidence to suggest that class consciousness is even less deeply embedded in

[38]The arts in China were viewed as a forum for heightening the class consciousness of the masses during Mao's time. The revolutionary operas and ballets were typically based on the class-struggle themes.

the beliefs of the Soviet and East European peo- ples. Every Soviet student can explain in class terms the Great Patriotic War or race relations in Africa; the same holds true for Yugoslavs and the East Europeans. However, in contrast to Mao's China, where class enemies were perceived to abound and where class warfare was said to rage endlessly, there is a much more relaxed atmosphere concerning the idea of class struggle in the European Communist Party states. The attitudes of the Soviet people concerning class consciousness are no doubt influenced by the official doctrine that says that the USSR has long since reached socialism and has eliminated antagonistic classes. Whatever the causes, the typical Soviet citizen, along with his or her counterparts in Eastern Europe, do not seem to be particularly conscious of the class struggle as Marxist theory would have it.

4. *Ideological study.* Ideological study in Mao's China meant the study of Mao Zedong's political writings, the works of Karl Marx, Friedrich Engels, and Joseph Stalin, and contributions by certain other Chinese party officials. Before Mao's death, schoolchildren and elderly adults alike were often seen reciting the thoughts of the Great Helmsman from his *Little Red Book*. The model Chinese citizen was to have the correct ideological outlook, which was to be derived from almost unceasing study of Chinese Communist ideology. However, the almost exclusive emphasis on ideological study has been sharply curtailed in the post-Mao period. Now, study of science, technology, and traditional academic disciplines is given more attention. The ideologically infused but poorly educated Chinese populace has a considerable amount of catching up to do to contribute fully to the Four-Modernizations Program.

Although revolutionary study was a pulsating enterprise very much a part of Mao's China, it has become passe in most all Communist Party countries. Rather than serving as an intimate part of one's everyday life, it tends to be a course one studies in school. When watching these courses being taught, one gets the impression that both teachers and students are simply going through the motions. In many respects, it resembles a course in American high school civics; there is some material to be covered and a test at the end, but the most important concern to students is the grade one receives at the end.

In the early 1970s, Tito and the Yugoslav Communists feared that even this minimal amount of ideological study was fading further from the school curriculum. As a response, they inaugurated a campaign to bring Marx and Lenin back in the classroom and to renew the ideological indoctrination of the Yugoslav populace. Even after the campaign, one gets the impression—in Yugoslavia and elsewhere in Eastern Europe—that ideological study is something to be done but nothing about which to be overly committed.

5. *Labor and production.* The new Communist citizen in China is expected to thrive on, and enjoy, manual labor. All students during the Maoist period, for example, were required to engage in productive labor for the state in addition to their normal study. Schools and universities, Chen notes, were to become centers of production as well as centers of learning. Mao's China was a picture of men and women at work; peasants marching in the fields, students and laborers working side by side in the factories.

Both men and women are working in contemporary China, and there is a strong trend toward specialization. Requirements on manual labor for students and professionals have disappeared. The enlightened Chinese citizen of today is attempting to become an expert in computers or energy technology and is likely to become more removed from the ideals of production and labor.

In 1958, Secretary Khrushchev proposed a set of far-reaching reforms for the Soviet educational system, part of which would establish a work/study program somewhat like those in Mao's China. Khrushchev's recommendations for a combined work/study experience for students were resoundingly defeated; a number of influential groups critically questioned the advisability of the proposals. "How can we compete with the United States in the development of science and technology when our best students are required to spend part of the day in the factory?" the scientific leaders asked. "How can we meet our quotas," asked the factory directors, "when we have to put up with these immature students?" The defeat of Khrushchev's proposals and the continued separation of work and study in the USSR today does not mean that the leaders are unconcerned with labor and production. Rather, there is a feeling that modern economies require specialization and that it is unreasonable to expect trained professional or aspiring nuclear physicists to spend part of their day in a factory or on a collective farm. As a result, political cultures in contemporary Eastern Europe and the Soviet Union reflect growing divisions among workers and professionals. The "enlightened" citizen of these countries is likely to be well educated, highly specialized, and ill-disposed to taking part in manual labor.

6. *The Red/expert blend.* The enlightened socialist citizen in most contemporary Communist Party states is to be both committed to Communist ideology (*i.e.*, Red) and an expert with specific skills and talents that will contribute to the construction of Communism. The different blends of Redness and expertness, however, illustrate some significant contrasts among the various Communist Party states. Mao's China invariably placed greater emphasis on the ideological side (Red) and less on the technical, scientific aspects (expert) of socialist construction. During the 1960s, Yugoslavia was at the other extreme on the continuum and had allowed expert to assume predominance over Red. This trend in Yugoslavia generated a highly educated technocratic sector that, although largely Communist, viewed the question of socioeconomic growth in developmental and scientific rather than ideological terms.

The Chinese and Yugoslavs have traditionally occupied the two extremes on the Red/expert continuum, whereas the Soviet Union has assumed a more conservative, middle-of-the-road position. Although the Soviet leadership has not emphasized the value of extreme Redness, neither has it allowed the more unfettered development of the technocratic experts. What it has done is to insist on both. That is, the new enlightened citizen should be not only ideologically committed but also trained and educated to bring the most advanced skills and training available to his or her work setting. Some individuals do indeed approximate this model citizen, but most have deficiencies in one, or more likely, both categories. There is little evidence to support this hypothesis, but it seems that the higher the level of training and education, the lower the level of Redness, and *vice versa*. If this relationship is indeed correct, the problem of assuring ideological purity and commitment will be an increasingly difficult one as the process of modernization and enlightenment continues. The recent Four-Modernizations Program in China will provide an interesting test of this hypothesis.[39]

## SUBCULTURES

We can think of Communist Party states in terms of their dominant political cultures, but we should recognize that this is a major simplification of reality. Because most Communist-run societies are complex and heterogeneous, they contain a variety of subcultures within their broader populations. Although these subcultures are likely to share certain values with the dominant political culture, they also hold many distinct values of their own.

Subcultures are based on a diverse set of characteristics. We can divide populations geographically (*e.g.*, the North and South in the United States) and find distinct subcultures; we can also divide societies by social or occupational attributes, ethnic differences, and so forth. Another meaningful and useful way to explore subcultures is by dividing societies into political elites and masses. The Chinese masses, for example, hold values that are in some respects quite different from those held by the political élites.[40]

[39]For an examination of political socialization and educational policy in the post-Mao era, see Suzanne Pepper, "Chinese Education After Mao: Two Steps Forward, Two Steps Back and Begin Again," *The China Quarterly, 81* (1980), pp. 1–65; also, see the recent articles written by various Chinese officials, observers, and scholars in the journal, *Chinese Education.*

[40]For a study that uses the mass/elite distinction, see James D. Seymour, *China: The Politics of Revolutionary Reintegration* (New York: Thomas Y. Crowell, 1976), pp. 25–66.

In addition, workers in urban, industrial centers hold values that often contrast with those in isolated villages; and the political culture of the inhabitants of Beijing, the capital in the north, tends to vary in important respects from the populations in the more business-oriented south.

The dissidents in the Soviet Union—such as the noted physicist Andrei Sakharov, who was instrumental in developing the Soviet A-bomb; groups of courageous young people; Jewish and religious activists; and others—represent significant subcultures at odds with the official party line. Because their ideas and values oppose the existing system, they are viewed as threats and have been harrassed, banished, and imprisoned. When compared with the West, Communist leaders display a high level of intolerance toward groups in opposition to the dominant culture.

Frederick C. Barghoorn has also distinguished different political subcultures in the Soviet Union on the basis of social structure.[41] Thinking of Soviet society in terms of intelligentsia, workers, and collective farmers, Barghoorn has identified attitudes and behaviors that distinguish each group from one another and from the dominant political culture as well. According to his study, different orientations about politics are largely defined by one's position in the social structure. Because the intelligentsia are a somewhat privileged strata in Soviet society, they have higher levels of education and sometimes expect higher levels of power, respect, and well-being than the less privileged "unenlightened" sectors. Different opinions, such as those about the proper distribution of values, have resulted in a variety of intense policy disputes over the years.

Nationality is also an important determinant of subcultures in the USSR. The Ukrainians, Jews, Crimean Tatars, the Baltic nationalities, and others, all evidence different attitudes and values having an impact on politics. Teresa Rakowska-Harmstone has written that nationalism in such groups challenges the central Soviet Government in three important areas: (1) pressure for broader political autonomy, (2) pressure for greater allocation of resources in local areas and more autonomy in managing local affairs, and (3) pressure for greater freedom to promote local national cultures.[42] Another leading expert on Soviet nationalities writes, "Far from having solved the nationalities question, Soviet leaders must consider it as among the most salient issues on the political agenda."[43]

The national differences between Serbs, Croats, and other national and ethnic groups define a diverse set of subcultures in Yugoslavia. Based on cultural, religious, lingual, and economic differences, these groups hold political orientations that contrast, and often conflict, with some important areas of Yugoslav political life. Some of the groups (e.g., the Macedonians and Albanians) who inhabit less developed national areas of Yugoslavia feel that the state should do more to equalize the level of well-being among different national regions.[44] Because their levels of well-being are considerably below those in the developed regions, they feel funds should be taken from the developed regions and invested in their areas to aid social and economic development. These and other differences of opinion associated with ethnicity in Yugoslavia are reflected in both elite and mass political cultures and on many occasions have resulted in political conflict pitting one republic or a group of republics against another.

After having viewed the pre-Communist cultures, the desired political cultures, and the dominant political cultures and subcultures, we might conclude by assessing what it all means. Have the strategies of political socialization been successful? Have the Communists succeeded in creating new ideas and values, a new mentality and a new socialist person? Although one does observe a certain level of conformity among the people throughout most of the Communist Party

[41]Barghoorn, *op. cit.*, pp. 48–86.

[42]Teresa Rakowska-Harmstone, "The Dialectics of Nationalism in the USSR," *Problems of Communism* 33 (3) (1974), p. 12.

[43]Brian D. Silver, "Soviet Nationality Problems: Analytic Approaches," *Problems of Communism,* 38 (4) (1979), p. 71.

[44]The autonomous province of Kosovo, inhabited primarily by Albanians, was rocked by rioting and demonstrations in 1981 as Albanians sought a greater share of resources in the Yugoslav federation.

states and even some level of acceptance and support of the ideals and values of the regime, it seems apparent that there is no "new man." In their book on political culture and political change in Communist Party states, Archie Brown, Jack Gray and others summarized the results of considerable research on this question.[45] In all of the countries examined, there is little evidence to suggest that human nature and political culture have been changed in a fundamental way. Although recognizing that the amount of time devoted to Communist change has been relatively brief in the course of human history and, therefore, recognizing that more fundamen-

tal changes may still come about, our conclusion raises some important implications for the question of politics to which subsequent chapters will now turn. Namely, because Communist leaders have been unsuccessful in creating a totally new political culture, they must make decisions in an environment blessed with less than total agreement on the distribution of such values as power, respect, well-being, and enlightenment. This means that policy will be made in a politicized environment where different groups and individuals will prefer different decisions and policy outcomes. Like the historical and socioeconomic forces reviewed in Chapters One and Two, the attitudinal and behavioral forces reviewed here are environmental determinants of considerable importance to politics and the political system.

[45]Archie Brown and Jack Gray, eds., *Political Culture and Political Change in Communist States* 2nd rev. ed. (New York: Holmes & Meier, 1979).

# Suggestions for Further Reading

Brown, Archie and Jack Gray, eds., *Political Culture and Political Change in Communist States*, 2nd rev. ed. (New York: Holmes & Meier, 1979).

Chang, Parris H., "Children's Literature and Political Socialization," in Godwin Chu and Francis Hsu, eds., *Moving a Mountain: Cultural Change in China* (Honolulu: The University of Hawaii Press, 1979), pp. 237–256.

Chen, Theodore Hsi-en, *The Maoist Educational Revolution* (New York: Praeger, 1974).

Dewitt, Nicholas, *Education and Professional Employment in the USSR* (Washington, D.C.: U. S. Government Printing Office, 1961).

Fagen, Richard R., *The Transformation of Political Culture in Cuba* (Stanford, Calif.: Stanford University Press, 1969).

Grant, Nigel, *Soviet Education*, 3rd ed. (Baltimore: Penguin, 1972).

Harasymiw, Bohdan, ed., *Education and the Mass Media in the Soviet Union and Eastern Europe* (New York: Praeger, 1976).

Hollander, Gayle Durham, *Soviet Political Indoctrination* (New York: Praeger, 1972).

Hu, Chang-tu, *Chinese Education Under Communism* (New York: Columbia University Press, 1962).

Kassof, Allen, *The Soviet Youth Program* (Cambridge: Harvard University Press, 1965).

Lifton, Robert J., *Thought Reform and the Psychology of Totalism: A Study of "Brainwashing" in China* (New York: Norton, 1961).

Liu, Alan P., *Political Culture and Group Conflict in Communist China* (Santa Barbara, Calif.: Clio Press, 1976).

Metzger, Thomas A., *Escape from Predicament: Neo-Confucianism and China's Evolving Political Culture* (New York: Columbia University Press, 1977).

Mickiewicz, Ellen P., *Soviet Political Schools: The Communist Party Adult Instruction Program* (New Haven, Conn.: Yale University Press, 1967).

Price, R. F., *Education in Communist China* (New York: Praeger, 1970).

Solomon, Richard H., *Mao's Revolution and the Chinese Political Culture* (Berkeley: University of California Press, 1971).

Volgyes, Ivan, ed., *Political Socialization in Eastern Europe* (New York: Praeger, 1975).

Welsh, William A., ed., *Survey Research and*

*Public Attitudes in Eastern Europe and the Soviet Union* (Elmsford, N.Y.: Pergamon, 1980).

White, Stephen, *Political Culture and Soviet Politics* (New York: St. Martin's, 1979).

Zukin, Sharon, *Beyond Marx and Tito: Theory and Practice of Yugoslav Socialism* (London: Cambridge University Press, 1975).

# CHAPTER FOUR
## The Communist Parties: Structures and Personnel

Of what importance are Communist parties in our study of the allocation of values in the Second World? What do we know about these mysterious organizations? Are they staffed with dull-witted, paunchy bureaucrats and how do they affect the cause of human dignity in the Communist world?

It is the Communist Party and its singular effect on the political process that most distinguishes Second World policy making from that found in the two or multiparty systems of the First World. Called by its leaders the "vanguard of the people" and the "fount of political wisdom," the Communist Party dominates the policy-making process in all Second World states. Characteristic of a one-party state is a policy process much more centralized and much less open to outside influence than that found in the United States or many of the West European democracies. This difference is, in part, a result of the historical origin and subsequent evolution of the Communist Party of the Soviet Union (CPSU).

### HISTORICAL SETTING

Karl Marx and Friedrich Engels provided their heirs precious little guidance concerning the proper organization of the postrevolutionary Marxist state. "Now that we've won, what do we do?" Vladimir Ilyich Lenin and Leon Trotsky asked themselves after the Bolshevik victory in 1917. How should they organize political activity to solve the pressing social, economic, and political problems facing the Russian state?

Lenin was neither naïve nor unprepared when it came to the question of political organization. As one leading scholar puts it:

> One trait that made [Lenin] a pioneer of twentieth-century politics was his insight into the crucial role of organization. Lenin realized that . . . all human activities . . . are carried out in and through organizations and associations.[1]

In what is perhaps his most important work, *What Is to Be Done?*, Lenin recognized the need for a particular type of organization that could be used to speed work toward the revolutionary goal of socialist construction. Years before the Russian Revolution, Lenin's political organization, the Communist Party, evolved into a highly centralized, authoritarian, and militant "party of a new type,"[2] one that became the sole guardian of organized political rule.

[1] Alfred G. Meyer, *Communism*, 3rd ed. (New York: Random House, 1967), p. 43.

[2] For an excellent discussion of Lenin's "party of a new type," see Bertram D. Wolfe, "Leninism," in Milorad M. Drachkovitch, ed., *Marxism in the Modern World* (Stanford, Calif.: Stanford University Press, 1965), pp. 76–84.

Under Lenin's leadership, the Communist Party represented the key institution for consolidating power and forging the subsequent construction of Communism. Using great organizational and leadership skills and adhering to the pragmatic principle that "the ends justify the means," Lenin concentrated policy-making power within the organizational structure of the party. What was initially viewed by the Bolsheviks as the dictatorship of the proletariat became, for all intents, a dictatorship of the party. During the Leninist and Stalinist stages of development, the party grew into a dictatorial bureaucratic organization that controlled the goals, actions, and policy outcomes governing the Soviet political process.

Lenin attempted, however, to combine democratic values with the party dictatorship by adopting the principle of democratic centralism. This formula represents an intended merging of both democratic and centralistic (or dictatorial) powers in which members of the party are encouraged to debate policy matters freely until the point of decision. Once a vote has been taken and a decision is made, however, centralism is required and further discussion and debate are forbidden. Although this principle does allow some level of democratic debate within the party and although it is not clear to what extent subordinates are successful in challenging the policy preferences of superiors, it does not alter the underlying primacy of party rule, in which a small minority of the state's population monopolizes the primary institution of political power. One-party rule administered according to the principle of democratic centralism is the single most distinguishing characteristic of the Soviet and other Communist political systems.

Assuming a dominant position in the political system alongside the party is the state or government system itself, discussed more fully in Chapter Five. Early Marxist-Leninist doctrine posited that the state would "wither away" with the construction of Communism and that "rule over men" would give way to the "administration of things." After 60 years of Soviet Communism and better than a quarter century of Communist rule in most other Second World na-

tions, the states seem to be growing rather than withering. As reflected in Leon Fischer's famous quotation, "What began to wither away was the idea of withering," contemporary Communist leaders seldom speak of the inevitable dissolution of the state. Dissolving the state would mean tearing down the elaborate bureaucracy on which Communist Party rule so heavily depends. Accordingly, the withering of the state appears to be a gamble Communist leaders are unwilling to take.

Another reorientation in doctrine in most Communist Party states that has to do with party rule involves the use of the phrase, dictatorship of the proletariat. Because of the contradiction between the party monopoly of power and the "official" policy of a proletarian dictatorship and because of the shrinking proletarian sector within the modernizing population, the proletarian-state concept slipped from usage in the USSR and was replaced in the 1977 Constitution by the "state of socialist toilers," in which the CPSU serves as "the leading and guiding force."

At the 25th Party Congress, General Secretary Leonid I. Brezhnev exclaimed:

> The Soviet people are aware that where the Party acts, success and victory are assured! The people trust the Party. The people whole-heartedly support the Party's domestic and foreign policy. This augments the Party's strength and serves as an inexhaustible source of energy.

With minor and generally insignificant exceptions, the leading roles of the Communist parties in the other Marxist-Leninist states are described similarly. One partial exception, however, is Yugoslavia; during the 1960s, the League of Communists of Yugoslavia (LCY) talked of "removing itself from power" by assuming a less central role in the political process.[3] In the resulting power vacuum, the fragile political balance maintained by the LCY was upset when national (ethnic) conflict in the early 1970s threatened the unity and stability of the Yugoslav state. Fearing

[3]At the 6th Party Congress in 1952, the Yugoslav Communist Party changed its name to the League of Communists. This was a symbolic change related to the leaders' desire to alter the dominating role of the party to that of arbiter.

a factionalized and a possibly disintegrating state, Josip Broz Tito and the LCY leaders moved decisively to reassert the leading role of the party in the government process.[4] The LCY is still less centralized and authoritarian than the CPSU and the Chinese Communist Party (CCP), but it has now assumed a considerably more orthodox "Leninist" position on the question of party rule.

In view of the high level of societal complexity and the growing diversity of political interests in most of these states, the monolithic dominance of the Communist parties is somewhat surprising and viewed by some Western observers as retarding national development. These observers contend that high levels of social pluralism and complexity require political expression and representation and that social and political development in modernizing industrial societies is facilitated by a more open, less controlled political process than that found among the Communist Party states. This point of view is widely held in the West, but it is heatedly challenged and denied in the Communist world.

Among the reasons for the Communist leaders' (particularly Soviet leader's) overriding concern with maintaining centralized party rule is their general distrust of foreign and internal hostile, anti-Communist forces. Externally, they view the capitalist West, particularly the United States, as an aggressive, imperialistic power that, if not challenged and checked, will exploit peoples and nations throughout the world. The best defense against this Western threat, in the eyes of the Communist leaders, is strength at home; this is a capability that they believe can be guaranteed only through strict party rule.

There is also a distrust of forces at work within their own countries. Remnants of the presocialist system, and signs of the continuing class struggle and bourgeois ideas are often considered present and require the vigilance of the Communist Party to keep them in check. There exists in this outlook a messianic vision that the party knows best, that it is really acting in the best interests of the working class; if the people will only give their unswerving support, the party will facilitate and hasten the eventual construction of Communism. Although some party leaders occasionally register cynical, antiparty remarks in private, most are dedicated true believers convinced of the validity of this political philosophy and of their right to rule.

## THE PARTY: MEMBERSHIP AND COMPOSITION

Who belongs to these Communist parties? As Table 4.1 indicates, only 6.3 percent of the Soviet people, 3.9 percent of the Chinese, and 8.4 percent of the Yugoslavs belong to the Communist parties in their countries. In other countries, membership ranges from a high of 13.3 percent in Romania to a low of 0.2 percent in Cambodia (Kampuchea).[5] As one expert points out, the fact that only a minority of the populations in the Soviet Union and the other socialist states are party members does not mean that the majority are anti-Communist or opposed to the regime, rather:

> Party membership is demanding, and it is not easy to join. Nor does membership bring tangible rewards, although it does open some career opportunities that are virtually closed to non-Communists. Membership in the party may, indeed, bring with it some hardships. Theoretically, a member puts himself at the party's disposal when he joins; he may find himself summoned to a political meeting or given some political assignment when he would rather do something else. Moreover, party members are supposed to provide a model for other Soviet citizens to follow; therefore, the Communist may find his private life scrutinized and his behavior called into account.[6]

---

[4]In a collection of speeches prepared for both domestic and foreign consumption, Tito and other LCY leaders outlined the LCY's revitalized policy role. High LCY official, Stane Dolanc, did so in particularly blunt terms: "We communists are in power in this country. . . . This, comrades, must be openly stated, for there was a time [1960's] when it was shameful to admit this to anyone." *Ideological and Political Offensive of the League of Communists of Yugoslavia* (Belgrade: Secretariat for Information, 1972), p. 46.

[5]As a result of the war waged in Cambodia (Kampuchea), Laos, and Vietnam in 1980, the party figures for these states may not be accurate indicators of membership.

[6]Darrell P. Hammer, *USSR: The Politics of Oligarchy* (Hinsdale, Ill.: Dryden, 1974), p. 166.

**TABLE 4.1**  Communist Party Membership

| Country | Party Name | Total Communist Party Membership | Communist Party Membership as Percent of Population |
|---|---|---|---|
| China | Chinese Communist Party | 37,000,000 | 3.9% |
| USSR | Communist Party of the Soviet Union | 16,630,000 | 6.3 |
| Vietnam | Vietnamese Communist Party | 1,533,000 | 2.9 |
| Poland | Polish United Workers' Party | 3,080,000 | 8.7 |
| Yugoslavia | League of Communists of Yugoslavia | 1,855,638 | 8.4 |
| Romania | Communist Party of Romania | 2,930,000 | 13.3 |
| East Germany | Socialist Unity Party | 2,127,413 | 12.7 |
| North Korea | Korean Workers' Party | 2,000,000 | 10.7 |
| Czechoslovakia | Communist Party of Czechoslovakia | 1,473,000 | 9.7 |
| Hungary | Hungarian Socialist Workers' Party | 797,000 | 7.4 |
| Cuba | Communist Party of Cuba | 200,000 | 2.0 |
| Bulgaria | Bulgarian Communist Party | 817,000 | 10.3 |
| Cambodia | Khmer Communist Party | 10,000 | 0.2 |
| Laos | Lao People's Revolutionary Party | 15,000 | 4.1 |
| Albania | Albanian Party of Labor | 101,500 | 3.9 |
| Mongolia | Mongolian People's Revolutionary Party | 67,000 | 4.1 |

SOURCE: Richard F. Staar, ed., *Yearbook on International Communist Affairs* (Stanford, Calif.: Hoover Institution Press, 1980).

Therefore, the low percentage of party membership may not be surprising at all. With the hardships involved, it is surprising that anyone belongs. There are a number of different factors, however, that lead people to join the party, and three are significant. First, some individuals are particularly achievement oriented and have high aspirations for success. Joining the party, as Hammer noted, can open doors that might otherwise be closed. Others join the party because of the political influence it gives them. If one wants to pursue a career in politics or in some other line of government service, membership in the party is practically mandatory. Finally, there are those who join because of a spirit of conviction. Committed to the Marxist-Leninist doctrine, they perceive that their best opportunities for promoting Communism and the betterment of the society are within the organizational structure of the party. In many respects, the motivations for joining are similar to those found for becoming involved in partisan politics in the United States.

Although citizens with such expectations continue to join, Communist parties are unlikely to become mass parties in the Western sense.

One overriding reason for this results from the attitudes of the party leaders themselves. They prefer minority parties that include only the most dedicated, ideologically committed and "pure" citizens. This makes it easier to maintain party "correctness" and to ensure its role as the revolutionary vanguard of society. Because the parties are viewed as performing such a crucial and significant role in society, the leaders want to keep them small and to keep standards for party members high.

The parties attempt to attract members from all sectors of their societies although many states have difficulties keeping the peasant and workers' ranks sufficiently high to justify the toilers orientation. At one time or another, most of the parties have undertaken campaigns to increase the number of peasants, workers, and minority nationalities among their members. The substantial increase (over 8 percent) in worker representation in the CPSU between 1957 and 1980 was the result of a campaign begun by Nikita S. Khrushchev and continued by his successors to increase proletarian involvement.

Table 4.2 reveals that workers represent a

**TABLE 4.2** Social Composition of the CPSU, LCY, and CCP

|  | CPSU USSR (1976) | LCY Yugoslavia (1975) | CCP China (1957) |
|---|---|---|---|
| Workers | 42% | 31% | 14% |
| Peasants | 14 | 6 | 67 |
| Technical intelligentsia | 20 | 6 | 15 |
| Others[a] | 24 | 57 | 4 |

[a]Others include humanistic intelligentsia, white-collar workers, those involved in education, the military, and a few other smaller sectors. This category is more inclusive in the Yugoslav figures and draws from some of the more narrowly defined peasant and technical intelligentsia groups.

SOURCE: *Current Digest of the Soviet Press*, 28, (8) (1976), p. 24; Richard F. Staar, ed., *Yearbook on International Communist Affairs* (Stanford, Calif.: Hoover Institution Press, 1976), p. 92; *Area Handbook on China* (Washington, D.C.: U.S. Government Printing Office, 1967).

sizeable portion of the party membership in the Soviet Union (42 percent) and Yugoslavia (31 percent). Peasants and collective farmers are still the most underrepresented groups in these two countries, a trend reversed in China. The CCP has a high percentage of peasants and a relatively low percentage of workers. This reflects and results from the higher proportion of peasants in the occupational structure of Chinese society.

In all countries, however, the parties earnestly strive to ensure broad representation of all social classes. It is important to have communication channels linking the leadership to all sectors of society; this goal is best served by having party representatives drawn from all sectors of society.

Procedures governing entrance into the parties vary somewhat from country to country and, in some cases, from region to region. The procedures followed in the Soviet Union, however, are fairly representative and illustrate the strict standards that are maintained. When an individual wants to join the CPSU, he or she must be recommended by three persons, each of whom must have been a party member for five years and known the candidate well for one year. Once the application is prepared and brought before the local primary party organization, a two-thirds majority vote is required for admission as a candidate member. After serving for one year in this provisional status—a period when the candidate's work is closely monitored by peers—the application is again voted on by members of the local primary organization. If the individual receives a two-thirds vote, his or her file is sent to the next higher party level (usually city or district) where it is normally approved.[7]

## ORGANIZATIONAL STRUCTURE

### PRIMARY ORGANIZATIONS

Figure 4.1 illustrates the typical organization of a Communist Party from the lowest level primary organization (what formerly were called the local party cells) to the highest level party leader. The organizational structure of the party approximates a pyramid at the bottom of which are thousands of primary organizations based in factories, schools, collective farms, and the like. When an individual joins the party, it is this local organization that receives and processes the application. Recruitment of new members and ideological work (spreading official propaganda, political education, and so on) are major responsibilities of the primary organizations. These organizations also serve as an ideological caretaker within factories, schools, and other institutions to ensure that attitudes and behavior correspond with the party's expectations. By linking with every social, economic, and territorial unit within the state, the primary organizations provide the central party with a communication network that reaches to the grass roots of their societies. There are approximately 390,000 primary organizations in the Soviet Union today.

The structure and organization of each cell varies somewhat according to the size of the organization and the country in which it is found. Typically, small organizations, such as those in stores or schools, elect a secretary who assumes a part-time role of directing the cell's party activities. Larger organizations, such as those in factories and universities, have a full-time secretary, an elected committee, and assorted assistants who serve the secretary in carrying out his or her

[7]For a more detailed account of the Soviet selection procedures, see Hammer, *op. cit.*, pp. 176–177.

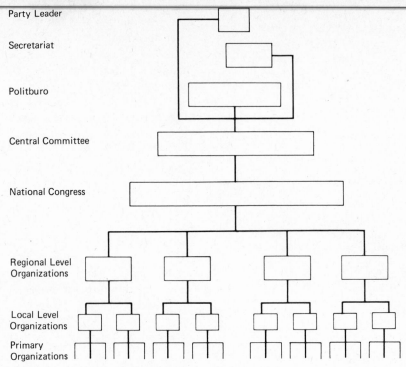

Party Leader

Secretariat

Politburo

Central Committee

National Congress

Regional Level
Organizations

Local Level
Organizations

Primary
Organizations

**Figure 4.1** Communist Party organizational structure.

work. To link these party cells to higher level organs, each primary organization elects a delegate (frequently the secretary) to represent the cell at the next highest level, usually the city or local district. This system of representation applies throughout the entire pyramid and has been called by some the dictatorship of the secretariat.

## REGIONAL AND LOCAL-LEVEL ORGANIZATIONS

The vast majority of party members work in part- and full-time capacities within the regional and local-level networks. The central party organization provides the regions with a relative degree of autonomy in the administration of party affairs. These regional organizations typically coordinate their own party conferences and have leadership organs that closely correspond with the national organization.

The regional-level party organizations in the Soviet Union are based on a federal structure. At the regional level, the parties of the 15 Soviet Union republics have the highest status. They hold party congresses once every two years. Next in order of importance are the regions and areas within the Soviet Union republics, followed by the towns, rural and urban districts, and so on down the list. Each of these organizational units has its own party networks, including full-time committees, officials, and elected delegates to represent the unit at the next highest level.

The CCP is also divided into regional and local party networks. The degree of regional party autonomy has been subject to the shifting desires of the central party leaders, however, and has been relatively limited at all stages of Chinese Communist development. During the Great Proletarian Cultural Revolution (GPCR) (1966–1969), for example, the provincial party structures were assaulted by both the national leaders and such grass roots groups as the Red Guards. More recently, the provinces have regained some semblance of regional autonomy and are becoming a stronger force in making policy within their regions. Many of the new leaders emerging in the post-Mao era gained their experience in the regional organizations. Before assuming Mao Zedong's post as chairman of the CCP in 1976, Hua Guofeng was the head of the party organization in the province of Hunan.

The Yugoslavs have the most formalized and autonomous regional party organizations. Each of the six republics and two autonomous provinces have regional congresses, central committees, and the usual executive party organs. Meeting regularly, these organs and their members have considerable power in determining regional party policy. In fact, when the central party organization withdrew partially from the political arena in the 1960s, the regional party organizations grew in status and power. Their vigorous pursuit of regional interests resulted in a high level of interregional conflict during this period, leading many to remark that Yugoslavia had a *de facto* multiparty system.

## NATIONAL PARTY CONGRESS

In all Communist Party states, delegates from the regions and lower level organizations tend to gather every four or five years to attend the national party congress. Called the All-Union Party Congress in the USSR and the National Party Congress in China and in Yugoslavia, these large and highly ceremonial meetings are filled with considerable party fanfare. As indicated in Figure 4.2, the meetings draw great crowds of delegates and, although they differ in many important respects from the national party conventions of the Democratic and Republican parties in the United States, they hold some interesting similarities. In addition to the attendance of delegates from every section of the country and the pomp and circumstance (not to mention cocktails and parties) characteristic of the American conventions, the Communist Party congresses are also blessed with the speeches of the contemporary

party dignitaries.[8] The ranking party leader typically opens the Congress with a stirring call to arms that applauds the party's accomplishments and draws attention to its future goals.

Also bearing a certain similarity to American political party conventions is a statement of the party's platform, outlining the policy goals and directives that will guide the party's work until the next congress. To an even greater extent than in the United States, however, hammering out the platform is the right and responsibility of party leaders and is usually completed far in advance of the formal congress.

The most significant difference between Communist Party congresses and American political party conventions is the conspicuous absence of opposition, debate, and healthy political rancor. All proposals, all candidates, and all speeches are met with a uniform unanimity of opinion (and applause).[9] Although the rank and file's attendance at these meetings is an exciting event that few would want to miss, when it comes to political influence, they might as well have stayed home. The primary function of the delegates is to ratify the policy proposals of the leaders rather than to have any significant impact on the proposals themselves. Centralization of power is an undeniable fact of Communist political rule, and it is given clear expression in the functioning of the national congresses.

In theory, the delegates also come to the national congresses to elect the new central committee that will serve until the next congress. In fact, however, the slate of candidates is typically prepared in advance by the leaders themselves, which results in the unanimous election of the of-

[8]The congresses are colorful and festive occasions with workers and intellectuals, city dwellers and peasants, and members of national minorities in traditional dress rubbing shoulders in crowded reception halls. To emphasize the parties' worker orientation, welders, collective farmers, and other common folk grace the official program with presentations alongside those of the party leaders.

[9]The speeches of dignitaries are interrupted even more frequently than their counterparts in the West. Newspaper accounts of the speeches find them interspersed with notations of "applause," "prolonged applause," or even "stormy, prolonged applause."

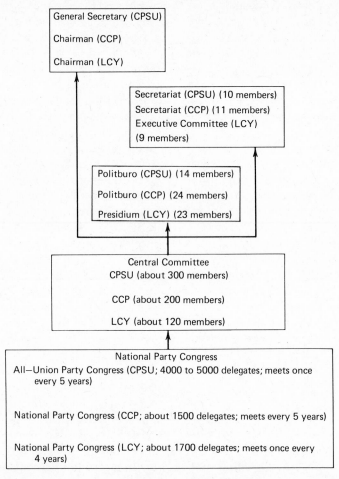

**Figure 4.2** National Communist Party organizations, Soviet Union (CPSU), China (CCP), and Yugoslavia (LCY)—all figures are approximate and change periodically.

ficial slate. Rank-and-file delegates have little, if any, effect on the selection of their highest leaders. The content of the speeches, the selection of the central committee, and the congress in general is carefully orchestrated by the top party leadership.

## CENTRAL COMMITTEE

Because of their great size, the infrequency of their meetings, and the general lack of expertise and information among the rank-and-file dele-

gates, the national party congresses have little meaningful power as policy-making bodies. Although affected by some of the same factors, the central committee is a far more influential body. The central committees are large, generally ranging between 100 and 300 members within the different states, but not nearly so enormous as the bodies that supposedly elect them. Meeting periodically, usually every few months or so, the central committees are theoretically considered the most important party organization within their states. The Central Committee of the CPSU has its role outlined in the party statutes:

> The Central Committee . . . directs all the activity of the Party, and of the local organs, selects and appoints leading personnel, directs the work of central governmental and public organizations of toilers through Party groups within them, creates various Party organs, agencies, and enterprises of the Party, and directs their activities, appoints the editors of the central newspapers and magazines operating under its control, allocates funds from the Party budget and controls their use.

In reality, however, the bulk of these responsibilities are reserved for higher organs within the various parties, organs to which we now turn.

## POLITBURO, SECRETARIAT, AND PARTY LEADER

Although the central committees in theory hold enormous power, they delegate the bulk of it to the bodies and individuals they typically elect— the politburos, the secretariats, and the party leaders (see Figure 4.2).[10] The politburo is an exceedingly important decision-making institution with a great deal to say concerning who gets what in Communist Party states. Meeting at least weekly, this group of party members transacts the highest level and most important business on the nation's agenda. The sizes of these groups vary considerably over time and among the countries. Yet they are generally small enough to transact political business. Similar to cabinets in the First World states, the politburos are considered the most significant and powerful policy-making bodies in Communist Party states.

Formal power to make policy is given to the politburo, but the secretariats have considerable power and important responsibilities of their own. The Soviet Party statutes note that the CPSU Secretariat is "to direct current work, mainly in . . . the organization and supervision over the fulfillment of Party decisions." As the organizational arm of the politburo, the secretar-

iats supervise the implementation and execution of party policies. Meeting almost daily, these bodies have occasionally overshadowed the politburos, particularly in times of crisis, by making policy proposals, issuing decrees, and ensuring administrative execution. The Secretariat of the CCP Politburo was abolished in 1967 and reestablished in February 1980. During that period, the Standing Committee of the CCP—often thought of as the Secretariat but, in fact, much more than an administrative body—was even more powerful than the CCP Politburo and was, indeed, the topmost decision-making body in China. During the unstable period following Mao's death in 1976, for example, the Standing Committee of the CCP convened an enlarged Politburo session and undertook a number of important actions of great consequence to the future course of Chinese politics. Perhaps the most important was the purging of Mao's wife, Jiang Qing, and three additional members of the CCP Politburo, the so-called Gang of Four. Because of the relative absence of formal rules outlining the use of power in the upper party echelons as well as a general disregard for statutes and rules during times of crisis, the power relationships between the politburo and the secretariat can become rather fluid.

As a result of their heavy supervisory, implementation, and execution functions, the various secretariats control and rely on large bureaucracies to assist them in these tasks. The bureaucracies are divided into departments organized according to broad policy areas (defense, agriculture, etc.). Generally, each member of the secretariat is in charge of certain departments and specializes in these policy areas. In overseeing the policy implementation and execution in these different departments, the secretaries have a major impact on the policy process.

Also elected by the central committees, the party leaders have traditionally been the highest ranking officials in their states, outranking the top government officers, such as the President or the Premier. The first among equals in their states and in their parties, the party leaders preside over the work of the politburos, control the cen-

---

[10]Because some of the counterpart institutions are named differently in the three countries, the Soviet designation is used when referring to the general institution.

tral party apparatus, and act as the primary spokespersons for the party and for the state.

## THE PARTY PERSONNEL

With approximately 37 million party members in China, over 16.5 million in the Soviet Union, and nearly 2 million in Yugoslavia, roles and personalities within the party structures are numerous and diverse. Beginning at the top of the party hierarchy (illustrated in Figure 4.1), we consider some of the officials, ranging from the highest ranking party leader in the nation's capital to secretaries of the primary organizations in the outlying hinterland.

### PARTY LEADERS

Lenin was the supreme leader of Russia from 1917 to 1924.[11] After Joseph Stalin's assumption of power (he became General Secretary of the party in 1922), the position of party secretary soon overpowered all other political offices, including the leading government positions. In his so-called testament, Lenin warned his comrades that Stalin had already become too powerful and did not use his power with sufficient caution. Shortly before his death, Lenin added a postscript to his testament, suggesting that Stalin be removed from his post. As history shows, Stalin was not dislodged; rather, he moved decisively to increase his power within the role of General Secretary. Under his administration, this role of party leader became the dominant position in Soviet politics. This pattern is also reflected in all other Communist Party states through the present day.[12]

On Stalin's death in the spring of 1953, a power struggle between Nikita S. Khrushchev and a number of high CPSU officials ensued. Having a solid political base by virtue of being a member of both the Secretariat and Politburo, Khrushchev soon became the dominant figure and had his title upgraded to first secretary.[13] Unlike Stalin's leadership as General Secretary, however, Khrushchev's was never as autocratic. Not only was he less powerful, but his reign of power was relatively short lived. In the fall of 1964, while on vacation in the Crimea, Khrushchev was summarily summoned back to party headquarters in the Kremlin and ousted from his job. As Khrushchev learned, central committees elect party secretaries—but they also can fire them. Because of shortcomings in his agricultural policy, embarrassment and failure in the Cuban missile episode, and other alleged shortcomings, the free-spirited, impulsive Khrushchev's career was abruptly brought to an end.[14] Replacing Khrushchev as head of the CPSU was Leonid I. Brezhnev, who has now headed the party for almost two decades longer than both Lenin and Khrushchev. Beginning his stewardship of the CPSU under Khrushchev's former title of First Secretary, Brezhnev assumed Stalin's upgraded title of General Secretary in 1966 and the state presidency in 1977. Brezhnev has been considered the "first among equals" on the collective CPSU Politburo, as signified by other officials speaking of "the Politburo headed by Brezhnev."[15]

Until September 1976, the People's Republic of China had known only a single leader of the CCP. As one of the founders of the CCP in 1921, Mao Zedong held a variety of positions in the party before becoming its head during the period of the Long March (1934–1935). When the People's Republic was proclaimed in October 1949,

---

[11]Lenin was referred to as Premier, ruled as Chairman of the Council of People's Commissars and also as a member of the Politburo, which at that time had no formal head.

[12]Stalin ruled in the dual position as head of both party and state. Although the tendency in most states during the post-Stalin era has been to divide these posts, General Secretary Leonid I. Brezhnev combined them once again in 1977 by assuming the ousted Nikolai V. Podgorny's role as President.

[13]Georgi M. Malenkov initially replaced Stalin as head of both party and state. His leadership evolved into a triumvirate in which he shared power with Vyacheslav M. Molotov and Lavrenti P. Beria. Beria's arrest and Khrushchev's ascent to increased power in 1953 led to Khrushchev's election as first secretary (it was not capitalized until 1955) in September 1953.

[14]Khrushchev lived out the remaining years of his life in retirement on the outskirts of Moscow, in a *dacha* ("country home") supplied by the state.

[15]For an excellent review of the Brezhnev era, see Jerry F. Hough, "The Man and the System," *Problems of Communism*, 25 (2) (1976), pp. 1–17.

Mao became Chairman of the Republic as well as Chairman of the CCP. The Chairman of the People's Republic is considered the head of state and is in charge of a number of executive and ceremonial responsibilities. Giving up the head of state role in 1959, Mao remained the reigning head of the CCP until his death. Although choosing Mao's successor was a favorite pastime of many Sinologists, most were surprised when Hua Guofeng, a relatively unknown party official from the province of Hunan, assumed the party leadership on Mao's death. Hua, earlier designated as Premier to replace Zhou Enlai, who had died in January 1976, assumed the dual roles of Chairman of the CCP and Premier of the State Council. The role of Premier was passed on to Zhao Ziyang in 1980. In 1981, Hua's power was further diminished when he was forced to pass the party leadership on to Hu Yaobang, a 65-year-old moderate.

In the same tradition as Mao, Tito was an organizer of the Yugoslav Communist Party and rose to the position of party leader before World War II. When the Yugoslav Communists assumed power in the postwar period, Tito became the head of both party and state. Tito had his special status written into the 1974 Constitution:

> In view of the historic role of Josip Broz Tito . . . and in line with the expressed will of the working people and citizens, nations and nationalities of Yugoslavia—the S.F.R.Y. [Socialist Federal Republic of Yugoslavia] Assembly may . . . elect Josip Broz Tito for an unlimited term of office.

Although Tito, like Mao, was not particularly active politically in the latter years of his career, he assumed a high level of official power through his dual role as head of the LCY and the state. On Tito's death in 1980, the LCY chairmanship was rotated on a yearly basis, and Yugoslavia moved to a more collective form of rule.

Table 4.3 shows that most party leaders have had an unusually lengthy term of office. It has proven exceedingly difficult to unseat a party leader in view of the leader's control over information, the military, and political power. Al-

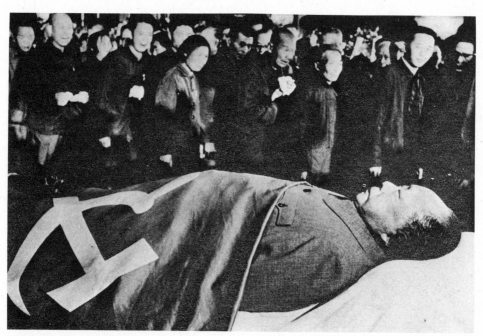

Chinese mourners file by Mao's body, at his funeral in September, 1976. At that very moment, an intense struggle for succession was underway. It resulted in the elevation of Hua Guofeng to take Mao's mantle and the purging of the "Gang of Four," which included Mao's wife, Jiang Qing.

**TABLE 4.3** Communist Party Leaders

| State | Initial Leader | Initial Leader's Fate | Present Leader | Years as Leader (1981) |
|---|---|---|---|---|
| Albania | Enver Hoxha | Still in office | Enver Hoxha | 40 |
| Bulgaria | Georgi Dimitrov | Died in office | Todor Zhivkov | 27 |
| Cambodia | Pol Pot | Ousted[a] | Heng Samrin | 2 |
| *China* | Mao Zedong | Died in office | Hu Yaobang | 0 |
| Cuba | Fidel Castro | Still in office | Fidel Castro | 23 |
| Czechoslovakia | Klement Gottwald | Died in office | Gustav Husak | 13 |
| East Germany | Walter Ulbricht | Retired | Erich Honecker | 10 |
| Hungary | Mátyás Rakosi | Ousted | Janos Kadar | 25 |
| Laos | Kaysone Phomvihan | Still in office | Kaysone Phomvihan | 7 |
| Mongolia | Khorloin Choibalsan and Sukhe-Bator | Died in office | Yumjaagiyn Tsedenbal | 24 |
| North Korea | Kim Il Sung | Still in office | Kim Il Sung | 36 |
| Poland | Wladyslaw Gomulka | Ousted | Wojciech Jaruzelski | 0 |
| Romania | Gheorghe Gheorghiu-Dej | Died in office | Nicolae Ceausescu | 16 |
| *Soviet Union* | Vladimir Ilyich Lenin | Died in office | Leonid I. Brezhnev | 17 |
| Vietnam | Ho Chi Minh | Died in office | Le Duan | 12 |
| *Yugoslavia* | Josip Broz Tito | Died in office | (rotates yearly) | – |

[a]In 1975, the Vietnamese Communist Party asserted control over large portions of Cambodia and drove the Pol Pot regime from Phnom Penh. In 1980, guerilla war between Pol Pot and his forces and those of the pro-Vietnam Heng Samrin (a Pol Pot deserter) continued.

though Khrushchev's ouster and Edward Gierek's and Stanislaw Kania's forced retirements in Poland demonstrate that it is not impossible, party leaders generally command widespread support among other high-level leaders and the mass populace; when they lose this support, the challengers still face considerable odds in mounting a movement that will successfully unseat the incumbent. The ouster of Khrushchev was successful because of his increasing unpopularity among the Politburo members and their ability to win the Central Committee's support of their anti-Khrushchev plot. The uncertainty of political succession, the lack of a regularized circulation of leaders at the highest party levels, and the general absence of any formal, constitutional provisions for replacing party leaders are unresolved shortcomings of Communist political rule.[16]

[16]Although the party statutes typically call for the election of a new party leader on the termination or death of the previous one, the struggle and jockeying for power within the highest level of the party makes this a rather contentious, conflict-ridden process.

## THE HIGH OFFICIALS: POLITBURO AND SECRETARIAT

The highest party organs are staffed by individuals (usually men) who have generally worked their way up, step-by-step, from regional to the national center of political power. Because of the great diversity of policy issues dealt with at this level of policy making, members of the Politburo generally have greater expertise and special responsibilities in certain, specialized policy areas. Andrei A. Gromyko's considerable experience in international relations and his position as Minister of Foreign Affairs make him a natural expert in the field of foreign policy. In policy discussions concerning relations with the West or Soviet involvement in the Third World, Gromyko's opinions are likely to have considerable weight even though all issues are decided through collective decision making. Others, such as Yuri V. Andropov (in the policy areas of security and intelligence) and Mikhail A. Suslov (in ideology and culture), have their own areas of policy expertise and influence. When the members of the

Politburo assemble to discuss a particular issue, years of direct and extensive expertise in the various matters weigh heavily in the decision-making process.

The long years of party experience are also reflected in the members' ages. In 1981, the average age of the Soviet Politburo member was 69, making it one of the "oldest" national leadership bodies in the world. Because the CPSU General Secretary is normally drawn from the Politburo, future Soviet leaders are also likely to be men in their 60s or 70s. Many observers suggest that the advanced age of the Soviet Party leaders is reflected in the general conservatism of their policies. This conservatism was reflected once again at the 26th Party Congress. The 1981 Congress was an affirmation of the *status quo*. There were few new policies and no new leaders at the Politburo level. It was the first time in a half century that a party congress ended without introducing new blood into the upper echelons. The 26th Congress also brought about little turnover within the Central Committee where less than 10 percent of the old members retired or lost their jobs.

The Secretariat, like the Politburo, has no fixed number of members. Although the number of party secretaries in the CPSU Secretariat was 10 in 1980, there have been as few as three in the past. Unlike the nonsecretary members of the Politburo who often hold high positions in the government, members of the Secretariat hold no other position than that of party secretary. Charged with supervising the work of the CPSU, these full-time professionals rely heavily on the departmental personnel under their administration. These individuals are professional administrators responsible for the implementation and execution of policies adopted by the national party and government organs.

The mid-1970s through the early 1980s were years of enormous turmoil and change within the highest leadership bodies of the CCP. Mao Zedong spent his last 10 years searching for a successor in hopes of preparing a stable succession that would follow his passing. Mao lost faith in two successors in the last decade—Liu Shaoqi and Lin Biao—and entered the mid-1970s with

no clear heir apparent.[17] Although Mao did not consider Zhou Enlai (his second-in-command in the 1970s) as an heir to the chairmanship mantle, he did hope to have Zhou oversee an orderly succession after his death. However, on January 8, 1976, Zhou Enlai succumbed to the advances of old age and Mao's succession plans suffered another setback.[18]

As the fall of 1976 approached, it was clear that the life of the fading Mao was nearing its end. Dignitaries who visited Beijing were permitted only brief sessions with the octogenarian and on September 9, 1976 the Great Helmsman died. Although silence initially surrounded the succession, news began to leak that called attention to a power struggle within the CCP Politburo and Standing Committee. Amidst the turmoil and within days after Mao's passing, the Politburo selected Hua Guofeng as Mao's successor. Moving decisively to consolidate his uncertain position, Hua and his moderate associates purged four of Mao's most ardent and prominent followers, the so-called Gang of Four. Accused of a variety of crimes against the Chinese people and Mao, the "four dogs" were vilified in wall posters that appeared throughout the country describing the culprits' antiparty plot. Some posters accused the zealots of "tormenting . . . vexing . . . and nagging" Mao to death. Still others flatly referred to Mao's wife as his "killer." Hua's reign at the top of the party hierarchy was short lived. Even though Hua engineered the coup that ousted the Gang of Four, many Chinese blamed Hua for collaborating with the radicals prior to Mao's death. This and other developments led to Hua's downgrading and to the rise of Deng Xiaoping and the moderates in the early 1980s.

The ascent to a position on the politburo or secretariat is usually a long and arduous process, yet a member's downfall can sometimes occur with surprising speed. After being revealed as

[17]Liu was dismissed for being a "capitalist roader" during the GPCR in 1968 and Lin was reportedly killed fleeing to the USSR following an abortive anti-Mao plot in 1971.

[18]For a discussion of this period, see Parris Chang, "China's Politics and Policies. Mao's Last Stand?" *Problems of Communism*, 25 (4) (1976), pp. 1–17.

# CPSU Politburo and Secretariat
## Positions and Responsibilities

| | Name | Birthdate | Total Years Tenure | | Present Position (Date of Election or Appointment) | General Responsibilities* | |
|---|---|---|---|---|---|---|---|
| | | | As Full Member | As Candidate Member | | Domestic | Foreign |
| Full Members | Yu. V. Andropov | 15 Jun 14 | 7 | 6 | Chmn, KGB (May 67) | Security, Intelligence | Intelligence |
| | L. I. Brezhnev | 19 Dec 07 | 23 | 2 | General Secretary (Oct 64); Chmn, Supreme Soviet Presidium (Jun 77) | General Supervision, Defense, Security, Legislature | General Supervision, General Foreign Relations |
| | K. U. Chernenko | 24 Sep 11 | 2 | 1 | Party Secretary (Mar 76) | Politburo Staff Work | |
| | M. S. Gorbachev | 2 Mar 31 | 0 | 1 | Party Secretary (Nov 78) | Agriculture | |
| | V. V. Grishin | 18 Sep 14 | 9 | 10 | Moscow City First Secretary (Jun 67) | Moscow Party Supervision | |
| | A. A. Gromyko | 18 Jul 09 | 7 | 0 | Minister of Foreign Affairs (Feb 57) | | General Foreign Relations |
| | A. P. Kirilenko | 8 Sep 06 | 18 | 4 | Party Secretary (Apr 66) | Party Organization, Industrial Management | |
| | D. A. Kunayev | 12 Jan 12 | 9 | 5 | Kazakh First Secretary (Dec 64)** | Kazakh Party Supervision | |
| | A. Ya. Pel'she | 7 Feb 99 | 14 | 0 | Chmn, Party Control Committee (Apr 66) | Party Discipline | |
| | G. V. Romanov | 7 Feb 23 | 4 | 3 | Leningrad Oblast First Secretary (Sep 70) | Leningrad Oblast Party Supervision | |
| | V. V. Shcherbitskiy | 17 Feb 18 | 9 | 7 | Ukrainian First Secretary (May 72) | Ukrainian Party Supervision | |
| | M. A. Suslov | 21 Nov 02 | 25 | 0 | Party Secretary (Mar 47) | Ideology, Culture | International Communism (Including PRC) |
| | N. A. Tikhonov | 14 May 05 | 1 | 1 | Premier (Oct 80) | Economic Administration, Industry | |
| | D. F. Ustinov | 30 Oct 08 | 4 | 11 | Minister of Defense (Apr 76) | Defense, Space | Military Aid, Foreign Military Support |
| Candidate Members | G. A. Aliyev | 10 May 23 | | 4 | Azerbaydzhan First Secretary (Jul 69) | Azerbaydzhan Party Supervision | |
| | P. N. Demichev | 3 Jan 18 | | 16 | Minister of Culture (Nov 74) | Culture | |
| | T. Ya. Kiselev | 12 Aug 17 | | 0 | Belorussian First Secretary (Oct 80) | Belorussian Party Supervision | |
| | V. V. Kuznetsov | 13 Feb 01 | | 3 | First Deputy Chmn, Supreme Soviet Presidium (Oct 77) | Legislative Agencies | General State Relations |
| | B. N. Ponomarev | 17 Jan 05 | | 8 | Party Secretary (Oct 61) | | Relations with Non-Ruling Communist Parties |
| | Sh. R. Rashidov | 6 Nov 17 | | 19 | Uzbek First Secretary (Mar 59) | Uzbek Party Supervision | |
| | E. A. Shevardnadze | 25 Jan 28 | | 2 | Georgian First Secretary (Sep 72) | Georgian Party Supervision | |
| | M. S. Solomentsev | 7 Nov 13 | | 9 | RSFSR Premier (Jul 71) | RSFSR Economic Administration, Finance | |
| Secretaries who are not in Politburo | V. I. Dolgikh | 5 Dec 24 | | | Party Secretary (Dec 72) | Heavy Industry | |
| | I. V. Kapitonov | 23 Feb 15 | | | Party Secretary (Dec 65) | Party Staffing | |
| | K. V. Rusakov | 31 Dec 09 | | | Party Secretary (May 77) | | Communist Bloc Liaison |
| | M. V. Zimyanin | 21 Nov 14 | | | Party Secretary (Mar 76) | Culture | |

*General policy responsibilities have been assumed on the basis of public activities and backgrounds.
** Excludes a previous stint in this position.
Information available as of 1 April 1981 has been used in preparing this chart.

**Figure 4.3** Positions and Responsibilities of CPSU Politburo and Secretariat (Source: Adapted from U.S. Department of State).

two of the "persons in authority who are taking the capitalist road" during the GPCR, Liu Shaoqi and Deng Xiaoping lost the CCP Politburo's support and confidence and were dropped from its membership. Liu was banished from politics. Deng, on the other hand, made a comeback and was appointed Vice Premier and named to the CCP Politburo in 1973. Much to the chagrin of those who rehabilitated him, Deng proved to be an "unrepentant capitalist roader" after all, was purged from the political arena once again in 1976—only to return again in 1977 to become the most powerful political actor during China's modernization program.[19]

Abrupt downfalls have been experienced in both the highest CPSU and LCY leadership bodies. Tito's earlier heir apparent, Aleksandar Ranković, was ousted from his leading party and government positions in 1967 for committing a number of inexcusable transgressions, not the least of which was the bugging of Tito's private quarters. Two members of the CPSU Politburo, Pyotr Y. Shelest and G. I. Voronov, lost the support of their colleagues and were expelled in 1973 from their positions for assorted policy shortcomings. In 1977, Nikolai V. Podgorny, a member of the CPSU Politburo and President of the Soviet Government, also lost the support of his comrades and was dismissed from both official positions. In contrast, Aleksei N. Kosygin's resignation from both the Communist Party and his government posts in October 1980 resulted from ill health; a few months later he died.

Because the politburos and secretariats are collective bodies and have no formal procedures for rotating and replacing their members, it is the collective membership that determines the fate of an individual member. Although the party leader usually has somewhat more influence than the others, all members are of critical importance when it comes to leadership changes. If a certain individual loses the confidence of a majority of the body's membership, his or her future is cast in doubt. This leads to the inevitable in-fighting

and contentious behavior associated with bureaucratic politics. In view of the possibilities for conflict, the relatively harmonious relations in the Soviet and Yugoslav bodies during the 1970s have been quite surprising, but probably more of an exception than a rule. The extremely high level of conflict characterizing the CCP leadership organs in the 1970s was also an exception generated by the uncertainties surrounding Mao's death. The possibility of such power struggles in Yugoslavia will be an interesting question in the post-Tito period.

Finally, it should be noted that politburos and secretariats have had quite different relationships to the party leaders at different times and in different countries. Stalin intimidated members of the CPSU Politburo during the 1930s and 1940s and clearly dominated the meetings and the general policy-making process. Members of the Politburo were often summoned to Stalin's home in the middle of the night where the pathological leader would criticize and ridicule them. John A. Armstrong and Darrell P. Hammer note that Stalin was even able to have some Politburo members shot during his leadership of the CPSU.[20]

If Stalin's Politburo was characterized by intimidation and the monopolization of power, the contemporary CPSU Politburo under Brezhnev is one inclined toward sharing and collective rule. In the words of one American scholar, "Brezhnev has been in an extremely strong position, but . . . he has deliberately chosen to delegate a great deal of authority to subordinates."[21] The picture painted of Brezhnev is one of a popular, effective leader who has taken care not to dominate the work of the Politburo. Brezhnev's gregarious personality seems to put others at ease in even the most formal settings and is conducive to a cooperative rather than an intimidating work environment.

---

[19]Under Deng's leadership, Liu Shaoqi was also rehabilitated posthumously in the post-Mao period.

[20]John A. Armstrong, *The Politics of Totalitarianism* (New York: Random House, 1961), pp. 14, 48, 200. Hammer, *op. cit.*, p. 193.

[21]Jerry F. Hough, *op. cit.*, p. 5.

If we were to gather the leading national and state government officials as well as the officials of the political parties in the United States and if we were to include a sampling of leading representatives of the diplomatic, military, labor, and scientific communities as well, we would have a body fairly similar to the central committees found in Communist Party states. The central committees are diverse groups that draw representatives from virtually every social and geographic sector in the country. The convening of the central committee is a gathering of the power elite of the state, a meeting of powerful figures who, to a great extent, have the formal (not *de facto*) responsibility for making policy decisions for the entire populace.

Because the central committees elect the politburos and secretariats from among their own ranks, representatives of these two bodies are automatic members of the central committees. The largest bloc of members in the central committees are the party secretaries from the territorial party organizations. In 1980, approximately one third of the 271-member CPSU Central Committee were secretaries of the republic and *oblast* ("regional") party organizations.[22] The next largest bloc typically comes from the central government institutions discussed in Chapter Five. These members represent heads of the central ministries, various departments, and committees.

Another large group of central committee members are drawn from the military. This is particularly true in China, where the People's Liberation Army (PLA) has played a central role in politics. As Yugoslavia prepared for the Tito succession in the 1970s and became more concerned with the problems of continuity and political stability, the number of representatives from the Yugoslav People's Army (YPA) swelled within the LCY Central Committee.

Also represented in the central committees are members of the diplomatic corps, the highest officials from the provincial governments, and a number of special groups. Typically included are representatives of the scientific communities and intelligentsia, heads of trade unions and other official national organizations, and a few token representatives from blue-collar and peasant communities.

This collection of individuals usually works closely with the politburo and secretariat. There have been exceptions, however, as represented by Stalin's purging of the CPSU Central Committee in the 1930s. Khrushchev once played the Central Committee against the CPSU Politburo, only to have it side some years later with the Politburo to bring about his removal. Theoretically, the central committees could play a much more influential role vis-à-vis their party leaders and leading organs. Possessing the power to hire and fire, they could pressure the leadership into accepting policy positions they might not otherwise support. This is an infrequent phenomenon, however, and unlikely to be followed much in the future. The central committees meet only infrequently, are not as well organized as the politburos and secretariats, and find it difficult from an organizational viewpoint to challenge these higher bodies. In addition, the up-and-coming status of a majority of their members might be ruined in an unsuccessful assault on the leaders who control their destinies.

## THE PARTY PROFESSIONALS: *APPARATCHIKI*

Proceeding down the party hierarchies, we encounter an important sector (approximately 2 to 3% of all party members) who are engaged in full-time party work. These are the so-called *apparatchiki*, the paid party functionaries who serve in the central, regional, and local party offices. Although they do not possess decision-making powers at the national level, they often have influential positions in the areas of policy implementation and execution.

These officials are also up-and-comers in the sense that many aspire to, and may attain, higher levels within the party network. Holding ministerial and cabinet positions in the nation's bu-

[22]By 1980, 25 of the original 287 Central Committee Members appointed at the 25th Congress had died or retired; 9 new members were elected during the same period.

reaucracy or in the party newspapers, journals, and publishing houses, these officials are often a step away from the central committee. At the regional and local levels, the *apparatchiki* have powerful positions within their respective political jurisdictions.

The *apparatchiki* represent a variety of social and occupational backgrounds. Although the bulk of these officials in the immediate post-revolutionary years were individuals who fought in the revolution and were awarded their positions as a result of their participation, there is now a trend toward increased professionalism among the middle-class *apparatchiki*. Now, most have attended special party-training schools; in addition, most have completed secondary educations and many have earned a university degree.

### THE RANK-AND-FILE ACTIVISTS

The largest bloc of party members are at the bottom of the hierarchy and represent those millions of rank-and-file volunteers at the disposal of the party. Although some may receive part-time pay for their party activities, the majority volunteer for work out of a sense of civic duty. Drawn from all sectors of the population, they are decidedly less "middle class" than the *apparatchiki* and higher level party officials. In China and the Southeast Asian Communist Party states, the majority of these volunteers are peasants; in the USSR and Eastern Europe, many are industrial workers drawn from the skilled and unskilled ranks. Some are apathetic and unenthusiastic, but the majority attend the meetings of the primary organizations and carry out the responsibilities expected as a part of their membership. These rank-and-file activists represent a local power élite who predominate in the leadership roles within their communities, workplaces, and social organizations. But, with increased influence and status come the risks of increased responsibility and political accountability. Those who would rather spend their evenings watching television or talking with friends and family avoid joining the party because they are aware of the many burdens of membership. As in states throughout the world, these represent the great mass of the population, the silent majority who are willing to leave politics in the hands of others.

### PARTY RULES AND PRACTICES

Unlike American political parties, Communist parties require more from their members than occasional financial contributions, verbal support, and turnout at key elections. What is expected of party members is made abundantly clear in the CPSU rules[23]:

1. To fight for the creation of the material and technical base of communism, to serve as an example of the Communist attitude toward labor, to raise labor productivity, to take the initiative in all that is new and progressive, to support and propagate advanced experience, to master technology, to improve his [the party member's] qualifications, to safeguard and increase public, socialist property—the foundation of the might and the prosperity of the Soviet homeland;

2. To carry out party decisions firmly and undeviatingly, to explain the policy of the party to the masses, to help strengthen and broaden the party's ties with the people, to be considerate and attentive toward people, to respond promptly to the wants and needs of the working people;

3. To take an active part in the political life of the country, in the management of state affairs, and in economic and cultural construction, to set an example in the fulfillment of public duty to help develop and strengthen Communist social relations;

4. To master Marxist-Leninist theory, to raise his [the party member's] ideological level and to contribute to the molding and rearing of the man of Communist society. To lead a resolute struggle against any manifestations of bourgeois ideology, remnants of a private-property psychology, religious prejudices, and other survivals of the past, to observe the principles of Communist morality and to place public interests above personal ones;

5. To be an active proponent of the ideas of socialist internationalism and Soviet patriotism among the masses of the working people, to com-

[23]*The Current Digest of the Soviet Press*, 13 (47) (1961), pp. 1–8; 18 (15) (1966), pp. 9, 43. Cited in Jerry F. Hough and Merle Fainsod, *How the Soviet Union Is Governed* (Cambridge: Harvard University Press, 1979), pp. 320–322.

bat survivals of nationalism and chauvinism, to contribute by work and deed to strengthening the friendship of peoples of the USSR and the fraternal ties of the Soviet people with the peoples of the socialist countries and the proletariat and working people of all countries;

**6.** To strengthen the ideological and organizational unity of the party in every way, to safeguard the party against the infiltration of persons unworthy of the lofty title of Communist, to be truthful and honest with the party and the people, to display vigilance, to preserve party and state secrets;

**7.** To develop criticism and self-criticism, to boldly disclose shortcomings and strive for their removal, to combat ostentation, conceit, complacency, and localism, to rebuff firmly any attempts to suppress criticism, to speak out against any actions detrimental to the party and the state and to report them to party bodies, up to and including the Central Committee of the CPSU;

**8.** To carry out unswervingly the party line in the selection of personnel according to their political and work qualifications. To be uncompromising in all cases of violation of the Leninist principles of the selection and training of personnel;

**9.** To observe party and state discipline, which is equally binding on all party members. The party has a single discipline, a single law for all Communists, regardless of their services or the positions they hold.

**10.** To help in every way to strengthen the defensive might of the USSR, to wage a tireless struggle for peace and friendship among peoples.

This is obviously a formidable set of rules, far more than is expected of Democrats in the United States or Social Democrats in Italy. Those who do not fulfill their responsibilities and obligations are subject to dismissal. Hough surveys CPSU admission and dismissal policy over a 60-year span and illustrates that the leaders are committed to ensuring a party membership supportive of regime goals.[24] For example, the Brezhnev regime "cleansed" the CPSU ranks a number of times in the 1970s to ensure a cadre of dedicated and responsible party members. Brezhnev announced at the 25th Party Congress in 1975 that around 347,000 persons "did not receive new party cards" as a result of these exchanges (the leaders emphasized this was an exchange of party documents and not a purge). Hough quotes *Pravda* in noting that these were persons "who had deviated from the norms of party life, infringed discipline, or lost contact with party organizations."[25]

The CCP is also guided by certain rules and obligations. In 1980, the Central Committee reissued the following basic principles for CCP members:[26]

**1.** To adhere to the Party's political and ideological line of Marxism-Leninism-Mao Zedong thought.

**2.** To uphold collective leadership and oppose the making of arbitrary decisions by individuals.

**3.** To safeguard the party's centralized leadership and strictly observe party discipline.

**4.** To uphold party spirit and eradicate factionalism that undermines the party's unity.

**5.** To speak the truth, match words with deeds, and show loyalty to the cause of the party and to the people.

**6.** To promote inner-party democracy and to take a correct attitude towards dissenting views.

**7.** To guarantee that the party members' rights of criticism, policy formulation, and implementation are not encroached upon.

**8.** To provide genuine democratic elections within the party and give full expression to the voter's wishes.

**9.** To criticize and fight against such erroneous tendencies as factionalism, anarchism, and extreme individualism and evildoers such as counter-revolutionaries, grafters, embezzlers and criminals.

**10.** To adopt a correct and positive attitude toward comrades who have made mistakes.

**11.** To accept supervision from the party and the masses and to see that privilege seeking is not allowed.

**12.** To study hard and become both red and expert in order to contribute to the four modernizations.

Just because the above are called Communist Party rules does not mean they are realities. Although there are certain principles suggested

[24]Hough and Fainsod, *op. cit.*, pp. 323–340.

[25]*Ibid.*, p. 336.
[26]"Guiding Principles for Inner-Party Life," *Beijing Review*, 23 (14) (1980), pp. 11–20.

by the rules, one needs to examine them in the light of practical experience. Both the Soviet and Chinese parties reveal important practices, and some interesting similarities and differences.

*Collective leadership* is a fundamental practice of both Soviet and Chinese Communist Party rule and, with a few marginal exceptions, of all other contemporary Communist Party states. Decision making in party organs at all organizational levels is a collective exercise that usually involves more than a few people. Although party secretaries may be the first among equals, they still must gain the support of their peers. The so-called one-man rule under Stalin, Mao, or Tito was never really a reality; and, in the absence of such powerful leaders, all three countries have more fully embraced the principle of collective rule.

*Democratic centralism* is another important practice at work in the Communist parties of the Second World states. Developed by Lenin to reconcile both freedom and discipline, democratic centralism is based on the following principles: (1) election of all party bodies, (2) accountability of party bodies to their organizations and higher bodies, (3) strict discipline of the minority to the majority on all decisions, and (4) decisions of higher bodies are binding on lower bodies. As one can see, there are both democratic and centralistic elements in these principles. Some interesting differences exist among Communist parties, both between states and over time, concerning the blend of these two elements. The Communist parties under Stalinist and Maoist rule emphasized the centralistic elements. The parties in the 1970s under Brezhnev, Hua, and Tito gave the democratic principles more importance. And, the CCP in the late 1970s flirted openly with much higher levels of inner party democracy than had been previously known. The Chinese experiment with greater democracy even found its way outside of the party to the banners posted on Democracy Wall. The bottom line is, however, that the party never loses ultimate control. If democracy goes too far and threatens the dominating role of the party, as it did in Yugoslavia at the end of the 1960s, the party can and (perhaps inevitably) will move to tip the balance

toward centralism. Although there are elements of both democracy and centralism, or freedom and unity, in Communist Party life today, the emphasis is decidedly on the side of centralism.

Another practice or set of practices is noteworthy, partly because of the general absence of party rules. This concerns the problems of *circulation and rotation* of party leaders, and the issue of *succession* once leaders die or are removed. The Yugoslavs have done the most in formalizing both rotation and succession of party leaders. At least in the immediate post-Tito period, the process by which successors were named to Tito's party and government roles went smoothly and as had been constitutionally established prior to his death. In the post-Tito period, the two most powerful LCY positions, the party chairmanship and secretaryship, were to rotate on a yearly and biyearly basis, respectively.[27] Efforts of most other states to formalize turnover within party organs have been ineffective or shortlived. For example, at the 23rd Congress of the CPSU in 1966, Brezhnev and his colleagues abolished the requirement (adopted at the previous Congress in 1961) that there would be a regular, specified turnover in party leadership bodies. The requirement was intended to avoid the election of the same leaders time after time and to bring some new blood into decision-making circles. This Soviet principle of systematic renewal, or anything like it, has not been observed in the USSR or any other Communist Party organization. What often results is what some have called ossified or petrified leadership bodies that are isolated and insensitive to the constituencies that elect them. Although party leaders recognize the problem and criticize its negative features, they have done little to resolve or reform it.

The question of *political succession* within party bodies raises similar problems. Based on

---

[27]In 1978, Tito suggested that yearly rotation should be applied to almost all LCY organs from the commune to the SFRY. In 1979, the Central Committee endorsed the practice. It will be interesting to see if it is observed in the post-Tito era. See Stephen L. Burg, "Decision-Making in Yugoslavia," *Problems of Communism, 29* (2) (1980), pp. 1–20.

formal rules, there is considerable uncertainty and political conflict once a leader dies or is removed. The succession periods can generate considerable turmoil, as the Mao succession of 1976–1977 revealed. The impending Brezhnev succession is likely to present a severe test for the Soviet system. The lack of formal rule for the circulation, rotation, and succession of elites, then, is a glaring shortcoming in Communist Party practice.

Another significant practice, proclaimed by all and practiced by few, concerns the principle of *criticism and self-criticism*. The CPSU rules require such behavior, but Soviet party leaders from the Politburo in Moscow down to local party secretaries often seem reluctant to engage in critical assessments of their own or their body's performance. About the only criticism one sees is that directed toward lower bodies or ousted colleagues who have been purged from the leadership ranks. In contrast to the Soviets, the Chinese Communists (initially under Mao and now under Hu) seem much more prepared to recognize their mistakes and try to improve through self-criticism. A major thrust in the Four-Modernizations Program is to recognize shortcomings and to learn from one another as well as from other countries.

The final practice we will address here is called *nomenklatura. Nomenklatura* refers to a list of positions, both in the party and in society at large, that the party maintains and for which party approval is necessary before personnel changes, removals, or replacements can be made. The *nomenklatura* list in the USSR includes such diverse high positions in the military, in scientific organizations, and in the mass media. This practice allows the CPSU to control appointments to key positions throughout Soviet society. CPSU party officials have actively used the *nomenklatura* practice to remove undesirables and select officials who meet party standards. Although less is known about this practice in China, available evidence calls attention to its importance there as well. Finally, the importance of the *nomenklatura* practice is much less and is still decreasing in much of Eastern Europe and particu-larly in Yugoslavia. In environments with weaker parties and stronger social institutions, the power of the party's *nomenklatura* practice is reduced. The consequence in these countries is a lower level of party control.

## THE PARTY: PAST, PRESENT, AND FUTURE

Although the Communist Party is one of the most significant political inventions of the twentieth century, a variety of disputes have arisen concerning its proper role and functions. Even before the Bolshevik takeover, Leon Trotsky expressed fears concerning the Leninist conception of the party: "The party takes the place of the working class; the party organization displaces the party; the Central Committee displaces the party organization; and finally, the dictator displaces the Central Committee." Under Lenin and Stalin, the revolutionary, militant, centralized party evolved in a fashion surprisingly parallel to Trotsky's prediction.

During the postrevolutionary decades, the role of the party continued to be a question of considerable concern. Stalin recommended a party role that would provide general direction to socialist development. During Khrushchev's years of party leadership, he moved the CPSU toward a specialized role of technical functionalism in which the party was to perform a more direct, specialized role in the administration and management of the country's economic and social life. The Brezhnev regime has returned the party to its more general leadership role although a considerable dose of technical functionalism still remains.

In all contemporary Second World states, however, the Communist Party performs a number of common functions. First, the Communist Party organizations perform an important role regarding international organization and control. Although the nonaligned Yugoslavs and isolationist Chinese have tended not to participate, the CPSU has established close communication links with other Communist Party organizations, particularly those in Eastern Europe.

The Soviet Party leaders utilize these links to coordinate and sometimes dictate on such policy matters as defense, relations with the West, trade and revolutionary strategy in the Third World, and so forth.

The Communist parties also perform some important domestic functions. Perhaps most important, the party has served to preserve the political system and to protect the incumbent regime. From the immediate postrevolutionary days through the current period, the party has controlled power in a manner that disallows both domestic and foreign challenges. Although internal rebellions have developed on occasion and although outside forces have threatened the existence of some systems, none of the Communist Party states have been overturned. In an age of great domestic and international turmoil, this is indeed a significant fact.[28]

Communist parties have also performed the important function of social control. In large and diverse countries, such as the Soviet Union and China, the propensity for internal conflict and civil strife is great. Occasional eruptions have dotted the years of Communist rule, but few have been of major significance. Of course, assuring domestic order and stability has often meant considerable infringements on civil liberties and personal freedom. Communist leaders apparently feel these are necessary policies at this stage of development. To preserve their own rule as well as to provide social services, domestic and international security, and other desired values, these leaders have chosen to use authoritarian Communist parties to direct or administer their societies—an approach to social control we often consider in conflict with basic human rights.

Finally, Communist parties have been used to order and organize the political process in a manner that the leaders consider in the best inter- ests of the general society. The leaders have vested the most important political functions (policy initiation, policy making, and policy implementation) within the structure of the party. Chapter Five illustrates that government organs participate and share in these functions. Yet, we should recognize that the government is staffed primarily by Communist Party members. This means that political processes in Communist Party states are carried on in an arena relatively free of the organized political opposition found in the two- or multi-party systems of the First World. Obviously, there are different interest groups and government organs that sometimes disagree and challenge party policy; however, there is little freedom to mount a serious political challenge to the ruling position of the incumbent Communist Party and even less opportunity to replace it with another.

The privileged and unassailable position of Communist parties has been criticized from both within and outside the Second World. The most stunning critique of all, however, came from a dedicated revolutionary and former Communist leader in Yugoslavia. In 1953, Milovan Djilas, President of the Yugoslav National Assembly, Vice-President of the Republic, and ranking party official, denounced the dictatorial role and privileged practices of Communist Party officials. After being relieved of his official duties and quitting the party, Djilas published his famous indictment, *The New Class*.[29] This exposé argued that although the Communist elite had struggled to end class exploitation, they themselves had become a new class, placed in a privileged position over the rest of society.

Djilas's critique was followed in the 1960s by considerable discord among the leaders of the Soviet Union, China, and Yugoslavia. Mao Zedong and other CCP officials were the most outspoken and accused both the USSR and Yugoslavia of phoney communism and of fostering

---

[28]The 1973 toppling of the Salvador Allende Gossens regime in Chile is an exception resulting from both domestic and foreign (United States) involvement. At the same time, it should be noted that there may have been major changes in Eastern Europe (*e.g.*, Czechoslovakia in 1968) if it were not for Soviet involvement under the terms of the Brezhnev Doctrine.

[29]Milovan Djilas, *The New Class* (New York: Praeger, 1957). Djilas suffered several periods of imprisonment for his persistent criticism of the party. Throughout the 1970s, however, he was free and living comfortably on a government pension in Belgrade.

the exploitative new class character of their parties.[30] Khrushchev responded by defending the historic and orthodox role of the CPSU and denigrating the revisionist character of both the CCP and the LCY. Although tending to be less acrimonious than the Chinese and Soviet leaders, the Yugoslavs defended their party and the Yugoslav approach to building Communism. Soviet criticism of the Chinese has softened somewhat, yet the Chinese continue to rebuke the Soviet leaders and the CPSU. The Sino-Yugoslav acrimony of the 1960s seemed to fade by 1980 as the contentious Mao and Tito passed from the political scene and the Yugoslavs moved their LCY back into a more orthodox, Leninist position. The peculiarities and unique features of the Communist parties may evolve in slightly different ways, but none are likely to relinquish their leading political roles.

In conclusion: Do Communist parties have any significant impact on human dignity? They certainly do although the weighing of costs and benefits and the overall record is not easily established. Many observers contend that although the party leaders have done much to develop their countries economically and to provide education, health care, and other social services for their people, the authoritarian way in which they have gone about it has involved great cost to the human spirit. How one weights these costs and benefits is a question we will return to in Chapter Seven.

In conclusion, then, the Communist parties are the dominant institutions in the Second World states. Using Hough and Fainsod's description of the CPSU, we can apply it to all Communist Party states and say the real prime minister is the party General Secretary, that the real cabinet is the Politburo, and the real parliament is the Central Committee.[31] Owing to these roles, the parties dominate the allocation of values and have a powerful impact on the level of human dignity.

# Suggestions for Further Reading

Armstrong, John A., *The Soviet Bureaucratic Elite: A Case Study of the Ukrainian Apparatus* (New York: Praeger, 1959).

Barton, Allen H., Bogdan Denitch, and Charles Kadushin, eds., *Opinion Making Elites in Yugoslavia* (New York: Praeger, 1973).

Beck, Carl, *et al.,Comparative Communist Political Leadership* (New York: David McKay, 1973).

Bialer, Seweryn, *Stalin's Successors: Leadership, Stability, and Change in the Soviet Union* (Cambridge: At the University Press, 1980).

Djilas, Milovan, *The New Class* (New York: Praeger, 1957).

Farrel, R. Barry, ed., *Political Leadership in Eastern Europe and the Soviet Union* (Chicago: Aldine, 1970).

Fischer-Galati, Stephen, ed., *The Communist Parties of Eastern Europe* (New York: Columbia University Press, 1979).

Gehlen, Michael P., *The Communist Party of the Soviet Union: A Functional Analysis* (Bloomington: Indiana University Press, 1969).

Hough, Jerry F., *Soviet Leadership in Transition* (Washington, D.C.: Brookings Institution, 1980).

Houn, Franklin W., *Short History of Chinese Communism*, rev. ed. (Englewood Cliffs, N.J.: Prentice-Hall, 1973).

[30]*On Khrushchev's Phoney Communism and Its Historical Lessons for the World* (Beijing: Foreign Languages Press, 1964).

[31]Hough and Fainsod, *op. cit.*, p. 362.

Huntington, Samuel P. and Clement H. Moore, eds., *Authoritarian Politics in Modern Society* (New York: Basic Books, 1970).

Janos, Andrew C., ed., *Authoritarian Politics in Communist Europe* (Berkeley, Calif.: Institute of International Studies, 1976).

Lewis, John Wilson, ed., *Party Leadership and Revolutionary Power in China* (Cambridge: At the University Press, 1970).

Rush, Myron, *How Communist States Change Their Rulers* (Ithaca, N.Y.: Cornell University Press, 1974).

Rusinow, Dennison, *The Yugoslav Experiment, 1948–1974* (Berkeley: University of California Press, 1977).

Ryavec, Karl W., ed., *Soviet Society and the Communist Party* (Amherst: University of Massachusetts Press, 1978).

Scalapino, Robert A., ed., *Elites in the People's Republic of China* (Seattle: University of Washington Press, 1972).

Schapiro, Leonard, *The Communist Party of the Soviet Union* (New York: Random House, 1971).

Schulz, Donald E., and Jan S. Adams, eds., *Political Participation in Communist Systems* (New York: Pergamon, 1981).

# CHAPTER FIVE

## Government and Institutional Actors in Communist Party States

If Second World societies are ruled by Communist parties, what are the functions of their governments? Are the party and government organizations distinguishable in any important ways? Which is more important in shaping the overall policy process and in influencing policy outcomes? This chapter uses institutional analysis to consider the part played by formal government structures and other institutional actors in Communist political systems.

Although Communist constitutions recognize the leading role of the Communist Party, they also outline a complex set of government structures of significance to the policy process. For example, all states have representative assemblies that have constitutionally prescribed legislative authority. All have a collegial or collective head of state, usually called a presidium, that also possesses legislative authority in addition to its presidential functions. Finally, all have executive or ministerial bodies, typically called the council of ministers, which are entrusted with the functions of policy implementation and execution. Although the Communist Party organizations outlined in the Chapter Four overshadow these government bodies, a discussion of the policy process would be incomplete if it did not include the government sector.

Perhaps the most important role of the gov-

ernment organs in the policy process involves the legitimation of party actions. If one assessed the influence of legislative assemblies on the initiation and formulation of policy decisions and programs in Communist Party states, one would be forced to conclude that their power is minimal. This leads to the often cited rubber stamp description of Communist assemblies.[1] However, if one were to assess the importance of the assemblies in legitimating the party's policies in the eyes of the people, the role of the legislatures would be considerably more significant. These and other government institutions do a great deal to gather mass support for party decisions concerning the allocation of values and, in so doing, ensure more compliant, supportive citizenries.

Generally speaking, although the Communist Party can be viewed as the source of policy, the government is its constitutional executor. The government bodies take the policy directives of the party and translate them into the rules and regulations that organize socialist life. Having rejected the idea of the separation of powers as a bourgeois theory, the responsibilities of the party, assemblies, presidiums, and councils are often intermeshed and ill defined.

[1]H. Gordon Skilling, *The Governments of Communist East Europe* (New York: Thomas Y. Crowell, 1966), p. 116.

To better understand the poorly defined setting in which the policy process takes place, we begin by describing the basic government structures and institutional actors in these states. Then, we explore their relationships with the Communist parties to determine the ways in which the highest party and government organs interrelate and overlap in the execution of their political functions. Last, we will examine the roles of other important institutional actors in the political process. The leaders of these states have meticulously prepared constitutions and party statutes to delineate the rights and responsibilities of the various organs, yet we will learn that the boundaries and relationships between them are very murky indeed. Before exploring these more complex issues, however, we begin with a basic overview of key government institutions.

## THE SOVIET UNION

In 1977, the Soviet Union adopted a new constitution replacing the Stalinist version of 1936. Perhaps the most surprising feature of the new constitution, the fourth since the Bolshevik uprising, is its close resemblence to its Stalinist predecessor. Serving a number of functions, including the legitimation of party policy and propaganda, the constitution also outlines basic law and the government structure of the Soviet state. The body that approved the new constitution, the Supreme Soviet, is the nominal legislative organ of the Soviet Government.[2]

### THE SOVIET ASSEMBLY: THE SUPREME SOVIET

As indicated in Figure 5.1, the Supreme Soviet is a bicameral legislature consisting of the Soviet of the Union and the Soviet of Nationalities. Neither of these two Soviets is a significant policy-making body that initiates and independently decides on legislation.[3] Rather, the Supreme Soviet

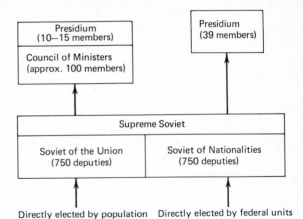

Figure 5.1  The structure of the Soviet Government.

is a government organ whose primary function is to enact the legislation sent to it by more powerful policy-making bodies. The political impotence of these two Soviets is indicated by the unusually short time they are in session; each house meets twice yearly, usually for only two to four days during each session.

The Soviet of the Union is elected according to the population density of territorial administrative units with 1 deputy elected per 350,000 inhabitants. The second chamber, the Soviet of Nationalities, is comprised of deputies elected by the federal units. The 15 Union Republics are each allotted 32 deputies, the 20 Autonomous Republics 11, the 8 Autonomous Regions 10, and the 10 National Areas 1 each. The system of representation results in chambers of about 750 deputies, bringing delegates from all sections of the country and representing all national and ethnic groups.

The two houses of the Supreme Soviet are constitutionally prescribed equal status and rights. Although they normally conduct their business jointly, unlike the U.S. House of Representatives and Senate, they do vote separately by a simple show of hands. If differences between the houses arise, the Soviet constitution prescribes their arbitration and resolution by a joint conciliation commission; failing that, the Presidium can dissolve the Supreme Soviet, send the

[2]For an analysis and the text of the constitution, see Robert Sharlet, *The New Soviet Constitution of 1977* (Brunswick, Ohio: Kings Court, 1978).

[3]The word, soviet, means council in the Russian language.

delegates home, and call for a new election. In fact, however, all votes are unanimous; the two chambers never disagree on any matter of legislation. These facts, taken together with the unusually short legislative sessions, illustrate that the Supreme Soviet is not an important, independent policy-making body. Rather, its chief functions are to ratify policy proposals of the smaller, more powerful party organizations, such as the Politburo, to legitimate the actions of the Communist Party of the Soviet Union (CPSU) in the eyes of the Soviet people as well as influence future policy.

Hough provides some insights into the work and role of the Supreme Soviet. Describing the activity surrounding a bill concerning the Soviet educational system, he calls attention to the appeals and policy recommendations of the various deputies.[4] Some deputies appealed for more funds for their own localities or for various educational programs. Other deputies raised more basic policy issues concerning the very nature of the Soviet educational system. Still others attacked an important CPSU decision, an earlier Central Committee/Council of Ministers decree on educational financing. Although the various appeals, suggestions, and attacks within the Supreme Soviet had almost no impact on the law under consideration, Hough contends that the important function and objectives of the exercise was to affect future policy and appropriations. At the conclusion of the session, an official said, "all these proposals and remarks will be attentively examined by the government, and also by corresponding ministries and departments."[5]

Deputies are elected to the Supreme Soviet every four years on the basis of universal suffrage (over 18 years) and secret printed ballots. Even though only one name appears on the ballot for each official position, 99.9 percent of the Soviet population vote in national elections, a surprising figure that remains relatively constant year after year.[6] One might wonder why so many Soviet citizens go to the polls when no meaningful choices are afforded. Soviet doctrine considers voting an obligation as well as a right; everyone is expected to go to the polls regardless of health, income, or preoccupation. To "get out the vote," criminals are required to vote in their prisons; the infirm vote from their hospital beds; ocean-going passengers cast votes on their ships; and so forth. Societal pressures are great and everyone votes as a matter of civic responsibility and national pride. Voters can cross off names on a ballot although a candidate for the Supreme Soviet has never been denied election as a result of such votes. On the other hand, some candidates at the provincial and local levels have been so denied on occasion.

The more important stage in selecting deputies, however, occurs *before* the election. Selection of the official slate that appears on the ballot begins with the nomination of candidates by public organizations, such as schools, factories, and the like. These nominees are subsequently discussed at public preelection meetings where choices are made on the candidates to be supported. Although the rank-and-file citizen can have some input at this stage of the process, the nomination is not entirely open and democratic; names forwarded to the electoral commission to be placed on the ballot are still very much determined by the appropriate CPSU officials.

Deputies to the Supreme Soviet represent an interesting cross section of Soviet society. Although far more of the deputies are party members (around 75 percent) than are found in the society at large and although approximately 40 percent are professional party bureaucrats (all members of the CPSU Central Committee are Supreme Soviet members), the remainder represent almost every conceivable occupational and ethnic group in the country. Approximately one quarter of the Supreme Soviet members are

[4]Jerry F. Hough and Merle Fainsod, *How the Soviet Union Is Ruled* (Cambridge: Harvard University Press, 1979), pp. 368–369.

[5]*Ibid.*, p. 370.

[6]For an illuminating study of Soviet elections, see Jerome M. Gilison, "Soviet Elections as a Measure of Dissent: The Missing One Percent," *American Political Science Review*, 62 (3) (1968), pp. 814–826.

workers of one sort or another; another quarter are from collective farms. The most typical occupation of American representatives and senators is the law, yet less than 1 percent of the deputies of the Supreme Soviet are lawyers. In addition, the USSR has a far greater representation of women in its national legislative chambers (around 25 percent) than the United States. It also has a strong sampling of ethnic and racial minorities.

Being a deputy in the Soviet Union is not a lucrative enterprise because delegates receive an allowance barely covering their official expenses. Turnover is high and most nonprofessional deputies do not serve a second term in office. Although this has the benefit of providing more citizens with the opportunity of participating in the national government, it also means that the nonprofessional deputies lack the experience, contacts, and information developed by additional terms in office. These less experienced representatives find it difficult to participate effectively and competently with those experienced party professionals who spend term after term in the halls of the Kremlin.

Considerable evidence suggests that the Supreme Soviet is controlled by powerful personalities who hold high positions in the CPSU hierarchy. For example, high party leaders control appointments to two important bodies, the Presidium and the Council of Ministers. The Supreme Soviet is constitutionally prescribed to make such appointments.[7] Darrell P. Hammer quotes the official text of a Supreme Soviet meeting in 1966; this provides a rather clear picture of how the Soviet's appointments are handled.

1. General Secretary Brezhnev took the floor, said he was speaking "in the name of the Central Committee," and proposed the election of Podgorny as chairman of the Presidium. Podgorny was elected unanimously.

2. Podgorny then was recognized. Announcing that he was acting "on the instructions of the party group," he nominated the other members of the Presidium, who were likewise elected.

3. The next speaker was Premier Kosygin, who presented a list of proposed members of the Council of Ministers. He noted that the list has been "approved by the Central Committee of the Communist Party." The list was then approved by the Supreme Soviet.[8]

The power of the CPSU party leadership was brought to bear unexpectedly once again in 1977. Wanting to enhance his own power at the top of the government, party leader Leonid I. Brezhnev, engineered a movement that stripped Nikolai V. Podgorny of his chairmanship of the Supreme Soviet Presidium (which Brezhnev assumed one month later) as well as his seat on the CPSU Politburo. The Supreme Soviet had no prior knowledge and nothing to do with the ouster. Therefore, real appointment power to the Presidium and Council of Ministers remains in the hands of the CPSU leaders.

Unlike the Supreme Soviet, the Presidium is a relatively influential policy-making body within the Soviet Government. Much more professional and less heterogeneous than the Soviets, the 39-member Presidium, still headed in 1981 by party leader, Brezhnev, has the right to conduct legislative affairs and make decisions while the Supreme Soviet is not in session. As a result of the short and infrequent meetings of the Supreme Soviet, this provides the Presidium with considerable policy-making responsibility and power for most of the year. Throughout this period, the Presidium undertakes a variety of policy actions, including issuing decrees later approved by the Supreme Soviet and promulgated as official statutes. The Presidium also has the power to interpret what the statutes mean, a right reserved for the Supreme Court in the American system of government.

[7] The Soviet Constitution also gives the Supreme Soviet the right to appoint members of the Supreme Court, the Procurator General (a national administrative and legal agency that has no counterpart in the United States), and other national commissions. Because these institutions are of little relevance to the policy-making process, they receive no attention here.

[8] *Pravda*, August 4, 1966, cited in Darrell P. Hammer, *USSR: The Politics of Oligarchy* (Hinsdale, Ill.: Dryden, 1974), pp. 261–262.

The executive arm of the Soviet Government, the Council of Ministers, includes the heads of all Soviet ministries, chairpersons of the Union of Republic Councils of Ministers, and chairpersons of important state committees. Ministries are the functionally organized departments in charge of foreign affairs, agriculture, and so forth. The Chairman of the Council of Ministers, Nikolay A. Tikhonov, is legally head of the Soviet government. (Aleksei N. Kosygin held this post until his resignation in 1980.) Because this body totals around 100 members, a smaller body, the 10-to-15 member Presidium of the Council of Ministers (not to be confused with the Presidium of the Supreme Soviet) often acts in the Council's name.

The Council of Ministers is an extremely important government institution, both in theory and reality. It is constitutionally prescribed the powers and responsibilities for issuing decrees in a fashion similar to the Presidium of the Supreme Soviet, that is, directing and coordinating the work of the All-Union ministries and carrying out the economic plan of the CPSU. Hough examined the most important collection of Soviet laws and decisions, *The Handbook of the Party Official*,[9] to determine who issued policy concerning the economy, living conditions and wages, education, law and order, and so forth. Of those promulgated between 1964 and 1976, 21 were laws of the Supreme Soviet, 86 were decrees of the Supreme Soviet, whereas 207 were Council of Minister decisions. Another 139 were decisions of the Council of Ministers in conjunction with other bodies.[10] Most Council of Minister decisions were probably taken by the body's Presidium. In addition to these policy-making functions, the Council is entrusted with the responsibility of maintaining law and order, conducting foreign affairs, organizing the armed forces, and setting up and coordinating the work of impor-

tant state committees. In its role as both a policy maker and chief executor of the party's policy, it has the capacity to shape policy outcomes significantly. The Council has been referred to as a collective head of government, a title it justly deserves in view of its many important functions.

Although we usually conceive of the Council of Ministers as the bureaucratic and executive arm of the Soviet Government, its legislative powers are also of considerable importance. David Lane calls attention to these powers when he notes, "In practice, the Council and its Ministries are the main sources of legislation and issue decrees and regulations governing the whole of economics and social life."[11] As we will see when examining the policy process in Chapter Six, the boundaries of policy-making power become extremely fuzzy when the functions of the party Politburo and Secretariat, the government Supreme Soviet and its Presidium, and the Council of Ministers and its Presidium are considered with respect to specific policy issues and programs. Although in theory these institutions have specific powers and functions, in practice the realities of power politics have made their jurisdictions subject to change and influence by the party élite.

## CHINA

The People's Republic of China is a clear example of how individuals can shape, and even eclipse, the roles of formal political institutions. The institutional fabric of the Chinese political system has been very much influenced by the strong personalities of such leaders as Mao Zedong and Zhou Enlai. These men viewed political institutions as necessary administrative tools, but when institutions obstructed revolutionary politics or became archaic they were simply ignored. Liu Shaoqi, for example, was Chairman of the People's Republic from 1950 to 1966 and then he fell into the party's disfavor and was ousted at the outset of the Great Proletarian Cultural Revolution (GPCR). Liu's official position was ignored

[9]*Spravochnik partiinogo rabotnika (The Handbook of the Party Official)*, 6th to 16th eds. (Moscow: Politizdat, 1966–1976).

[10]Hough and Fainsod, *op. cit.*, pp. 380–381.

[11]David Lane, *Politics and Society in the USSR* (New York: Random House, 1971), p. 149.

and went unfilled for over nine years until it was finally dropped from the government structure with the adoption of the new constitutions of 1975 and 1978. It is hard to imagine the presidency of the United States or even the chairmanship of the Soviet Presidium remaining vacant for almost a decade. But although the importance of Chinese government institutions should not be overemphasized, neither should they be ignored. If China continues its policy of modernization and adopts a more orthodox political strategy in the post-Mao years, as many observers expect, the role and significance of government institutions in the Chinese political process are likely to increase.

## NATIONAL PEOPLE'S CONGRESS (ASSEMBLY)

In constitutional terms, the National People's Congress (NPC) represents the highest organ of state power. The 1954 and 1975 constitutions accorded it this same status, but it had been dormant for a decade until its meeting in 1975! Although it is supposed to convene yearly, the Constitution provides the nation's leaders with considerable flexibility for canceling or postponing meetings of this highest legislative organ. The NPC meets less frequently than the Supreme Soviet in the USSR, but its sessions are somewhat longer, normally running two or three weeks.

The 3459 representatives to the 1978 NPC were elected for five-year terms by the provincial-level congresses, the armed forces, and the overseas Chinese, (see Figure 5.2). The NPC elections are indirect in the sense that rank-and-file citizens do not cast ballots for specific candidates. The nomination, selection, and election of delegates in China is handled through organizations even more party dominated than in the Soviet Union. What has resulted in the past has been a nonprofessional congress easily dominated by the party leadership. A Chinese publication noted that of the 2864 deputies attending the 1975 Congress, 72 percent were workers, peasants, and soldiers; 22 percent were women; and 54 minority nationalities were represented. This diverse group, however, has no real power in the policy-making process. James R. Townsend de-

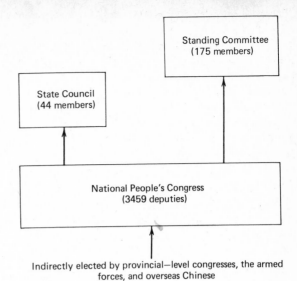

Figure 5.2    The Structure of the Chinese Government.

scribed its roles and significance during the Maoist period:

> Essentially, the NPC has been a forum for learning about, supporting, and ratifying actions of the central leadership; it symbolizes the popular base of the regime and honors the politically favored deputies elected to it, but it has no real political power.[12]

Although the evidence is incomplete, there appear to be no major changes in the Chinese assembly in the post-Mao period.

Like the Supreme Soviet's Presidium, the People's Congress elects a 175-member Standing Committee empowered to act on behalf of the NPC when not in session. Although it met quite regularly during Mao's reign, Townsend notes that "There is no evidence to indicate . . . that the Standing Committee . . . played a significant role in policy initiation or decision-making."[13]

However, the 1978 Constitution provides the NPC Standing Committee with many functions, including the conducting of NPC elections,

[12]James R. Townsend, *Politics in China* (Boston: Little, Brown, 1974), p. 85.

[13]*Ibid.*, p. 85.

interpreting the Constitution and laws, and supervising the work of the State Council. Moreover, the Standing Committee headed by Ye Jia-
nying has become more active and important
since 1979. This changing role makes it more like
the Presidium in the USSR where the Chairman
and his colleagues take an active role in policy
formation and execution.

## STATE COUNCIL (EXECUTIVE)

The head executive body in the Chinese government is the State Council. Since its inception in
1954, this counterpart to the Soviet Government's Council of Ministers had been headed by
Premier Zhou Enlai. On Premier Zhou's death in
January 1976, Hua Guofeng became the new Premier and leader of the State Council. In 1980,
Hua passed the Premiership on to Zhao Ziyang,
a protégé of the promodernization leader, Deng
Xiaoping.

The State Council took on added importance in the post-Mao period partly as a result of
the dynamic modernizer Deng. Deng has had a
remarkable up and down career in Chinese politics. Purged during the GPCR, his return to
power in the mid-1970s triggered intense resistance among the Maoists and resulted in his second purge in 1976. However, at the 5th NPC in
February 1978, Deng was named First Vice-Pre-
mier of the State Council and became the leading
advocate of the Four-Modernizations Program.

As the highest executive body, the State
Council directs and supervises the Chinese administrative structure. Assuming many of the
same functions as the Council of Ministers in the
USSR for fleshing out the party's policy proposals and for coordinating the economy and foreign and domestic affairs, the State Council
shares political power with the CCP Politburo
and Standing Committee. Many of the high party leaders simultaneously hold positions on the
State Council. Composed of the Premier, about
13 influential vice premiers, and approximately
30 heads of ministries in 1980, the Council performs the primary function of policy implementation and execution in the Chinese Government.

## YUGOSLAVIA

In February 1974, the Yugoslav assembly
adopted the fifth constitution in the country's
short lifespan of less than 30 years. Showing a
flexible attitude toward constitutional revision,
the Yugoslavs most current constitution is a far
cry from the 1946 version modeled after Stalin's
1936 Soviet Union Constitution. Designed to formalize the unique system of one-party rule and
self-managing socialism, the 1974 Constitution is
one of the longest and most complex in the
world. Outlining an intricate system of constitutional rights and responsibilities, the Yugoslavs
have moved farther in the direction of constitutionalism, a movement toward legal/judicial
rule, than any contemporary Communist Party
state.[14]

### THE FEDERAL ASSEMBLY

As indicated in Figure 5.3, the bicameral Yugoslav Assembly is composed of a Chamber of
Republics and Provinces and a Federal Chamber.
The Chamber of Republics and Provinces is based on the concept of territorial or federal
representation, much like the U.S. Senate. With
indirect election by the republic and provincial
assemblies, this system of delegate selection
demonstrates the powerful and important role
played by the republics and provinces in the
federal Yugoslav system. An accepted fact of Yugoslav politics is that the federal government
cannot act without the advice and consent of its
territorial jurisdictions.

The Federal Chamber, on the other hand,
demonstrates the equally strong position of the
local units (municipal, community, and work organizations) in the political system. The 220 delegates in this chamber are chosen from local self-
managing organizations and communities and
are elected by local assemblies; 30 delegates are
elected from each of the republics and 20 from
each province.

[14]Winston M. Fisk, "The Constitutional Movement in Yugoslavia: A Preliminary Survey," *Slavic Review, 30* (2) (1971),
pp. 277–297.

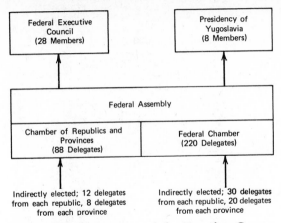

Federal Executive
Council
(28 Members)

Presidency of
Yugoslavia
(8 Members)

Federal Assembly

Chamber of Republics and
Provinces
(88 Delegates)

Federal Chamber
(220 Delegates)

Indirectly elected; 12 delegates
from each republic, 8 delegates
from each province

Indirectly elected; 30 delegates
from each republic, 20 delegates
from each province

**Figure 5.3** The Structure of the Yugoslav Government.

Elections to the two federal Chambers and to the regional and local assemblies are controlled by the Socialist Alliance, a broad-based mass organization sponsored by the League of Communists of Yugoslavia (LCY) and designed to mobilize and encourage popular participation in sociopolitical affairs. Although the majority of delegates in the Federal Assembly are members of the LCY, most delegates to local assemblies are *not* Communists. Elected to serve four-year terms, but limited to two consecutive terms, the local-level delegates are characteristically rank-and-file members of society. In 1974, over 700,000 Yugoslavs—*approximately 1 out of every 20 voters*—served in an assembly at some level in the political system.

In contrast to the Soviet Union and China, the Yugoslav Federal Assembly is a relatively influential branch of the federal government. Programs and proposals are vigorously debated, amendments to government policies are frequently made, and legislation relatively free of party control is produced within the chamber halls. Although the Assembly does not have sufficient stature to block official LCY policy, it plays a meaningful participant role in the policy-making process. Without a doubt, the Yugoslav assemblies, from the federal to the local levels, are the most influential legislative institutions with the Second World.

In addition to his role of party leader, Josip Broz Tito (1892–1980) was President of the Yugoslav Republic throughout his career. On his death in 1980, he was replaced by a collective executive, as called for in the 1974 Constitution. The Presidency of Yugoslavia is composed of representatives from the six republics and two autonomous provinces who are elected by secret ballot from their regional assemblies. They are elected to five-year terms and can serve no more than two consecutive terms. The positions of President and Vice President rotate annually among the eight representatives of the state Presidency.

The idea of constitutionally establishing a collective head of state is a unique and risky experiment. Collective leaderships often degenerate into highly competitive power struggles in which one participant normally emerges as the victor. The Yugoslav planners are willing to take this chance, however, because of their unique situation. With no successor to Tito who has widespread support from all of the national and ethnic groups that comprise Yugoslavia, they are forced to compromise with a collective executive comprised of representatives from all these different groups. The collective leadership body is a very important key to the future of Yugoslavia. If it works well, the country may have found an answer to the difficult leadership problem it faces in the post-Tito era. If it fails and the collective arrangement degenerates into partisan squabbles among the regional leaders or results in a situation where one regional leader emerges who can neither win the support of the other members or the nationalities they represent, then, the Yugoslav future may be bleak.

Delegated by the Constitution with a host of important government functions, the collective Presidency could become a powerful government institution in the Yugoslav political arena. It is entrusted with the typical head-of-state functions, including the conduct of international security and foreign affairs, command of the armed forces, and the proclamation of law by decree. As yet untried and untested, this unique institution will face many tests in the years ahead.

The Presidency of Yugoslavia met on March 5, 1980 to discuss the country's foreign activity and efforts to affirm the principles of nonalignment in international relations. Pictured from left to right are: Josip Vrhovec, Federal Secretary for Foreign Affairs; Veselin Djuranovic, President of the Federal Executive Council (Premier); Vidoje Zarkovic and Fadilj Hodza, members of the Presidency and Lazar Kolisezski, Vice President of the Presidency who presided over the meeting

## FEDERAL EXECUTIVE COUNCIL

Like the State Council in China and the Council of Ministers in the Soviet Union, the Yugoslav Federal Executive Council is the chief executive organ of the government. Elected for four-year terms by the Assembly in conformity with the principle of equal representation among the republics and provinces, the Premier of the Federal Executive Council, his Vice Premiers, and the federal secretaries are in charge of such federal administrative agencies as defense, foreign affairs, and justice.[15] Serving as key advisors to the Presidency, Premier, and other national leaders, the ministers oversee the bureaucratic hierarchies in their specialized areas. Unlike their counterpart councils in China and the USSR, members of the Federal Executive Council serve four-year terms in office. Although they are permitted to

[15]The Yugoslavs refer to the Premier and Vice Premiers of the Federal Executive Council as President and Vice President. To avoid confusion, we will reserve these designations for the Presidency.

serve an additional term if reelected by the Assembly, the Yugoslavs' emphasis on the rotation of public office holders insures a higher circulation of officials than found in most other Communist Party states.

## COMPARATIVE OVERVIEW

When we compare the basic government institutions of the three states, we find a high degree of structural similarity among them. All three have (1) an assembly, (2) a collegial head of state, and (3) a ministerial council entrusted with the administration of government policy. Examining the different institutions more closely, however, reveals a number of noteworthy contrasts.

The assemblies in the USSR and China are extremely large, meet infrequently for very brief periods, and are not independent legislative institutions as we know them in the West. The two Chambers of the Yugoslav Federal Assembly, however, are considerably smaller (roughly the size of the U.S. House of Representatives and

Senate), meet frequently and sometimes for extended sessions, and have become active and reasonably powerful legislative bodies. Yugoslavia is a notable exception from the general rule of rubber stamp legislatures in Communist Party states. Although the constitutions of these states uniformly call the assemblies the "highest organ of state authority," most are in fact quite weak in policy-making power.

Because of the infrequent meetings of the Supreme Soviet and the NPC, the assemblies "elect" organs to act in their names while they are not in session. Even this body in China—the 175-member Standing Committee—has little political power and is no test for the stronger Chinese Communist Party (CCP) organs. The Presidium in the USSR is considerably more powerful, and the collective state Presidency in Yugoslavia seems to be the most powerful of all.

Finally, each Assembly appoints an executive council to supervise and control the national bureaucracy and to oversee the execution of party policy. As the administrative sector of government grows with the development of the state, the role and importance of this executive branch has increased. The Council of Ministers in the USSR, the State Council in China, and the Federal Executive Council in Yugoslavia are all vital organs that ensure the functioning and coordination of the bureaucracy. Headed by high party officials with strong administrative experience— such personalities as Aleksei N. Kosygin, Zhou Enlai, and, more recently, Zhao Ziyang—these councils make sure that the government operates effectively and in a manner that corresponds with the desires of the party elite.

The governments of other Communist Party states correspond with the general descriptions outlined above. Most East European governments have national assemblies that approximate the influence and roles of the Supreme Soviet. Like their Soviet counterpart, these assemblies also have executive committees and administrative councils that assume many of the functions constitutionally prescribed to the assemblies. Relatively little is known about the government structures of the new Southeast Asian Communist Party states or, for that matter, even about

those of North Korea and Albania. What we do know is that all assume some features of both the Soviet and Chinese government systems and that the party tends to dominate the government institutions in all.

## OTHER INSTITUTIONAL ACTORS

There are other institutions of significance to policy making in addition to the Communist Party and the government structures we have outlined. Among the most important are the state ministries and committees (the bureaucracy), the military, and the scientific, intelligence, and security communities.

Communist bureaucracies are big. Convinced of the leading role of the Communist Party in social and economic development, the leaders have established massive bureaucracies to carry out their messianic vision. Figure 5.4 illustrates the many commissions, councils, ministries, and committees under the umbrella of the Soviet Council of Ministers. Each of these bodies have their own bureaucracies with hundreds and often thousands of additional offices, committees, and assorted bodies. Many employ hundreds of thousands of civil servants and have administrative structures that stretch throughout the country.

The Soviet Council of Ministers has a number of important commissions, such as the Military-Industrial Commission (VPK), which cut across ministry or departmental lines. The VPK is in charge of the defense industry, a very high priority sector in the Soviet economy and must work with other ministries and bodies to ensure Soviet preparedness in the defense sector. The interagency commissions on Foreign Economic Questions and the Council for Mutual Economic Assistance (CEMA or COMECON) Affairs have similar responsibilities in coordinating government activities to ensure international economic cooperation.

In addition, the Council of Ministers includes many ministries, like Foreign Affairs, Defense, Agriculture, and Health with their own areas of responsibility and specialization. Each is headed by a highly trained and specialized minis-

## Ministries

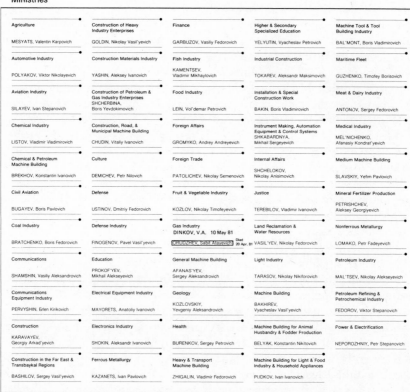

| | | | | |
|---|---|---|---|---|
| **Agriculture**<br>MESYATS, Valentin Karpovich | **Construction of Heavy Industry Enterprises**<br>GOLDIN, Nikolay Vasil'yevich | **Finance**<br>GARBUZOV, Vasiliy Fedorovich | **Higher & Secondary Specialized Education**<br>YELYUTIN, Vyacheslav Petrovich | **Machine Tool & Tool Building Industry**<br>BAL'MONT, Boris Vladimirovich |
| **Automotive Industry**<br>POLYAKOV, Viktor Nikolayevich | **Construction Materials Industry**<br>YASHIN, Aleksey Ivanovich | **Fish Industry**<br>KAMENTSEV, Vladimir Mikhaylovich | **Industrial Construction**<br>TOKAREV, Aleksandr Maksimovich | **Maritime Fleet**<br>GUZHENKO, Timofey Borisovich |
| **Aviation Industry**<br>SILAYEV, Ivan Stepanovich | **Construction of Petroleum & Gas Industry Enterprises**<br>SHCHERBINA, Boris Yevdokimovich | **Food Industry**<br>LEIN, Vol'demar Petrovich | **Installation & Special Construction Work**<br>BAKIN, Boris Vladimirovich | **Meat & Dairy Industry**<br>ANTONOV, Sergey Fedorovich |
| **Chemical Industry**<br>LISTOV, Vladimir Vladimirovich | **Construction, Road, & Municipal Machine Building**<br>CHUDIN, Vitaliy Ivanovich | **Foreign Affairs**<br>GROMYKO, Andrey Andreyevich | **Instrument Making, Automation Equipment & Control Systems**<br>SHKABARDNYA, Mikhail Sergeyevich | **Medical Industry**<br>MEL'NICHENKO, Afanasiy Kondrat'yevich |
| **Chemical & Petroleum Machine Building**<br>BREKHOV, Konstantin Ivanovich | **Culture**<br>DEMICHEV, Petr Nilovich | **Foreign Trade**<br>PATOLICHEV, Nikolay Semenovich | **Internal Affairs**<br>SHCHELOKOV, Nikolay Anisimovich | **Medium Machine Building**<br>SLAVSKIY, Yefim Pavlovich |
| **Civil Aviation**<br>BUGAYEV, Boris Pavlovich | **Defense**<br>USTINOV, Dmitriy Fedorovich | **Fruit & Vegetable Industry**<br>KOZLOV, Nikolay Timofeyevich | **Justice**<br>TEREBILOV, Vladimir Ivanovich | **Mineral Fertilizer Production**<br>PETRISHCHEV, Aleksey Georgiyevich |
| **Coal Industry**<br>BRATCHENKO, Boris Fedorovich | **Defense Industry**<br>FINOGENOV, Pavel Vasil'yevich | **Gas Industry**<br>DINKOV, V.A. 10 May 81<br>ORUDZHEV, Sabit Atayevich  Died 20 Apr. 81 | **Land Reclamation & Water Resources**<br>VASIL'YEV, Nikolay Fedorovich | **Nonferrous Metallurgy**<br>LOMAKO, Petr Fadeyevich |
| **Communications**<br>SHAMSHIN, Vasiliy Aleksandrovich | **Education**<br>PROKOF'YEV, Mikhail Alekseyevich | **General Machine Building**<br>AFANAS'YEV, Sergey Aleksandrovich | **Light Industry**<br>TARASOV, Nikolay Nikiforovich | **Petroleum Industry**<br>MAL'TSEV, Nikolay Alekseyevich |
| **Communications Equipment Industry**<br>PERVYSHIN, Erlen Kirikovich | **Electrical Equipment Industry**<br>MAYORETS, Anatoliy Ivanovich | **Geology**<br>KOZLOVSKIY, Yevgeniy Aleksandrovich | **Machine Building**<br>BAKHIREV, Vyacheslav Vasil'yevich | **Petroleum Refining & Petrochemical Industry**<br>FEDOROV, Viktor Stepanovich |
| **Construction**<br>KARAVAYEV, Georgiy Arkad'yevich | **Electronics Industry**<br>SHOKIN, Aleksandr Ivanovich | **Health**<br>BURENKOV, Sergey Petrovich | **Machine Building for Animal Husbandry & Fodder Production**<br>BELYAK, Konstantin Nikitovich | **Power & Electrification**<br>NEPOROZHNIY, Petr Stepanovich |
| **Construction in the Far East & Transbaykal Regions**<br>BASHILOV, Sergey Vasil'yevich | **Ferrous Metallurgy**<br>KAZANETS, Ivan Pavlovich | **Heavy & Transport Machine Building**<br>ZHIGALIN, Vladimir Fedorovich | **Machine Building for Light & Food Industry & Household Appliances**<br>PUDKOV, Ivan Ivanovich | |

## Agencies of the Council of Ministers Without Ministerial Status

| | | | | |
|---|---|---|---|---|
| **Academy of Sciences**<br>ALEKSANDROV, Anatoliy Petrovich | **Committee for Physical Culture & Sports**<br>PAVLOV, Sergey Pavlovich | **Main Administration for Foreign Tourism**<br>NIKITIN, Sergey Sergeyevich | **Main Administration for Safeguarding State Secrets in the Press (Glavlit)**<br>ROMANOV, Pavel Konstantinovich | **State Commission for Stockpiling Useful Minerals**<br>BYBOCHKIN, Aleksey Mironovich |
| **All-Union Bank of Financing Capital Investments (Stroybank)**<br>ZOTOV, Mikhail Semenovich | **Committee for Supervision of Safe Working Practices in Industry & for Mine Supervision**<br>MEL'NIKOV, Leonid Georgiyevich | **Main Administration of Geodesy & Cartography (GUGK)**<br>KUTUZOV, Il'ya Andreyevich | **Main Archives Administration (GAU)**<br>DOLGIKH, Filipp Ivanovich | **State Committee for the Utilization of Atomic Energy**<br>PETROSYANTS, Andronik Mel'konovich |
| **Committee for Lenin & State Prizes in Literature, Art, & Architecture**<br>MARKOV, Georgiy Mokeyevich | **Council for Religious Affairs**<br>KUROYEDOV, Vladimir Alekseyevich | **Main Administration of the Microbiological Industry**<br>RYCHKOV, Rostislav Sergeyevich | **State Board of Arbitration (Gosarbitrazh)**<br>ANISIMOV, Yevgeniy Vasil'yevich | **Telegraph Agency of the Soviet Union (TASS)**<br>LOSEV, Sergey Andreyevich |
| **Committee for Lenin & State Prizes in Science & Technology**<br>ALEKSANDROV, Anatoliy Petrovich | **Higher Certification Commission (VAK)**<br>KIRILLOV-UGRYUMOV, Viktor Grigor'yevich | | | |

Information available as of 1 April 1981
has been used in preparing this chart.

**Figure 5.4** Organization of the USSR Council of Ministers (*Source:* Adapted from U.S. Department of State).

# Presidium

| | |
|---|---|
| Chairman | TIKHONOV, Nikolay Aleksandrovich |
| First Deputy Chairman | ARKHIPOV, Ivan Vasil'yevich |

**Deputy Chairmen**

| | |
|---|---|
| ANTONOV, Aleksey Konstantinovich | |
| BAYBAKOV, Nikolay Konstantinovich | Chairman, State Planning Committee (Gosplan) |
| BODYUL, Ivan Ivanovich | |
| DYMSHITS, Veniamin Emmanuilovich | |
| KATUSHEV, Konstantin Fedorovich | Chairman, Commission for CEMA Affairs |
| KOSTANDOV, Leonid Arkad'yevich | |
| MAKEYEV, Valentin Nikolayevich | |
| MARCHUK, Guriy Ivanovich | Chairman, State Committee for Science & Technology (GKNT) |
| MARTYNOV, Nikolay Vasil'yevich | Chairman, State Committee for Material & Technical Supply (Gossnab) |
| NOVIKOV, Ignatiy Trofimovich | Chairman, State Committee for Construction Affairs (Gosstroy) |
| NURIYEV, Ziya Nuriyevich | |
| SMIRNOV, Leonid Vasil'yevich | Chairman, Military-Industrial Commission (VPK) |
| TALYZIN, Nikolay Vladimirovich | |

# Commissions

Commission of Presidium for Foreign Economic Questions

Commission of Presidium for CEMA Affairs

KATUSHEV, Konstantin Fedorovich

Military-Industrial Commission (VPK)

SMIRNOV, Leonid Vasil'yevich

# State Committees

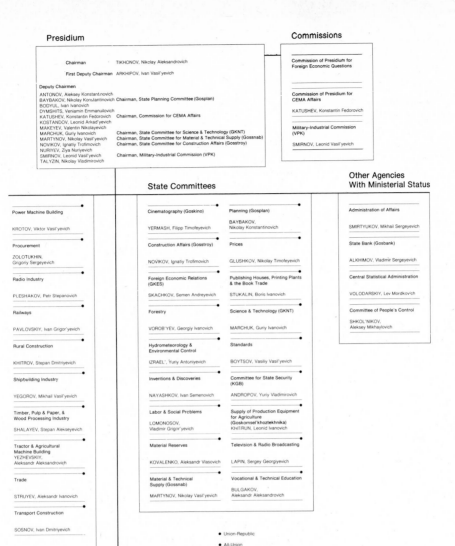

**Power Machine Building**
KROTOV, Viktor Vasil'yevich

**Procurement**
ZOLOTUKHIN, Grigoriy Sergeyevich

**Radio Industry**
PLESHAKOV, Petr Stepanovich

**Railways**
PAVLOVSKIY, Ivan Grigor'yevich

**Rural Construction**
KHITROV, Stepan Dmitriyevich

**Shipbuilding Industry**
YEGOROV, Mikhail Vasil'yevich

**Timber, Pulp & Paper, & Wood Processing Industry**
SHALAYEV, Stepan Alekseyevich

**Tractor & Agricultural Machine Building**
YEZHEVSKIY, Aleksandr Aleksandrovich

**Trade**
STRUYEV, Aleksandr Ivanovich

**Transport Construction**
SOSNOV, Ivan Dmitriyevich

---

**Cinematography (Goskino)**
YERMASH, Filipp Timofeyevich

**Construction Affairs (Gosstroy)**
NOVIKOV, Ignatiy Trofimovich

**Foreign Economic Relations (GKES)**
SKACHKOV, Semen Andreyevich

**Forestry**
VOROB'YEV, Georgiy Ivanovich

**Hydrometeorology & Environmental Control**
IZRAEL', Yuriy Antoniyevich

**Inventions & Discoveries**
NAYASHKOV, Ivan Semenovich

**Labor & Social Problems**
LOMONOSOV, Vladimir Grigor'yevich

**Material Reserves**
KOVALENKO, Aleksandr Vlasovich

**Material & Technical Supply (Gossnab)**
MARTYNOV, Nikolay Vasil'yevich

---

**Planning (Gosplan)**
BAYBAKOV, Nikolay Konstantinovich

**Prices**
GLUSHKOV, Nikolay Timofeyevich

**Publishing Houses, Printing Plants & the Book Trade**
STUKALIN, Boris Ivanovich

**Science & Technology (GKNT)**
MARCHUK, Guriy Ivanovich

**Standards**
BOYTSOV, Vasiliy Vasil'yevich

**Committee for State Security (KGB)**
ANDROPOV, Yuriy Vladimirovich

**Supply of Production Equipment for Agriculture (Goskomsel'khoztekhnika)**
KHITRUN, Leonid Ivanovich

**Television & Radio Broadcasting**
LAPIN, Sergey Georgiyevich

**Vocational & Technical Education**
BULGAKOV, Aleksandr Aleksandrovich

# Other Agencies With Ministerial Status

**Administration of Affairs**
SMIRTYUKOV, Mikhail Sergeyevich

**State Bank (Gosbank)**
ALKHIMOV, Vladimir Sergeyevich

**Central Statistical Administration**
VOLODARSKIY, Lev Mordkovich

**Committee of People's Control**
SHKOL'NIKOV, Aleksey Mikhaylovich

- Union-Republic
- All-Union

Union-Republic organizations operate locally through corresponding organizations on the republic level.
All-Union organizations have no such regional counterparts.

# Chairmen of the Republic Councils of Ministers

| | | | |
|---|---|---|---|
| **Armenian SSR** | **Georgian SSR** | **Lithuanian SSR** | **Turkmen SSR** |
| SARKISYAN, Fadey Tachatovich | PATARIDZE, Zurab Aleksandrovich | SONGAYLA, Ringaudas-Bronislovas Ignovich | KARRYYEV, Chary Soyunovich |
| **Azerbaydzhan SSR** | **Kazakh SSR** | **Moldavian SSR** | **Ukrainian SSR** |
| SEIDOV, Gasan Neyman ogly | ASHIMOV, Bayken Ashimovich | USTIYAN, Ivan Grigor'yevich | LYASHKO, Aleksandr Pavlovich |
| **Belorussian SSR** | **Kirgiz SSR** | **RSFSR** | **Uzbek SSR** |
| AKSENOV, Aleksandr Nikiforovich | DUYSHEYEV, Arstanbek Duysheyevich | SOLOMENTSEV, Mikhail Sergeyevich | KHUDAYBERDYYEV, Narmakhonmadi Dzhurayevich |
| **Estonian SSR** | **Latvian SSR** | **Tadzhik SSR** | |
| KLAUSON, Val'ter Ivanovich | RUBEN, Yuriy Yanovich | NABIYEV, Rakhman N. | |

ter—for example, Andrei A. Gromyko is the Minister of Foreign Affairs—and a thousand or so officials. There is little mobility from ministry to ministry as there is among departments and agencies of the United States. Government officials, such as Gromyko, are usually knowledgeable specialists who work their way up the bureaucratic ladder within a particular ministry. The primary function of these ministries is to coordinate policy in their specialized areas and supervise activities at the regional and local levels.

A particularly important ministry in the USSR is GOSPLAN, or the Ministry of Planning. GOSPLAN's primary responsibility is much like the Office of Management and Budget (OMB) in the United States, that is, to balance and meet ministerial needs and requests for resources in view of national goals. A large ministry with nearly 20 deputy ministers, GOSPLAN has a heavy responsibility in planning and coordinating the complex and cumbersome, centrally controlled economic system.

Although China has a substantially smaller bureaucracy and fewer ministries, the State Council also includes numerous ministries comparable to those of the soviets. One of them, the State Planning Commission, was established in 1952 as the Chinese counterpart to GOSPLAN. The Chinese bureaucratic system has been characterized by much higher levels of provincial power than has the Soviet system. During various Maoist movements, such as the Great Leap Forward, the GPCR, and the anti-Deng campaigns, decentralization to the provincial levels made some provinces and municipalities into what were called independent kingdoms.[16] Both the national ministries and provincial organs, then, can serve as powerful actors in the Chinese policy-making process.

Yugoslavia has also delegated considerable political and bureaucratic power to the regional levels of government. In the 1970s, however, the Federal Executive Council in the capital city of Belgrade and the various ministries within it have been increasing their power at the expense of the regional levels. Stephen L. Burg notes that this results from the federal bureaucracy's "near monopoly over the scientific, technical, and bureaucratic resources of the state and over the agenda of federal decision-making."[17] Although the republics and provinces of these Communist Party states can be important actors within the political process, they tend to be less powerful than the federal institutions and bureaucracies in the state capitals.

The military can be considered a significant actor in Communist political systems if for no other reason than that it is the only institution with the power to overthrow the government and regime. Although the military is a powerful participant in Soviet politics, the CPSU has taken care to keep the military establishment, including the Ministry of Defense, under party control.[18] The military is likely to remain active and powerful in Soviet politics in view of the high priority on defense in contemporary Soviet policy. Military leaders are well represented in the party bureaucracy (the Minister of Defense, Dmitriy F. Ustinov, is a member of the Politburo), the size of the military bureaucracy is vast, and the money allocated to defense continues to rise.

The Chinese military, the People's Liberation Army (PLA), has traditionally played a more important role in Chinese politics than has the Red Army in Soviet politics. During the civil war years, the CCP and the PLA were indistinguishable; during Mao's reign, the PLA was clearly the most powerful bureaucracy in politics. More recently, however, the PLA has been de-emphasized, made clearly subordinate to the party, and assumed what most experts call a pressure group role. Because of their role in protecting national security, the military will remain

---

[16]The January 14, 1977 issue of the *People's Daily* spoke of the Gang of Four and their supporters usurping power in the municipality of Shanghai and the province of Liaoning.

[17]Stephen L. Burg, "Decision-Making in Yugoslavia," *Problem of Communism,* 29 (2) (1980), p. 15.

[18]Roman Kolkowicz refers to the Communist Party and the military as the two most powerful bureaucracies in the USSR. Roman Kolkowicz, *The Soviet Military and the Communist Party* (Princeton, N.J.: Princeton University Press, 1967).

influential actors in all Communist political systems.

The scientific communities are playing increasingly important roles in the politics and policy of Communist systems. Scientific personnel are found within universities and within various ministries, committees, and scientific academies. The Soviet Academy of Sciences with nearly 300 different institutes represents a vast network of specialists expected to improve the scientific basis of Soviet development. Involving such diverse areas as earth sciences, space technology, and foreign policy, scientific personnel play an important role in Soviet planning. Both party and government bodies make use of their expertise by requesting and drawing on position papers and studies that address issues of technical and scientific importance. In addition, although the scientific communities are diverse and represent a variety of different opinions, groups within the larger establishment are purported to serve as pressure groups influencing party and government policies.

The role and influence of the scientific community is quickly changing in contemporary China. With the rapid expansion of the modernization program, more expertise is required in making decisions concerning Chinese development. Party leaders in the post-Mao era have called attention to the important role to be played by the scientific community and have shown greater attention to the reports and recommendations of scientific personnel.

Other institutions, such as trade unions, mass organizations [like Komsomol (Communist Youth League)], and security organizations play significant roles within the political process. Owing to Communist sensitivity to internal security, such organizations as the Soviet's Committee for State Security (KGB) have a special role in Soviet politics, certainly greater than that of the Federal Bureau of Investigation (FBI) and the Central Intelligence Agency (CIA) in the United States. Yuri V. Andropov, chairman of the KGB, is a member of the Soviet ruling elite, the CPSU Politburo. As Chapter Six on the policy-making process points out, under certain conditions these and other institutional actors can take on important roles in the formulation and implementation of policy.

## GOVERNMENT/PARTY RELATIONS

Many observers have called attention to the close relationship between the party and government and have described them as interlocking directorates. According to Darrell P. Hammer, two principles govern party/government relations in the USSR. The first concerns the paramount position of the party and the subordination of the government and the bureaucracies to its official line. He quotes an authoritative Soviet text: "No important decision is ever taken by an organ of government, or by an administrative organ, without corresponding instructions from the Party."[19] The second principle is that, although the party provides guidance, it does not replace the government organs or totally dominate their administrative work. Hammer cites another Soviet source, "The central Party organs give guiding instructions to the ministries . . . while not restricting their operational independence."[20] These principles underline the fact that, in the Soviet Union, the party leads and the government executes.

To ensure proper execution from the party's point of view, the CPSU places high-level party officials in the various government institutions. At the national level, for example, members of the Politburo head the Supreme Soviet Presidium (Brezhnev) and the Council of Ministers (Kosygin). As high-level officials in the CPSU and as the top officials (Chairman and Premier) in their government organs, these party leaders are able to assure a close working relationship between party and government.

This interlocking relationship (illustrated in Figure 5.5) applies at all levels of Soviet governance. From the All-Union level down through the local villages, party officials simultaneously staff the organs of government and administration.

[19]V. A. Vlasov, *Sovetskii gosudartvennyi apparat* (Moscow, 1959), p. 361. Cited in Hammer, *op. cit.*, p. 278.
[20]I. N. Ananov, *Ministerstva v SSSR* (Moscow: 1960) p. 22. Cited in Hammer, *Ibid.*, p. 277.

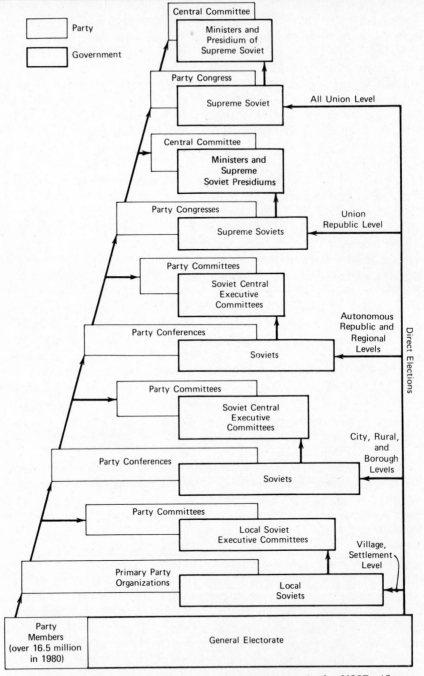

**Figure 5.5** Interlocking party and government structures in the USSR. (*Source:* Adapted from V. Aspaturian, "The Soviet Union," in R. C. Macridis and R. E. Ward, eds., *Modern Political Systems: Europe,* 2nd ed. (Englewood Cliffs, N.J.: Prentice-Hall, 1963).

As noted in the diagram, however, there is much more overlap at the highest levels and less overlap further down the hierarchy. This means that, although party leaders dominate the highest government levels, there is considerably more separation of function and power at the provincial levels and even more at the local levels of government.

The overlapping party/government relationship applies also for China, Yugoslavia, and other Communist Party states. Organizational charts listing the members of the Standing Committee of the Chinese NPC and the State Council and its ministries contain many names that appear in the CCP Politburo and Central Committee. As one proceeds downward from the national through the provincial to the local levels, the dual roles continue although, as in the Soviet case, they become less frequent.

The LCY attempted to end the interlocking directorate and divorce themselves from government power in the 1960s by prohibiting the simultaneous holding of party and government positions.[21] In the early 1970s, however, the LCY leaders perceived that the party was losing political control and decided to reassert their leading role. In 1980, the Yugoslav system once again had a relatively small number of elites holding the highest level party and government posts.

A short case study of the adoption of the USSR's 10th Five-Year Plan (1976) provides a simplified idea of the interrelationship between party and government organs and the role of other actors at the national level of policy making. In the mid-1970s, members of the party Politburo commissioned their personal economic advisors and government economic planners to prepare a set of guidelines for governing the future course of Soviet economic development. At one of the regular weekly sessions of the CPSU Politburo in 1975, a draft plan was brought before the assembled body, debated, and then discussed over a series of meetings. The heads of the appropriate government planning organizations within the Council of Ministers— the Ministry of Planning (GOSPLAN) responsible for identifying economic needs and determining what resources are available to meet them; the Ministry of Material and Technical Supply (Gossnab) and other relevant government organizations—were then summoned to Politburo meetings to share their research with the party officials. A set of economic guidelines was then drafted by the government agencies and returned to the party Politburo where they were reviewed, amended, and approved. At that stage in the decision-making process, the Politburo recommended its final draft of the economic plan to the CPSU Central Committee and the government's Supreme Soviet for their stamp of approval. After receiving the predictable and unanimous ratification of the Supreme Soviet, the new economic plan was given the force of law. The plan then became the responsibility of the Council of Ministers to implement and to see that the guidelines and directives were fulfilled at the different government levels. To ensure proper execution, the national CPSU Secretariat assumed the function of evaluating the implementation of the plan and intermittently reported to the Politburo the content of their findings.

The handling of the 10th Five-Year Plan portrays the way in which party and government bodies and personnel interrelate in the making of Soviet policy. Their respective functions result in a back-and-forth, cooperative sort of relationship where the functional divisions among party, government and other institutions become extremely blurred. Although the general principle of party determination and government execution applies in most policy matters, leeway exists that allows personnel from both hierarchies to step outside the normal lines of responsibility. Furthermore, because most high officials perform both party and government roles, the structural division between party and government can become extremely blurred.

The formal separation of party and government functions is even less pronounced in China. During many phases of Chinese development, institutional responsibilities were simply ignored as the top CCP leadership moved to decide and im-

[21]See the article by the former leading LCY official, Krste Crvenkovski, "Divorcing the Party from Power," *Socialist Thought and Practice,* 69 (7) (1967), pp. 40–49.

plement their directives. During the GPCR, for example, Mao and a few close advisors disregarded both party and government organs as they sought to rekindle the revolutionary spirit of Chinese society. In the aftermath of this chaotic period, which often approached a state of general anarchy, both party and government organs had to be rebuilt as China moved into the more orderly and moderate developmental phase of the 1970s. In this period, party and government organs interacted in a more cooperative and predictable way.

Like the Soviet example we have described, the power of initiation and establishment of general policy guidelines in China rests with the party leadership. In the Soviet case, the party Politburo usually is the primary initiating institution at this phase of the policy process; in Mao's China, however, where power was more fluid and concentrated among a few key officials, the smaller Standing Committee of the Politburo assumed a more influential role. The nature of the Standing Committee/Politburo relationship in the post-Mao era is still unclear, but it appears that the role of the Politburo has been enhanced under Chairman Hu's leadership.

Once the top CCP organs establish the general policy guidelines, the State Council expands them into programs and policies that are eventually formalized into government statutes and directives. As the key executive arm of government, the State Council supervises their execution through the central economic ministries and provincial and subprovincial layers of government and administration. Both the party's Standing Committee and the government State Council intermittently evaluate implementation at all levels to ensure execution in accordance with the CCP's intent.

Although we tend to know more about both party and government organs in Yugoslavia, their relationships are also clouded because of their relative newness and the uncertainties surrounding the Tito succession. We do know, however, that there are four key government organs—the state Presidency, the Assembly (with its Federal Executive Committee), the provincial governments, and the LCY Executive Commit-

tee—whose interrelationships will define the policy process in the post-Tito phase of Yugoslav development.

In the post-Tito period, the LCY Executive Committee remains the central policy-making body in the Yugoslav system. Functioning on a day-to-day basis, the Executive Committee is in a better position to remain abreast of policy matters than the leading government bodies that meet less frequently and regularly. However, the interrelations between party and government bodies in Yugoslavia exhibit a higher level of sharing and cooperation than do their Soviet and Chinese counterparts. The National Assembly meets more frequently, for longer sessions, and conducts more policy-relevant business than either the Supreme Soviet or the NPC. Although it lacks some of the independence of Western parliaments, the Yugoslav Assembly is nonetheless an important and influential political institution.

As the primary executor of government policy, the Federal Executive Council exhibits considerable autonomy as it goes about its work. The interagency and government working relations approximate those with which we are familiar in the West. In Yugoslavia, the executive arm of government has a base of power and a set of policy responsibilities independent of the domain of the party organs.


SUMMARY

It should be clear that government organs and institutional actors do play indispensable roles in the policy process. In the area of economic planning and policy making, for example, government officials work with the party leaders in preparing guidelines, formulating plans, and executing policy decisions. Although the party heads may initially prepare and debate policy guidelines among themselves and their advisors, the heads of government planning in the relevant ministries provide extensive comments and review and redraft the guidelines with the help of their own expert staffs. The party heads consider the revised drafts, amend them, and pass them on to the national assemblies for ratification. It is, therefore, the responsibility of the government ministries to execute the plans that have been arrived at by this long and intricate process of give and take between party and government hierarchies. There are certain variations on this general party/government relationship in different issue areas (for example, the party organs tend to be even more influential in the area of foreign policy), but the pattern is one that tends to hold across issue areas in all of the Second World states.

Because of their close and overlapping relationship, trying to determine which hierarchy is more important at a particular stage of the policy process is a very difficult task. It is fair to say, however, that the party tends to make policy in all Communist Party states and that the party organs at the summit—the politburo and the secretariat—are the most influential political bodies at the stages of policy initiation and formulation. This is not to say that they make policy in a vacuum and disregard the advice and counsel of others. Rather, they tend to have final authority in initiating policy proposals and deciding on those that come before the decision-making bodies.

Once these crucial decisions are made, the government organs tend to take over and assume their primary roles of ratification, implementation, and execution. After the CPSU Politburo decides the basic guidelines of a new five-year plan or a set of policies toward the Third World, it is up to the government actors to put them into practice and to see that they are properly executed. A loyal, dedicated government bureaucracy, from the highest national executive down to the local commune, is an extremely valuable political asset. In addition to legitimating public policy, a loyal government can promote decisive, effective action. Because the policy process is such an important key to the question of value distribution, and to the cause of human dignity in general, we examine it in greater detail in the pages ahead.

# Suggestions for Further Reading

Armstrong, John A., *Ideology, Politics, and Government in the Soviet Union*, 4th ed. (New York: Praeger, 1978).

Barnett, A. Doak, *Cadres, Bureaucracy, and Political Power in Communist China* (New York: Columbia University Press, 1967).

Cocks, Paul, *Controlling Communist Bureaucracy* (Cambridge: Harvard University Press, 1977).

Colton, Timothy J., *Commissars, Commanders, and Civilian Authority: The Structure of Soviet Military Politics* (Cambridge: Harvard University Press, 1979).

Hazard, John N., *The Soviet System of Government*, 5th ed. (Chicago: University of Chicago Press, 1980).

Hinton, Harold C., *An Introduction to Chinese Politics*, 2nd ed., (New York: Praeger, 1978).

Hough, Jerry F., and Merle Fainsod, *How the Soviet Union Is Governed* (Cambridge: Harvard University Press, 1979).

Ionescu, Ghita, *The Politics of the European Communist States* (New York: Praeger, 1967).

Lindbeck, John M. H., *China: Management of a Revolutionary Society* (Seattle: University of Washington Press, 1971).

Nelsen, Harvey W. *The Chinese Military System: An Organizational Study of the Chinese People's Liberation Army* (Boulder, Colo.: Westview 1977).

Oksenberg, Michel C., and Frederick C. Teiwes, eds., *The Chinese Communist Bureaucracy at Work* (New York: Praeger, 1972).

Osborn, Robert J., *The Evolution of Soviet Politics* (Homewood, Ill.: Dorsey, 1974).

Schapiro, Leonard, *The Government and Politics of the Soviet Union* (New York: Random House, 1965).

Schurmann, Franz, *Ideology and Organization in Communist China,* 2nd ed., (Berkeley: University of California Press, 1968).

Skilling, H. Gordon, *The Governments of Communist East Europe* (New York: Thomas Y. Crowell, 1966).

Staar, Richard F., *Communist Regimes in Eastern Europe,* 3rd ed., (Stanford, Calif.: Hoover Institution Press, 1977).

Vanneman, Peter, *The Supreme Soviet: Politics and Legislative Process in the Soviet Political System* (Durham, N.C.: Duke University Press, 1977).

Waller, Derek, J., *The Government and Politics of Communist China* (Garden City, N.Y.: Doubleday, 1971).

Wang, James C.F., *Contemporary Chinese Politics: An Introduction* (Englewood Cliffs, N.J.: Prentice-Hall, 1980).

# CHAPTER SIX

## The Policy Process in Communist Party States

If Communist parties are so powerful and if governments and bureaucracies are structured to assure their rule, is the policy process a highly rational and organized effort based on carefully studied goals? Or have the increasingly complex and bureaucratized party and government structures resulted in the same sort of muddling through policy-making process so characteristic of the developed states in the West? In other words, what do we know about policy making in the one-party systems of the Communist world?

### MODELS OF COMMUNIST POLITICS

The question of power and policy in Communist Party states has long intrigued Western scholars. Does the party leadership share power as a collective decision-making body? Is the party head the first among equals? What power do other groups and actors have? Are these groups able to influence the policy process? To help address such questions, political scientists often use models, that is, some simplified representation (*e.g.*, a diagram or a verbal description) of reality.

Until the 1960s, the *totalitarian model* guided most studies of Communist systems. This model drew attention to a highly organized, dic-

tatorial political process where individuals and groups outside of the top party leadership had no significant political power. Two leading proponents of this model, Carl Friedrich and Zbigniew K. Brzezinski, argued that the totalitarian system involves an unavoidable compulsion on the part of the rulers to absorb or destroy all social groups obstructing its complete control.[1] Although this widely used model drew attention to some very important features of Communist political systems, an increasing number of scholars began to feel that it also obscured some equally important aspects of reality. H. Gordon Skilling, for example, contended that the totalitarian model focused too much attention on outputs (the decisions made by the party leadership) and too little on inputs.[2] Skilling argued that groups and actors outside the formal party leadership can and do influence inputs (the structure of

[1]Carl Friedrich and Zbigniew K. Brzezinski, *Totalitarian Dictatorship and Autocracy* (Cambridge: Harvard University Press, 1956). The authors outlined the five essential features of a totalitarian system as an official ideology, a single mass party, a monopoly of control of all means of armed combat, a monopoly of control of mass communication and terroristic police control.

[2]H. Gordon Skilling, "Interest Groups and Communist Politics," *World Politics, 18* (3) (1966), pp. 435–451.

demands and supports) that affect the political process.

This viewpoint resulted in new concern with the input side of the policy process and brought increasing attention to the competing interests and bargaining that goes on prior to the formal making of decisions. Scholars with these interests began to use *group or pluralist* models to study power and policy in Communist systems. For example, utilizing a group model, Joel J. Schwartz and William R. Keech explain how a number of significant interest groups—teachers and administrators, higher education and scientific personnel, parents and factory managers—in Soviet society overrode First Secretary Nikita S. Khrushchev's suggestions for education reform in 1958.[3] Many other scholars began to use the group model to draw attention to the important roles that groups play in the Communist political process.[4] Other studies illustrate the importance of political participation, conflict and competition.[5]

By the 1970s, most scholars felt that increasing numbers of groups and political actors both inside and outside the party hierarchy were becoming influential in the policy process. With the decline of terrorism following Stalin's death; the increasing complexity of social, political, and economic decisions; and the growing expertise of different sectors of society, the conditions were set for a more open, sometimes pluralistic process. Jerry F. Hough contended, for example, that these tendencies had become so prevalent that a new pluralist model of Communist politics was

needed.[6] Although many scholars continued to use the totalitarian model and although some were critical of the group and pluralist models,[7] nevertheless, these newer approaches brought attention to the presence of interest-group competition and to at least some measure of political pluralism in Communist-run societies.

Other models and approaches also have had an impact on the study of politics in Communist systems. Some leading scholars argued that Communist studies ought to be brought more into the mainstream of contemporary political science and that greater use should be made of the techniques and concepts of modern behavioral science.[8] A number of efforts resulted from this development including studies of structural-functionalism,[9] leadership and élites,[10] organizational[11] and administrative[12] behavior. All these studies called attention to a form of policy making that was more complex than the centralized, party-controlled process identified by the totalitarian model.

At the same time, some scholars expressed concern that the new models and approaches were detracting attention and study from the

---

[6]Jerry F. Hough, "The Bureaucratic Model and the Nature of the Soviet System," *Journal of Comparative Administration,* 5 (2) (1973), pp. 134–167; and "The Soviet System: Petrification or Pluralism?" *Problems of Communism,* 21 (2) (1972), pp. 25–45.

[7]William E. Odom, "A Dissenting View on the Group Approach to Soviet Politics," *World Politics,* 28 (4) (1976), pp. 542–568; and Andrew C. Janos, "Interest Groups and the Structure of Power: Critique and Comparisons," *Studies in Comparative Communism,* 12 (1) (1979), pp. 6–20.

[8]Frederic J. Fleron, Jr., ed., *Communist Studies and the Social Sciences* (Chicago: Rand McNally, 1969); Roger E. Kanet, ed., *The Behavioral Revolution and Communist Studies* (New York: Free Press, 1973).

[9]Frederick C. Barghoorn, *Politics in the USSR,* 2nd ed., (Boston: Little, Brown, 1972).

[10]Carl Beck, *et al., Comparative Communist Political Leadership* (New York: David McKay, 1973); R. Barry Farrell, ed., *Political Leadership in Eastern Europe and the Soviet Union* (Chicago: Aldine, 1970).

[11]Alfred G. Meyer, *The Soviet Political System: An Interpretation* (New York: Random House, 1965).

[12]Jerry F. Hough, *The Soviet Prefects* (Cambridge: Harvard University Press, 1969).

[3]Joel J. Schwartz and William R. Keech, "Group Influence and the Policy Process in the Soviet Union," *The American Political Science Review, 62* (3) (1968), pp. 840–851.

[4]See, for example, the different studies reported in H. Gordon Skilling and Franklyn Griffiths, eds., *Interest Groups in Soviet Politics* (Princeton, N.J.: Princeton University Press, 1971).

[5]Barbara Jancar, "The Case for a Loyal Opposition Under Communism: Czechoslovakia and Yugoslavia," *Orbis,* 11 (2) (1968), pp. 415–440; D. Richard Little, "Mass Political Participation in the US and USSR: A Conceptual Analysis," *Comparative Political Studies, 8,* (4) (1976), pp. 437–460; Richard C. Thornton, "The Structure of Communist Politics," *World Politics,* 24 (4) (1972), pp. 498–517.

critical features of Communist politics. Franklyn Griffiths noted, for example, that "it seems apparent that interest group activity cannot be regarded as the central phenomenon in Soviet policy-making."[13] Although bringing attention to a host of interesting and, in some respects, significant phenomena concerning pluralism and interest-group activity, the newer approaches tend to lose sight of the most important feature of Communist policy making—the dominant role of the party hierarchy. Griffiths goes on to suggest a *systems* model that stresses the importance of the hierarchical party system and its role in the articulation of values as well as the formation and execution of policy. Paul Cocks also supports the systems model and notes, "Though generally not used by Western analysts of Soviet affairs, the systems approach is equally if not more useful than group theory as a guide and aid in understanding recent developments in the politics of oligarchy in the USSR."[14] Before deciding which of these models might be most useful in our study, it will be instructive to consider how Communist leaders see the question. For example, how would they like to make policy?

In his illuminating essay on the policy process in the Soviet Union, Cocks argues that Soviet leaders would like to make policy according to the *synoptic* or rational-comprehensive mode.[15] On the basis of this mode:

1.   The policy makers review all information and specify the needs confronting their system.

2.   The policy makers identify goals related to the resolution of these needs and rank them according to a thorough listing of priorities.

3.   All possible actions, or policy alternatives, for meeting social needs and fulfilling the specified goals are examined.

4.   The costs and benefits of each alternative are carefully reviewed and compared with those resulting from other policy options.

5.   The probable outcomes of each policy alternative are evaluated.

6.   Finally, the policy makers select that action or set of actions that maximize the probabilities of achieving the desired goals.

The synoptic policy-making process involves careful and thorough planning and the analysis of all available information. Although this process is comprehensive and rational and preferred by policy makers both inside and outside the Communist world, it is difficult to apply.

The *incremental* process of policy making, considered a more accurate description of what really happens in most systems, is described in terms of the following features:[16]

1.   The policy makers consider only a limited range of goals that differ only marginally (*i.e.*, incrementally) from previous goals.

2.   The policy makers consider only some of the actions for attaining the specified goals, which will differ only marginally from existing policies.

3.   The specification of goals and selection of policies are closely intertwined, with selection sometimes determining specification.

4.   The total costs and benefits of each alternative action are not carefully evaluated, and probable outcomes are not clearly understood.

5.   The policy makers select that action with which they can agree, a policy not necessarily the one that is most probable (scientifically speaking), to achieve the desired goal.

Incremental policy making, often called the process of muddling through, deals with policy matters as they arise on a more or less *ad hoc* basis and results in decisions that deviate from

---

[13]Franklyn Griffiths, "A Tendency Analysis of Soviet Policy-Making," in Skilling and Griffiths, eds., *op. cit.*, p. 335.

[14]Paul Cocks, "The Policy Process and Bureaucratic Politics," in Paul Cocks *et al.*, eds., *The Dynamics of Soviet Politics* (Cambridge: Harvard University Press, 1976), p. 157.

[15]*Ibid.*

[16]The discussion of the synoptic and incremental models draws on Charles Lindbloom's *The Intelligence of Democracy* (New York: Macmillan, 1964) and *The Policy-Making Process* (Englewood Cliffs, N.J.: Prentice-Hall, 1968).

present policy only marginally. This form of policy making is essentially short term, or remedial, and does not place much emphasis on long-range planning and analysis or the foresight necessary to promote future social and ideological goals.[17]

Which mode of policy making—incremental or synoptic—is preferred by Communist policy makers? How do they assess policy processes in their own systems? Do they see a rational comprehensive approach to attaining high priority goals or do they perceive a process of muddling through? Like the Soviets, other Communist leaders would prefer to make policy according to the synoptic mode. Michel C. Oksenberg describes the frustration of the synoptically oriented Mao Zedong as he battled with the short-sighted bureaucrats motivated by incrementalist goals and actions.[18] Although the Chinese bureaucrats considered only a limited range of policy alternatives designed to serve the interests of their government sectors, Oksenberg contends that Mao was guided by the following principles:

> A stress upon investigation of actual conditions: the necessity of remaining attuned to public opinion: the value of clarity, conciseness, and precision of expression; a distrust of highly institutionalized decision-making mechanisms; the need for open debate within Party committees followed by discipline after decisions were made: a belief that policy formulation and implementation are intertwined and hence the wisdom of fusing these two phases of the policy process.[19]

Oksenberg concludes that during Mao's rule, China combined elements of both the synoptic and incremental policy process. Like Mao, leaders throughout the rest of the Communist world are also disturbed by tendencies toward incrementalism. Despite the efforts of the party leadership to coordinate the planning process and their attempts to dominate decision making to move the society toward high-priority goals, the tendency has been toward incremental bargaining and negotiations. The political process is marked by a diversity of interests that result in clashes and compromises among the different leaders and agencies. Under these conditions, in the words of Jerry F. Hough, incrementalism has become the "hallmark of the system."[20]

What happened? How has the tightly controlled highly centralized leadership of Stalinist Russia evolved into a group of political brokers who mediate the competing demands of the different government and bureaucratic sectors? Changes have definitely occurred in Communist systems over the last few decades and they have had a major impact on the way policy is made. With the death of Joseph Stalin and the deconcentration of power that Khrushchev's rule ushered in, political power has devolved to a certain extent from the highest party bodies to different bureaucratic and state organs.[21] Although Khrushchev was an impulsive policy maker who would often take adventurous action to attain high-priority goals, his policies of liberalization and decentralization set the Soviet Union on a course that dispersed more autonomy and policy-relevant authority than had ever been accorded before.

Khrushchev's successors, Leonid I. Brezhnev and Aleksei N. Kosygin, moved the USSR even further in the direction of incrementalism. Basing their leadership on a system of collective rule, the post-Khrushchev leadership provided the specialized state, party, and scientific complexes with considerable policy-making autonomy in their fields. To avoid the loss of support that led to Khrushchev's ouster, the leaders have usually given all the various departments an incremental

---

[17]For a discussion of incrementalism in Communist systems, see Valerie Bunce and John Echols, "Power and Policy in Communist Systems: The Problem of Incrementalism," *Journal of Politics*, 40 (4) (1978), pp. 911–932.

[18]Michael C. Oksenberg, "Policy-Making Under Mao Tsetung, 1949–1968," *Comparative Politics*, 4 (2) (1971), pp. 327–328.

[19]*Ibid.*, pp. 327–328.

[20]Hough, "The Soviet System: Petrification or Pluralism," *op. cit.*, p. 29.

[21]T. H. Rigby, "The De-concentration of Power in the USSR, 1953–1964," in John D. B. Miller and T. H. Rigby, eds., *The Disintegrating Monolith: Pluralist Trends in the Communist World* (Canberra: Australian National University, 1965), pp. 17–45.

budgetary increase each year.[22] Although many terms have been used to describe Soviet politics over the past few decades—institutional pluralism, bureaucratic pluralism, participatory bureaucracy, and so on[23]—all draw attention to a sharing of political power in which ideas and actions flow up as well as down the traditional power hierarchy.

The 1970s witnessed a discernible change in Soviet decision making. The leadership became increasingly concerned and frustrated with their brokerage roles and decided that something would have to be done to stop the trend toward incrementalism. Cocks reports that the Soviet leaders may have reflected on the experience of the United States and borrowed a capitalist technique (modern systems theory) to move their policy-making process closer to the synoptic mode:

> Indeed, modern systems theory with its sophisticated analytical methodology, managerial technology, and centralizing bias has increasingly attracted Moscow's attention. . . . Like Washington in the sixties, the Kremlin in the seventies exhibits a peculiarly keen fascination with "technological forecasting," "scientific management," and the "systems approach." . . . Forces aiming at strengthening the capability of central authorities to plan, coordinate and implement national policies and program priorities have grown steadily since 1970.[24]

Although it is too early to evaluate the impact of these techniques, it is clear that they were adopted to inject greater rationality and planning into the cumbersome and fragmented Soviet policy process.

If the Soviet Union and China are both characterized as representing a blend of synoptic and incremental policy-making processes, Yugoslavia has moved considerably further in the direction of the latter. With the movement toward decentralization in the 1950s and 1960s, power was devolved both vertically and horizontally from the party center to regional and administrative complexes. Simultaneously, the role of national planning was severely curtailed, resulting in an unavoidable tendency toward *ad hoc*, remedial policy making. More and more, the Yugoslav leaders assumed the roles of political brokers in which they would mediate the competing demands of the various regions, different government bureaucracies, or interest groups.

Like the Soviets, the Yugoslav leaders also became concerned about the continuing trend toward incrementalism in the early 1970s. Viewing the lack of national planning, program development, and increasing interregional and government conflict as undesirable costs of incrementalism, the League of Communists of Yugoslavia (LCY) leadership decided to reemphasize centralization in planning, decision making, and policy implementation within the Yugoslav system. Placing greater emphasis on party leadership, democratic centralism, and government planning, the new policies represented what Dennison Rusinow so aptly called "a return to Leninism."[25] Although these policies were continued in the post-Tito period, the multiethnic composition and political structure of Yugoslavia makes her particularly susceptible to incrementalism.

What kind of policy-making process do we find in Communist systems? Because of the trends toward pluralism in the post-Stalin era, the deconcentration of power, and so forth, incrementalism has become a predominant feature of all Communist systems. At the same time, the continuing presence of centralized party rule with its emphasis on planning, coordination, and management assures the presence of some elements of the synoptic process.

[22]Jerry F. Hough, "The Brezhnev Era: The Man and the System," *Problems of Communism,* 25 (2) (1976), pp. 1–17.

[23]Hough, "The Soviet System: Petrification or Pluralism," *op. cit.,* pp. 27–29; Darrell P. Hammer, *USSR: The Politics of Oligarchy* (Hinsdale, Ill.: Dryden, 1974), pp. 223–256; Robert V. Daniels, "Soviet Politics Since Khrushchev," in John W. Strong, ed., *The Soviet Union Under Brezhnev and Kosigin* (New York: Van Nostrand Reinhold, 1971), pp. 22–23.

[24]Cocks, *op. cit.,* pp. 157, 163.

[25]Dennison Rusinow, *The Yugoslav Experiment, 1948–1974* (Berkeley, Calif.: University of California Press, 1977), p. 338.

If the policy process is characterized by both widespread interest group activity and centralized party rule, by pluralism and centralism, the model we use to study the process must draw attention to all these important phenomena. In addition, it should help account for changes in the various Communist systems and allow us to compare one with another. Unfortunately, no one model satisfies all these criteria. In the pages ahead, we utilize elements of both the *group* model, with its emphasis on bargaining and competing interests, and the *systems* model, with its emphasis on party control, to describe three important phases of the policy process.[26]

## PHASES OF POLICY MAKING

The policy process is a series of activities that can be viewed in different phases. For purposes of our study, it is divided into three major parts. *Setting goals* refers to the formulation of policy proposals as responses to ideological guidelines and social needs. *Taking action* embodies the decision phase where proposals are either approved or vetoed by the relevant authorities. *Producing outcomes* involves the implementation and execution of the policy decisions.

### SETTING GOALS

Goals can be derived from an ideology, such as Marxism-Leninism; from social needs that arise in a society in the course of national development; and from the sociopolitical experiences of leaders and masses. In Communist states, goals have all these origins.

The monumental study of Soviet politics, by Barrington Moore, Jr., deals with the impact of ideology on social and political change and *vice versa*. Moore outlines the complex interplay between ideology and policy in the following way:

> Once an ideology has been determined it enters in as a determining factor in its own right in subsequent social situations. It has an effect, sometimes slight, sometimes considerable, on the decisions

taken by those who hold it. In its turn, it is modified, sometimes slightly, sometimes considerably, by the impact of subsequent considerations.[27]

Historical events in the Soviet Union altered the goals of classical Marxist thought. For example, the equalitarian goals were modified as a result of Stalin's emphasis on variable income because of the need for rapid industrialization; the democratic goals were modified in favor of the authoritarian rule the leaders considered necessary for socialist construction. Moore refers to these more pragmatic ideas and considerations as an ideology of means. He contends that the Soviet ideology of means, as exemplified in the words and deeds of its leaders has had a greater impact on policy than the classical Marxist ideology of ends.[28]

Yet the ideology of ends continues to influence policy—at least, so the leaders would have the people believe. Brezhnev continues to speak of equality, democracy, respect, and well-being and acts as if these are the ideological goals that guide Soviet policy. Although it would be naïve to say that such idealistic goals are foremost in the leader's mind, it would be equally naïve to contend that they have no effect whatsoever. The typical result is a blend between political exigencies (ideology of means) and idealistic goals (ideology of ends). This blend is reflected in policy. Concerning political power, contemporary Soviet society shows both signs of a one-party dictatorship and a grass-roots democracy; concerning equality, we see both boring uniformities and glaring disparities; concerning respect, both brotherhood and a tragic disregard for human rights. This strange amalgam of policy outcomes reflects the conflicting goals guiding Soviet policy makers. Some result from the expedient ideology of means and others from the idealistic ideology of ends.

The ideology of means is related to the leader's perceptions of the needs of the people and the state. Vladimir Ilyich Lenin and Joseph Stalin ignored the democratic goals of classical Marx-

[26]Cocks recommends using both models in viewing the Soviet policy process, *op. cit.*, p. 175.

[27]Barrington Moore, Jr., *Soviet Politics—The Dilemma of Power* (Cambridge: Harvard University Press, 1950), p. 412.
[28]*Ibid.*, p. 403.

ism because they felt authoritarian rule within the party hierarchy was the best way to ensure Communist rule and national development. The Chinese Communists shared this basic assumption although they also recognized the great resources that could be provided by the hundreds of millions of Chinese people. Mao's emphasis on mass involvement and participation resulted from his perception that this was a way to bind the people to the collective and simultaneously mobilize the masses to attain otherwise impossible goals.

The Yugoslav's turn toward self-management and participatory democracy also grew out of political exigencies and the leader's perceptions of social needs. After the break with the Soviet Union in 1947, Josip Broz Tito realized that the Yugoslav regime would have to develop a high level of mass support to preserve their rule in the face of Soviet opposition. The Yugoslav leaders' emphasis on democracy, independence, and a more humanistic road to socialism served that purpose, changed the course of Yugoslav development, and, in the eyes of many observers, took the Yugoslavs closer to the ideals of classical Marxism. So, although it is true that ideology influences the setting of goals, it does not determine them in a vacuum. Sometimes the impact is great, at other times it is slight. Sometimes it is the more utopian ideology of ends, at other times, the more pragmatic ideology of means.

Finally, policy goals also result from the complex interplay between leaders and masses. Mao observed that it is the leadership's responsibility to turn the "scattered and unsystematic ideas of the masses into concentrated and systematic ideas" and to "synthesize their experience into better articulated principles."[29] Conventional wisdom in the West often assumes a shocking insensitivity among the Communist leaders to the needs and demands of their people, yet this feeling seems excessively harsh. Leaders realize that they must maintain the support of their people and that the chances of doing so are greater when they can provide the values the masses desire. They also recognize on occasion that some good can come from the ideas of the masses and that a two-way flow of communication can have valuable benefits. The history in a number of Communist Party states indicates that breakdowns in this communication flow and mass frustration among the populace can result in serious political difficulties for the leaders.[30] Perhaps not the major determinant, nevertheless, the needs of the society, as perceived and interpreted by the party leaders, have considerable impact on setting goals.

How are the different ideological, social, and personal considerations incorporated into an overall plan? Do the leaders set goals on a short-term, *ad hoc* basis or do they synthesize all the competing goals into a comprehensive plan? In the area of economics, where comprehensive planning appears most feasible, Communist Party states have shown remarkable difficulties. The Five-Year plans adopted throughout Soviet history and within most of the other Second World states seem unable to match societal needs with productive capacities. Either the plan falls short of the need or supply far exceeds demand.[31]

Considerable effort is made to plan in other areas of government activity. Giant bureaucracies are engaged in the study of regional development, in housing, education, health care, energy, the environment, and so on. The significant Soviet advance in space, defense, and some fields of science, indicates that long-range planning has freed some areas from the incrementalist muddling characteristic of most bureaucracies. Where goals have been clearly specified and agreed on, as they have in these few areas, major accomplishments are recorded. Yet, past experience has generally been far less than satisfactory and illustrates a long record of overly optimistic plans and unfulfilled goals.

The problems of long-range planning have become even more difficult in the past few dec-

---

[29]Mao Zedong, *Selected Works*, vol. 3 (Beijing: Foreign Languages Press, 1961), pp. 119, 158.

[30]For example, demonstrations of mass discontent in Poland led to the ousters of the party leader Wladyslaw Gomulka in 1970, his successor Edward Gierek, in 1980 and his successor Stanislaw Kania in 1981.

[31]Jan Marczewski, *Crisis in Socialist Planning*, trans. Noel Lindsay (New York: Praeger, 1974).

ades. With the partial devolution of power to various ministries and regional networks, more individuals are given a role in the planning process. In addition, different groups, often with competing interests in common policy areas, also want to participate in the goal-setting process. Goals desired by one ministry or group often conflict with those of another. Increased funding for space exploration or for defense investment must come at the expense of social programs. These are the guns-versus-butter issues important to the people and over which the party leaders must preside. The resultant bargaining indicates the forces of incrementalism, a trend that narrows the flexibility of the party leaders and limits their overall power and influence in the goal-setting process.

The extent to which the specification of goals is the right and responsibility of the party leaders is an issue of considerable and continuing importance in these states. Today, the general pattern is one in which the national leadership is struggling to maintain final control in the identification of developmental priorities and policy goals. At the same time, the leaders rely heavily on lower level agencies and complexes, including government organs, party committees, research offices, and so forth, that provide them with reports and recommendations on alternative courses of action. If a Soviet research institute on higher education recognizes certain difficulties in scientific education, for example, it will inform the Communist Party of the Soviet Union (CPSU) Central Committee's Department on Science and Educational Institutions of its concern and findings. These party officials, in turn, may report to members of the CPSU Politburo. Likewise, if a Yugoslav institute in charge of the study of self-management finds certain trends that will be of interest to the LCY leadership, it too will inform them of its specialized knowledge. The party leadership is then in a position to synthesize this more specialized information and include it in its consideration and ranking of national goals.

In contrast to the United States and First World states, national priorities and goals are usually established at the highest party and government levels. Although middle-level bureau-crats and private and social groups are often successful in placing items on the American political agenda, the process is more restricted and controlled in Communist Party states.[32] Inputs from these groups are sometimes articulated in Communist Party states, but they are typically made at lower levels and then incorporated into written reports prepared by research or government agencies before being forwarded to the appropriate party authorities. If the relevant authorities consider the issue sufficiently important, they will bring it to the attention of the party secretariat or politburo where it will be discussed and debated.

## TAKING ACTION

Once issues have been identified, they must be transformed into policy proposals. This also tends to be a function of the party leadership. Normally, the party leaders discuss policy options and alternatives with associates and advisors before they formally present them for debate and decision within the politburo. Often they will first make reference to the issues and policy options in public speeches to initiate newspaper coverage and some public debate of the issue. Questions of agriculture or educational reform, for example, may be addressed in the newspapers and discussed for some period outside the official party organs before official action is taken within the politburo. James B. Bruce's illuminating study of the politics of Soviet policy formation draws attention to a number of stages—policy proposal, decision in principle, policy controversy—preceding the formal decision process.[33] In his case study of the virgin-lands decision, Bruce found that different policy preferences were reflected in *Pravda* ("The Truth"), the official newspaper of the CPSU, and

[32]See Zbigniew K. Brzezinski and Samuel P. Huntington's comparison of policy formation in the Soviet and American systems, *Political Power: USA/USSR* (New York: Viking, 1965), pp. 202–223.

[33]James B. Bruce, *The Politics of Soviet Policy Formation: Khrushchev's Innovative Policies in Education and Agriculture* (Denver, Colo.: University of Denver, 1976), pp. 17–20. (Monograph Series in World Affairs)

*Izvestia* ("News"), the official newspaper of the government, some months prior to the formal decision. Similar developments have been found in other policy studies. During this period of debate and discussion, such special groups as interest associations, labor unions, research institutes, and so forth, can make their own preferences known. The exchange of ideas is not as open and freewheeling as in the United States, nevertheless, interested parties are likely to express their opinions by either consulting directly with the party authorities or by going through lower level organs or advisors. For example, a member of the politburo may request to meet personally with the head of a research institute to discuss policy options in some area of domestic or foreign affairs. Scientific complexes of all kinds do specialized government research and are at the disposal of the party leaders. Before the politburo or a close adviser meets to take some policy action, many hours of specialized research and consultation are conducted.

As the issues clarify and options become better defined, coalitions within the politburos often develop. It is at this time that the high concentration of power within the Communist policy-making process becomes most apparent. Although hundreds of individuals would still have considerable influence at this phase of the policy process in First World states, in Communist Party states, it now resides in the hands of a much smaller number of party members, most of whom hold positions within the politburo. At this stage, politburo members begin the process of persuasion and coalition building. To have their point of view supported, they lobby informally with one another and attempt to secure a voting majority within the politburo's membership.[34]

After this period of discussion and debate, alternative policy actions are formally brought before the members of the politburo. In the Soviet Union, China, Yugoslavia, and all other Second World states, ultimate decision-making power resides within the politburo. When members of these bodies seat themselves at the long tables within their party headquarters, they discuss, debate, and attempt to decide the course of action most likely to achieve their desired goals. Often debate on an important policy matter will carry far into the night or even over a series of long, interminable meetings. Sometimes an issue is dropped or postponed when the party leaders are unable to agree to a satisfactory action or resolution. Ultimately, most policy alternatives come to a vote and the politburo sets forth its official action.

The final decision process tends to correspond with the Leninist principle of democratic centralism. According to this principle, open discussion and debate takes place until the point of decision; then, the democratic nature of the process ends and centralism begins. Once the politburo members have voted and made a final decision, expression of alternative points of view is to cease. The principle of democratic centralism assures that different ideas are given expression before a vote is taken, but, once the decision is made, most politburo members abide by the principle of centralism and avoid publicly criticizing decisions with which they may disagree.

Although final decisive action is taken by a small number of people within the top party committee, a successful action still requires the support of a large number of other people. Ross suggests that key institutional actors in the hierarchy must be minimally satisfied before major decisions can be reached.[35] A policy action benefits from having the approval and support of officials from various government agencies and the central committee department most directly concerned with that particular area of policy. A successful action should also have the support of the government presidium.[36] If a particular policy program does not have the support of these people, it is likely to encounter difficulties and could be vetoed. Although the politburo membership can ultimately force an unpopular action through the policy-making process, it must remain sensitive to the preferences of these other individuals

[34]Dennis Ross, "Coalition Maintenance in the Soviet Union," *World Politics*, 32, (2) (1980), p. 258–280.

[35]*Ibid.*

[36]See Brzezinski and Huntington's discussion of the necessary support, *op. cit.*, pp. 217–218.

and groups. To maintain the support of their broader constituencies, the leaders attempt to operate in an atmosphere of cooperation and consensus.

## PRODUCING OUTCOMES

Once a decision has been taken within the high party organs, it is sent to certain party and government bodies for ratification and approval. The most important party organ is the central committee that normally meets every few months to review national party activity and the work of the politburo. Constitutionally recognized as the leading government organs, the Supreme Soviet in the USSR and National People's Congress (NPC) in China, are also expected to ratify the politburos' decisions and legitimize them by stamping them with the peoples' approval. Because they meet so infrequently, however, many decisions are made and implemented without their ratification or with the approval of the smaller executive bodies (*e.g.*, presidiums or standing committees) of the assemblies.

After a policy action is taken and ratified by the appropriate bodies, the government bureaucracy is responsible for seeing that it is implemented. Government agencies under the chief executive and administrative branch of government, the Council of Ministers or its counterpart, use a vast bureaucracy to ensure policy execution. Traditional ministries within the Council are in charge of executing the party's decisions in their areas of responsibility, including foreign affairs, defense, agriculture, education and culture, and so forth. Relying on their own bureaucracies, the ministers expect, but seldom get, prompt and efficient implementation down the administrative hierarchies. As we will shortly see, executing an idealistic decision is often more difficult than making it.

Although there is considerable party oversight, the government branch has great authority of its own at this stage of the policy process. H. Gordon Skilling notes that, "In the Communist Party countries of Eastern Europe, the administrative machinery has unparalleled authority . . .

administration has become a leviathan dominating the entire body politic."[37] The high level of administrative control has led some other observers to describe the Communist political process as one of "totalitarianism without terror" and the broader social system as an "administered society."[38] The stereotype of paunchy, dimwitted bureaucrats inflexibly carrying out party orders in the isolated hinterlands is a description not without fact. From the nation's capital to the outlying periphery, the Second World states have organized an elaborate but cumbersome and often inefficient network to carry out the party's directives.

In executing party policy, the government bureaucracies have policy-making powers of their own. Brzezinski and Huntington put it simply: "Those who execute policy can also make it."[39] Party directives are typically issued in imprecise and ideological language. The executors must attempt to interpret the meaning and intent of the party leaders. Usually, of course, they feel some compunction to apply the policies as they perceive the leaders intended them. However, they often have sufficient autonomy and independence of action to register their own preferences or those of the constituency they represent.

As a result, most observers agree that the bureaucracy has become extremely powerful and sometimes dominates the policy process. In evaluating the Soviet experience in which he originally participated, Leon Trotsky contended that bureaucracy assumed this dominant role as early as the 1920s when it "conquered the Bolshevik party . . . [and] defeated the program of Lenin."[40] A leading American scholar speaks of the USSR as a large complex bureaucracy and calls attention to the power of bureaucratic interest groups

[37]H. Gordon Skilling, *The Governments of Communist East Europe* (New York: Thomas Y. Crowell, 1966), p. 140.

[38]Allen Kassof, "The Administered Society: Totalitarianism Without Terror," *World Politics 16* (4) (1964), pp. 558–575.

[39]Brzezinski and Huntington, *op. cit.*, p. 220.

[40]Leon Trotsky, *The Revolution Betrayed* (New York: Doubleday, 1937), p. 93.

within the policy process.[41] Overall, the power and importance of the government bureaucracy in shaping outcomes is a widely accepted fact.

The elaborate bureaucratic structure provides the party with certain advantages in producing desired policy outcomes. As a result of the interlocking hierarchies of the party and government organizations illustrated in Figure 5.5, the party can maintain fairly close control over the execution function. The interlocking structure aids communication processes and allows the party direct input into the executive organs. Under these circumstances, the party can quickly mobilize the bureaucracy to carry out policy with a speed and ideological fervor that Western, democratic systems with nonpartisan bureaucracies can seldom muster.

Another important factor that contributes to the potential efficiency of Communist administrative branches is what many scholars have referred to as a politicized bureaucracy.[42] Administrative officials in Communist Party states, particularly in the more authoritarian and ideological ones, are expected to demonstrate a high level of commitment to the ideology and to the regime. Promotions and forms of monetary and symbolic rewards are often provided on the basis of political consciousness and commitment rather than on professional merit. Of course, commitment is sometimes suspect and problematical and varies considerably among administrative officials and among the various countries. Yet, Communist Party countries have a closer fusion of politics and bureaucracy than most of the world and, therefore, can more effectively utilize their politicized bureaucracy to ensure proper execution of the party's policy.[43]

At the same time, Communist bureaucracies in the execution process reveal certain disadvantages compared with the political systems of the West. The sheer size of the socialist public sector is so massive that the policy process in Communist Party states encounters inevitable problems of coordination and control. The state tries to do too much in administering the society. The huge bureaucracy this task requires encounters administrative overloads as it attempts to administer everything from space exploration to day care centers, from business trips to family vacations. Another factor that complicates the implementation and execution of policy involves the problems of regionalism and provincialism so prevalent in China, the Soviet Union, and Yugoslavia. Getting lower level, regional-oriented bureaucrats to execute national policy uniformly throughout the country is a difficult task that has no easy solution. Although new ideas are now being used to combat the problems of overload, coordination, and so forth, they are no panacea to the communication barriers that permeate these heterogeneous systems.[44]

A rather different disadvantage of the Communist's efforts to produce rational and effective policy outcomes involves the lack of autonomy and resistance within the politicized bureaucracies. If bureaucrats do disagree with party policy, they will sometimes repress their feelings or sabotage the execution process in an underhanded, damaging way. Instead of openly discussing the party's unreasonable expectations concerning industrial output in the Five-Year plans, for example, an official in charge of steel output might allow the production of a lower quality of steel simply to meet the production quota. The lack of full and open upward communication in the administrative networks of

[41]Meyer, *op. cit.*

[42]Ezra F. Vogel, "Politicized Bureaucracy: Communist China," in Lenard J. Cohen and Jane P. Shapiro, eds., *Communist Systems in Comparative Perspective* (Garden City, N. Y.: Doubleday, 1974), pp. 161–170. Anchor Books.

[43]Party control over the bureaucracies varies over time as well as among countries. See Trong R. Chai, "Communist Party Control over the Bureaucracy: The Case of China," *Comparative Politics*, 11 (3) (1979), pp. 359–370.

[44]The USSR is utilizing new hardware (*e.g.*, computers) and software (*e.g.*, managerial methods) in attempting to meet these organizational and structural problems. See Paul Cocks, "Rethinking the Organizational Weapon: The Soviet System in a Systems Age," *World Politics*, 32 (2) (1980), pp. 228–257.

~~these states is a widely recognized cost of the~~
politicized bureaucracy.

## EXAMPLES OF POLICY MAKING

To get a fuller picture of the roles of party, government, and other institutional actors in the policy process, we will now examine some studies of specific policy areas in China and the USSR.

Examining five policy issues in China during Mao's reign—the Twelve-Year Agricultural Program, administrative decentralization, the commune movement, the Socialist Education Campaign, and the ideological rectification campaign—Parris H. Chang makes substantial progress in determining how policy was made and who was making it in the 1950s and 1960s.[45] Chang found a variety of important actors in the decision-making process in addition to Mao, the Chinese Communist Party (CCP) Politburo, and the CCP's Standing Committee. Other actors included the party's Central Committee; party officials at the provincial and local levels; the People's Liberation Army (PLA); bureaucracy and extraparty forces, such as the Red Guard and revolutionary rebels. The actors involved, of course, varied according to the policy area. For example, Chang noted that those institutions connected with setting goals, taking action, and producing outcomes in the area of rural policies at the national level included at least the Ministry of Agriculture, the Agricultural and Forestry Staff Office, the CCP Central Committee Rural Work Department, and the CCP Secretariat, Politburo, and Central Committee.[46]

How, then, was policy made in Mao's China. Chang contends that:

> Policy in Communist China was not made by a few leaders alone; actors possessing different political resources participated, directly or indirectly, in each stage of the policy-making process and af-

~~fected in a variety of ways, the decision-output of~~ the regime.[47]

At the same time, Chang cautions, it is necessary to recognize the enormous power wielded by Mao. When Mao was most active—for example, during the second half of the 1950s—the policy-making process was more personalized and less routine. Mao used the other institutions and actors to initiate, accept, and carry out the policies he preferred. For example, when other party leaders favored a go-slow approach toward organizing collectivization in 1955, Mao argued vehemently for stepping up the tempo in a secret speech to provincial party secretaries. By skillfully using others, Mao was able to overcome the go-slow opposition and launch an intense nationwide campaign to accelerate agricultural collectivization.[48] In the 1960s, however, Mao became less active and the CCP Politburo and Central Committee handled decision making in most policy areas more routinely.

Chang summarizes the conclusions of his study in the following way:[49]

1.  Policy-making in China involved a complicated conflict and consensus-building process with many actors and many problems which—although distinctive in many respects—had some similarities to political processes elsewhere.

2.  Although Mao played an extremely important role in the system—different from the less important role he played after the early 1960s—he was frequently blocked and frustrated by other leaders, and he was not always "in command," as some scholars have maintained.

3.  When Mao maneuvered on various occasions to push his policies, he sought "outside" support to overcome his opponents at the center; consequently, the arena of political conflict was expanded, and more actors were drawn into participation in the resolution of conflict.

4.  Despite Mao's enormous power, policy was significantly influenced by debates and conflict among the leaders; the major shifts in policy followed an oscillating pattern between the conserva-

[45]Parris H. Chang, *Power and Policy in China*, 2nd and enlarged ed. (University Park, Pa: The Pennsylvania State University Press, 1978).

[46]*Ibid.*, pp. 186–187.

[47]*Ibid.*, p. 181.

[48]*Ibid.*, p. 189.

[49]*Ibid.*, p. 2.

tive and radical orientation, as a result of shifting coalitions and balance of power in the decision-making councils.

**5.** Leaders and cadres at the provincial and lower levels did have an effect on policy during the implementation phase in a variety of ways, although they may not have directly participated in its formulation.

The conflicts, disagreements, and involvement of actors outside the top party leadership became even greater in the post-Mao period. Although there is still much we do not know about this more recent period, everyone agrees that the moderates won the power struggle against the radicals. With the purging of the Gang of Four and others associated with their radical positions, Hua Guofeng, Deng Xiaoping, and the more moderate leaders participated in a collective, consensus-building decision-making process that was to set China on the road to modernization. In March 1978 the CCP officially embraced the Four Modernizations Program.

Of course, significant differences existed even among the so-called moderate modernizers. Deng and his supporters are known as the all-out modernizers, whereas Hua and his protégés are considered somewhat more conservative. When you get down to the specifics of modernization—for example, the amount of dependence on Western science and technology—real differences of opinion exist. Such differences are associated with factions and cleavages within the party and in the larger society. What we learned about conflict and consensus building during the Maoist period, then, is every bit as accurate and descriptive of the post-Mao years. Although the range of competing ideas may have been reduced somewhat with the defeat of the radical elements within the party, there are still sufficient differences and competing interests over the specific course of modernization and other issues to generate political debate, conflict, and competition.

In 1980, one leading observer described the new politics in China as the "pedestrian adjustment of interests."[50] Another called attention to

the "burgeoning leadership charged with determining priorities" and the "increasing diversification of governmental structures to facilitate the implementation of modernization programs."[51] Both suggest trends toward greater democracy, a government of laws, and constitutional guarantees. Although it may be premature to judge the significance and evaluate all the consequences of these trends, there does appear to be a higher level of incrementalism as well as intense leadership and policy conflict in contemporary Chinese politics.

We must remember when examining the policy process that to some extent what you find depends on where you look. The constellation of actors and structure of the process can vary significantly over time, between states, and across policy areas within the same state. Peter H. Solomon, Jr., has provided considerable insight into the area of criminal policy in the USSR.[52] By undertaking a number of case studies stretching from the late 1930s through the 1960s, Solomon uncovered a significant growth of the participation and influence of specialists in policy making during the post-Stalinist years. Solomon's work provides some valuable insights into the roles of scientists and specialists in the policy process, a phenomenon that apparently is growing in other Communist states as well.[53]

One of Solomon's case studies deals with the issues of alcoholism and hooliganism. (Hooliganism is defined in the Soviet criminal code as "intentional actions violating the public order in a coarse manner and expressing a disrespect for society."[54]) These two issues correspond with two distinct approaches for dealing with the problem of increasing crime in Soviet society. One approach attacks the root of the crime problem, alcoholism. The second addresses the conse-

[50]Ross Terrill, "China in the 1980s," *Foreign Affairs*, 58 (4) (1980), p. 921.

[51]Joyce K. Kallgren, "China in 1979: On Turning Thirty," *Asian Survey*, 20 (1) (1980), pp. 4–5.

[52]Peter H. Solomon, Jr., *Soviet Criminologists and Criminal Policy: Specialists in Policy-Making* (New York: Columbia University Press, 1978).

[53]The following discussion draws heavily on Solomon, *Ibid.* pp. 81–90.

[54]Solomon, *Ibid.*, p. 194.

quences of excessive drinking, hooliganism. The story begins in the winter of 1965 when the Soviet Supreme Court, at the urging of the head of its criminal division, proposed to the Presidium of the Supreme Soviet a compulsary treatment program for alcoholics. Solomon found that the Supreme Soviet reacted favorably to the Supreme Court's proposal but also decided that it was time for a comprehensive consideration and treatment of the issue. Accordingly, the Presidium established an investigative commission, including representatives of many government agencies and scholarly institutions, to study the issues.

During the summer and spring of 1965, the commission collected studies and other submissions from the relevant ministries and academic institutions. In the summer, a major public discussion of the issues took place. Among other things, *Izvestia* printed stories, commentaries, and letters, and there was a series of round-table discussions. In the fall, the Presidium of the Supreme Soviet asked for a draft law on the fight against alcoholism. The law was drafted by the Procuracy Institute, approved by the commission, and forwarded to the Presidium of the Supreme Soviet. Subsequently, the draft law received favorable discussion and press. It appeared that the leaders were going to adopt the alcoholism strategy as a response to the problem of Soviet crime.

Early in 1966, however, the alcoholism proposal was apparently in trouble; there was a mysterious silence about the legislation. Indeed, in April, *Izvestia* published an article by the Minister of Defense of the Social Order, V. S. Tikunov, calling for increased repression of hooliganism. This was a clear hint that someone was considering the antihooliganism strategy rather than the alcholism response as the way to deal with the problem of Soviet crime. Suddenly, in June, with little public discussion, the Presidium of the Supreme Soviet appointed another commission (actually, a subcommission of the Commission on Legislative Suggestions of the Supreme Soviet) to prepare a finished legal draft of antihooliganism legislation. On July 26, 1966, the Supreme Soviet passed a new law on hooliganism.

Solomon asks what happened. Why did minister Tikunov's proposal on hooliganism prevail over the carefully prepared and publicly acclaimed legislation on alcoholism? Apparently, three major reasons exist: (1) the high personal stature of Tikunov, (2) the political clout of his ministry, and (3) a conservative backlash against the post-Stalinist liberalization of law, which the alcoholism legislation was considered to be. In retrospect, it appears that the Soviet leadership was vacillating between two possible responses to the problem of crime. Just as it appeared that alcohol prevention would prevail, Minister Tikunov intervened with his attack on hooliganism and the political leadership went along. Like the Chinese cases described earlier, Solomon's study indicates that the policy-making process can be quite fluid, can involve diverse actors with conflicting interests, and can be influenced by those outside the immediate party leadership.

A study by Donald R. Kelley supports these notions and calls attention to the participation and influence of three important groups at various phases of environmental policy making in the USSR.[55] First, there are the industrial and commercial lobbies who have considerable power and influence at all phases because of their high bureaucratic standing and close relationship to the CPSU apparatus. Second there are the less powerful environmental protection agencies who do not have access to the upper echelons of the CPSU. The weakest group is the public conservation organizations and *ad hoc* coalitions of environmentalists. After examining the roles of these groups concerning the pollution of Lake Baikal (the world's deepest and one of its largest lakes), Kelley found that all these groups played important roles at some stage of the policy process. For example, the environmental lobbies were instrumental in bringing the problem to the attention of the political élites. The industrial and

[55]Donald R. Kelley, "Environmental Policy-Making in the USSR: The Role of Industrial and Environmental Interest Groups," *Soviet Studies, 28* (4) (1976), pp. 571–589.

commercial lobbies were powerful resisters to stricter environmental policies. Interestingly, Kelley's case study uncovered many dynamics that are characteristic of environmental policy making in Western, non-Communist systems.

These and other case studies call attention to the complex forces at work in Communist political systems. Having reviewed some of these studies, what can we conclude about policy making in Second World states? To what extent has there been rational-comprehensive planning or, on the other hand, signs of rampant incrementalism?

## COMPARATIVE OVERVIEW

Perhaps to an extent unparalleled in all other political systems, the Soviet leaders have attempted to articulate their plan for the future. In the visions they outlined at their party congresses and through other forums, three long-range goals have special significance: continued party leadership, continued industrialization and development of the defense sector, and a rise in the standard of living. After considering the options to the authoritarian form of CPSU rule, the party leaders decided that party-committed, centralized policy making is a necessary prerequisite to other Soviet goals. In attempting to build a strong socialist state, the leaders chose to follow an ideology of means, with its centralizing bias, rather than the classical Marxist ideology of ends, with its emphasis on democratic rule.

Given their dominant role in policy formation, the CPSU leaders were able to select the other two primary goals governing the Soviet future, that is, continued industrialization and heavy defense spending. These represent more of the same, a continuation of the policies of the past. As a result of careful study over the last decade, however, policy planners have decided that more will need to be done for the Soviet citizen. In the last two Five-Year plans, there has been, symbolically at least, greater emphasis placed on increasing the standard of living while continuing the process of rapid industrial and military development.

When comparing Soviet policy making with the muddling through so prevalent throughout the world, one must be impressed with their dedication to the synoptic mode of decision making. Although we can disagree with their goals and the values on which they are based, we can also understand the leaders' judgments concerning the most effective methods for pursuing their high-priority goals. Proceeding with single-minded dogmatism in following the specified plan, policy makers have disallowed either internal dissidents or Western critics to detract them from their objectives. Although a certain amount of muddling through is present, the leaders obvious distaste for the politics of incrementalism and their actions to discourage it provide evidence of how they intend to go about making policy in the future. Stressing technological forecasting and systems theory, the Soviets would like to follow a "scientific" process of decision making and management to fulfill the Soviet vision. Yet, Communist planners in the Soviet Union and other Marxist-Leninist systems often acknowledge that they have not achieved synoptic planning and policy making.

The goal-setting process in Maoist China showed a greater emphasis on ideology, both the means and ends varieties, than in either the USSR or Yugoslavia. The Chinese Communists approached the task of national development through a perspective very different from our own. Mao and his associates studied the Chinese dilemma over many decades and finally decided on a revolutionary, peasant-oriented strategy of development. Ignoring the Soviet model of heavy industrialization as well as the more consumption-oriented approach of the West, Mao attempted to forge a distinctively Chinese road to socialism.

In this process, Mao played the roles of arbiter and synthesizer. After evaluating alternative courses of policy, Mao attempted to take actions he judged were in the collective interest. It is here, Michel C. Oksenberg noted, that Mao encountered the incrementalist intrusions of the self-interested bureaucrats.[56] According to Ok-

[56]Oksenberg, *op. cit.*, pp. 323–360.

senberg, Mao strove to operate according to the synoptic mode, whereas specialized interests drove China toward incrementalism. This leads Oksenberg to observe: "The Chinese policy process combines elements of two separate models . . . the 'synoptic' and the 'incremental' policy processes."[57]

In the post-Mao period, there has been a further trend toward incrementalism. Lacking the personal stature of Mao, the new leaders (Hu Yaobang, Deng Xiaoping, Zhao Ziyang, and their colleagues) are involved in the pedestrian adjustment of interests with all of the conflict, compromise, and consensus building that implies. The overriding theme of politics in the post-Mao period has been the continuous and often intense conflict beneath the facade of leadership unity. However, if the present leaders can reach a higher level of agreement on the specifics of the modernization program and gain the widespread support of an increasing number of actors, the possibility for more rational-comprehensive policy making exists.

One of the features that has distinguished the Yugoslav form of decentralized socialism over the last few decades has been the relative absence of long-range planning. Although the result has been the most pluralistic and democratic system in the Communist world, it is also the site of considerable incrementalism. Alternative courses of action are examined, but rarely is the policy selected that is most likely to serve the national interest. Rather, decisions are made to reach agreement in the contentious and conflict-ridden state and seldom to select the optimal policy. Policy programs are rarely executed in correspondence with a long-term plan, either because a plan does not exist or, if it does, it tends to be so ill defined and vague that administrative discretion is inevitable. The leaders attempted to recentralize the fragmented system and reassert the leading role of the party in the 1970s, but the trend toward incrementalism will continue and probably increase in the post-Tito era.

The policy processes of the other Communist Party states reflect more of the same. The more developed states of Eastern Europe display blends of rational-comprehensive decision making and incrementalism, which are characteristic of other First and Second World systems. If there were a reduction in the level of authoritarian party leadership, the states would probably move in the direction of the rampant incrementalism found in Yugoslavia. The Southeast Asian states [Cambodia (Kampuchea), Laos, and Vietnam], although considerably more authoritarian than most Second World states, do not make policy in a synoptic and comprehensive way. Their error-prone processes suffer from incomplete and careless planning, dogmatic decision making, and corrupt administration. Whether they can develop an efficient system of decision making before their societies sink further into the depths of underdevelopment is a question currently impossible to answer.

In summary, which systems make policy according to the preferred synoptic mode and which tend toward the incremental? Of the three comparative cases, the Soviet Union is clearly the most synoptic. China has represented a blend of both decision-making modes, but in the post-Mao era, has moved considerably in the direction of incrementalism. Yugoslavia, the most open and democratic system, has been characterized by the most incrementalist policy process and is likely to move even further in that direction in the absence of Tito.

It is interesting to note that relative to First and Third World states, the Communist-run states of the Second World may be better equipped to make policy according to the synoptic mode. Centralized political leadership within an authoritarian system of government facilitates long-term planning, coordinated decision making, and effective implementation and execution. A small group of decision makers are relatively free to weigh competing goals, study alternative actions to attain them, and decide on those that appear to be in the collective interest. At the same time, excessive centralization can rule out valuable information and contribute to the costs of group think, that is, the state where individuals are reluctant to challenge prevailing opinions. Compared to non-Communist systems in the

[57]*Ibid*, p. 324.

contemporary world, then, the Second World states should be in a relatively good position to plan, make, and execute policy according to the synoptic model. If they now choose to open the process to the freer exchange of ideas and information without becoming bogged down in the excesses of incrementalism, they could enjoy the best of both the centralized and pluralist policy-making worlds.

Now that we have some understanding of the way political actors behave and how they formulate, make, and execute public policy, we can consider what power and policy mean to the people.

# Suggestions for Further Reading

Aspaturian, Vernon V., ed., *Process and Power in Soviet Foreign Policy* (Boston: Little, Brown, 1971).

Bruce, James, B., *The Politics of Soviet Policy Formation: Khrushchev's Innovative Policies in Education and Agriculture* (Denver, Colo.: University of Denver, 1976). (Monograph Series in World Affairs).

Brzezinski, Zbigniew K. and Samuel P. Huntington, *Political Power: USA/USSR* (New York: Viking, 1965).

Chang, Parris H., *Power and Policy in China*, 2nd and enlarged ed. (University Park, Pa.: The Pennsylvania State University Press, 1978).

Conquest, Robert, *Power and Policy in the USSR* (New York: Harper, 1967).

Friedgut, Theodore H., *Political Participation in the USSR* (Princeton, N. J.: Princeton University Press, 1979).

Hough, Jerry F., *The Soviet Prefects* (Cambridge: Harvard University Press, 1969).

Hough, Jerry F., and Merle Fainsod, *How the Soviet Union Is Governed* (Cambridge: Harvard University Press,1979).

Juviler, Peter H., and Henry W. Morton, eds., *Soviet Policy-Making: Studies of Communism in Transition* (New York: Praeger, 1967).

Lampton, David M., *The Politics of Medicine in China: The Policy Process*, 1949-77 (Boulder, Co: Westview Press, 1977).

Marczewski, Jan, *Crisis in Socialist Planning*, trans. Noel Lindsay (New York: Praeger, 1974).

Morton, Henry W. and Rudolf L. Tokes, eds., *Soviet Politics and Society in the 1970's* (New York: Free Press, 1974).

Ploss, Sidney I., ed., *The Soviet Political Process* (Waltham, Mass.: Ginn, 1971).

_____ *Conflict and Decision-Making in Soviet Russia* (Princeton, N.J.: Princeton University Press, 1965).

Rusinow, Dennison, *The Yugoslav Experiment, 1948-1974* (Berkeley, Calif.: University of California Press, 1977).

Schapiro, Leonard, ed., *Political Opposition in One-Party States* (London: Macmillan, 1972).

Skilling, H. Gordon, and Franklyn Griffiths, eds., *Interest Groups in Soviet Politics* (Princeton, N. J.: Princeton University Press, 1971).

Solomon, Peter H., Jr., *Soviet Criminologists and Criminal Policy: Specialists in Policy-Making* (New York: Columbia University Press, 1978).

Stewart, Philip D., *Political Power in the Soviet Union* (Columbus, Ohio: Bobbs-Merrill, 1968).

Townsend, James R., *Politics in China* (Boston: Little, Brown, 1974).

# CHAPTER SEVEN
## Political Performance in Communist Systems

One year after Karl Marx's death in 1883, Friedrich Engels, using Marx's research notes and materials, wrote:

> Democracy in government, brotherhood in society, equality in rights and privileges, and universal education, foreshadow the next higher plane of society to which experience, intelligence and knowledge are steadily tending. It will be a revival, in a higher form, of the liberty, equality and fraternity of the ancient gentes.[1]

But what progress, if any, have Communist states made toward this higher plane of society called Communism? To what extent have they furthered democracy, brotherhood, equality, and universal education? What do their records tell us about the cause of human dignity? Although most political science textbooks, including the bulk of this one, deal with Communist political systems from the top down, it seems reasonable to ask what the system has meant to the rank-and-file citizen. Therefore, this final chapter focuses on performance to attempt at least a partial assessment of what Communist states have accomplished for their people thus far.

When we evaluate Communist systems, we should be aware that we have far less statistical data than we need and would like. Ideally, we should have statistical indicators describing the amount and distribution of each of the values in all Communist societies. Although we do have useful, albeit incomplete, indicators for most of the values, data shortcomings will force us to leave many of the questions unanswered. Some judgments will be left for the reader to make and others will be made more satisfactorily sometime in the future.

We should also caution readers to be sensitive when evaluating and comparing systems at different levels of economic and political development. Whereas the Soviet Union is clearly an industrialized state and has had over 60 years to develop socialism, China is more backward economically and younger politically. Factors such as these influence what states have been able to accomplish and certainly affect their contemporary performance levels. Although we can not qualify all of our judgments, readers should be aware of, and sensitive to, these facts.

As outlined in our introduction, we evaluate the political performance of Communist Party

[1]Friedrich Engels, "The Origin of the Family, Private Property and the State," reprinted in Robert C. Tucker, ed., *The Marx-Engels Reader* (New York: W. W. Norton, 1972), p. 659.

states in two different respects. First, we attempt to *appraise* the leaders' and systems' general records in allocating the four values. Have their goals and actions resulted in democracy or dictatorship? In respect or suspicion? In welfare or poverty? In enlightenment or ignorance? Then, we try to *explain* why the values have been allocated in the ways that they have and why these allocations have resulted in particular outcomes.

## POWER AND POLICY: DEMOCRACY OR DICTATORSHIP?

Democratic power relationships are viewed as important and necessary features of both socialism and Communism by Marxist-Leninist leaders. Vladimir Ilyich Lenin once went so far as to say that socialism could not be successful and Communism would not be achieved unless "full democracy" was implemented. But what have Communist Party states done to promote the form of socialist democracy that they so fervently espouse? What *goals* were set, what *actions* taken, and what *outcomes* experienced in the Soviet, Chinese, and Yugoslav cases?

A number of *goals* have motivated Soviet policy makers concerning the distribution of power. Some goals involve the encouragement of more mass and expert involvement in the decision process, goals that seem to promote movement toward both increased democracy and incrementalism. However, the primary goal—the maintenance of Communist Party control over a centralized decision-making process—seems to be much less democratic in nature. In a sense, then, the goals are conflicting. The primary goal has been fairly constant throughout the entire Soviet experience and aims to ensure the Communist Party of the Soviet Union's (CPSU's) leading role in the political system. Even after 60 years of Soviet socialism, the CPSU is unwilling to allow organized opposition to challenge its privileged role in the political arena.

At the same time, party leadership appears to be increasingly cognizant of some of the major costs of excessively centralized rule. One impor-

tant cost involves the loss of decision-making expertise that exists among different specialized groups and individuals in the society; the second concerns the apathy, alienation, and lack of political support that can develop among a noninvolved citizenry. As a result of this awareness, the party leaders have advanced two other goals concerning the distribution of power within the Soviet system. The first involves the expansion of the influence of ministerial and scientific centers and organs in the policy process. Aware that the central party leadership is not the repository of all expertise and knowledge in the modern era, party leaders have attempted to increase the involvement of these specialized scientific complexes in the policy-making process by delegating increasing power to these lower level institutions. By drawing new actors into the policy process, they hope to make the decision-making process more efficient and scientific.

Another important goal involves increasing the level of mass political participation. Although prohibiting political activity in opposition to party policy, the leaders recognize the benefits of an active, participant society and, therefore, encourage the involvement of every citizen in the building of Communism. Encouraging citizen participation in a broad range of social and political tasks is viewed by the Soviet elite as a valuable strategy for increasing support and commitment to the system.[2]

The Soviet leaders have undertaken a variety of actions to achieve these basic goals. They have prohibited any challenges to the leading role of the CPSU; they have sought and encouraged the advice of specialized government and scientific complexes; and they have promoted mass involvement in the political system. For the most part, the party's actions have met with success. The CPSU has not been challenged. Its powerful, dominating role is as secure as ever. In addition, considerable evidence suggests that government and scientific experts have been given a wider role in policy making and have had

[2]See Theodore H. Friedgut, *Political Participation in the USSR* (Princeton, N. J.: Princeton University Press, 1979).

**TABLE 7.1** Political Participation in the Soviet Union, 1954–1976

| Group | 1954–1955 (in millions) | Percent Increase 1954–1963 | 1963–1964 (in millions) | Percent Increase 1963–1976 | 1975–1976 (in millions) |
|---|---|---|---|---|---|
| Adult population | 120.8 | 16% | 140.0 | 17% | 163.5 |
| Party members and candidates | 6.9 | 51 | 10.4 | 51 | 15.7 |
| Deputies to local soviets | 1.5 | 27 | 2.0 | 13 | 2.2 |
| Trade union members | 40.2 | 60 | 68.2 | 57 | 107.0 |
| KOMSOMOL members | 18.8 | 17 | 22.0 | 59 | 35.0 |
| Controllers | apparently 0 | – | 4.3 | 118 | 9.2 |
| Activists in independent organizations | ? | – | 20.0 | 55 | 31.0 |
| People's auxiliary police (druzhinniki) | 0 | – | 5.5 | 27 | 7.0 |

SOURCE: Adapted from Jerry F. Hough, "The Brezhnev Era: The Man and the System," *Problems of Communism*, 25 (2) (1976), p. 10.

a significant impact upon policy.[3] Finally, the data presented in Table 7.1 illustrate that the state has expanded the level of political participation among the Soviet population over the last two decades. After spending three years as chief of the Moscow bureau for the *Washington Post*, Robert G. Kaiser observed that, "there is probably no society in the western world with as large a percentage of politically active citizens."[4] Yet, although many citizens are politically active, they are expected to participate within bounds prescribed by the CPSU. At the same time, we should not underestimate the meaning and significance of this activity. Like citizens throughout the world, most Soviet people support their government and are quite satisfied to participate in the activities available to them.[5]

The Chinese Communists have also been guided by the primary goal of maintaining the party's leading and unopposed political role. This has not always been the case however. During the Great Proletarian Cultural Revolution (GPCR) in the late 1960s, Mao Zedong set aside

this goal and allowed the Chinese Communist Party (CCP) and many of its leading officials to be challenged by critical groups and individuals, such as the radical Red Guard. During this tumultuous period of Chinese development, Mao's goals of increased participation and equality came into conflict with the party's leading role. A number of specific actions, such as mass demonstrations, assaults on party officials who were taking the bourgeois line, and the dismissal of ranking party élites challenged the unchecked CCP leadership role. In addition, a series of actions leading to higher levels of power decentralization to the provincial and local levels, including the factories and workplaces, resulted in a major flattening of the traditional power hierarchy.[6]

China's record on the power value during the Maoist period and more recently suggests elements of both democracy and dictatorship. Although party dominance remains, we should not overlook evidence of genuine participation. A leading expert put it in the following way:

> Organizational, social, and political constraints notwithstanding, significant nonritual participation does take place in China, under conditions well

[3]See, for example, Peter H. Solomon, Jr., *Soviet Criminologists and Criminal Policy: Specialists in Policy-Making* (New York: Columbia University Press, 1978).

[5]For a critical and provocative review of the power and democracy question in the USSR, see Roy A. Medvedev, *On Socialist Democracy* (New York: Knopf, 1975). Although Medvedev is an uncompromising Russian dissident, he remains a Marxist and believes the only possibility for satisfactory change lies within the existing system.

[6]During the GPCR, increased worker participation in management was accompanied by increased management participation in production. Managers were expected to assume part of the manual workload just as workers shared in the management of the enterprise. See, for example, Mitch Meisner, "Report from China: The Shenyang Transformer Factory—A Profile," *China Quarterly*, (52) (1972), pp. 717–737.

During the Maoist period political study and participation did not take place solely in classrooms and government buildings. After a day's work in the rice fields, young farmers from the Popular Commune of Shinhua gathered for political discussions.

understood by all participants. Although there appears to be infrequent use of formal "democratic" instruments, and although mobilization instruments do not often serve as effective input channels, alternate forums allow for important, if limited, forms of genuine participation.[7]

Victor C. Falkenheim goes on to suggest that informal lobbying and personal networks constitute the basic techniques by which citizens pursue their goals.

The mass-line idea, one of Mao's important inventions, continues to influence citizen/party power relations in the post-Mao era. The mass line is a pattern of reciprocating communications between party members and the masses. Although some experts are far more critical, Phyllis M. Frakt contends that the mass-line idea does contain important features of the Western concept of representation.[8] Although this concept reserves primary decision-making power for the party and does not allow meaningful popular in-

fluence at the national level, it may provide the masses some minimal level of input and facilitate mass influence at lower levels of government. Because of the way the mass-line idea links masses with the party leadership, it aids the process of policy implementation at all administrative levels.[9]

Yugoslav leaders appear dedicated to their experiment in self-governing socialism, an innovative and serious effort to develop equalitarian democratic power relations in their society.[10] Basing the self-management system on the goal of decentralized, democratic administration of social, economic, and political affairs, the Yugoslavs have taken numerous actions to implement their experiment, at least at the local level of government. Beginning in the 1950s with workers' councils in factories and, then, expanding them over the years to include democratic forms of administration in other organizations, the Yu-

[7]Victor C. Falkenheim, "Political Participation in China," *Problems of Communism*, 27 (3) (1978), pp. 31–32.

[8]Phyllis M. Frakt, "Mao's Concept of Representation," *American Journal of Political Science*, 23 (4) (1979), pp. 684–704.

[9]See James R. Townsend, *Political Participation in Communist China* (Berkeley, Calif.: University of California Press, 1969).

[10]Branko Horvat *et al.* eds., *Self-Governing Socialism*, (2 vol) (White Plains, N. Y.: International Arts & Sciences Press, 1975).

In Yugoslavia's system of self-management, citizens are encouraged to participate in the affairs of all social, political, and economic organizations. Here is a meeting of a workers' council in a machinery factory near Belgrade.

goslav Constitution of 1974 *requires* self-management in all social, economic, and political bodies. Every school, factory, and organization is required by law to manage its own affairs. Yet, levels of participation and influence are certainly less than the ideology calls for.[11] Additionally, ultimate policy-making power at the federal level is still reserved for the central organs of the party. After partially withdrawing from power in the 1960s—only to witness a dangerous rise in interregional political conflict—the League of Communists of Yugoslavia (LCY) reasserted the party's leading role and now views itself as the primary political power. "We Communists are in power in this country" proclaimed a leading official of the LCY: "As the most responsible, progressive and most conscious part of the working class, the League of Communists holds the power in its hands."[12]

Yugoslav leaders have been guided by two primary and conflicting goals concerning the distribution of power in their political system. Although earnestly pursuing the democratic ideals of self-governing socialism, they have been

unwilling to relinquish the party's leading role, which would be required in a system of genuine democracy. Yugoslav leaders want *both* self-management *and* party rule and have undertaken actions to pursue these conflicting principles. Although it is conceivable that the post-Tito leadership will continue to pursue both goals simultaneously, many observers call attention to the inherent contradiction between the two and contend that genuine democracy can never be attained when one group of party élites is allowed a privileged and more powerful role in the political system.

The outcomes in Yugoslavia have reflected these competing and conflicting goals. Self-management has made considerable inroads into power relations within the society. Many of the authoritarian arrangements of the past have been replaced with more democratic processes involving large and varied groups of people. But the process of democratization is still incomplete and is likely to remain that way as long as the LCY maintains its dominating role.

In comparative terms, we can conclude that the national policy process in each of the Second World states is carefully orchestrated by the Communist party. No organized opposition is permitted; there is little open and free public debate of political issues outside of the party organs; and there are no truly competitive elections where national leaders can be selected by the broader populace. Yet, although it would be misleading to label the political process democratic, it would be equally unfair to call it dictatorial. Communist Party states are not dictatorships in the sense that a small group of people dictate every policy outcome. At the regional and local levels, political choices are often the consequence of a wide variety of debates and discussions. Even at the national level of government where the party leadership takes greatest interest and is most closely involved, the leaders probably aggregate and arbitrate competing interests just as much or even more than they dictate. As Mao observed, it is the leadership's role to synthesize. In this process of arbitration and synthesis within the party and government machinery, the participation of diverse groups

[11]See Gary K. Bertsch and Josip Obradović, "Participation and Influence in Yugoslav Self-Management," *Industrial Relations, 18* (3) (1979), pp. 322–329.

[12]*Ideological and Political Offensive of the League of Communists of Yugoslavia* (Belgrade: Secretariat for Information, 1972), p. 46.

and political actors within the bureaucracy is often extensive and intense. <u>Alternative policy actions are discussed and debated and, in some cases, the party leaders see their policy preferences defeated.</u>

The term, dictatorship, is inaccurate, but so too is the term democracy, if unqualified. It is true that there are some democratic features in the policy processes of Communist Party states, particularly at the local levels of government. Taking the lead in experimentation and innovation, the Yugoslav experience in self-management exhibits many forms of participatory democracy and is a genuine effort to devolve some policy-making powers and responsibilities to industrial organizations, to lower levels of government, and to the mass populace in general. Although other Communist Party states have at times criticized the Yugoslav's revisionism and continue to view it with reluctance and suspicion, different forms of self-administration and worker participation within their own centralized state and economic systems are creeping in. The Chinese were once the most critical of the Yugoslavs experimentation, but now they too are experimenting with self-management.[13] Even the Soviets note that "the objective need to consolidate and improve centralized management of production is coupled with a search for ways and means of improving the democratic forms of economic management."[14] Closely tied to the Soviet Union, the other East European states also appear to be carefully and discretely searching for ways to encourage democratic forms within their one-party systems of government.

Finally, at issue here is what exactly is meant by the term, democracy. With the typical conception of rule by the people in mind, the Communist leaders contend that their high levels of citizen participation qualify them as socialist democracies. True, most all these states are characterized by high levels of participation in sociopolitical affairs, but most participation is still restricted and constrained by general party policy and does not encourage the free thought and choice that genuine democracy presupposes.

Why do Communist Party states have political systems that are neither full dictatorships nor genuine democracies? What determinants have caused this? In the environmental realm there are a number of historical, cultural, and socioeconomic factors that have pointed the countries away from democracy. First, the historical traditions of most of the countries had a very weak democratic base. Most were states characterized by autocratic, imperial rule in which élitist, nonparticipant political cultures developed among the leaders and masses alike. The autocratic rule of tsarist Russia, imperial China, and Yugoslavia, for example, promoted a culture and set of traditions that did not prepare the countries for democratic rule. Robert C. Tucker and Alfred Meyer have pointed out that the Communist systems derive their values, including their political values, as much from their cultural past as from the tenets of Marxism.[15] Hence, it was relatively easy and not particularly surprising that the new Communist regimes carried on in the undemocratic tradition.

Once in power, the Communists typically found war-ravaged and economically bankrupt countries that had to undergo great and rapid change to catch up to the threatening Western world. Deciding that centralized rule was the most appropriate development strategy, the Communist leaders mobilized all resources behind the party-inspired reconstruction plans. Both historical forces and postrevolutionary realities steered the Communists away from democracy and toward a system of centralized, one-party rule.

Individual factors—that is, real live humans—have also affected this developmental experience. Lenin and Joseph Stalin were leaders willing to forego democratic ideals to achieve

[13]"Self-Management Enlivens Enterprises," *Beijing Review,* 23 (12) (1980), pp. 25-26.

[14]B. Topornin and E. Machulsky, *Socialism and Democracy* (Moscow: Progress Publishers, 1974), p. 102.

[15]See, for example, Robert C. Tucker, "Culture, Political Culture and Communist Society," *Political Science Quarterly, 88* (2) (1973), pp. 173-190; and Alfred Meyer, "Communist Revolutions and Cultural Change," *Studies in Comparative Communism, 5* (4) (1972), pp. 345-372.

developmental objectives. During the early, formative years of Communist development, their totalitarian rule left a deep indelible imprint on the nature of Communist politics. The new Communist states of Eastern Europe and Asia adopted an ideology and form of government that was developed under the Stalinist regime. Furthermore, the leaders who headed these new governments were, for the most part, trained in the USSR of Stalin. They, too, were unwilling and unprepared and, because of Soviet influence, were unable to adopt a system of more democratic rule.

Furthermore, the people of these new Communist Party states were not fully capable of accepting the responsibilities of democracy. Residing in economically deprived and less developed states and growing up under autocratic systems of government, the mass populace was ill equipped to undertake the type of participation a democratic government requires. Over the last few decades, however, great changes have taken place among these populations. Today, they are uniformly literate (with some exceptions among the Asian states) and have the education and training necessary to become able participants in the political process. Party leaders, however, continue to be reluctant about providing the mass populace with more meaningful and far-reaching political choices. True, they have encouraged higher levels of participation, but the participants' freedoms of choice and action continue to be restricted by the principles of centralized party rule. Some observers predict that, as new leaders with higher levels of education and possibly less ideological world outlooks assume the top party posts in these states, there may be greater willingness to make meaningful movements in the direction of genuine democracy.

Finally, there are also structural factors that help us explain power relations in the Communist Party states. First, the system of one-party rule is a powerful factor that impedes the development of more democratic political rule. Because it is extremely unlikely that the Communist parties will relinquish their leading roles, power concentrations within the one-party system will continue. Yet, it is possible that semi-institutionalized competition within the single parties will evolve as the less authoritarian Second World states seek more effective ways of weighing policy alternatives.

Examples of political structures that could contribute to a broader sharing of power and, as a result, more equalitarian power allocations in the political process, are legislative institutions, like the Supreme Soviet in the USSR; the National People's Congress (NPC) in China; and the national assemblies of the East European states. Conceivably, these legislative bodies could evolve over the years to assume more powerful policy-making roles like that of the Yugoslav National Assembly. Also, lower level representative bodies (local soviets) and work organizations could also evolve in the direction that Yugoslavia has taken. Although there is little evidence of impending change in most of the Communist world, recent events in both China and Poland may be noteworthy. At the behest of Deng Xiaoping and other party moderates, the Chinese experimented with a variety of democratic reforms in the late 1970s and early 1980s. In Poland, quite differently, the people demanded more power and democracy. Although these were dramatic and important developments, their impacts and real significance are still unknown.

## RESPECT: COMMUNITY OR CONFLICT?

Westerners often suspect a general lack of concern among Communist leaders for their people. We tend to think that leaders are primarily interested in production quotas, military competition with the West, or foreign affairs. Such thoughts are, at least in part, misconceptions; Communist leaders recognize the great importance of people in national development and have shown concern for developing the personal traits necessary to facilitate their overriding goals. But to what extent have they succeeded in promoting secure and supportive relationships among their people and between the political authorities and the broader populace?

Lenin realized that the class divisions and ethnocentrism that plagued and contributed to the collapse of tsarist Russia would have to be resolved if he and the Communists were to be successful in developing a unified Soviet commonwealth. Social and national cleavages were deeply cast in the old Russian state; radical goals and policies were required to overcome them. The initial goal that guided the postrevolutionary leaders was that of state survival, which required at least a minimal level of societal cohesion and political integration. Over the longer run, Stalin, Nikita S. Khrushchev and the contemporary leaders have sought to establish respect, trust, and a spirit of comradeliness among the diverse Soviet peoples. These traits, the leaders hoped, would contribute to the goal of a unified Soviet state.

To encourage the development of these traits, the leaders emphasized the common struggles of the Soviet peoples, the deep bonds that unite them, and the importance of cooperation and friendship among the different ethnic and national groups. The policies adopted by the Soviet leaders have reduced the rampant Great Russian chauvinism of the past and have done much to facilitate friendship and end discriminatory relations against and among the non-Russian peoples. Although evidence of ethnocentrism and some forms of discrimination still appear, one has to be impressed by the great changes that have taken place over the years.

Goals resulting in less impressive actions concern the respect the leaders and government provide their people and, conversely, the trust and respect the people accord their government. When examining the espoused goals of the leaders, it is quite clear that they have recognized the significance of encouraging the support and trust of the masses. As we will see shortly, however, the Soviet leaders show little inclination to trust and support their own citizens.

The most significant action taken by the Soviet authorities concerning the promotion of the interpersonal and group respect involves the reduction of gross inequalities in the income and status hierarchies of the society. After a thorough study of an extensive body of data, the British economist, Peter Wiles, asserts that, "the statistical record since Stalin is a very good one

indeed. I doubt if any other country can show a more rapid and sweeping progress towards equality."[16] Although more equal income and status systems have been established in the USSR, we should not assume that Soviet society is a homogeneous mass of tolerant and like-minded people. There is still considerable diversity of social characteristics and a good deal of the interpersonal and intergroup suspicion and particularism that these differences tend to generate. At the same time, however, the Soviet record in reducing those more negative features of social differentiation is an impressive one, particularly when compared with the experience of other multiethnic nations of the world.

One outcome that is not so impressive is the system's general disrespect for human rights and personal freedoms. Although requiring respectful and trustful relations among the Soviet people and toward the Communist Party and Soviet Government, the leadership has been reluctant to extend these relations to their people. Even though the majority of the population appear to support their system of government and their leaders, the leaders continue to treat the mass populace with a strong dose of disrespect, mistrust, and suspicion. Freedom of speech, travel to the West, and so on, are basic human rights the Soviet people richly deserve, but rights the leaders remain reluctant to accord them.[17]

The 1977 Constitution contained no basic legal changes concerning the rights and freedoms of the Soviet citizen. It elaborates in detail the citizen's economic guarantees that form the centerpiece of the Soviet definition of human rights: the right to housing (still in short supply), education, work, leisure, medical care, and maintenance in old age. Less prominent and heavily qualified are the political rights including freedom of speech, press, assembly, demonstration in the streets, religion, and privacy. The Con-

[16]Peter Wiles, *Distribution of Income: East and West* (Amsterdam: North Holland Publishing Company, 1974), p. 25.

[17]In 1974, the Soviet Union was one of 35 signatories to the so-called Helsinki Accord, an agreement that, among other things was to ensure the free exchange of ideas and people. To this day, the Soviet leaders have been unwilling to honor this aspect of the agreement.

stitution dilutes these rights by declaring that they are granted only "in conformity with the interests of the working people and for the purposes of strengthening the socialist system." An explicit limitation aimed at dissidents notes that, "The exercise of rights and freedoms shall be inseparable from the performance by citizens of their duties."

The very presence of dissident movements associated with nationality, religion, and other interests in the USSR indicates that some individuals and groups perceive a lack of respect and other important values. Considerable evidence, including the way the authorities treat these groups, suggests that their perceptions are well founded. Although the various groups are far too numerous to mention here, a few examples are illustrative. The Jewish movement gained momentum after the Middle East Six-Day War in 1967 and has actively pursued the right of Jewish citizens to emigrate. Although Jewish emigration has increased over the past decade, Soviet emigration policy is still exceedingly restrictive. Religious protest and dissent by Orthodox, Catholic, and Protestant groups have called attention to the lack of religious freedom and lack of a separation between church and state. Finally, a group of citizens intent on monitoring Soviet conformance with the Helsinki accords on human rights have called attention to the gap between Soviet pledges and practice. This group has been severely treated by Soviet authorities. Although Soviet accomplishments on the value of respect should not go unrecognized, neither should the shortcomings that are so courageously raised by these and other groups.

As a result of the deep social and regional cleavages that divided traditional China, the goal of societal integration also received a high priority in postrevolutionary China. To unify the society and polity, Mao and the Communist leaders set out to transform the Chinese populace by developing a new socialist person. Emphasizing the themes of respect, equality, and comradeship, the actions of the leadership in the area of political socialization played a major role in uniting the Chinese people.

Perhaps the most significant outcome of Mao's policy was the impressive level of equality now evident in the Chinese system. In a society with a long and strong tradition of élitist, hierarchical relations, Mao's actions altered in a period of less than 30 years a social characteristic that many observers thought impossible to change. Workers participate in management; managers participate in production. But along with this trend toward increased equality in production came reductions in economic efficiency and development. A major question confronting China in the post-Mao era is what balance it will strike on the equality/efficiency continuum.

The low level of corruption and criminal behavior in contemporary China, in comparison with the USSR, testifies to the great strides the Chinese have made in establishing relations based on respect and trust.[18] Once the sin city of the Orient, contemporary Shanghai is now a bustling metropolis of industrious workers and shows few of the violent features associated with present-day cities in both the East and West. Like the Soviets, however, the Chinese incurred significant costs in terms of human rights and civil liberties as the leaders attempted to mold a population based on equality and conformity.

A major question confronting the contemporary Chinese leaders involves the extent to which they will guarantee secure and supportive relationships among their people in the political realm. Articles in unauthorized magazines and posters on Democracy Wall in the late 1970s and 1980 demanded due process under the law and a less oppressive, more open political and intellectual atmosphere. Although a leading party slogan in 1979 was "Everyone is equal under the law," many dissidents question this and continue their demands for greater constitutionalism. The issue of human rights and the respect of political authorities for the rights of their citizens in China is one of the questions that will have to be answered in the future.

In trying to achieve a secure and supportive

[18]Crime and corruption are continuing problems in Soviet society. See Peter H. Juviler, *Revolutionary Law and Order: Politics and Social Change in the USSR* (New York: Free Press, 1976).

community from a diverse grouping of nationalities and ethnic groups inhabiting their traditionally explosive area of Europe, the Yugoslav policy makers pursued goals rather similar to the Soviet and Chinese leaders. While pursuing the common goals of integration and unity, however, they adopted policy actions that showed greater respect for human rights and local autonomy. Yugoslav socialization policies were less coercive, more respectful of the people, and more patient concerning the considerable time required to bring about the desired changes. Government actions in the area of federalism and self-management, which granted high levels of political and economic autonomy to the various national groups and local organizations, reflected a higher level of respect for the interests and concerns of the diverse Yugoslav peoples.

Although the Yugoslav policy makers may have followed higher ideals in allocating respect to all groups and regions on the basis of universalistic norms and principles, the regional groups, such as Serbs and Croats, have often been unwilling to accord respect and trust to one another. When faced with difficult political choices that critically affect the national republics and provinces—such as whether to take the profits of the richer republics to subsidize the development of the poorer—the leaders have tried to decide in the collective or Yugoslav interest. Some regional leaders, however, are still unwilling to place Yugoslav interests before the interests of their own national or ethnic group. As a result, political decisions often degenerate into nationalistic squabbles pitting one nationality against another.

The relatively higher level of ethnonationalism and interregional conflict exhibited in Yugoslavia is also due to the more open political environment. The Soviet and Chinese leaders do not encourage public debate of regional rivalries and are more likely to punish a citizen for disrespectful or uncomradely behavior, yet the more open atmosphere in Yugoslavia allows such behaviors to surface. Many observers consider this feature a positive characteristic of more open societies and believe that the more repressive Soviet approach forces conflicts below the surface. Once repressed issues reach the surface, however, they tend to be more critical and explosive than those that bubble up before they reach the critical stage.

The more open political environment in Yugoslavia has had both costs and benefits. It has given greater attention to individual choice and freedoms. Yet, many Yugoslav citizens live in a less secure and more uncertain environment than their Soviet or Chinese counterparts. Although full employment is almost guaranteed in these two systems, high unemployment in Yugoslavia has forced many Yugoslavs to find work abroad. Many of them note, however, that the freedom to travel abroad and seek employment far outweighs the benefits of guaranteed employment.

In an age of global conflict and turmoil, Communist Party states have attempted to portray pictures of domestic peace and comradely cooperation. Compared to the religious warfare in Northern Ireland, and the tribal and racial conflict in Africa, for example, most Communist societies have been remarkably peaceful and stable in the 1960s and 1970s, at least on the surface. To promote the ideals of community and comradeliness, Communist leaders have emphasized the common, collective interests of their people and attempted to minimize their differences. Although there have been some notable exceptions over the years, such as the Soviet treatment of Jews, their performances in allocating equal respect and deference to all national and ethnic groups comprising their states have been impressive. Research conducted by Western scholars has tended to show general equality and lowering levels of ethnocentrism and intergroup conflict between the diverse social and ethnic groupings comprising Communist societies.

At the same time, there have been periodic uprisings and demonstrations of national discontent. These signs of discord have resulted from what some individuals and groups perceive as unjust allocations of the values affecting the national groups. The revival of Croatian and Serbian nationalism and other displays of interethnic conflict in Yugoslavia during the late 1960s and early 1970s and the Ukrainian problem and underground national movements in the Soviet

Union are examples of such perceptions. These and other flaws in the performance of the governments continue to mar what is generally an impressive record of community building.

More serious than the intergroup conflict within the states, perhaps, is the international tension between and among them. The Soviet Union, through the Warsaw Treaty Organization (WTO) and the Council for Mutual Economic Assistance (CMEA or COMECON) seeks to play a major role in promoting secure and supportive relationships among the East European countries. Although WTO has brought a certain amount of military security, there is reason to doubt how supportive the military and economic relationships really are. Anti-Soviet demonstrations and national movements broke out in East Germany, Poland, and Hungary in the mid-1950s and continue to simmer. The Czechoslovak liberalization movement in 1968 was in part an anti-Soviet movement and was ended abruptly by Soviet and WTO military intervention. Athough the dominating Soviets profess equalitarian and comradely relations among socialist states, there continues to be a Soviet lack of respect for the full sovereignty and autonomy of the East European nations. The Soviet Union remains an imperialistic power in Eastern Europe. Many observers contend that this fact suggests continued tension and turmoil for the region.[19]

When searching for answers to the continuing problems of ethnocentrism and national tensions among the states, environmental factors, such as culture and geography, play major roles. Historical evidence of Great Russian chauvinism, Chinese warlordism, and nationalism within Europe and Asia indicates that intergroup distrust and hostilities are not of recent origin. In fact, when viewing the fratricidal past, the present levels of respect and cooperation are quite surprising.

The individual forces, such as the behavior of the political leadership and changes in the at-titudes and behaviors of the masses, have had a good deal to do with the improved relations of the contemporary period. Leaders, like Mao Zedong and Josip Broz Tito were guided by the ideals of socialist brotherhood and unity, and they undertook a wide variety of actions to transform their ideals into realities. Basing their developmental strategies on universalistic ethics and emphasizing the common interests of different groups within the larger collective, the attitudes and policies of the leaders have done much to promote more equalitarian and respectful relations within their states.

Although the attitudes of ethnocentrism are difficult to transform and although there are still pockets of particularism and distrust in many Communist Party states, the overall change in belief systems is quite remarkable. The majority of all citizens within these states enjoy secure and supportive relationships with others and reflect at least some of the attributes of a genuine political community. Personal attitudes concerning interstate (e.g., Sino-Soviet and Soviet-Czechoslovak) relations, however, are not nearly so amicable and will continue to be a source of tension in the future.

Some structural factors have contributed to the growth of community, whereas others have generated feelings of intergroup hostility. The high level of political and economic decentralization under the Yugoslav system of federalism has protected national rights and autonomy and given the South Slavic nationalities a greater feeling of security within the Yugoslav union. The lower level of decentralization within the Soviet system is a source of insecurity among many of the non-Russian nationalities and ethnic groups. For example, one of the structural factors prohibiting a higher level of integration among many of the Soviet nationalities is the fear of forced assimilation into the Russian language and culture combined with a corresponding loss of their own national or ethnic heritage. Because the Russian nationality dominates Soviet economic and political life and the Russian language has become the common language of the Soviet people, the continued threat of Russian domi-

[19]Ernst Kux, "Growing Tensions in Eastern Europe," *Problems of Communism, 29* (2) (1980), pp. 21–37.

nance tends to generate distrustful attitudes among many non-Russian peoples.

The fear of Soviet dominance among the smaller East European nations has a similar effect on the attitudes of their peoples. Hoping to find their own place in the international community of nations, the East European states desire inter-Communist relations based on the concepts of national sovereignty and noninterference. The Soviet's use of the socalled Brezhnev Doctrine of Limited Sovereignty, which was used to justify the intervention in Czechoslovakia in 1968 and Afghanistan in 1980, allows the East European leaders little freedom in the pursuit of their ideals.

In attempting to unite the socialist commonwealth, the Soviet leaders have relied on both the arts of persuasion and coercion. Their strategies have met with general success, but there are definite costs to the more coercive approaches. The Soviet's experience in Afghanistan is illustrative of this. Although you can force a nation to assume an "orthodox" role in the socialist commonwealth, tactics of this nature often breed rebellion and discontent. These are not characteristics corresponding to the ideals of brotherhood and unity and do not represent respect and equality either among humans within a common society or among nations of the Second World.

## WELL-BEING UNDER SOCIALISM: WELFARE OR POVERTY?

The value of well-being represents the area of social policy to which the Communist Party states attach great importance and in which they take great pride. Improvements in the standards of living have been quite impressive in some of the countries, yet the absence of expected progress relative to the West has been a source of discontent in others.

In his speech to the 24th CPSU Congress in 1971, General Secretary Leonid I. Brezhnev identified the country's principal goal as raising the standard of living. At the 25th Congress in 1976, he reemphasized the goal by pledging

a further increase in the Soviet people's well-being, the improvement of their living and working conditions and significant progress in public health, education, and culture.

Later in his speech, he pledged further increases in housing and in the production of consumer goods for the long-deprived and increasingly material-conscious Soviet citizen. At the 26th Congress in February 1981, Party leaders reemphasized that the CPSU is committed to an increase in the level of social and personal well-being.

When examining the actions and outcomes, we encounter a mixed picture. In many respects, it is apparent that much has been done in the area of social services. The Soviet Union is a welfare state that places a high premium on the well-being of its people. Housing is exceedingly cheap although often in short supply; medical care, health services, and education are free; employment is guaranteed. Yet, when comparing the average Soviet citizen with a West European counterpart, he or she is clearly deprived of many goods and services associated with a higher standard of living. First, housing is still scarce, forcing families sometimes to share apartments or to wait for years to be provided an apartment suited to their needs.[20] Second, consumer goods are still in critically short supply. Although the average family eats and drinks reasonably well, Soviet department stores show a short supply and limited variety of modern appliances, clothing, and other consumer goods. True, the Soviet leaders continue to speak of altering this situation, but the extent to which change is possible under the present conditions of exorbitant defense spending is a matter of some contention. Most observers believe that improvements in the consumer sector will be slow and flawed as long as the USSR continues its present level of defense procurement. The question for the Soviet policy makers is one of guns versus butter and no one should be more aware

[20]See, for example, Henry W. Morton, "Who Gets What, When and How? Housing in the Soviet Union," *Soviet Studies*, 32 (2) (1980), pp. 235–259.

Although Soviet cities are the scene of constantly growing apartment complexes, demand still far exceeds supply. Shown here is a "circle house" with enclosed shopping and entertainment facilities in the Gagarin district of Moscow.

of the importance and meaning of this choice that the Soviet people. The leaders seemed to recognize this reality and problem in the economic system at the 26th Party Congress when

Industrialization in the urban centers has drawn millions of workers from the countryside to the sprawling apartment complexes surrounding the older cities. Here, on the outskirts of Yugoslavia's federal capital, is a section of "new" Belgrade where many workers live.

they were uncharacteristically frank in calling attention to social and economic shortcomings.

Even though the Soviet consumer fares poorly in comparison to consumers in the West, the average citizen is relatively content. Comparing living standards with the past and recalling the hardships and great deprivation suffered during World War II, the more elderly consumer recognizes improvements and is generally optimistic about the future. The younger generation is less likely to recognize the improvements and is more skeptical about the sincerity of Brezhnev's promises. One accomplishment of the Soviet leaders has been to keep mass expectations in line with the state's capabilities to meet demands. One reason for the strict limitations on international travel is to prohibit comparisons with living standards in the West. As long as the Soviet population bases its expectations on what can be realistically attained in their country rather than on what they see others enjoying in the West, the leaders are given additional time to raise living conditions to compete with Western standards. If the disappointing record of the

1970s is an indication of the future and if predictions of a further downturn in Soviet economy in the 1980s come true, Brezhnev's promises will ring increasingly hollow.

Because of the lower level of economic development and the much greater number of people, the problem of providing all citizens with a reasonable level of well-being has been much more severe in China. Accordingly, the primary goal guiding the Chinese policy makers in the postrevolutionary period was the provision of a minimal level of economic security.

These provisions in a historically underdeveloped area require high rates of economic modernization and industrial production. Although the Great Leap Forward and the GPCR created major discontinuities in the overall economic progress, industrial production grew at an average of 13 percent during the years 1949–1974. However, economic performance in the more recent periods has been more problematical; although the average rate of growth during the period 1949–1960 was 22 percent, the rate for 1960–1974 was only 6 percent.[21] Recognizing the importance of the task before them, the post-Mao leadership has sought to put China on a more stable and moderate course that will raise the rates of economic modernization and industrial growth to higher levels. Economic growth is clearly the nation's highest priority.

Although the present-day contrasts between Chinese and Western standards of living and levels of consumption are even much greater than in the Soviet Union and Eastern Europe, the Chinese populace has witnessed considerable advancements over the last two decades. Even more isolated from the West than the Soviet populace and, therefore, largely unaware of Western affluence, the Chinese are relatively content with their present levels of social and personal well-being. Unlike the Soviet leadership, the Chinese leaders are making few promises about expanding markedly the availability of consumer goods. Although the Chinese leaders

have generally met Mao's "five guarantees" of "enough food, enough clothes, enough fuel, an honorable funeral, and a decent education,"[22] the likelihood of significantly higher levels of mass consumption in the next decade is highly improbable. One significant development in contemporary China, which will have consequences for the value of well-being, concerns the apparent movement from equality to equity. Although China's former social policy emphasized an equal distribution of well-being, there is now more emphasis on equity—reward on the basis of contribution. This means that inequalities are likely to increase within the rural sectors, among provinces, and between the countryside and the cities.[23]

Perhaps the most significant advancement in Communist China remains in the area of health care. Between 1952 and 1972, the number of doctors increased from approximately 39,000 to an estimated 457,000 (3200 persons per doctor).[24] Using paramedics (called barefoot doctors) to spread medical care to even the most remote village, the Chinese health system has made impressive strides and represents a model that many of the less developed states of the Third World would do well to emulate. In the words of one American expert:

> The accomplishments of the "sick man of Asia" [traditional China] in the face of severely limited resources and overwhelming problems are, after twenty-three years, unmatched in the history of the world. The accomplishments are evidence of what can be done when a goal is set and the population mobilized to do it.[25]

Although Yugoslavia is also a welfare state, in the sense that the public sector plays a primary

[21]U.S. Congress, Joint Economic Committee, *China: A Reassessment of the Economy*, (Washington, D. C.: US Government Printing Office, 1975), p. 149.

[22]Jan Myrdal and Gun Kessel, *China: The Revolution Continued* (New York: Pantheon, 1970), pp. 50–55.

[23]David M. Lampton, "New 'Revolution' in China's Social Policy," *Problems of Communism, 28* (5–6) (1979), pp. 16–33.

[24]E. Grey Dimond, "Medicine in the People's Republic of China: A Progress Report," *Journal of the American Medical Association, 222* (9) (1972), p. 1158.

[25]Victor W. Sidel, "Medicine and Public Health," in Michel C. Oksenberg, ed., *China's Developmental Experience* (New York: Academy of Political Science, 1973), p. 119.

Preventive medicine is doing much to heal the country once known as the "Sick Man of Asia." Here, young and old gather for daily exercises in front of an import-export firm in Peking.

role in providing social services for the people, the Yugoslav system has allowed greater individual opportunity with regard to increases in personal well-being. Evidence of this freedom of opportunity is everywhere; automobiles crowding the streets of even the most provincial cities; private homes being built in villages and towns

Factory workers' flats usually consist of one room inhabited by parents and child. Kitchens and bathrooms are generally shared with other families. Although this space seems inadequate by western standards, it is a tremendous improvement over the pre-revolutionary period.

and summer homes in the mountains and along the Adriatic. The policy makers have taken specific actions to make this possible. For example, the level of allowed income inequality is considerably greater than in other East European states. In addition, laws allow Yugoslav workers the opportunity to travel to, and work in, the capitalist countries of Western Europe. After a period of a few years, these workers are in a position to return home with a new auto and the cash required to build a comfortable private home on the city's outskirts.

The policy makers have also undertaken other actions affecting the allocation of well-being among the Yugoslav populace. One crucial decision involved the adoption of a competitive, market-oriented economy that promotes competition among firms and that also features some of the less desirable concommitants of Western economies, including embarrassing income inequalities, spiraling inflation, unemployment, and worker strikes.[26] Although Chinese and Soviet society exhibit a drab uniformity in con-

[26]Although Soviet and Chinese leaders pride themselves on full employment in their countries, unemployment in Yugoslavia fluctuated around 10 percent in the 1970s. During this same time, Yugoslav consumer prices climbed at rates of 15 to 30 percent per annum.

sumer goods, housing, and social services, Yugoslavia is a picture of contrasts. Poverty and affluence exist side by side. A peasant's deteriorating cottage is bordered by a beautiful new house built with Deutschmarks sent home by an enterprising Yugoslav worker abroad. Mercedes share crowded streets with horse-drawn wagons and archaic trolleys. In a land of traditional contrasts, Titoist social and economic policies added a mark of their own.

Well-being is one of the values that is more amenable to quantitative evaluation and comparison. A useful way of examining and comparing government actions, for example, is to see where they spend their money. Table 7.2 indicates how much money each government spends annually per person for the military, education, and health. Examining military spending first, the USSR spends far more per person (and overall) than any other Communist Party country. Although it spends somewhat less per person than the United States, it spends far

more as a percentage of the gross national product (GNP). The two superpowers are clearly the big spenders in the defense sector. China has comparatively little to expend and does invest less per capita in the military sector than any of the East European states.

Turning to education and health expenditures, the USSR and East Germany are the clear leaders, along with Czechoslovakia in the health sector, although all spend substantially less than the United States. The expenditures of the Laotians, Vietnamese, and North Koreans are extremely low and, as we will see later, explain the low quality of health care and schooling found in these countries. When combining health and education expenditures and comparing them with military expenditures, some interesting findings appear. Whereas the United States, for example, spends $465 per person a year on defense and $861 on health and education, the Soviets spend $348 and $239 respectively. U.S. defense spending per capita may surpass the Soviet's, yet the United States does invest comparatively more in other social sectors.

Actions in terms of government expenditures are of course related to policy outcomes. Table 7.3 provides a number of indicators of such outcomes, describing levels of health care, nutrition, and the physical quality of life in Communist Party states. First, when examining the number of people per physician in the first column, we find that the Soviet Union has the best ratio in the world (346 physicians for every 100,000 people). With the exception of the Albanians, the European Communist Party states also do very well on this indicator. The Asians, particularly the Cambodians (Kampucheans) and Laotians, do very poorly. The second column, describing the number of hospital beds reflects the same trends. Viewing the next two columns, East Germany has the best record on the infant-mortality and life-expectancy indicators among Communist Party states. The Soviets, East Europeans, and Cubans do quite well on these indicators, whereas the records of the Asians, with the exceptions of the Chinese and North Koreans, are extremely poor. Clearly, these indicators of health care corre-

**TABLE 7.2** Public Expenditures per Capita: Military, Education, Health

| Country | Military (U.S. $) | Education (U.S. $) | Health (U.S. $) |
|---|---|---|---|
| Albania | 55 | 33 | 10 |
| Bulgaria | 68 | 110 | 57 |
| Cambodia | na[a] | na[a] | na[a] |
| China | 22 | 15 | 6 |
| Cuba | 45 | 76 | 32 |
| Czechoslovakia | 126 | 128 | 135 |
| East Germany | 190 | 204 | 112 |
| Hungary | 69 | 119 | 74 |
| Laos | 9 | 2 | 1 |
| Mongolia | 78 | 70 | 12 |
| North Korea | 59 | 19 | 2 |
| Poland | 108 | 111 | 117 |
| Romania | 45 | 70 | 48 |
| Soviet Union | 348 | 169 | 70 |
| Vietnam | 16 | 3 | 1 |
| Yugoslavia | 96 | 110 | 81 |
| USA | 465 | 557 | 304 |

[a]Not available.

SOURCE: Adapted from Ruth Leger Sivard, *World Military and Social Expenditures, 1980* (Leesburg, Va.: World Priorities, 1980), pp. 21–29.

**TABLE 7.3**   Health, Nutrition, and Physical Quality of Life (PQLI)[a] Indicators

| Country | Physicians per 100,000 Population | Hospital Beds per 10,000 Population | Infant Mortality[b] Rate per 1000 | Life Expectancy | Calorie Supply[c] per Capita | Protein Supply[d] per Capita | Percent of Population with Safe Water | PQLI[e] |
|---|---|---|---|---|---|---|---|---|
| Albania | 104 | 649 | 87 | 70 | 2,624 | 76 | na[f] | 75 |
| Bulgaria | 226 | 872 | 24 | 72 | 3,594 | 104 | na[f] | 91 |
| Cambodia[f] | 7 | 106 | 150 | 46 | 1,857 | 45 | 45 | 40 |
| China | 33 | 185 | 65 | 64 | 2,439 | 63 | na[f] | 69 |
| Cuba | 94 | 413 | 23 | 72 | 2,636 | 69 | 56 | 84 |
| Czechoslovakia | 254 | 1,229 | 20 | 71 | 3,450 | 98 | 78 | 93 |
| East Germany | 190 | 1,065 | 13 | 73 | 3,610 | 99 | 82 | 93 |
| Hungary | 230 | 690 | 26 | 70 | 3,494 | 91 | 44 | 91 |
| Laos | 6 | 98 | 175 | 40 | 1,979 | 54 | 41 | 31 |
| Mongolia | 209 | 1,067 | 70 | 63 | 2,510 | 94 | na[f] | na[f] |
| North Korea | 40 | 59 | 70 | 63 | 2,730 | 80 | 47 | na[f] |
| Poland | 166 | 767 | 24 | 71 | 3,647 | 110 | 47 | 91 |
| Romania | 135 | 919 | 31 | 70 | 3,368 | 101 | na[f] | 90 |
| Soviet Union | 346 | 1,213 | 28 | 70 | 3,443 | 103 | na[f] | 91 |
| Vietnam | 18 | 343 | 115 | 62 | 2,032 | 51 | 14 | 54 |
| Yugoslavia | 131 | 603 | 35 | 69 | 3,469 | 100 | na[f] | 84 |
| USA | 176 | 630 | 14 | 73 | 3,537 | 106 | 98 | 94 |

[a]PQLI = physical quality of life index.

[b]Deaths under one year per 1000 live births.

[c]Per capita supply of food, including fish, in calories and grams of protein per day.

[d]Protein supply figures from Ruth Leger Sivard, *World Military and Social Expenditures, 1979.*

[e]The PQLI is based on three indicators: infant mortality, life expectancy, and basic literacy.

[f]Not available.

SOURCE: Adapted from Ruth Leger Sivard, *World Military and Social Expenditures, 1980* (Leesburg, Va.: World Priorities, 1980), pp. 27–29; and Morris David Morris, *Measuring the Conditions of the World's Poor* (New York: Pergamon, 1979), pp. 128–135.

spond with the health expenditures described in Table 7.2.

When examining the three indicators of nutrition in Table 7.3, the Soviets and Europeans do quite well once again, whereas the Asians lag far behind. Cambodia (Kampuchea) and Laos are among the few states in the world with calorie-supply-per-capita levels below 2000. Cambodia (Kampuchea) suffered tragic losses in the 1970s through starvation and war. In 1975, the country had a population of approximately 8 million. By 1980 as many as 4 million had died. No nation on earth suffered more in the past decade than this once tranquil and fertile land.

The final column in Table 7.3 contains data purporting to indicate the physical quality of life. Claimed to be an unbiased nonideological and nonethnocentric index "reflecting important elements that should be included in a humane existence," the indicator is based on infant mortality, life expectancy, and basic literacy data.[27] Rankings of countries worldwide range from a high of 97 for Sweden to lows of 12 for Guinea-Bissau and 18 for Afghanistan.

According to this indicator, Communist Party states reflect some important differences in the physical quality of life. The Asian states rank very low and appear to have physical quality of life standards similar to many states in the Third World. The USSR and East European states rank considerably higher and compare well with the industrial states of the First World.

Although the measure is useful in assessing the physical quality of life around the globe, it is not very helpful in discriminating among the more industrial countries of East and West and between the United States and the USSR. We are all aware of some important differences in the quality of life that the measure simply does not reflect.

Although all Communist leaders are committed to improving the quality of life of their people, the way in which they go about it and the priority given this goal in relation to others, such

as national defense, is a matter of differing interpretations. There are some leaders and many citizens in these states who are in favor of reducing the level of defense spending and perhaps, the level of industrial investment so that spending in the consumer and social services sectors can be expanded. Although these points of view have been registered by articulate and respected spokespersons, the concern with national defense and industrial development apparently remains paramount in the minds of the majority of Soviet policy makers. Conceivably, arms agreements between the East and West and expanding trust and cooperation could lead to reduced defense spending and a corresponding increase in investments related to the well-being of the populace.

Communist policy makers are also confronted by other difficult questions of socialist economics. For example, how do you establish a welfare state, ending exploitation and reducing income and status hierarchies, while simultaneously stimulating higher levels of production and economic output. The performance record of most socialist states is mixed in these respects and all have had particular difficulties with the second objective. The record is quite impressive in the welfare area—that is, most all citizens eat well, are adequately clothed and housed, and enjoy reasonable health care—yet the productive output in the socialist states has suffered. Soviet agricultural production in the 1970s, for example, was not that much greater than it was at the turn of the century. The Chinese economy continues to fall farther behind the growth and development of the economies of the Western world. Unless major advances are made in the area of production, Communist leaders are going to find it increasingly difficult to attain the advanced level of social well-being they so earnestly desire.

The basic question confronting the policy makers is how to stimulate the productive output of the individual worker and the firm without relying on the capitalist system of monetary rewards—which, the Communists argue, results in exploitation and injustice. Can Communist leaders find reward structures and general economic mechanisms that will ensure or surpass

---

[27]For a discussion of the index, see Morris David Morris, *Measuring the Conditions of the World's Poor* (New York: Pergamon, 1979), pp. 20–40. Of course, there are many other factors that are important to and effect the "quality of life."

The bustle of traffic in downtown Budapest suggests the impact of consumerism on Hungarian society.

the productive output of the Western systems without accepting some of their less desirable features? Obviously, the present system of restricted monetary rewards combined with symbolic recognition, such as medals and other forms of commemoration, for outstanding work are not doing the job. Not only does the output lag considerably behind the West, but so does the quality of the goods produced. Brezhnev's emphasis on quality and efficiency at the 25th CPSU Congress attests to the leadership's concern with the problem as well as their sensitivity to its impact on the general level of social and individual welfare.

Obviously, Communist success in the welfare area is quite satisfactory when compared to the experience of much of the Third World. Nowhere in the Second World (with the exception of some of the new Communist Party states of Southeast Asia) does one encounter the utter poverty, degradation, and mass injustice found in many of the less developed states of Africa, Asia, and Latin America. Of course, the USSR and East European states began at much higher levels of economic development than the Third World states. Yet most Communist Party states

fare well in comparisons with some of the Western countries that began the post World War II era on similar levels of development. In a systematic empirical comparison of postwar economic growth and its welfare effects in Bulgaria and Greece, for example, one scholar found that Communist Bulgaria did considerably better than its non-Communist Balkan neighbor.[28] At the same time, it is apparent, in view of the great human and physical resources within the Second World states, that they are still performing below their potential.

In attempting to account for the lingering difficulties of the Second World states in the welfare area, the environmental, individual, and structural explanatory factors are useful. One important environmental factor is the general level of economic underdevelopment found in most states before the advent of Communism. Only in Czechoslovakia and East Germany did the Communists encounter economic settings that resembled Marx's expectations of economic

[28]Hans Apel, *An Inter-system Comparison of Postwar Economic Growth and Its Welfare Effects: Bulgaria and Greece.* Unpublished manuscript, University of Michigan, 1975.

abundance. In every other state, with the partial exceptions of some of the other East European states, the picture was one of primitive, agrarian economies, many of which had barely entered the industrial age. Even in the more developed states, the economies were devastated by World War II and had to be rebuilt by the postwar leaders with little outside assistance. Although the Marshall Plan greatly aided the reconstruction of Western Europe, the Communist Party states chose to manage on their own.[29] The plight of some of the East European states was worsened as the Soviet Union undertook the wholesale movement of factories and productive equipment to the USSR in payment for wartime damages. Therefore, the postwar starting points for the Second World states were considerably below much of the First World. Yet, when pairing countries with similar economic starting points—for example, East Germany and Czechoslovakia with West Germany and Austria or the USSR and other East European states with Japan, Italy, and the Iberian states—it appears that the Western states have outperformed the East according to most indicators in the economic and welfare sectors.

Individual determinants have also affected the level of economic development and the state's capacities for providing the value of well-being. The leaders of all the countries were initially committed to increasing the economic output of their states through a strategy of forced savings and industrialization. Although Yugoslavia and China departed somewhat from this approach in the 1950s and 1960s, the general strategy was one in which the industrial sector was emphasized at the expense of the welfare and consumer realms. This developmental strategy did boost industrial potential, but the advancements came at great human costs. The construction of heavy industries often meant shortages in medical care or in consumer goods. These countries did not have the capacities to meet both industrial and welfare needs and decided to emphasize the former. The

leaders were willing to incur these costs over the short run to develop the industrial capacity to protect their states, and then, hopefully, they would begin to meet human needs over the long run. The workers did not always support the regime's economic policies and vented their misgivings through absenteeism, low output, and inefficiency. Now that the USSR and East European countries have reached a relatively high level of industrial capacity, and may expand the consumer realm, the potential for higher levels of output and efficiency may be met. This human element affecting the performance of the economy is of considerable importance in the coming decades.

The economic system itself must be considered as a structural determinant affecting levels of well-being within the Communist-run states. The command type, socialist system adopted in most of the states allows the leaders considerable control in allocating such resources as income, housing, and health care among the population. The centralized socialist economy has also served, in some respects, to impede higher levels of well-being. Tending to thwart some of the initiative and competition found under private ownership, the economic systems have not permitted the societies to produce to their full capacities. If higher and more efficient levels of production could be achieved, the system would be in a position to enlarge allocations to the welfare sector, and, as a result, improve the level of well-being among all its citizens. The unfulfilled promises and shortcomings of Communism became poignantly apparent in Poland in the 1970s and early 1980s. The Polish people grew increasingly dissatisfied with their economic situation.

At least partially aware of the shortcomings of the command-type system, policy makers and their advisers in Poland and elsewhere are searching for new economic forms that may help rectify present problems and inadequacies by borrowing some of the more desirable features of other systems. Yugoslavia has been in the forefront in economic experimentation, as evidenced by their adoption of a system of self-managed, market socialism. Although it is too early to

[29]The Soviet leaders denounced the Marshall Plan as a device to control Europe, refused to participate in the program, and denied participation to the East European states.

evaluate all of its effects, this more decentralized, competitive system appears to alleviate some of the costs of the Soviet model by stimulating higher levels of output and by making production more responsive to the laws of supply and demand. Some of the other East European states have carefully followed the Yugoslav experience and have adopted some economic innovations on a limited scale. As a result of the Soviet's intervention in Czechoslovakia in 1968, which was largely intended to stop the Czechoslovaks' movement toward decentralized, market socialism, East European leaders are proceeding with caution and keeping a close eye on their counterparts in Moscow.

## ENLIGHTENMENT: ERUDITION OR IGNORANCE?

Policy choices concerning the nature and distribution of enlightenment—what one should know about oneself, one's work, and one's world—have been the focus of considerable controversy and debate in political systems throughout the world. Should the goal be the development of a broadly trained citizen in the humanistic, liberal tradition or the development of a more narrow, ideologically trained citizen? Should enlightenment be spread among the entire populace or concentrated in a smaller sector? These and other choices also confront policy makers in Communist Party states as they attempt to mold populations likely to facilitate their overriding objective, the construction of Communism.

Soviet policy makers have been guided by the goal of what they call the molding of a new man. Brezhnev defined this individual in his speech to the 24th CPSU Congress as someone with "a high level of culture, education, social consciousness, and inner maturity." The proper policies for ensuring the development of such a citizen have been the subject of numerous policy debates. In April 1958, for example, First Secretary Khrushchev criticized the Soviet educational system and demanded fundamental and far-reaching changes. In September of that year, Khrushchev published a memorandum on school

reorganization that proposed, among other things, that continuous academic education be abolished and that all students be required to combine work with study. Finally, in December 1958, a set of educational reforms was adopted and—surprisingly—departed from Khrushchev's earlier proposals "not only in detail but in basic principles."[30] According to scholars who have studied the policy debate, Khrushchev was overruled as a result of the influence of a variety of individuals and groups who disagreed with his proposals. This example illustrates the high level of concern with education policy and also exhibits the importance of political debate and the influence that specialized interests can have on the making of policy.

Contemporary Soviet education attempts to provide both ideological and more traditional academic and cultural training. The Soviet people are uniformly literate (99 percent), have a solid basic education, and are challenging the West in many areas of scientific inquiry. However, with the strong emphasis on strict and narrow ideological training, the vast majority of the people are woefully lacking in accurate information and perspective about life and politics in other parts of the world.

The total revolution envisioned by Mao and his colleagues abolishing the old and establishing the new, required the widespread allocation of what might be called a Maoist conception of enlightenment among the Chinese people. Mao thought all Chinese citizens should be selfless, imbued with a collective spirit, and willing to endure personal hardships in service to the public good. They should possess a keen class consciousness and be both a Red and expert in their workplace. Mao and the CCP leaders undertook a variety of actions to develop these new minds, new outlooks, and new behaviors. They adopted a strategy of political socialization that utilized indoctrination in the schools, mass media, and the arts. The printed and spoken word was to serve the revolution, and the goal of a politically

[30]Joel J. Schwartz and William R. Keech, "Group Influence and the Policy Process in the Soviet Union," *The American Political Science Review, 62* (3) (1968), pp. 840–851.

conscious populace was a necessary ingredient leading to victory.

The outcomes of the Maoist period were mixed. Some groups, such as the Red Guards, exhibited a sense of revolutionary dedication and exuberance that bordered on fanatical devotion. Yet, one wonders about the stability and fragility of this revolutionary devotion. Was it deeply embedded into the psychological and behavioral makeup of these young citizens? Or, was it a passing fancy that will weaken with middle age or transfer to another ideology or other political symbols? Among some sectors of the Chinese populace, old habits, patterns, and attitudes tend to persist. Mao's concept of enlightenment was not equally distributed among the populace, not so much because the leaders did not try but rather because many resisted the new thoughts, new hopes, and new policies.

Enlightenment in contemporary China has come to mean something quite different than it did during the Maoist period. Today, there is more emphasis on a Western-style education. Training in the sciences, humanities, and other fields has taken on an equal, or even more important, position alongside politics and ideology. With the new conception of enlightenment comes new challenges for the Chinese. Because advanced education can not be guaranteed to all, some sectors of the population will no doubt become more highly educated than others. Who makes these choices and on the basis of what criteria? Although some policy actions are still to be taken, the present emphasis seems to be on merit and achievement, a criteria that may promote development and modernization while contributing to increasing inequalities in the Chinese system. One thing is clear however. If the present policies continue, the enlightened Chinese citizen at the end of the next decade will look far different than his counterpart did at the end of the last decade.

Over the last few decades, the Yugoslav leaders have attempted to promote an educational system that would, as stated in their education laws:

Contribute to the building up of an all-around personality, of an independent and a critical spirit possessing intellectual, high character, and moral and working qualities of the citizen of a socialist community.[31]

To an extent greater than any other Communist Party state, the Yugoslavs have encouraged the development of an all-around personality, an endeavor that has required a much more open, less ideological educational environment. The style and content of instruction is very similar to what we know in the West.

In attempting to develop the system of self-managing socialism, the Yugoslav leaders have been guided by the overriding goal of developing a citizen trained for self-management. The 1970 resolution on education states the goal explicitly in noting that young people must "become fit for direct decision-making on the conditions and results of their own work," and that they should have "a fully developed personality, educated and capable to perform its functions in the complex conditions of life and work."[32]

To implement these goals, the leaders have followed a strategy of political socialization and instituted an educational system intended to prepare the society for self-management.[33] Like other social organizations, schools are to be self-managed and provide students with first-hand experience in participatory democracy. Although the socialization experience is decidedly focused on youth, actions have been taken to prepare older sectors of the population for the responsibilities of self-management. Workers' universities and in-service training are provided to better equip them to help administer the affairs of their firm or other place of work.

Although there is much we do not know about the outcomes of the Yugoslav approach (as

[31]Vera Tomich, *Education in Yugoslavia and the New Reform* (Washington, D. C.: U. S. Government Printing Office, 1963), p. 109.

[32]*Resolution on the Development of Education on Self-Management Basis* (Belgrade: 1971), p. 9.

[33]For an excellent account of the Yugoslav strategy and an appraisal of its success, see Susan Lampland Woodward, "Socialization for Self-Management in Yugoslav Schools," in Gary K. Bertsch and Thomas W. Ganschow, eds. *Comparative Communism: The Soviet, Chinese, and Yugoslav Models* (San Francisco, Calif.: W. H. Freeman, 1976), pp. 307–319.

it's true with the Soviet and Chinese approaches), most observers agree that the Yugoslav populace is generally committed to the principles of self-management even though they are sometimes reluctant to assume the responsibilities participation requires. By most Western standards of enlightenment, the Yugoslavs are the most enlightened of all the Second World societies. The less coercive actions of a more open educational system, a freer exchange of ideas and opinions, and a high rate of international travel have resulted in a surprisingly well-rounded, sophisticated populace in this historically backward area of the Balkans.

Comparatively speaking, what kind of citizen will contribute most to the supreme goal of all Second World leaders, the construction of Communism. Might it be the ideological zealot of the Maoist period? Or, is the more well-rounded, less dogmatic Yugoslav citizen more likely to possess the blend of political consciousness, knowledge, and patriotism conducive to developmental goals? Or, will it be the "new Soviet man" who seems to be somewhere in between the Chinese and Yugoslav extremes? Ultimately, the leaders of the Second World states must determine who is really enlightened and, furthermore, whether their conceptions of enlightenment will really contribute to a higher level of human dignity and societal well-being.

We should not conclude without recognizing some of the major advancements recorded in this value area. At the turn of the century, education was a value reserved for the privileged few in Russia, China, and many other Second World societies. Today, it is a right guaranteed to all citizens. Educational opportunity in Communist states is probably as open and as nearly equal as anywhere else in the world today. Second, we must recognize the great impact education has had on development in these states. The rapid transformation of backward, traditional countries into powerful states can in large part be attributed to advancements in the educational sector.

The data presented in Table 7.4 gives us a clearer idea where Communist countries stand. Cuba and East Germany have as good a teacher to population ratio as does the United States. The USSR's is only slightly poorer. Although the East European states compare favorably with the Western world, the Asians lag considerably behind. Cambodia (Kampuchea) and Laos rank extremely low on all of the indicators of educational performance. In Laos, for example, around 65 percent of their school-age children are *not* in school, few of their women are in universities, and barely over one quarter of their people are literate. According to most all conceptions of enlightenment, the Laotians are in dire straits.

The last four columns in Table 7.4 summarize communication indicators and also call attention to the differences between the European and Asian Communist states.[34] China ranks low on all indicators and has the lowest number of television sets per capita in all of the Second World. The Soviet Union and East European states rank extremely high, even higher than the United States, on newspaper circulation. The governments have invested heavily in getting the party's word before their publics.

Although education and communication represent a relatively free and open search for truth and understanding in most Western countries of the world, they remain strictly disciplined activities in Communist-run states. Television, the press, and educational curriculums are all carefully controlled by party authorities. These same authorities take part in and condone systematic distortions of history. Whether these policies are conducive to long-term developmental goals is a problematic question that depends very much on one's personal attitudes concerning freedom and control, creativity, and conformity. For those adhering to Western value systems, there is considerable reason to be critical in this area of policy and performance.

In conclusion, we can ask: What environmental factors, such as ideology and culture, influence what Communist citizens know about the world and the process by which they come to know it? Most of these populations inherited

---

[34]Interestingly, Albania displays the communication characteristics of an Asian state.

**TABLE 7.4**  Education and Communication Indicators

| Country | Teachers per 1000 School-age Population | Percent of School-age Population in School | Percent of Girls in Total High School Enroll- ment | Literacy[a] | Phones per 1000 | Radio Sets per 1000 | TV Sets per 1000 | News- papers[b] |
|---|---|---|---|---|---|---|---|---|
| Albania | 29 | 64 | 47 | 75 | 5 | 71 | 1.8 | 46 |
| Bulgaria | 30 | 57 | 53 | 95 | 107 | 262 | 168 | 232 |
| Cambodia | na[c] | na[c] | 31 | 48 | 1 | 14 | 3.3 | 10 |
| China | 18 | 65 | 40 | 70 | 28 | 16 | 0.6 | 8 |
| Cuba | 43 | 75 | 49 | 94 | 33 | 224 | 64 | 95 |
| Czechoslovakia | 30 | 60 | 62 | 99 | 190 | 265 | 245 | 300 |
| East Germany | 43 | 66 | 53 | 99 | 171 | 356 | 307 | 472 |
| Hungary | 36 | 55 | 47 | 98 | 103 | 243 | 223 | 233 |
| Laos | 14 | 35 | 34 | 28 | 2 | 38 | na[c] | 3 |
| Mongolia | 21 | 56 | 52 | 95 | 25 | 79 | 2.4 | 78 |
| North Korea | 13 | 61 | na[c] | 85 | na[c] | 40 | na[c] | 20 |
| Poland | 27 | 54 | 55 | 98 | 84 | 237 | 179 | 248 |
| Romania | 30 | 64 | 45 | 98 | 51 | 146 | 120 | 129 |
| Soviet Union | 37 | 58 | 55 | 99 | 75 | 461 | 208 | 397 |
| Vietnam | 24 | 62 | 49 | 75 | 1 | 121 | 26 | 29 |
| Yugoslavia | 26 | 60 | 46 | 85 | 71 | 193 | 132 | 89 |
| USA | 43 | 85 | 50 | 99 | 744 | 1,882 | 571 | 287 |

[a]Represents percent of adult population (over 15) able to read and write.

[b]Daily newspaper circulation per 1000 population.

[c]Not available.

SOURCE: Adapted from Ruth Leger Sivard, *World Military and Social Expenditures, 1980* (Leesburg, Va.: World Priorities, 1980), pp. 21–29; *Reader's Digest Almanac and Yearbook 1980* (New York: Norton, 1980), pp. 472–477.

cultures that were historically denied free access to information and ideas. The present policies of ideological training and party control are not practices, therefore, that represent a sharp break with the past. Rather, the states' control of the socialization process and educational policy are features of thought control to which most of these populations have long been accustomed.

When examining individual factors, however, we find that the present-day leaders are committed to promoting mass education and have been willing to pay the high cost that this task requires. Most Communist policy makers have been generous in their spending on education, as illustrated by their expenditures devoted to education (see Table 7.2). Communist Party countries tend to allocate a higher percentage of their GNP to education than most countries in either the First or Third World.

In the eyes of the leaders, the major human obstacles to their conceptions of enlightenment have been the reluctance of some sectors of the population to fully support the system's ideology and to display their support in acceptable forms of political activity. The undesirable attributes of apathy and alienation are still apparent among many sectors, including the young, and will have to be eradicated before enlightenment policy can be called an unqualified success.

Lastly, structural factors, such as state controlled educational systems and party domination of the mass media, explain a good deal of Communist policy and performance in this value area. Educational policy, although not immune from competing interests and debates over financing and so forth, is one area where long-term, rational-comprehensive planning is possible. On the basis of these plans, policy makers have undertaken major programs and provided massive funding to establish the socializing institutions capable of developing a new socialist citizen. From sports arenas to ballet theaters, from day care centers to workers' universities and scientific institutes, the Communist Party states' investment in promoting their concept of human development is one generally unparalleled in the contemporary world.

## COMMUNIST POLITICS, VALUES, AND HUMAN DIGNITY

Is politics of any significance in explaining the allocation of values and their impact on human dignity in Communist sytems today? Can any of the variations in the distributions of values or the plight of human dignity be attributed to political factors? Does the ideology, nature of political leadership, or policy-making system make a difference? First, we ought to recognize that considerable research has indicated that economic development may be the most powerful determinant of policy and, particularly, government expenditures. As demonstrated in Table 7.2, richer countries such as the USSR and East Germany have more to spend per capita on health, education, and defense than such poorer countries as China, Cuba, and Vietnam. But once we accept this fact, does the type of political system have any significant impact on either the amount of expenditures invested in different policy areas (*e.g.*, defense versus health) or on the distribution of policy outcomes (*e.g.*, education and health care) among different sectors in the society?

Concerning the impact of the type of political system (*e.g.*, Communist or non-Communist) on expenditure patterns, some research has shown the influence of the political system to be weak if not nonexistent. For example, after examining expenditures for national security and a variety of social and domestic programs in six Communist Party and six capitalist countries, Frederick C. Pryor concluded that political systems provide essentially the same types and levels of public expenditures and services for their people.[35] On the other hand, some have suggested that the type of political system does make a difference. Classifying political systems into three regime types (established democracies, innovative-mobilizational or Communist autocracies, and traditional autocracies), Alexander J.

[35]Frederick C. Pryor, *Public Expenditures in Capitalist and Communist Nations* (Homewood, Ill.: Richard D. Irwin, 1968).

Groth argues that their policies are substantially different from one another.[36] In a more recent analysis of 59 countries, including 11 Communist Party states, Groth concludes that ideologies and political systems do make a difference:

> The findings reflect not merely higher social welfare benefits among socialist states—at generally lower direct cost to the worker—but also more consistent, more homogeneous levels of benefits among these states, as compared with states at similar levels of development.[37]

Research exists, therefore, suggesting that political systems and political factors do and do not have influence on the policy process.

Although recognizing that the level of economic development is probably the most powerful determinant of policy, we feel there is good reason for concluding that political systems do have some significant influence on the pattern of expenditures, the distribution of values within a society, and the human dignity of individual citizens. For example, Table 7.2 suggested that the pattern of expenditures varies significantly between the USSR and the United States. The USSR invests considerably more per capita in its military relative to health and education than does the United States. Other comparisons suggest differences in expenditure patterns that seem to be related to political forces. Furthermore, ideology and political systems appear to be even more powerful in determining how values are distributed within systems. That is, expenditure data suggest how much a government spends in a particular policy area, like health, but it does not reveal what sectors in a society enjoy the health care.

Data on the distribution of values tells you who gets what and how much. In the Second World states, most governments have eradicated the extreme haves and have nots. Although the Chinese spend relatively little on health care, for example, all Chinese are guaranteed free access to medical care regardless of their social position. Most other Communist Party states do the same. Finally, by influencing government expenditures and the distribution of values, political factors have a powerful impact on the human dignity of the people. By determining where monies are spent and who gets what and how much, Communist Party governments have a powerful impact on the lives of their citizens.

On the basis of our study, three political factors seem of major importance in Communist systems. The first of these—Marxist-Leninist ideology and the national adaptations of this doctrine—serves as a major political force in all the Communist Party states. Although interpreted and used somewhat differently among the various systems, the ideologies of means have served as general frames of reference, or guides to action, and are used by the leaders as they confront the challenges of our age. The interpretation and application of the ideologies; the flexibility, dogmatism, or self-righteousness in their uses; and the emphasis on one set of ideological values versus another—all have a clear and powerful impact on the allocation of values and the course of human dignity.

The second important political feature of Communist systems influencing the distribution of values is the nature and structure of strong personal leadership. Individual leaders like Lenin, Mao, and Tito were powerful, revolutionary leaders who presided over political processes that changed the course of Soviet, Chinese, and Yugoslav history. In addition, the power élites with whom they worked, and by whom they were replaced, were dedicated social and political engineers devoted to the construction of Communism and to using the means required to bring about progress toward this end. They were permitted this power, and the opportunities it provided, because of the third political factor we consider. This factor is the centralized structure of policy making in the one-party state. Operating within a centralized, comparatively closed environment, Communist leaders have

[36]Alexander J. Groth, *Comparative Politics: A Distributive Approach* (New York: Macmillan, 1971).

[37]Alexander J. Groth, *Worker Welfare in the Marxist-Leninist States: A Comparative Perspective, c. 1975.* Paper presented at the meeting of the International Political Science Association, Moscow, USSR, 1979.

Antiaircraft missiles on display in Moscow's Red Square at the anniversary celebration of the Great October Revolution. Although heavy spending in the military sector has moved the USSR into "superpower" status, it has meant considerable deprivation for the consumer.

been relatively free to set goals, adopt policies, and, then, mobilize human and nonhuman resources to attain them. The centralized structure of politics within the one-party system, in other words, has proven to be a powerful determinant influencing the allocation of values and overall government performance.

These three factors—ideology, leadership, and a centralized policy-making process—are in some respects the strengths of Communist systems. They allow a political process that can sometimes move with vigor and efficiency to address and resolve some of the pressing needs and problems of modern life. When examining the performance of Communist systems in some of these areas, such as education and health care, areas in which the Communists place high priority and can utilize the three political attributes to attain them, we find satisfactory, if not outstanding, performance records. But—and this is very important—although ideology, leadership, and centralized policy making have great strengths, paradoxically, they also have great weaknesses.

In their fervent efforts to tackle the pressing problems of modern life, Communist élites have often violated the interests and dignity of the primary objects for which they labored: the men and women of socialist life. In struggling to industrialize, wipe out illiteracy, provide medical care, tasks in which they have often succeeded admirably, they have ignored some of the other needs and rights of humanity. As a result, when we examine performance records in other value areas related to human dignity, such as the leaders' willingness to accord their people trust and respect or to allow them meaningful participation in the decision-making process, their records are found wanting. The picture, in other words, is mixed; there are great accomplishments alongside tragic costs.

In evaluating the Soviet Union, Zbigniew K. Brzezinski and Samuel P. Huntington note:

All the strong points of the Soviet system—in ideology, in leadership, in policy-making—would be impossible to duplicate in a society which protects the liberty of the individual.[38]

Therefore, the ideology, leaders, and centralized policy process that have encouraged significant advancements in some performance areas have by their very nature brought about significant costs in others. Although the denial of Western standards of liberties and democracy have allowed Communist systems to advance in ways non-Communist systems sometimes find difficult, this has often come at considerable sacrifice to the cause of human dignity.

## CONCLUSION

We will conclude by returning to our central concern in this study: both the allocation of values in the Soviet, Chinese, Yugoslav, and other Communist-run systems as well as the impact of these value outcomes on the issue of human dignity. When judging performance in terms of the general Communist conception of human dignity—a political community of democratic rule, trust, and respect; equality and well-being; and enlightenment and comradeship—it is clear that all the states are still far removed from the ideals of Communism. Where they stand today seems to result from certain environmental factors, particularly the level of economic development, and each state's particular blend of ideology, leadership, and degree of centralization. The Soviet model, with its more "orthodox" ideology, conservative leadership, and centralized policy process, has made undeniable advancements; its people are better fed, better clothed, and better cared for than at any other time in the country's history. Some experts are predicting, however, a period of decelerating growth or even stagnation in the 1980s and "an environment in which diverse claimants must compete for shrinking marginal increments of resources."[39] Alongside

these advancements, we find a bureaucratized party monopoly and a trend toward increasing conservatism within its ranks. Some observers contend that these trends are accompanied by continuing, if not increasing, repression, a denial of meaningful citizen participation, continuing centralization, and, possibly, a form of neo-Stalinism. Others strongly disagree. In evaluating trends in the Soviet Union, Jerry F. Hough argues:

> [It] has not been a period of growing repression of individual freedom; it has not been a period of declining citizen participation; it has not been a period of greater privileges accorded to the "New Class" in comparison with other strata of society; it has not been a period of recentralization of the Soviet political system. On the contrary, the trend in policy has been in the opposite direction in these areas.[40]

As students of politics, we should recognize that we have no crystal ball and that wise men and women may disagree. The trends and outcomes are never as clear as we would like them to be. But, although there is not complete agreement on the nature or direction of change in the Soviet Union and other Communist Party states, there is agreement on the basic and significant fact that these societies are changing. Some see a return to Stalinism, or neo-Stalinism; others see a more just and democratic state. We cannot adequately cover all of the different viewpoints on Soviet change in this short book, yet we would err by not drawing attention to the diversity of opinion on this topic and encourage you to stay abreast of these issues and attempt to make some judgments of your own.

Although predicting trends in the Soviet Union is fraught with certain difficulties, forecasting the future of China may be one of even greater uncertainty. Will the new Chinese leaders continue their developmental strategy and the program of four modernizations? If so, what will come with modernization? Some have

---

[38]Zbigniew K. Brzezinski and Samuel P. Huntington, *Political Power: USA/USSR* (New York: Viking, 1963), p. 413.

[39]Seweryn Bialer, "The Politics of Stringency in the the USSR," *Problems of Communism*, 29 (3) (1980), p. 19.

[40]Jerry F. Hough, "The Brezhnev Era: The Man and the System," *Problems of Communism*, 25 (2) (1976), p. 8.

suggested that as ideological tensions subside, new sociological tensions are bound to intensify.[41] Problems of dissatisfied youth, city/rural cleavages and regional assertiveness are but a few of the potential problems on the Chinese horizon.

Finally, we come to the more humanistic approach to building Communism followed by Yugoslavia. Here, the interplay of features of strength and weakness encountered in the Soviet Union and China seem paradoxically rearranged. In the USSR, a conservative ideology, a dominant and aging set of élites, and a centralized policy-making process contributed to progress in some areas of development (primarily material) but also incurred great costs in others (primarily human). In Yugoslavia, a more flexible ideology and more decentralized leadership structure and policy-making process resulted in rather different value outcomes. Compared with China and the Soviet Union, we found much more democracy in Yugoslavia and considerably greater respect and trust between the mass populace and the political leaders. However, in policy areas that required the decisive and efficient action of a centralized authority, the performance of the more decentralized Yugoslav form of self-managing socialism was often found deficient. Caught in the incremental process of muddling through, the Yugoslav system increasingly reflected the pluralistic nature of the heterogeneous society within which it operated and, in doing so, was often bogged down in the give and take of competitive, factionalized politics. What happens in the emerging post-Tito era will provide another interesting chapter in the Yugoslav story.

The Communist Party states of Eastern Europe, Asia, and Cuba are carefully viewing the developments in these three countries as they search for alternatives in their own developmental programs. The East European countries will continue to follow the Soviet Union but will simultaneously search for greater autonomy in the hope of making more of their own choices in both domestic and international spheres. In 1980, Southeast Asian states were still involved in fratricidal warfare and had little time for long-range planning. In most states, however, there will be a continuing search for policies to meet the needs of their people and to improve the quality of life under socialism. At times, the emphasis will be on economic growth and material rewards and incentives; at other times, policies will promote equality and the collective good. Sometimes the process of policy making will be rational and comprehensive, at other times, short term and incremental. But, in all cases, the approaches will never be cost free. A more centralized Soviet approach may facilitate greater decision-making efficiency; the radical Chinese approach may be able to mobilize the masses to strive toward high-priority goals; the more humanistic Yugoslav approach may show greater respect for human rights and democracy. It seems an unfortunate but inevitable law of politics that all these strengths have accompanying weaknesses. A high level of centralization, with its emphasis on efficiency, generally means limitations on individual freedom and initiative; an expansion of more humanistic values and increasing personal choice, on the other hand, brings about costs in the centralized coordination of the system. How leaders decide to apportion these strengths and weaknesses explains the great diversity of politics one finds among Communist Party states in the Second World today.

# Suggestions for Further Reading

Baum, Richard, ed., *China's Four Modernizations*, (Boulder, Colo.: Westview, 1980).

[41]Ross Terrill, "China in the 1980s," *Foreign Affairs*, 58 (4) (1980), pp. 932–933.

Bowers, John Z., ed., *Medicine and Society in China*, Josiah Macy Foundation, (New York:) 1974.

Chalidze, Valery, *To Defend These Rights:*

*Human Rights and the Soviet Union* (New York: Random House, 1974).

**DiMaio, Alfred John, Jr.,** *Soviet Urban Housing* (New York: Praeger, 1974).

**Field, Mark G.,** ed., *Social Consequences of Modernization in Communist Societies* (Baltimore: Johns Hopkins University Press, 1976).

**Frolic, B. Michael,** *Mao's People* (Cambridge: Harvard University Press, 1980).

**Hanson, Philip,** *The Consumer in the Soviet Economy* (Evanston, Ill.: Northwestern University Press, 1968).

**Kaser, Michael,** *Health Care in the Soviet Union and Eastern Europe* (Boulder, Colo.: Westview, 1976).

**Kelley, Donald R.,** *Soviet Politics in the Brezhnev Era* (New York: Praeger, 1980).

**Kirsch, Leonard Joel,** *Soviet Wages: Changes in Structure and Administration Since 1956* (Cambridge: MIT Press, 1972).

**Lane, David,** *The Socialist Industrial State* (Boulder, Colo.: Westview 1976).

————, *The End of Inequality? Stratification Under State Socialism* (Baltimore: Penguin, 1971).

**Lardys, Nicholas R.,** *Economic Growth and Distribution in China* (New York: Cambridge University Press, 1978).

**Lasswell, Harold, Daniel Lerner, and John D. Montgomery,** *Values and Development: Appraising the Asian Experience* (Cambridge: MIT Press, 1976).

**Medvedev, Roy A.,** *On Socialist Democracy* (New York: Knopf, 1975).

**Mieczkowski, Bogdan,** *Personal and Social Consumption in Eastern Europe* (New York: Praeger, 1975).

**Oksenberg, Michel C.,** ed., *China's Developmental Experience* (New York: Academy of Political Science, 1973).

**Osborne, Robert J.,** *Soviet Social Policies: Welfare, Equality and Community* (Homewood, Ill.: Dorsey, 1970).

**Pryor, Frederic L.,** *Public Expenditures in Communist and Capitalist Nations* (Homewood, Ill.: Richard D. Irwin, 1968).

**Wesson, Robert,** *The Aging of Communism* (New York: Praeger, 1980).

# PART THREE

## Power and Policy
## in the Third World

# CHAPTER ONE

## The Impact of Colonialism on Third World Politics

In all probability, historians of the next century will look back on the period from 1500 to 2000 as the time of one of the most remarkable and significant events in world history: the expansion of Europeans beyond their continent to explore, populate, and dominate most of the rest of the world and to bring with them the ideologies, technologies, and institutions of modernity. The period of European domination of the globe was, historically, relatively brief. By 1776, less than 300 years after it began, the tide of European expansion began to ebb in the Western Hemisphere, first in the north, with the American Revolution, and then, 30 to 40 years later, in the south, with the breakup of the Spanish Empire. The reversal of colonialism is lasting about as long as its launching, but the rapid dissolution of empire around the world since 1945 seems to establish the trend quite firmly. By 2000, it seems, most legal colonial relationships will be eliminated, and national self-determination will be worldwide.

Nevertheless, for all of its brevity, European colonial domination of less advanced peoples must be the point of departure in our journey to the Third World because it was the European influence that initiated the spread of industrialization and modernization around the world. With-

out the colonial experience, most of the nations of the Third World would not even exist, at least in the form that we know them today; indeed, entire regions, such as Latin America and Indochina, would certainly carry different labels when we locate them on a map. The European colonial influence brought to the peoples of the Southern and Western hemispheres the social, intellectual, and material inventions that had allowed Europe to break out of its own Dark Ages; the introduction of these cultural innovations would prove to have much the same effect on the so-called backward peoples of the globe. That the introduction of these inventions has not brought to the Third World similar levels of material prosperity and political progress as it did for Europe is due partly to the colonial experience itself, partly to its remnants, which still characterize Third World relationships with the industrialized West, and partly to the inability of Third World political élites to exploit the enormous value of European ideas.

### THE COLONIAL PERIOD

By some accounts, premodern life was brutal, savage, unpredictable, and ignoble. The population  was divided into two groups: the landed

A small boy carries water to his home in a remote village in Ecuador. The boy's clothing and the materials used in building the dwellings identify the village as traditional. Millions of citizens of Third World countries continue to live in similar villages despite the modernization of their country's major cities.

Enveloping all these communities (of peasants) there is a sense of life robbed of all significance. Man is both degraded and mocked. The peasantries are all haunted by the fear that the earth will lose its fertility. . . . They are obsessed by an almost panic concern to maintain the size of their populations. Surrounded by malignant demons and spirits, threatened by the unruly forces of nature and society, they were led to seek the intervention of occult powers whom they must try to propitiate or coerce by means of offerings, spells, worship, to protect their precarious though unchanging position in the natural and social order . . . war, famine and disease desolated them, conquerors swept over them, tax collectors . . . robbed them, but these villages remained unchanged and unaffected, always ready to resume the old burdens and to submit tamely to the same degrading routine.[1]

By other accounts, life in premodern societies although certainly hard physically was stable and secure and provided people with what they needed most—a sense of belonging, a feeling of one's place in the universe. Society was divided into two classes, a poor majority and a wealthy élite. But the aristocracy cared for and looked after the peasants or serfs and managed their lives in a remarkably efficient manner, given the overall scarcity of goods for society generally. Furthermore, the fact that traditional society lived in extended families spread out into clans made it possible for individuals who suffered from some particular problem to be supported by the psychic resources of the entire community. According to this way of looking at things, premodern societies were internally consistent and logical and, above all, their system worked. Because their village political system was closely linked to their village social system, the two functioned in harmony. If food and shelter were not available in abundance, at least they were adequate to meet the needs of the villagers. Land was usually owned and cultivated in communal style. The actual land was the property of the village, and the fruits of the

gentry who controlled the only real source of wealth, the land, and the peasants who tilled the land for their masters. Traditional populations were uniformly rural, agrarian, ill educated or illiterate, cut off from all external influences, and subject to the ravages of famine, pestilence, war, plagues, and natural disasters. Life spans were short, personal civility was lacking, the social order was shot through with suspicion and distrust, and there seemed to be little opportunity for members of the society to realize any of their higher ambitions short of obtaining enough food to get through the day.

I. R. Sinai has painted for us a dramatic picture of the life of Asian peasants in *The Challenge of Modernization*.

[1] I. R. Sinai, *The Challenge of Modernization* (New York: Norton, 1964), pp. 34–35.

harvest belonged more or less equitably to all members of the community. Perhaps most important, there was stability and consistency in the lives of traditional people. The continuity of their traditions sustained them in times of trouble and taught them in times of plenty not to expect much improvement in the future.[2]

Political scientist John H. Kautsky, has chosen to analyze traditional societies in terms of their social and economic class structure as well as their fragmented and isolated physical setting. For Kautsky,[3] traditional societies are those that are entirely unaffected by the impact of modernization and that are composed minimally of an aristocracy and several primitive agrarian societies under its rule.

Kautsky notes that the societies of traditional countries were highly decentralized. That is, they consisted of numerous small villages spread throughout remote valleys or along winding rivers, with little central control or direction of their lives. Because communications were restricted to face-to-face conversation and transportation was limited to that powered by humans and animals, remote villages enjoyed the luxury (or suffered the disadvantages) of being fairly free from control by central government authorities, despite what the theoretical powers of that political authority might have been.

The economic basis of traditional society was overwhelmingly agricultural. As much as 80 to 90 percent of a traditional society's labor force was employed in tilling the land and in related activities (the comparable statistic for a modern industrial society, such as the United States, is 5 to 7 percent). Because land was the basis for the society's economic structure, ownership of the land was the basis of power. Power, in turn, was very unequally distributed between a landed aristocracy, who owned the land and who received most of the benefits from its use, and a massive, poor peasant class. Government for the

aristocrats was little more than a device to manage the subordinate classes, to extract what surplus there was from agricultural pursuits, and to spend that surplus in the time-honored aims of the aristocratic classes: making war, amusing themselves, and fighting with other aristocrats for the privilege of maintaining their position. They did not envision any societal change, but they surely would have opposed such change if they could have imagined it. They opposed the spread of capitalism to their jurisdictions, and they sought to keep the lower rural classes bound to them in every way.

The peasant class generally accepted this arrangement, because they, too, benefited from the system. They did not benefit in a material sense as we in the modern world would understand it. Their lives were poor or, better yet, impoverished, and they lacked even a semblance of the advantages of a wealthier society: health care, housing, and entertainment for instance. But, in their complex relationships with the upper classes, the peasants enjoyed a security that emerged from a stable place in the constellation of social units within which they lived. To change this would have implied movement, from a village to a larger town, as well as social movement to another kind of unit. Societal modernization would have meant submitting oneself to the impersonal control of the economic work unit. All of these changes would have been not only unfavorable and unlikely to the peasant but also threatening and frightening. As long as the society remained traditional, neither peasants nor aristocracy had anything to fear because the fatalism and apathy of rural premodern life prevented the lower classes from even imagining an improvement to their lives.

Like traditional societies, traditional people differed markedly in their make-up from those with more modern perspectives. As we will discuss in greater detail in Chapter Three, the set of attitudes and values that defines the traditional way of life emphasizes fatalism, apathy, suspicion of strangers, and the choice of low-risk alternatives to the solving of life's problems. We will have more to say later about how these at-

[2]Robert E. Gamer, *The Developing Nations: A Comparative Perspective* (Boston: Allyn & Bacon, 1976), chap. 2.

[3]John H. Kautsky, *The Political Consequences of Modernization* (New York: Wiley, 1972), chap. 1.

titudes and values affect, and are affected by, the modernization process.

Around the world, traditional societies have been under the influence of modernization for at least several generations. It would be an error, however, to conclude that traditional ways of life have crumbled and eroded, leaving only modern societies in their place. In every instance in which a traditional society has been affected by modernization, the result has been an amalgamation of the two forces, a social order that is more or less modernized but with significant traces of traditionalism still intact and still important. Despite the apparent disparity between the physical and economic power of traditional and modern societies, the former has shown the resilience and absorptive capacity to withstand the influence of the latter in each case in which they have been in contact.

Europeans first encountered the traditional world in the Western Hemisphere or, to be more specific, in the island chains that cross the Caribbean Sea and in the littoral washed by its waters. Spreading inland through Mexico, Central America, and south through Peru and Chile, the Spanish *conquistadores* carried the power of Spain abroad in the name of the king and of the Roman Catholic Church. On the eastern side of the South American continent, separated from the Spanish colonies by a line confirmed by the pope in 1506, Portuguese explorers emulated their fellow Iberians and established their hold over what would become Brazil. (In addition, during the sixteenth century, the Portuguese established their rule over Angola and Mozambique in Africa as well as over the Spice Islands and the East Indies.)

Spanish rule in Latin America (and, to a great extent, in the Philippine Islands) was characterized by its legalist basis, its centralist allocation of powers, and its authoritarian treatment of dissent. Despite the distances separating Madrid from its colonial holdings and the time required to traverse them, Spain insisted on maintaining tight control over its various political dependencies. At the same time, Spain's insistence on the rigid fulfillment of the law to its exact letter encouraged local *de facto* autonomy

accompanied by a good deal of cynicism about the need to obey the laws issued from Madrid. Finally, there were no opportunities for dissent to be lodged from the colonies, despite the early growth of local settler colonies in several major cities, including Buenos Aires, Caracas, Lima, and Mexico City. Local political participation was regarded as radical and upsetting by the Spanish monarchy. Thus, in 1810, when the Spanish colonies began to cut away from Spain in the aftermath of the Napoleonic wars, there was little heritage of local self-government and practically no indigenous business or political élite interested in pursuing the objective of enhancing human dignity; instead, there were the still-rigid cultural artifacts of traditional society.[4]

After the decolonization process was completed in Latin America in the early 1820s [with the exception of the Caribbean countries of Cuba, Haiti, and Santo Domingo (now the Dominican Republic), which would come to independence later], the former Spanish-Portuguese colonial domination was replaced by a neocolonial (or quasicolonial) relationship between Latin America and Great Britain and, later, between Latin America and the United States. In these relationships, the important currency of power was not law or constitutional prerogative but money and its material products: trade, commerce, raw-material extraction, manufacturing, and the attendant social changes. As a consequence of differential rates of industrialization, Latin American countries became the suppliers to Great Britain and the United States of industrial raw materials and exotic consumer goods while serving as a market for the manufactured products exported from the two industrializing countries.

Other European countries began their process of expansion somewhat later; and other parts of the world were exposed to European influence only at the beginning of the eighteenth century or later. During the seventeenth and eighteenth centuries, the principal expansionist countries were

[4]Claudio Veliz, "Centralism and Nationalism in Latin America," *Foreign Affairs*, 47 (1) (1968), pp. 69–83.

Great Britain, France, Belgium, and the Netherlands. Their efforts at expansion were turned first toward South and Southeast Asia and, later, toward sub-Saharan Africa.

The entry of Great Britain and the Netherlands into the colonial arena differed greatly from the entry of Spain and Portugal. The Iberian influence had been spread first by soldiers and, subsequently, by agents of the Church; in the case of the British and Dutch, trade and political and strategic advantage were the foremost concerns. Accordingly, the two governments formed joint public-private companies to trade with newly discovered areas. In 1600, the British East Indies Company was founded, followed 2 years later by the Dutch East Indies Company. Other European powers followed suit and, throughout Asia in the eighteenth century and throughout Africa later, trading posts and economic enclaves sprang up, injecting Western currencies, influence, and thought into traditional societies.[5]

Through the first three quarters of the nineteenth century, colonial influences spread primarily by informal means and in accord with economic, political, and strategic impulses. The colonial powers sought to penetrate the traditional regions of Asia and Africa by means of trade, and they negotiated commercial agreements or treaties with tribal chieftains or village heads. Western control was strong but still informal. The system of informal trade penetration had an inherent bias toward expansion of control and toward more formal dominance of the remote areas. As each trading area was secured, the local commercial official in charge became responsible for the maintenance of order in the region, including the frontier regions that marked the area off from neighboring, still uncivilized zones, where traditional societies lay untouched by the colonial system. At the first sign of disturbance on the border, the colonial power seized the opportunity to expand its influence and to establish new boundaries around

its zone of influence. In this act, however, the authorities unwittingly lengthened the boundary to be secured and magnified the possibilities for additional disturbances in the future, which would necessitate even further encroachment into previously unsettled lands. The expansionist imperative of colonial trading arrangements was unmistakable.

By 1870, the pressures for formal political control over colonial preserves had mounted to such a degree that the European powers launched a series of expansionist moves that effectively divided up almost all of the remaining unclaimed land area of the globe. From 1870 to 1900, the European colonial states added to their direct political control abroad more than 10 million square miles of territory and about 150 million people (about 20 percent of the earth's land area and about 10 percent of the world's population). Great Britain was the largest beneficiary of this expansion: nearly half of the land area and nearly 60 percent of the people brought under colonial rule became subjects of the British Government. The British Empire stretched from the Indian subcontinent westward to Egypt, the Sudan, Uganda, Kenya, and other areas of Africa to British Guiana in South America and to Malaya and Burma in Southeast Asia. The French were second in the scramble for colonies, claiming 3.5 million square miles and about 26 million persons, mostly inhabitants of Africa and Southeast Asia. Germany, Italy, and Belgium also acquired significant colonies in Africa; in the Pacific, Japan and the United States joined in the expansion drive. The hardest hit region was Africa. In 1870, only about 10 percent of the continent was under alien control; by 1900, only 10 percent remained independent.

Traditional societies in the Middle East remained isolated from European colonization efforts until after World War I. The war brought about the destruction of the Ottoman Empire, and the Versailles Peace Conference of 1919 was the scene of unscrupulous bargaining and division of the spoils of war in the area. Under the League of Nations mandate system, Great Britain and France established control over most of the Middle East, excluding Turkey, Iran, and Saudi

[5]Benjamin J. Cohen, *The Question of Imperialism: The Political Economy of Dominance and Dependence* (New York: Basic Books, 1973), chap. 2.

Arabia. Syria, Iraq, and Lebanon were designated as mandates, and Palestine was established as the special responsibility of Great Britain, despite the protestations of the Palestinian Arabs.

One of the ironies of the entire colonial experience involves the role of the great wars in extending the system and in bringing it to a close. World War I was fought by the United States as a struggle for the right of self-determination of all peoples, but it resulted in the expansion of colonial empires into areas previously saved from colonialism. In contrast, World War II had little to do with self-determination as a cause, yet, it left in its wake the conditions that led directly to the dissolution of nearly all the formal colonial possessions around the world. In 1945, the Japanese had been driven out of all of their colonial holdings, as had Italy. Germany had been denied expansion once again. In addition, Great Britain, France, Belgium, and the Netherlands had all been so weakened by the war that they were unable to maintain control over their possessions for more than a decade or two. The year 1945 would mark the definitive beginning of the end of Europe's 500-year-long domination of the world. As European power receded, it left behind the emerging political systems of the Third World as well as, many would say, a lingering system of informal, neocolonial influence and control.

## AN ASSESSMENT OF COLONIAL RULE

What do we mean by a colonial relationship? A typical dictionary definition of colonial is "a relationship between two groups of people characterized by a highly unequal distribution of power." A colonial relationship is one between a very strong group and a very weak group in which the weak are dependent and the strong dominant. To apply that idea to this discussion, let us further assume that (at least) the strong group is formally organized into a national state; the weak, dependent group may or may not be so organized.

The exact nature of the colonial relationship derives from the various ways in which each side may perceive its links with, and its privileges and obligations toward, the other. The powerful, dominant nation may wish to absorb the people of the weak nation and make them citizens in their own society with full privileges and responsibilities; or, conversely, the strong nation may wish to keep the weak group at arm's length, extracting the benefits from the relationship without incurring any of the costs. The former case can be exemplified by the United States with regard to the American Indians, former black slaves, Mexicans living in California, and Hawaiians. The French also tried to assimilate colonial peoples into their society, as in the case of the Algerians and the Vietnamese; they even granted them seats in the national legislature and positions in the national cabinets. The Portuguese did likewise in their colonies in Africa, Angola and Mozambique. On the other hand, the Dutch in Indonesia practiced the rule of cultural relativism. They allowed native rulers to continue in power more or less undisturbed and made no effort to transform Indonesians into citizens of the Dutch nation. The British fell somewhere in between. They were interested primarily in the maintenance of order; where native rulers could accomplish this task, they were left alone; where native rule faltered, the British substituted their own bureaucracy. In each case, the British objective was to implant the rule of law and government by representative institutions without necessarily intending for all colonial peoples to become Britons or even loyal British subjects.

From the point of view of the weaker side, however, the colonial bond was inherently an unstable one. If the weak found the relationship to their liking, they moved closer to the mother country and eventually were absorbed into it; this happened with Alaska and Hawaii. At times, this took place even if the weak peoples were not particularly fond of the colonial regime, if they thought they had no choice, or if they perceived long-run benefits to be derived from closer association with their powerful benefactor. For many years, the quasicolonial relationship between Panama and the United States was of this type although that is no doubt changing. In most cases, however, the weaker peoples were unhappy with their subordinate relationship, and they became more so as the waves of modernization and nationalism swept through the Third World. The obvious outcome in these cases has been guerilla insurgency, terrorism, and wars of national liberation. Such violence marked the passage to national independence of virtually all of Latin America, Algeria, Israel, Angola, Bangladesh, Indonesia, Vietnam, Malaya, Kenya, and other states. The success of these independence movements can be traced partially to the declining value of the colony to the economic and political goals of the mother country. To a large degree, however, the struggles were successful because of the distance between the insurgent colony and Paris, London, or Madrid. In instances where the colonial peoples live on the same territory with the dominant peoples, separation may be much more difficult and violent because the central authority will fight much harder to retain control over the separatists.

An accurate assessment of the colonial experience should weigh all of the things the Europeans brought to their colonies, both the good things and the bad, both the benefits of colonialism and the costs.[6]

The most obvious contribution of the Europeans to traditional countries has been modern technology. This does not imply that all technologies are either good or bad or that Western technology introduced into traditional societies always has had either a good or bad impact. Instead, technology for the Third World has been a mixed blessing, just as it has been for the areas where it originated, Western Europe and North America.

Some specific examples of technology as introduced into traditional countries will help to clarify the costs and benefits of such a contribution. Transportation technology, including railroads, highways, and small airports, has obviously contributed greatly to the opening up of remote interior portions of many Third World countries. An analysis of the spatial spread of modernization within a newly independent country would reveal that the impact of modernization is heavily influenced by the transportation infrastructure built by the colonial power and left behind after its departure.[7] The control of the new government over its jurisdiction is shaped strongly by the existing rail, air, and road facilities constructed by the mother country. Frequently, however, the metropolitan country constructed the transportation network to serve some existing economic necessity that had little to do with the overall development of the colony. Because Third World areas usually served the industrialized world as sources of raw materials and exotic tropical food products, the transportation facilities were built primarily to facilitate the exportation of these commodities. The remaining needs of the colony for internal lines of communication and transportation, for instance, were ignored. In some Central American countries today, for example, the only railroads in existence are those constructed by the banana companies to move their produce to the seaports and, from there, to markets in North America and Europe. Any relationship to the internal needs of the host country was purely coincidental. The same kind of conclusions can be drawn about communication facilities, including telephone, telegraph, radio, television, and print media (newspapers, magazines, and postal services).

A second important kind of technological contribution made by European colonizers to the Third World lies in the area of hygiene and health care. Through the introduction of mass innoculations; public health clinics; prenatal and postnatal care; food shipments under programs, such as "Food for Peace"; and other advances, the Western world has succeeded in altering the death rates of many Third World countries. No doubt this is to be applauded. Yet, as we will learn in Chapter Two, the combination of falling

[6]For a detailed discussion of the same theme, see Rupert Emerson, *From Empire to Nation: The Rise to Self-Assertion of Asian and African Peoples* (Cambridge: Harvard University Press, 1960).

[7]Peter R. Gould, "Tanzania 1920–63: The Spatial Impress of the Modernization Process," *World Politics,* 22 (2) (1970), pp. 149–170.

death rates, as a consequence of Western health-care techniques, and of stable birthrates, as a consequence of rigid social structures, attitudes, and mores, has produced a frightening population explosion in the Third World.

Still another area of Western technology that has had mixed blessings for Third World countries has been that of manufacturing and agriculture. With little thought for their total impact, Western business representatives have pressed backward areas to adopt Western techniques in manufacturing (mass production, assembly-line techniques) and in farming (heavy use of equipment, pesticides, fertilizers). This has had a variety of effects. These technologies have improved the individual worker productivity in many traditional countries and, thereby, have made more products available on the market, perhaps even at a reduced price. But there have been costs to these innovations. Modern manufacturing techniques have reduced the need for labor and have thrown many potential workers out of a job, thereby reducing the aggregate purchasing power of the society. The same thing has happened on the farm. Fewer workers are needed to produce more food so that aggregate demand falls and more and more heads of families are out of work. Furthermore, the Third World countries are discovering that the adoption of Western manufacturing technologies makes them more vulnerable to external pressures instead of less vulnerable. The use of modern industrial facilities makes the economy more dependent on foreign sources of raw materials and energy, especially petroleum. In the agricultural area, the use of petroleum-based fertilizers has cost many Third World countries a great deal because the cost of crude oil has risen.

A fourth kind of technology introduced by the European states was in the form of weapons and other military equipment. Western domination over traditional societies was facilitated greatly, if not actually made possible, by their use of firearms and other lethal technologies to force the more backward peoples to submit to their rule. Later, as the natives learned to turn this new technology against their masters and as the number of weapons available in the developing world increased enormously, modern-weapons technology helped to accelerate the destruction of the European colonial empires. Yet, after helping emerging nations to gain their independence, modern-weapons technology is certainly making political life in the Third World more difficult. These weapons of radically increased lethality make local disputes much more costly in terms of human life and property, as the evidence from the Lebanese civil war of 1975–1976 will attest. As the Western powers freed their colonies, they left behind not only the military equipment of a modern army but also the military organization needed to use it. After a while, the new military leaders frequently came to power in these nations, determined to impose on them the order and discipline of the barracks. As we note in Chapter Five, military intervention in politics has been one of the most serious problems Third World states have had to deal with since 1945. In addition, the adoption of military technology from the Great Powers or from other industrialized states tends to make the recipient countries dependent on the countries of origin for training, ammunition, and replacement parts; this perpetuates the dominant-dependent relationship even after it has formally ended.

Perhaps the most significant aspect of the introduction of Western technology through the colonial system has been in the attitudes of Third World citizens with regard to nature. We will discuss more extensively in Chapter Three the question of the prevalent personality structures and attitudes in both traditional and modern countries. Traditional persons usually possess what behavioral scientists call a fatalistic view of life, which means that they usually do not believe that human beings can change nature but, instead, must adjust to nature's vagaries. Modern persons, however, feel that they can change nature through technology. Generally, the technology brought to traditional societies by colonists may have wrought its most important change in the minds of heretofore traditional peoples.

Another important European contribution

to the traditional lands of the Third World has been education.[8] By education we mean a formal, school-based transmission of knowledge as well as the more informal socialization techniques based on family, kin groups, and, in many instances, the mass media. All of these educational media will be considered at length in Chapter Three.

In most instances, when Europeans arrived in the traditional societies of Latin America, Africa, or Asia, they found no native educational systems. Traditional communities utilized the family and other village-based organs of communication to transmit certain essential lessons to their growing young; beyond that, these cultures were simply not organized to make education a formal, institutionalized endeavor.

It was not until after World War II that most colonial administrations began to take any measures to improve public-supported education in their territories. Prior to the 1940s, the support of the colonial government for public education had been very scanty and had depended more on local funds than on any allocations from the wealthy mother country. For example, in 1942, Indonesia, with a population of more than 70 million, could count fewer than 1000 natives who had completed a college education. During British control of Egyptian education, which came nominally to an end in 1922, illiteracy remained constant at more than 90 percent of the total population. In Tunisia in 1945, under the French protectorate, less than 10 percent of the eligible children were attending primary schools. Even in nations that had shaken off colonial rule earlier, such as Latin American nations, the remnants of an underfinanced and mismanaged educational system left 80 percent of the population illiterate at the close of World War II.

If the overall quantity of European-supported education can be severely criticized, it is still true that in certain very specific qualitative terms, the impact of European education has been enormous throughout the Third World. Western education, especially higher education in Paris or London, eventually created the articulate, activist, nationalist leaders of the native middle class, the intelligentsia of the local societies, and these people provided the leadership and the ideas for the dissolution of colonial ties.

Beyond the leadership élites of Third World nationalist movements, Western education had an equally important impact on the masses of Africa and Asia, primarily by heightening their awareness of their own ethnic and national identities. Citizens of established Western nations often forget just how modern the notions of nationalism, national identity, and ethnic self-determination are. Only since the end of the eighteenth century have people started to think of themselves as members of a national group, a set of citizens whose boundaries were larger than, and transcended, those more narrow enclosures of language, ethnic heritage, village grouping, clan, or something else altogether different. Western-introduced education, with civics training directed from the mother country, aided by textbooks with Western-style national maps and other symbols, helped to divert young attentions away from traditional identifications and toward the broader self-image. Many traditional areas acquired their present national, territorial label only as a result of the decisions of their colonial rulers. In the Western Hemisphere, ancient kingdoms were destroyed and replaced by colonial administrative structures, which, in turn, gave way to independent nation-states. The Incan Empire fell to the Spanish conquerors who established the viceroyalty of Lima, which eventually became the nation-state, Peru. In West Africa, the British grouped together tribes that had literally nothing in common, and they called their creation Nigeria. The same process was repeated in the Indian subcontinent. After termination of the British rule, the nation of Pakistan was created to shelter the religious freedoms of millions of Muslims who felt that if they were included in a larger unit with predominantly Hindu India, their rights to worship would be suppressed. The label, Indochina, is

[8]A useful compendium of articles on this subject is James S. Coleman, ed., *Education and Political Development* (Princeton, N.J.: Princeton University Press, 1965).

itself of European origin, as were the various subregional identities forced on the Vietnamese people by the French. Despite the artificial character of these national identities, nationalist leaders in the Third World have discovered that the symbols of nationhood are powerful weapons to wield against their former European masters. The typical citizen of, say, Nigeria, might not have known what Nigeria stood for in the late 1950s, but he or she at least knew that it stood against continued British rule and, therefore, merited support and allegiance. Once independence is achieved, the uniting force of nationalism becomes thin and fragile and separatist movements have frequently aggravated what is, at best, a very difficult process of nation building. But, with all its weaknesses, the idea of the nation as the core of one's identity has proven to be one of the most powerful motivating forces in modern world politics.

Another major European colonial contribution to the Third World is the modern system of commerce and trade; this includes the ways in which this system disrupted traditional methods of relating individuals to one another and to some broader social unit.[9]

Whatever else might be said about traditional societies as they were on the eve of European intrusion, they at least fed themselves relatively satisfactorily. As noted, traditional society was agricultural in character; the overwhelming majority of its workers were employed in growing food for the community. The land was generally owned by some sort of communal arrangement although the exact nature of the land-tenure system obviously varied widely across the Southern Hemisphere. Private ownership constituted the exception and not the rule. Land was dedicated to the cultivation of one of the three kinds of crops from which traditional peoples could maintain a more than subsistence diet: cereal grains (wheat, maize, and rice); tubers (sweet potatoes, potatoes, and yams); and legumes (beans, lentils, and peas). These were the only foods that satisfied the nutritional and commercial requirements of traditional peoples before colonialization; the evidence shows that they were all grown and cultivated extensively throughout the area now known as the Third World. Virtually all of a community's food needs were self-met; there was little need for, or interest in, trading and little surplus available to be traded.

With the arrival of the Europeans and their ideas of trade and commerce, the traditional techniques of farming, the traditional forms of land tenure, and the traditional crops were all cast aside in favor of more modern ways to employ the great agricultural riches of the Third World. First, the intruding colonial powers altered traditional forms of landownership and allowed private citizens to purchase large plots of land, to enclose this land, and to plant on it whatever they wished. In Latin America, the Spanish Government went one step further and rewarded the adventurers and conquistadores with huge grants of land; the grants included ownership of the native Indians who happened to reside in the villages on this land. In Asia and Africa, the colonial countries first confiscated the land from village or communal ownership, then sold it to private companies or individual citizens who were supposed to use the land productively. This usually meant that the land was not to be used to grow crops for local consumption but for trade to the colonial countries. Because Europe was already rich in cereal grains, tubers, and legumes, the lands of the Third World were turned to the production of crops that had little nutritional value but that commanded high prices in the developed markets of Europe and North America. Thus was born the agricultural system of the colonial world, the dedication of rich farmland to the cultivation of coffee, cocoa, sugar cane, pepper, hemp, bananas, rubber, peanuts, and tobacco. In other instances, if land contained rich mineral deposits, it was exploited, not for what it could grow but for what lay under it; the flow of minerals also began to mark trade patterns between the industrializing countries and their colonies to the south. During the nineteenth century, copper, tin, iron, nitrates, and coal were all shipped from the colonial em-

[9]Celso Furtado, *Economic Development of Latin America: A Survey from Colonial Times to the Cuban Revolution* (Cambridge: At the University Press, 1970).

pires to the industrial center. In the twentieth century, these flows have been joined by perhaps the most important raw material for an industrial society, petroleum.

Most of these linkages have mattered little economically to the industrialized countries, but they have been catastrophic to the Third World. Instead of land being used to grow food to feed the communities that till the soil, we see land used to grow exotic, tropical crops for shipment abroad to grace the tables of Europeans or Americans. Instead of communal ownership of the land, with an equitable distribution of its fruits, we see the concentration of the land in the hands of a few favored entrepreneurs and resultant impoverishment of the remainder of the people. Instead of the steady and secure working of the soil for what it gives to the community, we see the extension of the cash nexus to the workers, linking them precariously to the whims of a market system not only beyond their control but also literally beyond their comprehension.[10]

Clearly, modernization of the techniques for owning and exploiting the soil is not, in itself, destructive of the ways in which people live. Every modern state of Europe experienced the same transformations in their drive to modernity. The rural, agrarian classes had to be pushed in the direction of capitalist exploitation of the soil; property had to be enclosed and private ownership adopted for the incentives of the market to compel full and efficient use of the land; and the rural working class had to be forced off the land and into the cities for an urban industrial class to come into existence to support modernization. The way in which these transformations took place in a country like Great Britain was beneficial and helpful for the overall development of the society.

In the colonized areas, however, the intrusion of modern trade and commerce has destroyed traditional lifestyles without substituting, or aiding in the development of, alternatives. Agricultural and mining products did not remain in the community or even in the nation but, instead, were sent abroad. The modern commercial sectors of the traditional countries constituted economic enclaves, separate and isolated communities; they were cut off from the colony and had their own set of laws and social services. The benefits of these enclaves rarely were extended to the larger community. The proceeds from the sale of these products were usually kept in the financial system of the mother country or, at best, were returned to the enclave to improve its standard of living but without touching the lives of the great majority of native citizens. Rural workers were forced from their communal lands and were made to labor for European owners and managers at highly unstable wages. They worked at jobs that depended not on natural forces, like the weather—which could be seen and felt—but on distant forces, like the international market economy—which were neither experienced firsthand or understood. Bert N. Adams writes that in Africa, colonists used both political coercion, conscription, slavery, and economic coercion (the head or hut tax) to force natives to leave the land and provide the human raw material for Western economic ventures in mines and factories.[11] Local industry did not grow because the enclaves imported what they needed for their own use. Worker productivity did not rise because the enclaves were not faced with local competition and, therefore, did not need to lower production costs. Social services were not provided and wages were not stabilized or improved because native workers had not mastered the skills of labor organization and collective bargaining. The colonial system created many economic inequities by needlessly disrupting traditional modes of economic cooperation without replacing them with more stable, more productive arrangements that would spread the benefits of modernization evenly throughout the world.

The introduction of European forms of agriculture, trade, commerce and manufacturing had the additional important effect of altering the already existing traditional class structure,

---

[10]This idea is explored extensively in Jeffrey M. Paige, "Inequality and Insurgency in Vietnam: A Reanalysis," *World Politics*, 23 (1) (1970), pp. 24–37.

[11]Bert N. Adams, "Kinship Systems and Adaptation to Modernization," *Studies in Comparative International Development*, 4 (3) (1968–1969), p. 50.

which, as we have seen, was limited primarily to a small land-owning aristocracy and a large rural agrarian lower class. The arrival of the colonial economic system caused the emergence of a new socioeconomic class, a small but growing commercial and industrial middle class whose principal advantage was their ability to deal effectively with the representatives of the foreign power. The members of this growing middle class achieved their special status by virtue of their ability and willingness to leave behind their distinctive traditional languages and culture and to embrace the new European languages and customs. As a consequence, this new class rose rapidly in the economic and social structure of the new state, leaving behind their more intransigent ethnic colleagues. It is for this reason that contemporary struggles for national liberation from colonial rule quite often have a class origin as well as an ethnic and linguistic stimulus. As Third World nationalists struggle to throw off foreign domination, they are also fighting to unseat from power those ruling groups who had succeeded in adapting to the colonial or neocolonial system. This additional class dimension of these struggles helps us understand more fully why the conflicts over national liberation in the Third World are as violent as many of them have become and why they seemingly pit native against native during the early phases of the struggle.

The final result of European domination of the Southern Hemisphere was a cultural inferiority complex—a belief inculcated in the colonial peoples that Europeans were superior to them in economic and political relationships and, therefore, deserved to rule them. When the Europeans began their conquest and colonization of the traditional peoples of the Third World, they regarded their new charges as little children, too primitive to be trusted with their own fate. Because, the conquerors reasoned, it was obvious which group was the more powerful, it was obvious which group should rule and which should submit. The dominant colonial administration managed to justify its own arrogance by reference either to religious superiority (as in American President William McKinley's agoniz-

ing decision to assume responsibility to bring Christianity to the Philippines), to race (as in Rudyard Kipling's reference to "the white man's burden"), or to a general cultural superiority (as in the French insistence on their civilizing mission). The British held only the utmost contempt and disregard for the abilities of the Indians. Lord Cornwallis is quoted as saying, "every native of Hindustan is corrupt," and Lord Wellesly described Indians as "vulgar, ignorant, rude, familiar and stupid." As late as 1934, Indians were considered genetically inferior and, therefore, not qualified to hold jobs on a par with the British.[12] Whatever the origin, this feeling of religious, racial, or cultural superiority naturally conveyed itself to the natives, both in the formal sense (through the colonial education system) and in the countless informal tensions that characterized the prevailing master-servant relationship.

Ironically, it was also the European introduction of the psychological attributes of modernity, particularly their emphasis on self-rule and self-determination, that eventually led to the creation of a class of nationalist intellectuals who manifestly rejected the idea of European superiority and who determined to expel the light-skinned invaders from their country. Psychologists have learned that a culturally modern person accepts ultimate responsibility for the successes and failures of life and that external powers or forces cannot assume this intensely personal duty. Consequently, the more modern people become in attitudinal terms, the more they are inclined to reject external attempts to rule them and to assert their own responsibility for self-governance. Apparently, within the group of Western-educated nationalists who have led the struggle against European domination in the Third World, this assertion of personal responsibility has assumed great importance. This has resulted in the demand of colonial states that they be permitted to rule themselves, even if the outcome is not necessarily com-

[12]Saleem Qureshi, "Political Violence in the South Asian Subcontinent," in Yonah Alexander, ed., *International Terrorism: National, Regional and Global Perspectives* (New York: Praeger, 1976), p. 160.

fortable or fruitful. As they often state, "We would rather be governed like hell by ourselves than well by someone else."

After centuries of seeing their country governed from abroad, aided many times by members of their own group who were willing to cooperate with the foreigners, ardent nationalists, like Juan Bosch of the Dominican Republic, can only agonize over the desire for independence and self-control of their nation's destiny. Bosch's cry of anguish must stand for similar expressions heard throughout the Third World since World War II.

> [For the American Ambassador], dealing with me was no easy matter. . . . I was sensitive to anything that might affect Dominican sovereignty. My poor country had had, from the first breath of its life as a republic, a string of political leaders who had dedicated all their skills and resources to looking for any foreign power on which to unload our independence. . . .
>
> I felt wounded, as if it were a personal affront, at the spectacle of so many men without faith in the destiny of their own country. In my childhood, I had seen the Dominican flag coming down from the public buildings to give way to the U.S. banner. No one will ever know what my seven-year-old soul suffered at the sight. . . .
>
> Perhaps I love my little Antilles country so passionately because when I became aware of it as a nation, I realized that it was not that at all, but a dominion. This caused me indescribable pain, and often kept me awake a long time after I had been sent to bed. . . . By the time I was ten, I was ashamed that Santana, who annexed the country to Spain in 1863, and Baez, who wanted to turn Samana [Bay] over to the United States, were Dominicans. As the years passed, that pain and that shame became transformed into passionate patriotism.[13]

As a consequence of these dramatic attitudinal changes in developing countries, one discovers that the leaders of the nationalist movements in the Third World look toward modern industrial society with a complex mixture of love and hate, fear and admiration. On the one hand, they ardently desire to liberate

their countries and their people from the suppression of foreign domination, but they realize that to accomplish this feat, they must modernize their societies and industrialize their economic structures. In short, they must turn their backs on the traditional ways of doing things and embrace modernity with all of its pitfalls and shortcomings. The symbols of industrial society, such as steel mills and modern capital cities, become more than that—they are transformed into the very expression of national independence. On the other hand, these nationalist intellectuals try desperately to retain the essence of their traditional ways and to avoid the flaws of modern industrial society. They laud the "golden age" of their peoples before the arrival of the Europeans, and they seek ways to preserve the fragile and intricate social structures of the traditional village-based communal life, which is under constant assault from modernization. Not surprisingly, these attempts to blend modern and premodern ways of life generate substantial tensions in political ideology and everyday life among many Third World peoples.[14] We will consider the psychological and cultural implications of this phenomenon in Chapter Three.

## THE DECOLONIZATION PROCESS SINCE 1945

As observed earlier, 1945 and the end of World War II signaled the end of Europe's formal domination of its far-flung empires. The devastation of the war left the major colonial powers battered and exhausted; they had little interest in renewed struggle over their fringe territories. The early victories of Japan, on the other hand, had shown the world's nonwhite races that a non-European power could defeat a predominantly white nation in combat; this restored a great deal of self-confidence in the Third World's peoples. Finally, the principles of self-determination, as taught in the Western schools and as enunciated in the United Nations Charter, began to have an effect on the nationalist elites of Africa and Asia.

[13]Juan Bosch, *The Unfinished Experiment* (New York: Praeger, 1965), pp. 162–163.

[14]Mary Matossian, "Ideologies of Delayed Industrialization: Some Tensions and Ambiguities," *Economic Development and Cultural Change, 6* (3) (1958), pp. 217–228.

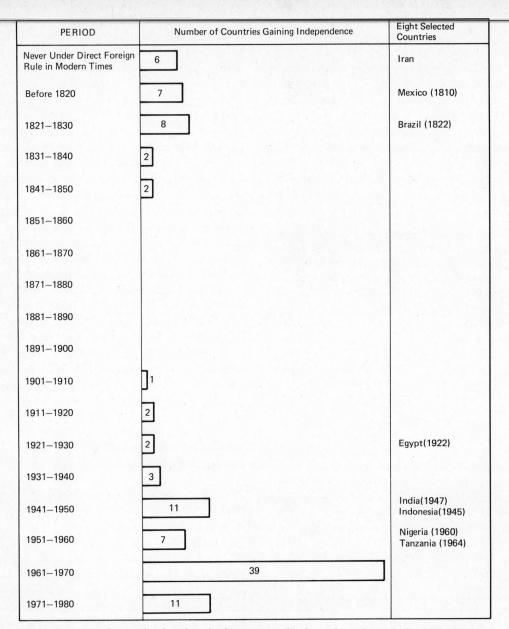

| PERIOD | Number of Countries Gaining Independence | Eight Selected Countries |
|---|---|---|
| Never Under Direct Foreign Rule in Modern Times | 6 | Iran |
| Before 1820 | 7 | Mexico (1810) |
| 1821—1830 | 8 | Brazil (1822) |
| 1831—1840 | 2 | |
| 1841—1850 | 2 | |
| 1851—1860 | | |
| 1861—1870 | | |
| 1871—1880 | | |
| 1881—1890 | | |
| 1891—1900 | | |
| 1901—1910 | 1 | |
| 1911—1920 | 2 | |
| 1921—1930 | 2 | Egypt (1922) |
| 1931—1940 | 3 | |
| 1941—1950 | 11 | India (1947) Indonesia (1945) |
| 1951—1960 | 7 | Nigeria (1960) Tanzania (1964) |
| 1961—1970 | 39 | |
| 1971—1980 | 11 | |

**Figure 1.1** Distribution by decades of achievement of independence by 101 Third World countries with specific years for eight selected countries. (George Thomas Kurian, *Encyclopedia of the Third World* (2 vols.) (New York: Facts on File, 1978).

The result was a swelling surge of anti-imperialist sentiment that rocked the European colonial powers and forced them to reconsider their imperial pretensions.

In 1945, the largest empire in the world was Great Britain. More than one fourth of the world's population, about 600 million people, were governed from London. By 1948, about two thirds of this total were living in independence. In these years, the nations of South Asia—India, Pakistan, and Ceylon (now Sri Lanka)—were created. Burma, Egypt, Iraq, and

Jordan also successfully asserted their independence. Following the partition of Palestine, Israel claimed its independence and, by the early 1950s, informed British opinion recognized the inevitability of the disintegration of its empire. In 1956 and 1957, the granting of independence to the Sudan, Malaya (Malaysia), and Ghana initiated the process of emancipation in large scale. Today, the British Empire consists of a few scattered islands in the Western Hemisphere (such as Bermuda) and a handful of strategic points that Great Britain refuses to yield (Gibraltar and Hong Kong are the most important). The second largest empire in 1945 was France and, although France fought much harder than Great Britain to retain its colonial holdings, the outcome was the same. In the mid-1940s, Syria and Lebanon were given their independence and, in 1954, after the disastrous French-Indochina War, Cambodia (now Kampuchea), Laos, and the two halves of Vietnam left the French sphere. In 1956, Tunisia and Morocco were freed after agitation and guerilla war. In 1958, after Charles de Gaulle's return to power, France's African holdings were reduced—first Guinea (1958) and later (1960) the remainder of her French Equatorial and West African possessions as well as Madagascar were liberated. Algeria was the possession that France was most reluctant to release, probably because of its proximity to the mother country and because of the many French citizens living in Algeria. But, by 1962, the violence and destruction of the Algerian war had so weakened French resolve that the nation's possessions there were terminated as well. As of the middle of the 1970s, French possessions include some scattered holdings in the Western Hemisphere (French Guiana, Guadeloupe, and Martinique) and some islands in the Pacific.

The same story applies to the smaller colonial systems still in existence in 1945. The Japanese Empire was divided among the victors of the war: the United States, the Soviet Union, and China. Korea was partitioned and granted its dual independence. Italy's overseas possessions—Ethiopia, Libya, and Somalia—were quickly freed. In 1946, the United States granted independence to the Philippines and statehood

was granted in 1959 to two other possessions—Alaska and Hawaii. Okinawa was returned to Japan in 1972. The Dutch lost Indonesia almost immediately after the war; and Belgium gradually loosened its hold on its African possessions—the Belgian Congo (now Zaire), Burundi, and Rwanda.

The Third World empires that lasted the longest were those that belonged to countries that lived under dictatorial rule at home, Spain and Portugal. However, even in these cases, inevitable changes in the mother country (the deaths of Francisco Franco and Antonio Salazar) have brought new governments to power; the result has been a rapid decolonization of the Spanish Sahara (now under control of Morocco) and of Portugal's possessions: Angola, Guinea, and Mozambique.

## CONCLUSIONS: ETHNONATIONALISM AND HUMAN DIGNITY

Formal, legal control of the Third World from Europe and North America seems to be definitely coming to a close.

However, this does not indicate a lessening of the tensions of ethnonationalism, the belief that people should be governed only by others of their same ethnic group.[15] When we consider that dozens of self-aware ethnic groups are compressed into the boundaries of about 150 distinct national entities, we see immediately the revolutionary potential of ethnic pride and self-defense.

In the Third World, the phenomenon of decolonization, with all its ramifications, has yet to run its course. Two special problems emerge. First, the trend toward ethnic self-consciousness in newly created nations has a momentum of its own, a momentum that has led to the fragmentation of several of the nations left behind by the former European colonial powers and to unsuccessful threats to the stability of several others. At the beginning of the decolonization period in Africa, secession attempts, such as those of Katanga (in the Congo) and Biafra (in Nigeria), failed; many other African states may feel that

[15]Walker Connor, "The Politics of Ethnonationalism," *Journal of International Affairs*, 27 (1) (1973), pp. 1–21.

Guerilla fighters of the Eritrean Liberation Front (ELF) raise their weapons in celebration of a victory in the struggle against the government of Ethiopia. The ELF is one of the many ethnic and regional separatist movements given impetus by the spread of decolonization around the world since World War II. Note that the fighters are holding both AK–47 rifles, manufactured in the Soviet Union, and American-made M–14s, thus, indicating their ability to receive aid from both of the superpowers.

they have successfully weathered the storm. In South Asia, on the other hand, Bangladesh (formerly East Pakistan) has successfully separated itself from Pakistan (itself a separation from India), and the potential in Southeast Asia for fragmentation continues to be severe. We should expect more such upheavals in the future as previously submerged peoples attempt to build a political order that is more rational and more responsive to ethnic feeling than that imposed by foreign rulers. We will return to this theme in Chapter Two.

The second residual problem is the continued struggle against economic and other forms of domination still exercised by the industrialized nations over Third World peoples. As we will discuss in greater detail in Chapter Two, the poor nations can be expected to take more and more forceful steps to redress the balance of resources and wealth distribution around the world. The abortive efforts of Chile's late President Salvador Allende to bring his nation's resources under Chilean control and the oil embargo of 1973 were only the opening shots in this new phase of the decolonization struggle.

Indeed, many of the policy decisions made by the governments of Third World countries can best be understood as part of the very long process of undoing what was done to them by the colonial experience. You may find it easier to understand politics in the Third World in the 1980s by remembering that these events and policies owe their origins to hundreds of years of foreign rule with all of its benefits and imperfections.

# Suggestions for Further Reading

**Black, Cyril E.**, *The Dynamics of Modernization* (New York: Harper & Row, 1966).

**Cohen, Benjamin J.**, *The Question of Imperialism: The Political Economy of Dominance and Dependence* (New York: Basic Books, 1973).

**Deutsch, Karl W.**, and **William J. Foltz**, eds., *Nation-Building* (New York: Atherton, 1963).

**Easton, Stewart C.**, *The Rise and Fall of Western Colonialism* (New York: Praeger, 1964).

**Emerson, Rupert**, *From Empire to Nation: The Rise to Self-Assertion of Asian and African Peoples* (Cambridge: Harvard University Press, 1960).

**Foster, George M.**, *Traditional Cultures, and the Impact of Technological Change* (New York: Harper & Bros., 1962).

**Furnivall, J. S.**, *Colonial Policy and Practice* (Cambridge: At the University Press, 1948).

**Furtado, Celso**, *Economic Development of Latin America: A Survey from Colonial Times to the Cuban Revolution* (Cambridge: At the University Press, 1970).

**Hodgkin, Thomas,** *Nationalism in Colonial Africa* (London: Muller, 1956).

**Hunter, Guy,** *Modernizing Peasant Societies: A Comparative Study in Asia and Africa* (New York: Oxford University Press, 1969).

**Kautsky, John H.,** *The Political Consequences of Modernization* (New York: Wiley, 1972).

**Mannoni, Dominique O.,** *Prospero and Caliban: The Psychology of Colonization,* trans. Pamela Powerland (New York: Praeger, 1956).

**Seton-Watson, Hugh,** *Nations and States: An Enquiry into the Origins of Nations and the Politics of Nationalism* (Boulder, Colo.: Westview, 1977).

**Wallerstein, Immanuel,** ed., *Social Change: The Colonial Situation* (New York: Wiley, 1966).

**Wolf, Eric R.,** *Peasants* (Englewood Cliffs, N.J.: Prentice-Hall, 1966).

# CHAPTER TWO
## Social and Economic Problems in the Third World

From the vantage point of the political leaders of the Third World, the question of how to enhance human dignity through public policies quickly focuses on one central issue: inequality. Third World leaders who desire to raise the level of human dignity of their citizens must face the fact that the desirable goods, services, and values of life are distributed in a grossly unequal way among the earth's inhabitants. Public policies aimed at enhancing human dignity must deal with this inequality and find ways to redistribute the world's wealth and power more nearly equitably, both across national boundaries and within their nations. If this could be accomplished, they believe, other indicators of human dignity would be improved accordingly.

Throughout this textbook, we will deal with the concept of the Third World and, at times, if we are not careful, it may appear as if all of the states of the Third World formed one homogeneous whole. For our purposes, the nations of the Third World are all of the independent nation-states of Central and South America and the Caribbean, the Middle East and North Africa, sub-Saharan Africa, and Asia and the Pacific. We exclude from our definition all the nations in these regions that have adopted clearly and unequivocally the development pattern of either the industrial Westernized democracies or

of the centrally directed authoritarian regimes inspired by Marxist-Leninist philosophy. Thus, we will eliminate not only the Communist Party states of the regions listed, such as North Korea, Vietnam, Cambodia (Kampuchea), Laos, and Cuba, but those that are clearly in the camp of the Western democracies: Israel and Japan. Some states are apparently inclined strongly in one direction or another; a similar listing made a decade from now might not even include them in the Third World at all. These states might include Marxist-oriented countries, such as Angola and Libya, as well as those firmly established as Western democracies, such as Mexico and Venezuela. It is still too early to locate these countries without question outside the Third World boundaries; so, we continue the customary practice of including them in the Third World region until the outlines of their political style become somewhat clearer. Organized and defined in this way, the Third World consists of 101 nations: 23 in Latin America, 18 in Asia and the Pacific, 19 in the Middle East and North Africa, and 41 in Africa south of the Sahara.

The Third World category is a residual category, made up of nations whose only common link is that they do not fit cleanly into either of the other two categories of nations. Third World nations are neither Western industrialized democracies nor authoritarian Marxist regimes. But exactly what are these nations? The Third World category contains a very wide variety of social, historical, economic, political, and ethnic dimensions; only some of them can be indicated here.[1] Take the question of size for example. In the Third World, we find huge states, such as Brazil (more than 3 million square miles—larger than the United States, excluding Alaska) and Argentina and India (more than 1 million square miles each). We also find some very tiny nations that are only small islands, like São Tomé, or cities that have separated themselves from their surrounding country, like Singapore. Third World states differ widely in population, too, all the way from mammoth India, whose 672 million people make her the second most populous nation in the world, down to some of the tiny oil-rich states in the Arabian peninsula, such as Qatar with a population of only about 180,000. The Third World has landlocked countries, like Bolivia, and long island chains, like Indonesia. There are nations that are rich agricultural areas, like the rice areas of Southeast Asia, and there are regions where the wealth is derived from the minerals drawn from beneath the ground, such as the oil areas of the Middle East. The Third World has nations that have been independent and active members of the international system for more than 150 years, like Argentina, and it has nations that have existed for barely a few months and are almost completely ignored by the rest of the international community, like Papua New Guinea, formerly a member of the British Commonwealth administered by Australia. And, as we will note shortly, the states of the Third World do not even share their condition of poverty; a few nations in the region possess some of the highest per capita incomes in the world.

Table 2.1 summarizes some of the more important demographic and economic indicators of the Third World—its four regions in general and eight of its countries in particular. Throughout this book, in the presentation of tabular data as well as in other kinds of illustrative examples, we will use these eight countries (Brazil, Egypt, India, Indonesia, Iran, Mexico, Nigeria, and Tanzania) to highlight certain key points about Third World politics. These eight countries, all significant members of the international community in their own right, were selected to represent the Third World only in a most general sense. It would be arbitrary to try to reduce the diversity of the Third World down to only eight examples. The countries are offered as "typical" developing states although, no doubt, others could have been chosen that would have portrayed somewhat different characteristics of the Third World.

## DIMENSIONS OF INEQUALITY

Consider carefully Tables 2.2 and 2.3. You will notice in Table 2.2 that the world's population in 1972 amounted to slightly more than 3.8 billion persons who lived in 130 separate and independent nations. The area we call the Third World contained 92 of these nations and slightly more than 1.8 billion persons, or about 48 percent of the world's population. We have divided the states not only into the First, Second, and Third Worlds but also according to their gross national product per capita (GNP per capita). Poor countries are those with GNP per capita ranging from $275 to $1425 per annum. Middle income states range from $1425 to $3500 annually; whereas rich states have GNP per capita levels from $3500 to more than $5000 per year. You will see that the Third World's nations are divided as follows: more than 1.8 billion people live in 90 low-income nations, whereas only 2 nations (Libya and Kuwait) with a total population of about 3 million are classified as middle-income or high-income states. The GNP per capita of the 90 poor nations is only $238 per year. Kuwait and Libya, with per capita GNP levels of $4222 and $1952 respectively are of course major oil-exporting countries. Thus, their high classification does not reflect self-sustaining economic and political development.

[1]A good source of factual information about all the world's political systems is Arthur S. Banks, ed., *Political Handbook of the World: 1980* (New York: McGraw-Hill, 1980). See also, George Thomas Kurian, *Encyclopedia of the Third World* (New York: Facts on File, 1978).

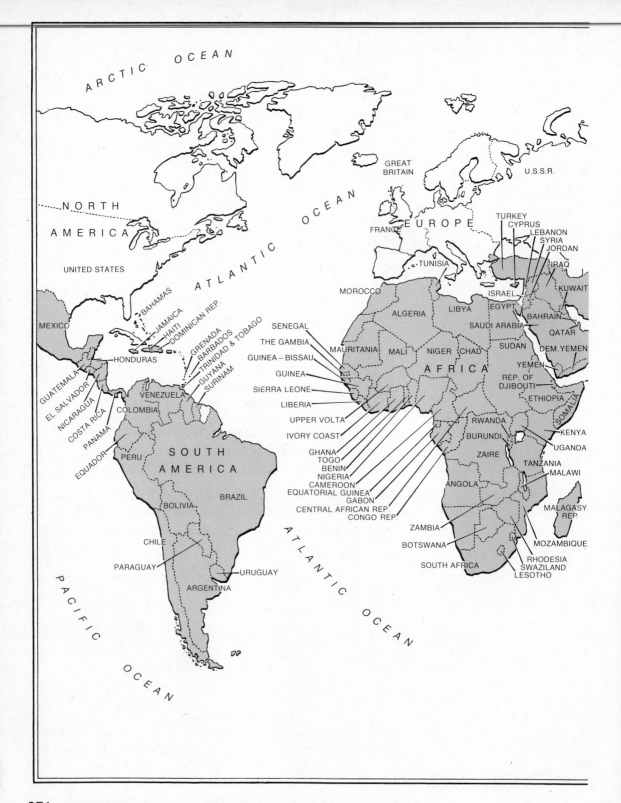

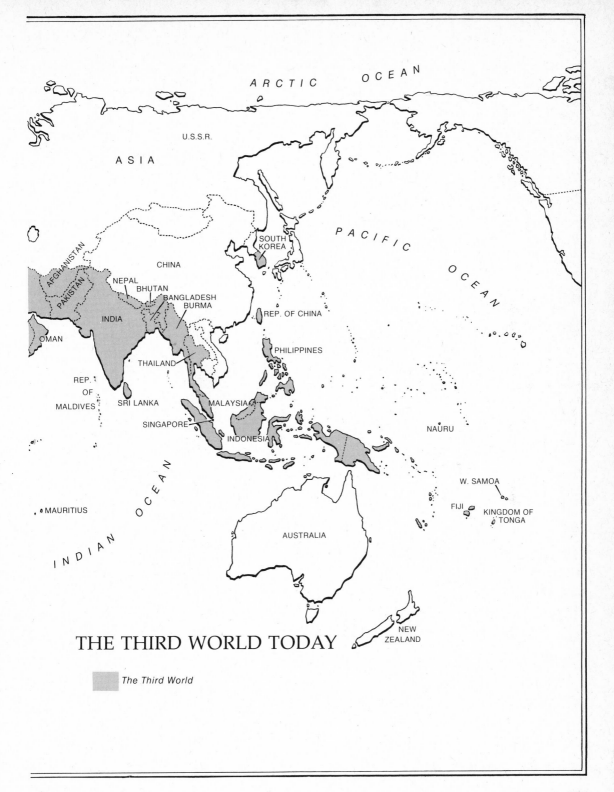

# THE THIRD WORLD TODAY

The Third World

**TABLE 2.1**  Profile of the Third World and Eight Selected Countries, 1976

| Region/Country | Area (Thousand Square km) | Population (Millions) | GNP[a] (Billions $U.S.) | GNP[a] per Capita ($U.S.) |
|---|---|---|---|---|
| Africa (41 countries) | 27,012 | 333.3 | 122.1 | 366 |
| Nigeria | 924 | 64.8 | 31.2 | 482 |
| Tanzania | 945 | 15.8 | 2.6 | 165 |
| Asia (18 countries) | 9,464 | 1,158.0 | 238.5 | 206 |
| India | 3,288 | 632.4 | 86.1 | 136 |
| Indonesia | 1,904 | 138.7 | 30.1 | 217 |
| Latin America (23 countries) | 20,292 | 318.8 | 354.2 | 1,111 |
| Brazil | 8,512 | 115.4 | 125.6 | 1,088 |
| Mexico | 1,972 | 61.6 | 82.6 | 1,341 |
| Middle East/North Africa (19 countries) | 11,914 | 199.3 | 267.6 | 1,343 |
| Egypt | 1,001 | 37.8 | 14.5 | 383 |
| Iran | 1,648 | 36.0 | 65.6 | 1,820 |
| Total Third World (101 countries) | 68,682 | 2,009.4 | 982.4 | 489 |

[a]GNP = gross national product.

SOURCE: Ruth Leger Sivard, *World Military and Social Expenditures, 1979* (Leesburg, Va.: World Priorities 1979), Table 3.

**TABLE 2.2**  Distribution of Gross National Product (GNP) Among Three Worlds, 1972

| GNP per Capita | First World | Second World | Third World | Total |
|---|---|---|---|---|
| Poor: (less than $1425) | 3 nations $62.3 billion GNP $1193 GNP per cap 52.2 million pop | 7 nations $168.7 billion GNP $180 GNP per cap 937.0 million pop | 90 nations $433.8 billion GNP $238 GNP per cap 1819.7 million pop | 100 nations $664.8 billion GNP $237 GNP per cap 2808.9 million pop |
| Middle: ($1425 to $3500) | 11 nations $703.8 billion GNP $2658 GNP per cap 264.8 million pop | 7 nations $801.6 billion GNP $2278 GNP per cap 351.9 million pop | 1 nation $4.1 billion GNP $1952 GNP per cap 2.1 million pop | 19 nations $1509.5 billion GNP $2439 GNP per cap 618.8 million pop |
| Rich: (more than $3500) | 10 nations $1875.8 billion GNP $4969 GNP per cap 377.5 million pop | | 1 nation $3.8 billion GNP $4222 GNP per cap 0.9 million pop | 11 nations $1879.6 billion GNP $4967 GNP per cap 378.4 million pop |
| Total | 24 nations $2641.9 billion GNP $3804 GNP per cap 694.5 million pop | 14 nations $970.3 billion GNP $753 GNP per cap 1288.9 million pop | 92 nations $441.7 billion GNP $242 GNP per cap 1822.7 million pop | 130 nations $4053.9 billion GNP $1065 GNP per cap 3806.1 million pop |

SOURCE: Ruth Leger Sivard, *World Military and Social Expenditures, 1974* (New York: Institute for World Order, 1974); GNP per capita rating system from K. K. S. Dadzie, "Economic Development," *Scientific American*, 243 (3) (1980), pp. 60–61.

**TABLE 2.3** Distribution of Gross National Product (GNP) Among Three Worlds, 1977

| GNP per Capita | First World | Second World | Third World | Total |
|---|---|---|---|---|
| Poor: (less than $1425) | | 7 nations $403.1 billion GNP $376 GNP per cap 1071.9 million pop | 77 nations $681.6 billion GNP $373 GNP per cap 1827.2 million pop | 84 nations $1084.7 billion GNP $374 GNP per cap 2899.1 million pop |
| Middle: ($1425 to $3500) | 5 nations $359.4 billion GNP $3122 GNP per cap 115.1 million pop | 6 nations $1139.3 billion GNP $3197 GNP per cap 356.4 million pop | 12 nations $365.8 billion GNP $1716 GNP per cap 213.2 million pop | 23 nations $1864.5 billion GNP $2723 GNP per cap 684.7 million pop |
| Rich: (more than $3500) | 19 nations $4598.5 billion GNP $7596 GNP per cap 605.4 million pop | 2 nations $149.0 billion GNP $4686 GNP per cap 31.8 million pop | 6 nations $102.8 billion GNP $8094 GNP per cap 12.7 million pop | 27 nations $4850.3 billion GNP $7463 GNP per cap 649.9 million pop |
| Total | 24 nations $4957.9 billion GNP $6881 GNP per cap 720.5 million pop | 15 nations $1691.4 billion GNP $1158 GNP per cap 1460.1 million pop | 95 nations $1150.2 billion GNP $560 GNP per cap 2053.1 million pop | 134 nations $7799.5 billion GNP $1842 GNP per cap 4233.7 million pop |

SOURCE: Ruth Leger Sivard, *World Military and Social Expenditures, 1980* (Leesburg, Va.: World Priorities, 1980); GNP per capita rating system from K. K. S. Dadzie, "Economic Development," *Scientific American, 243*, (3) (1980), pp. 60–61.

Turning to Table 2.3, we see that the global inequities of wealth have not really been affected much by the worldwide energy crisis and resulting economic depression of the mid-1970s. By 1977, the 4.2 billion people in the world were divided into 134 nations, of which 95 were located in the Third World. The Third World's population of slightly more than 2 billion is still about 48 percent of the total. Of the total Third World population, 89 percent still live in poor countries, whereas the other 11 percent live in 18 countries, most of which are either oil-exporting states or the source of other highly valued minerals—these include Bahrain, Gabon, Iran, Kuwait, Libya, Oman, Qatar, Saudi Arabia, United Arab Emirates, and Venezuela.

It is true, of course, that the number of Third World states with relatively high incomes has increased noticeably with the shift in oil prices after 1973. However, this increase in well-being has not been shared to any marked degree with other Third World states, whose status continues to decline relative to the industrialized countries. From 1972 to 1977, GNP per capita of the poorest Third World states grew from $238 to $373, whereas that of all Third World states grew from $242 to $560. However, in the same period, the richest group of First World states saw an increase in GNP per capita from $4969 to $7596, an increase of well over 10 percent per year during the period.

This, then, is the economic dilemma confronting the Third World today. The industrialized West, beginning from a much higher economic base, continues to register large gains, whereas the still-poor Third World can look forward to only the most modest of increases for the remainder of this century. For all but a few oil-rich states, it certainly seems to be the case that, "The rich get richer and the poor get poorer."

Comparisons of economic growth of developed and less developed countries by means of GNP per capita figures are apt to be somewhat superficial for several reasons. First, a considerable portion of the population of the Third World lives and works outside the money economy so that their economic transactions will be less likely to appear on the balance sheets of national-accounts statistics prepared in the capital city. Second, we should not lose sight of the importance of inflation, a force that has accounted for so much of the change in GNP figures during the last half of the 1970s and that probably caused the income figures of the industrialized countries to rise faster than those of the less developed world. Finally, the Third World could actually be registering faster growth of GNP per capita in percentage terms than the industrialized countries and still be dropping behind in absolute terms because of the relatively larger initial base of the developed economies.

Behind these dry statistics, however, are real human beings, most of whom live in constant anxiety about the stability of their jobs and incomes. A recent worldwide Gallup Poll found, for example, that two thirds of all respondents in Latin America, Africa, and Asia say that they worry "all" or "most of the time" about meeting family expenses. Half of them report insufficient money to provide their families with food, and an even higher percentage say there are times when they cannot afford to buy their families clothes. About half are unable to pay for the simplest medical care. As a consequence of such material poverty, only 28 percent of Latin Americans, 8 percent of Africans, and 6 percent of Indians interviewed considered themselves fully satisfied with their lives.[2]

Economic inequality is the easiest kind to document, but the unequal distribution of wealth around the world is felt by human beings in ways that directly affect their health and well-being. In developed countries, life expectancy is about 72 years, whereas it is only about 57 years in the less developed world, 49 years in Africa, and 51 years in southern Asia. More than 90 percent of the population of the developed countries have access to safe drinking water, whereas in the less

[2]George H. Gallup, "What Mankind Thinks About Itself," Reader's Digest (October 1976), pp. 132–136. For a good discussion of poverty in the Third World from the vantage point of specific country case studies, see Charles Elliott, Patterns of Poverty in the Third World (New York: Praeger, 1975).

developed world, the figure is less than 40 percent. The countries of the developed world spend more than $200 annually per capita on health services; in the developing world, the figure is only $7. In 52 Third World countries, more than 15 percent of the population were undernourished by the standards of the United Nations Food and Agricultural Organization, a standard that specifies only 1600 calories per day, whereas the typical diet of the developed world averages about 3100 calories per day. In 1975, the average rate of energy consumption was about 2 kilowatts per person per year; in the United States, each citizen consumed about 11 kilowatts that year; in the Third World, the average was less than 1 kilowatt per year.

Any textbook discussion of the quality of life in the Third World must somehow attempt to communicate to American university students what it means to live, to work, and to die in the grinding poverty and dismal surroundings of poor countries. In both the huge cities and the small rural villages, from Asia to Latin America, what makes life in the Third World distinct for most of its poor is the sense of absolute despair and dreariness that is cast over their lives.

Consider, on the one hand, the life of a 29-year-old pedicab driver in one of Indonesia's larger cities, Jogjakarta. His name is Sarjono, and he pedals his cab more than 20 miles a day for daily earnings of about $3.20. One quarter of his earnings must go to rent his pedicab; the remainder is spent on food for the day (rice, less than a pound of fish, a few vegetables). Milk, eggs, fruit, meat, even clothes for his two children, are luxuries. He pays $45 a year to rent a dark, dirt-floored room on one side of a bamboo-walled hut owned by a second family that occupies the main part of the house. All four members of the family sleep in the same room, which also serves as the kitchen, living room, and dining area. For a toilet, Sarjono's family and neighbors all share a hole in the ground shielded by a partition from the rest of the shacks in the neighborhood. Sarjono is typical of literally tens of thousands of young Indonesian men and women whose desperation has driven them to this kind of minimal existence, an existence that frequently leads to a life of crime, prostitution, and drugs.[3]

If life in big cities is bad, rural villages in the Third World can seem even worse. Not much has changed in rural Latin America since the following description was written of Los Toldos, Argentina, the birthplace of María Eva Duarte, the famous wife of Argentine dictator Juan Perón:

No one who has not seen such a pueblo can imagine the dreariness of it. It lies like a worm cast on the platter of the plains, its squalid little buildings crumbling back into the dust from which they have been built. Dust lies everywhere, a foot thick on the unpaved road where a passing troop of cattle raises a white cloud that for a while stagnates in the hot air and then settles slowly on the earth again. Dust seeps into the small houses whose pink and yellow plastering has faded to the dun of dust; the grit of it settles on the food and on the clothes and on the skin and teeth and in the very heart of man. Dust and silence everywhere, a deathly stillness broken only by the mongrel dog crossing the road to scratch itself or an iron windmill that clanks as it turns which way to the wind. Flies buzz above offal cast out in a yard and men's voices are raised in momentary anger, or a woman scolds at a whining child.[4]

Such descriptions help us understand the true meaning, the human meaning, of inequality in the Third World.

## THE CAUSES OF INEQUALITY: SOME POPULAR THEORIES

Because global economic inequality is such an obstacle to human dignity in the Third World, it has received a great deal of attention from political leaders and scholars who have attempted to find the causes of the problem and, thereby, to discover a solution to it as well.

Many different theories have been proposed to explain the causes of poverty in the Third World. Some theories place the causes outside

[3]Paul Zach, " 'Low Quality' Job Earns Indonesian Pedicab Driver $3.20 a Day," *Washington Post*, October 10, 1980.
[4]Maria Flores, *The Woman with the Whip: Eva Peron* (New York: Doubleday, 1952), p. 15.

the Third World, for example, in the nature of the international system. Other theories locate the cause of poverty within the national political systems of Third World countries. If the theory focuses primarily on the world outside of the Third World nations, it may emphasize either the intentional thwarting of legitimate Third World desires by profit-hungry capitalism in league with imperialistic Great Powers or it may concentrate on the impersonal, relatively automatic workings of an international system composed of industrial and raw-material-exporting countries. If the theory deals with conditions inside the nations of the Third World, then, it may deal with some of these themes: resource deficiencies; rigidities in social structures (with special emphasis on the population explosion, on education, or on urbanization); ethnic, linguistic, or racial characteristics; psychological factors; or political structures and processes. Because this textbook is about politics, Chapters Four, Five, and Six examine these latter factors and take up in detail assertions that Third World nations generally lack the kind of political order necessary to bring about badly needed socioeconomic reforms. In Chapter Three, we will discuss the political culture and socialization processes of Third World countries in general, and we will examine the psychological factors included in the preceding list. In this chapter, we summarize the remaining theories concerning the causes of poverty in the Third World.

## INTERNATIONAL SOURCES OF THIRD WORLD POVERTY

One of the most prominent theories used to explain the poverty of backward peoples has been the one that states that the rich nations exploit and suppress the poor nations. The motivation of the wealthy nations varies. In some theories, the villains are big corporations that manipulate politics behind the scenes in the wealthy countries. These corporations employ the great power of nations not only to secure markets for their products but also to exploit the poor nations as sources for needed raw materials. In other theories, the true mischief makers are not business

leaders but the government élites who establish Great Power influence throughout the poorer nations so that they can play the game of international power politics on the territory of states that cannot defend themselves from being used in this manner.

The best known of the economic theories are those associated with Karl Marx and Vladimir Ilyich Lenin. Their work has been interpreted and updated in our times by three prominent American economists, Paul Baran, Paul Sweezy, and Harry Magdoff.[5]

The imperialistic imperative of modern capitalist society, say these writers, derives from the inevitable tendency of monopoly capitalism to generate insufficient demand at home to absorb its surplus production. Lenin wrote of this as a problem of underconsumption that stemmed from the growing discrepancy between what workers produce (increasing worker productivity) and what they are allowed to consume (decreasing share of output to workers in the form of wages). Critics of traditional Leninist theorizing respond to this assertion by pointing to the vigor of the trade union movement in the industrialized countries and the consequent capacity of the workers to gain an increasing share of what they produce. In an effort to modernize Lenin's theory and bring it into line with twentieth-century, politicoeconomic realities in the capitalist states, Baran and Sweezy have altered conventional Marxist-Leninist theory to stress the tendency toward excess surplus that derives from the expansion or growth imperative of monopoly capitalism. That is, modern business philosophy in capitalist society condemns to extinction any firm or corporation that does not try to maximize its share of the market and, thereby, grow in the process. Hence, there develops the trend toward mergers and oligopolies within the industrialized states and the counterpart trend toward the spread of multinational firms abroad. Despite the growing proportion of industrial output diverted into the

[5]Paul Baran and Paul Sweezy, *Monopoly Capital* (New York: Monthly Review Press, 1966); Harry Magdoff, *The Age of Imperialism* (New York: Monthly Review Press, 1969).

hands of labor, profits (the equivalent of surplus in the Baran-Sweezy formulation) rise even faster and the investing class (the capitalist entrepreneurs) are at a loss to find ways to dispose of, or to absorb, these profits. The answer, say the Marxists, lies in the poorly developed markets of the Third World.

According to this reasoning, the capitalist monopolies and multinational firms of the industrial economies have spread abroad in an effort to use the purchasing power of the Third World consumers to drain off, or absorb, the excess production of the industrialized West. To do this, the multinational firms must maintain significant control over the economic and political fortunes and directions of the weak states of the Third World. The overseas outlets of the Western firms must be permitted to bring their products into the developing countries free of import restrictions, such as duties and licenses. Local Third World firms that might compete with Western products are to be discouraged from operating and should be denied the working capital they need to become established. The consumption tastes of Third World consumers must be manipulated through Western-dominated mass media, particularly motion pictures, radio, and television, to induce them to purchase exotic items from the United States and Western Europe, even if they cost more. Labor unions in Third World states are discouraged from putting undue pressure on the local factories and manufacturing installations of the Western firms so that the multinationals can take advantage of cheap labor costs abroad. Finally, the governments of the host nations in the Third World must not regulate the Western-based firms, tax their local profits, or otherwise interfere in their operations. To achieve such a docile operating environment abroad, it is argued, large Western corporations have cooperated with, and used, the governments of the Western powers, particularly that of the United States, to suppress local reform movements in Third World states that appeared to stand a chance of altering the privileged status of the foreign corporations. Proponents of the Marxist-Leninist theory of imperialism would use this argument to explain Western intervention against a number of radical Third World leaders, including Salvador Allende in Chile (1973), Jacobo Arbenz in Guatemala (1954), Mohammad Mossadegh in Iran (1953), Fidel Castro in Cuba (1961), and Gamal Abdel Nasser in Egypt (1958).

Although the Marxist-Leninist theory of imperialism has received a great deal of attention and support from Western intellectuals and Third World political leaders, its principal flaw lies in its assertion that all of the above things will inevitably happen, regardless of what Western leaders desire, simply because of the inherent flaws in the capitalist system. Benjamin J. Cohen in *The Question of Imperialism*,[6] has called into question not the possibility of such outcomes, but the inevitability of them. Is it not possible, asks Cohen, to find other ways of accounting for the dominant-dependent relationship between the powerful and the weak states in international relations? First, Cohen argues, monopoly capitalism does not necessarily lead to the production of an unabsorbable excess surplus (profit). Even in pluralist democracies in the larger Western states, labor unions have represented the working class sufficiently well so that profits as a percent of GNP have actually been gradually declining since the 1930s. Even if we admit the tendency toward the generation of excess profits, Cohen says, there are other ways in which these profits can be absorbed besides exploiting the Third World consumers. For one thing, businesses in the capitalist system may be induced to lower prices to increase consumption, especially if their sector of the economy is reasonably competitive, as many are. Second, the government can intervene in the economy to drain off these profits through transfer payments to the poor and middle-income citizens, thereby redistributing income and increasing consumption at home. Finally, the government may come to the rescue of the capitalists by absorbing these profits itself, primarily through expenditures on military equipment. Thus, says Cohen, imperial exploitation of the Third World markets is only

[6]Benjamin J. Cohen, *The Question of Imperialism: The Political Economy of Dominance and Dependence* (New York: Basic Books, 1973).

one possible outcome of monopoly capitalism; there are others, depending on the shape of domestic politics in the First World.

This variation on the Marxist-Leninist theme leads us to still another explanation of Third World poverty and weakness, one derived not from the economic imperatives of monopoly capitalism but from the military imperatives of the game of Great Power politics.[7] According to this version of imperialism, Third World nations are kept in a state of weakness, poverty, and dependence by the Western powers because of the way in which Great Power struggles are carried out. As a result of nearly 100 years of bloody struggle in Europe, the major world powers have learned an important lesson: when possible, Great Power confrontation should be carried out on the soil of an intermediate state, one that cannot prevent its own territory from being used as a battleground for foreign struggles. If anything, the shift to nuclear weapons and the exponential growth in the lethality of Great Power arsenals have reinforced this belief. In the late nineteenth and early twentieth centuries, Great Powers confronted one another directly and worked out the prevailing rules of the game of international politics through a direct-testing process. Today, the rules of the game emerge from a testing process carried out between proxies of the Great Powers on the soil of poor, weak states that have no stake in the larger struggle but whose leaders cannot defend their territory from these external interventions.

A brief review of the major confrontations of the Cold War reveals a recurring pattern. Korea, Vietnam, the Philippines, Malaya, the Middle East, Lebanon, the Suez Canal, the Congo, Nigeria, Angola, Rhodesia, Chile, Cuba, Guatemala, and the Dominican Republic have three things in common. They are (or were) Third World countries or regions with little if any stake in the global struggle between the capitalist and Marxist versions of historical destiny. Next, they are usually in the "seams" between the shifting monolithic worlds dominated by Washington and Moscow. Finally, they constitute what geopoliticians call shatter zones, regions that are unable to govern their own political directions and to control their own internal political processes. These shatter zones are usually prone to internal disturbances and violence, as first one force and then another struggles for, and gains, power. This disorder frequently offers the excuse for the Great Powers to intervene to restore order if only to forestall counterintervention by the adversary. The tendency of expanding economies to produce economic surplus, which is siphoned off into military expenditures, completes the theoretical circle by leading to the creation of large, standing military establishments, which, then, look for ways to be used.

Still another way of looking at the problem of global inequalities of wealth and power states that the poverty and dependence of the Third World stem not from any intentional policy decisions made in Washington, London, or Moscow but, instead, simply from the impersonal and automatic workings of an international system that is so constructed that raw-material-exporting nations are condemned to lose their share of the benefits of production. This theory is usually called the Prebisch thesis after its first exponent, Argentine economist Raul Prebisch. As Secretary General of the United Nations Economic Commission for Latin America (UNECLA), Prebisch wrote the seminal essay in this field in 1949, *The Economic Development of Latin America and Its Principal Problems.*[8] Although originally intended as an explanation of the causes of underdevelopment in Latin America, the Prebisch thesis has now been adopted by many radical but non-Marxist regimes throughout the Third World as the best way to explain their economic relations with the industrialized world.

For many years (centuries, in fact), classical economists have followed the *laissez-faire* position first articulated by Adam Smith in 1776, that the economic interests of all nations were best served under a system of free trade and

[7]Melvin Gurtov, *The United States Against the Third World* (New York: Praeger, 1974).

[8]United Nations Economic Commission for Latin America, *The Economic Development of Latin America and Its Principal Problems*, (Lake Success, N.Y.: UN Department of Economic Affairs, 1950).

economic specialization wherein each trading party performed the economic functions for which it enjoyed a relative (not an absolute) advantage. Smith and others of the free-trade school were able to demonstrate that each trading partner benefited most from such specialization because the sum total of the economic pie grew most rapidly under such a system. Even though some states obviously benefited more than others, economic specialization and free trade made all partners better off than they would be under any other kind of arrangement because they provided for the most rational allocation of resources throughout the system. In other words, states that manufactured things best exported manufactured items; states that possessed rich deposits of raw materials should export those. Governments should refrain from intervening in the process through such devices as tariffs, subsidies, and taxes; intervention would distort the natural workings of the system. This system has been called the "doctrine of harmony of interests" by the British historian, Edward H. Carr, because it asserts that all economic interests, worldwide, are in natural harmony, and that government interference can only make things worse.[9] Adam Smith referred to the system as the "invisible hand," meaning that the sum total of all individual private economic decisions was equivalent to raising the general welfare for all the parties to the system.

Prebisch's theory departs significantly from the classical *laissez-faire* approach. According to Prebisch, the free-trade system works against the interests of the nations that export raw materials (the periphery nations) and in favor of the interests of the industrialized, wealthy nations that export manufactured goods (the center nations). The reason for this stems not from any evil intent on the part of the center countries but from the very structure of the international economic system.

The prevailing distribution of economic functions around the globe allocates the benefits of economic interchange in an unequal fashion,

with the industrialized countries retaining more than their fair share of the benefits of trade. The center is able to retain a greater than fair share because of the impact of technology and social structure on economic productivity. In the center countries, their relatively greater access to manufacturing technology means that worker productivity can be linked to labor-saving devices instead of to increased employment. In addition, the organization of the workers into powerful unions means that the fruits of this increase in productivity are passed back to the workers in the form of increased wages; this leads, in turn, to increased savings, investment, and government revenues. Increases in productivity in the periphery, on the other hand, are lost through unnecessary consumption or through remittances back to the industrialized countries. We have already seen in other contexts some of the reasons for the inability of Third World countries to retain the benefits of increased productivity: the low state of development of labor unions means that the workers have little leverage to apply against the foreign companies; the few manufacturing installations that do exist are not tightly linked to the host economy (the enclave theory) so that there is little spillover into the local technological environment; and, finally, the host government is too weak to extract from the enclave industry any resources to devote to domestic development.

In addition to the problem of retention of the fruits of improved productivity, the raw-material-exporting countries also are hurt by the prevailing price structure in the international economy. Prices for manufactured goods are relatively rigid, both at home and abroad, because of the strength of labor unions in the center nations and because of the powerful position of multinational corporations and their ability to administer price levels or to control overall price structures for their products. The prices of raw materials and agricultural products, on the other hand, are very elastic and fluctuate wildly, creating alternate years of bonanza and depression. Thus, raw-material-exporting nations cannot plan adequately for the future without knowing more definitely the levels of financial resources

[9]Edward H. Carr, *The Twenty Years' Crisis, 1919–1939*, 2nd ed. (New York: St. Martin's, 1958).

on which they will be able to draw. Finally, the link between income levels and demand also works against the prices of raw materials. In general, as one's income rises, the percentage of income devoted to manufactured products rises at a faster rate than does the percent of income devoted to the purchase of raw materials and food. Because incomes are rising in both the center and the periphery countries, the demand for manufactured goods must rise more than the demand for unprocessed raw materials. In both instances, the outcome works against the countries that export raw materials.

There are other important aspects of Prebisch's theory that help to explain the causes of Third World poverty. Investment capital, for example, helps to perpetuate industrial control over the factors of production in the periphery nations by insuring that all local production installations are geared to the export trade. Local savings and, therefore, local investment remain small because of the workers' inability to raise their share of the surplus and because of the government's inability to tax the sectors where the excess is located: foreign businesses and local traditional economic groups, such as landowners and traders. Inflation is a persistent structural problem, not because of an excess of demand but because of the rigidities of supply: rigidities in agricultural production and transportation infrastructure; inadequacies in labor; and persistent pressure on the balance of payments because of the unpredictable changes in raw-material prices on the world market.

Prebisch, unlike the Marxists, finds the solution to the problem of Third World poverty not only in the international system but also at home. Internationally, Prebisch has recommended that the center countries give special treatment to the raw-material exports of the Third World and devote increased financial resources to aid Third World governments that are trying to reform their domestic economies but lack the funds to do so. But, asserts Prebisch, Third World governments must assume a major burden in reforming their internal economic structures to make them more responsive to demand pressures, to retain a greater share of the earnings of production within the country, to increase the taxation of possible sources of revenue to increase government income and, perhaps most important, to build up domestic industry to the point where the nation consumes its own locally produced manufactured products no matter what the cost. Only through such import substitution, claims Prebisch, can the Third World emerge from its peripheral status in the foreseeable future.[10]

An important variation of the Prebisch thesis, which has appeared in recent years, is called dependency theory. It is an approach that seeks to link Third World nationalism with Marxism to explain underdevelopment. Dependency theory goes beyond Prebisch to assert that the way the system works against poor countries on the international periphery is both global—in the sense that it affects all Third World countries wherever and however they launch their development effort—and intentional—in the sense that certain economic classes deliberately keep developing countries poor to advance their own fortunes. Based on many of the same ideas we have already discussed in connection with Marxist-Leninist theory and the ideas of Raul Prebisch, dependency theory holds that underdevelopment is the result of a dominant international capitalist system (embodied in multinational corporations) in league with local Third World élites who use their special advantages to maintain their privileged positions. Although the Third World cannot industrialize and develop economically so long as it is caught in the grip of a discriminatory international system, local élites cannot disengage from this system because to do so would imperil their own standing in their countries.

Many aspects of dependency theory will appear throughout this book, and many of its writers will be cited. If the theory has significant flaws, however, they lie in its attempt to explain complex social processes, like development or underdevelopment, by recourse to single factors.

[10]James D. Cockcroft *et al.*, eds., *Dependence and Underdevelopment: Latin America's Political Economy* (Garden City, N.Y.: Doubleday, 1972).

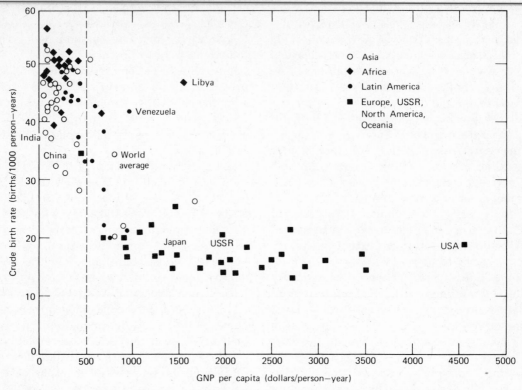

**Figure 2.1**   Crude Birth Rates versus GNP per Capita, 1971. (*Source*: Donella H. Meadows et. al., *The Limits to Growth*, New York: Universe, 1972, p. 112.)

Certainly, there are a number of important factors internal to Third World countries and specific to any one of them that will help us to a better understanding of underdevelopment. We discuss these factors at the appropriate point in the book. For now, however, let us pass to a brief examination of national sources of Third World poverty.[11]

[11]Many of the key writings in dependency theory have been collected in Michael Smith, Richard Little, and Michael Shackleton, eds., *Perspectives on World Politics* (London: The Open University, 1981), pp. 273–386. For additional readings, see Guy F. Erb and Valeriana Kallab, eds., *Beyond Dependency: The Developing World Speaks Out* (Washington: Overseas Development Council, 1975). For an excellent critique of dependency theory, see Tony Smith, "The Underdevelopment of Development Literature: The Case of Dependency Theory," *World Politics*, 31, (2) (1979), pp. 247–288.

## NATIONAL SOURCES OF THIRD WORLD POVERTY

**Population.**   Before 1700, world population grew very slowly, probably at the average rate of about 0.2 percent per year. As far as demographers can tell, the population of the world in 1750 was about 0.5 billion. World population began to grow more rapidly at about the time of the Industrial Revolution and, although it has declined in certain areas and during certain historical periods, the overall pattern has been one of exponential growth rates. By 1850, world population stood at about 1.3 billion; by 1900, it was 1.6 billion; by 1970, it was 3.6 billion; and, in the middle of the 1970s, world population exceeded 4 billion. Demographers now estimate that the world's population will continue to grow, although at a declining rate of increase,

This traffic jam in central Bombay, India, illustrates the effect of the uneven spread of industrialization to the large cities of the Third World. Rapid population growth and the increasing availability of automobiles even in poor countries have combined to overwhelm the road network of major cities, such as Bombay.

until sometime near the end of the next century when a stable population will be achieved at somewhere between 8 and 15 billion persons.[12]

The social phenomenon that we call the population explosion is caused by the demographic transition that occurs in countries that are experiencing modernization. During the first stage of the demographic transition—characteristic of traditional countries with a low standard of living—population levels are kept low and stable through a combination of high birth and high death rates. In traditional countries, the birth rate tends to be about 40 to 50 per 1000, the death rate is about 30 to 40 per 1000; the resultant population growth rate is about 1 percent annually, meaning that the population will double in about 70 years. As a country begins to make the transition from traditional to modern status,

however, it reaches stage two, in which advanced technology and increasing standards of living have a differential impact on birth and death rates. The introduction of advanced medical and hygiene technologies from the wealthy nations as well as an improved diet combine to reduce the death rate (particularly among infants) to perhaps 20 to 30 per 1000, but birth rates remain at their traditional level (because of the resistance of customs and mores concerning desired family size). Therefore, population grows at the rate of 2 to 3 percent per year. Under these conditions, population will double every 25 to 35 years. The third stage of the demographic transition appears in countries that are more or less completely modernized and industrialized. While death rates remain at about 20 to 30 per 1000, birth rates also drop to about the same level. Eventually, if this happens for enough years in succession (about two generations are required), population levels off.

[12]Tomas Frejka, "The Prospects for a Stationary World Population," *Scientific American, 228* (3) (1973), pp. 15–23.

**TABLE 2.4** Population Data from Eight Selected Third World Countries

| Country | Estimated Population 1978 (Millions) | Annual Population Growth Rate (1970–1975) | Estimated Population in Year 2000 (Millions) | Year When Stationary Population Will Be Reached |
|---|---|---|---|---|
| Nigeria | 67.5 | 2.7 | 154 | 2155 |
| Tanzania | 16.3 | 2.9 | 32 | 2160 |
| India | 649.4 | 2.1 | 958 | 2150 |
| Indonesia | 139.1 | 2.6 | 198 | 2165 |
| Mexico | 65.5 | 3.5 | 126 | 2075 |
| Brazil | 113.9 | 3.0 | 205 | 2070 |
| Egypt | 39.4 | 2.2 | 59 | 2100 |
| Iran | 34.8 | 2.9 | 60 | 2100 |

SOURCE: George Thomas Kurian, *The Book of World Rankings* (New York: *Facts On File,* 1979), Tables 8, 9, and 10; pp. 12–16.

Most Third World countries are in the second stage of demographic transition. Developed countries experienced population growth rates of less than 1 percent during the 1970s, but the underdeveloped countries showed rates ranging much higher, usually between 2.25 and 2.5 percent annually. The overall rate in Latin America was, and continues to be, the highest regional rate in the world: 2.9 percent. Taiwan's rate was about 3 percent during the early 1960s but it has dropped in recent years to nearer to 2 percent. In Thailand, the rate has exceeded 3 percent consistently since 1946. In Sri Lanka, the rate during the 1960s was about 2.5 percent, but it, too, has been dropping. (Also see Table 2.4.) At the beginning of the 1970s, the world's population was divided roughly 30:70 between the developed and less developed countries (both Communist and Third World). By 2000, if current rates of population growth hold steady, the ratio will change to 20:80. Asia will contain 40 percent of the world's population and Latin America and Africa 10 to 12 percent. Europe, on the other hand, will decline to 6 percent of the total, the Soviet Union to 4 percent, and North America to 4.5 percent.

High rates of population growth affect Third World poverty levels in several important ways. The addition of so many new people to the population absorbs much of the new productivity that the developing states manage to squeeze out of an inadequate industrial base, an inadequate agricultural sector, and an inadequate social infrastructure (schools, hospitals, housing, etc.). Although the rates of population growth seem small, the bulk totals of new population every year are staggering. At present rates of growth, 75 million new persons are added to the world's population every year. To feed the yearly increment requires nearly 20 million tons of additional grain each year, more than the entire Canadian wheat crop. The resources of Sri Lanka are presently inadequate to support its 13 million people, yet, in 80 years, by a conservative estimate, its population will exceed 30 million. To cope with its population increase, Egypt must build and equip a city the size of Washington, D.C., each year. India must build 10 such cities per year.

Population growth in developing countries occurs in a way that burdens economically productive sectors with new persons who are not immediately productive. Age distribution in a rapidly growing population shifts downward because the young segments of the population grow more rapidly than do the older ones. Thus, the proportion of the working-age population steadily declines. In the whole of Africa in 1965, the working-age population (ages 15 to 65) amounted to only 54 percent of the total population; in some countries, such as Algeria, Niger, and Chad, the percentage was even lower. Because not all working-age persons are actually economically productive, the proportion of the labor force to the total population in Africa declined to about 40 percent in 1970, and it is expected to drop even lower through the decade.

The other way in which rapid population growth increases the burden on the economically productive sectors is through the phenomenon of rapid urbanization. In every region of the Third World, cities are growing more rapidly than the general population. In Africa as a whole, from 1965 to 1970, the urban population grew at an annual rate of more than 6 percent, about twice the rate of population growth in general. At that rate, urban areas in Africa will double in size in less than 12 years. In Latin America, the same is true. From 1960 to 1970, Rio de Janeiro, Brazil, grew at the annual rate of 4.1 percent; Santiago, Chile, 4.1 percent; Mexico City, 4.5 percent; Lima, Peru, 5.8 percent; and Caracas, Venezuela, 4.7 percent. The sudden and dramatic rise in urban populations is presenting the Third World's countries with insurmountable problems in housing, food, medical care, sanitation, transportation, and public security.[13]

A third impact comes from the relationship between lowered birth rates and per capita income and between these two factors and resource consumption. Although demographers are not certain about this, it appears that out of all the possible factors that could cause birth rates to decline, the only factor that is predictable consistently is per capita income. That is, as a nation's per capita income rises, desired family size declines, probably because the cost-benefit balance of each additional child tends to discourage having large families. Figure 2.1 portrays this relationship. Therefore, although government programs encouraging birth control (as in Sri Lanka) or encouraging male sterilization (as in India) may have some local impact, in the long run and in general, the world's population will stabilize only when and if per capita wealth increases beyond subsistence levels.

The principal drawback to this solution lies in the third variable, resource consumption. As an individual's income increases, his or her burden on the earth's resources and on pollution-absorption capacity also increase. Of the total increase in energy consumption in the United States from 1947 to 1973, nearly 60 percent was due to increased affluence; only 40 percent was due to increased population. Thus, each wealthy person places a burden on the earth's resources about five times as great as his or her poor counterpart. Figure 2.2 illustrates this phenomenon on a worldwide basis.

From the vantage point of the Third World, the implications of these findings should be sobering. If birth rates can be reduced only by means of increasing per capita wealth, but if increased affluence spells a greater burden on already scarce resources, then the prospects for economic progress by the world's poor nations appear dim indeed.[14]

Recent press reports suggest that population growth continues to present major policy problems for Third World countries although there are signs that in a few nations the skyrocketing rates of the 1970s are beginning to abate somewhat. India's most recent census figures, released in March 1981, shocked government planners with the news that the country's population had climbed to 684 million, some 12 million more than projected. Despite nearly a billion dollars spent on population-control programs during the 1970s, India's growth rate has remained about the same as it was in the 1960s, nearly 2.5 percent. In Kenya, a population growth rate of 4 percent means that its 16 million population will double in 18 years. In 1981, there will be almost 650,000 more mouths to feed than in 1980. The average Kenyan woman has slightly more than eight children. On the other hand, in Brazil, the growth rate has declined from the predicted 2.7 percent to about 2.4 percent, principally because of increased literacy, more women working outside the home, and an increased exposure to modern urban lifestyles. Brazil, alone among

[13]Robert W. Fox, *Urban Population Growth Trends in Latin America* (Washington D.C.: Interamerican Development Bank, 1975).

[14]Nathan Keyfitz, "World Resources and the World Middle Class," *Scientific American*, 235 (1) (1976), pp. 28–35.

Jamaica is just one of many Third World countries where government leaders are much concerned about rising population pressures. Billboards, like this one, are part of a major government effort to persuade Jamaican couples to use birth control devices.

major Third World countries, has no population-control policy. On the contrary, some Brazilian political figures lamented the declining growth rates, apparently because it will now take longer for Brazil to overtake the United States as the most populous country in the Western Hemisphere. Nevertheless, Brazil now adds about 3 million people (about the population of Israel) to its ranks each year and its urban corridor from Rio de Janeiro to Saõ Paulo now holds more than 21 million people, which is projected to rise to 45 million by the year 2000.[15]

**Agricultural Production and Land Tenure.** A rapidly growing population would not be an undue cause for alarm if the society in question could somehow mobilize the resources to feed, house, and clothe its newly arrived members. This re-

quirement places heavy demands on the agricultural sector to grow the needed food, fibers, and lumber to meet this demand. Unfortunately, the record shows that agriculture in the Third World is, at best, holding even with population growth; in many instances, it is actually falling badly behind. From a base index number of 100, representing per capita agricultural production prior to World War II, per capita production levels from 1965 to 1966 declined to 94 in mainland Asia (excluding China) and to 92 in Latin America, increased slightly to 101 in maritime Asia and to 102 in Africa, and showed appreciable gains to 114 in the Middle East. Because Third World countries remain overwhelmingly agrarian in their labor force, with 50 to 70 percent of the economically active population still employed in tilling the land, these countries must look to this sector for major gains in worker productivity. Their failure to register major gains in agricultural production remains a major cause of Third World poverty and structural weakness.

The causes of underproduction in agricul-

[15]Stuart Auerbach, "Indian Census Spurs Call for Birth Control Plan," *Washington Post*, May 12, 1981; Jay Ross, "Kenya's 4% Birthrate Said to Create 'Mind-Boggling' Problems," *Washington Post*, June 20, 1981; Jim Brooks, "Brazil's Population Growth Rate Decreases," *Washington Post*, February 2, 1981.

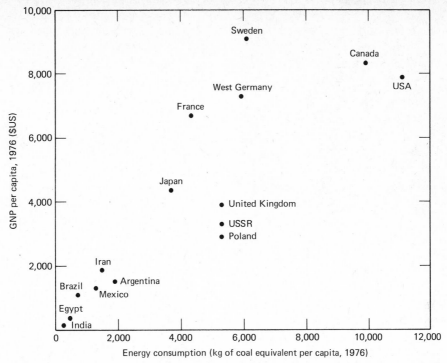

**Figure 2.2** Energy Consumption and GNP/Capita, 1974. (*Source*: GNP/capita—US ACDA, *World Military Expenditures and Arms Transfers, 1965–1974*, US GPO Washington, 1976. Energy consumption—UN *Statistical Yearbook*, 1974.)

ture in the Third World are both technological and socioeconomic.[16] On the one hand, per acre crop yields remain low because of the poor nations' inability to devote high levels of agricultural technology to their farming effort. Such technologies as improved seeds, pesticides, herbicides, fertilizer, irrigation, animal husbandry, marketing, transportation, and storage of crops remain substantially beyond the reach of the average small farmer in virtually all of the Third World. The ability of the industrialized world to apply modern technology to farming means that the gap between rich and poor nations has been widening in agriculture, just as it has been in manufacturing. From 1948 to 1965, while North America and Europe registered annual rates of improvement in yield of major crops (cereals,

tubers, oil seeds, cotton) of between 2.5 and 7.0 percent, Africa, Asia, and Latin America were able to achieve improvement rates of no more than 1.5 to 2.0 percent in most areas. This achievement by the industrialized countries explains how we in the West can consume between 3000 and 4000 calories per day and still dedicate only about 5 to 7 percent of our work force to agriculture, whereas people in the developing nations, with ten times as great a proportion of their work force in agriculture, still can consume only about 2000 calories per day (the minimum to maintain reasonably good health according to many nutritionists).

The second major reason behind the low agricultural productivity of the Third World lies in the land-tenure system, or the way in which land is owned and exploited. In most Third World nations, the rural sector remains that part of the nation most strongly wedded to traditional, anti-

[16]Gunnar Myrdal, *The Challenge of World Poverty* (New York: Random House, 1970), chap. 4.

Primitive farming techniques are still used in many parts of the Third World. This particular scene is from the Nile Delta region of Egypt. Since the construction of the Aswan Dam, the Nile doesn't flood this region, and irrigation is difficult without tools and technical assistance. Again, the uneven spread of industrialization creates imbalance that make life more difficult for poor inhabitants of the Third World.

modern ways of living, and this is reflected particularly sharply in the way in which landownership is determined. The exact system differs across the Third World, but the effects are usually the same: little incentive to maximize production, unstable land title, uneconomic size and distribution of parcels, and a highly unequal distribution of social power in rural areas based on landownership.

In Latin America, one of the areas with the greatest agricultural problems, the land-tenure problem is one of highly unequal distribution of land combined with uneconomical size of parcels.[17] This is the familiar phenomenon of the *minifundia*, the many extremely small parcels, existing along side the *latifundia*, the few extremely large holdings. In Peru in 1961, for example, 88 percent of the parcels accounted for about 7 percent of the land, whereas 1 percent of the holdings accounted for over 80 percent of the land. In Chile, 37 percent of the farms contained only 0.2 percent of the land, whereas 6.9 percent

of the parcels contained 81.3 percent of the land. Other nations outside Latin America also suffer from this problem. Even in Egypt, in 1961, after nearly 10 years of vigorous land-reform activity by a progressive regime, 5.6 percent of the farm owners held 45.2 percent of the land, 59 percent of the owners held 8 percent of the land, and more than three quarters of a million families, about 23 percent of the total, possessed no land at all.

In sub-Saharan Africa and in much of Asia, the problems of land tenure follow a somewhat different pattern. In Africa, much rural land is still owned communally, which means that individuals do not own the land but work it for the benefit of the entire village. Each villager is assigned a parcel to work, and the proceeds are shared by the general population. There is little emphasis on production for commercial purposes, and most of the food and fiber are consumed within the village. Much of this land is now being encroached on by commercial plantations, which grow food crops, such as cocoa and peanuts, for export. Young men leave their villages to join the flood of migrant farm laborers who move from plantation to plantation, trying to save money before returning to their villages. But, their savings are quickly dissipated in uneconomic consumption, and, when they do return to their villages, they form a part of the growing rural *lumpenproletariat*—underemployed, landless, and mired in poverty.[18] The few individuals who manage to obtain a small parcel of private property find themselves almost completely at the mercy of the swarms of intermediaries who control the farmers' access to the far-off markets: the brokers, the owners of the means of transport, the moneychangers, the mill and silo managers, and so forth. The undue control of the farmers by intermediaries has also aggravated rural poverty in South and Southeast Asia. In Thailand, for example, government plans to establish new groups of prosperous small farmers in the rich rice lands upcountry from Bangkok failed to break the hold of the ab-

[17]Celso Furtado, *Economic Development of Latin America: A Survey from Colonial Times to the Cuban Revolution* (Cambridge: At the University Press, 1970).

[18]Peter C. Lloyd, *Africa in Social Change*, rev. ed. (Baltimore: Penguin, 1975).

sentee landlords in the north and of the parasitic intermediaries in the other rice-growing areas.[19] As a consequence, although nonfarm GNP per capita has risen nearly 60 percent from 1960 to 1970, from $739 to $1156, the farm share of the same economic pie has grown only slightly, from $103 to $139 in the same period.

**Social Class Structure and Income Distribution.** Another severe social problem affecting levels of human dignity in the Third World is that of highly unequal social class structures and the way in which these structures affect political power, wealth, and economic development. French scholar, R. Gendarme, has outlined a typical social class structure of the sort frequently found in underdeveloped countries.[20] The following is based on Gendarme's formulation.

At the bottom of the social scale are what Gendarme calls the urban subproletariat, or urban dwellers who are only occasionally employed; rural folk only recently arrived in the city and not yet accustomed to city life; illicit street vendors; and people with minor service trades, such as shoeshine boys, porters, and rickshaw drivers. In addition, the urban lower class includes servants of the rich, who may account for as much as 10 percent of the urban population according to Gendarme. Rounding out the bottom of the social ladder are the masses of rural poor, landless farmers who work on an erratic basis and who live at a subsistence level. In Egypt, the landless rural population may amount to as many as 3.8 million persons, about 20 percent of the country's total rural population. In Iran, under the Shah (according to Gendarme), 60 percent of the country's rural families owned no land; in Ecuador, out of a total (rural and urban) population of about 3 million, 500,000 people receive no money income at all

and about 1 million receive only between $30 and $40 per year.

At the next level up the social ladder, we find the urban artisan and working-class groups. The artisans, still a powerful force in traditional societies, work as tailors, shoemakers, potters, blacksmiths, and weavers. The urban wage earners, on the other hand, work in factories, are accustomed to assembly-line discipline and regular employment, and are settled into an urban routine that means they are more or less modernized. Factory employees may account for no more than 30 percent of the total economically active population of an underdeveloped country, as opposed to 60 percent or more in an industrialized one.

The closest resemblance to a typical Western middle class one finds in the Third World consists primarily of civil servants, government bureaucrats, and army officers. Because the state is frequently the most progressive employer in a developing economy, large percentages of high school and college graduates can find work no other place and become absorbed into a very large bureaucracy. In Ghana, P. C. Lloyd reports, 40 percent of the workers are employed by the government; in other West African states, the figure is likely to be as high as half.[21] The armies of developing states, although very small by Western standards, have come to play an extremely important role in the development of their societies, partly because of their more modern outlook, partly because of their superior social discipline, and partly because of their monopoly of the armed forces in the country. We will examine the military's role in Third World politics in greater detail in Chapter Five.

At the top of the social scale come the bourgeois and aristocratic classes. Despite their high social standing and their high income levels, this is actually a very heterogeneous social grouping; some of the upper classes are decidedly modern in their attitudes, whereas others are staunchly committed to retaining the country's traditional way of life. Within the upper class, we are likely to find landlords (a tiny fraction of

[19]Brewster Grace, "Population Growth in Thailand, Part I: Population and Social Structure," *Reports* [American Universities Field Staff (Asia)], 22 (1) (1974), p. 7.

[20]R. Gendarme, "Reflections on the Approaches to the Problems of Distribution in Underdeveloped Countries," in Jean Marchal and Bernard Ducros, eds., *The Distribution of National Income* (London: Macmillan, 1968), pp. 361–388.

[21]Lloyd, *op. cit.* p. 120.

**TABLE 2.5** Income Distribution in Eight Selected Third World
Countries in the Mid-1970s

| Country | Percent of Income to Richest 5 Percent | Percent of Income to Poorest 20 Percent | Percent of Population Living in Absolute Poverty |
|---|---|---|---|
| Nigeria | na[a] | na[a] | 30 |
| Tanzania | 34.0 | 5.0 | 54 |
| India | 25.0 | 5.0 | 36 |
| Indonesia | na[a] | na[a] | 51 |
| Mexico | 36.0 | 4.0 | 10 |
| Brazil | 27.0 | 5.0 | 8 |
| Egypt | 20.0 | 4.0 | na[a] |
| Iran | 25.0 | 5.0 | 5 |

[a]na = not available.

SOURCE: George Thomas Kurian, *The Book of World Rankings* (New York: *Facts on File*, 1979), Tables 60, 61; pp. 85–86. Based on data from the World Bank.

the total rural population), who enjoy ownership of the vast majority of rural property; the old aristocracy, who can trace their origins back to precolonial days and frequently assert some sort of royal lineage; the educated, nationalist élite found mostly in the liberal professions, such as law, medicine, engineering, and architecture; and traders, business leaders, bankers, and other economic forces.

The data presented in Table 2.5 portray the distribution of income in selected Third World countries in recent years. Income is distributed in a highly unequal fashion in virtually every country for which we have reliable data. The top 20 percent of the population in each country earns as much as half of the country's income each year. The percentages decline sharply thereafter so that the bottom 20 percent in a typical Third World country earns from 3 to 5 percent of the total national income.

Moral considerations aside, in purely economic terms, unequal income distribution does not necessarily mean that the country is not progressive or developing. Income is distributed unequally in all of the industrialized democracies, including the United States, where the top 20 percent of the population earns about 40 percent of the national income. Moreover, it appears that inequities in income distribution

become sharper and gaps between rich and poor greater in rapidly developing nations. Income inequalities in developing countries appear to be much more of a social and political problem for at least three reasons. The low-income sectors of the population are so poverty stricken that the gap between rich and poor is greater than in the industrialized countries, the affluence of the upper-income groups becomes much more visible and the issue becomes politically much more volatile. Furthermore, because of the close links among income, education, and social power, the great disparities in income levels in the Third World also mean great disparities in power. One often hears radical regimes assert the need for land-tenure reform, not for economic purposes but to break the political power of the landed gentry. Also, much of the income, wealth, and social power in Third World countries is concentrated in the hands of traditional groups whose members, as we saw earlier, are not only not interested in modernization and industrialization but are determined to fight their introduction through public policies whenever and wherever they can.

**Cultural Schisms in the Mosaic Societies.** Third World countries have been characterized aptly as mosaic societies because they are made up of many separate pieces, each of which adds to the whole picture without being absorbed or assimilated into any other segment.[22] This is not a problem unique to the Third World, as the recent agonies in Ulster attest. One recent survey of the question of ethnonationalism—the belief that people should be governed only by others of their same ethnic group—tells us that there are only 14 nations in the world substantially free of at least one significant minority, that Japan is the only one of these that has a large population, and that only 4 percent of the world's population lives in a nation-state that corresponds closely to a single ethnic group. This same survey went on to assert that, as of 1973, 58 nations were "currently or recently troubled by internal discord predicated upon ethnic diversity."[23]

It is obviously difficult to generalize about such a problem, but it still seems that ethnic discord is a much more serious obstacle to national development in the Third World than it is in most of the industrial countries. There are several reasons for this. Many Third World countries, particularly in Africa and Asia, are enclosed by artificial boundaries that were imposed on the country by the departing colonial power and do not reflect true tribal or ethnic divisions. In addition, the struggle against the colonial power led many of the nationalist leaders to emphasize each person's inherent right to self-determination, an ideology that turns out to be a two-edged sword, which can be wielded by an ethnic minority against a newly created regime just as that regime used it against the colonial mother country. Also, the general trend of modernization seems to exacerbate tribal, ethnic, or linguistic feelings. Sharp increases in mass media expose countless thousands of people to new cultural symbols, awakening in them a cultural consciousness that leads to new ideas about the "them" and "us" of their world. Rapid social change frequently drives bewildered traditional peoples back into the comparative safety of mystical religions and tribal cults, which tend to emphasize the dividing lines in human society. Rapid economic change can produce sharp inequalities in the distribution of the gains of industrialization; not infrequently, these economic inequities correspond to some kind of ethnic division. Finally, we must note the comparative fragility of many of the Third World's nations, whose people have not yet become committed to the nation as a symbol of a going concern, one that deserves their loyalty and dedication. In such instances, ethnic divisions loom large as the cause of conflict, violence, and even the breakup of the state.

Third World nations are divided by the customary social faultlines seen elsewhere (see Table 2.6). Language is one such source of division. Ghana, with a population of 10 million, has 5 major languages; India has 15 major languages and over 1600 dialects. In the Philippines, no one language can be understood by as many as one third of the people. Nigerians speak 3 major languages; in Zaire, 4 languages are used for communication between Europeans and natives, 4 others are used in primary education, and 3 more are used only in certain localities.[24] Even in Latin America, where the nations have had much time to resolve these problems, Indian languages, such as Quechua and Guarani, present obstacles to communication in the Andean countries.

Religious ties and beliefs are also sources of conflict in the Third World. In the middle of the 1970s, the gravest instance of this was in Lebanon, where the population is divided into six principal socioreligious groupings: the Christian Maronites (about 23 percent of the total population), the Greek Orthodox (7 percent), the Armenians (5 percent), the Sunni Moslems (26 percent), the Shiite Moslems (27 percent), and the Druze (7 percent). The chief division in Sri Lanka is between the 2.5 million people of the Tamil Hindu minority and the 9 million Sinhalese Buddhist majority. In the former South Vietnam, conflict among the syncretic Christian

[22]W. Howard Wriggins, *The Ruler's Imperative: Strategies for Political Survival in Asia and Africa* (New York: Columbia University Press, 1969), p. 22.

[23]Walker Connor, "The Politics of Ethnonationalism," *Journal of International Affairs,* 27 (1) (1973), pp. 1–21.

[24]Rupert Emerson, *From Empire to Nation* (Cambridge: Harvard University Press, 1960).

**TABLE 2.6**  Ethnic/Linguistic Data from Eight Selected Third World Countries in the Mid-1970s

| Country | Number of Separate Languages Spoken (Principal/Secondary) | Number of Significant Discrete Ethnic Groups (Principal/Secondary) | Homogeneity Index[a] |
|---|---|---|---|
| Nigeria | 3/250 | 4/250 | 13 |
| Tanzania | 1/100 | 1/130 | 7 |
| India | 15/1600+ | 2–3/numerous | 11 |
| Indonesia | 1/250+ | 2–3/300+ | 24 |
| Mexico | 1/5–10 | 1/3 | 70 |
| Brazil | 1/3–5 | 1/3–5 | 93 |
| Egypt | 1/2 | 1/5 | 96 |
| Iran | 1/5–8 | 1/40–50 | 24 |

[a]Ranges from 0 to 100; 100 represents complete homogeneity of ethnicity.

SOURCE: The data on ethnic homogeneity are from George Thomas Kurian, *The Book of World Rankings* (New York: Facts on File, 1979), Table 32; pp. 44–46; the data on languages and ethnic groups are from George Thomas Kurian, *Encyclopedia of the Third World* (2 vols.) (New York: Facts on File, 1978).

faith; the Cao Dai; the Catholics; and the Hoa Hao (a Buddhist sect) further weakened the already shaky political order and contributed to the downfall of the U.S.-sponsored regime.

Racial differences and tribal allegiances compound the problem of national unity, especially in Africa and Asia. Nigeria and Zaire (at the time called the Congo) experienced severe challenges from separatist movements soon after gaining their independence, in both cases the source of conflict was tribal loyalties and feelings of persecution (often aggravated by outside intervention). The presence of many racially different overseas minorities has sparked conflicts, for example, the Indians in several East African countries and the Chinese in Malaysia and Singapore. Even though many Latin Americans may proclaim that their countries are more tolerant of racial differences, persons of European origins seem to enjoy greater advantages economically, socially, and politically than do persons of mixed racial ancestry.

Nigeria is one of the Third World countries that has experienced greatest strain from its ethnic diversity. Since independence from Great Britain in 1960, Nigeria has suffered three military coups, one bloody attempted coup, and a civil war, which lasted 2½ years (ending in 1970) and cost an estimated 1 million lives. For 13 years, from 1966 to 1979, the country lived under military rule—the armed forces are never far from the center of power. The principal cause of all this discord is the tribal animosities contained within the fragile and artificial nation. The civil war centered on the country's three major tribal groupings, the Yoruba of the west, the Hausa-Fulani of the north, and the Ibo of the east. After the breakdown of the shaky tribal coalition that had governed since independence, there followed a series of riots, charges of rigged elections, and two military coups that involved ethnic hostilities. Thousands of Ibos living in the north were killed and thousands more fled to their home region, which, then, seceded as the independent state of Biafra in 1967. Although the defeat of the Ibos resulted in the consolidation of Nigerian national identity, the Ibos have felt resentful ever since because of their treatment at the hands of the victors. Ibo property confiscated during the war still had not been returned as of 1980. Biafra's war wounded are not helped by the central government. Public works, such as roads and drinking-water supplies, have been left to deteriorate, and many badly needed projects remain uncompleted. It was not until late 1980 that Ibo civil servants from the days before the civil war had their federal government pensions restored. Much remains to be done to weld Nigeria's 250 ethnic groups into a single proud nation. In this respect, Nigeria resembles many other Third World countries experiencing ethnic strain and discord.[25]

## CONCLUSIONS: ECONOMIC AND SOCIAL BARRIERS TO HUMAN DIGNITY

As this brief discussion makes clear, Third World governments desirous of raising the levels of human dignity in their societies must first come to grips with a number of severe social and economic problems. The international economic system within which the Third World must live is one obvious source of difficulty. Multinational corporations and Great Powers use developing countries to further their own goals and ambitions; infrequently does this treatment redound to the benefit of the poor nations themselves.

Within each Third World nation, however, lies a set of social and economic problems that will be just as intractable as those of the international arena. Explosive population growth absorbs increased industrial and agricultural production, meaning that even the most prosperous Third World economies must run harder and harder just to stay in place. Social class structure and inequalities in income distribution create political conflict, economic waste, and the misallocation of scarce resources. Ethnic, tribal, linguistic, and racial differences complete the list

[25]See the series of articles by Leon Dash that have appeared in the *Washington Post*: "10 Years Later Ibos Still Feel Impact of Nigeria's Civil War," May 27, 1980; "Nigeria Acts to Conciliate Ex-Biafrans," October 2, 1980; "Nigeria Election Recriminations Revive Sensitivities of Civil War," December 28, 1980.

of the noneconomic obstacles to human progress.

The list is a formidable one. Even the most stable and creative of political systems would have difficulty in managing any of these problems in isolation, much less the entire set together. In the following chapters, we will examine governments in the Third World as they attempt to cope with problems that seem at times to be overwhelming in scope and intensity.

# Suggestions for Further Reading

**Agarwal, Amar Narayan,** and **S. P. Singh,** eds., *The Economics of Underdevelopment* (New York: Oxford University Press, 1963).

**Angelopoulos, Angelos,** *The Third World and the Rich Countries: Prospects for the Year 2000* (New York: Praeger, 1972).

**Baran, Paul,** and **Paul Sweezy,** *Monopoly Capital* (New York: Monthly Review Press, 1966).

**Bauer, P. T.,** and **Basil S. Yamey,** *The Economics of Under-Developed Countries* (Chicago: University of Chicago Press, 1957).

**Bhagwati, Jagdish N.,** ed., *Economics and World Order: From the 1970s to the 1990s* (New York: Free Press, 1972).

**Connor, Walker,** "The Politics of Ethnonationalism," *Journal of International Affairs,* 27 (1) (1973), pp. 1–21.

**Elliott, Charles,** *Patterns of Poverty in the Third World* (New York: Praeger, 1975).

**Erb, Guy F.,** and **Valeriana Kallab,** eds., *Beyond Dependency: The Developing World Speaks Out* (Washington: Overseas Development Council, 1975).

**Holt, R. J.,** and **J. E. Turner,** *The Political Basis of Economic Development* (New York: Van Nostrand, 1966).

**Hoselitz, Bert F.,** *Sociological Aspects of Economic Growth* (New York: Free Press, 1960).

**Johnson, Harry G.,** ed., *Economic Nationalism in Old and New States* (Chicago: University of Chicago Press, 1967).

**Kerr, Clark,** et al., *Industrialism and Industrial Man,* (Cambridge: Harvard University Press, 1960).

**Lloyd, Peter C.,** *Africa in Social Change,* rev. ed. (Baltimore: Penguin, 1975).

**Mountjoy, Alan B.,** ed., *The Third World: Problems and Perspectives* (New York: St. Martin's, 1978).

**Myrdal, Gunnar,** *Asian Drama: An Inquiry into the Poverty of Nations* (New York: Pantheon, 1968).
_____,*The Challenge of World Poverty* (New York: Random House, 1970).

**Smith, Michael, Richard Little,** and **Michael Shackleton,** eds., *Perspectives on World Politics* (London: The Open University, 1981).

**Vogeler, Ingolf,** and **Anthony de Souza,** eds., *Dialectics of Third World Development* (Montclair, N.J.: Allanheld, Osmun, 1980).

# CHAPTER THREE
## Psychological Aspects of Modernization

In Chapter Two, we outlined a number of major economic and social obstacles to raising the level of human dignity in the Third World. Much of what goes on in politics in developing countries is aimed at removing these obstacles by reforming the social, economic, and political structures. Despite the determined and, at times, heroic efforts of political leaders, only a few countries in the Third World seem to be making significant progress toward this goal. One reason for this difficulty may lie in the psychological features of the societies in question. If the attitudes, modes of thinking, and forms of interpersonal relationships are not supportive of political and economic reform, the changes will not endure no matter how well designed or financed they may be.

For this reason, many Third World regimes now spend significant resources on policies intended to alter or influence the traditional psychological characteristics of their people. They do this out of a conviction that traditional cultures impede the implementation of policies to raise the level of human dignity. In this chapter, we examine some of the principal features of traditional and modern ways of thinking[1] and discuss the links between these different modes of

thought and the enactment of public policy. All policies have their costs, however, and we must also consider the costs of government programs aimed at changing the way in which people think.

Some people in every society wish to preserve the old, the tried, and the tested ways of thinking and doing. They perceive, with justification, that modern ways of thinking have disadvantages as well as advantages. Perhaps, after reading this chapter, you will also decide that traditional values and habits should be conserved and that modernization of one's mental processes is too costly. Nevertheless, most Third World leaders who are trying to reform their societies believe that such reform must include some psychological changes. Whether or not this is wise, or even feasible, are questions you should be better prepared to contend with at the end of this chapter.

### FROM TRADITION TO MODERNITY: THE DIMENSIONS OF CHANGE

Psychological modernization is a multidimensional phenomenon, meaning that it is a process

---

[1]As we use the terms, traditional and modern, they stand for ideal types, or mental constructs, that illustrate our argument. They do not exist in the real world. All of us are mixtures of traditional and modern ways of thinking and acting. All cultures form a continuum from traditional to modern, none can be regarded as entirely of one type.

that affects many, if not most, of the mental structures of an individual. Human beings do not become modern only in certain parts of their personality but, apparently, must make the transition along a wide range of mental activities. In fact, if the changes do not take place across this wide range, the chances are greater that modernity will not become established within the individual's personality and a return to traditional modes of thinking, feeling, and acting will occur. More frequently what happens is that an attempt to reconcile traditional and modern mental structures within a single individual produces psychological strain or tension, leading to forms of behavior that are unstable or unhealthy for the broader society.

The changes involved in psychological modernization affect four areas of one's mental functioning: ego structures, attitudes, cognition (or the handling of information), and behavior.[2]

## CHANGES IN EGO STRUCTURE

At the very core of one's mental structures lie both the devices that the ego uses to guide and direct the personality in its encounters with the environment and the protective techniques (defense mechanisms) that are brought into play to shield the personality from threat and attack. These structures are deeply embedded in the personality and are the outcome of very early childhood experiences, especially those arising within the family setting. Until recently, many psychologists regarded these structures as being virtually unchangeable after adolescense, except under traumatic conditions. Thanks to the work of Erik Erikson, ideas about this are beginning to

[2]This analysis is based on the following works: Alex Inkeles and David H. Smith, *Becoming Modern: Individual Change in Six Developing Countries* (Cambridge: Harvard University Press, 1974); Joseph A. Kahl, *The Measurement of Modernism: A Study of Values in Brazil and Mexico* (Austin: University of Texas Press, 1968); (Latin American Monographs No. 12); Daniel Lerner, *The Passing of Traditional Society* (Glencoe, Ill.: Free Press, 1958); David McClelland, *The Achieving Society* (New York: Free Press, 1967); Kenneth S. Sherrill, "The Attitudes of Modernity," *Comparative Politics*, 1 (2) (1969), pp. 184–210.

change.[3] The dimensions of the ego that appear most relevant to psychological modernity are those that have to do with one's openness to change; with feelings of efficacy and optimism; with an ability to empathize with others; and with an inclination toward moderate risk taking.

A traditional person is inclined to be skeptical about change. In fact, the very definition of traditional would probably include reverence for the old and the tested and suspicion of the new and the untried. A modern person, on the other hand, is not only open and receptive to change but looks about for it, even at the cost of uprooting self and family and moving to a different location. A modern person's readiness for change extends to more than just job, home, or customs; he or she is also inclined to be receptive to new modes of production or of cultivation and to new political forms. Change, even when it comes rapidly, is usually not threatening or unmanageable for the modern person.

A traditional person relates to the natural environment with a feeling of resignation and with a sensation that he or she must accept what nature imposes without trying to alter the inevitable. This characteristic of the traditional person, which we call fatalism, is indicative of the degree to which the tradition-bound individual feels that life is controlled by external forces, beyond one's control. Typical of this sort of mentality would be the farmer who refuses to take resolute action to rid a crop of pests out of the belief that the pests are an act of God, against which the farmer cannot struggle. Modern people, on the other hand, act decisively to overcome nature and its obstacles. They believe that destiny is in their own control and that they can influence events that have a bearing on their lives. A modern person feels efficacious and capable of resolving many of the problems that confront daily life without resorting to spiritual or external assistance.

A third dimension of ego structure affected by modernization involves a person's dealings

[3]Erik Erikson, *Childhood and Society*, 2nd ed. (New York: Norton, 1963).

with others. A traditional person does not trust others, especially if they come from beyond the immediate circle of friends or kin groups; strangers are to be suspected, not dealt with openly. Relations going in the opposite direction are also difficult because a traditional person lacks the ability to empathize with others, to put himself or herself in their position and to imagine how the world looks from their vantage point. A modern person, however, possesses the opposite of both of these characteristics. Modernity communicates to an individual a trust in others, especially if he or she has some sort of rule or legal document to insure that the impersonal other can be expected to behave in a certain manner. Bureaucracy, that great social invention of the modern world, could not work if it were not for the tendency of modern people to trust others to conform to a written set of rules. A modern person also has the ability to empathize with others, to imagine the sorts of problems from which they may be suffering, and to adjust personal behavior to the feelings of others. Some social psychologists even assert that a modern person has greater respect for the dignity and worth of weak and poor people, of women and the aged, and of other groups that have been discriminated against until recent times.

Finally, a traditional person has a tendency to avoid taking risks in daily life. This fatalism, low sense of efficacy, and unwillingness to accept change combine to make a traditional person a low-risk person who tries to reduce all life choices to those guaranteed to come out successfully. New agricultural techniques, for example, are avoided unless they offer complete certainty of yielding a larger crop. Movement to the city, likewise, is avoided because to do so creates uncertainty and risk. A traditional person is not so much interested in achieving success as in avoiding failure; the best way to avoid failure is to attempt nothing unless success is guaranteed. In the real world, this is usually the equivalent of doing nothing. A modern person accepts a moderate amount of risk in life. He or she understands that certain tasks offer only a medium chance for success; but he or she feels that the

outcome of the task can be influenced by throwing skill and intelligence into the balance. A modern person wishes to achieve positive things, merely avoiding failure is not sufficient. Modern psychology leads to the creation of an entrepreneurial class as well as to highly motivated and well-trained workers. In many ways, this dimension is the key to the economic development of a society.

## CHANGES IN ATTITUDES

Moving away from the core of a person's mental activities, we come to a wide-ranging variety of social, economic, and political attitudes that mark an individual's day-to-day relationships with the world. As these attitudes and opinions are acquired somewhat later in life than the ego structures mentioned earlier, they are, in theory, more easily changed or discarded as new information about the real world becomes available. This is particularly true for individuals who are more modern and, therefore, relatively more open to change and new experiences.

There appear to be six major sets of attitudes that undergo change as a person makes the transition from tradition to modernity. First, the very propensity to form and hold opinions begins to broaden, thereby making it easier for a modernizing person to develop a wide and rich set of beliefs and feelings about new and unusual phenomena. A traditional person would be less likely to have numerous opinions about things far removed from daily life and more likely to answer, "I don't know" to an interviewer's questions about such issues. A modern person, in contrast, forms, changes, and discards opinions at a rapid pace that reflects the rapidly changing world.

Second, modern and traditional people differ in their attitude about time. Traditional persons, reared in primarily agricultural settings, gear their lives to much broader and vaguer notions of time requirements. Time for a rural dweller in a traditional country is linked to the seasons instead of to clocks or watches. Modern persons, however, are much more attuned to the formal requirements of clocks and watches. Schools, factories, businesses, and other complex institutions depend on their members arriving and departing more or less together or at specific times. The modern institution teaches its participants the importance of time, that is, if they have not already learned it.

Closely related to the attitudes they have on time are the feelings modern people have about planning. Modernity implies an ability to bring order out of chaos, to impose a rigorous framework of analytical thought over the otherwise unorganized data of our surroundings. A traditional person resists planning because what is going to happen will happen anyway without human intervention. A modern person, on the other hand, intervenes in the flow of events to plan, to develop preferred sequences of events, and to impose his or her own sense of order on the environment.

A modern person believes in the efficacy of science and the scientific method as a means for people to get nature under control. Some tradition-bound persons hold that the world is completely random with no structure and, thus, no predictability. Others hold that whatever structure may exist is unknowable to ordinary mortals and can only be reached through spiritual appeals to some divine power—efforts to apply rationality and science to real problems are doomed to failure. A modern person, in contrast, believes in the inherent rationality of the universe and, therefore, holds that science can be used to rid humanity of some of its worst problems. One interesting illustration of this dimension is in the area of birth control. A traditional person argues against artificial attempts to control or alter the conception of children; a modern person accepts not only the possibility of achieving this goal but also the desirability, if not the necessity, of doing so.

Modern and traditional people differ in their attitudes about how society should reward its members. Modern persons, who are more achievement oriented, assert that society should distribute its rewards according to only one criterion: how well individuals perform their soci-etally assigned task. Traditional people are more ascriptive, which means that they believe that society should reward its members according to some criterion (or criteria) other than role performance. Such criteria might include one's religion, race, language, ethnic group, gender, or age. Obviously, as society generally moves toward a more achievement-oriented means of rewarding its members, individual persons must abandon ascriptive modes of interacting with their fellow citizens.

Finally, we should mention the shift from particularism to universalism as an example of attitudinal change in a modernizing society. Particularism is the belief that a particular group has the right to promote its own specific interests without reference to the interests of any larger or more inclusive entity. Universalism implies a belief that one's ultimate loyalty should be directed toward a social or political entity larger than one's own narrow parochial grouping. When applied at the concrete level in a traditional society, particularism means the supremacy of one's clan, kin group, family, tribe, language group, religious order, or ethnic grouping. The explicit political application of universalism in a modern context means the granting of ultimate supremacy to the nation. Although some citizens in the industrialized West may have begun to shift their loyalty to transnational entities or even to some global entity (such as all of humanity), those residents of the Third World who are emerging into psychological modernity focus primarily on the nation as the political unit to which they attach their commitments.

## CHANGES IN INFORMATION AND BEHAVIOR

From attitudes, let us move to the outer mental structures where we find the cognitive dimension of the personality. The cognitive mental processes deal with what we know about the outside world as opposed to how we feel about it. In a political context, the cognitive dimension is closely related to the conative aspect of personality, or the behavioral side of mental functioning. For this reason, we will consider knowl-

**TABLE 3.1** Communications and Media Data from Eight Selected Third World Countries in the Mid-1970s

|  | Literacy Rate | Radios per 1000 Population | TV Sets per 1000 Population | Daily Newspaper Circulation per 1000 Population |
|---|---|---|---|---|
| Nigeria | 25% | 69 | 2 | 10 |
| Tanzania | 15 | 16 | na[a] | 4 |
| India | 29 | 25 | 0.5 | 16 |
| Indonesia | 60 | 39 | 1 | 16 |
| Mexico | 65 | 301 | 84 | 116 |
| Brazil | 67 | 60 | 83 | 39 |
| Egypt | 40 | 140 | 17 | 21 |
| Iran | 37 | 249 | 47 | 15 |

[a] = not available.

SOURCE: George Thomas Kurian, *The Book of World Rankings* (New York: Facts on File, 1979), Tables 267, 300, 302, 309; pp. 308–310, 347–348, 350–351, 358–359.

edge and behavior simultaneously with special emphasis on their political ramifications.

The single most important cognitive-behavioral aspect of psychological modernization is that having to do with information and how a person goes about getting it. A traditional person lives in a world largely lacking in simple bits of information. Furthermore, he or she has few resources that would permit seeking out needed information. Literacy rates are apt to be quite low in poor and developing countries, which indicates that many people are effectively cut off from a flow of information through the printed media that most of us in the industrialized countries take for granted. In addition, electronic forms of the mass media—telephones, motion pictures, radio, and television—are hardly developed in most emerging countries, with the likely exception of the country's capital city. Table 3.1 indicates the relative poverty of information within which Third World citizens live. Modern people, in contrast, not only possess large amounts of information but also devote significant resources to the search for more data that they can use to order their lives.

We see this transformation from traditional to modern most clearly when we consider the political behavior of the two types of individuals. Traditional persons typically do not have many political opinions, and they lack the

necessary information that would enable them to form opinions about an issue. Modern individuals, on the other hand, possess ample attitudes and opinions about political issues; they know where and how to go about getting the information they need to form an opinion on any new issues that might arise in their surroundings. The same generalization applies to the exchange of political opinions. Traditional people do not share opinions with others because conversation about things they cannot change (the regime in the far-off capital for instance) is a waste of time. Modern persons, however, appear quite ready to exchange opinions about political issues with each other, especially if the environment is supportive. There are, of course, many social settings within which it would be inappropriate or inadvisable for the holder of a minority opinion to engage the dominant majority in debate over some political issue; but, these exceptions aside, the exchange of political ideas in a modern society is much more frequent than in traditional surroundings.

As we move on to consider what modern and traditional persons actually do in politics, the contrast stands out even more starkly.[4] On the input side of politics, where citizens are supposed to bring their demands, grievances, and

[4]Gabriel Almond and Sidney Verba, *The Civic Culture* (Princeton, N.J.: Princeton University Press, 1963).

support to the attention of policy makers, traditional people are almost totally inactive. Their fatalism, their lack of faith in their own efficacy, and their inability to join with others in common enterprise makes them unable to mount an effective campaign to influence the political system. Their lack of information about politics makes them ignorant of how, where, and by what means to exert pressure, even if they were so inclined. Modern persons, on the other hand, possess not only the motivation, the activist spirit, and the interpersonal and organizational skills to advance their interests through the political input process but they also know how best to make their influence felt to achieve their goals. The gap between traditional and modern is somewhat less on the output side of the policy process, where people (and groups) are less concerned with influencing policy before it is made and more concerned with protecting themselves from its adverse effects during the implementation stages. People in traditional societies are apt to have a fairly well-developed set of skills that they can put to use to protect themselves from the impact of a given policy. In addition, there are always the ubiquitous intermediaries whose main job it is to obtain special treatment from the state bureaucracy for their clients. We will meet these intermediaries again as we move on in subsequent chapters to consider the government structures of Third World countries. In modern societies, however, the task of protecting a citizen or a group from the adverse impact of public policy falls more into the realm of legitimate interest-group activities and less into the jurisdiction of informal intermediaries or back-alley wheeler-dealers. All of this helps explain why, in modern political settings, we are more apt to find formal associations, interest groups, and political parties operating on both ends of the political process—to influence policy before it is made and to protect their members or clients afterward, when it is being implemented. Although such an arrangement appears to be largely institutional, it could not survive for long if the basic personality and political culture of modernity did not strongly support it.

## PSYCHOLOGICAL CONSEQUENCES OF RAPID CHANGE

If you consider the changes we have discussed as a complete set, or package, of mental transformations that a person must undergo as he or she makes the change from traditional to modern, it is obvious that we are talking about massive personality alterations. These alterations do not ordinarily come about easily or painlessly; in fact, there is usually considerable turmoil involved in psychological modernization. This problem begins to take on political ramifications whenever the personal turmoil suffered by modernizing men and women erupts into societal disturbances that cannot be contained within the prevailing social and political institutions. Nevertheless, governments and modernizing élites in Third World countries cannot afford to ignore the problem of psychological change or to treat it as a given in their human resources environment; if the basic personality[5] of a developing nation is not brought along in tune with the demands of a modern society, the process of political change may founder and slip backward.

The psychological effects of rapid modernization are a particular version of what Alvin Toffler calls future shock, or change at such a rapid pace that one's mental and physical resources are overwhelmed.[6] Toffler was writing about the impact of high-speed change in modern, industrial society, but his observations also apply to persons caught in the dizzying whirl of psychocultural modernization.

Making the change from tradition to modernity requires unlearning or discarding inappropriate behavioral tendencies, information, attitudes, and ego structures and replacing them with their modern counterparts. Modernizing people must reassess their repertoire of mental

[5]The term basic personality means "that personality configuration which is shared by the bulk of the society's members as a result of the early experiences which they have in common." Ralph Linton in the introduction to Abram Kardiner, et al., *The Psychological Frontiers of Society* (New York: Columbia University Press, 1945), p. viii.

[6]Alvin Toffler, *Future Shock* (New York: Bantam, 1971).

structures, determine which of these are inappropriate for a modern society, and cast them off in favor of others more attuned to the needs of modernity.

Human beings learn in one of four ways. First, our environment conditions our behavior in certain directions by the granting or withholding of rewards or by the application and withdrawal of punishments. Through repeated encounters with sets of such rewards and punishments, humans learn by the process of adding rewarded behavioral choices and discarding nonrewarded or punished ones. For more complex social activities, we rely on modeling (social learning), a process that enables us to learn entire packages of behaviors at once by observing others engaged in a particular action and, then, emulating them. In addition, we may transfer lessons learned in one sphere of activity to another area of our lives through the learning process known as generalization. And, finally, the process of exemplification allows us to internalize a rule or guideline of an institution and make it our own as a lesson for personal behavior. An example of this latter process would be seen in an individual who, after working in a factory that is run according to a set schedule of events, learned the value of scheduling personal events also. We can assume, then, that the process of psychocultural modernization within an individual will be less disruptive and will endure longer if (1) the person is rewarded substantially for having made the shift, (2) the environment provides ample models in the form of other modern persons who can be emulated, (3) the person has an opportunity to transfer the lessons of modernity from one sphere of life (school for instance) to another (business), and (4) if the person is placed in institutions or organizations that are run along modern lines and that provide ample opportunity to copy their behavioral principles.

Under the best of circumstances, psychocultural changes of this magnitude involve what some psychologists call object loss, a condition marked by a person's perception that he or she has been deprived of, or must do without, some object (another person, an aspect of one's own self-concept, a tangible resource, or a cultural abstraction) that is invested with emotion and that is culturally defined as valuable.[7] In this particular case, the object that is lost is the set of mental structures that were appropriate in a traditional setting but that are out of step in a modern surrounding. Some degree of object loss is inescapable. We all lose loved ones and valued objects as part of the normal process of living. Many such losses are well within the normal range of predictability, however, and society generally provides us with institutions, rituals, and compensation to cushion us against the shock. Occasionally, however, entire social aggregates, such as ethnic groups or social classes, may experience object loss together as the result of the sudden change of some important group characteristic such as land ownership or income level. When this happens, social buffer institutions are less effective because society itself had a stake in maintaining the *status quo ante*. Rapid psychocultural modernization of a developing country is one such instance.

As a very general term, object loss embraces two somewhat more narrow kinds of psychological disturbances that can affect the stability of developing countries. One of these is relative deprivation. This is a person's perception that there is a significant gap between the objects (goods, conditions of life, opportunities, symbols, etc.) to which he or she feels legitimately entitled (expectations) and the objects that he or she can reasonably hope to attain and keep (capabilities). The awareness of this gap is often called frustration, and the frequent outcome of a frustrating condition is the direction of aggression against a convenient and symbolic target.[8] A second kind of object-loss disturbance is called cognitive dissonance. Psychologist Leon Festinger asserts that one of the most important human drives is that which impels us to desire in-

[7]Fred Weinstein and Gerlad M. Platt, *Psychoanalytic Sociology* (Baltimore: Johns Hopkins University Press, 1973).

[8]Ted Robert Gurr, *Why Men Rebel* (Princeton, N.J.: Princeton University Press, 1970).

ternal consistency of opinions, perceptions, expectations, and the whole general range of mental structures. A human being in possession of contradictory mental structures feels uncomfortable, and this discomfort energizes the person to seek to correct the condition. The awareness of internal inconsistencies or contradictions in one's mental makeup is called cognitive dissonance, and actions taken to soften or eliminate these contradictions are called dissonance reduction.[9]

Up to now, we have dealt with object loss at a fairly abstract level. Let us now consider some problems of developing countries to see actual conditions of relative deprivation and cognitive dissonance at work. Consider, for example, the plight of the Indian intellectual caught between the traditional demands of the family and kin group, on the one hand, and the modern requirements of adult experiences, education, and profession, on the other hand. I. R. Sinai writes of the agony of this individual:

> People like me are heirs to two sets of customs, are shaped in our daily lives by dual codes of behavior. For example: my generation on the one hand declared its agnosticism and on the other tamely succumbed to the old rituals; we yearned for romantic love but were reconciled to marriage by the well-established method of matching horoscopes to a girl selected for us by our parents; outside our homes we smoked, consumed alcohol, and ate meat, when available, but at home we were rigidly puritan and vegetarian; we glibly talked about individual salvation although we belonged to a very closely knit joint-family system.[10]

Sinai is writing of cognitive dissonance; yet, relative deprivation can also produce disturbances in rapidly modernizing societies. In some cases, stable, tradition-bound groups try to hold fast to unchanging expectations but find their resources eroding away under the pressure of modernization. In the East African countries of Kenya and Tanzania, for example, small farming villages are caught between the unrelenting increase in population and the finite amount of land available for cultivation. Because the traditional methods of passing land from one generation to another are not adequate to resolve this problem, the inhabitants of these small villages see the average size of the agricultural parcel dwindle away to the point of not being economically viable. In other instances, more modernized groups, such as urban, middle-class political leaders, see a gap develop between their high (and rising) expectations of what can be accomplished under an independent, democratic, national reform government and their perceptions of what actually does happen: not reform, but corruption; not economic progress, but decay; not self-denying leadership, but self-indulgent abuse of power. The result in numerous instances has been for the most powerful modernizing élite, the armed forces, to intervene to restore order and begin anew the drive to development. We will return to this phenomenon again in detail in Chapter Five, when we consider government structures.

For the individual in Latin America, Asia, Africa, or the Middle East, who is caught in the midst of the turmoil of modernization, several broad kinds of mechanisms are available to help cope with the tensions of rapid change. Withdrawal, either partially through drugs or totally through suicide, offers one escape from modern life. Indeed, we often find that developing countries are experiencing increases in drug use and in suicide rates as they try to transform their cultures. For many individuals who look to the supernatural for aid, mysticism, witchcraft, and magic play an important role. In many countries of the Third World—Mexico, other areas of the Caribbean, West Africa, and Southeast Asia— the transformation of society from traditional to modern has been accompanied by an increase in popular belief in sorcery, voodoo, witches, spirits, and other agents of supernatural power. Some of the frustration of psychocultural change is expressed in social pathology. Homocides; divorces; crimes of passion, theft, and burglary; and other forms of socially disruptive aggression are on the increase as a frustrated and discontented individual, caught in the grip of forces

[9]Leon Festinger, *A Theory of Cognitive Dissonance* (Evanston, Ill.: Row, Peterson, 1957).

[10]I.R. Sinai, *The Challenge of Modernization* (New York: Norton, 1964), p. 64.

he or she cannot understand, strikes out against symbolic targets, usually in the family and the immediate circle of friends and kin groups. And, finally, mental illness may rise along with levels of modernization as many individuals succumb to the stress and tension of rapid change.

What we have described are the negative effects of psychological change, the consequences that disrupt society and one's personal life and divert a reform government's attention away from larger, more institutional problems. That these individual-level responses to modernization can mean the undoing of the national development efforts seems obvious. Governments in the Third World have found that they cannot simply leave the traditional political culture alone and expect it to change as the nation's institutions change. Neither can a modernizing regime ignore the danger signals contained in the rising rate of social pathology in its country: suicides, homicides, drug addiction, alcoholism, and the rest. Thus, whether they want to or not, modernizing governments have found themselves confronted with the need to intervene in the very subtle and elusive process of psychocultural change to smooth its adverse effects and to speed it up if they can.

## IRAN, ISLAM, REVOLUTION: CASE STUDY IN RELIGION AND POLITICS

People caught up in the turmoil of rapid political, economic, and social change are frequently left bewildered and confused by the destruction of traditional standards of thought and behavior with which they are apt to be most comfortable. In their search for a belief system to which they can anchor themselves in the midst of change, they will, at times, support the revival of religious fundamentalism, a return to the old values that had served them so well in the past. Such a development has been taking place in the Islamic world since the early 1970s, and it has been one of the most significant events in the Third World during that turbulent decade.

The Islamic revival of the 1970s has affected the peoples covering a broad band of the Third World, running all the way from Mauritania and Morocco on the northwest shoulder of Africa to Indonesia and the Philippines in the Western Pacific.[11] The revival has taken on many different forms. In ethnically strife-torn Mauritania, the universal adherence of the country to Islam is used by the government to override social schisms.[12] In violent Turkey, Islamic fundamentalism appears in the guise of revolutionary terrorist organizations and neo-Fascist political parties that challenge the secularism of Turkey's national development elite.[13] In Libya and Saudi Arabia, the revival accompanies efforts by these two regional powers to support allies and friends throughout the Middle East, and, indeed, the world. Libya, of course, uses Islamic fundamentalism to advocate revolutionary insurgency; Saudi Arabia, much more conservative, uses its immense wealth to support less well-off Islamic countries, primarily through such quiet methods as heavy donations to the Islamic Development Bank. In the Philippines, the Moro National Liberation Front, representing the Muslims of the southern island of Mindanao, has revived a centuries-old struggle against the central government, fighting both for autonomy for Muslims and against the settlement of Christians in their territories.

Of all the instances of the political impact of Islamic fundamentalism, however, the most dramatic and the best known to Americans has been the Iranian revolution and its aftermath. At the beginning of 1978, the Shah of Iran had seemed at the height of his power. He was undisputed ruler of his country, a position he had held formally since 1941 when his father abdicated in his favor and one that he had exercised vigorously since the failure of a nationalist revolution in 1953. At that time, and with increasing fervor

---

[11]Daniel Pipes, " 'This World Is Political!!' The Islamic Revival of the Seventies," in Steven L. Spiegel, ed., *At Issue: Politics in the World Arena,* 3rd ed (New York: St. Martin's, 1981), pp. 80–111.

[12]See two articles by Leon Dash in the *Washington Post:* "Torn Between Past, Present, Mauritania Lurches from Crisis to Crisis," May 24, 1981; "Tensions Mount in Mauritania's Delicately Balanced Caste System," May 31, 1981.

[13]Kevin Klose, "Turkey, Searching for Modernity, Offers Fertile Field for Terrorism," *Washington Post,* May 25, 1981.

from the early 1960s on, the Shah had attempted to lead his country through the turbulence of a massive social, economic, and political revolution without taking into account the disturbances that such a development would inevitably unleash. Especially after the increase in oil prices in 1973 produced a bonanza in foreign exchange, the Shah combined vigorous developments with the buildup of a major military force that would make Iran the dominant power in the Persian Gulf. Nevertheless, although development proceeded at a rapid pace, the Shah became intolerant of competing ideas and suppressed dissent with an increasingly heavy hand. Political repression and corruption spread rampantly, and crass Western materialism sickened the once devout Muslims of the country.

The opposition to the Shah stemmed from many different sources. The deterioration of the country's agriculture coupled with the failure of land reform 15 years earlier produced a peasantry dislocated to the city, where they swelled the ranks of the unemployed and discontented. Real growth declined after 1976, but the conspicuous gap between the wealthy few and the numerous poor grew ever wider. The urban proletariat, denied the right to protest and strike, soon joined the peasants as the mass of desperate lower class Iranians looked for an institution to which they could turn for help. That institution was the only familiar one remaining intact and vital; the mosque. The Iranian revolution took an Islamic form for several reasons. Islam stands for tradition and contrasts most sharply with the Western features of the Shah's rule. The clergy provided solace and a haven for the distressed of the big cities. Its dislike and distrust of foreigners (especially Americans) made it a likely core around which to mount anti-Shah propaganda. And the mosques and the mullahs offered the one institution capable of organizing a network of people who could be forged into a base for national political action.

For Iran, Islam and the anti-Shah movement were embodied in the Ayatollah Ruhollah Khomeini. He was not the only religious critic of the Shah, but he became the most powerful. He em-phasized traditional Islamic and Persian virtues. He was incorruptible in a land where corruption abounded. He refused to compromise with the Shah in contrast to many more moderate leaders. All of these characteristics caused the people to rally to him in large numbers after his move to exile in Paris (from Iraq) in October 1978.

The movement against the Shah grew to a violent crescendo during 1978. Rioting spread through most major cities during the first half of the year. Martial law was imposed in August, but to little effect. The final blow was the strike of oil-field workers late in the year, causing panic in the nation's economy. On January 6, 1979, the Shah appointed a moderate leader to head a new government and 10 days later, on January 16, left Iran on what was termed a vacation. In February, Khomeini returned from exile, the Iranian army buckled under the pressure, and the Shah's last government resigned. The Ayatollah's choice for prime minister was installed shortly thereafter and recognized by most governments of the world.

The Iranian revolution has been bloody but in 1981 was still far from being consolidated. During 1979, until a new constitution could be adopted, the country functioned under the control of Khomeini and a clergy-dominated Revolutionary Council. Shortly after the adoption of the constitution, in December 1979, the country began to function under a quasi-parliamentary system heavily dominated by Islamic leaders. The new constitution establishes Shi'ite Islam as the official state religion, places supreme power in the hands of the Muslim clergy, and names the Ayatollah as the nation's religious and political leader for life. Both an elected president and a unicameral legislature are provided for in the constitution, but they are subordinate to the Ayatollah. A Council of Guardians of the Constitution (destined to replace the Revolutionary Council) is empowered to nullify laws they consider contrary to the Islamic faith.

Shortly after the new government began to function, Abolhassan Bani-Sadr, a moderate Western-trained economist, was elected President of Iran with more than 70 percent of the vote in a field of six other official candidates. His government lasted 17 months. He was dismissed by the Ayatollah in June 1981, allegedly for counterrevolutionary acts and having been a puppet of Western interests. Even before his dismissal, Bani-Sadr had been in hiding to avoid capture and execution. His dismissal removed the last obstacle to a complete takeover of the country by Islamic fundamentalists and clergy who are determined to reverse the trend of modernization begun under the Shah. The costs in human terms have been heavy, just as they were under the Shah's regime. Religious fundamentalism in Iran proved to be as violent as its predecessor, and just as autocratic. Whether it would prove to be a more effective force for mobilizing the talent and energy of the Iranian people is a question that cannot be answered at this writing.

## PSYCHOCULTURAL MODERNIZATION: SOCIAL AGENTS AND PUBLIC POLICIES

As Figure 3.1 indicates, the various agents of psychological modernization can be arranged across a wide spectrum according to the type of mental activity they are designed to alter. At the far left of the spectrum we find the mental activities located at the core of one's personality, which we have labeled ego structures. In the center of the line fall the mental activities midway between the personality's core and its periphery, which we refer to as attitudes. At the far right of the scale we encounter the mental activities that are most superficial, which we refer to as cognitive, that is, having to do with information.

Arrayed in similar fashion below the spec-

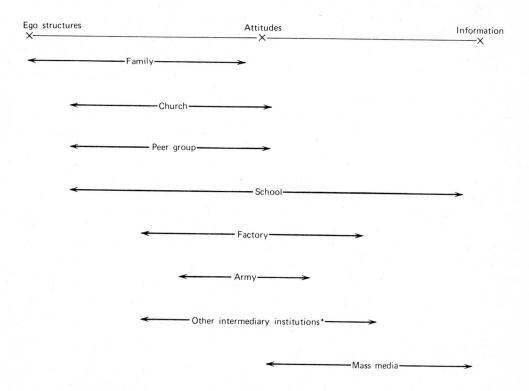

*Labor union, agricultural cooperative, neighborhood association.

**Figure 3.1** Impact of various modernizing agents on three levels of mental activity (length of arrow indicates approximate range of impact of each agent).

trum are the social institutions, or agents of modernization that have special impact on certain specified areas of one's psychological functioning. The family, for example, being the first socializing agent encountered by the young child, has most of its impact on the core of mental activity, the ego. However, many family-taught lessons also pertain to attitudes, values, and preferences. Churches and peer groups, such as youth gangs or Scout troops, primarily affect attitudes, but they also have considerable impact on ego structures. The school probably affects a wider range of mental activities because it conveys information, influences attitudes and value choices, and also has some ability to transform ego structures. Several intermediary institutions, such as the factory, military service, labor unions, or agricultural cooperatives, are of obvious importance to the modernization process. Most of the work of these institutions is performed in the changing of attitudes, whereas relatively less of their activity has to do with the transmission of information. Finally, the mass communications media, such as radio, television, motion pictures, and newspapers, have a great deal of influence in the transmission of raw and distilled information, and they may alter individual attitudes although their ability to change deep-seated ego structures is relatively small unless they are supported by other institutional arrangements.

Public policies designed to shape and direct the modernization process must take into account the nature of the political culture in most Third World countries, the interplay between levels of mental activity, and the character of the social change agents.

Let us begin at the lowest level of mental functioning. Traditional family practices, child-rearing practices, and peer-group pressures in Third World countries have been investigated in great detail by visiting Western social scientists. The results of these investigations generally point to real and major problems for any government seeking to modernize the ego structures of its country's basic personality. In brief, the evidence is that traditional child-rearing practices and other early childhood socialization techniques found in the Third World do not prepare the growing child to take an active and constructive role in modern politics. Although we cannot survey all of the many details of such widely varying techniques, let us focus on just a few typical characteristics to illustrate these conclusions. We will divide our survey into three periods of early socialization: child-rearing, social pressures of the extended family, and sex-role performance.

In many traditional cultures, such as those of Southeast Asia, child-rearing typically begins with much permissiveness, indulgence, and affection. Young children are allowed virtual autonomy within their tiny universe; their every demand is granted; and all of their siblings and older relatives (aunts, uncles) take great pains to respond to the crying infant or toddler. Suddenly, however, without warning or preparation, the young child or adolescent is plunged into the world of the adult, both socially and sexually. There is much pressure placed on the child at this point to perform at very high standards, and there is severe punishment for failure. Child-rearing practices that have been indulgent and affectionate to this point now turn sullen and teasing; the child begins to lose the confidence that had been his or hers as a 2- or 3-year old. This pattern of child-rearing has been called the betrayal syndrome because of its clear-cut tendency to teach the small child that he or she cannot trust anyone in a position of authority, not even mother, and that the world is an unpredictable and malevolent place to be endured but not to be changed.[14]

Antimodern lessons continue to be learned through peer-group pressures in many Third World areas, as exemplified by the social forces of the Arab world. The Arab child is not a free agent in his or her society but is bound and constrained by numerous social commitments, duties, and obligations. Many different social groupings of which he or she is a member take deep interest in the behavior of the member and regularly pronounce on this behavior. Many

[14]Lucian W. Pye, *Politics, Personality and Nation Building: Burma's Search for Identity* (New Haven, Conn.: Yale University Press, 1968).

This rural elementary school in El Salvador must hold classes outside because of a lack of available building space. Literacy rates in Third World countries generally range between 50 and 75 percent. One important reason is the scarcity of school facilities in rural areas.

areas of social contacts must be consulted before acting, and many different individuals must be placed in the act. Social punishment is turned against wayward, nonconformist members of the group and takes the form of scolding, ridicule, face-to-face insults, shaming, and other forms of intimidation. The consequence of this form of social pressure is a basic personality that takes its cues for behavior from external sources instead of measuring its behavior against inner standards of excellence. Persons who grow up in this sort of environment frequently exhibit tradition-bound behavior patterns as adults, such as scapegoating, distrust of foreigners, belief in conspiracies, and blaming unseen forces for failure. Clearly these do not contribute to psychological modernization any more than did the more deeply rooted family child-rearing practices examined earlier.[15]

We conclude this brief inquiry into traditional early socialization practices by mentioning the pressure on extreme sex-role performance under which young men grow to maturity in many Latin American countries. The drive to dominate others through the proving of one's

masculinity is almost the cultural imperative of many Latin American societies, including Mexico, Venezuela, and countries further south, such as Argentina. This cultural phenomenon is labeled *machismo*, after the Spanish word *macho*, or male. From an early age, a young boy's attention is directed to the size of his genitals and the aggressiveness of his sexual exploits. The boy's father emphasizes rapid sexual maturation and encourages the boy to explore his own sensuality, in most cases before the boy is physiologically or psychologically ready. This pressure leads to the establishment of goals of sexual performance far beyond the reach of most mature men and to sexual failure or inadequacy. The disappointment of Latin American men felt in this area is reflected in their defensiveness and aggressiveness in other social spheres as well in their manifest need to dominate others. A social order built on this kind of "lesson" will be one in which compromise and adjustment of interests will be seen not as moderation, but as weakness, and even as homosexuality.[16]

Although we have detailed several major

[15]Sania Hamady, *Temperament and Character of the Arabs* (New York: Twayne, 1960).

[16]Carl E. Batt, "Mexican Character: An Adlerian Interpretation," *Journal of Individual Psychology,* 25 (2) (1969), pp. 183–201.

ways in which traditional socialization practices leave antimodern residues in ego structures across the Third World, the fact is that most modernizing regimes in Latin America, Africa, and Asia simply cannot muster the kind of political power necessary to intervene actively into these intimate and very personal practices. Only in a few countries have governments sought to change the ways in which families shape the personality of their young; however, in most instances, these policies consist of removing children from the family environment before traditional lessons have been learned and placing them in state-run institutions, such as day care facilities, nurseries, or kindergartens. In this way, radical governments, such as those in Cuba or China, have succeeded in breaking the grip of the family on future generations. But only the most revolutionary governments (those of the Second World) have been able to bring to bear enough political power and public will to throw off the influences of tradition as it is exemplified in antimodern child-rearing techniques. This is not to say that changes in child rearing will not occur through the natural workings of economic, educational, and social modernization. Peter C. Lloyd reports that élite families in West African countries, such as Nigeria, are already applying modern child-rearing techniques to bring their offspring into the modern world as positive, activist, change-oriented, and achieving adults.[17] But, significantly, these changes are occurring apart from government policy, not because of it. As far as public policy is concerned, family and peer-group socialization practices are beyond the reach of most Third World governments.

We turn now to the intermediate socializing institutions: the school, the army, the factory, and other linkages, such as labor unions and agricultural cooperatives. In later chapters, we will return to an examination of the role these intermediate institutions play in channeling population participation into the political arena and in providing much-needed information for policy makers concerning the effects of their decisions.

In this section, however, we are most interested in the ways in which these institutions can be used to alter the basic personality of traditional groups.

Generally, modern institutions help to modernize the people in them by means of the learning principle we discussed earlier, exemplification. Modern institutions, of the sort we have just listed, are organized, maintained, and operated according to a set of principles that are based, in turn, on a modern outlook on life. They are bureaucratic in nature, emphasizing the impersonal and predictable meeting of responsibilities. They are regular and routinized, again stressing the ability of people to predict the behavior of their superiors, subordinates, and peers. The emphasis on rules and on the fair application of these rules leads people to become more trustful of their environment and of impersonal, unknown others. Modern institutions are achievement oriented, rewarding the people in them more for their performance of societally assigned roles than for some ascriptive characteristic, such as race or religion. In addition, many of these institutions, such as the armed forces, the factory, and the agricultural cooperative, offer to their members clear examples of people dominating nature. Members of these groups are taught to operate and maintain heavy equipment and machinery, to manipulate the natural world and to bend it to human needs, and to work productively with large amounts of energy and raw materials.

Completely traditional societies are, on the whole, institutionally impoverished, meaning that they have none or few of these institutional arrangements within which people can learn to apply the rules of modernity to their daily lives. Thus, in many developing Third World countries, the first decisions regarding social change are frequently aimed at establishing or encouraging such institutions. Schools are usually first on the list, not only because of their impact on traditional modes of thought but also because of their teaching of literacy to an illiterate populace.[18] In

[17]Peter C. Lloyd, *Africa in Social Change* (Baltimore: Penguin, 1975), pp. 181–190.

[18]James S. Coleman, ed., *Education and Political Development* (Princeton, N.J.: Princeton University Press, 1965).

Turkey, after the modernizing revolution of Mustafa Kemal (Atatürk) in 1919, not only were local schools and universities made the recipients of rapidly increased investments but also certain important philosophical changes in education were introduced. Village institutes were established to receive a select cadre of children who were removed from their family and village environment at the age of 14 and sent to special boarding schools for future teachers. Religious instruction in schools was terminated, as was the teaching of Arabic and Persian, so the contacts that had linked the traditional Islamic groups with the nation's youth were severed. From 1923 to 1941, the number of students in Turkish elementary schools grew from about one third of a million to nearly 1 million and college-level enrollment increased nearly fourfold.

The army is another intermediary institution that reform governments in the Third World have depended on, not only to educate large numbers of young recruits drawn from rural, traditional villages and low-income slums in big cities but also to provide the officer corps its training in modernity, which frequently leads to the creation of new, forward-looking officers. In Ghana, under the late Kwame Nkrumah, the government sponsored the creation of the paramilitary Worker's Brigade, a uniformed organization that absorbed unemployed and ill-educated youths who had been cut loose from family and tribal ties and turned these youths into a loosely disciplined construction unit, used particularly in public-works building. In addition to serving their country and supplying symbolic evidence of the government's existence and activity, the Workers' Brigade also provided its members with rudimentary education, health care, social coordination, discipline, and a sense of responsibility.

A third kind of intermediary institution designed to aid in the psychological modernization of traditional peoples is the government-sponsored agricultural cooperative, as exemplified by the Comilla experiment in Bangladesh (formerly East Pakistan). In 1959 and 1960, the Pakistan Academy for Rural Development was launched in the Comilla District as an effort to

eliminate rural backwardness in the region by means of a coordinated, comprehensive attack on many aspects of rural traditional agrarian society. Through the Academy, villagers and small farmers were first collected into cooperatives, which were linked together with each other and with the Academy as the central coordinating force. The cooperatives were shown the benefits of mutual agreement in the joint solving of problems. The Academy provided the cooperatives with substantial assistance in water development, operation and maintenance of tractors, marketing, and a number of important social services, such as midwife training and local elementary schools. But the key to the success of the Comilla experiment was the Academy's insistence on mass participation in the project. Each cooperative decided jointly on the communal need for resources and jointly guaranteed each individual loan made to its members. Instead of simply being the recipient of technical help by a group of élite bureaucrats from the capital city, the Comilla cooperatives were genuine schools of modernity for their members.

The examples discussed are important reflections of public policy in Third World countries, where governments have tried to construct the intermediate institutions so badly needed to bring the mental structures of modernity to their still-traditional peoples. Although these examples are impressive, they are characteristic of only a minority of reform regimes. Governments throughout the Third World are discovering tremendous obstacles to the building of institutional linkages between the modern and traditional sectors of their countries. Because this is a problem affecting mass popular participation in politics, we will postpone until Chapter Four any further discussion of the institutional aspects of political change.

The inability of nearly all governments to influence the formation of ego structures through family and peer socialization and of most governments to shape attitudes through intermediary institutions has led many regimes in the Third World to concentrate their efforts on the informational end of the spectrum: the creation and transmission of symbols, usually through

One of the most charismatic of contemporary Third World leaders, Libya's Col. Muammar el-Qaddafi, is shown acknowledging the enthusiastic response of a crowd of thousands in Lahore, Pakistan. Col. Qaddafi was in Pakistan for the second Islamic summit, held in February, 1974.

the mass communications media.[19] The fact that the mass communication of patriotic and modern mobilizing symbols has little impact on the more deeply rooted mental structures of traditional people apparently matters only slightly, if at all, to Third World leaders. What these leaders seek is, first, to dominate the media of communication with the symbols of their regime and frequently, of their person and, second, to prevent the mass media in their country from being used to criticize or dissent from government policies.

Many observers of politics in the Third World have commented on the tendency of leadership in these countries to be based on the personal appeal of a particularly charismatic figure, such as Juan Peron of Argentina, Gamal Abdel Nasser of Egypt, Sukarno of Indonesia, or Kwame Nkrumah of Ghana. In a country where the institutional forms of modern government were lacking or in disrepair, leaders such as these could offer to their people the symbol of action, of power, of the solutions to the many problems that assaulted them in their daily lives. No government in the world is fortunate enough to have tangible resources sufficient to distribute to each

citizen to meet his or her needs; so, each government is thrown back onto its symbolic resources. That is, each government must distribute psychic benefits to those people who do not receive material benefits from a given policy decision. Where tangible or material resources are in especially short supply (as is the case in any poor country) and where loyalty to the national government is fading or nonexistent, symbolic resources must fill the gap to buy time while the government tries to solve the countless material problems confronting it. This is the real meaning of symbolic or personalistic politics in the third World.

Far more serious for anyone concerned about the state of civil liberties in the Third World today is the increasing use of press censorship by governments in developing countries to prevent criticism of their policies and decisions (See Table 3.2). Reports reaching the West from various countries throughout the Third World indicate that the free press of these countries is under such an assault that it may not survive intact. A review of the state of freedom of reporting and of operations of the mass communications media in the Third World[20] suggests that private news media enjoy substantial freedom to investigate and report the news in only about 40 countries. But, even in these countries, there is an official news agency and government control of at least one medium of communication to ensure that the government's position is reported to the people.

In another group of about 40 countries, the private news media exist alongside the official, government-sponsored media. But the controls—both official and unofficial—placed on the private media are so strong that they constitute censorship. The style and degree of press censorship vary greatly within this group. In India, for example, news magazines and newspapers are required to submit all copy to government censors prior to publication. In Mexico and Peru, government control over the source of scarce

[19]Lucian W. Pye, ed., *Communications and Political Development* (Princeton, N.J.: Princeton University Press, 1963).

[20]George Thomas Kurian, *Encyclopedia of the Third World*, (2 vols.) (New York: Facts on File, 1979).

**TABLE 3.2** Indicators of Degree of Press Freedom in Eight Selected Third World Countries, 1980

| Country | Indicators of Degree of Press Freedom |
|---------|---------------------------------------|
| Nigeria | Newspapers publish relatively freely. The government maintains an official news agency and, since 1975, has controlled all radio and television broadcasting facilities. |
| Tanzania | The Newspaper Ordinance of 1968 empowers the president to ban any newspaper if he considers such action to be in the "national interest." The government has its own official news agency and owns and operates the two radio stations and the single television station in the country. |
| India | Although Indian news media had been among the freest in Asia, they were subjected to rigid government censorship following the declaration of emergency in June 1975. Most emergency legislation was rescinded in April 1977, and press freedom guarantees were written into a constitutional amendment in 1978. The government supervises both radio and television broadcasting, but commercial television was introduced in 1976. |
| Indonesia | Newspapers have been tightly controlled by the government since 1974, and several were banned in 1978. All broadcasting is government controlled, and the government also operates the principal domestic news agency. |
| Mexico | The press and broadcasting media are privately owned but operated under government regulation. The government does not censor newspapers but, instead, effectively controls what they write through its newsprint monopoly. |
| Brazil | Censorship of newspapers fluctuates according to the political climate, but the potential for government curbs on press freedom is very real. In 1977, for example, the government banned all political party statements on radio and television. Since 1978, censorship has been somewhat relaxed. Despite the government controls, Brazil's press has traditionally been vigorous and widely read. |
| Egypt | In theory, state supervision of the press was ended in 1978, but the government still owns all newspapers and television broadcasting stations. There is some commercial radio service. |
| Iran | All opposition newspapers were closed by government order in August 1979. The government maintains its own news agency and has expelled a number of foreign journalists. Television and radio are all government owned. |

SOURCE: Arthur S. Banks and William Overstreet, eds., *Political Handbook of the World: 1980* (New York: McGraw-Hill, 1980).

newsprint is sufficient to quiet potential criticism of government policies. In Tanzania, a 1968 law allows the president to ban any newspaper if he considers such action to be in the national interest. The constitution of Libya guarantees press freedom as long as it does not interfere with the principles of the Libyan revolution. In the Philippines, since the imposition of martial law in 1972, newspaper activity has been under the jurisdiction of the government's Mass Media Council. In Turkey, a nominally free press censors itself through a Press Council Court of Honor, aided by official favoritism in the placement of advertising. At the extreme, in Uganda, under now-deposed President Idi Amin there was jailing and torture of journalists who insisted on reporting their criticism of the Ugandan government.

In at least 19 countries, there is no private communications sector. All media of communication belong to the government.

In addition to controlling the news media in their own countries, many Third World governments are now seeking to restrict the news-reporting agencies in their countries to purely indigenous organizations and to exclude the Western-based international news agencies, such as Reuters, United Press International, and the BBC. These Western agencies, say Third World leaders, are an embarrassment to developing countries because they print only the bad news about local conditions, never bringing out the good aspects of Third World politics. Furthermore, and probably a much more serious problem, some international news agencies have been reported to be fronts for the Central Intelligence Agency (CIA) and other organizations run by Western governments. For example, prior to the fall of the government of Marxist Salvador Allende, the CIA sent a number of foreign reporters to Chile to bring back unfavorable material on the Allende regime to affect the opinion of influential political and business leaders in the United States regarding the Allende government. Whether or not these plans to control foreign news agencies will come to fruition will depend greatly on the ability of Third World governments to develop their own international news agency to replace the Western, biased journalists. In view of their inability to develop such news agencies on a purely national basis, one is inclined to doubt the capacity of the Third World countries to mount a more sophisticated transnational effort in the foreseeable future.

Beyond policies designed to control the private news media, however, Third World governments have done little, if anything, to stimulate the spread of mass communications into the traditional regions of their countries. In contrast with Communist regimes, such as that of Cuba, where television and radio are relied on heavily to exhort the public to be supportive of the government and of the revolution, Third World governments seem little inclined to exploit the great symbolic potential of broadcasting and telecasting. The case of India is instructive. In the mid-1970s, there were 25 radio receivers for each 1000 people in India, and television was virtually nonexistent. Yet, in the country's first Five-Year Plan, only 0.2 percent of total expenditures were allocated to develop broadcasting, whereas education expenditures were 60 times as great. The same allocation characterized the second Five-Year Plan. In its third Five-Year Plan, broadcasting expenditures slipped to 0.1 percent of total expenditures. Of course, actual expenditures ran considerably below those planned. In the area of mass communications, Third World policies to ease the strain of psychological modernization seem to be too little and too late to accomplish their goals.

Mexico is one country where the government is doing something to reach rural areas through the mass media. High in the Sierra Madre mountains near Mexico's southern border with Guatemala, *Radio Indigena* (Indigenous Radio), broadcasts daily in five separate Indian languages, all offshoots of Maya, because virtually no one in the region speaks Spanish. The content of the broadcasts is decidedly practical, positive, and nationalistic. The bulk of the station's programming consists of helpful hints for the Indians, such as how to cure snake and tarantula bites and how to practice birth control. Bad news, especially about political affairs, is never mentioned, and the emphasis is always on the bright side of the government's accomplishments. Finally, the station's messages are always aimed at integrating the Indians more firmly into the Mexican nation; the folk tales and songs are usually geared to this objective. One technician at the station was quoted as saying, "We don't do sensitive or sensational news. We have government propaganda, good news, and useful information." No one knows how many people listen to *Radio Indigena*, but one indicator was seen in 1981 when the station reported that in a distant state capital a meeting would be held for people interested in regularizing the titles to their land. Over 20,000 men showed up at the meeting. Many had walked and traveled on buses for two days to get there.[21]

## CONCLUSIONS: PSYCHOLOGICAL MODERNIZATION AND HUMAN DIGNITY

Human dignity begins in the minds of human beings. If a person is at peace with his or her surroundings and social order, outside observers should respect this peace. If a person believes that he or she enjoys a dignified existence, then, we must accord that view our respect even though the person's outward appearance may contradict it.

It is important to avoid equating tradition with bad and modern with good. Many aspects of traditional life, such as the conservation of natural resources or the solidity of the family circle, are of great value and should be preserved. Likewise, there are some features of modern value structures that degrade human dignity, such as the social disintegration of big-city slums and the widespread destruction and waste of natural resources.

But this is a textbook about politics and specifically about politics in the Third World. Regardless of what we may think of their decision, most reform-minded Third World political leaders believe that traditional modes of thought and behavior stand in their way, and they are determined to correct this problem. As far as we know, no society has ever set out on the journey to modernity and then subsequently decided to return to their traditional origins voluntarily; it is unlikely that any large group of individuals have ever done so either. In recognition of that fact, this textbook has adopted a working definition of human dignity that owes much to Western, modern ways of thinking. In making this choice, we seek not to pass judgment on the wisdom of Third World leaders who have directed their societies toward modernity but, instead, to evelute their methods of reaching that goal and to measure their success or failure. Given the nature of the goal (*i.e.,* modernity), certain aspects of traditional thought can certainly be regarded as obstacles or barriers. However, the costs of removing them will inevitably be high, and, because thinking is the most personal of all acts, each of us must decide whether the price is too high for the benefits to be derived.

# Suggestions for Further Reading

**Almond, Gabriel,** and **Sidney Verba,** *The Civic Culture* (Princeton, N.J.: Princeton University Press, 1963).

**Brokensha, David,** *Social Change at Larteh, Ghana* (Oxford: Clarendon, 1966).

**Bryant, Coralie,** and **Louise G. White,** *Managing Rural Development: Peasant Participation in Rural Development* (West Hartford Conn.: Kumarian Press, 1980).

**Coleman, James C.,** ed., *Education and Political Development* (Princeton, N.J.: Princeton University Press, 1965).

**Doob, Leonard, W.,** *Becoming More Civilized: A Psychological Explanation* (New Haven, Conn.: Yale University Press, 1960).

**Gurr, Ted Robert,** *Why Men Rebel* (Princeton, N.J.: Princeton University Press, 1970).

**Inkeles, Alex** and **David H. Smith,** *Becoming Modern: Individual Change in Six Developing Countries* (Cambridge: Harvard University Press, 1974).

[21]Marlise Simons, "Radio Brings the World to Mexican Indians," *Washington Post,* June 20, 1981.

Kahl, Joseph A., *The Measurement of Modernism: A Study of Values in Brazil and Mexico* (Austin: University of Texas Press, 1968). (Latin American Monographs No. 12)

Lerner, Daniel, *The Passing of Traditional Society* (Glencoe, Ill.: Free Press, 1958).

McClelland, David, *The Achieving Society* (New York: Free Press, 1967).

Nash, Manning, *The Golden Road to Modernity: Village Life in Contemporary Burma* (Chicago: University of Chicago Press, 1965).

Pye, Lucian W., ed., *Communications and Political Development* (Princeton, N.J.: Princeton University Press, 1963).

_____, *Politics, Personality and Nation Building: Burma's Search for Identity* (New Haven, Conn.: Yale University Press, 1962).

Pye, Lucian W., and Sidney Verba, eds., *Political Culture and Political Development* (Princeton, N.J.: Princeton University Press, 1963).

Redfield, Robert, *A Village That Chose Progress: Cham Kom Revisited* (Chicago: University of Chicago Press, 1950).

# CHAPTER FOUR

## Political Participation in
## the Third World

It is customarily assumed by the proponents of liberal democracy that there is a direct and causal relationship between the spread of mass participation in politics, on the one hand, and levels of human dignity, on the other. In other words, public policies designed to raise the level of human dignity in a society are the direct outgrowth of an increase in mass participation in the political process, primarily through voting in elections and exposure to mass communications.

In this chapter, we will examine this idea as it is applied to politics in the Third World. We are interested specifically in uncovering the connections between mass participation in politics and public policies in Third World countries. If an increase in mass political participation has not brought about an increase in the level of human dignity in many developing countries, the fundamental theoretical cornerstone of liberal democracy would certainly be of dubious validity in typical Third World settings. Furthermore, if we discover this to be the case, we must ask why the link between mass participation and human dignity seems to have been broken, at least in the case of many Third World polities. Let us consider, then, how in the Third World the individual citizen who is not a political professional relates to the government and how those relationships affect public policies.

## DIMENSIONS OF POLITICAL PARTICIPATION

The words political participation mean many different things to different people, depending on the political culture in which they live. We will use the meaning developed by political scientists Samuel P. Huntington and Joan M. Nelson: "activity by private citizens designed to influence governmental decision-making."[1] Political participation has to do specifically with overt, observable behavior or activity. In Chapter Three, we considered the more elusive, inner states of political actors, the attitudes of tradition and modernity. In this chapter, we move one step closer to the actual performance of political systems by examining the actions taken by citizens to influence their government's decisions. We are concerned with the behavior of private citizens, the individuals who do not make politics a profession but who engage in political behavior as an avocation or only intermittently. We will be examining only the activities intended to influence or alter some action or decision forthcoming from a government agency. Many

[1]Samuel P. Huntington and Joan M. Nelson, *No Easy Choice: Political Participation in Developing Countries* (Cambridge: Harvard University Press, 1976).

events have political ramifications, even if they are unintended. These may range from a natural disaster, such as an earthquake, to an act designed to influence some other area of human society (a strike or boycott for example) but that spills over into the political sphere unintentionally. We will limit our inquiry to the activities expressly intended by the actor to influence government policy. This aspect of the definition includes all forms of activity intended to alter public policy, including violent and nonviolent behavior and legal and illegal action.

Finally, we will discuss both autonomous and mobilized behavior in the political arena. This distinction has relatively little significance for Americans, but it is of major importance for citizens of the Third World. In brief, the distinction is this: political participation is autonomous when the actor intends his or her behavior to influence government decisions; it is mobilized when the action is intended by someone other than the actor to influence policy. In many traditional settings in the Third World, individual citizens engage in politically relevant behavior (such as voting or attending rallies) not because they believe that their actions will influence government policy but because some influential or powerful figure in their community (such as a village chief or a union boss) has instructed or otherwise encouraged them to undertake such activities. When we reach our discussion of the patron-client system in Third World politics, we will be referring extensively to the idea of mobilized political participation.

Many observers of traditional politics believe that we should not include mobilized participation in our study because it is not really participation inspired by an individual citizen's belief in his or her own efficacy. We believe, however, that a complete understanding of politics in the Third World cannot be gained without including this kind of participation. Mobilized participation may blend imperceptibly into autonomous action, either because the actor internalizes (that is, learns the action and incorporates it into the repertoire of political choices) or because what starts out as mobilized participation from the vantage point of the actor

may end up being regarded as autonomous by the policy makers who are on the receiving end of the participants' messages. Many Third World governments actively reach out to mobilize their own citizens through mass mobilization parties or other institutional linkages. These official mobilization efforts arise from a government's desire to show to potential opponents the popular support they enjoy, either generally or for a particular policy or decision. Because this aspect of politics is so profoundly important in the transitional societies of the Third World, we cannot ignore such behavior or its implications.

We have so far been using the term, political participation, as if it were a phrase that stood for or represented only one single kind of behavior. Actually, the concept of political participation covers a variety of behavioral patterns that encompass (1) electoral activity, including voting, working in campaigns, seeking to persuade others to vote for a given candidate or party, or otherwise trying to alter the outcome of an election; (2) lobbying, which means contacting government officials to influence their attitudes and behavior on issues that affect significant numbers of people; (3) organizational activity other than lobbying that is designed to influence the general climate within which policy making takes place (such as efforts to influence public opinion on a given issue); (4) individual contacting of public officials to express grievances on a matter relating to a single individual; and (5) violence, meaningful efforts to influence government decisions by doing physical damage to persons or property.

Even though most studies of political participation focus on voting behavior and other forms of electoral activity, we must understand that the other categories are widely used throughout all political systems. However, in any given political system, the precise mixture of forms of participation may vary considerably. A government that has outlawed elections and parties obviously is not encouraging much electoral activity. That simply means that we must look deeper to discover the ways its citizens are expressing their demands, their needs, and their opinions to the government.

## ELECTIONS IN THIRD WORLD POLITICS

The one kind of behavior in which most citizens engage is voting, so, we begin our survey of political participation in the Third World with a look at electoral behavior. Table 4.1 portrays eight selected Third World countries and the level of their citizens' participation in the voting process. Levels of voting vary quite widely. Although voting levels tend to be quite high in the Second World states and somewhat less so in the Western democracies, these levels fluctuate greatly in the Third World. As a general rule, however, about one third to one half of all citizens register to vote in the Third World and about 75 to 90 percent of those registered actual-

**TABLE 4.1** Indicators of Level of Political Participation in Eight Selected Third World Countries

| Country | Indicators of Political Participation |
| --- | --- |
| Nigeria | In presidential election of 1979, 10.6 million persons out of an estimated population of 73 million (about 14.5 percent) voted for the two major candidates. In 1964 elections, 28 percent of the eligible electorate voted. |
| Tanzania | In 1975, there were 5 million registered voters out of a population of about 16 million (about 31 percent). Because Julius Nyerere was elected President for life in 1962, there have been no recent presidential elections. |
| India | In 1971, the number of voters on the electoral roles was about 271 million out of an estimated population of 560 million (about 48 percent). In 1977, the percentage rose to nearly 55 percent registered. Voter turnout to cast ballots customarily runs about 60 percent of those registered. |
| Indonesia | In 1971 elections, 58 million persons registered to vote out of a population estimated at 120 million (about 48 percent); 94 percent of those registered voted. |
| Mexico | In 1975, about 48 percent of Mexico's population had been registered to vote. Voter turnout in most elections is about 30 percent. |
| Brazil | Registered voters are estimated at between 30 and 35 percent of the population as of 1978. Because the president is not elected by direct popular vote, data on voter turnout are not available. |
| Egypt | Voting is mandatory in Egypt, and failure to vote is punishable by fine. Voting for president is indirect. Specific data on registration and turnout percentages are unavailable. |
| Iran | In the 1980 presidential elections, about 14 million persons voted out of an estimated population of 37 million (about 38 percent). |

SOURCE: For Nigeria, Leon Dash, "Nigerian Election Recriminations Revive Sensitivities of Civil War," *Washington Post*, December 28, 1980; Arthur S. Banks and William Overstreet, eds., *Political Handbook of the World, 1980* (New York: Mc-Graw-Hill, 1980), p. 341. For Tanzania, George Thomas Kurian, *Encyclopedia of the Third World* (New York: Facts on File, 1978), vol. 2, pp. 1379, 1383. For India, Kurian, *Encyclopedia, op. cit.*, vol. 1, p. 635; George Thomas Kurian, *The Book of World Rankings* (New York: Facts on File, 1979), Table 37, p. 52; U.S. Department of State, *Country Reports on Human Rights Practices for 1979* (Washington, D.C.: U.S. Government Printing Office, 1980), p. 742. For Indonesia, Kurian, *Encyclopedia, op. cit.*, vol. 1, p. 662; For Mexico, Kurian, *World Rankings, op. cit.*, Table 37, p. 52; Kurian, *Encyclopedia, op. cit.*, vol. 2, p. 990. For Brazil, Kurian, *World Rankings, op. cit.*, Table 37, p. 52; Kurian, *Encyclopedia, op. cit.*, vol. 1, p. 188. For Egypt, *Encyclopedia, op. cit.*, vol. 1, p. 434. For Iran, *Washington Post*, June 23, 1981.

ly turn out. However, in a number of countries (including Brazil, Tanzania, and Egypt), where the election of the president is by means of indirect ballot, the number of persons who actually vote is apt to be misleading.

Electoral competitiveness and honesty are also qualities that are distributed unevenly across the Third World. According to the *World Handbook of Political and Social Indicators,* during the mid-1960s, 26 percent of Third World states held competitive and reasonably free elections; about 35 percent had elections that deviated significantly from the competitive and free norm; nearly 17 percent held elections that were markedly uncompetitive and in which there was widespread fraud; 5 percent held no elections at all; and 15 percent could not be judged for lack of data.[2] Unfortunately, we do not have more recent comparable data on which to judge the electoral behavior of other contemporary Third World states. We see no reason to believe, however, that electoral competitiveness and honesty are any more prevalent now than they were in the 1960s.

At least at the level of symbolic rhetoric, most Third World governments have committed themselves to the principle of popular sovereignty as expressed through universal suffrage, mass voting, regular elections, free competition, and honest counting of the ballots. In many Third World countries, mass voting is not only encouraged but also coerced. A survey of the 28 nations of the Third World for which comparable data are available indicates that an average of 62.6 percent of their adult populations voted in elections held at some point during the middle 1960s. The comparable figure for 20 Western industrial countries is 75.6 percent; for 8 Communist nations, it is 98.7 percent. And, as the data presented earlier indicate, only 5 percent of Third World countries failed to hold elections sometime during the 1960s.

As one might suspect, however, the gap between symbolic promise and tangible performance is wide. Elections in the Third World have been notorious for the way in which the dominant political forces have suppressed opposition parties, coerced illiterate peasants and city workers into voting for the approved candidates, used goon squads to harrass political rallies and to disrupt campaign headquarters, and miscounted ballots or conveniently lost entire ballot boxes in hostile precincts. The list of violations of honest election principles could continue at length. Although few outside observers are in a position to attest to this, national elections in most Third World countries fall far short of offering the voter an honest choice between two or more candidates, each of which has an unfettered opportunity to campaign freely, to see that the ballots are counted, and to take power if victorious. On more than one occasion, in fact, the army has stepped in to nullify elections after the vote showed an unacceptable candidate on the verge of winning (as in Peru in 1962) or to declare certain political groups or parties to be illegal and therefore not entitled to present candidates (as in Argentina several times over the previous decade).

The case of the 1981 Philippines presidential election offers us an interesting example of the ambiguous role of elections in Third World politics. In 1972, President Ferdinand Marcos—serving the third year of his second four-year term—imposed martial law on his country in a move some said was intended to keep himself in office. (The constitution of the Philippines, at that time, limited the president to two four-year terms, as is the case in the United States.) On January 17, 1981, eight years later, Marcos lifted the martial-law edict and initiated the process of changing the country's constitution to permit his reelection. The changed constitution was approved by the electorate in a referendum on April 7, which opponents labeled as a fraud. The amended constitution now allows a president a succession of six-year terms for as many times as he wants and the people approve. Unsurprisingly, Marcos presented himself as a candidate for another term under the new constitution. Against him were presented two token candidates, one of whom ran on a platform favoring American statehood for the Philippines. Opposi-

[2]Charles Taylor and Michael Hudson, eds., *World Handbook of Political and Social Indicators,* 2nd ed. (New Haven, Conn.: Yale University Press, 1972), Table 2.9 pp. 57–58.

tion groups again charged Marcos with fraud and attempted to organize a boycott of the elections. Election day, June 16, 1981, was marked with some violence (13 persons were reported killed in clashes with government troops), and arrests of 45 boycott leaders. The government asserted that 85 percent of Philippine voters had cast ballots; opposition groups argued the number was less than 60 percent. Marcos won overwhelmingly, with 86 percent of the vote.[3]

Even if elections were conducted in a spotlessly clean and scrupulous manner, we would still be concerned about the way in which the average citizen of the Third World views his or her role in elections or the electoral process. No matter how meaningful the elections might be, if they do not convey to the typical villager, peasant, or worker of the developing world a sense of efficacy, elections do not serve effectively the purpose of mobilizing traditional folk into a modern political process.

In his book on village life in Burma, Manning Nash describes the meaning of the electoral process for one set of Burmese villagers.[4] The process began, observes Nash, with a visit by the village headman and the local patron, the village's richest man, to the national capital for a talk with the organizers of the Union Party. Upon their return to the village, the word was passed around the village that the patron, U Sein Ko, had decided to join the Union Party and others from the village were expected to do likewise. The book to enroll new members was kept in U Sein Ko's house. Aspiring members passed by the house for a ceremonial visit and cup of tea; this was followed by enrollment in the party. There were no campaign activities, no mass-enrollment effort, and only one mass meeting (attended by about 40 men of the village) at which U Sein Ko's son was chosen to head the local party organization. On election day, U Sein

Ko's prestige and power as the local patron were sufficiently strong to mobilize 90 percent of the villagers to vote for the Union Party candidate. They voted not out of a conviction that they were influencing policy but out of a complex set of traditional Burmese cultural mores: that society was organized around a local man of power, that followers joined this powerful figure to enjoy his protection from outside forces, and that voting for the Union Party candidate entitled the villagers to receive U Sein Ko's protection from government policies. Thus, we can see that voting plays a very special role in the lives of Burmese villagers, a role that may have little or nothing to do with the policy process or with politics generally.

## VIOLENCE IN THIRD WORLD POLITICS

Violence in Third World politics also must receive special attention in the overall treatment of mass political participation. There seems little doubt that, compared to the rest of the world, the developing countries of Latin America, Asia, and Africa suffer from high incidences of politically relevant violence, such as riots, military coups, assassinations, guerrilla war, and terror-

Helmeted riot police are seen in action quelling a protest demonstration against high prices and unemployment in Lahore, Pakistan. This demonstration took place in April, 1977. Although the government and the army attempted to prevent such assemblies and demonstrations, the continued political unrest added to Pakistan's economic woes throughout 1977. Such turbulence is typical of the tension and instability of politics in Third World countries beset by intractable economic problems.

[3]See the two reports in the *Washington Post* by William Branigan, "Marcos Trying to Thwart Plans for Election Boycott as Voting Nears," June 14, 1981; and "Marcos Easily Wins a Six-Year Term; Vote Is Marked by Opposition Boycott," June 17, 1981.

[4]Manning Nash, *The Golden Road to Modernity: Village Life in Contemporary Burma* (Chicago: University of Chicago Press, 1965), chap. 3.

ism.[5] One important study of political violence from 1955 to 1961 ranked 74 nations on a scale of 0 to 700; 700 represented the highest amount of instability in any country. The 50 nations of the Third World averaged an instability score of 457.5, 10 Communist nations averaged 393.5, and the 24 nations of the Western bloc were scored at 277.3. That same study discovered a close relationship between political instability and level of modernization (as measured by a number of socioeconomic indices, such as mass media and health services). Modern nations had a mean instability score of 268, transitional countries scored 472, and traditional countries achieved a mean score of 470. Still another study of the period from 1961 to 1965 ranked 112 nations according to an empirical index called the Magnitude of Civil Strife (a complex indicator taking into account the number of events of political violence, their duration, and their intensity). The highest score was 48.7, and the mean for the entire sample was 9.08. The 80 nations of the Third World had a mean civil strife score of 14.3, the 10 nations of the Communist world scored 4.9, and the 22 nations of the West averaged 5.3. As of January 1, 1980, 36 nations in the Third World harbored significant insurgent activity, such as guerrilla war or terrorism, or contained at least one clandestine, illegal, opposition group.[6]

According to *The Defense Monitor* (see Table 4.2), there were approximately 37 major and minor armed conflicts raging around the world in late 1979. Of this list, 29 involved Third World states in one way or the other.

In Chapter Three, we discussed the psychological disturbances arising from object loss in rapidly changing societies, such as those we typically find in the Third World. Rapidly changing ideas about political participation also result in heightened levels of disorder and strife, primarily as a consequence of the uneven penetration of modern institutions into a society. Education, government propaganda, and the mass media are the first elements of modernity to impinge on the consciousness of traditional folk; their aspirations and expectations are raised thereby, and they begin to hope that they can achieve some improvement to their lot through government action. However, the other institutions of modernity that we have described—the political party, the associational interest group, the agricultural cooperative, the neighborhood association—all appear much later in the modernization process, and they often fail to appear at all. We have here the classic revolution of rising expectations. Ideas about what people think they should be achieving in politics begin to outreach the institutions available to help them achieve these objectives. The results are frustration, anger, aggression, and a generally increased level of political instability.

One should not conclude, however, that high levels of instability necessarily are associated with political reform. One of the most important features of a developing society is the disjunction between the rural, traditional segment and the modern segment. This absence of an articulating link between traditional and modern is paralleled by a similar gap between those who have power and those who do not. This means that there seldom are linkages between political violence and the actual making of public policy. The high level of political violence witnessed in many Third World countries does not actually affect the prevailing political structures because the violence takes place in a distant arena that is sealed off from the centers of power. As long as the forces of law and order (the police and the army) remain loyal to the government, isolated outbreaks of rioting, terrorism, or guerrilla war can be contained remarkably easily without having much impact on public policy making. Of course, when the army *does* lose confidence in the regime in power, it is a relatively simple matter for it to intervene to overthrow

[5] Ivo K. Feierabend, *et al.*, eds., *Anger, Violence and Politics: Theories and Research* (Englewood Cliffs, N.J.: Prentice-Hall, 1972). The specific articles from this collection that are discussed are Ivo K. Feierabend and Rosalind L. Feierabend, "Systemic Conditions of Political Aggression: An Application of Frustration-Aggression Theory" (chap. 9): and Ted Robert Gurr, "A Causal Model of Civil Strife: A Comparative Analysis Using New Indices" (chap. 10).

[6] Based on a survey of the data in Arthur S. Banks and William Overstreet, eds., *Political Handbook of the World: 1980* (New York: McGraw-Hill, 1980).

**TABLE 4.2**  Armed Conflicts in the Third World in 1979

| Location of Conflict | Date Conflict Began | Warring Parties | Number of Troops (estimated) | Foreign Support | Type of Foreign Support | Number Killed (estimated) | Notes |
|---|---|---|---|---|---|---|---|
| | | MIDDLE EAST AND PERSIAN GULF REGION | | | | | |
| Western Sahara | 1975 | Morocco vs. Polisario guerrillas | 40,000 / 7,000 | U.S., France / Algeria, Libya | Arms & Economic aid / Arms, Economic aid and base camps | N.K.[b] (1,000+?) | High potential for greater U.S. involvement. |
| Lebanon | 1975 | Christian Lebanese vs. Muslim Lebanese & Palestines | 100,000 (all factions) | Israel / Arab & Communist States | Arms / Arms | 50,000 killed | There are also 30,000 Syrian and 6,000 U.N. peace keeping forces in country. |
| Israel | 1948 | Israel vs. Palestinian guerrillas | 174,000[a] (active military & police forces) / 20,000[a] (mainly in Lebanon) | U.S. / Arab & Communist States | Arms & Economic aid / Arms & Economic aid | N.K.[b] (Low-less than 1,000) (1977-79) | Most deaths are in Southern Lebanon and result from Israeli counterattacks |
| Iraq | 1979 | Iraqi government vs. Kurdish & Shiite Muslim guerrillas | 212,000[a] (active military forces) / Several thousands? | U.S.S.R. / Israel (for Kurds) | Arms & Economic aid / Arms | N.K.[b] (Low) | Low level action |
| Syria | 1979 | Syrian government vs. Sunni Moslem rebels | 227,500[a] (active military forces) / Several hundred | U.S.S.R. | Arms & Economic aid | N.K.[b] (Low less than 300 killed in 1979) | |
| Turkey | 1974 | Turkish government vs. Left- and right-wing guerrillas | 686,000[a] (total military & police force) several hundred | U.S. | Arms & Economic aid | 3,000+ (1977-79) only | Most political violence in form of religious rioting and shootings |
| Iran | 1978 | Revolutionary government vs. Left-wing & separatist guerrillas | 200,000+?[a] / 20,000+? | | | N.K.[b] (several thousand) | Serious potential for super-power involvement |
| Pakistan | 1973 | Pakistan government vs. Baluchi guerrillas | 540,000[a] (total military & para-military forces) / 5,000 | U.S. / Afghanistan | Arms & Economic aid / Arms | 3,000+ killed | Currently in a state of truce |
| Afghanistan | 1978 | Afghanistan government vs. Islamic guerrillas | 90,000 / tens of thousands | U.S.S.R. / Pakistan (?) Iran (?) | Arms & Economic aid & Troops/Advisors Arms (?) | 100,000 to 250,000 killed | Most active conflict in the region. Major potential for massive Soviet intervention. |
| North & South Yemen | mid-1950's | North Yemen vs. South Yemen | 36,600[a] / 20,800[a] | U.S., Saudi Arabia / U.S.S.R., Cuba, East Europe | Arms, Economic aid & advisors / Arms, Economic aid & advisors | N.K.[b] (Low) | Currently in a state of truce. |

**TABLE 4.2** (continued)

| Location of Conflict | Date Conflict Began | Warring Parties | Number of Troops (estimated) | Foreign Support | Type of Foreign Support | Number Killed (estimated) | Notes |
|---|---|---|---|---|---|---|---|
| | | | | SUB-SAHARA AFRICA | | | |
| Chad | 1965 | Chad government VS. Islamic rebels | 5,000+ several hundred? | France Libya | Arms, Economic aid and 1,800 French troops arms aid, 3,000 Libyan troops | N.K.[b] N.K.[b] | Libya has occupied 44,000 square miles of Northern Chad |
| Angola | 1975 | Angolan government VS. Anti-Communist guerrillas | 60,000 (Angolan & Cuban forces) 30,000 rebels | U.S.S.R., Cuba & East Europe S. Africa, Zaire, France | arms aid 20,000 troops, 9,000 advisors Arms & Economic aid | N.K.[b] | |
| Ethiopia | 1961 | Ethiopian government VS. Eritrean & Ogaden guerrillas | 230,000[a] (military & para-military forces) 50,000+ | U.S.S.R., Cuba East Europe Somalians & Arab States | Arms, Economic aid and 17,000 soldiers and advisors Arms & Economic aid | N.K.[b] (tens of thousands) | Oldest on-going war in Sub-Sahara region. |
| Namibia | 1968 | South Africa VS. Namibian rebels | 28,000 3,000 | Angola South Africa | Arms & Base camps Arms & Economic aid | N.K.[b] (Low) | |
| Zimbabwe-Rhodesia | 1965 | Zimbabwe government VS. Black guerrillas | 80,000 (military & para-military forces) 20,000+ | African & Communist States | Arms & Economic aid & Base Camps | 20,000+ | Bloodiest War in Africa 500+ a week are killed. |
| Mozambique | 1978 | Mozambique government VS. right-wing rebels | 25,000[a] (total active force) a few hundred | U.S.S.R., Cuba East Europe South Africa | Arms & Economic aid & advisors Arms | Low 200+ | |
| South Africa | Mid-1970s | White regime VS. Black nationalist rebels | 570,000[a] (active & reserve military & police forces) a few hundred | African & Communist states | Arms, Economic aid | N.K.[b] (Low) | |
| | | | | LATIN AMERICA | | | |
| Argentina | 1976 | Argentine government VS. Left- and right wing urban guerrillas | 175,000[a] (active military & para-military) several hundred | U.S. | Arms | 5,000+ (1976–79) | |
| Colombia | 1978 | Colombian government VS. Leftist urban guerrillas | 117,500[a] (active military & para-military) several hundred | U.S. | Arms & Economic Aid | N.K.[b] (Low) | Much of the violence is related to drug trade. |
| El Salvador | 1977 | El Salvadoran government VS. Leftist elements | 10,000[a] (active military & para-military) several hundred | U.S. | Arms & Economic aid | N.K.[b] (Low) | |
| Honduras | 1970's | Honduran government VS. Leftist elements | 14,300[a] (active military & para-military) several hundred | U.S. | Arms & Economic aid | N.K.[b] (Low) | Most guerrilla activity against property. |
| Mexico | 1960's | Mexican government & local land owner VS. Leftist elements | 100,000[a] (active military) several hundred | U.S. | Arms & Economic aid | N.K.[b] (Low) | Social banditry has a long history in southern Mexico |
| Guatemala | 1967 | Guatemalan government & right-wing elements VS. Leftist elements | 21,000+[a] (active military & para-military) less than 1,000 | U.S. | Arms & Economic aid | 22,000+ | |

**TABLE 4.2** (continued)

| Location of Conflict | Date Conflict Began | Warring Parties | Number of Troops (estimated) | Foreign Support | Type of Foreign Support | Number Killed (estimated) | Notes |
|---|---|---|---|---|---|---|---|
| | | | | ASIA | | | |
| Northeast India | 1947 | Indian government VS. Naga & Mizo separatist guerrillas | 150,000 (military & para-military) 2,500 to 5,500+ rebels | China & Burmese Communists | Arms | N.K.[b] (Low) | |
| Philippines | 1972 | Philippine government VS. Islamic & Communist guerrillas | 185,000[a] (total military & police forces) 25,000 | U.S. Libya | Arms & Economic aid Arms | 30,000+ | Level of war increasing, could develop into full scale civil war. |
| Malaysia | 1945 | Malaysian government VS. Communist guerrillas | 77,500[a] (total military & para-military force) 3,000 | U.S., Australia | Arms & Economic aid | N.K.[b] (Low) | Guerrillas are losing |
| Burma | 1948 | Burma government VS. Communist and separatist guerrillas | 242,500[a] (total military & para-military forces) 20,000+ | | | N.K.[b] (Low) | |
| Thailand | 1965 | Thai government VS. Communist and ethnic guerrillas | 282,000[a] (military & para-military forces) 2,000+ | U.S. | Arms & Economic Aid | N.K.[b] (Low) | |
| Indonesia | 1962 | Indonesian government VS. Separatist guerrillas | 351,000[a] (active military & para-military) several hundred? | U.S. | Arms & Economic aid | 100,000+ | |

[a]Not all troops are engaged in combat.

[b]N.K. = not known.

SOURCE: Center for Defense Information, *The Defense Monitor*, 8, 10 (November 1979), pp. 10–11.

the government and to install a military dictatorship. We will consider this phenomenon in detail in Chapter Five.

## INCREASED PARTICIPATION: THE INSTITUTIONAL DIMENSION

Political participation is something that individual persons engage in; political institutions exist merely as the psychological and cultural context within which individuals interact, in politics as well as in any other area of society. When we say, for example, that a certain political party supports a specific candidate or demands a certain kind of policy, we are actually engaging in a sort of shorthand to describe these events. The party as an institution can support or demand nothing; these activities are undertaken by specific individuals who act and speak in the name of the party, a privilege given to them by other members of the party and conferred on them symbolically by granting to them a certain role (party chairperson for example). Thus, although only individuals act, the institutional context within which they act is all-important because it determines how others will react to their behavior.

Political leaders of the Third World are confronted with a major problem in their efforts to mobilize previously traditional groups and to weld them tightly into the modernizing political system. In Chapter Three, we saw some of the difficulties they encountered in designing institutions that would convert traditional personalities into modern ones with a minimum of disruption. In this chapter, we see the same kind of difficulties experienced in a somewhat different context, that is, how to mobilize previously inert citizens and make them active citizens, without disruption or political decay.[7]

Many Third World nations suffer from what anthropologist, Manning Nash has called multiple societies.[8] The multiple society is a divided social order consisting of two separate social systems that are bound together by a single set of economic, political, and legal bonds. One social system of this divided society is national in scope, is urbanized (usually living in the capital city), identifies with the nation as an abstract concept, maintains relations with other nations, and is in touch with the trends of modernity around the world. The national segment supplies the nation with its political, economic, and intellectual élites. It has access to resources of economic and political power and is the arena within which the contests over the use of these resources is focused. The other social system (or systems) of the multiple society is region based or village based. It lives in the countryside, small towns or villages, or in big-city slums and rarely identifies itself as a part of the nation. It is traditional in attitude but may be undergoing certain aspects of the transition to modernity, particularly in the economic sphere. Its only resources are regional in nature, and even these are tiny when compared with the resources of the national élite.

The tension of political modernization arises from the difficulties encountered in attempting to link together these two halves of the multiple society. The two halves are poorly connected. The national segment is the planner, the organizer, the decision maker for the nation; the rural, village segment is rarely more than the raw material for political purposes. Communications rarely pass freely between the two segments.

Three devices, or social forms, have been used to link together the two segments of the multiple society. These are (1) the mass communications media; (2) modernizing political institutions, such as the political party and the interest group; and (3) the patron-client system.

We have already discussed in another context government use of the mass communications media (see Chapter Three).[9] We found, as you may recall, that the mass media had little lasting effect on the more substantial dimensions of attitudinal change. In the same way, we find that

---

[7]Samuel P. Huntington, *Political Order in Changing Societies* (New Haven, Conn.: Yale University Press, 1968).

[8]Manning Nash, "Southeast Asian Society: Dual or Multiple," *Journal of Asian Studies*, 23, 3 (May 1964), pp. 417–431.

[9]Lucian W. Pye, ed., *Communications and Political Development* (Princeton, N.J.: Princeton University Press, 1963).

the mass media are of little value in providing the linkages needed to mobilize the village-based segment of the multiple society and to give it a vigorous role in policy making at the national level. There are several reasons why the mass media are inefficient instruments for mobilizing mass participation. Use of the mass media requires an investment of something of value, such as money, time, energy, or attention span. In the rural and low-income areas of the Third World, all of these things are in extremely short supply, and there is rarely little surplus left to expend on an activity for which there is so little demonstrable reward. The mass media are of value only in communicating information and in providing people with an intellectual framework that they can use to make sense of their surroundings. We have been stressing here the institutional context of participation because, among other reasons, the institutions of participation act as a sort of school of modernization by making traditional peoples aware of the countless demands of interpersonal exchanges and dealings. In providing traditional peoples with only information, the mass media offer only one dimension (and by far the least important one) of political participation. Without the institutional surroundings of the political group or party, the new participants will not learn the valuable lessons of how to get things accomplished by working with others in politics.

Perhaps the most significant reason why the mass media cannot mobilize rural folk is that they tend to be channeled through the single source of power and authority in each village or neighborhood. In a moment, we will encounter the patron-client system so prevalent in Third World local politics, and we will begin to get some idea of how politics is carried on in the day-to-day life of traditional peoples. For now, let us just observe that the political boss, or patron, of each village, tribe, or neighborhood effectively controls the mass media, just as he or she controls everything else of value. What the people know of the mass media is usually what the patron wants them to know. In the remote Mexican village of Cham Kom, for example, anthropologist Robert Redfield found that only two or three

men regularly read a newspaper; among them was the village patron, Don Eus.

> The knowledge that other people in Cham Kom have of the matters reported or urged in these papers comes to them largely as Don Eus, having read the paper, explains the contents as the men sit together in the plaza in the evening.[10]

Manning Nash found much the same sort of situation in small villages in Burma where, at least in one case, the village patron received a copy of the city newspaper and left it in a special place outside his home for others in the village to peruse at their convenience. No one else in the village received the publication, leaving the village chief in virtually complete control over the mass media exposure of the people of the village.[11] Because traditional culture states that the validity of an item of information is determined by its source and not by the degree to which it conforms to some abstract standard of scientific correctness, traditional society cannot use the mass communications media as a tool to transform its people into active, mobilized citizens.

This brings us to the set of modernizing institutions considered so important by Western scholars: the political party and the associational interest group, the agricultural cooperative and the labor union, the neighborhood civic association, and the ethnic interest group. (See Table 4.3 for description of status of political parties and interest groups in eight selected countries.)

## POLITICAL PARTIES

Historically, political parties have appeared in political systems under one or more of three conditions.[12] First, in the older parliamentary systems of Western Europe and North America, parties were preceded by the emergence within parliament of factions that organized themselves

[10]Robert Redfield, *A Village that Chose Progress: Cham Kom Revisited* (Chicago: University of Chicago Press, 1950), p. 144.

[11]Nash, *The Golden Road to Modernity, op. cit.,* p. 283.

[12]Joseph LaPalombara and Myron Weiner, "The Origin and Development of Political Parties," in Joseph LaPalombara and Myron Weiner, eds., *Political Parties and Political Development* (Princeton, N.J.: Princeton University Press, 1966), pp. 3–42.

**TABLE 4.3** Data on Political Parties and Labor Unions in Eight Selected Third World Countries as of 1979–1980

| Country | Status of Parties, Labor Unions |
| --- | --- |
| Nigeria | 1966 ban on parties lifted in 1978. Parliamentary democracy restored in 1979. All unions belong to a single labor federation which represents about 3 million workers. Most unions have the right to strike and bargain collectively. |
| Tanzania | The sole legal political party is the Chama Cha Mapinduzi (CCM), the Revolutionary Party of Tanzania, formed in 1977. About 4 percent of labor force represented by the sole official union. All other unions banned. Strikes are illegal. |
| India | Multiparty system with most ideological viewpoints represented by legal parties, including Marxist. About 2.5 percent of the labor force is unionized but unions are divided and their influence is weak. Strikes are legal but rare. |
| Indonesia | There are three official parties, all created and sponsored by official agencies of the government, including the armed forces. Less than 10 percent of the labor force is unionized. All unions are weak. Strikes are rare. |
| Mexico | Officially a multiparty system, but the ruling party, the PRI (Institutional Revolutionary Party) customarily wins more than 90 percent of the vote. About one quarter of the labor force is unionized. Unions are relatively free, but industrial disputes are submitted to compulsory arbitration by the government |
| Brazil | In 1979, the officially sanctioned two-party system was abolished and replaced with an apparently more open multiparty system. However, to qualify for approval as a legal party, groups must pass a rigorous set of rules. Nearly half the labor force is unionized, but industrial disputes are controlled by Ministry of Labor. |
| Egypt | The sole official party, the Arab Socialist Union (ASU), was founded in 1962. No other parties are permitted. The sole labor union permitted is closely tied to ASU. |
| Iran | Parliamentary system established following overthrow of Shah, but parties must conform to concept of Islamic Republic to be approved. Multiple parties contested presidential elections in January 1980. Unions not organized on independent basis, but oil workers have demonstrated considerable power to hurt economy through strikes. |

SOURCE: George Thomas Kurian, *Encyclopedia of the Third World*, (2 vols.) (New York: Facts on File, 1978); Arthur S. Banks and William Overstreet, eds., *Political Handbook of the World: 1980* (New York: McGraw-Hill, 1980); and U.S. Department of State, *Country Reports on Human Rights Practices for 1979* (Washington, D.C.: U.S. Government Printing Office, 1980).

internally and, then, turned their attention to the winning of electoral support from within the broader populace. Clearly, the development of parties under these circumstances had to be accompanied by the growth of the electorate, which, in turn, was linked to reforms in the electoral law. In the Third World, the only area where this development had a chance to occur was in the more advanced regions of Latin America, particularly Argentina and Chile. There, Liberal and Conservative parties came into being during the mid-nineteenth century. However, where these groupings did emerge, they failed to enlist popular support and became stunted in their growth, either because they were unable to relate to the needs of the masses or because their unprincipled exploitation and manipulation of the electoral laws caused a wholesale degeneration of public morality, which led eventually to military rule, as in Argentina.

Parties can also emerge during a specific developmental crisis that has to do either with the legitimacy of the regime, with the establishment of an integrated national society, or with the channeling of large numbers of newly mobilized persons into political activity. In the new nations of Africa and Asia, the struggle against the colonial rulers provided the setting for the creation of nationalist parties. Their main function was to mobilize popular support for the battle against the metropolitan country and to convince everyone concerned (including themselves) that their nation had the right to exist as a separate social and political entity. Where large unassimilated ethnic groups declined to pay homage to the new national entity, it was expected that the nationalist mobilization party would provide them with the new identification they needed. There are several classic examples of such a party: the Congress Party of India, the Convention People's Party in Ghana, and the Tanganyika African National Union (TANU) of Tanganyika (now Tanzania). In other cases, parties like Malaysia's Alliance Party or the Democratic Party of the Ivory Coast (PDCI) have been particularly effective in overriding ethnic and regional loyalties and in mobilizing disparate peoples into a single, embracing national system.[13] In those instances where a single nationalist party was not formed prior to independence, such as in Nigeria, much greater latitude was given to the unassimilated ethnic and tribal minorities; consequences for national unity in Nigeria have been quite negative.

Another condition accompanying the formation of political parties has to do with the social modernization of the country and the need to harness the unleashed social forces and turn them to some political benefit. In this case, political parties emerge from a society that is being assaulted by the forces of modernization—communications, economic development, mass education, the disruption of traditional social forms and attitudes—and that lacks the organizational framework to discipline itself. The alternative appears to be chaos; men and women are uprooted psychologically and lack social and political reference points. The modernizing nationalist reform party, then, is created, not to lead the nation to independence (that has already been accomplished) but to help establish order in a disorderly world. There are a few clear-cut examples of such a party, particularly in Latin America: Accion Democratica in Venezuela, the Institutional Revolutionary Party ["*Partido Revolucionaro Institucional*" (PRI)] in Mexico, and the National Liberation Party of Costa Rica. In other areas of the Third World, modernizing parties would include the Republican People's Party of Turkey and the Destourian Socialist Party of Tunisia.

Regardless of the social or political origins of parties in the Third World, they seldom perform exactly the same kind of functions that are carried out by their counterpart organizations in Western democracies. In the United States, we are accustomed to thinking of political parties as possessing four characteristics (at least in theory): (1) organizational continuity, a lifespan that outlasts the life of the current leadership; (2) an organizational structure that is permanent and that extends down to the local level; (3) a leadership determined to capture and hold decision-making power, not simply to influence the exercise of such power; and (4) an effort to persuade voters to vote for their candidates.

Political parties in the Third World are, at the same time, both more and less than this formulation. The more successful parties are well organized down to the local block level. Tunisia's Destourian Socialist Party has more than 1000 cells with an average of 100 to 400 members each and operates effectively at the lowest precinct sphere of local politics. In addition, the party has formed close working alliances with the country's only labor union and has formed within itself an artisans' and shop-

[13]Richard E. Stryker, "A Local Perspective on Developmental Strategy in the Ivory Coast," in Michael F. Lofchie, ed., *The State of Nations: Constraints on Development in Independent Africa* (Berkeley: University of California Press, 1971), pp. 134–135.

keepers' section, a farmers' union, a student group, a youth section, a scout organization for young boys, and a women's organization. Some of the older, successful parties, such as Mexico's PRI, have managed to transfer leadership and power to several younger generations without breaking the organizational continuity of the party. Effective modernization parties, such as Accion Democratica of Venezuela, provide social services for their members that go far beyond the mere mobilization of voters. A typical local office of one of these parties could be expected to provide information on jobs to an unemployed member, housing for a newly arrived person, or recreation for the member who wishes to spend his or her idle hours with friends.

But, if some political parties do more than their Western counterparts, many (perhaps most) do considerably less. Most organizations that call themselves parties in fact only faintly resemble what we would recognize by that name. Many are only the personal creations of a specific individual or family, and they will fade away after that person's death or loss of interest in politics. Many others have some ideological base but lack the organizational basis to carry through the periods out of power. Most parties are underfinanced and understaffed, and they suffer from a lack of experienced personnel who can manage complex bureaucracies.

Probably the most significant difference between Third World parties and their counterparts in the First World is that Third World parties are not necessarily organized to organize and mobilize voters, to win elections, and to hold power for some recognizable political purpose. In perhaps a majority of the cases, Third World parties exist not to compete with other parties for votes but to link the newly mobilized citizens to the modern segment of the multiple society. These parties operate in a noncompetitive situation. They are the only party permitted by law. About one third of all Third World states, including Algeria, Burma, Egypt, Kenya, the Philippines, Tunisia, and Zaire permit only one official party to exist. Many others (the exact number would be impossible to to determine) are legally multi party states, but are *de facto* one-party systems because of the legalized dominance of one party over all the rest. Mexico is the best-known example of this phenomenon; other examples include Costa Rica, Indonesia, and Taiwan. In these systems, the dominant or single party exists not to mobilize the voters to win elections but, instead, to act as a communications and educational channel that hopefully will tie together the rural, traditional section of society with the modern, urban segment.[14]

## INTEREST GROUPS

Going beyond the political party, we find a wide variety of associational interest groups. For ease of discussion, let us categorize these interest groups according to whether or not the rationale for their existence is economic or not.

Generally, countries that are still relatively traditional in their economic and social makeup are also countries where the most active associational interest groups are those that cut across economic lines and are based on noneconomic criteria for membership. In many emerging African countries, urban neighborhoods are frequently organized by tribal or ethnic associations that exist to serve the social needs of their kinfolk recently arrived in the city from the countryside. According to Peter C. Lloyd, these ethnic associations assist recent arrivals to find housing and employment, incorporate them into a group that shares their culture and their language, and act as an informal conflict-resolution device for disputes between members of the association.[15] Local government ties with these associations will usually be limited to some sort of informal advisory status but, occasionally, the associations will assist the local municipal administration by acting as a law enforcement authority in the local neighborhood. Other traditional, noneconomic interest groups might revolve around such criteria as religion, language, or kinship patterns. One would expect that, as a society modernizes, the bases for such grouping would erode consid-

[14]Henry Bienen, "Political Parties and Political Machines in Africa," in Lofchie, *op. cit.*, chap. 9.

[15]Peter C. Lloyd, *Africa in Social Change* (Baltimore: Penguin, 1975).

The city of Caracas, Venezuela, must house a population of over two million, about one-fifth of the nation's total. Slum dwellings, called "ranchos," cover the mountains surrounding the city and contrast sharply with the city's modern skyscrapers. The government would like to destroy the shantytowns and move the slum dwellers into the nearby high-rise apartments, but the modern buildings cannot be erected fast enough to accommodate the city's exploding population.

erably; but the activity of distinct ethnic groups in American politics, such as the activity of people of Italian or Polish origin, should make us aware that noneconomic criteria for human association persist in even advanced states of modernity.

As a nation's economic system modernizes, it also becomes more differentiated. This means that its members begin to take on tasks and role assignments that are more and more specialized and that require specialized knowledge and working conditions. This is the basis for the growth of associational interest groups based on economic self-interest. Of these, the most important politically is the trade or labor union.[16]

Trade unions in Third World countries differ substantially from their Western counterparts. Although Western (particularly American) unions concentrate on their economic needs first and leave formal political activity aside, in the Third World, trade union activity has become distinctly political, with little interest in pursuing a specifically economic approach. Because trade unions in the Third World are especially weak compared with Western trade unions, they rely much more on official or political party support and nurturance; such support frequently leads to control and political dominance.

The sources of trade union weakness in developing countries can be summarized quickly.

[16]Bruce H. Millen, *The Political Role of Labor in Developing Countries* (Washington, D.C.: Brookings Institute, 1963); Everett M. Kassalow, "Trade Unionism and the Development Process in the New Nations: A Comparative View," in

Solomon Barkin *et al.*, eds., *International Labor* (New York: Harper Row, 1967), pp. 62–80. Everett M. Kassalow, ed., *National Labor Movements in the Postwar World* (Evanston, Ill.: Northwestern University Press, 1963).

The still-traditional state of the country's economy means that many, if not most, of the workers will be employed in jobs that are hard to unionize: subsistence agriculture, service tasks in urban areas (domestic servants, street vendors), and so forth. Rural farm workers are difficult to organize because of their geographical isolation. Consequently, trade unions rarely represent more than a small fraction of the workers in any given country. At least 10 states in the Third World have no unions whatsoever, another dozen or so have only one officially recognized union to which few workers belong, and the remainder have tiny, fragmented unions that represent 1 to 20 percent of the workers. To give some examples, the percentage of the work force represented by unions in Algeria is 17 percent; in India, 2.5 percent; in Colombia, 13 percent; and in Iran, Iraq, and Nicaragua only about 1 percent.[17] A second source of weakness for Third World unions is their lack of regular financial support. Most of the workers in low income areas lack the means to contribute regularly to union treasuries. Strike funds and other financial accoutrements of modern union activity must either be obtained from official sources, from sources outside the country (the competing American and Soviet-sponsored international trade union movements), or must be done without. In many countries, such as Zambia and Malaysia, prevailing ethnic or tribal allegiances cut across the working class and split the labor movement into quarreling factions. Add to these problems the lack of administrative personnel and the rampant graft and corruption within Third World unions, and one can see why the working class is only weakly represented, if at all, in these countries.

A second reason for the increased politicization of Third World unions has to do with the level of economic development of the country. During a country's early stages of development, there is a great need for investment capital, which can only be gotten from two places. Either foreign sources must supply the financial aid through government loans or through private investment (both of which are distasteful to Third World governments) or there must be an economic surplus created within the country itself. If the latter strategy is adopted, the citizens of the country must be forced or persuaded to produce more than they consume, at least for the first decade or two of the development plan. This objective runs exactly counter to the rationale for trade unions, that is, to obtain increasing financial returns from the economic system for their members. This conflict is often referred to as the struggle between the consumption and savings imperatives of economic development. Although some economists assert that there is no necessary conflict between the two, most governments persist in their belief that there is such a conflict and that the only way to resolve the struggle is by persuading the working classes to accept a certain sacrifice for the initial period of the development effort. Peasants are not usually affected by this call for sacrifice because they produce and consume so little already that they could have little impact on development no matter what they do. Most upper- and middle-income groups are likewise little affected, because their political power makes them immune to such government confiscatory taxation policies. Obviously, few free and independent trade unions would accept such a bargain and most union members would overthrow any leadership that tried to impose such an arrangement on the members. Thus, governments in developing countries must bring unions under their official jurisdiction to make them compliant members of the national development effort.

As a consequence of these factors, trade unions in the Third World are much more tightly controlled by politically organizations than in the West. They are rarely free and independent in the sense that American unions are free. Instead, they are usually directly controlled by the country's Ministry of Labor or they are merely a union sector integrated into the single or dominant political party. Either way, the trade union offers little opportunity to mobilize apathetic lower-income or working-class persons into political activity.

[17]The World Factbook: 1974 (Acton, Mass.: Publishing Sciences Group, 1974).

Until the 1980s, governments in the Third World had been fairly successful in preserving peace in the industrial labor movement. There are some early warning signs, however, that labor unions in key developing countries are becoming restive and impatient. In Mexico, despite the prestige and power attributed to the Mexican Workers' Federation (CTM), younger leaders are beginning to challenge the older leadership, and charges of corruption and selling out to Mexican industry are having the effect of weakening the strength of the labor bureaucrats. In Brazil, Latin America's most dynamic and popular labor leader, Luis Ignacio da Silva, has come to offer such a strong challenge to the military regime that they have succeeded in convicting him of leading an illegal strike and have sentenced him to three-and one-half years in prison. In Nigeria, the socialist-leaning leadership of the Nigerian Labor Congress has rejected pleas from the government that they restrain wage-increase demands, and, in fact, the unions in 1980 demanded three times as great an increase as the recommended rise offered by the new president, Shehu Shagari. These are clear signals that the economic cramp of the 1970s may well lead to major explosions in the 1980s in the major industrial countries of the Third World.[18]

Roughly, the same degree of underdevelopment in trade union organization is seen in Third World organizations that represent middle-class professional and business interests. Perhaps as many as half the countries in the Third World report having something like a Chamber of Commerce but, in most intances, these business organizations are just small clubs that operate in the capital city. Only a few countries possess highly differentiated business-sector interest groups that cover the entire range of a modernizing economy. Even in a relatively advanced country like Chile, where the private business sector is well represented by interest groups of

long standing, only a minority of business leaders actually bother with the work of such groups, out of indifference, the press of business, or a feeling that political action is not likely to produce tangible benefits for business interests.[19] Because of their relatively high level of development and because of the high degree of American business influence, Venezuela and Mexico have developed very large, well-financed, and well-organized business- and manufacturing-interest associations that have a great deal of influence with their respective governments. But these two countries are definitely in a tiny minority among Third World states.

The wealthy members of a nation's economy have ways of making their influence felt without the assistance of formal organizations or interest groups. Wealthy landowners, industrialists, and the representatives of foreign corporations are usually able to get the attention of the president or other top officials of a country merely by virtue of their strategic location in the system, apart from any special organization representation they may enjoy. The wielding of influence by Western multinational corporations, such as Lockheed Aircraft or International Telephone and Telegraph, to gain special favors in the developing world is already well known. Other examples of such foreign business intervention in Third World politics would be Gulf Oil Company's payment of $460,000 to Bolivian President, René Barrientos, from 1966 to 1969 to obtain special favors for their operations in Bolivia or United Brands' payment of $1.25 million to Honduran military dictator, Oswaldo Lopez Arellano, in return for exemptions from Honduran export taxes. Such tactics for gaining influence are equally well employed by the wealthy within the nation. Even governments that profess a radical and uncompromising hostility to the traditional business and agrarian élites of their countries are usually found to be doing business with them behind closed doors,

[18]Marlise Simons, "Labor Patriarch Is Key Figure in Evolving Mexico," *Washington Post*, December 28, 1979; Jim Brooke, "Union Leader Vexes Brazil's Military Leaders," *Washington Post*, March 4, 1981; Leon Dash, "Restive Unions Pose a Threat to Nigeria's Plans," *Washington Post*, December 27, 1980.

[19]Dale L. Johnson, "The National and Progressive Bourgeoisie in Chile," in James D. Cockcroft *et al.*, eds. *Dependence and Underdevelopment: Latin America's Political Economy* (Garden City, N.Y.: Doubleday, 1972), pp. 201–206.

reformist rhetoric to the contrary notwithstanding.

In addition to the groups already mentioned, there are at least three other kinds of interest groups that span both economic and noneconomic criteria for membership; these are students, peasants, and neighborhoods. Student groups in all parts of the world came into prominence during the 1960s as the source of unrest and disorder as well as the voice for radical changes in many societies. In a few countries, such as Korea and Venezuela, students came close to disrupting society sufficiently to bring about the downfall of the government. In Latin America, particularly, where the principle of the inviolability of a university campus had been used for generations to protect student protestors, the role of students in politics has been especially important. Many prominent Latin American political leaders, such as Fidel Castro of Cuba and Romulo Betancourt of Venezuela, got their start as leaders of student political groups.

In several countries, in addition, peasant groups or leagues have been formed to represent the needs and demands of the low-income, landless workers of the soil. Sometimes peasant leagues are created by government agricultural ministries or by political parties as mobilization devices to gain political support (as in Venezuela) or as administrative devices to assist in the implementation of land reform programs (as in Egypt). At other times, as in Brazil, peasant leagues have been formed essentially free of offical control, in which case they are usually suppressed by government action. In either case, they are seldom the channel for the mass mobilization hoped for by Western observers.

Finally, in many cities there are neighborhood associations whose objective it is to force government attention to persisting urban problems that they cannot solve by themselves—garbage collection, crime control, water, housing, paved streets, and so forth. In most Third World countries, but especially in Latin America and South Asia, a prime urban problem is that of the squatters, the illegal residents of urban slums or shantytowns. In cities like Lima or Caracas, the squatters have formed associations to establish some primitive organizational framework to administer their neighborhoods and to pressure the national government into granting them legal title to their lands. In many cases, where these association have been careful to limit their demands to very narrowly stated aims and where they have been willing to resort to disruptive action to achieve their objectives, they have been reasonably successful.

## PATRON-CLIENT POLITICS: THE FAILURE OF INSTITUTION BUILDING

Institutions are the key to increased political participation in rapidly modernizing societies. Yet, the record shows relatively few effective modernizing (and modern) institutional linkages between traditional, low-income peasants and urban workers, on the one hand, and the modern, nationalistic city élites, on the other—a mass mobilization political party in Mexico or Venezuela, the village institutes in Turkey, an agricultural cooperative in Pakistan, ethnic or tribal associations in Nigeria or Ghana. The scarcity of these few examples shows how thinly modernization is penetrating into the Third World in an institutional sense.

Why are so many Third World political leaders unable to build the institutional bridges out to the traditional folk of their countries? For one thing, many members of the modern, well-educated élites in developing countries cannot understand the ways in which traditional, lower-status people calculate the costs and benefits of their daily lives. The Westernized education received by the modernizing élites has often blinded them to the essential rationality of the traditional style of life. They have forgotten, if they ever knew, the ways in which the elemental forces that play on the lives of traditional people impel them toward personal calculations that appear irrational to Western-trained observers. Often, the city élites in Third World countries cannot even speak the same language spoken by rural villagers; if they do share the same language, they do not speak similar dialects. In any case, communication of the simplest sort is rendered difficult, if not impossible. The urban, modern élites, in the shape of the visiting bureaucrat, planner, or agricultural extension agent, cannot empathize with, or even communicate with, the intended client.

Even where the bureaucrats of the national government are committed to a style of reform in the countryside that is intended to benefit the peasants, they frequently expect the peasants to respond to their plans as if some sort of modern class consciousness existed among the rural workers. When the peasants refuse to respond favorably to these plans and institutions, the bureaucrats become exasperated with their backward or childlike clients and impatiently decide to coerce the peasants into actions and decisions that are manifestly in their own interest. In Chile, during the reformist regime of Salvador Allende, bureaucrats from the capital swarmed over the countryside intent on building a more modern and just social order. Land was to be expropriated from the large landowners and placed in collectives to be worked communally by the peasants. The proceeds would be pooled and, then, redistributed equally, with a percentage going to the state to pay for the whole enterprise. Naturally, but to the surprise of the modernizing bureaucrats, the peasants would silently nod their assent to the project and, then, quietly go about the business of sabotaging the collectives. The bureaucrats were astounded at the lack of consciousness of their clients; frequently, they were provoked into using coercion to motivate the peasants to act more according to their own rational interests (of course, as those interests were defined by the bureaucrats.)[20]

As a consequence, élites cannot construct institutional arrangements that can induce, support, and reinforce modern behavior and attitudes. The characteristics of such arrangements, such as new farming techniques or novel methods for selecting a village chief, depend to a large extent on shared standards of rationality; these, in turn, derive in essence from the ideas of modernity. Remove these ideas and the shared standards of rationality and the institutional arrangements will collapse because of the unwillingness of the people to internalize their lessons and to assimilate them into their daily lives. The problem is aggravated when the agents of social and technological change are merely temporary vistors in a rural area. A few months after bringing some innovation to the village, they may return to the comfort of the city, abandoning the villagers to their fate with the new equipment, seeds, medicines, or books. Small wonder that the villagers are reluctant to commit themselves to an unknown factor in their struggle to eke out a bare subsistence from the soil. Experience with the new miracle grains in Asia showed that the only farmers who were willing to adopt the new methods and seeds were those who were already wealthy and could afford to risk a bad crop. Those who lived perpetually on the edge of starvation were unwilling to risk any departure from the prevailing norms.

Traditional peoples in the Third World also lack what the nineteenth-century, French social observer, Alexis de Tocqueville, called the "art of associating together," by which he meant the ability of people to join together in common enterprises. In traditional parts of the world, we find many people unwilling to join with others, especially if the others are not of their kin group or ethnic circle. After all, where everyone lives so close to the margin of survival, there is little reason to trust one another, especially in the context of a formal institution, such as a political party. In modern institutions, trust is derived from formal, impersonal features, like laws, rights, obligations, and constitutional provisions. In traditional institutions, trust derives from personal familiarity, thereby limiting sharply the number of people who will meet the requirements of mutual trust in any consensus-based political organization.

Finally, and perhaps most important, reform governments in the Third World frequently fail to construct modernizing institutions in traditional areas because, in each case, some powerful traditional political force is present to resist such institutionalization. These traditional

[20]David Lehmann, "Agrarian Reform in Chile, 1965–1972: An Essay in Contradictions," in David Lehmann, ed., *Peasants, Landlords and Governments: Agrarian Reform in the Third World* (New York: Holmes & Meier, 1974), p. 109.

forces may be religious (priests, witch doctors, shamans), political (village chiefs), or economic (large landowners, peasants). Whatever the source of their power, these individuals resist modernizing institutions because they understand clearly that the introduction of these institutions into their community will undermine their power, their privileges (where they have them), and their accustomed way of life. Not surprisingly, they will fight back with the tools and weapons at their disposal, such as money, graft, bribes, rural insurgencies, refusal to implement the law, and voodoo and other ritualistic devices. And, in most places in the Third World where this confrontation is taking place, the forces of tradition are winning or, at least, holding their own.

As a consequence, mass local politics in the Third World has fallen under the control of numerous patron-client systems or what John Duncan Powell calls "clientelist politics."[21] These patron-client relationships stand midway between the tribal chieftancies of the traditional, precolonial era, on the one hand, and the modern, bureaucratic, rule-oriented authority relationships of urban, industrial politics. The patrons in question may be people of immense power, such as large landowners and priests, or they may be persons of modest influence, such as money lenders, ward bosses, and other kinds of intermediaries. Their clients may be poor, illiterate peasants, small shopkeepers, or even urban workers. But, however they are constructed and wherever they are, patron-client political systems are extremely important to Third World politics for several reasons: (1) they constitute the primary (and, often, the sole) channel for rural and urban poor to be involved in political activity, (2) they have great influence over the ways in which public policies are implemented at the local level, and (3) they are (or can be) valuable sources of information for modernizing élites who are attempting to formulate a policy to solve some recurrent problem. In the terms of

this chapter, however, patron-client politics is most significant because of what it says about the failure of Third World elites to construct modernizing institutions to guide the newly mobilized citizen into productive and constructive political participation.

## CONCLUSIONS: POLITICAL PARTICIPATION AND HUMAN DIGNITY

Mass populations in the Third World are not the inert and helpless lumps of clay as they are often depicted in Western literature. In some ways, citizens participate in politics to as great a degree as they do in modern, industrialized nations; in a few instances, they may even participate more than their Western counterparts. Yet, this increased political participation does not translate evenly into public policies that are aimed at enhancing human dignity. It is almost as if there were a short circuit in the connection between mass participation and public policy in many developing countries.

In this chapter, we have identified the causes of this break in the link between participation and policy. The mass media are seen as an insufficient mobilizing agent because they fail to involve the citizen in an active role in the political process. The various institutions of political participation—parties, associational interest groups, and the like—exist only in fragmentary form and are often coopted by the very government that they exist to influence. Even well-meaning reformist bureaucrats have difficulty in constructing the institutions of mass participation because of cultural and economic reasons we presented earlier.

In the absence of these other channels for involvement, Third World citizens are mobilized (if that is the correct word in this case) by patron-client systems or they are provoked by their frustration into unstructured violence. The aggressive features of political life in developing countries have been fully documented and seem to stem from the unsettling experiences of change unrelieved by any opportunity for the citizen to intervene in the process of modernization. The patron-client system exists not to influence pol-

---

[21]John D. Powell, "Peasant Society and Clientelistic Politics," *American Political Science Review*, 64 (2) (1970), pp. 411–426.

icy but, instead, to confer on a selected powerful few the privileges of an élitist society while maintaining the rhetoric of liberal democracy.

In sum, mass participation in Third World politics frequently fails to elicit progressive public policies because there are few institutions whose purpose it is to transmit popular needs and demands and to link together the mass of the village and the slum with the national élites in the capital city.

# Suggestions for Further Reading

**Alba, Victor,** *Politics and the Labor Movement in Latin America* (Stanford, Calif.: Stanford University Press, 1968).

**Davies, Ioan,** *African Trade Unions* (London: Penguin, 1966).

**Feierabend, Ivo K., Rosalind L. Feierabend,** and **Ted Robert Gurr,** eds., *Anger, Violence and Politics: Theories and Research* (Englewood Cliffs, N.J.: Prentice-Hall, 1972).

**Galenson, Walter,** ed., *Labor in Developing Countries* (Berkeley: University of California Press, 1962).

**Hodgkin, Thomas,** *African Political Parties* (London: Penguin, 1961).

**Huizer, Gerrit,** *The Revolutionary Potential of Peasants in Latin America* (Lexington, Mass.: D. C. Heath, 1972).

**Huntington, Samuel P.** *Political Order in Changing Societies* (New Haven, Conn.: Yale University Press, 1968).

**Huntington, Samuel P.** and **Joan M. Nelson,** *No Easy Choice: Political Participation in Developing Countries* (Cambridge: Harvard University Press, 1976).

**LaPalombara, Joseph,** and **Myron Weiner,** eds., *Political Parties and Political Development* (Princeton, N.J.: Princeton University Press, 1966).

**Leiden, Carl,** and **Karl M. Schmitt,** *The Politics of Violence: Revolution in the Modern World* (Englewood Cliffs, N.J.: Prentice-Hall, 1968).

**McKenzie, William J. M.** and **Kenneth Robinson,** eds., *Five Elections in Africa* (Oxford: Clarendon, 1960).

**Millen, Bruce H.,** *The Political Role of Labor in the Developing Countries* (Washington, D.C.: Brookings Institute 1963).

**Smith, T. E.,** *Elections in Developing Countries* (London: Macmillan, 1960).

**Vega, Luis Mercier,** *Guerrillas in Latin America: The Technique of the Counter-State* (New York: Praeger, 1969).

**Weiner, Myron,** *Party Politics in India: The Development of a Multi-Party System* (Princeton, N.J.: Princeton University Press, 1957).

# CHAPTER FIVE

## Government Structures in the Third World

The historical, psychological, social, cultural, and economic features of a society provide the setting within which official government structures must operate. We have already seen the ways in which the setting of politics influences policies designed to increase human dignity. It is now time to examine some of the typical political institutions likely to be found in the Third World. We are concerned with uncovering links between kinds of formal institutions and levels of human dignity in a given country and across the Third World. Or, to put it another way, are the government structures that are typical of the Third World capable of undertaking policies that vigorously enhance human dignity in their societies? If not, how can we identify and explain major flaws in the political structures of developing countries?

### POLITICAL IMPLICATIONS OF DELAYED INDUSTRIALIZATION

Most countries in the Third World possess what some scholars have called regimes of delayed industrialization.[1] This means that these countries

typically began their industrialization process considerably after the nations of Western Europe and North America. The reasons for this delay and its consequences are central to an understanding of the prevailing Third World government structures.

Industrialization as a social process is never cheap. In fact, where the process has more or less run its course, the costs are seen to have been extremely high. Although the costs of industrialization are always high, regimes vary widely along other important dimensions of the industrialization process, for example, which social classes will pay the costs, which will receive the benefits, and how rapidly will the overall process be carried out. The process of industrial growth seems to require a good deal of social coercion, but whether or not it explodes into revolutionary violence or class warfare depends on how a polity answers these questions.

The high costs of industrialization stem directly from the massive shifts in human values, attitudes, resources, and behavioral propensities that accompany the change from a preindustrial to an industrial society.[2] Income must be trans-

[1]Mary Matossian, "Ideologies of Delayed Industrialization: Some Tensions and Ambiguities," *Economic Development and Cultural Change, 6* (3) (1958), pp. 217–228. This important article has been reprinted in several places, including

Claude E. Welch, Jr., ed., *Political Modernization* (Belmont, Calif.: Wadsworth, 1967), pp. 332–334.

[2]Walt W. Rostow, *The Stages of Economic Growth* (Cambridge: At the University Press, 1960).

ferred from those who spend unproductively (on luxuries) to those who will spend productively (on capital equipment). Current consumption must be held down in favor of future investment. Unproductive agrarian classes (mostly peasants) must be encouraged or forced to leave their land and move to the cities where they form the large pool of potential laborers.[3] The commercialization of agriculture and the shift of agrarian resources into food and away from export crops make possible the growing of enough food to maintain the urban working classes in a state of health and vigor that is adequate to make them productive workers. To cite Barrington Moore, Jr., the policy challenge of industrialization amounts " . . . to using a combination of economic incentives and political compulsion to induce the people on the land to improve productivity and at the same time taking a substantial part of the surplus so generated to construct an industrial society. Behind this problem there stands a political one, whether or not a class of people has arisen in the society with the capacity and ruthlessness to force through the changes."[4]

Nations that began their drive to industrialization relatively late must modernize under much more difficult conditions than such early industrial states as Great Britain or the United States. For the latecomers, internal social structures are not conducive to such far-reaching changes. Language, race, religion, class, and ethnic divisions present seemingly insurmountable obstacles to rapid development. Abroad, the special position enjoyed by the already-industrialized states blocks the developing countries from reaping the benefits of the international trade system. As traditional social structures and attitudes crumble under the strain of modernization, Westernized intellectuals agonize over some new kind of ideology that can guide their people toward a new brand of social cohesion. When industrialization is delayed, the tendency is for the process to take place in an atmosphere of intense

feeling, hostility, passion, class and national prejudices, and there is little inclination to preserve the rights of the individual citizen.

Some late industrializers, including the Soviet Union, China, and Cuba, have chosen to deal with these obstacles by means of the model of development called (by political scientist A. F. K. Organski) the Stalinist alternative.[5] Stalinist regimes are characterized by the violent destruction of the premodern rural classes—both landed aristocracy and peasantry—and the accumulation of massive coercive power in the hands of an industrial élite. This élite uses its power to squeeze all possible surplus out of both the urban and the agrarian working classes and fuels the industrialization effort with this surplus. Peasants are driven from the land by collectivization, and the gentry by confiscation. Although the cost in terms of human suffering is high, the results of forced-draft industrialization are impressive.

Most of the other late industrializers, including a majority of the countries of the Third World, have followed still another path to development. Syncratic politics is the term coined by Organski to describe this model. The chief characteristic of the syncratic model is how the government attempts to handle the inevitable conflict between the old landlord class and the rising industrialists. In liberal democracies, such as Great Britain, the conflict dissolved slowly as the agrarian sector modernized and became commercialized. In Stalinist countries, the industrial élites smashed the antimodern classes, frequently using the peasants as shock troops against the landlords, only to dismantle the peasant class itself once the revolution was consolidated. In the syncratic model, however, agrarian interests are too powerful, or industrial sectors too weak, to permit either of these solutions. The result is a shaky compromise that involves completely different kinds of bargains, payoffs, and protective devices. In sum, syncratic politics refers to the style of governance that emerges in late industrializing countries when the agrarian class is too

[3] Barrington Moore, Jr., *Social Origins of Dictatorship and Democracy: Lord and Peasant in the Making of the Modern World* (Boston: Beacon, 1966).

[4] *Ibid.*, pp. 385–386.

[5] A. F. K. Organski, *The Stages of Political Development* (New York: Knopf, 1965).

strong to be destroyed or converted by the industrial élite, and, so, must be brought into some sort of broad coalition to preserve the special premodern conditions of the countryside.

Although they are both members of their nation's economic élite, the landed aristocracy and the industrialists are actually divided from one another by a number of inescapable economic schisms. For one thing, agrarian and industrial élites frequently come from different regions of the country or are members of different ethnic, racial, linguistic, or religious groups. These noneconomic differences may aggravate emerging class distinctions. More important, the economic roles of the two classes are antithetical. Industrialists exist to save, invest, and produce; landlords exist to consume and to withhold resources from production. Urban élites value work and self-sacrifice; agrarian élites regard manual labor as demeaning. Industrialists need a large, mobile, well-educated, disciplined, and motivated work force and will seek to lure farm workers into the cities to fill this need; landlords want to keep their peasant class docile, traditional, and poorly educated so that they will not wish to upset the clientelist system. The industrialists intend to squeeze the agricultural sector of its surplus production through taxation and to use the resources to advance the state's industrial base; the landlords quite naturally will try to resist being used in this manner.

In a few instances, the rural and industrial élites have managed to cover over their differences enough to cooperate in governing the country, usually through the mechanism of a semiparliamentary, authoritarian regime that, although strong, would still fall short of a military dictatorship. In most cases, however, economic crisis or foreign threat causes internal conditions to deteriorate. As the previously quiet lower classes clamor for change, the coalition loses its nerve and submits either to a syncratic party or to a military dictator who can impose order and establish the conditions necessary for industrialization to continue.

Once in power, a syncratic regime typically undertakes a set of reform measures designed to industrialize the country without disturbing the social structures of the countryside. Traditional territorial divisions, local peculiarities, and internal barriers to trade are suppressed, and strong central government agencies are put in charge of the nation's economic fortunes. The mass of citizens must be brought into the modern social order by means of the expansion of literacy and technical skills. Antimodern loyalties to region, clan, religion, or ethnic kin are overridden. Steps are taken to stimulate latent industrial potential. Government incentives, including protective tariffs, are used to aid native manufacturing. Where the private sector is unwilling or unable to invest in a needed project, the state itself will mobilize the needed capital. Because it appears that these early measures favor the industrial élite, a syncratic regime discovers it must now provide benefits to the other partner in the coalition. Agricultural élites are kept in the partnership through three types of policy. First, they are permitted a great deal of freedom to perpetuate their exploitation of the countryside, and the central government stands ready to suppress rural rebellion where it should occur. Second, by using the threat of revolution, the regime may convince the conservative, traditional élites that they have little choice but to side with the state in the struggle. Finally, industrial workers are kept under control by the enactment of increasingly liberal welfare measures and by the use of corporatist labor organizations that bind the urban proletariat into the structure of the state economic system.

The special compromises struck by the syncratic state mean that the costs of industrial development are allocated much differently than in the liberal bourgeois or Stalinist models. Because the landed upper classes are protected by the syncratic compromise and their hold over the land is left unmolested, the surplus for reinvestment (forced savings) must come from some other source. Occasionally, these resources may be derived through foreign aid from one of the wealthy states in the international system, but this is a weak and insecure support on which to rest the industrialization policy. Eventually, the syncratic state must turn to the only remaining source of capital: the fledgling industrial sector itself. To cite Organski:

> Under a syncratic system, the savings for investment in industry are squeezed primarily out of the industrial sector itself, not gathered from the entire country. To a very large extent, the savings in the industrial sector are created by increases in productivity in the modern portion of the economy and by decreases in the living standard of the industrial proletariat.[6]

The 10½-year (1958 to 1969) military regime of General Mohammed Ayub Khan of Pakistan offers a clear example of a syncratic regime in action.[7] The Ayub government took power in Pakistan in October 1958, following a period of prolonged instability, unrest, and violence under the former parliamentary system. The 1958 proclamation of martial law lasted for almost 4 years, until March 1962. Pakistan lived under martial law for 8 years between 1958 and 1971. During the period that Ayub was the chief executive of the country, Pakistanis had little access to open or free government; the executive branch of the government controlled all aspects of the country's political life. The 1962 constitution legitimized one-man rule by placing all political functions—legislative, executive, and judicial—into the hands of Ayub.

From 1958 to 1969, Pakistan's economy experienced a strong growth trend, with gross national product (GNP) rising at the average rate of 6 percent per year during the 1960s. A new business and industrialist class was fostered by government stimulus, but little was done for the urban proletariat or for the landless rural workers. An extremely small number of wealthy families continued to enjoy control of the growing industrial power of the nation, but income inequalities increased during Ayub's regime instead of diminishing.

The rhetorical dimension of Ayub's so-called revolution illustrates the syncratic govern-

ance style in action. In the case of land reform, the government responded to a critical problem by creating the Land Reform Commission in 1958. The Commission's report, issued in early 1959, contained only the mildest kind of recommendations for Ayub but was still accepted by him with only minor changes. Few large land-owners lost land; few, if any, peasants received any land. Apparently, Ayub was unwilling to risk losing support from the wealthy rural sector by imposing forced expropriation of agrarian lands. In other areas, such as equal rights for women or education, far-reaching laws were passed, but little attention was paid to implementation or to the financial burdens of such legislation. The result was that a large set of unenforced (probably unenforceable) laws developed that merely specified desirable goals, but left unanswered the question of how to reach them.

This gap between rhetoric and reality was not the product of ignorance or incompetence on the part of Ayub Khan and his colleagues; instead, it was the calculated effort on his part to build a governing coalition made up of both élites: the modernizing, urban-based nationalists and the tradition-bound, rural aristocracy. In the cities, Ayub not only sought to stimulate industrial development but also turned government policy toward strengthening the army, both as a modernizing bureaucracy and as the ultimate arbiter of Pakistan's fate in any armed clashes. In the countryside, as we have seen, Ayub's rule was more notable for what it did not achieve than for what it did. The privileges of the landed élites were maintained and, perhaps, even strengthened.

Ayub was not without his opponents and, in the end, the disturbances caused by these opposition sectors unseated his government. The major forces against the regime were the disaffected intellectuals of the universities and the professions, religious leaders, the urban middle class, and the urban and rural workers. Toward the end of Ayub's regime in 1968, these groups began to express their displeasure with the fact that they were being asked to carry more than their fair share of the development burden. The result was

---

[6]Organski, *Ibid.*, p. 139.

[7]Robert LaPorte, Jr., "Pakistan and Bangladesh," in Robert N. Kearney, ed., *Politics and Modernization in South and Southeast Asia* (New York: Wiley, 1975), pp. 122–135.

a series of street clashes between rioting workers and students and the army and police. By 1969, matters had worsened to the point that the army insisted that Ayub step down and allow a successor regime to try to restore order. Faced with these realities, Ayub resigned his office in March 1969 and appointed another general to take his place.

Recent reports of political unrest and government repression in Pakistan illustrate well the continuing agony unleashed by the syncratic approach to politics. In early 1981, after more than three weeks of student riots, the martial-law government of President Mohammed Zia ul-Haq launched an intensive crackdown on dissidents, jailing at least a dozen opposition leaders who had been demanding an end to his three-and-one-half-year rule. Zia had come to power in 1977 by overthrowing (and later arresting and executing) President Zulfikar Ali Bhutto. When he seized power, Zia had promised prompt elections and a return to democracy, but, in October 1979, he canceled voting scheduled for that fall. Pakistan's inability to find a formula for long-term solutions to its pressing problems typifies the Third World in many respects.[8]

The syncratic political style is both a cause and a consequence of a social phenomenon we have noted before: the uneven penetration of modernization through various layers of a traditional society. On the one hand, uneven rates of modernization in a traditional society allow the rural élites to retain their stranglehold on the political system despite the progressive modernization of the industrial sector in the cities. At the same time, the syncratic state perpetuates this uneven penetration of modernity simply because it exists by relying on two antithetical social groupings. For these reasons, the syncratic political style is an integral part of the central characteristic of Third World social, economic, and political systems today. They are separated into dual societies: one modern, rational, secular, urban, and nationalistic; the other traditional, religious (or mystical), rural, and particularistic.

Binding together all of these features of Third World politics is a three-tier institutional arrangement that we will now consider in detail. At the top is what we will call (following Robert Gamer[9]) the major network. The major network consists of the power élite of the country, the national government ministries, the civil and military bureaucracy, and the industrial-entrepreneurial leaders. These individuals are almost always located in the nation's capital city, cut off from the vast majority of the country. The major network extracts political support, obedience, labor, and agricultural commodities from the general populace with whom they are linked by the second level of institutions (the many minor networks). The minor networks consist of the middle-echelon patrons, the leaders of patron-client systems both in the cities and in the countryside. These patrons receive personal rewards for their service that are at least adequate to maintain a satisfactory lifestyle. Below these minor networks lies the vast bulk of the population, usually unorganized and unrepresented in the power structure by any forces other than their patrons. The masses supply the national system with labor and with commodities, and they participate in the system more or less regularly by means of symbolic exercises like voting for similar candidates in fraudulent elections. The patrons maintain their clients in a state of commitment to the system by a variety of means that we will examine shortly.

## MINOR NETWORKS: PATRON-CLIENT POLITICS

In the small, remote Honduran village of Tocoa lives a very powerful man named Carlos Bascha. Señor Bascha does not derive his power from any formal elective office, his ownership of large areas of land, or any special religious or ethnic status. Señor Bascha is, instead, simply the freight agent for the Honduran national airline, which operates (irregularly) a DC-3 flight into Tocoa, the only link between the village and the

[8]Stuart Auerbach, "A Dozen Pakistani Leaders Arrested After Student, Political Unrest," *Washington Post,* February 26, 1981.

[9]Robert E. Gamer, *The Developing Nations: A Comparative Perspective* (Boston: Allyn & Bacon, 1976), chap. 4.

outside world. Tocoa was at one time situated on a rail line constructed by the United Fruit Company many years ago. With the onset of a blight, the land in the vicinity was rendered useless for growing bananas, so, the company took up the line, leaving Tocoa almost completely isolated from the rest of Honduras. All commercial activity, such as the movement of locally cultivated agricultural produce, depends on the air service provided by the government. Because Señor Bascha controls that service, he rather completely controls the town. Preferential freight rates tie certain influential villagers to his goodwill, and Bascha's general store (the only one in town) is allowed to dominate the village's local commerce. Señor Bascha is, in our terms, a patron; the people of Tocoa are his clients.

In remote villages of Burma, Manning Nash reports, the patron may or may not be the elected village headman. In some cases, such as in the village of Nondwin, another man, more powerful than the headman, may be regarded as the local patron. In Nondwin, this local power, named U Sein Ko, was not only the richest man in the village but the person with whom everyone had to check in case of any dispute or political question. His power derived from the almost mystical aura of *pon*, the Burmese concept of control, which implies one's possession of the ability to make others conform to one's wishes. U Sein Ko had this ability; no one else in the village did. Therefore, the village population clustered around him to bask in the warmth of his power and to receive protection from it.[10]

Patron-client systems are very important features of urban politics in Third World countries as well. In large cities throughout the Third World, such as Lima or Caracas, the festering slums and impoverished neighborhoods have produced squatters' associations to protect the land rights of the residents. These usually come under the jurisdiction or control of local patrons who defend the interests of their clients and receive deference and respect (as well as more material rewards) from them in return. Several observers of the work of political parties in African cities have likened them to the big-city machines in the United States and other Western countries, especially as they operated before World War II. In Africa, these political machines rarely operate on the basis of ideology or political theory but more often win their support as patrons win support from clients by using an intricate mixture of coercion, prestige, material benefits (spoils), bribes, cajolery, and ceremony.[11] Other modern interest groups, such as labor unions, often find themselves infiltrated by tribal-based patron-client systems that use tribal, ethnic, and linguistic cleavages to fragment the unions and render them helpless. The presence of traditional patron-client relationships within their organizations helps explain the weakness of the otherwise powerful copper miners' union in Zambia or the rubber workers' union in Malaysia.[12]

Latin American specialist John Duncan Powell has observed that the patron-client system is marked by three characteristics. First, the tie between patron and client develops between two parties who are unequal in status, wealth, and influence. Second, the formation and maintenance of the relationship depends on the reciprocal exchange of goods or services. Finally, the development and maintenance of the system depends largely on face-to-face contact between patrons and their clients.[13] In his study of Thailand, Clark D. Neher writes,

> The ideal superior acts as a patron and is expected to protect, aid, complement, and give generously to those whose status is inferior. In return, the subordinate, or client, is expected to act deferentially to the superior, who is his patron. He is expected to

[10]Manning Nash, *The Golden Road to Modernity: Village Life in Contemporary Burma* (Chicago: Chicago University Press, 1965), pp. 73–93.

[11]Henry Bienen, "Political Parties and Political Machines in Africa," in Michael F. Lofchie, ed., *The State of the Nations: Constraints on Development in Independent Africa* (Berkeley, Calif.: University of California Press, 1971), chap. 8.

[12]Henry L. Bretton, *Power and Politics in Africa* (Chicago: Aldine, 1973), p. 258; Gordon P. Means, "Malaysia," in Kearney, *op. cit.*, p. 202.

[13]John Duncan Powell, "Peasant Society and Clientelistic Politics," *American Political Science Review, 64* (2) (1970), pp. 411–425. See also Rene Lemarchand, "Political Clientelism and Ethnicity in Tropical Africa: Competing Solidarities in Nation-Building," *American Political Science Review, 64* (1) (1972), pp. 68–90.

perform tasks efficiently and with the least amount of trouble for his superior. The subordinate maintains his inferior position by not challenging the superior or undermining the latter's position.[14]

Patron-client relationships can be classified according to the kinds of values that pass in exchange. Those that are of greatest relevance to the political order involve power, trust, and loyalty. The clients of such a system support their patrons' choices for public office; in return, they receive government services and personal security.

Patron-client systems are crucial to developing countries as links between the national, urban-based modernizing élites, on the one hand, and the mass of urban and rural laborers, on the other hand. Most patron-client systems can be viewed as existing at two levels. At the lowest level, in the rural village or the big-city neighborhood, clientelistic politics involves a relationship between large numbers of low-status persons and a single powerful patron who defends the interests of his or her clients and who receives deference or more material rewards in return. This patron, however, is also a member of another, higher level patron-client system but this time as a client to a member of the national, urban élite. The intermediary depends on an élite patron to deliver special treatment to his or her clients, but the intermediary also provides valuable services to the urban élites, particularly by mobilizing the low-status clients for mass manifestations of loyalty to the regime, such as demonstrations and elections. Patron-client systems at the village or neighborhood level are institutions that lean backward toward tradition instead of looking forward toward modernity. At the lowest level of operation, patron-client systems usually do not contribute to the modernization of the nation-state but, instead, detract from this process. In the case of patron-client links that tie intermediaries to national élites, however, the resources and values that are exchanged come closer to characterizing what we think of as modern politics: money, power, and all of the

symbolic and tangible manifestations of these (votes, land, and so on).

Because of this dual nature, patron-client political systems can be regarded either favorably or unfavorably for their impact on the overall process of political development. Some observers, such as Robert E. Gamer,[15] are quite critical of clientelistic politics. As they see it, such political processes always work a hardship on the mass of clients at the very bottom of the pyramid. According to this view, patron-client systems owe their origin to the uneven penetration of modernity through the several layers of a traditional social order. The modern nation-state has enough power and organizational ability to reach down into the traditional sectors to manipulate the masses and to mobilize them to perform the symbolic functions of politics, such as voting; but the two-way institutions that are truly indicative of modern politics—political parties and associational interest groups—are simply lacking in most Third World countries. In the absence of parties and interest groups, patrons are brought to the fore to facilitate communication (mostly of a top-down nature) between élites and masses. In the course of this communication process, however, the intermediaries extract their due (and more) from the exchange and the minor networks end up receiving much less in terms of material well-being than they should. Accordingly, only the creation of truly modern, mass-based institutions, such as political parties, can do away with the exploitative patron-client systems and extend modernity all the way down to the very lowest level of society.

However, another way of looking at the question (as exemplified by John Duncan Powell[16]) holds that, at the middle level of operation, patron-client systems offer the potential for being transformed into modernizing institutions. Powell cites as an example the various peasant leagues that were created by the Venezuelan reformist political parties, primarily Acción Democrática. These leagues were not, at the outset,

[14]Clark D. Neher, "Thailand," in Kearney, *op. cit.*, p. 228.

[15]Gamer, *op. cit.*
[16]Powell, *op. cit.*

what we would regard as modern institutions. They were still operating on the basis of patron-client principles: unequal status, exchange of goods and services, obedience and deference, loyalty and security, a face-to-face communications system, and so forth. Yet, the leaders of Accion Democratica relied on these leagues for the mobilization of the peasants as potential voters, and they used their vigorous land-reform program to attract peasant voters to their standard. Thus, Accion Democratica transformed the clientelistic peasant leagues into modernizing institutions capable of linking the peasant (and, subsequently, the middle-class farmer) into the national political system in a way that meets the needs of the low-status members of the network.

The Venezuelan experience, although not unique, is certainly the exception rather than the rule. In the majority of Third World countries, low-status persons, whether in the city or in the country, simply have no other way to communicate with their government other than through their local patron. Transportation and communication gaps cause rigidity in the links between the government and its people; the absence of mass-based, modernizing institutions, such as parties and interest groups, likewise contribute to blocking effective communication. For good or ill, in most developing countries, patron-client systems (the minor networks of Robert E. Gamer) are almost the only connection between the nation and the mass of citizens.

## MAJOR NETWORKS: THE DOMINANT EXECUTIVE

The cornerstone of the American system of government is expressed by the phrase, separation of powers. During the Republic's formative years, the new American colonial élite were so eager to prevent government from abusing the rights of the citizens that they devised a simple formula for keeping the central government weak: divide power and authority into so many hostile and competing institutions that the constant struggle between and among these agencies will occupy their attention and drain their resources so that

there will be little of either left over to direct toward the average citizen in private life. John Taylor, a noted liberal writer of the period, expressed the thought this way:

> Power is divided by our policy, that the people may maintain their sovereignty. . . . Our principle of division is used to reduce power to that degree of temperature, which may make it a blessing and not a curse. . . . We do not balance power against power. It is our policy to reduce it by division, in order to preserve the political power of the people.[17]

But it was James Madison, the principal author of the Constitution, who expressed the classic argument in favor of separation of powers:

> But the great security against a gradual concentration of . . . powers in the same department consists in giving to those who administer each department the necessary constitutional means and personal motives to resist encroachments of others. . . . Ambition must be made to counteract ambition. The interest of the man must be connected with the constitutional rights of the place. . . . If men were angels, no government would be necessary. If angels were to govern man, neither external nor internal controls on government would be necessary. In framing a government which is to be administered by men over men, the great difficulty lies in this: you must first enable the government to control the governed; and in the next place oblige it to control itself. A dependence on the people is, no doubt, the primary control on the government; but experience has taught mankind the necessity of auxiliary precautions.[18]

Indeed, much of American political history can be seen as a struggle between and among Madison's auxiliary precautions: the various states against the national government, the legislature against the President, the courts against each of the others, and so on.

Because the principle of separation of powers is so deeply embedded in the American political system, it may seem strange to note that

[17]John Taylor, *Inquiry into the Principles and Policy of the Government of the United States* (New Haven, Conn.: Yale University Press, 1950), pp. 171, 356.

[18]Alexander Hamilton, John Jay, and James Madison, *The Federalist* (New York: Random House, 1937), p. 337.

few other countries in the world share our aversion toward centralizing power in the hands of a single institution or person. Among the Third World countries, almost none have political institutions and constitutional structures that try to divide powers among several competing agencies or sources of authority. In Latin America, the Spanish and Portuguese tradition of centralized power in a monarchy was transmitted to the New World in undiluted form, and was amalgamated with the indigenous political systems, which were similarly inclined toward centralization of power.[19] In Africa and Asia, the native, precolonial political systems were usually of the centralized and unified type. The introduction of European power did nothing to alter this situation. The practice of direct rule employed by France, Holland, and other continental colonial powers lodged power in the mother country. British indirect rule merely confirmed authority in the local rulers (tribal chieftains, village headmen, and so on) who had been the beneficiaries of centralized power for centuries. Thus, the countries of the Third World came to independence and began their drive to development with little in the way of historical preparation for, or appreciation of, governance by means of separation of powers.

At the same time, Third World leaders confronted problems quite different from those faced by Washington, Madison, Hamilton, and Jefferson. The new country of America came into being determined to free the individual from government interference and, thus, to reduce government power, but the new states of the Third World find that they must *increase* government power to meet the critical problems created by the dual processes of industrialization and modernization. Instead of limiting government's power, what the élites of the Third World want to do is break the substantial constraints on their power so that they might better cope with the social and economic difficulties of which America's founding élite could have been only dimly aware.

Finally, in the industrialized West, we have a tendency to look at government not as a party to a given dispute but as the reconciler of conflicting interests, the ultimate recourse for the resolution of conflict. This view depends, however, on the prior existence of a rich and accessible network of modern institutions that are essentially outside government: political parties, interest groups, and many different kinds of voluntary associations, such as the Rotary or the Kiwanis. These institutions are notably lacking in most Third World countries. Voluntary associations are almost completely unknown in many developing countries; where they do exist, they are weakened by the traditional mistrust with which such associations are viewed by low-status individuals in poor countries. Parties and interest groups are frequently controlled by the government itself, and they are used not to channel messages upward from the populace but to channel commands and rhetoric downward from the regime. In this context, government becomes more than a reconciler of interests, it becomes a party to the dispute. Consequently, there is great pressure on the government to adopt a unified position, to employ decision-making techniques that accelerate action and suppress dissent. The result is an inclination to override whatever institutional separation of powers there might have been to begin with.

The notion of separation of powers actually has two different meanings. The first meaning has to do with the separation of powers within the policy-making body of government. (The second meaning will be discussed shortly.) Regardless of the form that government may take, there are three more or less distinct functions that must be performed in the course of the policy process: legislation (the adoption of general principles and the statement of general goals); execution (the translaton of these principles and goals into politically acceptable actions); and adjudication (the judgment of the fairness of the application of the general principles in specific cases where a party is thought to be damaged). In the United States, we like to think of these three functions as being assigned primarily to the three corresponding institutions: the Congress, the

[19]Claudio Veliz, "Centralism and Nationalism in Latin America," *Foreign Affairs*, 47 (1) (1968), pp. 69–83.

President, and the Supreme Court. (In reality, the dividing lines are much fuzzier in practice than they are in theory.) But, in the Third World, they tend to be performed by the same institution or, in some extreme cases, by the same individual. That latter phenomenon we call the principle of executive dominance. In the struggle among and between competing institutions of government in the developing world, it is the executive power that has won.

Let us consider some concrete manifestations of the executive-dominant system in the Third World. Most observers of politics regard an independent legislature or parliament as the surest check on the power of the executive. A survey of the 101 Third World nations in 1980 reveals that in 30, the legislative branch has been summarily dismissed, dissolved, or suspended indefinitely. In many others, the legislature consists solely or largely of persons appointed by the president or military ruler. In instances where the legislature is freely elected, it usually has such little real power that it is reduced to the task of ratifying the decisions made by the executive power.

Another indicator of executive dominance is the degree to which incumbents manipulate or suspend the constitution or engage in other electoral irregularities to remain in power beyond the end of their legally prescribed term of office. In 1980, at least 32 Third World countries were operating either without any constitution or with their basic law suspended or bypassed by the executive. And more than half of the countries (54) experienced significant electoral irregularities (or even no elections at all in a few cases) during the period from 1960 to 1976.

Not all examples of executive dominance are extralegal or unconstitutional. Many Third World executives enjoy extraordinary powers as a consequence of a constitutional grant of authority. The 1962 Republic of Tanganyika Act provided that, "except as may otherwise be provided by law, in the exercise of his functions, the President shall act at his own discretion and shall not be obliged to follow advice tendered by any other person." Following this broad grant of authority, President Julius K. Nyerere acted unilaterally to end discrimination against non-Africans

in the civil service; to unite Tanganyika with Zanzibar (creating Tanzania); to introduce a one-party state, making the Tanzania African National Union the sole legal party in the country; to break diplomatic relations with Great Britain in 1965; and to create completely new agencies, such as the Village Resettlement Agency (1963).[20]

Other Third World executives enjoy similar powers. The President of Brazil can constitutionally appoint state governors and the mayors of municipalities, and dissolve the Brazilian Congress if it disagrees with his decisions. The Prime Minister of Singapore has imposed one-party rule, jailed political opponents and held them for years without trial, closed down newspapers, and otherwise suppressed public dissent, and all within the boundaries of the country's Constitution. For 17 months, from late 1975 through early 1977, India's Prime Minister, Indira Ghandi, ruled her giant country under the provisions of emergency law, which permitted her to censor the press and jail her opponents for simple acts of dissidence. In all, at least 100,000 dissidents were imprisoned during this period. In parliamentary elections in March 1977, Mrs. Ghandi was defeated. She has since returned to power and in mid-1980 sought once again to impose emergency police measures in India to suppress unrest in rebellious Assam State. Again, as in the other instances cited above, Mrs. Ghandi's acts were all decreed by her as Prime Minister and were within the bounds imposed by the Indian Constitution.[21]

Executive dominance is also reflected in the relatively high degree of administrative centralization that exists in most Third World countries. The nation's chief executive dominates legislative and judicial colleagues at the national level, and, because of the concentration of administrative power in the hands of the national government

[20]R. Cranford Pratt, "The Cabinet and Presidential Leadership in Tanzania: 1960–1966," in Lofchie, op. cit., pp. 96, 112, 116.

[21]See two Washington Post articles by Stuart Auerbach, "Indian Government Increases Powers," September 24, 1980; and "Gandhi in Crisis as Her Leadership Is Being Openly Questioned," October 16, 1980.

he or she also dominates local, provincial, and municipal governments.

In his excellent analysis of local administration in Thailand,[22] Clark D. Neher has identified three separate but closely interrelated patterns of authority that apply to local populations in that country. The territorial or provincial administration, which receives its power and resources from the central government in Bangkok, is the most powerful of the three systems. Briefly, this administrative system consists of the Minister of Interior, 71 provincial governors, and 530 district officers. The Minister of Interior appoints, removes, and transfers both the provincial governors and the district officers; these subordinate officials are, consequently, responsible to the Interior Minister in all that they do. All major decisions are referred to the Minister. The provincial governors are powerful only in a sort of derivative sense, that is, they have no resources themselves but derive power from carrying out central government decrees. District officers' authority seems to be restricted primarily to the supervision of the Ministry's local employees and to the filling out and submission of an almost endless number of forms and reports. The second pattern of authority consists of some 50,000 villages that, in turn, are clustered into about 5000 communes for some limited purposes of self-government. Each village elects a headman who, as we saw in the example drawn from Burma earlier, may have considerable social and economic power in addition to his formal political authority. But the actual powers of the village and commune are restricted to making arrests in criminal cases, settling petty disputes and quarrels, submitting reports and information to higher authorities, and deciding how to spend the meager sums distributed to the villages from the central government. The third pattern of authority, called local self-government units, is the weakest system of the three. It consists of provincial councils, municipal councils, and sanitation districts. The first two bodies are purely deliberative institutions; all substantive policy decisions remain in the hands of the central government.

Sanitation districts are charged with responsibilities in such fields as garbage collection, street paving, street and house lighting, slaughterhouse regulation, water and sewage facilities, and health centers. These units are notoriously inefficient and lack adequate funds for their many operations.

Most local authority in Third World countries lies effectively in the hands of the national governments, primarily in the various ministries of interior and their subordinate units. In instances where local units actually have authority, however, a serious lack of resources prevents them from taking advantage of this constitutional delegation of power. Henry Bretton reports that local self-government in many African countries is hampered by a lack of locally obtained and locally expended funds.[23] Local governments either do not have the authority to collect their own taxes or, if they do have such authority, they lack the trained personnel to apply the authority efficiently. In addition, where power resides so solidly in the national government and local governments lack the financial resources to cope with local problems, the obvious strategy for patron-client systems is to bypass the local administrators and go straight to the pertinent ministry in the capital. Such a development further weakens local government and strengthens the central administration's ties over local patrons in a vicious circle of progressive local debilitation. This sort of circumstance seems to be a significant reason why state governors and municipal mayors in Mexico are bypassed by local patrons and interest-group leaders who feel that the only place their problem can be handled is in Mexico City.

## MAJOR NETWORKS: THE MILITARY BUREAUCRACY

As noted earlier, one meaning of separation of powers involves the division of the legislative, executive, and judicial functions of the policy-making process among these separate institutions. The second meaning involves separating

[22]Neher, op. cit., pp. 233–237.

[23]Bretton, op. cit., pp. 141–145.

the institutions that make policy from those that implement it, that is, the civil and military bureaucrats that put the political decisions into effect. It is usually assumed by observers of Western democracy that the individuals who administer or implement policy must be separated from those who make policy because of the need to identify clearly the lines of political responsibility. At least in theory, those who make policy are somehow to be more or less directly responsible to the electorate who can judge the policies and change them if they desire simply by electing a different group of policy makers. Bureaucrats, on the other hand, are invulnerable to voter pressure; they are not supposed actually to make policy but, instead, should simply apply the decisions of the political officials in successive specific cases. To the degree that bureaucrats, either civil or military, stray across the line from policy implementation to policy making, they are acting in an antidemocratic fashion because they are putting into effect policy decisions over which the sovereign public has no control.[24]

Problems connected with the operations of the civil bureaucracy in the Third World (corruption, lack of training, clientelism) will be discussed in Chapter Six, "Policy Making in the Third World." In this section, we concentrate on the intervention of the armed forces into the policy-making process in the developing world.

It is true that, on occasion, some democratic governments in the Third World have welcomed military intervention in politics to restore order to political life. Yet, in the larger sense, military intervention in civilian politics constitutes a major barrier to Third World political development. Military intervention in politics has been a major problem of Latin American governments ever since the nineteenth century. During the 36-year period from 1930 to 1965, there were 106 illegal and unscheduled changes in the heads of state in the countries of Latin America; all but a tiny portion of these changes were initiated and carried out by the military although frequently with ci-

vilian support and encouragement. There were many observers, however, who believed that the nations of Africa and Asia that became independent after World War II would be spared this dismal history and would demonstrate that civilian constitutional regimes could meet the severe problems of development in a stable and responsive manner without succumbing to military rule. Such hopes have been destroyed by military coups in most of the countries in Africa, the Middle East, and Asia and by continued military rule in 32 of them. Table 5.1 indicates the extent of military intervention throughout the Third World. These data show that a coup or attempted coup occurred once every 4 months in Latin America (from 1945 to 1972), once every 7 months in Asia (1947 to 1972), once every 3 months in the Middle East (1949 to 1972), and once every 55 days in Africa (1960 to 1972)!

The degree of military rule in effect in the Third World today attests to the instability and ineffectiveness of civilian regimes since World War II. As Tables 5.2 and 5.3 indicate, military rule is spread evenly and thickly across all four regions of the Third World. In Table 5.2, we see that in 40 nations officers of the armed forces actually occupy the position of chief executive, usually without leaving active military service. Africa and Latin America are the two regions most susceptible to this sort of institutional decay, but it is not unknown in the Middle East or

[24]Fred W. Riggs, "Bureaucrats and Political Development: A Paradoxical View," in Joseph LaPalombara, ed., *Bureaucracy and Political Development* (Princeton, N. J.: Princeton University Press, 1967), chap. 5.

**TABLE 5.1** Military Coups in the Third World for Selected Periods, 1945–1972

|  | Successful | Unsuccessful | Total |
| --- | --- | --- | --- |
| Latin America (1945–1972) | 53 | 28 | 81 |
| Asia (1947–1972) | 21 | 21 | 42 |
| Middle East (1949–1972) | 41 | 42 | 83 |
| Africa (1960–1972) | 32 | 46 | 78 |
| Total | 147 | 137 | 284 |

SOURCE: Gavin Kennedy, *the Military in the Third World* (New York: Scribner's, 1974), pp. 337–344.

Turkish army troops are shown patrolling a street in Ankara, Turkey, following a military takeover of the government in September, 1980. The army intervened in politics when the civilian leadership proved incapable of maintaining order in the country. Throughout the Third World, street scenes like this are frequent reminders to the civilian population of the fragile nature of their political system.

Asia. In Table 5.3, we see that an additional 18 countries have military establishments that, although not actually occupying the seat of power, exercise substantial influence in areas beside those traditionally assigned to the armed forces. In many of these countries, the nonmilitary rulers must assume that a military-coup attempt is being plotted virtually constantly. These nations' leaders are fully aware that any deterioration in public order or the financial status of the nation could bring the military into control. In some states, the incumbent regime is headed by a former military commander who rose to power at the head of a coup, then resigned his military status to be elected more or less democratically to be the chief executive of a newly established constitutional order. These two categories of military rule together account for 58 nations in the Third World.

One can learn almost as much about Third World politics by studying countries in which the military is not dominant. For this, we can turn to

**TABLE 5.2**  Third World Nations in Which Armed Forces Occupy Chief Executive Position as of January 1, 1980 (N = 40)

| | Latin America (9) | Middle East (6) | Africa (18) | Asia (7) |
|---|---|---|---|---|
| Military Control Not Yet Ratified by Constitutional Process | Argentina<br>El Salvador<br>Honduras<br>Nicaragua | | Benin<br>Burundi<br>Congo<br>Equatorial Guinea<br>Ethiopia<br>Mauritania<br>Niger | Afghanistan<br>Pakistan |
| Military Control Ratified by Constitutional Process | Brazil<br>Chile<br>Paraguay<br>Peru[a]<br>Uruguay | Algeria<br>Egypt<br>Iraq<br>Libya<br>Syria<br>Yemen Arab Republic | Angola<br>Guinea-Bissau<br>Madagascar<br>Mali<br>Mozambique<br>Rwanda<br>Somalia<br>Sudan<br>Togo<br>Upper Volta<br>Zaire | Bangladesh<br>Burma<br>Indonesia<br>Republic of Korea (South Korea)<br>Thailand |

[a]Replaced by civilian regime in 1980.

SOURCE: Arthur S. Banks and William Overstreet, eds., *Political Handbook of the World: 1980* (New York: McGraw-Hill, 1980).

**TABLE 5.3**  Third World Nations with Weak Civilian Regime and Strong Potential for Military Intervention as of January 1, 1980 (N = 18)

| Latin America (7) | Middle East (2) | Africa (8) | Asia (1) |
|---|---|---|---|
| Bolivia[a]<br>Dominican Republic<br>Ecuador<br>Guatemala<br>Haiti<br>Panama<br>Suriname[a] | Iran<br>Turkey[a] | Chad[b]<br>Ghana<br>Liberia[a]<br>Mauritius<br>Nigeria<br>São Tomé and Príncipe<br>South Africa<br>Zimbabwe | Philippines[c] |

[a]Regime overthrown by military during 1980.

[b]In midst of civil war in 1979–1980.

[c]Under martial law until January, 1981.

SOURCE: Arthur S. Banks and William Overstreet, eds., *Political Handbook of the World: 1980* (New York: McGraw-Hill, 1980).

**TABLE 5.4**  Third World Nations in Which Armed Forces Offer Little Threat of Intervention as of January 1, 1980.[a] (Traditional Monarchies and Civilian One-Party States) (N = 24)

| | Middle East (10) | Africa (11) | Asia (3) |
|---|---|---|---|
| **Traditional Monarchies** | Bahrain[b] <br> Jordan <br> Kuwait[b] <br> Morocco <br> Oman[b] <br> Qatar[b] <br> Saudi Arabia <br> United Arab Emirates[b] | Lesotho[b] <br> Swaziland[b] | Bhutan[b] <br> Brunei[b] <br> Nepal |
| **Civilian One-Party States** | People's Democratic Republic of Yemen <br> Tunisia[b] | Cameroon <br> Gabon[b] <br> Guinea <br> Ivory Coast <br> Kenya <br> Malawi <br> Sierra Leone <br> Tanzania <br> Zambia | |

[a]There are no Third World nations that fall into this category in Latin America.

[b]Population less than 2 million in 1977.

SOURCE: Arthur S. Banks and William Overstreet, eds., *Political Handbook of the World: 1980* (New York: McGraw-Hill, 1980).

**TABLE 5.5**  Third World Nations (Civilian Multiparty Democracies) in Which Armed Forces Offer Little Threat of Intervention, as of January 1, 1980[a]. (N = 16)

| Latin America (7) | Africa (3) | Asia (6) |
|---|---|---|
| Colombia <br> Costa Rica <br> Guyana[b] <br> Jamaica <br> Mexico <br> Trinidad and Tobago[b] <br> Venezuela | Botswana[b] <br> Gambia[b] <br> Senegal | India <br> Malaysia <br> Papua New Guinea <br> Singapore <br> Sri Lanka <br> Taiwan |

[a]There are no Third World nations that fall into this category in the Middle East.

[b]Population less than 2 million in 1977.

SOURCE: Arthur S. Banks and William Overstreet, eds., *Political Handbook of the World: 1980* (New York: McGraw-Hill, 1980).

Tables 5.4 and 5.5. We can see that 40 Third World states have so far managed to escape military rule, or, as in the cases of Mexico and Venezuela, have actually produced civilian regimes that have defeated military insurgents. Of these 40 countries, however, 15 are quite small (population of less than 2 million in 1977) and consist largely of former British island colonies (Jamaica, Trinidad and Tobago), and underdeveloped traditional monarchies (Bhutan, Swaziland). Of the 25 states that have a population of more than 2 million in 1977 and that have also escaped military rule, 4 (Jordan, Morocco, Nepal, and Saudi Arabia) are autocratic, traditional monarchies, and most of the remainder have one-party civilian regimes that have achieved a poor record in the field of human rights (see Chapter Seven, "Policy Making in the Third World"). Thus, of the entire range of 101 Third World nations, only a comparative handful (Costa Rica, Kenya, Mexico, Sri Lanka, Tanzania, Tunisia and Venezuela) can be said to have faced successfully the challenges of governing a large, rapidly developing country under a more or less open and constitutional process and, at the same time, to have managed to avoid giving the military a reason and an opportunity to intervene.[25]

A brief review of the massive literature on the role of the military in Third World politics reveals that the following arguments have been advanced to explain the intervention of a nation's armed forces into politics.[26]

1.   A sharp decline in the prestige of the government or of the ruling political party. This causes the regime to use increasing amounts of physical coercion to maintain order and to stress the imperative of national unity in the face of crisis, leading consequently to a suppression of dissent.

2.   Schisms between or among political leaders, causing military commanders to doubt the continued ability of the civilian regime to govern effectively.

3.   A low probability of external intervention by a major world power or by neighboring states in the event of a coup.

4.   Contagion from military coups in neighboring countries.

5.   Domestic social antagonisms, most obviously occurring in countries governed by a minority group (Ibos in Nigeria, Arabs in Zanzibar).

6.   Economic crises, leading to austerity policies that affect the organized, urban sectors of society (labor unions, civil servants).

7.   Corruption and inefficiency among government and party officials or a belief that civilian officials are on the verge of selling out the nation to some foreign group (Peru, in the case of Fernando Belaúnde; Chile, in the case of Salvador Allende).

8.   A highly rigid class structure that makes military service the only possible avenue for a poor boy to move from low to high status.

9.   A growing belief among the military that they are the only social class with enough discipline and enough commitment to modernization to move the country out of its traditional ways.

10.   Foreign influences. These could include the military representatives of foreign governments, experiences gained in foreign wars (e.g., the Colombian battalion in the Korean War) or in foreign training centers, or foreign aid in the form of equipment and weapons.

11.   Defeat of the military in a war with another country, especially when the military are convinced that the civilian government betrayed them by negotiating disadvantageous peace terms or by mismanaging the war effort behind the front lines (Bolivia in the 1940s).

Any one or any combination of these causes could constitute an impressive bill of particulars

[25]Three of the 101 nations in the Third World were either too new or too unstable in 1980 to fit into one category or another without question. In addition, some readers may disagree with the subjective judgments that place a given country in one category or another. I have tried to give civilian rulers the benefit of the doubt where possible, so, if anything, some countries could be moved from low to high military influence (Venezuela is one example).

[26]Claude E. Welch, Jr., "Cincinnatus in Africa: The Possibility of Military Withdrawal from Politics," in Lofchie, *op. cit.*, chap. 10. See also Robert P. Clark, *Development and Instability: Political Change in the Non-Western World* (Chicago: Dryden, 1974), pp. 185–186.

to lay at the doorstep of the ousted civilian government. No doubt, some military leaders have intervened in politics primarily (or even solely) out of a desire to advance personal prestige or power. The regimes of Idi Amin in Uganda or of Rafael Trujillo in the Dominican Republic seem to have brought to their respective countries not prosperity and peace, but suppression of human rights in the most brutal fashion and economic stagnation, all for the greater glory of "The Dictator." The evidence seems to indicate, however, that the Idi Amins and the Trujillos are in the minority as far as military governments are concerned. The majority of military regimes in the Third World are in place not primarily because of a desire for personal power but for the same reason people strive for political power anywhere: to improve the public sector's capacity to solve persistent and annoying (or even critical) problems.

And how well do military regimes perform that function? How effective have military regimes been in their search for economic prosperity and social order? One sort of evidence lies in both the life and the death of military governments. On the one hand, most military governments are most reluctant to give power back to civilian authorities, apparently on the assumption that the same circumstances that prompted their original intervention are still present. The civilians can simply not be trusted with power until the country's stability is assured. On the other hand, most military regimes end the way they began: at the hands of another coup launched by a hostile faction within the military. Gavin Kennedy asserts that of all the precipitating factors that might bring the military into power in the Third World, the most important is simply that the incumbent regime is also a military government that gained power illegally.[27] In other words, the more military coups a country has, the more it is likely to have. The first is the most difficult; they become progressively easier as the military become accustomed to

holding power. But this observation also suggests that military governments rarely solve the problems they say motivated their entry into politics in the first place.

In recent years, political scientists have begun to assess the economic growth performance of military and civilian regimes in the Third World.[28] In general, their findings suggest that there is really rather little difference between the two kinds of regimes, especially when other such factors as national wealth are held constant. R. D. McKinlay and A. S. Cohan assessed the performance of military and nonmilitary regimes in 101 countries over the period from 1961 to 1970.[29] Their findings revealed that, although there was considerable difference between the two kinds of regimes in political terms (such as the dissolution of legislatures or the banning of opposition political parties), there was relatively little significant difference between the two types of regime in the areas of military policy and economic growth rates. That is, the economies of the countries in question grew rapidly or slowly in response to other factors (their endowment with strategic raw materials for instance) apart from the kind of regime they possessed.

Our own investigation of this subject is reported in the data contained in Table 5.6. Here, 80 selected Third World countries are compared along two axes: one axis measures the degree of military influence in each country, drawn from Tables 5.2 to 5.5; the second axis measures the growth rate of each country's per capita GNP for the period 1960 to 1978. As our discussion would suggest, clear cut patterns do not emerge from Table 5.6. Countries with low degrees of military influence and strong constitutional traditions (e.g., Colombia, Taiwan) are mostly high growth economies (3 percent and above),

[27]Gavin Kennedy, The Military in the Third World (New York: Scribner's, 1974), pp. 23–30.

[28]For a summary of these studies, see Sam C. Sarkesian, "A Political Perspective on Military Power in Developing Areas," in Sheldon W. Simon, ed., The Military and Security in the Third World: Domestic and International Impacts (Boulder, Colo.: Westview, 1978), chap. 1.

[29]R. D. McKinlay and A. S. Cohan, "Performance and Instability in Military and Nonmilitary Regime Systems," American Political Science Review, 70 (3) (1976), pp. 850–865.

**TABLE 5.6** Third World Countries[a] Compared According to Degree of Military Influence in Politics and Growth Rate of GNP per Capita, 1960–1978

| Degree of Military Influence | GNP per Capita Growth Rate | | | | | |
|---|---|---|---|---|---|---|
| | *Less than 0.0* | *0.0-0.9* | *1.0-1.9* | *2.0-2.9* | *3.0-3.9* | *More than 4.0* |
| High Influence (Table 5.2) | Bangladesh<br>Madagascar<br>Niger<br>Somalia | Afghanistan<br>Benin<br>Mozambique<br>Sudan<br>Uruguay | Angola<br>Burma<br>Chile<br>Congo<br>El Salvador<br>Ethiopia<br>Honduras<br>Mali<br>Rwanda<br>Upper Volta<br>Zaire | Algeria<br>Argentina<br>Burundi<br>Nicaragua<br>Pakistan<br>Paraguay<br>Peru | Egypt<br>Mauritania<br>Syria | Brazil<br>Indonesia<br>Iraq<br>Libya<br>Republic of Korea<br>　(South Korea)<br>Thailand<br>Togo |
| Strong Potential Influence (Table 5.3) | Chad<br>Ghana | Haiti | Zimbabwe | Bolivia<br>Guatemala<br>Liberia<br>Panama<br>Philippines<br>South Africa | Dominican Rep.<br>Nigeria | Ecuador<br>Iran<br>Turkey |
| Low Influence, Weak Constitutional Base (Table 5.4) | Bhutan<br>Kuwait | Guinea<br>Nepal<br>Sierra Leone | Zambia | Cameroon<br>Ivory Coast<br>Kenya<br>Malawi<br>Morocco<br>Tanzania | | Lesotho<br>Saudi Arabia<br>Tunisia |
| Low Influence, Strong Constitutional Base (Table 5.5) | Senegal | | India | Jamaica<br>Mexico<br>Sri Lanka<br>Trinidad and<br>　Tobago<br>Venezuela | Colombia<br>Costa Rica<br>Malaysia<br>Papua New<br>　Guinea | Singapore<br>Taiwan |

[a]Countries not listed for lack of data: Bahrain, Botswana, Brunei, Central African Republic, Equatorial Guinea, Gabon, Gambia, Guinea-Bissau, Guyana, Jordan, Lebanon, Mauritius, Oman, People's Democratic Republic of Yemen, Qatar, São Tomé and Príncipe, Suriname, Swaziland, Uganda, United Arab Emirates, Yemen Arab Republic.

SOURCE: GNP per capita growth data is from World Bank, *World Development Report, 1980* (New York: Oxford University Press, 1980), pp. 110–111.

whereas countries with low degrees of military influence and a weak constitutional tradition (Bhutan, Kuwait, Nepal) are primarily low-growth countries (from negative growth rates to 0.9 percent). Most countries with high or potential military influence have moderate economic growth records (from 1.0 to 2.9 percent), although a few countries with high military influence also have some rather remarkable growth rates, especially Brazil, Iraq, and Libya. However, it appears that nations desiring to achieve a rapid rate of economic growth will not accomplish this goal by adopting a military form of government unless other economic, social, and political factors also favor rapid growth.

## CONCLUSIONS: GOVERNMENT STRUCTURES AND HUMAN DIGNITY

It seems that many Third World governments suffer from a number of important flaws that work to block them from making a maximum contribution to the enhancement of human dignity in their countries. Being comparative late-comers in the rush to industrialization, many Third World industrial élites have been too weak to absorb or defeat the traditional agrarian élites so that they have been forced to turn to the authoritarian rule of the syncratic regime, which manages to maintain order by refraining from attacking rural landlords and by suppressing mass demands for a better standard of living. Industrialization must proceed at a reduced pace because the rural élites oppose it and because the

industrial sector has difficulty in financing its own development. Whatever surplus there is must be extracted from the low-income city and village dwellers.

The ability of a syncratic regime to carry out this kind of policy depends largely on three sets of institutions, which we have considered in detail. The first set consists of the network of patron-client systems that link together the urban élites and the low-income citizens in a complex psychological bond that makes it possible for governments to ignore mass demands without provoking mass rebellion. The second set is the nation's dominant executive, the president and his or her circle of advisors and experts. Aided by both constitutional grants and extraconstitutional seizures of extraordinary powers, the chief executive can rule without serious challenge from outside interests or groups as long as the patron-client systems remain intact and as long as he or she can effect the industrialist-landlord coalition that supports the syncratic regime. Behind many of these regimes, however, stands the third set of institutions, the military, ready to intervene to restore order if the constitutional government should prove unable to govern. The comparative frequency of military interventions in politics in the Third World reflects the continuing inability of civilian, constitutional regimes to break through the barriers of syncratic politics and to master the industrialization process. Levels of human dignity are unlikely to rise greatly in countries where these three institutions remain powerful and unchallenged.

# Suggestions for Further Reading

**Anderson, James N. E.**, ed., *Changing Law in Developing Countries* (New York: Praeger, 1963).

**Ashford, Douglas E.**, *National Development and Local Reform: Political Participation in Morocco, Tunisia and Pakistan* (Princeton, N.J.: Princeton University Press, 1967).

**Braibanti, Ralph,** ed., *Political and Administrative Development* (Durham, N.C.: Duke University Press, 1969).

**Burke, Fred G.**, *Local Government and Politics in Uganda* (Syracuse, N.Y.: Syracuse University Press, 1964).

Janowitz, Morris, *The Military and the Political Development of New Nations* (Chicago: University of Chicago Press, 1964).

Johnson, John J., ed., *The Role of the Military in Underdeveloped Countries* (Princeton, N.J.: Princeton University Press, 1962).

Kennedy, Gavin, *The Military in the Third World* (New York: Scribner's, 1974).

Lieuwin, Edwin, *Arms and Politics in Latin America* (New York: Praeger, 1960).

_____, *Generals vs. Presidents: Neomilitarism in Latin America* (New York: Praeger, 1964).

Lloyd, P. C., ed., *The New Elites of Tropical Africa* (London: Oxford University Press, 1966).

Park, Richard L., and Irene Tinker, eds., *Leadership and Political Institutions in India* (Princeton, N.J.: Princeton University Press, 1959).

Sherwood, Frank P., *Institutionalizing the Grass Roots in Brazil: A Study in Comparative Local Government* (San Francisco: Chandler, 1967).

Simon, Sheldon W., ed., *The Military and Security in the Third World: Domestic and International Impacts* (Boulder, Colo.: Westview, 1978).

Tinker, Hugh, *Ballot Box and Bayonet: People and Government in Emergent Asian Countries* (New York: Oxford University Press, 1964).

_____, *The Foundations of Local Self-Government in India, Pakistan and Burma* (London: London University Press, 1954).

Younger, Kenneth, *The Public Service in New States* (London: Oxford University Press, 1960).

# CHAPTER SIX
## Policy Making in the Third World

In preceding chapters, we examined some important social, economic, and psychological dimensions of Third World political life and discussed the major institutions and structures of Third World political systems. The capacity of Third World governments to enhance human dignity in their countries depends largely on how these various ingredients come together to form an effective and creative policy process. The term, policy-making process, refers to the series of steps taken by a government to solve problems, make decisions, allocate resources or values, implement policies, and, in general, to do the things expected of them by their constituents. We cannot appreciate the connections between levels of human dignity and politics until we have analyzed the nature of the policy process in a typical Third World setting.

There is obviously some risk involved in making generalizations about 101 different political systems in an area of social behavior that is so poorly defined. The chapter offers an outline of a policy-making process that many observers think characterizes most governments in the Third World regardless of their social and economic circumstances or their colonial heritage. The principal components of this process derive largely from the nature of traditional society and personality, from the scarcity and unpredictability of funds needed to carry out government policy, and from a shortage of modernizing institutions to assist governments in making and implementing public policy choices.

## POLICY MAKING IN THE THIRD WORLD: AN OVERVIEW

Several years ago, Yale University economist Albert O. Hirschman published the first of a series of books and articles in which he attempted to outline what he understood to be the major reasons that developing countries so frequently fell short of their goals, particularly in the field of economic well-being. Based on his experiences as an economic advisor to the government of Colombia and a number of in-depth studies made in other Latin American countries, Hirschman's analysis eventually focused on what he terms the failure-prone policy process in the less developed world.[1]

Hirschman begins by considering the fundamental problem of less developed countries—the inability to make decisions that will induce development, specifically, development of the economy. For Hirschman, the prevailing inability of development élites to make these decisions can be traced back to certain psychological and

[1] Albert O. Hirschman, *Journeys Toward Progress: Studies of Economic Policy Making in Latin America* (New York: Twentieth Century Fund, 1963); Albert O. Hirschman, *The Strategy of Economic Development* (New Haven, Conn.: Yale University Press, 1961).

social structural inadequacies that inhibit the decision makers of the country from bringing to bear the needed amount of knowledge and commitment to make the proper judgments about the allocation of resources. In the face of this recurring inability to meet development problems, struggling groups within the society begin to grow desperate at their failure to penetrate the decision-makers' attention screen and attract attention to their problems. As the problems become more and more aggravated, groups are pushed toward acts of violence to attract attention. The consequence is usually an impulsive policy decision taken in the heat of debate or passionate confrontation and without adequate understanding of what is required to solve the problem. The result, not surprisingly, is failure.

The fatal flaw, according to Hirschman, now appears in the decision-making styles of developing countries. Instead of learning from their mistakes, Third World élites typically compound the problem by what Hirschman calls *la rage de vouloir conclure*, a phrase taken from Gustave Flaubert that means (approximately), "the mania for wanting to be done with it." At the point of

Steel production in this mill in Sao Paulo, Brazil, is impressive. Yet, production of steel in Brazil almost never reaches predicted levels. Repeated failures of major programs or projects to achieve their goals or targets are depressing to the morale of Third World technicians and political leaders. Government legitimacy must be won through performance, and the failure of many Third World regimes to meet their own stated goals makes them appear incompetent in the eyes of their own citizens.

recognizing failure, a great cry arises from the country's intellectuals who call for a comprehensive total attack on the problem. Earlier solutions are decried for being piecemeal, partial, fragmented, less than total, and generally inadequate. Fundamental change must be introduced, anything less will certainly fail. The reformist élites of the country cannot tolerate any further delay in attacking the problem. Now, very few countries possess governments with the policy-making apparatus adequate to the task of producing a comprehensive program dealing with a major issue in a span of months; and, certainly, the Third World countries are more poorly equipped in this regard than most other governments. Therefore, calls for comprehensive solutions are met in the only possible way: by introducing policy solutions from abroad. The history of Third World attempts to solve domestic problems is littered with examples of poorly related solutions borrowed from the industrialized states. Successful policy solutions, like the Tennessee Valley Authority (TVA), have been copied all over the Third World to solve problems in agrarian reform, flood control, land reclamation, power generation, pest control, as well as many other issues for which a particular policy tool might actually be inappropriate. Likewise, international agencies, like the World Bank and the International Monetary Fund (IMF), are frequently called on to send professional advisors to struggling Third World countries to prescribe an instant remedy for ills that are centuries old.

Not only do the foreign solutions usually fail to resolve the immediate problem but also their very use tends to have an adverse effect on future efforts. For one thing, the nation's intellectual leaders are inhibited from acting on a local problem as long as some foreign miracle is being developed. Anyone who has worked in the field of solving public policy problems knows that before a person can really solve a problem, he or she must interact with the problem, become immersed in its very nature, and come to know the problem intimately. There must be, to quote Hirschman, "that long confrontation between man and a situation" before creativity emerges.[2] By introducing foreign solutions on a poorly thought-out crash basis, Third World élites deprive themselves and their intellectuals of any chance to master the problem on their own terms. In addition, the continued failure to solve a given problem begins to sap the morale and weaken the resolve of a national political cadre. They begin to believe that they merit the title, failure prone; they deprecate the national style; and they either escalate the ideological battle considerably or drop out by resigning themselves to mediocrity or going into self-imposed exile. Each time this sequence is repeated, it erodes the scant supply of problem-solving talent with which Third World political leaders have to work. The long-term consequences of failure-prone politics are to lead the country into a vicious circle of one disaster after another until some authoritarian force, usually the army, steps in to impose discipline on the nation and attempts to reassure the people that they are in control of their destiny once again.

## POLICY MAKING IN THE THIRD WORLD: GOALS, ACTIONS, OUTCOMES

### SETTING GOALS

The policy-making process begins with the setting of goals. For the average American, the idea of setting national goals is alien, because our system of separation of powers and our cultural predilection against long-range planning obscure the setting of goals in our government. There is, for example, no single document in the U.S. Government that could be called, "National Goals for 1980." The closest thing we have to that would be the federal government budget for any given fiscal year. Similarly, we do not have any single agency responsible for devising the nation's goals for a specific period. The closest agency to this would be the Office of Management and Budget (OMB) located within the Office of the President. The ability of OMB to influence the structure of our national political goals derives almost entirely from its role as the coor-

dinator of the executive branch's budget proposal, which is sent to the Congress for approval each year. Probably before the end of the century, even the U.S. Government will adopt formal goal-setting procedures for its operations. As of 1981, however, we are practically the only country of any significance that still believes that single sets of national goals should not be imposed on our heterogeneous population.

In the Third World, in contrast, there is usually great emphasis placed on goal-setting exercises and planning agencies. In Mexico, for example, according to Bo Anderson and James D. Cockcroft, there are four national goals: political stability, economic growth, public welfare, and Mexicanization.[3] The goal of political stability consists of three components: basic institutions that are viewed as legitimate by the population; decision makers who are regarded as having the right to make binding decisions for the polity; and the mode of transferring power from one person to another that is accepted by most people. Economic growth in the Mexican context means approximately what it means elsewhere, an increase in the industrial productivity of the nation and in gross national product (GNP) per capita. The public-welfare goal involves the raising of the material and cultural level of the country's masses, especially in the rural sector; Mexicanization refers to the policy of gaining control of the major corporations and other economic activities in the country, either for private Mexican citizens or for public agencies.

Morocco's first Five-Year Plan (1960 to 1964) listed two chief goals: (1) to lessen the country's dependence on foreign technicians, capital, and markets and (2) to integrate the traditional sectors into the national economy.[4] These two broad goals led to the establishment of specific programs to increase the number of technicians and other qualified personnel by emphasis

[2]Hirschman, *Journeys Toward Progress, op. cit.*, p. 240.

[3]Bo Anderson and James D. Cockcroft, "Control and Cooptation in Mexican Politics," in James D. Cockcroft *et al.*, eds., *Dependence and Underdevelopment: Latin America's Political Economy* (Garden City, N.Y.: Doubleday, 1972), pp. 221–225.

[4]Albert Waterston, *Planning in Morocco* (Baltimore: Johns Hopkins University Press, 1962), pp. 28–29.

on education and training; to stimulate traditional agriculture by giving top priority to agricultural reform and the introduction of modern technology into the rural areas; to establish basic steel and chemical industries by promoting private investment if possible but by state intervention if necessary; and to facilitate the implementation of both plans by reforms in government administration and organization and by the Morocconization of the civil service. This last objective appears to have much the same meaning as Mexicanization has for Mexico, that is, gaining control of national agencies for national personnel.

Pakistan's first Five-Year Plan (1953 to 1958) listed these major objectives: (1) to achieve the greatest increase possible in national income and the standard of living; (2) to increase health, education, housing, and social welfare services justified primarily on grounds other than increasing the national income; (3) to improve the nation's balance of payments by increasing exports and import substitution; (4) to increase opportunities for useful employment; and (5) to increase rapidly the rate of development in East Pakistan and other relatively less developed zones of the country.[5] Although the first four objectives presented problems that were primarily technical in nature, the fifth objective—showing favoritism toward the relatively less developed East Pakistan—was the subject of intense controversy. The controversy was never resolved; East Pakistan seceded from the rest of the nation in 1971 to form the new nation of Bangladesh.

Where are goals typically formulated in Third World countries? In a very few instances, such as in Mexico, nations with very strong official political parties may employ the inner councils of their parties to discuss alternate goals and to formulate a final list for state action. In an equally small number of traditional monarchies, like Saudi Arabia, the setting of goals amounts to little more than an expression of the personal convictions of the monarch and the monarch's closest advisors. However, in most Third World republics, central economic and social planning agencies have been created and charged with the task of setting goals for public policy makers to follow. In a 1965 study, Albert Waterston lists central-planning institutions in over 100 Third World independent nations and (at that time) soon-to-be independent colonies.[6] Although the degree of sophistication and state control obviously vary considerably from one example to another, the list of those Third World countries that are, at least, formally committed to some kind of central planning is clear evidence of the strength of the idea of rational government ordering a society's priorities.

Planning in the Third World has usually followed one of three models, depending on the colonial heritage of the country, the type of planning used by the former colonial mother country, and, most important, the specific economic and social structures in the developing state.[7] (See Table 6.1 for planning data from eight selected countries.) At one end of the spectrum are the states that engage in detailed central planning of both the private and the public sectors of the economy. Typical of this style is India, whose civil servants were strongly influenced by the Fabian socialists under whom they studied in Great Britain. India's brand of socialism is rather unconventional, because over 90 percent of the country's business enterprises remain in private hands. This means that the government must undertake to set detailed goals and objectives for the businesses in the private sector if the overall goals of the national economic plan are to be realized.

At the other end of the planning spectrum lie the states that are basically committed to reliance on the private sector to achieve the broad goals of the national economy. These countries, of which Malaysia, Pakistan, and the Philippines are the best examples, typically restrict their planning to the formulation of the broadest goals

[5]Albert Waterston, *Planning in Pakistan* (Baltimore: Johns Hopkins University, 1963), pp. 44, 102.

[6]Albert Waterston, *Development Planning: Lessons of Experience* (Baltimore: John Hopkins University Press, 1965) Appendix 3.

[7]John C. Honey, *Planning and the Private Sector: The Experience in Developing Countries* (New York: Dunellen, 1970), Part I.

| Country | Development Planning: Institutions and Objectives |
|---|---|
| Nigeria | Economic planning began with an eight-year plan to cover the period 1962–68, a four-year plan for 1971–74, and the plan currently in effect, for 1975–80. The principal goal of the current plan is to raise Gross Domestic Product growth rate to 11.7 percent. Major projects include an iron and steel plant, two liquefied natural gas plants, a petrochemical complex and two new refineries. Principal source of funding is the nation's petroleum production. |
| Tanzania | Development planning began in 1947, when country was a United Nations Trust Territory, and included a second plan for the 1955–60 period and a three-year plan for 1961–64. In 1964, the government began a series of five-year plans covering the period up to 1980. Principal source of outside aid is the People's Republic of China. |
| India | Planning is carried on by the autonomous Planning Commission, established three years after independence and responsible only to the Prime Minister. Its draft plans are presented for approval to various policy making bodies, including ultimately the parliament. Planning is done on a five-year cycle. The current plan (1978–83) projects an economic growth rate of 4.7 percent, and assumes that foreign assistance will account for only 5 percent of plan expenditures. |
| Indonesia | Responsibility for planning vested in the National Development Planning Council, established in 1969. The second five-year plan, for 1974–79, placed most emphasis on meeting pressing social needs through construction, consumer good production and employment. Its target was to increase GNP by 7.5 percent per year. From 65 to 82 percent of the plan's expenditures were to come from national revenues, particularly from natural gas and oil. |
| Mexico | Although the national government is directly involved in setting goals for economic development, there is no formal national planning organization as such. Centralized planning limited to regional and sectoral development. Planning policies are determined in the Ministry of the Presidency, but plans are not formally adopted or published as government policy. The Mexican Development Institute, established in 1974, coordinates investment programs and formulates long-term economic goals. |
| Brazil | Economic planning began in the 1940s, and was expanded and made more comprehensive in 1970 with the publication of an overall ten-year plan for the 1970s. This plan was supplemented with series of sectoral plans, as well as with plans for shorter time spans, the last of which covered the period 1975–79. This last plan sets targets of growth rate of 10 percent per year and a per capita GNP of $1,000. Overall planning goes on at the national level, as well as in most states and even a few coordinated regions, such as Brazil's very poor northeast zone and the Amazon River area. |
| Egypt | Development planning coordinated by the Ministry of Planning, the National Planning Committee and the Permanent Council for the Development of National Production. First plan issued for period 1960–65; subsequent plans have been plagued with problems, and some have been left unimplemented for various reasons. The 1976–80 plan aims to raise national income by 7 to 10 percent, reduce the balance of payments deficit, and increase consumption and savings. Foreign aid of about $5 billion will be required to cover the deficits in the plan. |
| Iran | Under the Shah's rule, development planning was the responsibility of the Plan Organization, created in 1947. Objectives of the 1973–78 plan were to improve living standards, education and training. Aided by huge oil revenues, the country was expected to show an annual economic growth rate of about 15 percent, and to raise the GNP to $80 billion by 1978. Since the revolution, instability has prevented any long-term planning. |

SOURCE: George Thomas Kurian, *Encyclopedia of the Third World* (2 vols.) (New York: Facts on File, 1979).

possible (called macroplanning). Thus, a planning document in one of these countries might set as a goal the achievement of an increase of 3 percent in per capita income over the next year without specifying exactly how such a goal is to be accomplished. Then, the plan is augmented through budgetary and other procedures to grant special incentives to the private sector to undertake projects whose overall result will be the fulfillment of the national-plan goals. Accordingly, the state does not become involved in direct industrial activity unless there is clearly no alternative and unless the project in question is badly needed. Another feature of macroplanning is its tendency to encourage and rely on regional planning institutions. As in Malaysia, the national plan is frequently little more than the regional plans collected under one cover.

In the middle of the planning spectrum are the countries that have adopted the French consultative planning method, these include Chile (before 1970), Morocco, Tanzania, and Tunisia. The French method of planning involves careful consultation between the public sector's planning officials and representatives of the private sector. As a result of this planning style, private industry and commerce leaders leave the consultations knowing (and accepting) what is expected of them in the way of investment and production decisions. The state, for its part, undertakes to provide support for economic activities that conventionally are not financed by private industry: social infrastructure, such as roads and schools, and large projects that cannot pay for their costs of construction, such as huge dams, and so forth.

Regardless of the exact model followed by planning agencies in Third World countries, these nations have exhibited a serious tendency to set unrealistic goals, which frequently are followed by failure and a decline in public morale. Hirschman has observed that government decision-making can fit into one of two categories: (1) either capabilities outrun motivation (the technical solution to a problem surfaces before the problem becomes critical), in which case the goals adopted are usually within the reach of government power or (2) motivation outruns capabilities (as when a problem becomes critical rapidly), in which case the outcome is usually failure. Goal setting in the Third World tends to be of the second type, thus, helping to account for the failure-prone political style noted earlier.

Brazil, according to an old saying, has a great future—and always will have! Brazilians are accustomed to seeing their government plan in dreamlike confidence about the realizability of grandiose projects. It almost seems as if the enormous size of the country has encouraged its leaders to imagine that they can accomplish miracles. Press reports coming out of Brazil revealed however, that several key projects are seriously behind schedule, contributing even more to disbelief and cynicism in Brazilian and foreign private economic circles.[8] In 1970, for example, Brazil announced that it would increase steel production from 5.4 million ingot tons to 20 million tons by 1980. Shortly thereafter, the goal was raised to 24 million tons and then to 35 million tons by 1985. Actual performance was disappointing. Figures for 1975 showed steel production reaching 8.3 million tons. Most observers admitted that the goal of 35 million tons was totally beyond the country's capacity. Another fantastic project envisioned by Brazilian planners was the Northern Perimetral Highway, a space-age highway intended to link Brazil's northern Amazon region with Venezuela, Colombia, and Peru. Construction was begun in 1973, and completion was promised by 1977. But, in the middle of 1976, only 400 miles of the highway's 2600-mile length had been completed and construction was proceeding so slowly that the jungle was reclaiming parts of the completed roadway. But, as the Brazilian Finance Minister was quoted as saying, "It's better to plan for too much than for too little. If your original goals are too high, you can always change your plans. But, if they're too low, progress could become strangled."[9] Perhaps the minister would be correct were it not for the serious blows to national confidence and morale that are suffered each time the government defaults on a promise.

Another example is the huge Helwan steel mill in Egypt. Begun in 1955 by a West German firm, the Helwan iron and steel works was nationalized by the Egyptian Government in 1961. As a consequence, Egypt needed continued aid from the Soviet Union to complete Helwan, to

[8]Bruce Handler, "Brazil: Big Projects but Big Delays," *Washington Post,* July 20, 1976.
[9]Ibid.

expand it, and to keep it running in the face of mounting operation and maintenance problems. Total capital investment in Helwan, one of the largest industrial enterprises in the Middle East, reached $1 billion. Despite Egypt's political break with the Soviet Union, there were in 1976 still 500 Soviet technicians working at Helwan who were supplemented by a team of consultants and advisors from U.S. Steel and from the United Nations.

All of these foreign advisors were needed simply because nothing ever seemed to go right at Helwan. Originally designed to be producing 1.5 million tons of steel products by 1976, the plant's current output was more like 500,000 tons. Although export sales reached $21 billion in 1975, Egypt spent more than that amount on imports—coal, spare parts, vehicles, and other equipment—needed to keep the plant running. Egyptian iron ore has a very high salt content, which corroded the plant's machinery. Although Helwan had its own plant for converting coal into coke, the coal had to be imported, and was frequently delayed in the country's snarled port facilities. Staffing was a huge problem. There were 20,000 workers, far too many for the plant's needs, but political considerations made layoffs impossible. Low salaries made it difficult to retain middle-level managers and engineers. Many managers spent more time in their offices than they did supervising operations on the plant floor. Alleged corruption and kickback deals caused plant supplies to lag behind requirements. Improper use of equipment caused much breakage and many maintenance problems. One piece of expensive equipment, designed to last ten years, was broken in four days at Helwan. Finally, the Egyptians depended almost completely on foreign capital and technology to make the plant function properly. In an effort to reduce the cost of importing coal, Egypt tried to convert some of the equipment to run on natural gas, which the country has domestically. Amoco Oil Company ran a pipeline to the plant but could not complete the task because the U.S. law inhibits American companies from participating in projects funded by the Soviet Union. The USSR, for its part, refused to connect the

pipeline to plant facilities because of its running feud with the late Egyptian President Anwar Sadat. And Helwan stumbled along consuming more wealth than it produced.[10]

Industrial projects are not the only examples of failure to meet unrealistic goals. Massive agricultural developments also have fallen short of high expectations. In the early 1970s, following the increase in world oil prices, the combination of Arab petrodollars, Western technology, and local manpower was supposed to turn the Sudan into the agricultural mainstay of the Arab world. The wide open spaces and favorable climate of the country were thought to be ideal for cattle raising and wheat farming. The region could become the breadbasket of the Arabs, offering them the promise of food self-sufficiency. After less than a decade of effort, the project is bankrupt for all intents and purposes. With imports running more than $1 billion ahead of exports each year, the Sudan quickly ran up a huge foreign debt, which in the early 1980s had mounted to more than $2 billion. Arab money sources dried up in the face of the magnitude of the problems. Many of the specific projects were simply too great for the country's overtaxed infrastructure. Western salespersons delivered outdated and unsound equipment. Government tax, employment, and nationalization policies worked against the very developments they sought to advance. There was no overall planning and little accountability for money borrowed abroad. At the rate the project is moving, it may not be completed until the end of this century.[11]

The Third World inclination to set unrealistic goals has its economic disadvantages in that it distorts the efficient allocation of resources. From our vantage point, the most disturbing consequences of this tendency are political and psychological. Most Third World governments lean on shaky popular support under the best of circumstances. Few governments in the develop-

[10]Thomas W. Lippmann, "Egypt's Large Steel Plant Is Economic Embarrassment," *Washington Post*, October 11, 1976.

[11]Jonathan C. Randal, "Debt-Ridden Sudan Mocks Former Promise as Arabs' Breadbasket," *Washington Post*, May 16, 1981.

ing world enjoy such popular acclaim that they can maintain their legitimacy in the face of repeated failure. Thus, when failure comes, as it inevitably must if goals are set unrealistically high, one serious effect is to weaken mass confidence in their ruling élites.

Why do Third World political élites set such high goals for themselves and for their political systems? A review of the policy-making literature in developing states suggests at least four reasons. First, political debate in the Third World is carried on with such intensity and fervor that appeals to moderation have little impact. The role of inspirational, charismatic leaders was highly useful during the struggle against the colonial masters when a lethargic populace had to be roused into heroic actions to gain national (and personal) liberation. But, once independence is obtained and the state must settle down into the routine of managing complex economic and social problems, charisma loses its usefulness. Legitimacy must be based on real achievement, and regimes based on inspiration and promises do not long survive, as the fate of Sukarno of Indonesia or Kwame Nkrumah of Ghana can attest.

A second source of unrealistic goal setting derives from the general non-Western cultural inclination to deal in the comprehensive and the total, leaving the marginal and the partial to the pragmatic (but, they say, the unprincipled) Western capitalists. Such cultural predelictions certainly reinforce the already-present institutional tendencies toward global and grandiose projects and goals (what some call grand-design politics).

Third, unrealistic goals are established largely because decision makers lack reliable information on which to base their calculations. The problem of insufficient information is partly derived from inadequate data-gathering services and national statistical agencies. Too often, bureaucrats in developing countries simply cannot obtain complete and reliable data. Even more symptomatic of political underdevelopment, however, is the way in which empirical data are distorted for political purposes. In nations where the population is narrowly balanced between competing and hostile tribal or ethnic groups, such as in Lebanon or Nigeria, even outwardly simple statistical exercises, such as conducting a national census, become the cause of much concern lest the new data reveal that the balance of demographic power has shifted. In Nigeria, this fear became so great that in 1975 the military dictator, Brigadier General Murtala Ramat Muhammad, simply declared the 1973 census to be inoperative and proclaimed that the 1963 census would be used henceforth for planning purposes. A similar example can be seen in Pakistan. The first Five-Year Plan (1955 to 1960) was drafted on the assumptions that (1) the GNP would rise by 20 percent during the period; (2) the population would increase 7.5 percent (a rate of only 1.5 percent annually); and (3) consequently the GNP per capita would grow 12.5 percent. As Waterston reports, according to the Deputy Chairman of the Planning Board, it was believed that population was actually growing much faster than 1.5 percent but that it was felt that the growth rate of population had to be understated in the plan "to keep despair away."[12]

The final cause of incorrect goal setting involves the suppression of dissent in most Third World regimes. In a study of foreign policy decision-making in the U.S. Government, Irving Janis discovered that policy makers were most disposed to make serious errors of judgment whenever the social cohesion of the group imposed a sort of dissent-free atmosphere over the deliberations so that contradictory opinions were suppressed, often by those who held them.[13] Janis labels this phenomenon groupthink. Any group that is wrestling with a particularly complex problem should take pains to insure that dissent is protected and encouraged, even institutionalized, to avoid as many errors as possible. In most Third World regimes, however, just the opposite is true. Dissent is suppressed and ideological conformity is imposed during all stages of decision making. The certain consequence of this practice is to lead the government into making

[12]Waterston, *Planning in Pakistan, op. cit.*, p. 46, footnote 29.
[13]Irving Janis, *Victims of Groupthink* (Boston: Houghton Mifflin, 1972).

numerous errors of judgment and into setting unreasonably high goals.

## TAKING ACTIONS

Clearly, our discussion about the setting of unrealistic goals would not be necessary if Third World governments somehow found the ability to carry through their plans and to implement the policy choices they have made. Yet, when we come to this second phase of the policy-making process, we find that many Third World governments must operate under administrative, economic, and political constraints that virtually guarantee failure at the point where the policy is applied to the society.[14]

It is not easy to generalize about problems of policy implementation in countries as different as those of the Third World. One recent book, edited by political scientist Merilee S. Grindle, highlights a number of factors that affect the ability of Third World governments to implement policies.[15] Some of these factors stem from the content of the policy, such as who wins and who loses from the policy, the type of costs and benefits associated with the policy, and the extent of change called for by the policy. Other factors have to do with the power, interests and strategies of the parties involved, or the willingness of the people affected by the policy to comply with its provisions. As they attempt to implement policy, most Third World governments are constrained by three special sets of problems: administrative, economic, and political.

The first kind of constraint on Third World policy actions comes from the administrative sphere. Here we note the numerous problems connected with the administration of development plans and specific projects: long delays in execution of the plan (some plans, such as those of Pakistan, were not put into effect until the plan period was more than half over), increased costs over the projected costs because of delays and inflation, inferior construction, low yields on investment, unnecessary dispersal of resources among a number of small and uncoordinated projects, and so forth. There are at least three sources of administrative confusion and incompetence. The first is the most obvious, the lack of trained experts to administer the complex programs and projects so vital to economic development. This severe shortage of expertise brings on poor project preparation, especially in crucial areas, such as economic feasibility (cost-benefit) studies and engineering supervision of the project once under way. A second problem stems from the lack of political support for civil servants and bureaucrats. From Tanzania, for example, we have the report that the cabinet officials were so opposed to the basic provisions of that nation's first Five-Year Plan that, even after the plan had been put into effect, they fought for, and secured, major changes in the program. The changes benefited their ministries but eroded the administrators' enthusiasm for the plan. A similar phenomenon was observed in Pakistan where the planning agency's own analysis for the reasons for plan failure began by accusing the political élites of failing to enforce the plan's provisions. Finally, we must again note the casual way in which Third World bureaucrats manipulate statistical data to conform to political requirements. This point brings to mind the story told by the American political scientist and State Department official Roger Hilsman at the time of America's involvement in the Vietnam war. During the early years of that struggle, Americans were still trying to develop statistical indicators to measure our progress in the war. To which one of the Vietnamese generals replied, "Ah, les statistiques! Your Secretary of Defense [Robert S. McNamara] loves statistics. We Vietnamese can give him all he wants. If you want them to go up, they will go up. If you want them to go down, they will go down."[16]

[14]On this general subject, see Immanuel Wallerstein, "The Range of Choice: Constraints on the Policies of Governments of Contemporary African Independent States," in Michael F. Lofchie, ed., *The State of the Nations: Constraints on Development in Independent Africa* (Berkeley, Calif.: University of California Press, 1971), chap. 2.

[15]Merilee S. Grindle, ed., *Politics and Policy Implementation in the Third World* (Princeton, N.J.: Princeton University Press, 1980).

[16]Roger Hilsman, *To Move a Nation* (Garden City, N.Y.: Doubleday, 1967), p. 523.

The second kind of constraint on policy implementation is an economic one, the severe lack of funds available to pay for the many projects and programs that all Third World governments would like to establish. Immanuel Wallerstein[17] has shown that in virtually every independent nation in Africa expenditures have exceeded receipts at least in the long run (more than two or three years). Even where some sort of windfall makes new revenues available unexpectedly, as with the negotiation of new arrangements between the Zambian Government and the international copper companies, increased needs absorb the new revenues as fast as they become available. Even such oil-rich states as Venezuela and Nigeria found themselves in financial straits only a few years after the oil embargo and the rise in oil prices brought them close to the point of luxury for Third World countries.

There are only a limited number of sources from which a development-minded élite can extract the money needed to pay for their programs. The industrialized states, such as the United States and countries in Western Europe, can provide official government-to-government loans or grants; but these sources attach significant conditions to this money, and such strings usually infringe on the power of the developing nation. No Third World nation likes to find itself in the situation of India where 30 percent of the entire income of the third Five-Year Plan had to come from foreign aid. Many Third World countries have sought financial relief by controlling the sale of export commodities, either by administering these sales entirely through some sort of export marketing board (as with cocoa in Ghana) or simply by levying an indirect tax on the exported items. In extreme cases, such as those of oil in Venezuela or copper in Chile, the exporting country's government will actually nationalize or expropriate the commercial, mining, or industrial enterprises so that all foreign exchange from export sales will accrue to the government. Dependence on foreign sales of raw materials is a shaky source of support for government policy because prices are so volatile that it is difficult to

predict far in advance exactly what government revenues are likely to be. Furthermore, many Third World countries are based on monocultural economies, meaning that one single commodity or product dominates the export picture. Fluctuations in the price of that commodity can have disastrous effects on the nation's over-all economy.

When a development élite turns to its own national resources, the picture is not too bright. Some governments have chosen to avoid the problem of insufficient funds by simply creating money to pay at least their domestic bills. In cases like that of Chile in the 1960s, inflation was used by the government to avoid a clash between economic sectors that were not predisposed to compromise. Inflation was a substitute for taxation and expenditure of real resources. As subsequent events in Chile testify, that kind of policy cannot be maintained for long without tragic results. Only a regime that already maintains a reputation with its people for honesty and legitimacy can afford to run budget deficits and to meet the difference in created money. Governments that do not enjoy legitimacy with their people or with significant disadvantaged sectors do not usually have this option. In addition, inflation by creating money at home does not solve the equally severe problem of shortage of foreign exchange, which a government needs to purchase greatly needed imported items for industrial and agricultural modernization.

Thus, development élites are forced to consider the most critical of all financial policies, the levy of taxes on private, personal, and corporate income. During the 1950s and early 1960s, the less developed countries typically took between 8 and 15 percent of their GNP to finance government operations. The average for 24 developing countries in the 1953–1955 period was 11.8 percent. In contrast, the average during that same period for 15 industrialized countries was 26.2 percent, several collected more than 30 percent of the GNP in taxes. Since that time, Third World governments have been making great strides in their ability to tax their own nations' wealth. During the period 1972–1976, the same 24 developing countries averaged 16.3 percent of

[17]Wallerstein, *op. cit.*

their GNP in taxes, an increase of 38 percent. By comparison, after about two decades of development, the poor countries were still taking out of their national economies less than half of the percentage taxed by industrialized countries, whose figure for the 1972–1976 period stood at 36.2 percent. Moreover, since 1975, tax ratios in developing countries have not increased. A 1980 World Bank report found that "the scope for raising taxation is less now than it was 20 years ago."[18]

As we can see from Table 6.2, governments in the Third World differ markedly in their ability to rely on income taxes to finance public expenditures. Those that are relatively highly developed, and that have capable tax-collection agencies and a relatively high level of public loyalty, such as Mexico, account for nearly half of their government revenues from income taxes. Others that lack these advantages derive a relatively small proportion of government revenues from income taxes (e.g., India, 15 to 17 percent; Egypt, 19 to 22 percent). Industrial democracies, such as Canada, France, Great Britain, or the United States, typically receive more than 50 percent of government revenues from personal income taxes. The average for 83 countries of the Third World for which we have comparable data (excluding those petroleum-exporting nations that do not separate their petroleum revenues from other income tax) is less than 20 percent.

As might be expected, the typical Third World government's inability to tax income properly stems from several defects in the political and economic systems: the highly unequal distribution of income combined with the close connection between income distribution and political power; the regressive nature of most Third World tax systems (tax rate goes *up* as income goes *down*); the tendency for the wealthiest sectors of Third World economies to derive their income from inaccessible sources, such as rents and land; and the bureaucratic in-

**TABLE 6.2** Percentage of Central Government Budget Derived from Income Tax in Eight Selected Third World Countries with an 83-Nation Average, 1967 and 1973

| Country | 1967 | 1973 |
|---|---|---|
| Nigeria[a] | 8.4% | 4.0% |
| Tanzania | 22.8 | 24.8 |
| India | 17.4 | 15.7 |
| Indonesia[b] | 27.9 | 53.0 |
| Mexico | 43.5 | 47.3 |
| Brazil | 17.2 | 22.8 |
| Egypt | 19.1 | 22.2 |
| Iran | 8.5 | 10.6 |
| 83-Nation Average[c] | 18.0 | 19.0 |

[a]Excludes petroleum revenues.

[b]Includes petroleum revenues.

[c]Excludes all petroleum-exporting countries that do not report petroleum revenues separately from other income tax.

SOURCE: World Bank, *World Tables, 1976*, Series 2 (Baltimore: Johns Hopkins University Press, 1976).

adequacies that make levies, such as land taxes, easy to evade.

This last observation brings us around to a consideration of the political constraints of policy implementation, which will be subsumed under Gunnar Myrdal's phrase, the soft state.[19] According to Myrdal, all underdeveloped countries are, to one degree or another, soft states. This means that they suffer from social indiscipline, which manifests itself in deficiencies in legislation and, in particular, in law observance and enforcement; a widespread disobedience by public officials of rules and directives handed down to them; and often the collusion of public officials with powerful persons and groups whose conduct they should regulate. Singapore's former Minister for Foreign Affairs and Labor, S. Rajaratnam, has called this government by kleptocracy. In specific terms the soft state includes corruption, racketeering, bribes, payoffs, smuggling, kickbacks, black-market profits, arbitrary enforcement of the law, lax or nonexistent enforcement of the law, and abuse of power, especially on the local level.

Political and commercial corruption can

[18]World Bank, *World Development Report*, 1980 (New York: Oxford University Press, 1980), Table 6.1; p. 73. See also, Nicholas Kaldor, "Will Underdeveloped Countries Learn to Tax?" *Foreign Affairs, 41* (2) (1963), pp. 410–419.

[19]Gunnar Myrdal, *The Challenge of World Poverty* (New York: 1970), chap. 7.

alter the quality of life in Third World countries in many different ways, ranging from the trivial to the critical. In Lima, Peru, one of the more vexing public policy problems for city officials during the first half of 1981 was what to do about the hordes of street vendors who thronged the city's main avenues selling all manner of consumer products, from clothing to cooking utensils. No one seemed to know just how many such vendors there were. Estimates ranged from 20,000 to 200,000, with the city's official census counting 4,000. What everyone knew, however, was that they were operating illegally. In the decade or so that the street vendors had been working the area, however, there had grown up an intricate underground support structure, including license kickbacks and illegal protection rackets. With such a supporting social system, it seemed unlikely that the city government could take the action needed to remove the vendors without a show of armed force. Half way around the world, in Nigeria, the issue was much more critical: the price of rice, a staple of the Nigerian diet. Because Nigeria does not produce enough food to feed its own population, the government issues permits to private firms to import 200,000 tons each year. Despite these imports, rice was hard to find during the last half of 1980, and prices continued to rise. The reason, many observers alleged, was that the government had been distributing licenses only to its friends and political allies and that the amount was kept low to keep prices and profits high. Government officials countercharged that their opponents had been buying up the rice as soon as it got to the country, causing prices to rise and artificial scarcities to develop. As so often is the case, the truth was impossible to ascertain. But, for typical Nigerian citizens, it was imperative that some solution be found to the problem if they were to have enough rice to feed their families.[20]

Before we discuss the specific causes for the soft state, we must discard two erroneous notions. The first is that political corruption in the

Third World has something to do with the form of government. Actually, many Third World regimes are soft, lax, and corrupt regardless of whether the chief of state is a military dictator or an elected president or whether parties and press function freely or are suppressed. The second erroneous idea is that political corruption has something to do with inferior standards of morality. The morality of Third World citizens and public officials is about what it is in most political systems and probably higher than the public morality exhibited by political bosses in some of America's larger cities. If we want to understand the causes of political softness in developing countries, we must learn to look for it in the nature of political power in a less developed political system.

For one thing, we must attempt to put ourselves into the place of the citizens of most Third World countries. Often, low-status and low-income persons from these countries, whether they live in urban or rural areas, have grown up in an environment where the government was feared or hated, and rightly so. In many cases, the precolonial administrations were only slightly benevolent dictatorships; their successors, the colonial regimes, only exceeded their predecessors in the extent to which they could abuse power. Manning Nash's description of politics in a remote Burmese village is significant in this regard.

> Government [to the people of Nondwin village] is one of the five traditional enemies, along with fire, famine, flood and plague. . . . From the days of arbitrary demands from the royal city to the British colonial administration, through the Japanese occupation and the civil disorders following independence, political power in the shape of government has been something alien, demanding, and usually capricious or enigmatic. Government is identified with the unrestricted use of force. Nondwin villagers seek means to avoid or subvert the force of government, except when there is a local man who also has the kind of power that governments are thought to have.[21]

[20]Cynthia Gorney, "Lima's Hordes of Street Vendors Enraged by Plan to Relocate Them," *Washington Post*, June 6, 1981. Leon Dash, "Nigeria Rice Prices Fuel Political Feuding," *Washington Post*, December 27, 1980.

[21]Manning Nash, *The Golden Road to Modernity: Village Life in Contemporary Burma* (Chicago: University of Chicago Press, 1965), p. 75.

The effect of this ancient tradition of mistrust of government is to encourage local villagers to look the other way when smuggling or bribery occurs and to engage in passive resistance when the national government enters their village. It seems as if peasants the world over have learned much the same kind of defense against government intruders: stare at the bureaucrats with a passive, noncommittal look and, then, wait for them to leave, secure in the knowledge that nothing of consequence will really change, for good or ill.

A second cause of political corruption in the Third World can be traced to the administrative style of many of these countries. Despite a notable lack of real political power and authority, Third World governments have legislated an amazing array of official restrictions and regulations that amount to an open invitation to bribery and payoffs. In Burma, the state attempts to control most retail merchandising by requiring merchants to sell their wares through state-run stores. However, visitors to the official stores find them virtually empty, whereas street vendors a few feet away from the stores display a wide variety of consumer goods—all illegally sold of course. The customary insistence on a seemingly endless series of forms, permits, licenses, and other devices allow administrative discretion at a very low level, encouraging bureaucrats to take advantage of the helpless business people or consumers. In addition, many Third World countries try to regulate citizen behavior by offering financial subsidies for certain kinds of private decisions—rental of an apartment for example—which burdens the administrative apparatus and offers further opportunity for abuse. Add to this apparatus the notoriously low salaries earned by civil servants in poor countries and you have a situation open to abuse, corruption, and bribery. Some of the worst offenders appear to be foreign multinational corporations, which regard the bribes they pay to public officials as a normal cost of doing business in developing countries.

A third cause of the soft state lies in the highly unequal distribution of political power in the Third World. We have already seen that Third World governments frequently make use of the syncratic style of governance as they attempt to modernize and industrialize their countries without seriously altering the privileges and special powerful status of the traditional sectors of the country. This effort leads, in turn, to the promulgation of laws, decrees, and proclamations that are more honored in the breach than in the observance. Third World regimes have enacted numerous laws intended to reform the land-tenure patterns of their countries, to curb abuses of power, to grant security of property to peasants, to establish a minimum wage for urban laborers, or to provide free health care for the poor, and so on. What happens to these laws? Most of the provisions of these laws are designed to please either low-status interest group representatives or foreign governments trying to urge local reforms before external assistance is granted. But the really powerful of the country know that the law will contain enough escape provisions (loopholes) so that they themselves need never feel the adverse impact of the law. Despite the radical sounds emanating from many national capitals in the Third World, little in the way of radical change ever really takes place because of the élites' ability to block effective enforcement of the law. Thus, we see a growing gap between the symbolic pronouncements of the political leaders and the tangible significance of the regime's actions. There is not a government in the world that does not distribute at least a little symbolism instead of tangible benefits to its people. That is, no government has enough control over real goods (money, food, housing, health care) that they can distribute a satisfactory quantity to each person; so, each government has to concentrate on making its people feel happy instead of enjoying material well-being. All governments do this, but the evidence suggests that Third World governments do it more than most other political systems. Again, as in the case of unrealistic goal setting, the real difficulty arises from a growing class consciousness of low-income persons who are coming to realize that one cannot live on symbols indefinitely and that, eventually, governments must turn to the real issues of power, wealth, and their unequal concentration.

One final point needs to be made regarding corruption in the soft state. It appears as if the real hidden cause of political softness and public immorality in the Third World lies in the comparatively underdeveloped state of countervailing powers in these societies. Perhaps the chief characteristic of Third World power systems is the relative lack of power anywhere in the system. Coercion, force, and authoritarian rule are all present in abundance, but power is a genuinely scarce commodity. Little power exists outside of the local-level patron-client networks and the international influences, which bear on the national network from both sides. (This theme will be examined in greater detail later.) But, at the national level, individuals are not organized into collectivities that can exercise power efficiently. There are few freely operating opposition political parties or independent judiciary systems. Most legislatures are of the rubber stamp variety. Interest groups are primitive and are mostly under the control of the government itself. Press freedom is rare. In other words, there are few checks on the unrestrained and abused power of a dominant executive (civil or military) and its representatives. Laws are made or unmade and enforced or unenforced not according to some master guide, such as a constitution, but according to the whim of the administrator and the special access enjoyed by traditional élites. The founders of the U.S. system did not assume that political leaders were especially moral people. The opposite seems true because they created the system in such a way as to pit one force against another, each with enough power to defend itself and none with enough power to overwhelm the others. Through the years, that system has been subjected to many threats, but the essential soundness of the principle appears to have emerged intact. This lack of a system of countervailing powers paradoxically encourages Third World leaders to try to accumulate more and more force and authority. It is paradoxical because even as they violate their own laws and

abuse their own supporters to gain more power, in the long run, they condemn themselves to further weakness and softness.

## EVALUATING OUTCOMES

To complete the picture of the failure-prone policy-making process, we must examine how Third World governments evaluate the outcomes of their policy choices. We will find that the defects of the first two stages of decision making (setting goals and taking actions) are compounded by an inability to evaluate policies quickly and accurately, to locate mistakes, and to remedy those errors to avoid serious adverse consequences.

Several concepts are particularly useful here. We have already encountered the idea of feedback, information about past or present system performance that can be used to improve future system performance. Feedback in the political context means any information about the impact of past and present policy choices to make new decisions about future policy directions. When feedback is lacking, political systems in an environment of rapid change cannot respond to mistakes quickly enough to avoid their adverse consequences. If certain environmental factors, such as population, change by means of a percent increment each year instead of by a fixed quantity (e.g., population growth of 2 percent per year instead of 1 million persons per year), we say that these factors are growing exponentially. In contrast to linear growth, when the increments are always of a fixed quantity, exponential growth makes quantities grow surprisingly fast because the base for growth expands so rapidly. Third World political systems are particularly vulnerable to exponential growth because of their poor facilities for evaluating policy outcomes (feedback), their penchant to make mistakes in the first place, and their limited resources to rectify their errors once detected. When environmental factors change so fast that a mistake cannot be detected until it is too late to avoid its adverse consequence, we say that the system is in a condition of overshoot. When overshoot is experienced often enough, in enough sectors of the society, and to a strong-enough degree, the policy-making mechanism of the system collapses under the burden of repeated failures. This is the situation facing many Third World governments today.

We have discussed some of the characteristics of Third World societies and political systems that contribute to an inability to evaluate policy outcomes. Certainly, the limited communications media available in less developed systems inhibit the free flow of information that is so vital to policy makers in attempting to understand their own societies. Third World governments' policies to constrain a free press also play a key role in undermining their own self-analysis efforts. Political culture, especially in the mass of urban and rural poor, is another important obstacle faced by developing governments. In examples drawn from countries as far apart as Burma and Chile, we have already noted the prevailing peasant response to mistaken policies advanced by bureaucrats from the national government: "They rarely say no; they prefer to nod their heads in agreement, so that the long-winded officials will depart soon, and so that they can continue to pursue their interest in their own way."[22] No government can evaluate its own policies as long as the supposed beneficiaries of these policies remain mute about their defects.

But of all the causes of poor policy evaluation in the Third World, perhaps the most serious is, again, the institutional flaw in developing political systems. There simply are not enough autonomous associations and institutions at work in Third World societies to obtain information about the impact of policies on their members, to assess the costs and benefits of this impact, and to communicate this information to public officials. The policy-evaluation tools that heve become so familiar to American observers—think tanks, university research facilities and laboratories, and investigative journalism—

are virtually unknown in the developing countries. And the more conventional feedback mechanisms, such as political parties and interest groups, either are fragmented, not trusted by their constituents, or controlled or ignored by the government. Robert Scott, for example, points out that most Latin American governments have found it exceedingly difficult to respond to the multiple dislocations brought about by rapid social and economic change because of their lack of accurate information about their societies.[23] Most governments in that region have discounted the benefits to be derived from nurturing and encouraging a multiparty system stocked with reform-minded, modernizing political parties. Instead, they have preferred to proceed on the institutional basis of an expanded bureaucracy (civil and military) and the artificial creation of captive interest groups that represent industry, commerce, and agriculture at a minimum. Yet, Scott continues, these awkward and stilted feedback mechanisms simply are not up to the demands of rapid development. Bureaucrats, whether civil or military, tend to see development where there is none—and have the data to prove it. Even in countries where interest groups are nominally independent of government control, as in Chile before 1970, the majority of the business sector declined to participate in the activities of their interest group; they felt the group to be ineffective and too subservient to government dictates.[24] Finally, where the government sets out to create feedback institutions, as in Pakistan's basic democracies experiment, the regime's opponents quickly learn that dissent within the controlled institutions is permitted only up to the point where it begins to be effective. In other words, the institutionalization of dissent is done more for theatrical purposes than for the purpose of obtaining badly needed information about the state of affairs in remote areas. (The

[22]David Lehmann, "Agrarian Reform in Chile, 1965–1972: An Essay in Contradictions," in David Lehmann, ed., *Peasants, Landlords and Governments: Agrarian Reform in the Third World* (New York: Holmes & Meier, 1974), p. 109.

[23]Robert Scott, "Political Parties and Policy Making in Latin America," in Joseph LaPalombara and Myron Weiner, eds., *Political Parties and Political Development* (Princeton, N.J.: Princeton University Press, 1966), pp. 365–367.

[24]Dale L. Johnson, "The National and Progressive Bourgeoisie in Chile," in Cockcroft *et al.*, eds., pp. 201–206.

proof of this flaw lies in Pakistan's inability to sense the depth of grievances in East Pakistan until it was too late and secession was inevitable.) The Tanzanian example seems particularly typical.

> [Other than the National Executive Committee of the ruling Tanganyika African National Union (TANU) Party,] there were few other ways for the government to inform itself of popular reactions to its proposals. Parliamentary discussion was none too vigorous and members were very cautious with any criticism they might wish to make of government policies. The newspapers were either controlled by the party or were extremely timid. The trade union movement had been brought increasingly under tighter government control. Within both the civil service and the party bureaucracy the upward flow of information on popular reactions to government policies was sporadic and inadequate.[25]

Myron Weiner writes on one of the key differences between developed and less developed political systems:

> A modern political system has no single mechanism, no single procedure, no single institution for the resolution of conflict; indeed, it is precisely the multiplicity of individuals, institutions and procedures for dispute settlement that characterizes the modern political system—both democratic and totalitarian. In contrast, developing societies with an increasing range of internal conflict, typically lack such individuals, institutions and procedures. It is as if mankind's capacity to generate conflict is greater than his capacity to find methods of resolving conflict; the lag is clearly greatest in societies in which fundamental economic and social relationships are rapidly changing.[26]

## CONCLUSIONS: POLICY MAKING AND HUMAN DIGNITY

As a generalization, let us conclude this analysis by outlining the consequences of the Third World policy-making style: unrealistic goals, ineffectual and underfinanced actions, and poorly evaluated outcomes. Policies designed to enhance human dignity often suffer from the tendency of many Third World states to swing wildly back and forth between two polar extremes, the conservative and the radical approaches, which are drawn here in abstract and general terms. In this analysis, we follow the work of Immanuel Wallerstein on styles of governance in Africa.[27]

The conservative regime, according to Wallerstein, desires above all to maintain a relatively open economy and national society. This has usually meant keeping the country within the zone of some international currency (dollar, pound, franc); maintaining few economic restrictions, such as import quotas, tariffs, or controls, over the transfer of capital; and permitting (and encouraging) foreign private capital investment. At home, agitation from the left is suppressed and human rights do not flourish. As the years pass, the initial difficulties of the conservative regime stem from its growing international problems with consequent pressure on the government's budget. Declining prices on the world market for the country's raw-materials exports cause the nation's foreign-exchange situation to become critical. Much of the national income is spent on imported luxury items, worsening the nation's balance of payments and not contributing to domestic production. Free transfer of capital leads to capital drain or flight, typified by the opening of Swiss bank accounts by the country's élite. Steady expansion of the nation's educational system produces too many over-educated persons for the small number of jobs available in the contracting economy, but the government finds that it cannot do anything to reduce school enrollments. Universities become centers of agitation against the government's hiring policies. Unemployment grows, particularly among the urban lower classes and the young intellectuals, creating an explosive coalition of disaffected masses and restive articulate leaders.

---

[25]R. Cranford Pratt, "The Cabinet and Presidential Leadership in Tanzania: 1960–1966," in Lofchie, *op. cit.*, p. 100.

[26]Myron Weiner, "Political Integration and Political Development," *The Annals*, 358 (1965), p. 60.

[27]Wallerstein, *op. cit.*, pp. 28–32. See also James D. Cockcroft, "Last Rites for the Reformist Model in Latin America," in Cockcroft *et al.*, eds., pp. 118–119.

Foreign interest in supporting the government declines, either as a result of lessening international tensions (the decline of the Cold War) or because of the decline in the return on foreign investment in domestic enterprises. In the face of growing unemployment, rising prices, and declining government services, the lower class begin to believe charismatic leaders who offer them simplistic explanations for their plight. In Latin America, these leaders may come from universities or from the trade union movement; in Africa, from tribal leadership positions; and in Asia, from plantation unions or from the élite professions (law, medicine, journalism). Popular pressure on the government provokes considerable suppression of individual rights and reshuffling of the cabinet, but the basic causes of the government's discomfort—economic cramp magnified by international pressure—refuse to go away. As popular rebellion grows, the armed forces are provoked once again to enter the political arena, less for their own benefit (although military budgets *will* increase once they take power), than for a growing realization that the civilian leaders cannot set things aright.

Wallerstein's typical radical regime begins with an entirely different set of assumptions. Instead of openness in the economy and polity, they seek to close off the national system from disturbing and imperialistic influences. At the international level, this means breaking ties with the former colonial country's currency zone and establishing strict currency controls. Heavy constraints are placed on imports, currency transactions, and the movement of convertible currencies abroad. Internally, although the growing commercial and industrial bourgeoisie is limited in its development, private foreign investment is not inhibited until it becomes apparent that such investment comes working against the best interests of the nation. Then, it is usually confiscated or expropriated by the government, sometimes with compensation (oil companies in Venezuela), sometimes without adequate compensation. In the international political sphere, the radical regime usually adopts an anti-Western, neutralist position, supporting the national liberation movements in the still-colonized areas of the Third World (southern Africa especially) and the radical opposition parties in conservative states. Internally, the one-party state comes into being, and dissent from the right is suppressed. Human rights are denied, as they were by conservative regimes. Despite the many differences between radical and conservative regimes, however, their undoing commonly comes from the same place: growing budgetary deficits combined with inflation and economic policies that alienate key political groups. In the case of radical regimes, budget deficits grow because of the desire to spend larger amounts to provide needed social services as well as to create employment. With sufficient jobs, the urban working classes are kept relatively quiet. The problem comes from the taxation side of the equation. To pay for growing government programs, the regime tries to tax the traditional and progressive élites, the cash-crop farmers, the urban middle class, and the urban workers. Government bureaucrats are asked to do more with less in the name of fiscal austerity. Luxury imports are restricted, leading to higher domestic prices for inferior goods and angering the middle class. The leftward shift of the government brings about economic retaliation from the West, as manifested by pressures by the World Bank, the IMF, and the U.S. Government. Foreign sources of capital begin to dry up. Once again, the dreary picture of instability is displayed. Rising costs, declining incomes, loss of government control over events, and so forth, all lead to growing unrest, disorders, turbulence, the threat of even more radical policies from the far left and, at last, intervention by the armed forces.

And, so, for the past two decades, the nations of the Third World have swung back and forth between these two alternative governance styles. Sometimes the period between regimes is marked by military government; sometimes the military takes power permanently and attempts to establish its own style or approach to meeting the nation's problems. The exact sequence of events or the exact labels on all the key participants are not important. What does matter is that each regime lacks the sensory mechanisms necessary to let it know when disaster looms in enough time to pull back from mistaken policies. What we see are a series of experiments in failure as the Third World oscillates from conservative to radical and back again, never finding its own solid path to development and failing to emulate the models from the First and Second Worlds.

# Suggestions for Further Reading

**Dror, Yehezkel,** "Public-Policy-Making in Avant-Garde Development States," *Civilisations, 13* (4) (1963), pp. 395–405.

**Grindle, Merilee S.,** ed., *Politics and Policy Implementation in the Third World* (Princeton, N.J.: Princeton University Press, 1980).

**Heidenheimer, Arnold J.,** ed., *Political Corruption* (New York: Holt, Rinehart & Winston, 1970).

**Hirschman, Albert O.,** *Journeys Toward Progress: Studies of Economic Policy Making in Latin America* (New York: Twentieth Century Fund, 1963).

_____, *The Strategy of Economic Development* (New Haven, Conn.: Yale University Press, 1961).

**Honey, John C.,** *Planning and the Private Sector: The Experience in Developing Countries* (New York: Dunellen, 1970).

**Ilchmann, Warren F.,** and **Norman Thomas Uphoff,** *The Political Economy of Change* (Berkeley, Calif.: University of California Press, 1969).

**LaPalombara, Joseph,** ed., *Bureaucracy and Political Development* (Princeton, N.J.: Princeton University Press, 1963).

**Mason, Edward,** *Economic Planning in Underdeveloped Areas* (New York: Fordham University Press, 1958).

**Montgomery, John D.,** and **William J. Siffin,** eds., *Approaches to Development: Politics, Administration and Change* (New York: McGraw-Hill, 1966).

**Riggs, Fred,** *Administration in Developing Countries* (Boston: Houghton Mifflin, 1964).

**Waterston, Albert,** *Development Planning: Lessons of Experience* (Baltimore: Johns Hopkins University Press, 1965).

_____, *Planning in Morocco* (Baltimore: Johns Hopkins University Press, 1962).

_____, *Planning in Pakistan* (Baltimore: Johns Hopkins University Press, 1963).

**Wraith, Ronald,** and **Edgar Simpkins,** *Corruption in Developing Countries* (New York: Norton, 1964).

# CHAPTER SEVEN
## Political Performance in the Third World

Politics is a struggle under the best of circumstances, but the Third World does not enjoy the best of circumstances or even anything approaching the best. Nevertheless, the political life of a community must go forward, for better or worse. The pressure of events is relentless. Our concern as students of comparative politics is to assess the degree of success or failure experienced by Third World regimes in responding to these pressures.

Inquiries such as this are always susceptible to distortions caused by ethnocentrism or the disposition to judge foreign groups by reference to one's own cultural and political customs, institutions, and standards. We have examined Third World governments as they allocate four values: power, well-being, respect, and enlightenment. Although the simple listing of these four values may seem objective enough, the way in which we interpret each of the four may make a great deal of difference in our findings. Consider, for example, the value of respect. In the industrialized democracies of Western Europe and North America, respect means the guarantee of individual human rights against the pressure of the group or the coercion of the state. In countries inspired by Marxist or Maoist philosophy, respect may mean comradeship or the feeling of

being accepted by the ruling group. In many Third World countries (but by no means all), Western norms of individualism are less important. In these countries, respect may mean the domination of one ethnic group by another or the prestige enjoyed by the government in international or regional organizations.

As we go about the task of applying the four-value framework to political performance in the Third World, we must try not to define values and goals solely by Western norms. Many developing countries have adopted the goal structure of modern, industrialized nations, even if only superficially or partially. Yet, in most instances, the transfer of Western values took place under duress or coercion when the recipient colony could not defend itself and its culture against European influence. Understandably, many Third World leaders are caught uncomfortably between their desire to match the economic and political power and well-being of the industrialized nations, on the one hand, and their need to return to the cultural tradition that characterized their peoples before the arrival of the Europeans. The result has been the emergence of mixed traditional-modern philosophies and ideologies to guide the new nations of the developing world. In the 1930s, Victor Raúl Haya de la Torre of

Peru began to articulate the doctrine of *aprismo* in an attempt to link together the urban, modernizing elites of his country and the poor Indian villagers of the remote interior. Similarly, Julius K. Nyerere in Tanzania espoused *ujamaa* socialism as the best way to combine traditional village communal values with the benefits of the modern welfare state. Whether any of the mixed ideologies will survive their founders cannot be known this early. At this juncture of history, we can only note the dangers of ethnocentrism, observe the efforts of Third World leaders to define their own goals in terms to which they can relate, and, then, use these same goals as yardsticks against which to measure their performance.

## GOALS, ACTIONS, OUTCOMES: POWER

We begin our discussion of political performance in the Third World with the value of power because of the central role of power in any plan to maximize or distribute any of the other values. Possession of power is, by itself, no guarantee that individuals or governments will really try to enhance human dignity in their societies. But, without power, no individual or government can do much to advance this goal.

Power in the Third World can best be visualized as existing in three more or less separate realms: the international, the national-modern, and the local-traditional. Most national governments in Latin America, Asia, Africa, and the Middle East are caught in a squeeze between two largely autonomous power centers, neither of which is much interested in promoting the power of the national regime. One power center lies outside the Third World, that is, the governments of the developed nations (both the industrialized democracies of the West and the Communist states); the private, multinational corporations located primarily in Western Europe and North America, many of which are richer and more powerful than entire nations in the Third World; and the international institutions that represent the industrial countries (the United Nations and its subordinate agencies; the International Monetary Fund (IMF); the World

Bank; and the many separate institutions that control the marketing of raw materials). As long as the international economic, military, cultural, and political systems continue to intrude into their national arenas, the Third World's latitude for reform will be defined by what the international system will permit.

The other competing source of power is just as much an obstacle to national development as the international system, but it usually is harder to locate and identify. This second power center consists of the traditional élites of the countryside and the patrons of both the city and the village who manipulate their clients to protect them against an encroaching national government. We have already discussed the agents, money lenders, plantation owners, slum bosses, local chieftains, village heads, and the many other petty political powers, each guarding his or her province from the national authority and each benefiting from the respect and privilege received from clients.

In view of the fact that both the international and the clientelist power sources are in agreement about the necessity to limit the power of the national government, it is not surprising that we occasionally find them in alliance to undermine a particular reformist élite or to weaken its policies that are designed to strengthen national power. Examples of these alliances are difficult to find in the open literature because they are usually clandestine and are denounced by the government as illegal when they occur. Nevertheless, there are enough cases openly admitted to suggest that such alliances are fairly common in the Third World. Agencies of the U.S. Government, for example, have entered into working relationships with local traditional élites to weaken or unseat reform-minded national regimes on several occasions in Latin America (Chile, Guatemala, Peru). Review the arguments about the reasons behind such actions in Chapter Two, "Social and Economic Problems in the Third World." Here, we simply want to illustrate the informal ties that exist between the international power triad (national governments, multinational corporations, international institutions) and local patrons and other traditional leaders. Together and separately, they render many progressive, reformist regimes in the Third World powerless to carry out their intended transformations of their societies.

Accordingly, the first order of business for reform-minded élites in the Third World must be to concentrate on the accumulation of power at the national level. In the first instance, this means seizing the institutionalized power of the state; in the second, it means securing that power and expanding it to reach into areas of the country and the society previously beyond the control of central authority. Power has been seized in the Third World in many different ways. A few regimes still in existence can trace their legitimacy back through previous rulers, handed down to them by inheritance. These include the traditional monarchies of Jordan and Saudi Arabia. The fate of Ethiopia reveals what happens to this fast-disappearing type of political order if it delays modernization too long. In a second type of regime, also represented by comparatively few cases, the present rulers were handed power peacefully by the departing colonial regime. A few such regimes, such as that of Julius K. Nyerere in Tanzania, are still in power. The great majority, however, have been removed one way or another by successor regimes. Still another way of achieving power is through violent revolution against a stubborn colonial authority, as in Algeria and Indonesia and (much earlier) in most of the states of Latin America. For most Third World countries, however, the transfer and acquisition of power have now settled down into one of two techniques: either peacefully through democratic procedures, including open elections (Costa Rica, Mexico, Sri Lanka, Venezuela), or violently and extralegally, often through a military coup but also through a civilian seizure of power (as in India prior to the 1977 elections).

Once in power, however, most Third World regimes find that they must devote major resources to the task of remaining there. Of course, simply staying in power is not enough to enable a government to enhance human dignity. The regime must accumulate enough extra power so that some may be diverted to making badly needed changes in the country's society, economy, and culture. Although different strategies are used by different regimes to accumulate power, in essence they all boil down to one significant fact: virtually all of the country's leaders and most of its mass population must regard the incumbent regime as having the authority to make decisions on behalf of the entire nation or the coercive force necessary to require acceptance of these decisions, or both.

Power in this sense can be thought of as a commodity. Power can be exchanged or traded, like money, and it can be taken from one person or group and given to another, like land. In the short run, however, it can not be increased in absolute terms for an entire society. As a regime increases its power, the power of other groups in society or outside its boundaries must decline by an approximately equivalent amount. If, for example, the government of Peru were to develop the country's industrial base sufficiently to be relatively impervious to the international economy, then, the power of the IMF to influence Peruvian politics would decline accordingly. Internally, as the power of the government of India to set a national policy regarding languages increases, the power of various minority linguistic factions must be reduced by the same degree. To the extent that national governments succeed in accumulating and consolidating power, they do so only by influencing competitors to relinquish their power and to transfer their loyalty to the central regime. This is the goal with regard to power.

For regimes that lack control over tangible resources, reliance on the charismatic leader quickly becomes a cornerstone of policies designed to increase power.[1] Charisma has been defined as the ability of a person to make others feel more powerful in his or her presence.[2] In politics, charisma involves a complex psychocul-

---

[1] This discussion leans heavily on Howard W. Wriggins, *The Ruler's Imperative: Strategies for Political Survival in Asia and Africa* (New York: Columbia University Press, 1969).

[2] David McClelland, "The Two Faces of Power," *Journal of International Affairs*, 24 (1) (1970), pp. 29–47.

tural relationship between a leader and the masses who are led to believe themselves more powerful simply by being in the presence of the great ruler. The entire process, then, feeds back into itself. The ruler, by enjoying the enthusiastic support of the mass of followers does indeed become capable of great things and can lead the country on to high achievements.

Charisma has several functions in a developmental setting. Aided by the apparatus of modern mass communications, the charismatic leader bypasses the traditional bosses, chieftains, and heads of the local areas and reaches out to enter the consciousness of the low-income and low-status citizens who previously were shielded from national politics by their patrons. Thus armed, the charismatic leader can persuade the masses to undergo sacrifices, to unite in national movements to carry out grand schemes, and to feel themselves part of a larger enterprise—the work of a nation. On the foreign scene, a charismatic leader personifies the nation in its relations with other states and can, when necessary, direct the sentiment of the people against foreign enemies or to meet external threats.

If the individual leader is not particularly well endowed with charisma, a frequently used substitute is leadership through ideology. Many people in the developing world live in a confusing state of rapid change. One way to secure their support and loyalty is to make rapid change understandable and rational to them. An ideology, in its cohesive and comprehensive picture of the world, makes sense to the populace and enables them to grapple with a world that is more and more threatening. Moreover, the leadership as the custodian of the official ideology is given the authority to carry the ideological prescriptions out to their logical policy conclusions.

Child psychologists tell us that one of the most important early tasks of a mother is to make a child's deprivations and frustrations understandable and rational in a world that the child does not at first grasp. Ideologies and charismatic leaders do much the same sort of thing for illiterate and poor citizens in rapidly changing societies. If the élites perform this function effectively, the masses respond by following

them, by obeying their orders, and by quietly enduring the sacrifices imposed on them.

Regimes that rest their power on the personality of a single leader or ideology are in a weak position; individual leaders grow old and die and ideologies lose their significance in the face of rapid change and repeated crisis. Reforming élites who want to endure in power must turn their attention to ways to institutionalize their rule. To institutionalize a particular political phenomenon, such as power, means to depersonalize it, to embed it in a regularized set of interactions and activities that are identified with the name or label of an organization, not with the name of an individual. Any mass of politically aware people must be given a feeling that the enterprise in which they are engaged has a life of its own, that it existed before they joined it, and, most important, that it will persist after they have left so that their contributions will not have been in vain. In the United States, political leaders seek to identify themselves and their followers with the ancient sages and leaders of another era (Thomas Jefferson and Andrew Jackson among the Democrats; Abraham Lincoln among the Republicans) to give members of both parties a sense of the historical ties that bind them not only to earlier generations but also to future ones.

Institution building also has to do with predictability and reliability. Feelings of unpredictability and discontinuity often characterize politics in newly created nations. There is little tradition of the essence of politics: how power is transferred, how ordinary citizens can relate to political leaders, what kind of morality one can expect from élites, and so forth. Political organizations, in performing the same tasks over and over, lend predictability to the political process, and the people soon learn what to expect from élites and from their fellow citizens.

Institutions can also improve communications in a society. Rulers can transmit messages to subordinates and, hence, to mass followings, and they can be reasonably certain that the message that was sent will be the one that arrives. At the same time, the channels of communication are available for the masses to respond, either through acceptance or through protest and dissent. Leaders are well advised to pay attention to the reverse flow of information through institutions because these channels are likely to be the only ones available.

With comparatively few exceptions, political parties, interest groups, and the other institutions of a modern, developed polity have simply not emerged in the Third World. Where they have emerged, as in Sri Lanka, Tunisia, or Venezuela, progressive political leaders have made good use of them to pursue policies that consolidate the power of the ruling élite and that enhance the level of human dignity of the masses of the society. Where they have not emerged, regimes rarely last long enough to embark on fundamental reform or they are so preoccupied with mustering coercive force to suppress dissent that there is little in the way of resources, energy, or time left to devote to bettering the lot of their citizens.

No regime can endure long if it depends solely or even largely on the charismatic charm of a single leader or on the organizational strength and flexibility of a party. At some point, regimes must try to alter certain aspects of the political environment, either inside the country or abroad. At least four kinds of policies have been used by developing regimes in their quest for power: economic development, expansion of political participation, encouragement of ethno-nationalism, and foreign relations.

Economic development is one of the most important policies for the maintenance of a regime in power. In societies where many people live at or near subsistence levels, expansion of the overall economic pie is a prerequisite for distribution of income or wealth to the poor. Monuments, sports stadia, or public works symbolize the presence and the strength of the regime. Communications and transportation media not only facilitate movement of people from the countryside to the cities (thereby throwing off the domination of the local patrons) but also permit extension of central government authority into previously inaccessible regions. National industrial strength enables a developing country to resist international economic pressures, especially as they affect its balance of payments and rate of inflation. Certainly, policies of economic development have their drawbacks because it is difficult to finance their costs and benefits appear only after a long waiting period. But few regimes can last for long if they do not have the industrial and agricultural potential for material well-being in their countries.

A second kind of public policy designed to consolidate a regime's power involves the expansion of political participation. Several of the more progressive élites in the Third World have come to power supported by sectors of the population that previously had been politically inactive. The new regime reached down into the inert layers of traditional society and awakened groups that had never tried to exert their influence before. The regime must, then, reinforce the inclination of these new groups to participate by being genuinely responsive to their needs and wishes. Where this has happened, as with the peasants in Venezuela or the rural villagers in Sri Lanka, the political system undergoes a genuine transformation and is never quite the same again.

At times, however, the mobilization of new actors in the political drama takes on an ugly overtone. Regimes may seek to take advantage of smoldering ethnic animosities to secure their power position in society. By pitting one ethnic group against another or by representing themselves as the protectors of formerly oppressed ethnic groups, regimes may purchase some time in the race to develop and modernize their countries. We have already seen that ideologies are used at times to help define "the enemy" and, quite often, that "the enemy" turns out to have a different skin color, speak a different language, or worship a different god. The cost of such policies can only be excessive. The hatred and hostility generated by ethnonationalistic chauvinism may produce solidarity behind the regime for a time, but it is a weak reed on which to rest an entire national government.

Finally, the international environment offers two different kinds of resources that can be directed toward securing domestic power. First, tangible resources, particularly money and mil-

**TABLE 7.1**  Ranking of Eight Selected Third World Countries as of 1977 by Ray Cline's World Power Assessment

| Country | Rank[a] | Total Power Capability[b] | Critical Mass[c] | Economic Capability | Military Capability— Strategic | Military Capability— Conventional | National Strategic Purpose | Will to Pursue National Strategy |
|---|---|---|---|---|---|---|---|---|
| Nigeria | 17 | 65 | 60 | 5 | 0 | 0 | (0.4) | (0.4) |
| Tanzania | 42 | 30 | 30 | 0 | 0 | 0 | (0.5) | (0.5) |
| India | 9 | 97 | 90 | 4 | 0 | 3 | (0.3) | (0.3) |
| Indonesia | 11 | 85 | 80 | 4 | 0 | 1 | (0.5) | (0.5) |
| Mexico | 13 | 74 | 70 | 4 | 0 | 0 | (0.2) | (0.4) |
| Brazil | 10 | 94 | 85 | 7 | 0 | 2 | (0.5) | (0.8) |
| Egypt | 16 | 65 | 55 | 1 | 0 | 9 | (0.5) | (0.6) |
| Iran | 12 | 80 | 60 | 12 | 0 | 8 | (0.9) | (0.7) |

[a]Out of 76 countries ranked. The United States ranked 1st, with total power capability of 468; the Soviet Union 2nd, with 402.

[b]Total power capability is calculated by adding critical mass and economic and military capabilities. Strategic purpose and will are important factors but are not added to the capability index.

[c]Critical mass is population plus territory.

SOURCE: George Thomas Kurian, *The Book of World Rankings* (New York: Facts on File, 1979), Table 36, pp. 50–51.

itary aid, can be of great use to an economic- and political-development effort, especially if the donors of such aid can be kept at arm's length. Some developing nations have found that they can form regional alliances, free-trade associations, or raw-materials cartels, and, thereby, come to one another's aid in staving off the threat of great power interference in their economies. In addition, the international system offers many important symbolic resources to a struggling, young regime. Membership and a speaking platform in the United Nations and related agencies are taken as proof of the nation's acceptance as an equal member of the world community. Foreign enemies can also be conjured up to provide justification for solidarity behind the regime. These foreign enemies may be industrial states, like the United States, or they may be regional neighbors that profess differing ideologies (Kenya and Uganda for example) or that claim the same territory (Bolivia, Chile, and Peru for example). Although this facet of the in-

ternational system may turn out to be a disadvantage if hostilities flare into real war (as former Indonesian President Sukarno found out in his confrontation with Malaysia), a sort of psychological mini Cold War may actually help to consolidate political power on both sides of the border.

National power is a most elusive concept, one not easily quantifiable. Table 7.1 suggests one way of portraying such a concept, based on the World Power Assessment project of Ray Cline.[3] According to Cline's formulation, national power is a product of population, territory, economic capability, strategic and conventional military capabilities, strategic purpose, and the will to pursue national objectives. Assessed in this way, the power of the Third World does not appear to be quite as low as one would expect. Of the top 10 states in Cline's list of 76,

[3]Ray Cline, *World Power Assessment, 1977* (Boulder, Colo.: Westview, 1977).

there are 2 that are from the Third World: India (9th) and Brazil (10th). Moreover, 8 of the next 10 countries are Third World states: Indonesia (11th), Iran (12th), Mexico (13th), Argentina (14th), Egypt (16th), Nigeria (17th), Turkey (18th), and Pakistan (19th). Finally, countries from the First World and Second World also appear toward the bottom of the list—5 of the bottom 10 countries are from the First World [Greece (68th) and Portugal (71st)] or the Second World [Bulgaria (67th), Cuba (69th), Albania (73rd)].

Lest the reader draw erroneous conclusions from these data, two important points should be kept in mind. First, although many Third World states appear high on the power list, in fact, the gap between the major world powers and the rest of the world is substantial. Although India's total power capability score is 97 and Brazil's is 94, that of the United States is 468, the Soviet Union 402, and China 171. No other nation even begins to approach these three in power. Second, Cline's scale of power is very sensitive to territory and population. Indeed, it is almost entirely on the basis of their large areas and populations that such Third World states as Brazil and Indonesia rank as high as they do. Their scores on other dimensions of power are near or at 0. Without substantial economic and technological capability, however, large territory and populations may prove to detract from national power rather than to enhance it. The poor nation with many mouths to feed and large areas to control without roads or other transportation means is actually less powerful than a relatively small nation with fewer demands on its scarce resources.

With so many state actions available to accumulate and consolidate power at the national level, it is remarkable that in 1981, 30 years after the Third World came into being, there is still so little real national power in the region. There remains an abundance of coercive force and personal abuse of power, but the stable, progressive development of power is still a slippery goal that eludes more Third World regimes than have mastered it. Numerous case studies and articles attest to the continued dominance of the international system in the economies of developing

states.[4] There is less firm evidence of the continued power of patrons and antimodern élites, but the fate of radical reformers, such as Chile's Salvador Allende or the leaders of the Palestinian Liberation Organization (PLO), reveal that the forces of the *status quo* retain their stranglehold over development policies throughout most of the Third World. Several countries seem to have broken through these obstacles to develop strong, flexible sources of power that are independent of the international and local spheres. Venezuela, aided by its enormous oil deposits, or Sri Lanka, with its relatively high level of education, or Tanzania, with its extraordinarily astute leader, lead the way. But few of their fellow Third World states follow.

## GOALS, ACTIONS, OUTCOMES: WELL-BEING

After the seizure, accumulation, and consolidation of power, the next important goal of most developing countries is to enhance the value of well-being. The principal distinguishing feature of the Third World is its grinding and dehumanizing poverty, which is accompanied by a high infant mortality rate, malnutrition, unemployment, lack of housing, social disintegration, and illiteracy. To combat its poverty, almost without exception, nearly every government in the Third World, radical or conservative, must be committed to improving the well-being of its citizens.

Looked at in global terms, the economic growth picture of the Third World for the decade of the 1970s was not especially unfavorable (see Table 7.2). During the decade, developing countries saw their economies grow at the rate of about 5.3 percent per year, compared with a growth rate of only about 3.1 percent for the industrialized countries.[5] This record compared favorably with the rate of growth of the 1960s when the Third World economies expanded at a rate of about 5.6 percent, whereas the in-

[4]James D. Cockcroft *et al.*, eds., *Dependence and Underdevelopment: Latin America's Political Economy* (Garden City, N.Y.: Doubleday, 1972).

[5]Hobart Rowan, "World Bank: Next Ten Years May Be Worse," *Washington Post*, September 22, 1980.

**TABLE 7.2**  Summary Indicators of Economic Performance of Eight Selected Third World Countries

| Country | Average Annual Growth Rate (Percent) | | | | |
|---|---|---|---|---|---|
| | GNP per Capita 1960–1978[a] | GNP 1970–1978[a] | Industry 1970–1978 | Agriculture 1970–1978 | Manu-facturing 1970–1978 |
| Nigeria | 3.6 | 6.2 | 10.3 | −1.5 | 13.4 |
| Tanzania | 2.7 | 5.0 | 2.3 | 4.5 | 4.5 |
| India | 1.4 | 3.7 | 4.5 | 2.6 | 4.6 |
| Indonesia | 4.1 | 7.8 | 11.2 | 4.0 | 12.4 |
| Mexico | 2.7 | 5.0 | 6.2 | 2.1 | 6.2 |
| Brazil | 4.9 | 9.2 | 10.1 | 5.3 | 9.5 |
| Egypt | 3.3 | 7.8 | 7.2 | 3.1 | 7.6 |
| Iran | 7.9 | 7.4 | 4.0 | 5.2 | 16.1 |
| 38 Low-Income Countries | 1.6 | 3.6 | 4.5 | 2.0 | 4.2 |
| 52 Middle-Income Countries | 3.7 | 5.7 | 7.1 | 3.1 | 6.8 |
| 5 Oil-Exporting Countries | 7.1 | 6.0 | 4.0 | 5.2 | 16.1 |

[a]GNP = gross national product.

SOURCE: World Bank, *World Development Report, 1980* (New York: Oxford University Press, 1980), Tables 1, 2, pp. 110–113.

dustrialized countries expanded at the slightly smaller rate of about 5 percent. These simple figures, however, mask some genuinely critical flaws in the economic growth of the Third World, flaws that will doubtless grow more severe as the decade of the 1980s proceeds.

Despite the rather favorable overall growth rate, the true picture of Third World economic progress is altered significantly by the chaos that has afflicted the world's petroleum market since 1973. Whatever shocks there have been to the economy of the United States and other industrialized countries, the Third World has felt them more often and more severely.[6]

First, we must note that the positive picture painted by the growth rate of more than 5 percent for the 1970s holds true solely for the petroleum-exporting countries and a small handful of other successfully developing countries,

[6]Don Oberdorfer, "'Me Decade' Looms for Oil Users," *Washington Post*, March 23, 1980.

principally Brazil, Mexico, and South Korea. Virtually all other Third World states experienced severe growth problems during the 1970s (which will probably continue into the 1980s). Many of these problems are related to soaring energy costs and their directly linked problems of inflation, unemployment, and massive foreign debt. The following are some specific examples of the impact of the energy crisis on several Third World countries:

1. Brazil has accumulated a foreign debt of more than $50 billion and is forced to spend virtually all of its export earnings just to service the debt and pay for imported petroleum.

2. The bill each year for imported petroleum in South Korea has more than doubled to $6 billion annually, nearly 10 percent of the country's entire annual production of goods and services.

3. In Turkey, as in Brazil, payments of interest on foreign loans plus the cost of imported

oil are about equal to the country's entire foreign-exchange earnings each year.

4. Oil import costs consume about 50 percent of the foreign-exchange earnings of the Philippines.

Significantly, each of these countries is plagued with political instability and the threat or actuality of military governments. The Turkish military overthrew the constitutional regime in 1980, Brazil and South Korea have lived under military dictatorships for some time; and the Philippines was under martial law for eight years, from late 1972 to early 1981.

Although the bill for imported oil grew in the industrial world from $13 billion in 1973 to $29 billion in 1979, in the Third World [excluding the Organization of Petroleum Exporting Countries (OPEC)], the costs rose from $8 billion to $39 billion. The total foreign debt of non-OPEC Third World countries has grown from about $77 billion in 1973 to more than $250 billion in 1979, and it was expected to increase another $80 billion in 1980 alone. Faced with these grim realities, the oil-importing nations of the Third World will be fortunate to make it through the 1980s with an overall growth rate of 3 percent, a sharp decline from the relatively strong performance of the 1960s and early 1970s. If population continues to grow at about 2 percent or more, then per capita growth will stagnate at about 1 percent or less. In other words, as the 1980s near their end, we may see the Third World decline to a growth rate of 1 percent or less per capita.[7]

The economic growth potential of any state is a product of both industrial and agricultural strength. Any overall development effort mounted by a Third World government must deal with both of these important elements. To get a clearer picture of economic development in the Third World, then, we must examine both industrial and agricultural policies and accomplishments over the past two decades.

The industrial goal of most developing states is twofold: (1) to increase the amount of inputs available to the industrial sector (capital, energy, raw materials, trained labor, and infrastructure improvements such as roads and telephone service); and (2) to increase the number of outputs received per unit of input (i.e., the productivity of the various production factors). In addition, Third World states would like to channel industrial production away from the extraction of raw materials and toward the manufacture of finished goods, away from industrial systems that were designed with Western societies in mind and toward systems more in keeping with local traditions and resources, away from the manufacture of Western-influenced goods and toward the production of goods that will satisfy real (not manipulated) native demand.

To accomplish these objectives, Third World governments have a wide variety of alternate policy choices available: the regulation of national currency and foreign exchange; the expropriation of private property for public uses; the control of monetary flow and currency levels; propaganda efforts to exhort the citizens to sacrifice for the industrial effort; the power to levy tariffs on imported goods, to tax (or to exempt from taxes) certain industries or firms, or to create money and credit; investment in social and economic infrastructure (roads, electric power, potable water); the granting of credit and technical assistance to productive enterprises; direct investment in productive activity; negotiation of contracts with foreign businesses; and price stabilization of major export commodities.[8]

Governments across the entire ideological spectrum try to stimulate industrial production through many of the same public policies.[9] In India, the nation's industrial sector is divided into three spheres: industries reserved for public ownership (mostly strategic industries, such as

[7]Jonathan Power, "After Decade of Growth, Third World Faces Grim Future," *Washington Post*, June 6, 1980.

[8]Charles W. Anderson, *Politics and Economic Change in Latin America: The Governing of Restless Nations* (Princeton, N.J.: Van Nostrand, 1967), Table 1, pp. 64–65.

[9]This discussion based on John C. Honey, *Planning and the Private Sector: The Experience in Developing Countries* (New York: Dunellen, 1970), especially Chapter 6. See also Stanley A. Kochanek, "India," in Robert N. Kearney, ed., *Politics and Modernization in South and Southeast Asia* (New York: Wiley, 1975), pp. 86–89.

iron and steel, and public utilities); industries in which private capital is expected to supplement public investment (machine tools, drugs, aluminum, transport); and industries reserved for the private sector and guaranteed against national expropriation. Even though India professes to be a socialist state, 90 percent of the nation's industrial productivity remains in private hands. The Indian Government, through its central economic planning mechanism, seeks to direct private investment decisions in directions desired by the government. However, the government's paramount position in the country's financial and credit institutions together with the conventional government monopoly of certain taxing and spending functions means that much stimulation of industrial growth occurs in the form of traditional incentives, including the licensing of new industrial facilities; in the potential for assuming management of facilities if conditions warrant; and in the control over supply, distribution, and price of a company's production. The Indian government also gives incentives in the form of tax holidays to firms it desires to attract to the country and otherwise provides substantial advisory services for prospective industries. Finally, because of the nation's recurring severe balance-of-payments problems, India has had to apply sharp restrictions on imports, contributing, thereby, to national industrial development through import substitution.

Throughout the 1960s and early 1970s, industry and manufacturing were relatively bright spots in the economic picture of developing countries.[10] In 38 low-income countries, industrial production grew at the rate of 6.1 percent from 1960 to 1970 and 4.5 percent from 1970 to 1978. In these same countries, manufacturing rose at the rate of 6.6 percent and 4.2 percent during the same periods. In 52 middle-income countries (a category that includes a few non-Third World countries, like Greece, Portugal, and Spain) industrial output rose 7.8 percent and 7.1 percent during the two periods measured. Manufacturing increased 7.6 and 6.8 percent

during the same time spans. These figures compare favorably with industrial and manufacturing data from the industrialized world (6.1 and 3.4 percent; 6.2 and 3.3 percent). Yet, the strength of the Third World industrial and manufacturing base was spread most unevenly, with a few countries like Brazil, Nigeria, and South Korea achieving spectacular growth rates, but with many countries (including Chile, Ghana, and Uganda) actually declining during the 1970s.

There are signs that some of the ill effects of rapid industrial growth are beginning to be felt in some Third World countries. For some years, Third World leaders have deemphasized the prospects for environmental pollution or energy deficiencies as their countries moved ahead toward industrial status. It would appear that some of the more successful Third World states will now have to consider the adverse impact of their forced-pace industrial programs. Just a few miles outside the industrial city of São Paulo, Brazil, Latin America's largest petrochemical complex has turned the surrounding area into what residents call "the Valley of Death." Air pollution is so bad that the suspended particulate count per cubic meter of air is twice that identified by the World Health Organization as causing excess mortality; monitoring devices installed to measure the contaminants in the air overloaded and broke down. According to the city health director, theoretically, by the level of pollution, "there shouldn't be life there." In Mexico, the issue is nuclear energy, specifically whether or not the government should move ahead with its plans to build a nuclear reactor on the shore of scenic Lake Pátzcuaro, not only one of the most beautiful spots in the nation but also one where many peasants fish to sustain themselves and their families. The coming of the reactor, they fear, will kill the lake's fish population with thermal pollution. In Nigeria, the nation's ambitious $125-billion development plan stands in jeopardy because of the oil glut that developed around the world in 1980 and 1981. Because of Nigeria's great dependence on petroleum exports for foreign exchange, the projected $3-billion loss that the country faces during 1981 will force some reversals in the country's industrial devel-

[10]World Bank, *World Development Report, 1980* (New York: Oxford University Press, 1980), Table 2, pp. 112–113.

opment. In Sri Lanka, the rapid pace of development from 1978 to 1981 produced such an influx of consumer appliances, such as television sets, electric stoves, and air conditioners, that the country's electric grid was overloaded. The government responded with planned power shortages for five-and-one-half hours each day until the seasonal rains filled the reservoirs of the hydroelectric plants. In these and many other ways, development élites throughout the Third World are learning what the industrialized world already knew: that development without planning and precautions inevitably brings severe problems and unforeseen costs that eventually must be met if the national quality of life is not to suffer.[11]

The second half of the problem of poverty lies in agriculture. Here, Third World regimes begin with what seems to be a fairly simple overall objective: to increase the food supply available to their people, to avoid famine, to lower rates of malnutrition and, generally, to raise overall levels of health and physical well-being in their populations. There are, however, two competing strategies for accomplishing this broad objective.

The first strategy, which emphasizes the continued interrelationships between the developing world and the dominant international economy, is based on the maintenance of the agricultural *status quo* in the Third World. According to this dependence strategy, the Third World will continue to cultivate export crops, such as bananas, coffee, sugar, and cocoa. The foreign exchange gained from these overseas sales will, in turn, be used to purchase food supplies, principally wheat and rice, from the major international sources: Australia, Canada, the United States, and (to a much lesser extent)

Argentina. In times of crisis, Third World recipients of food can assume that the world's grain-exporting nations will give them free food or sell it to them at highly subsidized prices, not necessarily out of humanitarian concerns but to guarantee high returns to their own farmers, who constitute a powerful domestic interest that must be treated kindly. The dependence strategy has a few good features. It insures that food prices will be kept low in the urban areas of the Third World; hopefully, these low prices can be subsequently translated into social peace and support for the incumbent regime. Foreign business enterprises that own plantations are also reassured that they will be treated fairly and profitably.

By all measures, however, the costs of the dependence strategy outweigh the supposed benefits. For one thing, the strategy practically guarantees that the nation's rural areas will remain backward, not only economically but also socially and politically, without the financial incentives that accompany production for the national market. Inflation in the grain-exporting countries means that the purchase price for wheat and rice will continue to rise, draining the Third World of badly needed foreign exchange. Finally, oscillating prices on the world's raw-materials markets mean that secure income cannot be predicted and national economic planners in developing countries must be prepared for foreign-exchange shortfalls from year to year. The results of all these factors in recent years have been growing food shortages, starvation, and malnutrition on a planet that theoretically could support 40 billion people at an acceptable level of caloric intake.

Confronted with the defects in the dependence strategy, more and more Third World countries, principally Brazil, India, Mexico, Pakistan, and the Philippines, have now turned their attention to a strategy of self-sufficiency. Most, if not all, Third World countries were at one time food exporters or, at least, produced enough food for their own needs. Many would like to return to that status; some actually show promise of being able to do so. The self-sufficiency strategy requires an increase in the productivity of land presently under cultivation as well as bringing

[11]Michael J. Eden, "Environmental Hazards in the Third World," in Alan B. Mountjoy, ed., *The Third World: Problems and Perspectives* (New York: St. Martin's, 1978). Also, from the *Washington Post*: Jim Brooke, "Industrial Pollution Scars Brazil's 'Valley of Death'," May 10, 1981; Christopher Dickey, "Scenic Mexican Reactor Site Entangles Indians, Unions, Nationalists," May 18, 1981; Leon Dash, "Oil Glut Spurs Nigerian Cutback, Loss of $3 Billion," July 13, 1981; Stuart Auerbach, "Sri Lanka Discovers Capitalism's Benefits and Pitfalls," May 9, 1981.

new lands under cultivation. For political and technological reasons, the second objective is proving to be more difficult to accomplish than the first. Some presently cultivated land is being used for nonfood export crops but to bring that land into food production would put the government on a collision course with powerful foreign commercial enterprises, such as United Brands (bananas) and the various international coffee companies. Underutilized haciendas contain much land kept out of production either because of the cautious mentality of the owner or the absence of sufficient price incentive; to bring this land into production would require policies aimed at breaking the power of the landed gentry. There is much land lying in remote areas of many Third World countries that is essentially untouched; to bring this land under the plow would require enormous investments in infrastructural improvements (especially roads and irrigation) and other agricultural technologies. One authority on the subject has estimated that more than $46 billion would be needed to modernize 50 million hectares of arable but unused land in India. At this same expenditure rate, more than $700 billion spread out over 30 or more years would be required to bring all arable land in developing countries under cultivation.[12] To put this sum into perspective: the same amount is spent on military purposes by the North Atlantic Treaty Organization (NATO) and the Warsaw Pact countries in less than two years.

For these reasons, most developing countries have concentrated their efforts on increasing the agricultural productivity of each unit of land already being used for the cultivation of food. To put into context the actions taken to reach this goal, we must understand the nature of the development process in agricultural production. Generally, agricultural development takes place in four relatively well-defined stages. Each step represents a definite intermediate goal that must be reached and passed through to make subse-quent stages feasible. The first stage, traditional agriculture, was marked by reliance on conventional hand-wielded implements, rudimentary cultivation and ground-breaking practices, and rainfall for water. Land cultivated this way typically yields less than 1 metric ton of rice per hectare. Most of rural Africa and substantial parts of Latin America (especially in the Andean and Central American mountains) are still farmed in this manner. The second stage is characterized by the introduction of land improvement through irrigation and drainage, the enhancement of soil nutrients through improved incorporation of organic materials, and by better timing of crop production through improved cultivation techniques. Rice yields typically reach 2 tons per hectare. Nearly all of South and Southeast Asia and much of the remainder of Latin America fall into this category. In the third stage, scientifically developed techniques are introduced, thus, raising rice yield to the range of 2.5 to 4 metric tons per hectare. During this stage, improved varieties of seed, fertilizers, pesticides, and improved storage and transportation facilities are introduced. Very few countries in the Third World (Malaysia, Mexico, Taiwan, with Brazil and Venezuela soon to enter) are in this category yet. Finally, during stage four, institutional and structural reforms are introduced, thus, changing the very nature of agricultural production. Institutions, such as research and development laboratories, credit banks, farmers' cooperatives, tractor stations, and farm extension services begin to dot the countryside, making improved food production a regularized and institutionalized matter instead of a question of providence and good weather. Countries fortunate enough to achieve this stage typically produce as much as 6 tons of rice per hectare, and often more. Only South Korea has reached this stage among Third World countries.[13]

The actions required for a developing country to move its agrarian sector from stage two to stage three are contained in the handy but over-

---

[12]Roger Revelle, "The Resources Available for Agriculture," *Scientific American, 235* (3) (1976), pp. 165–178, especially p. 172.

[13]W. David Hopper, "The Development of Agriculture in Developing Countries," *Scientific American, 235* (3) (1976), pp. 197–205.

worked phrase, the Green Revolution. Ever since 1970, when Norman E. Borlaug won the Nobel Peace Prize for developing a miracle strain of wheat that promised food self-sufficiency to developing countries, the Green Revolution has been looked to for the salvation of hungry millions. Actually, the Green Revolution is simply a summary term for the many different scientific and technological advances that were being introduced into farming in several developing countries at that time. Foremost among these innovations were the new, high-yield strains of rice and wheat that allowed farmers to irrigate and fertilize their crops to degrees never before possible. But, as many farmers came to understand, the Green Revolution consists of a more or less complete package of techniques, each of which must be applied efficiently and in conjunction with the others. The absence of any of these other significant factors could erode the gains brought about by the miracle strains of rice and wheat. These additional technologies include improved fertilizers (which, because of their petroleum base, make for increased imports from the oil-exporting countries); wells, pumps, ditches, and embankments for better irrigation; improved harvesting and cultivating machinery; improved facilities to store, transport, and market the additional output; and new pesticides to keep down the rodents and other pests that infest the fields. In addition, certain social factors have to be present as well. The nature of cultivation of the miracle strains require more labor for a more regular period of time; so, the character of rural employment had to change. Finally, because the investment required to acquire all of these innovations is substantial, progressive farmers have to be guaranteed a satisfactory return on their investment which, in turn, means the introduction of guaranteed high prices or subsidies, or both. In any event, major government intervention in both the rural areas and the urban markets seems inevitable with the Green Revolution.[14]

[14]Zubeida Manzoor Ahmed, "The Social and Economic Implications of the Green Revolution in Asia," *International Labour Review, 105* (1972), pp. 9–34.

To what extent have these government policies succeeded in actually raising the level of food production in the Third World? Certainly, no one can doubt that some amazing achievements have been recorded by certain individual countries. India, for example, one of the leading exponents of the Green Revolution, has raised its rate of increase in farm output from 2.5 percent during the period from 1947 to 1965 to about 3.3 percent during the 1965 to 1971 period. From 1961 to 1976, India's food production grew annually at the rate of 2.6 percent, exceeding slightly the country's population growth rate of 2.4 percent. Pakistan, another important Asian agricultural state, increased its rice and wheat production by more than 30 percent from 1966–1967 to 1968–1969. From 1966 to 1970, production of rice in Asia as a whole rose from 232.4 million metric tons to 260 million metric tons; wheat rose from 61.8 million metric tons to 71.4 million metric tons. Similar advances were registered in maize and barley.

Nevertheless, when taken as a whole, the record of the Third World in food production has been poor, and it is probably going to get worse before any improvement is noted. Let us consider gross production indicators from 1963 to 1973. During this 11-year span, world food production climbed at an average annual rate of 2.8 percent; in the developing countries, the rate was slightly lower, 2.5 percent. In Africa, the worst record was compiled, 1.5 percent annually; Latin America and Asia registered increases of about 2.5 percent; in the Middle East, production climbed about 3 percent. These increases, however, do not take into account population growth. World food production per capita from 1963 to 1973 remained almost stable with an increase of only 0.6 percent. In the developing world as a whole, per capita food production actually declined by two tenths of 1 percent as a result of Africa's disastrous record (−1 percent) and relative stability in the other three regions. Of the 71 developing nations for which data are available from 1953 to 1971, food production failed to keep pace with population growth in 24; in 17 more nations, growth in food production fell short of the increased demand for food (a combined result of increased population and rising personal incomes). Thus, in only 30 nations from this sample did food production manage to equal population growth and increased demand. Even in Mexico, where Borlaug developed the miracle strains of wheat, the Green Revolution appears to have run its course, but population growth continues at the rate of 3.5 percent. Mexico was actually exporting wheat, corn, and beans from 1966 to 1969, but, by the early 1970s, the country had to import between 15 and 20 percent of its basic food grains. Despite almost heroic measures in some countries and continued effort in most of the rest, population growth is eroding what little increase in food production there is in the Third World.

Looked at over a somewhat longer time span, the picture of agriculture in the Third World is still fundamentally disappointing. From 1961 to 1976, according to the United Nations Food and Agricultural Organization (FAO), food production in 94 developing countries grew at a rate of 2.6 percent per year, thus, barely staying abreast of population growth. Despite the fact that food production exceeded population growth in 24 of these countries, the FAO estimated that more than 23 percent of the people in 86 countries with a total population of 1.9 billion were undernourished. The FAO definition of undernourishment means, however, a daily caloric intake per person of only 1600 calories, a figure regarded by many experts as minimal for maintaining existence but not high enough to permit any kind of strenuous exertion. Studies undertaken of agricultural workmen in the tropics suggest that 3500 calories per day may be required in these areas. If this threshold of undernourishment is used, then, more than one fourth of the world's population is undernourished. The results of the FAO estimate are stark enough however—in the mid-1970s in 52 developing countries, the undernourished population exceeded 15 percent.[15] (See Table 7.3 for some additional indicators of well-being in eight Third World countries.)

[15]Nevin S. Scrimshaw and Lance Taylor, "Food," *Scientific American*, 243 (3) (1980), pp. 78–88.

## GOALS, ACTIONS, OUTCOMES: ENLIGHTENMENT AND RESPECT

Third World governments generally accord a higher priority to power and well-being policies and goals than they do to enlightenment and respect. The relative poverty of the Third World in both power and material comfort dictates that any progressive government must attend to these needs first, relegating enlightenment and respect goals to a second level of importance. Where enlightenment and respect policies do receive great attention, it is usually to serve the goals of power and well-being first. Only secondarily do policies bearing on enlightenment and respect have any intrinsic worth.

We will shortly examine some data regarding the performance of Third World regimes in the fields of enlightenment and respect. Be aware that we have entered areas of human behavior that resist quantitative analysis. We will look at some numerical indicators of performance, but readers should treat all such data with a certain degree of skepticism. At best, the data reflect general orders of magnitude instead of precise levels of performance.

### ENLIGHTENMENT

In a different context (see Chapter Three, "Psychological Aspects of Modernization"), we considered what Third World governments attempt to do in the field of enlightenment to increase the value of national power. Turn back to the section on control and censorship of the mass media of communications; you should realize now that what Third World regimes intend with their policies is to manipulate the media to advance the causes of national unity, integrity, loyalty, and legitimacy. In the conclusions from Chapter Three, we found that the majority of Third World governments exercise some form of control over their nation's news media, especially in radio, film, and television. Even in the print media, newspapers and magazines, many Third World regimes exert what amounts to *de facto* censorship in an effort to shape the information given to the mass population.

| Country | Public Expenditures per Capita on Health[a] | Physicians per 100,000 Population | Infant Mortality Rate[b] | Life Expectancy[c] | Calorie Supply per Capita | Percent of Population with Safe Water | Physical Quality-of-Life Index (PQLI)[d] |
|---|---|---|---|---|---|---|---|
| Nigeria | 7 | 7 | 160 | 45 | 2291 | na[e] | 25 |
| Tanzania | 4 | 20 | 160 | 47 | 2089 | 39 | 33 |
| India | 2 | 26 | 122 | 51 | 1949 | 31 | 41 |
| Indonesia | 2 | 7 | 114 | 48 | 2115 | 11 | 50 |
| Mexico | 8 | 57 | 60 | 65 | 2668 | 62 | 75 |
| Brazil | 13 | 59 | 109 | 62 | 2522 | 55 | 68 |
| Egypt | 8 | 92 | 98 | 54 | 2716 | 93 | 46 |
| Iran | 33 | 39 | 104 | 52 | 3193 | 51 | 38 |

[a]Per capita public expenditures on health expressed in $U.S.

[b]Infant mortality rate expressed in deaths under one year of age per 1000 live births.

[c]Life expectancy expressed in years.

[d]PQLI is an index developed by the Overseas Development Council. It is a composite index based on life expectancy, infant mortality, and literacy. All countries are ranked from 1 to 100, with Sweden holding the highest rank of 100 and Guinea-Bissau having the lowest score of 10. These data are from 1973.

[e]na = not available.

SOURCE: All data, except that for the PQLI, are from Ruth Leger Sivard, *World Military and Social Expenditures, 1980* (Leesburg, Va.: World Priorities, 1980), Table III, pp. 24–29; PQLI data are from George Thomas Kurian, *The Book of World Rankings* (New York: Facts on File, 1979), Table 247, pp. 286–287.

The fate of Mexico City's great newspaper, *Excelsior*, in 1976 illustrates the unmistakable trend toward increasing government control of the news media in the Third World. In July 1976, a splinter faction of dissidents and toughs took over the cooperative-run newspaper, while Mexico's President, Luis Echeverria, looked on with disinterest. For many months, the Mexican Government had been carrying on a running feud with the world-famous and prestigious *Excelsior*, not only for the paper's criticism of government policies but also because of its attacks on the military dictatorships that came to power in Chile and Uruguay during the early 1970s. From late 1975 to the middle of 1976, the Mexican Government lashed out at the *Excelsior* editor-in-chief, Julio Scherer Garcia, and his staff for allegedly undermining public confidence in the government through its attacks. In June, a mob of slum dwellers was bused by the government to a 90-hectare property owned by the newspaper and began to squat illegally on the land. Government officials refused to take action to evict them. Matters worsened until the tumultuous meeting of July 8, when a gang of thugs shouted down the Scherer supporters in an illegal meeting of the *Excelsior* cooperative; they also threatened Scherer with bodily harm if he did not leave the newspaper's building. Once evicted from the premises, Scherer was removed from his position, and the paper passed into the control of pro-government editors and reporters. Scherer's subsequent efforts to launch another newspaper in Mexico City have been harassed by government agencies, which have denied Scherer the newsprint he needs to start printing. In effect,

The plenary session of the 1976 meeting of the United Nations Educational, Scientific, and Cultural Organization (UNESCO) convened in Nairobi, Kenya. At this meeting, Third World representatives sharply criticized the news media from the industrialized countries for their biased reporting of events in developing countries.

all free-press criticism of the Mexican Government has been stifled by the *Excelsior* coup.[16]

Third World governments have demonstrated resolutely that they have the power to close down critical newspapers and magazines internally, but they have still not been able to do much about the persistent criticism emanating from the international wire services and other news agencies, such as Reuters or United Press International (UPI). During 1975 and 1976, many developing countries, led by Mexico, began to urge the creation of a Third World news agency to be based in Mexico City. This new agency would foster the publication of news

reports favorable to the Third World to counteract the bad impressions left by the critical international news agencies. In October 1976, the issue came to a head at the meeting of the United Nations Educational, Scientific, and Cultural Organization (UNESCO) in Nairobi, Kenya. At the UNESCO meeting, Third World delegates sought to pass a resolution that would go beyond the news-pool idea, and they asserted that governments are responsible for the activities in the international sphere of all mass media under their jurisdiction, a proposition that runs exactly counter to the notion of press freedom.

Since the 1976 meeting in Nairobi, the Third World has acted to establish its own international news service, an information pool operated by a number of nonaligned news agen-

[16]Armando Vargas, "The Coup at *Excelsior*," *Columbia Journalism Review*, (1976), pp. 45–48.

Bodies bearing placards hang from the gallows in downtown Damascus, Syria, in September 1976. The three men (and an accomplice who was killed) had seized a hotel the previous day and held hostages before they were captured by Syrian troops. Thousands of people crowded to within 50 yards of the hanging, the first held publicly in Damascus since the 1965 execution of an accused Israeli spy.

cies that report on events throughout the developing world and send the stories to seven regional centers, the most important of which are Belgrade, Havana, and New Delhi. From there, the reports are disseminated to media editors and staffs throughout the Third World for subsequent publication. The new service has not prospered for a number of reasons. Many of the developing countries distrust each other almost as much as they do the West, and reports emanating from Third World countries are frequently censored by the affected governments just as if they had been broadcast or written by Western news agencies. The Third World is still largely dependent for the transmission of their stories on the communications technology that is dominated by the Western wire services. In addition, the field of journalism is still a rather new and untested one in many Third World countries; admittedly it is not particularly easy for a journalist to write an engaging and dramatic story about rice production in the Philippines or housing problems in India. Leaders of this news-dissemination effort reply in defense, however, that,

since the founding of the pool, the major Western news services—such as Reuters and the Associated Press (AP)—have begun to devote more time to development news, a trend that by itself justifies the creation of the pool.

Restrictive policies toward the news media have the effect of promoting national unity and, thereby, strengthening national governments; such policies, however, will also concentrate power into fewer and fewer hands. As the opposition élites that formerly occupied positions of responsibility in the media are forced out and replaced by government representatives, power will be redistributed toward a single national élite that is directly beholden to government agencies. The prevailing trend in the Third World is to undertake policies in the field of enlightenment that will encourage the growth of power at the national level but that will also distribute that power even more unequally than had previously been the case.

Our consideration of policies that have a bearing on enlightenment must lead us to look at educational policy in the Third World. Third

**TABLE 7.4** Summary Indicators of Educational Policy in Eight Selected Third World Countries, mid-1970s

| Country | Percent of GNP[a] to Education | Percent of Public Expenditures to Education | Public Expenditures per Capita on Education[b] | Percent of School-Age Population in School | Teachers per 1000 School-Age Population |
|---|---|---|---|---|---|
| Nigeria | 4.7 | 21.2 | 23 | 22 | 7 |
| Tanzania | 4.4 | 15.5 | 10 | 36 | 7 |
| India | 3.2 | 11.1 | 5 | 42 | 13 |
| Indonesia | 1.4 | 8.9 | 7 | 39 | 14 |
| Mexico | 4.0 | 11.1 | 56 | 64 | 19 |
| Brazil | 2.8 | 17.8 | 33 | 51 | 25 |
| Egypt | 5.5 | 18.4 | 27 | 44 | 13 |
| Iran | 5.4 | 14.1 | 118 | 51 | 20 |

[a]GNP = gross national product.

[b]Per capita public expenditures on education expressed in $U.S.

SOURCE: Percent of GNP to education and percent of public expenditures to education are from *UNESCO Statistical Yearbook, 1978–1979*, Table 6.1, pp. 625–651; the remaining indicators are from Ruth Leger Sivard, *World Military and Social Expenditures, 1980* (Leesburg, Va.: World Priorities, 1980), Table III, pp. 24–29.

World élites have been greatly influenced by the favorable effects of large expenditures on public education in developed countries. Despite the obvious differences between the economic and cultural environments in developed and less developed countries, Third World leaders are convinced that they can make massive improvements in the economic potential of their countries by investing heavily in the human capital of their society, and that means investing in education. Table 7.4 illustrates the level of effort being made by selected Third World governments in the field of education.

Beyond the bare statistics of educational expenditures lie several major areas of dispute over educational priorities. Boiled down to its essentials, the dispute amounts to a difference of opinion whether to stress low-level education to raise literacy rates or to stress high-level education to provide the managers and skilled professionals to run a developing economy. To some degree, the dispute changes focus, depending on the relative stage of development of a given country. Nations that are still rather backward and traditional are faced with a major problem in communications. No matter how much they spend on the electronic media (radio and television), there are still many significant kinds of information that can only be communicated by the written or printed word. In an urban setting, well over half of all information is conveyed by written media, according to one study by a communications expert.[17] A society that enjoys general literacy among its adult population possesses the potential for a completely different kind of economic and social organization—one that emphasizes bureaucratic rule making and the transmission of formal, written messages as well as one that can be relied on to perform routine tasks efficiently by individuals with a minimum of personal supervision. The drive for adult literacy in devel-

[17]Richard L. Meier, "The Measurement of Social Change," in *Proceedings of the Western Joint Computer Conference*, San Francisco, 1959.

| Country | Adult Literacy Rates | | | | |
|---|---|---|---|---|---|
| | 1947–1951 | 1960 | 1970 | 1975 | 1977 |
| Nigeria | — | — | — | — | 25 |
| Tanzania | — | 10 | — | 66 | 37 |
| India | 18 (1951) | 28 | 36 | 36 | 36 |
| Indonesia | — | 39 | 56 | 62 | 62 |
| Mexico | — | 65 | 84 | 76 | 80 |
| Brazil | 49 (1950) | 61 | 68 | 76 | 70 |
| Egypt | 26 (1947) | 26 | 40 | 44 | 44 |
| Iran | — | 16 | 37 | 50 | 50 |

SOURCE: *United Nations Statistical Yearbook, 1955* (New York: United Nations, 1955); World Bank, *World Tables, 1976*, pp. 522–523; World Bank, *World Development Report, 1980*, (New York: Oxford University Press, 1980), Table 23, pp. 154–155. Ruth Leger Sivard, *World Military and Social Expenditures, 1980* (Leesburg, Va.: World Priorities, 1980), Table 3, pp. 24–29.

oping countries goes far beyond the need for an individual citizen to be able to read a newspaper. It has an impact on the organizational potential of a society. Inasmuch as we have repeatedly stressed the need for Third World countries to enhance their institutional power, both politically and economically, we see that increased literacy is an indispensable component of this approach.

In Table 7.5, we can see the result of literacy policies in the eight countries we have selected for examination. Obviously, many of these figures are rough and unreliable, especially those for the earlier period. Nevertheless, very few countries exhibit any remarkable breakthrough in literacy. Those nations, like Mexico, that enjoyed high literacy rates two decades ago improved slightly on their performance. A few, like Tanzania, managed to double their percentage, but the very low point of departure means that they are still basically illiterate nations for most purposes. The remainder demonstrated only slight improvement. Despite massive infusions of technical assistance and capital into literacy programs, rapid population growth, especially among the rural and urban poor, robs the policy of much of its impact.

At the opposite end of the spectrum are the advocates of policies that would stress upper-level training to prepare people to staff a complex society and its institutions. Here, the data are clearly inadequate and are merely suggestive of the magnitude of the problem. In the United States, for example, approximately 1.25 percent of the total population is employed as scientists, engineers, or technicians, whereas about 0.3 percent of the population works in fields that deal with scientific research and development. In typical Third World countries, the figures are likely to be about one tenth of these levels. In India, a country relatively well endowed with educational facilities, scientists and engineers constitute about 0.25 percent of the total population, whereas research and development tasks occupy 0.017 percent. In Ghana, comparable figures are 0.2 percent and 0.04 percent. The same holds true for most Latin American countries.[18]

The gravity of the problem is clear to all interested observers, yet, policy solutions are consistently falling short of success for several reasons. For one thing, upper-level training of this sort has been found to be extremely expensive, especially when compared with lower-level, primary grade education. Although post secondary education in the United States may cost per

[18]Calculated from data in the *United Nations Statistical Yearbook: 1975* (New York: United Nations, 1975).

pupil about twice what it costs to educate a student in the primary grades, the data indicate that in developing countries the ratio may be 1:40. Pressed by the scarcity of funds, Third World governments may succumb to the apparent bargain they purchase by investing in primary education. A second problem stems from the relatively great prestige of higher education in such fields as the humanities, law, and the social sciences, whereas what developing countries need are students in fields like the physical and natural sciences, engineering, and agronomy. The distortion in university enrollments often means that many students flood the market in law and the humanities and become disgruntled when they fail to find employment. The interaction of an expanding educational system and a stable or contracting economy brings about the third problem in educational policy, the phenomenon of the brain drain—the migration of highly trained professionals from developing countries (where they are needed in theory but where there are often too few real jobs available) to the more highly developed markets of Europe and North America. Finally, we must note the effects of educational policy on equality in the Third World. As Charles Elliott[19] points out, Third World educational programs frequently aggravate the tendency toward differentiation because a certain few individuals are chosen to move up the social, economic, and political ladder by means of a highly selective policy that relegates the vast majority to a continued life of poverty. Educational policies as they are implemented in the Third World usually skew the distribution of income and power even more than would be the case if the government allowed market forces to operate freely. Government loans and scholarships, decisions about where to build schools, teacher assignments, informal ties to certain racial or religious groups that smooth their access to educational resources, and other policies operate to accelerate the rise of a very few individuals at the expense of leaving behind the great bulk of their fellow citizens. We find that educational policies emphasize growth while operating to accentuate inequity.[20]

## RESPECT

During his first campaign for the Presidency in 1976 and, subsequently, in the opening months of his administration, Jimmy Carter moved quickly to make clear the concern of the U.S. Government over the plight of political prisoners and over the fate of human rights generally, not only in the Soviet Union but also in many Third World states. The expressions of concern were not limited to rhetoric; foreign military assistance was reduced or eliminated entirely if the recipient was judged to be in violation of human rights and if the aid reduction did not adversely affect America's defense posture. Some of the Third World countries affected were Chile, Ethiopia, and Uruguay. Others, such as Brazil, rejected American aid if it was to be accompanied by lectures about human rights.

During the 1980 American Presidential campaign, one of the major points of disagreement between President Jimmy Carter and Ronald Reagan involved American policy toward friendly regimes that violated the human rights of their citizens. Once in office, President Reagan made it clear that he would draw a distinction between adversary nations, like the Soviet Union, and those allied with the United States, such as Argentina or Chile, when the violation of human rights was at issue. Further, the President and his Secretary of State confirmed their view that it was more effective and proper to work through private diplomatic channels to secure more favorable treatment of prisoners in other countries than to use highly visible and dramatic techniques, such as those favored by Carter. The differences of opinion between these two American leaders reflect the challenging and divisive nature of the human rights issue in international politics and in the conduct of American foreign policy.

[19]Charles Elliott, *Patterns of Poverty in the Third World* (New York: Praeger, 1975), chap. 9.

[20]Many of these issues are discussed in greater detail in Bert F. Hoselitz, "Investment in Education and Its Political Impact," in James S. Coleman, ed., *Education and Political Development* (Princeton, N.J.: Princeton University Press, 1965), chap. 16.

Few policy areas are as difficult to assess as those having to do with human rights violations, and the difficulties are compounded when the region of concern is the Third World. Let us consider first the problem of information. We must recognize the extreme sensitivity of most governments to matters of this sort. Are governments really interested in evaluating policy outcomes or in measuring political performance in this field? Past experiences and common sense suggest that they are not. Nearly every state in the Third World is a signatory of the United Nations Declaration on Human Rights, yet, many of them systematically violate that Declaration. Most governments are reluctant to admit any deviation from their professed goals and objectives. Can we expect any less when the issue of concern is so controversial and sensitive? Then, there is the problem of unbiased news reporting in the Third World. Most of the information that we have about human rights violations in the Third World comes from one of two sources: Amnesty International and other international human rights reporting agencies, and Western news agencies. Both of these agents of information have come under fire for extreme biases in their reporting. Critics of Amnesty International complain that it only criticizes right-wing dictatorships, such as Argentina and Chile, and never (or seldom) charges left-wing regimes with suppression of human rights. On the other side of the ledger, as we have already seen, so many Third World governments have complained of reporting by the Western news agencies (such as UPI and Reuters) that they have replaced these services with a Third World news network. In such an emotion-charged area of human relations, can we ever expect to obtain information that would meet scientific standards for objectivity, methodological rigor, and verifiability? The answer seems highly doubtful.

Even if the information problem could be solved, however, we must still deal with the philosophical question of how to interpret news about Third World violations of human rights. Are these events really all that uncommon? We know that many countries that now enjoy a democratic tradition once suppressed dissent and freedom of political thought in the interest of public order and economic progress. Is the Western tradition entirely applicable here? Perhaps the poverty and illiteracy of many Third World countries work to make freedom of political expression an unacceptable luxury at this early stage of their development. And, are there no long-term benefits to be derived from the near-term suppression of human rights? At one time or another, nearly every country on earth, including our own, has denied free expression to certain groups of people in the interest of increasing or preserving the well-being of the remainder.

For their part, many Third World leaders claim that human dignity can be guaranteed and protected without building the intricate structure of institutions and laws that characterize the Western approach to human rights. On the contrary, they argue, many Western traditions actually work to deny individuals their rights in a developing setting. Political parties, for example, only aggravate conflict and institutionalize class strife. Elections polarize opinion and foster disunity when what a country needs is an integrating force. A free press merely serves to enflame passions. Irresponsible demagogues take advantage of free speech to whip up the masses and provoke them to rebellion. Many non-Western societies, such as Indonesia, place greater emphasis on mass, public consensus as a prelude to decision making than they do on dissent and adversary proceedings so important to pluralist democrats in the West. Most important, many Third World leaders assert that public order is required to preserve private rights. Those who would dissent and who would disrupt the public order must be suppressed to protect the rights of those who are loyal to the state.

We may admit the validity of more than one approach to this most complex question, but we may not retreat into ignorance and fuzzy generalizations about human rights. Instead, what we have attempted to do is to survey several sources of information about the status of human rights around the world and categorize the various Third World regimes according to the actions they have taken in this field. The reader must, then, determine for himself or herself what this information signifies in our overall appraisal of Third World political performance.

We will consider government policies that have to do with political rights, that is, the liberties that a person is thought to enjoy regardless of political opinion, partisan affiliation, or attitude. For a political system to be considered a democracy, three criteria must be satisfied. First, there must be safeguards for each individual to speak and to organize according to his or her political beliefs. Governments that seek to suppress these rights censor or otherwise control the media of mass communications, imprison persons for their beliefs in the political realm, and infringe on the rights of representative assemblies (legislatures, parliaments, congresses) to articulate dissenting opinions. Second, in a democracy, safeguards must exist for the freedom of individuals to remove the existing regime through elections and to replace it with one more to the liking of the people. Furthermore, this freedom must be protected through the creation of appropriate institutions so that exercise of this freedom does not depend on the whim of a single individual. Regimes that intend to suppress these freedoms concentrate their policies on preventing free and open elections, on the prohibition of some or all political parties, and on overriding the constitution by some extralegal procedure. Third, in a democracy, individual citizens must be able to live in peace without fear that the state will terrorize them or allow others to do so for political reasons. Regimes that do not uphold these freedoms practice torture and other inhuman prison practices and encourage vigilante-type groups to engage in illegal but unpunished assassinations of dissenting political leaders.[21]

Table 7.6 reveals our findings about the extent of human rights violations in the Third World.

The rankings used to classify Third World countries in Table 7.6 are a composite of two scales issued annually by Freedom House of New York City since 1972. The first measure, dealing with political rights, ranks countries according to the extent to which the people are able to play an active role in choosing their leaders and in determining the laws under which they live. States ranked either 1 or 2 have a respected electoral procedure, multiple parties, free elections, and political participation by all segments of society. States ranked 3 or 4 have unfair electoral systems that ban opposition parties. States ranked 5 have poor electoral procedures but some opposition. States ranked 6 have electoral systems that are manipulated by ruling parties. States ranked 7 do not permit any legal opposition or open elections. The second scale deals with civil rights and also ranks states from 1 to 7, depending on how well they protect four critical rights (freedom from censorship, open public discussion, maintenance of rule of law, and freedom from government terror) and four subsidiary rights (economic independence of the media; freedom of movement; freedom of choice, including religious freedom; and freedom of property). The rankings in Table 7.6 are achieved by adding together the scores of both scales for each of the 96 countries on which data are available. Thus, countries with a 7 on both the political rights and the civil rights scales have a score of 14 in Table 7.6. (A score of 1 would not be possible because we are combining two scales, the lowest score on each of which is 1.)[22]

It is obvious from Table 7.6 that the state of human rights in the Third World leaves much to be desired. Only 19 of the 96 states surveyed fall below the midpoint of the scale, and 10 of these are in Latin America. The scores from 11 to 14 indicate really serious violations of human rights because each country in these groups must have scored near the bottom of the scale on at least one of the two measures of human rights per-

[21]This discussion is based on Rupert Emerson, "The Prospects for Democracy in Africa," in Michael F. Lofchie, ed., *The State of the Nations: Constraints on Development in Independent Africa* (Berkeley, Calif.: University of California, 1971), chap. 11. See also the important collection of studies in Willem A. Veenhoven, ed., *Case Studies on Human Rights and Fundamental Freedoms: A World Survey*, 2 vols. (The Hague: Martinus Nijhoff, 1975).

[22]Data are drawn from George Thomas Kurian, *Encyclopedia of the Third World*, 2 vols (New York: Facts on File, 1979).

**TABLE 7.6**  Composite Political and Civil Rights Scores of 96 Third World Countries Based on Freedom House Ratings in 1977

| 1 | 2 | 3 | 4 | 5 | 6 | 7 |
|---|---|---|---|---|---|---|
|  | Costa Rica | Venezuela | Gambia | Botswana | El Salvador | Dominican Republic |
|  |  |  | Jamaica | Colombia | Guyana | Guatemala |
|  |  |  | Papua New Guinea | India |  | Madagascar |
|  |  |  | Suriname | Mauritius |  | Malaysia |
|  |  |  | Trinidad and Tobago | Sri Lanka |  |  |
|  |  |  |  | Turkey |  |  |

| 8 | 9 | 10 | 11 | 12 | 13 | 14 |
|---|---|---|---|---|---|---|
| Bhutan | Brazil | Bahrain | Argentina | Algeria | Afghanistan | Benin |
| Lebanon | Egypt | Bolivia | Bangladesh | Angola | Burundi | Central African Republic |
| Mexico | Honduras | Ecuador | Congo | Burma | Chad | Guinea |
|  | Lesotho | Indonesia | Ivory Coast | Cameroon | Equatorial Guinea | Iraq |
|  | Pakistan | Kenya | Kuwait | Chile | Ethiopia | Mali |
|  |  | Liberia | Nepal | Gabon | Libya | Mozambique |
|  |  | Morocco | Paraguay | Ghana | Malawi | Peoples Democratic |
|  |  | Nicaragua | Republic of Korea | Guinea-Bissau | Niger |   Republic of Yemen |
|  |  | Nigeria |   (South Korea) | Haiti | Panama | Somalia |
|  |  | Peru | Sierra Leone | Iran | Togo | Uganda |
|  |  | Philippines | Tunisia | Jordan | Zaire |  |
|  |  | São Tomé and | Yemen Arab | Mauritania |  |  |
|  |  |   Príncipe |   Republic | Oman |  |  |
|  |  | Senegal |  | Rwanda |  |  |
|  |  | Singapore |  | Saudi Arabia |  |  |
|  |  | Swaziland |  | Sudan |  |  |
|  |  | United Arab |  | Syria |  |  |
|  |  |   Emirates |  | Tanzania |  |  |
|  |  | Upper Volta |  | Thailand |  |  |
|  |  | Zambia |  | Uruguay |  |  |

SOURCE: George Thomas Kurian, *Encyclopedia of the Third World*, 2 vols (New York: Facts on File, 1979).

formance. More than half of the countries surveyed (51) appear on these upper scales, a sad commentary on the way in which human rights have been abused in developing countries in the late 1970s.

## CONCLUSIONS: ENHANCING HUMAN DIGNITY IN THE THIRD WORLD

In the preceding pages, we have assessed the performance of the 101 governments of the Third World as they struggle to improve the level of human dignity in their countries. Not surprisingly, the record is a mixed one. Scattered throughout the developing world are significant cases of impressive success and even of heroic triumph over the obstacles to development. In Colombia, Costa Rica, Sri Lanka, and Venezuela, among others, progressive governments have the development process in hand, and they have achieved this without serious suppression of individual freedoms. In other countries, including some that once offered great promise of success, the results have been decidedly negative, even bordering on disastrous. Ethiopia, Ghana, Uganda, and Uruguay typify these countries. In general, however, we simply do not know at this stage in their development how most countries will fare in the struggle. Many countries exhibit wide variations in performance from year to year, and most are highly vulnerable to factors beyond their control, such as the condition of the international economy or the weather. With the exception of the older countries of Latin America, most Third World states have not been independent long enough to demonstrate a track record, so, it is too early to make any firm judgments about their future.

As most Third World élites know only too well, however, many of the important determinants of human dignity look more like obstacles than opportunities. Power remains divided among three competing forces: local, tradition-bound élites; national governments; and powerful international agencies. Economic development is being advanced somewhat in the industrial sphere, agricultural production has stagnated throughout the area, and exponential population growth threatens to erode progress in both sectors. Enlightenment policies dwell excessively on interference with the free flow of ideas, particularly when they offer criticism of the existing regime, whereas educational expenditures are too little and too late to keep up with the challenge of population growth. And a growing number of Third World regimes are leaning toward the denial of human rights in an effort (usually futile) to keep order and accelerate economic growth. In sum, the balance sheet of human dignity in the Third World looks mixed but with signs of deterioration over the decade of the 1980s.

The preceding chapters have focused on the separate threads of Third World politics. It is time now to pull these threads together into a coherent picture to explain why many Third World countries find themselves in such difficulty today. Our explanation must deal with three factors: the environment, the individuals who occupy important political roles, and the structural setting within which the political drama is acted. Just as the surface area of a rectangle is a function of the interaction of its length and width, so, also, is Third World politics a function of the interaction of these three factors. No single factor can be isolated as being of paramount importance; each interacts with the other two in both cause-and-effect relationships.

First, let us consider the environment. The historical experience of colonialism has left a residue of attitudes and institutions that has proven intractable. The international political and economic systems work against the national interests of poor and developing states, quite apart from whether some evil force so wills it or whether the system is some kind of mammoth practical joke played by impersonal forces on struggling Third World countries. The privileged role enjoyed by traditional élites is also a severe obstacle to more progressive policies at home. The comparative scarcity of natural resources (and of financial ones, too) has aggravated the disadvantage suffered by developing states who are late arrivals on the path to industrialization. At times, it seems that even the weather and other natural forces conspire against the world's poor countries as droughts, monsoons, floods, and earthquakes seem to affect most those nations and peoples who can least protect themselves against their force. In short, the environment within which the Third World must act is mostly unfavorable for the improvement of human dignity.

The human resources of the Third World also offer their share of obstacles to progress. Low levels of health, nutrition, and literacy come together to sap the working class of its strength and productivity and, thereby, make it that much more difficult to launch a flourishing industrial effort with the necessary skilled labor. The prevailing personality structure that characterizes many non-Western societies seems ill suited to the requirements of incremental politics, compromise, joining with others for political gains, or valuing achievement. Many facets of the traditional personality do seem quite functional in the context of a struggle against colonial powers, for which heroic measures and enormous sacrifice are called. And compromise is equivalent to betrayal. But, once independence is won and the system settles into the day-by-day routine of meeting economic and social challenges, a new kind of personality is required, and traditional child rearing and socialization procedures seem badly equipped to shape such a personality. In addition, dimensions of a society, such as the way in which families rear their young, are beyond the reach of most Third World governments. Changes in basic personality may occur, but they will take place more as the result of the gradual impact of economic modernization than they will as the outcome of intentional public policy. Finally, the heavy reliance of mass populations on charismatic leaders makes it correspondingly more difficult for these same leaders to build the institutions so necessary for a developing country. Again, the charismatic leader is very valuable during the anti-colonial struggle, when public commitment must be raised to new heights. Eventually, however, charisma must yield to institutions as the motivating force for political change. Regretably, many charismatic leaders fail to sense the appropriate time to begin to ease the state to a

new foundation, one that will outlast the revolutionary leaders.

These comments bring us to the structural dimension of Third World politics. Readers who have followed our arguments through the book must now realize that the institutionalization of political change must receive top priority from reforming élites. The reasons for this are spelled out in greatest detail in Chapters Four, Five, and Seven. The institutional base left behind by colonial economics and politics contains both individuals and regularized relationships that resist and, eventually, undermine efforts to modernize and industrialize. Instead of dealing decisively with these antimodern forces, as has been done in both Western democracies and in Communist states, most Third World governments have opted for a sort of shaky compromise wherein the traditional élites are left alone and modernization is pursued in only a part of the nation. Not surprisingly, the costs of change are, then, borne by those individuals who cannot protect themselves from bearing the burden: the urban and rural poor. The institutions that have come to the aid of these classes in other regions in the past, political parties and interest groups, are notoriously ineffectual in most Third World situations, and they often are even captive of the very regimes whose actions they exist to influence. This is not to say that every country in the Third World must now adopt the two-party system and create a chamber of commerce. The particular institutional network created within each country must be closely related to that country's peculiar social, economic, and historical background. But, without the institutions to mobilize, organize, and shape the collective behavior of the Third World's masses, progress toward distribution of power, well-being, enlightenment, and respect will lag behind the expectations of the bulk of the population with disastrous consequences.

## WHY IS THERE SO LITTLE UPHEAVAL IN THE THIRD WORLD?

Given the massive discontent that we sense in developing countries, why is there so little actual revolutionary change in these nations? This text-book has tried to make the argument that the majority of developing nations are not appreciably better off today than they were 10 or 15 years ago. Even worse, the small gains of development are distributed in a highly uneven manner so that the average citizen of the Third World must surely note little real improvement in his or her life over the years. Yet, with few exceptions, there seems to be little support for radical change in these countries. Even in those few countries where radicalization has occurred, such as Cuba or Vietnam, the motivation was at least as much one of establishing national independence as it was raising the material standard of living of the mass of the people. Why do the poor of the developing countries accept their fate with so little resistance?

Several explanations have been suggested. Some Western observers point to the apathy, fatalism, and lethargy of the rural masses in traditional countries as a factor that robs them of the strength to rebel. Others claim that there is actually a great desire to rebel among the poor but that the cultural obstacles to common causes prevents them from organizing to achieve their goals. Still others assert that there is actually a great deal of violence in politics in the Third World but that the military and the police have so far been able to contain rebellion by sheer coercion and counterterror.

Still another cause of mass acceptance of what seems to be a manifestly unjust social system exists. The central feature of this explanation has to do with the difference between symbolic and tangible politics. We begin with a quote by Robert A. Dahl as he discusses ethnic politics in New Haven:

> Politicians who play the game of ethnic politics confer individual benefits like jobs, nominations, bribes, gratuities, and assistance on all sorts of individuals more or less according to ethnic criteria. But ethnic characteristics serve as a kind of comprehensive symbol for class and other criteria. Moreover, benefits conferred on an individual member of an ethnic group are actually shared to some degree by the rest of the group, for every time one member makes a social or economic

breakthrough, others are likely to learn of it, to take pride in his accomplishment, and to find it easier themselves to achieve the same sort of advance. The strategies of politicians are designed to confer specific benefits on particular individuals and thus to win the support of the whole group.[23]

What Dahl is describing with regard to ethnic politics in New Haven is just another specific example of the more general social institution that Charles Elliott calls the confidence mechanism.[24] The confidence mechanism is any social practice or structure that permits real resources to be distributed unequally but does so in such a way as to convince those who lose that the system is essentially fair and that they lost because of their own shortcomings. Any confidence mechanism consists of these six characteristics: first, there must be competition among the members of a group for individual enrichment; second, only a few members of the group are chosen to benefit from the enrichment process; third, the process of selection is biased away from natural abilities or merit and toward some ascriptive criterion, such as race or language; fourth, these selective biases are not obvious to those who compete; fifth, the system remains sufficiently open (at least to all appearances) to make the process seem legitimate to those who lose; and sixth, the overall process of enrichment is controlled by persons who benefit directly or indirectly from it.

Murray Edelman has drawn our attention to the central role of symbols in any political system.[25] In poor countries, symbolic capability may be the key to regime survival. Symbols have their greatest value in politics as media to bestow the psychic benefit of a given policy on those sectors or individuals who do not receive any material benefit from the policy and who did not have the opportunity to participate in its formulation. In other words, political symbols help

[23]Robert A. Dahl, *Who Governs? Democracy and Power in an American City*, (New Haven, Conn.: Yale University Press, 1961), p. 53.

[24]Elliott, *op. cit.*, chap. 1.

[25]Murray Edelman, *The Symbolic Uses of Politics* (Urbana: University of Illinois, 1964).

a government make its people feel good about a policy that does not benefit them materially in any way. In developing countries where there are not many material benefits to distribute, symbolic politics (as administered by confidence mechanisms) takes on heightened importance.

Does this line of analysis suggest that people who benefit from politics only symbolically are being deceived or duped? More radical commentators of Third World politics would certainly answer in the affirmative. To these people, the lower classes are being bought off by essentially worthless symbols, such as racial or ethnic pride, and they must experience an increase in class consciousness to attract more tangible benefits to their lives. On the other hand, argues Dahl, who are we to denigrate another person's values, which may include symbols instead of tangible goods and services. As he says,

> Terms such as benefit and reward are intended to refer to subjective, psychological appraisal by the recipients, rather than appraisals by other observers. An action can be said to confer benefits on an individual . . . if he believes he has benefited, even though, from the point of view of observers, his belief is false or perhaps ethnically wrong.[26]

After all, when people have lost all hope of gaining material rewards commensurate with their efforts, can anyone deny them the right to take refuge in symbols? One of the lasting contributions of Freud to our understanding of human consciousness was to show that our desires were inherently insatiable and, therefore, we must engage in psychological exercises to be able to live on a day-to-day basis with frustration and denial as our constant companions. Certainly, persons who have had their class consciousness raised and who are denied the sanctuary of symbolic gratification are frequently the fuel for the fires of revolution. Nevertheless, traditional identities based on race, religion, tribal affiliation, ethnic characteristics, or language are still powerful in the Third World. They should serve as a constant reminder to potential revolutionaries that the task of mobilization of the poor of their country has so far defied all but the most talented of leaders. Whether this continues to be the case or not is a secret locked in the minds and in the social institutions of the 2 billion people of the Third World.

# Suggestions for Further Reading

Adams, Don, and Robert M. Bjork, *Education in Developing Areas* (New York: David McKay, 1969).

Baranson, Jack, *Industrial Technology for Developing Economies* (New York: Praeger, 1969).

Carter, Gwendolyn, and William O. Brown, *Transition in Africa: Studies in Political Adaptation* (Boston: Boston University Press, 1958).

Froelich, Walter, ed., *Land Tenure, Industrialization and Social Stability* (Milwaukee: Marquette University, 1961).

Hermassi, Elbaki, *The Third World Reassessed* (Berkeley: University of California Press, 1980).

Hill, Kim Q., ed., *Toward a New Strategy for Development* (New York: Pergamon, 1979).

Hoselitz, Bert F., and Wilbert E. Moore, eds., *Industrialization and Society* (Paris, UNESCO, 1963).

Livingstone, Arthur, *Social Policy in Developing Countries* (London: Routledge & Kegan Paul, 1969).

Marchal, Jean, and Bernard Ducros, eds., *The Distribution of National Income* (London: Macmillan, 1968).

[26]Dahl, *op. cit.*, p. 52, footnote 1.

Schultz, Thomas W., *Transforming Traditional Agriculture* (New Haven, Conn: Yale University Press, 1964).

Schram, Wilbur, *Mass Media and National Development* (Stanford, Calif.: Stanford University Press, 1964).

*Scientific American, 243* (3) (1980). (Special issue on economic development.)

Sigmund, Paul E., ed. *The Ideologies of the Developing Nations* (New York. Praeger, 1963).

U.S. Department of State, *Country Reports on Human Rights Practices for 1979* (Washington, D. C.: U.S. General Printing Office, 1980).

Veenhoven, William A., ed., *Case Studies on Human Rights and Fundamental Freedoms: A World Survey*, 2 vols. (The Hague, Martinus Nijhoff, 1975).

Warriner, Doreen, *Land Reform and Development in the Middle East*, 2nd ed. (London: Oxford University Press, 1962).

World Bank, *World Development Report, 1980* (New York: Oxford University Press, 1980).

Wriggins, Howard W., *The Ruler's Imperative: Strategies for Political Survival in Asia and Africa* (New York: Columbia University Press, 1969).

# CONCLUSION
## Politics and Human Values in Three Worlds

As we conclude this introduction to the study of comparative politics, we want to draw together some of the central themes of the preceding chapters and summarize our findings about the major questions that face political leaders around the world today. It is in the nature of politics that few political issues are ever successfully resolved once and for all. Some issues gradually disappear from public awareness; some become aggravated and critical; most are simply managed and coped with from year to year, from one generation to another. So, if in our presentation we seem to leave a number of questions unresolved, we urge you to remember that politics is not a neat and tidy process wherein everything comes nicely to a conclusion at the appropriate time and place.

The key questions that remain to be dealt with here are:

1. How do concepts of human dignity vary in the three political worlds?
2. How do levels of political performance compare in our three worlds?
3. Is politics significant in assessing the levels of performance in each world; does politics matter to people trying to improve their lives and achieve their values?
4. What can we say about the state of human values in the future: in which direction(s) do the three worlds seem to be headed, and at what speed?

## CONCEPTS OF HUMAN DIGNITY IN THREE WORLDS

On the basis of our findings presented earlier, it seems that one central difference stands out in importance in any discussion of varying perspectives of human dignity. In the polyarchies of Western Europe—what we have called the First World—there is no single, official, centrally directed and mandated version of human dignity that all citizens must endorse, accept, and obey. Instead, the Western polyarchies encourage multiple concepts of human dignity, the public good, the national interest, and other ambiguous and contentious symbols of the political community. Communist states, on the other hand, do have such an official version of human dignity, and perspectives that challenge this version are not allowed to be disseminated or even held as opinions in some countries. In the Third World, matters are more complex. Many governments, perhaps even a majority of them, have an official view of human dignity, and they make efforts to have it accepted by the citizenry, either willingly or not. Evidence indicates, however, that many Third World citizens are not willing to accept their governments' official versions of the public good, and challenges to existing regimes have been frequent and sharp. Most Third World states do not have the legitimacy to persuade everyone to agree to the official view of human dignity or the power to force them to accept it. The consequence is, and will continue to be, a good deal of instability and turbulence in the Third World as its nations go through the difficult process of developing a national identity.

Let us consider some important differences in the ways governments in the three worlds look at the four human values that we have been discussing throughout this book: *power, well-being, respect,* and *enlightenment.*

When we think about differing versions of the value of power, we must consider three definitions of democracy. In the liberal states of Western Europe, democracy means pluralism, or a genuine respect for, and protection of, the right of each citizen to participate in the political process according to the dictates of his or her conscience. Such participation must be significant in that real issues (and not just symbolic ones) are at stake. Elections must be contested meaningfully; the votes must be counted fairly; and opposition parties must be allowed to rise to power if elected. Thus, in the Western view of democracy, politics is basically a form, or a structure, intended to guarantee maximum popular participation. The exact outcomes are not prescribed in the liberal definition of democracy; it is assumed that if the processes are correct, the outcomes must be also.

In Communist Party states, democracy is still a much used term, but the operational definition has changed. Instead of the freewheeling emphasis on mass participation in multiple parties that we see in Western Europe, the Communist Party states emphasize participation by those who share the official version of the public good (*i.e.*, those who do not challenge the right to rule of the Communist Party). Because the state's purported reason for existence is to promote social justice for the workers and because the Communist Party also exists for the same

purpose, to be loyal to the state is to be loyal to the Communist Party. There is no need for opposition parties to challenge the regime's policies or right to rule. All debate and dissent are to be carried out within the confines of the Communist Party—that which cannot does not deserve to persist because it betrays the functioning and the purposes of the state. Thus, even though there is extensive mass participation in most Communist Party states, it is participation channeled through and coordinated by the various Communist parties.

Democracy in the developing countries of the Third World is distinguished in two important ways from the definitions we have already considered. First, many governments in the developing countries cannot even consider the question of sharing power until they have created a set of centralized institutions that have power over their societies. Power is a scarce commodity in the Third World. National governments find themselves caught in a vise between an inhospitable international system and a set of local chieftains who resist modernization at every turn. Democracy in this context means first consolidating power at the national level, perhaps through coercion. Then, and only then, can the issue of sharing power be raised. The second major distinction concerns the democratic nature of public policy. In many cases, political leaders in the Third World think of democracy as being what a government does for the people (an output) instead of a set of procedures for organizing and protecting the right of the masses to participate (an input). Social justice and economic progress are more important indicators of democracy for these countries than the existence of competing parties, honest elections, and free news media.

A comparison of three views of well-being leads us to a discussion of what constitutes the good life in the three worlds. In Western Europe, most public policy emphasis is on the fine tuning of the economy, that is, how to manipulate the economy to avoid the gross excesses of either depression and unemployment or of inflation and financial chaos. All the governments of the industrialized West possess the ideology and the skills needed to direct the economy, to maintain growth momentum, and to provide jobs for a slowly growing work force. With the basic problems of production and consumption apparently under control, the industrialized democracies now confront the major issue of what to do about affluence: preventing pollution and the flow of hazardous substances throughout the environment; insuring a secure source of energy in the years ahead; and relieving the tensions and stresses of life in an urban, industrial society.

Communist Party states face much more pressing needs as they attempt to secure the good life for their people. Although most Communist Party states are relatively well developed economically, they still face fundamental problems of industrialization, increased food production, housing for an expanding population, and growing public demand for more consumer goods. In many states, such as the Soviet Union, heavy defense expenditures drain away much needed funds for social welfare projects and for consumer items, such as cars and refrigerators. Conditions are more severe in China. Despite impressive growth over the past generation, China is finding the Four Modernizations Program a difficult challenge.

Developing countries face an even greater challenge in defining the good life for their people; not only must they industrialize their economies and upgrade their agricultural production, but they must also experience wrenching psychological changes. Some leaders have suggested that it is possible for the Third World to modernize and industrialize and remain traditional at the same time. To date, no country has succeeded in achieving this goal although many continue to try. It is still too early to make a judgment, but historical experience does not make us optimistic about the Third World's ability to find a third way to economic well-being and progress.

An examination of the three worlds' perspectives on the human value of respect leads to a consideration of differing views about human rights. In Western Europe, governments encourage dissent although there are still some problems—even in countries famed for their tolerance, such as Great Britain. On the whole, however, there appears to be increasing respect for the rights of ethnic, regional, and linguistic minorities although the class struggle remains fierce in such countries as Italy, France, and Spain. Most important, Western Europe has not lost faith in the cornerstone of human rights: the belief that the rights of the individual are paramount and that the rights of the social collective and the state remain secondary, unless an exceptional crisis, such as war or natural disaster, endangers the continued existence of the community.

As the section on the Second World emphasized, Communist views of human rights differ sharply from those in Western Europe. Communist systems place relatively great emphasis on the rights of the collectivity, especially of the workers and their related communities and workplaces, over those of the individual. Individuals are not allowed to engage in behavior that would have socially adverse repercussions, such as disseminating antistate literature or advocating the right to strike. Instead, national unity and social cohesion are major objectives; the rights of the individual must be submerged. In place of the Western emphasis on the individual, Communist Party states stress the supportive role of the collectivity. Individuals are to find their greatest pleasure and psychological support when they place themselves within the context of a comradely group of fellow workers or citizens. Emphasis is placed not on the immediate gratification of one's personal desires but, instead, on sharing in a communal context.

In developing countries, human rights are relegated to a definitely secondary position. The weakness of most Third World governments dictates that power considerations must take first priority; the shaky nature of most Third World economies means that industrialization and agricultural modernization must receive second place in the goal structure. Thus, little time or resources are left to devote to shoring up the foundation of human rights in developing countries. On the contrary, the leaders in many developing countries insist that too much attention to human rights can block their governments from the actions they need to move their countries forward economically. Opposition parties cannot be allowed to enflame mob passions. The mass media must be harnessed to the needs of the state. Workers cannot be permitted to strike for higher wages when doing so would intensify inflation. In a political sense, human rights suffer (sometimes grievously) in rapidly developing countries. This does not mean, however, that Third World populations have been brutalized to the point of social atomization. There remains at the local, village level considerable concern for the welfare of others and for the maintenance of a warm and nurturant environment.

The issue of enlightenment can be usefully compared by considering the three worlds' views of education and knowledge, broadly defined. Because enlightenment in our inquiry means what a person knows about his or her world and the process by which he or she comes to know these things, we must examine how the three worlds deal with these vital questions.

Western European governments interpret the issue of enlightenment as involving the nature of public education. The key issues are the relative priority of education versus other social expenditures and the issues of mass versus élite education. Like all industrialized countries, the Western European states confront the problem of how to prepare their growing youth for responsible roles in managing a complex economy and society as well as how to live productive and useful lives. Much of the contemporary debate surrounds the question of whether quality education geared to a privileged minority should be sacrificed in favor of expanding educational opportunities for the many, the latter being a priority choice that the United States and a few other First World countries had made earlier.

The Communist Party states are much more ambitious in their approach to knowledge and the process of acquiring it. The governments of China, Cuba, and the Soviet Union want to go far beyond the simple requirements of education; they want to create a new Soviet (or Cuban, or Chinese) person, one who will welcome the burdens and special demands of life in a Communist Party state, who will accept the responsibilities imposed by the collectivity, and who will work productively within the framework established by other forces. A collective spirit must prevail in a Communist society, and the educational system is given the task of insuring that such a spirit will emerge. Of course, all other media of expression—the press, the arts, television, and radio—must fit within this same mold. Even the family is expected to do its part in changing the personality type that prevails in the culture.

The education goals of Third World states focus on mass education and on technical/vocational training to manage the nascent industrial base; but there is also an élite educational system (usually very large) that produces liberally trained professionals in far greater numbers than there are jobs available for them. Thus, the educational objectives of developing states must range from the eradication of illiteracy in remote villages to the management of great universities in large urban areas. To complicate matters, developing elites wish to modernize their countries while retaining the beneficial qualities of tradition: respect for the past, the extended family, social cohesion, and stability. The educational system is somehow expected to carry out these multiple objectives, despite their almost inherently contradictory implications. Finally, Third World regimes frequently seek to curb the liberties of the mass media to insure that the press will play a positive role in the overall developmental effort.

## POLITICAL PERFORMANCE IN THREE WORLDS

Considered in the very broadest of terms, the larger industrialized states of Western Europe—Britain, France, West Germany, and Italy—have been quite successful in creating centralized state power and in distributing it widely to citizens who desire access to the political process. Since World War II, these states have not only established effective administrative machinery in London, Paris, Bonn, and Rome, but they have also reaffirmed the traditional European commitment to widely shared access to these centers of power. Compared to the United States, power is concentrated to a greater degree in these four European countries; but, because of the rule of law and the self-restraint of bureaucrats at the national level, there is an underlying faith in the ability of government institutions to restrain the larger excesses of political leaders. Even in France, where the notion of an imperial leader has gone further than in the rest of Europe, there are fundamental institutional factors that protect the citizenry from being overwhelmed by the exercise of power from the center. In regard to the value of a widespread distribution of power, we must rate the governments of the First World high.

Governments of the Communist world have approached the problem of power and its distribution in a different way. The goal of the Soviet government has been to consolidate the power of the Communist Party and to insure that it can not be effectively challenged from opposition groups that might seek to betray the foundations of the state. Within that framework, the Soviet citizenry has experienced expanded opportunities to participate in politics and to have access to their government, certainly to a far greater degree than possible prior to World War I. The continuing uncertainties in the post-Mao era obscures political events in China, but, there, too, the Communist Party's institutional structure has greatly facilitated access of the average Chinese citizen to power of a scope and importance unknown before the advent of Communism. Finally, the high level of mass participation within the Yugoslav self-management system suggests major advances in the direction of participatory democracy. Thus, although Communist Party states do rate lower on the scale of power distribution than the industrialized Western European states, the differences may be largely relative ones, especially given the cultural and ideological context within which Communist governments operate.

The achievements of developing countries in the area of power have been concentrated on the creation of power, the consolidation of a particular regime, and the establishment of a set of institutions that can transcend the life of a specific set of élite members. Because of the peculiar fragmentation of power in the developing world (*i.e.*, the three-way split between international system, national government, and local power brokers), there have usually been formidable obstacles to the centralization of power in the national government's institutions. Very little has been done to move a step beyond this stage and to begin to grant some of the government's power to individual citizens. Indeed, some Third World regimes, such as Mexico, India, and Tanzania, have centralized power to a degree never before seen in these countries. Given the continuous hazards confronting developing regimes, the prospects for change seem quite remote.

An appraisal of political performance in the area of well-being involves two factors: (1) How do public policies contribute to the overall growth of the total economic pie of a country? (2) How do public policies affect the way in which the total pie is distributed, especially to the groups and classes that have previously received relatively little from the economic system?

In this regard, the countries of Western Europe have a mixed record. As a region, Western Europe has reached the postindustrial era in which it begins to face many new problems and difficulties. This fact alone is a sign of success because it indicates the achievement of sustained economic growth since the end of World War II. During the 1950s and 1960s, indicators reveal that Europe as a whole achieved surprisingly good economic growth records, with West Germany, France, and Italy scoring better than the United States (although behind the Soviet Union and Japan). The major worry in Western Europe in the past several years, however, has been the economy of Great Britain, which seems to be faltering because of a chronic balance of payments problem. All four countries are making moderate progress in income redistribution. Spending on social security and health care is higher in terms of percent of gross national product (GNP) in the four major states of Western Europe than in the United States, but there are other countries of Europe, such as Sweden, where the percentage is even higher. Despite the very good record of most Western European countries economically after World War II, worldwide inflation, unemployment, and energy scarcities are beginning to take their toll, and the economies are starting to slip in performance.

On the yardstick of well-being, the Communist Party states have achieved less than those of Western Europe, but Communist citizens are better off today than ever before. The picture in the Soviet Union is mixed. On the one hand, housing is cheap but scarce; medical care, health services, and education are free. On the other hand, the right to strike is curtailed. Soviet citizens seem content with what they have, perhaps because they can still remember the poverty and sacrifice of the period between the wars, especially during World War II. When a new generation of potential consumers and workers comes of age in the Soviet Union, will they be as tolerant of the economic shortcomings of their system? Will the recent demands of the Polish people spread to the USSR, other East European countries, and to China. Chinese welfare policy has tended to focus on an equal distribution of sacrifices and to ensure that everyone has enough to eat and wear. Here, too, an economic slowdown during the past several years has caused ambitious industrial plans to be revised downward. However, as in the Soviet Union, Chinese citizens appear supportive of the system and appreciative of what they regard as a comparatively bountiful existence.

Economic achievements have been poorest in the Third World for reasons that are political and economic. Industrial production from the mid-1960s on has managed to creep ahead slowly at the rate of about 3 percent per capita per year; but a large part of this increase took place in the Middle East, where oil reserves have supported impressive growth rates since the early 1970s. In many other parts of the world, however, where energy supplies are scarce and expensive, industrial growth has been halting. It is in agriculture, however, that the developing world has suffered most. With few exceptions, farm production has not even kept up with population growth over the past decade. This situation must surely

change before the Third World's citizens can begin to enjoy the standard of living seen in even the Communist Party states of Europe. The standards of living of the industrialized democracies of Western Europe and North America are quite beyond both their short-term and long-term expectations.

We now move to a comparison of political performance in human rights. Here the Western European countries have been impressive in their achievements, even if they have fallen short of their own high expectations in several instances. Given the authoritarian and oppressive background of the Benito Mussolini and Adolph Hitler dictatorships, Germany and Italy have gone far toward insuring fair and just treatment of all citizens regardless of their political beliefs. France's record has been equally as good. In Great Britain, the special strains introduced by the violence in Northern Ireland have been difficult to withstand, and there have been calls for reinstituting the death penalty against terrorists of the Irish Republican Army (IRA). In Northern Ireland itself, the British Army employed a policy of preventive detention without a trial, and there were even reports of torture of IRA members. It is a reflection of Great Britain's high standards in this field, however, that such reports are newsworthy in Great Britain, whereas, in countries with laxer standards, such matters pass unnoticed. We must give high marks to the Western European countries for their performance concerning human rights.

When viewing the Second World, the record of human rights in the Soviet Union and Eastern Europe has now become an issue of international public concern. Soviet dissidents have been placed under house arrest, jailed for long periods after trials of doubtful authenticity, or exiled for daring to write or speak their feelings. If there are no fewer reports from Southeast Asia and China, it is probably because the systems deal there even more severely with dissent or because the Western news media are prevented from observing repression of human rights in action. This development points out one of the growing number of differences between Soviet and Chinese Communism and the so-called Eurocommunism, as advocated by the Communist parties of Italy, France, and Spain. These latter parties assert that Communism is strong enough to permit dissent and opposition parties and that human rights must be respected in Communist Party states as they are in non-Communist Party states. So far, however, the much more cautious Soviet, East European, and Chinese leaders have been reluctant to relax their vigilence over dissenting opinions. Considering their historical experiences and the difficulties they had in achieving and holding on to power, it is not likely that we will see flourishing dissent in these countries for some time.

The more than 100 countries of the Third World span the entire range of possibilities in the treatment of human rights. At one end of the spectrum are several scores of countries that respect human rights to a remarkable degree. Included within this group are a number of small islands that were formerly British colonies, another testimony to the sanctity of human rights in the mother country. At the other end of the scale lie a half-dozen countries where torture, military rule, press censorship, and political imprisonment are the rule and not the exception; these include Argentina, Brazil, Chile, Iran, Iraq, Uganda, and Uruguay. In between fall most of the major states of the Third World. In these countries, dissent is limited, but not completely stifled. Some opposition parties may be permitted, but they are not expected to get out of line. Elections are held, but votes are not counted honestly. The press functions, but not too critically for it will be shut down or deprived of newsprint if it does. In brief, most Third World countries hover on the brink of serious suppression of human rights, and the merest disturbance or economic crisis may be sufficient to push them over the side. Certainly, there are few institutionalized barriers to dictatorship when and if the rulers decide to impose it.

The fourth human value to be considered is enlightenment, or the acquisition of knowledge and information. Our assessment of Western European achievements in this field is that they are reasonably good although the larger countries do not compare favorably with the United States, Canada, or several other Western European countries. The four major European states spend between 3 and 5 percent of GNP on education, whereas the United States spends about 6 percent and Canada and the Scandinavian countries have invested more than 7 percent. School enrollment figures confirm these conclusions. The four Western European states show between 15 and 20 percent of the total population enrolled in schools at all levels; in the United States, the figure is nearer 29 percent. Even greater differences are observed at the higher levels of education—Europe's educational systems begin to separate out students who are denied access to college because of poor performance in lower grades. In other areas of knowledge and information, however, Western European polities rate high. The mass media function freely and prolifically, and public criticism of the government is tolerated and protected.

Starting from a much lower base both economically and institutionally, the Communist Party states have recorded remarkable advancements in their educational systems. From an era when education was reserved for the privileged few, the Soviet Union and China have extended mass education down to the most remote village in an effort to make every citizen literate and an active member of the political community. Similar policies were initiated at a later date in Cuba and North Vietnam. In terms of numbers, the Communist educational systems have surely been successful, especially in technological and scientific areas, where they have transformed backward and traditional countries into world powers in less than 50 years. Has this transformation also produced the new person as the Communist leaders hoped? Although the data here are inconclusive and the records mixed, there appear to be serious problems in such countries as Poland. And, what have Communist socialization efforts done to the human spirit? Is the new person a well-rounded, self-actualized individual who enjoys life and can realize his or her full potential? Given the difficulty of doing research in these countries on such topics, we will have to leave such questions substantially unanswered.

What of education and information policies in the Third World? As earlier discussions indicate, the simple statistics seem to reflect a major effort by many developing countries to overcome their backwardness through crash education programs. Many countries in the Third World spend as great a percent of their GNP on education as do the Western European countries (3 to 5 percent), and many have as high a percentage of the population enrolled in schools (15 to 20 percent and higher). Yet, because of institutional rigidities, scarcities of qualified teachers and learning materials, and high rates of population growth, the majority of the developing countries are just barely managing to hold their own in the battle against illiteracy. Policies toward the mass media span the same range as those on human rights. Several dozen countries allow the press to operate freely, about a dozen suppress free press operations, and the remainder fit somewhere in between, neither allowing a free press nor suppressing it entirely, but using the media to support government policies and to reduce dissent and criticism of the government.

## EXPLAINING DIFFERENCES IN PERFORMANCE: DOES POLITICS MATTER?

It is good for observers of politics to be modest as they try to construct plausible explanations of complex social phenomena, such as differing levels of political performance in three widely varying kinds of political systems. In the explanatory comments that follow, we suggest several of the more important features of our previous analyses that might lead us to a better understanding of our three worlds.

The human dimension of politics in Western Europe has two facets. On the one hand, Western European countries possess an enormous advantage in the relatively well-educated, modernized, well-trained, and motivated labor force available to staff their industrial facilities and farms. Furthermore, the Western European populace participates actively in politics although exact levels vary widely from country to country and from one kind of activity to another. In recent years, however, some observers have pointed to a growing apathy among the youth of all Western countries as if to warn their political leaders that a new generation was finding politics a useless and deceptive enterprise.

The second facet of the human dimension in European politics involves leadership styles and patterns. Comparative analysis seems to indicate some correlation between vigorous but self-restrained leadership and progressive policies in one set of countries (e.g., West Germany and France) and less creative or assertive leadership as well as political immobilism in others (e.g., Great Britain and Italy). This fact should remind us that no matter what environmental advantages a particular country may start out with, little can be done with these assets without creative leadership to mobilize and direct resources toward valued public goals.

This observation leads us to some conclusions about the environment of Western European politics, an environment that contains both advantages and disadvantages. The historical residue of World War II, for example, was an advantage for Germany and Italy because they have struggled for a generation or more to wipe out the last vestiges of their social and economic systems that had made fascism possible. Great Britain seems to have emerged from the war shaken in her own self-confidence and puzzled about her role in a world now dominated by the two superpowers, the United States and the USSR. On the other hand, her long experience with the traditions of representative government have made possible the well-known British tolerance for dissent without slipping into excesses of rhetoric or repression. Most of the countries of Western Europe have enjoyed traditional restraints on the arbitrary use of power as well as economic abundance since World War II. However, in many areas, social cleavages and class struggle persist and make the search for social and political consensus more difficult.

In structural terms, the key to Europe's political moderation has been the growth of institutionalized restraints on power that do not exist anywhere else in the world. Courts, political parties, the mass media, and traditions of constitutional governance all can be brought to bear to keep a potential dictator under control. Public opinion as expressed through institutions, such as the press and voluntary associations, is also a powerful factor in Western European politics. Furthermore, many countries enjoy thoroughly professional bureaucracies that can restrain political leaders who might abuse power and that can provide leadership themselves when the political leaders are indecisive or weak. Finally, the pluralist style of governance in Europe insures that virtually all citizens will have access to the centers of power and that participation will be significant.

The human dimension of politics in Communist Party countries also exhibits some interesting interplay between elite-leadership styles and mass participation although the relationship is far different from that in Western Europe. Without question, the leadership abilities and styles of world figures, such as Vladimir Ilyich Lenin, Joseph Stalin, Mao Zedong, Josip Broz Tito, and Ho Chi Minh, have done much to determine the direction of Communist politics, quite removed from any ideological considerations. These men were all of a type: dedicated to the supremacy not only of their ideological system, but also of the party that propelled it into power; unwilling to permit opposition or dissent; and skilled craftspersons in the construction of institutions that have outlived the original leadership generation. Each had the ability to sense the needs of the people, to articulate these needs on a broader stage, and, therefore, to make politics a real and significant exercise for the many who had previously been excluded from the process. They were all violent men, but who can say whether history will remember them more for their violent rise to power or for the radical reconstruction of their societies later on?

The masses of ordinary citizens in Communist Party countries have generally adapted to the special demands of Communist politics; this results, at least partly, from the historical and cultural setting within which they were socialized. Prior to the Communist revolutions in Russia and China, the masses were given virtually no opportunity to participate in politics. Voices of dissent were stilled and political organizations were suppressed. Thus, the present Communist Party states have inherited as well as built on a relatively passive political community. Whether they will remain passive as Communist systems begin to open up to greater mass participation or become more active as they have in Poland, is one of the unanswered questions with which we must conclude this study.

Many environmental factors have conditioned contemporary Communist politics. As we have mentioned, the historical tradition of autocratic rule has facilitated state control of such institutions as schools and mass media. Cultural schisms and strong regional ethnonationalisms (especially in the Soviet Union and Yugoslavia) have sensitized many Communist leaders to the need for national unity. After World War I, the Soviet Union was buffeted by the turbulence of civil war, foreign intervention, economic crisis, depression, and, finally, the tragedy of World War II. Soviet leaders received a baptism of fire that would have undermined and destroyed weaker regimes and people. Their survival was due to their ruthlessness in smashing opposition internally, and the lessons they learned during this period have been hard to forget. Similar conditions have attended the birth of other major Communist Party states, including China, Cuba, and Vietnam, which have come into existence in the midst of an international system that regarded them with fear and hostility. Finally, although Karl Marx predicted that Communism would come first to the industrialized countries, the reverse has been true. Communism has become a method for underdeveloped countries to lift themselves up by mobilizing mass resources. Thus, new Communist states have come into being in backward and poor countries that require hard and forceful policies to wrench them from the past.

Two crucial structural features influenced the shape of Communist politics: one-party rule and state socialism. In every Communist Party country the key institution, without peer or tolerated opposition, is the Communist Party. The party controls access to the centers of power and most public discussion of government policies. It is the device for channeling communications between the élite and the masses and for mobilizing the masses into their participatory roles. The Communist parties of the Soviet Union, China, and Cuba are the envy of many developing countries whose élites would like to emulate the creations of Lenin. Few of them manage such a feat however. The other major institutional factor in Communist politics is the central government direction and management of the economy, including production and pricing decisions and broad investment allocations. Although many Western countries are gradually moving toward some kind of government-indicative planning for the economy, Communist governments intervene in almost every economic decision covering both industry and agriculture. Because the economic policies of a state are crucial in affecting the quality of life in the country, Communist governments exercise influence over their societies to a degree unmatched in the other two worlds.

The relatively unsatisfactory political performance of the developing countries of the Third World can be accounted for in terms of similar dimensions of comparison. At the level of the masses, individual preparation for modern participatory politics is poor. The masses of citizens are ill equipped educationally and physically. Many of these people are still illiterate and, thereby, dependent on the few people who control the source of information; and their physical well-being (health, income, housing, nutrition, clothing, medical care) is usually so precarious that they have little time or energy left over for political activity. In addition, many traditional cultures discourage behavior and attitudes that are important in politics: bargaining, compromise, a positive[*] and instrumental approach to one's environment and one's fellow workers, and a sense of efficacy and competence. On the contrary, traditional cultures and psychology encourage fatalism, apathy, and a feeling of inefficacy when dealing with authority figures. Such characteristics must be changed before traditional peoples are ready for roles in a modern participatory democracy.

Many developing countries are governed by charismatic figures whose major claim to power rests on their ability to sway the masses with their rhetoric. The chief problem with this style of governance lies in the personality of the charismatic leader. Charisma is a valuable leadership trait for countries that are called on for heroic measures and when compromise means defeat. Too frequently, however, charismatic figures cannot settle down to the routine of daily politics after the war is over or the revolution is won. The politics of moderation and compromise is not helped by charisma. Furthermore, charismatic leaders frequently fail to develop the institutional structures that can shape and guide the political process after they are gone. When the leader dies or is deposed, this lack of institutions leaves the state without the sense of predictability and regularity so badly needed in rapidly changing societies.

The environmental problems faced by developing countries are so numerous that we can only list a few of the more important ones. The historical legacy of colonialism has been, on the whole, disadvantageous even though colonial regimes did bring some beneficial aspects of European culture. Nevertheless, the sense of a native people's inferiority left behind by the colonial powers and the disruption of the native economic system have condemned developing states to many years of struggle as they try to catch up with the more developed countries. The international systems—both political and economic—work against the interests of the Third World in many different ways. A combination of scarce resources and late industrialization has meant that developing countries have few resources that they can call on to aid their citizens in achieving their values. Thus, a vicious circle of poverty (low income—low savings—low investment—poverty) affects not only the economies but also the political systems of developing countries.

Many of these environmental and human factors come together in the peculiar institutional makeup of the typical Third World country. The syncratic state is one that attempts to industrialize the country without disturbing ancient traditional privilege, a task that requires formidable political skills, large resources, and infinite patience. Most of the requisites are lacking in the Third World, which helps to explain why syncratic regimes (*e.g.*, Peron in Argentina or Ayub Khan in Pakistan) fail and are deposed by the country's military. Not only is the syncratic regime attempting the impossible but it also tries to accomplish it without building a suitable institutional base. Institutions are notoriously weak in developing countries, and the consequences are well documented—lack of access for the masses to policy making, absence of countervailing powers to prevent an abuse of authority by the political élites, and a lack of a sense of continuity and dependability so badly needed in developing states. Finally, because syncratic leaders lack the institutions or the resources to create real power and to distribute tangible benefits, they become addicted to politics by symbolism, and the people are drugged with empty slogans, ethnic hatreds, and the rhetoric of class struggle.

It should be evident by now from this comparative overview of our three worlds that politics does indeed matter and that political choices and styles are significant in determining whether or not—and to what extent—people can achieve valued goals and objectives in their lives. Certainly, the research and study of a number of other scholars suggest the importance of political forces. In *Modern Politics in Britain and Sweden*, Hugh Heclo describes political structural forces and characteristics that have produced different solutions and outcomes in these two countries.[1] Calling attention to the significance of

political factors, Douglas E. Ashford[2] points to the influence of parliamentary forces in Great Britain by noting that when "looking at a variety of policy developments over the past two decades, it is remarkable how each is affected in its conception, its evaluation, and its implementation by the needs of parliamentary government."[3] Other distinguished political scientists have called attention to the impact of politics and political forces on government actions and policy outcomes. Yet, we should recognize that domestic or national politics is not the sole determinant of the quality of life or human dignity in countries throughout the world. For example, a number of scholars have called attention to global and international forces impacting on nation-states. Such international crises as wars and economic developments—the Great Depression and current inflationary trends—have much to do with what goes on within states. In addition, foreign states can have a powerful impact on what goes on in other states. The influence of the Soviet Union on the quality of life and human dignity in Afghanistan, Poland, and other East European countries is one of numerous examples. The impact of the United States on Europe and Japan after World War II and the present-day impact of the superpowers on the Third World can not be denied. Accordingly, we must recognize that some of what occurs in nation-states is beyond their immediate control. Many contend that this is a growing phenomenon and will continue as countries become more interdependent. The impact of the international energy situation on the quality of life around the globe is a good current example of the power of global forces in the contemporary era.

Other scholars have called attention to the social and economic forces that affect politics and policy outcomes. Seymour M. Lipset examined the relationship between economic devel-

---

[1]Hugh Heclo, *Modern Politics in Britain and Sweden* (New Haven: Yale University Press, 1974).

[2]Douglas E. Ashford, "The Structural Analysis of Policy or Institutions Really Do Matter," in *Comparing Public Policies*, Douglas E. Ashford, ed. (Beverly Hills, Calif.: Sage, 1980).

[3]*Ibid.*, p. 86.

opment and democracy,[4] Han S. Park examined the relationship between socioeconomic development and democratic performance,[5] and Roger W. Benjamin and John H. Kautsky examined the relationship between economic development and Communism.[6] Others, such as Thomas R. Dye, Frederick C. Pryor, and Harold I. Wilensky have called attention to the powerful impact of socioeconomic forces on policy outputs.[7] Accordingly, we should recognize the power and significance that these forces have on the world in which we live.

Although domestic politics is not the sole determinant of human dignity nor even the primary one in many circumstances, it is still important and worthy of our study and consideration. Political decisions and political institutions do much to shape the world we live in, and they help and hinder us in our efforts to make it better. If each of us lived alone on a desert island or atop a mountain, there would be no need for the coordination of our desires and our behaviors with the desires and behaviors of others. Humans do not live alone, however, and somehow the things that people do to reach their goals must be subjected to a certain degree of social and political coordination. Goals must be established for the entire community; resources must be mobilized and deployed and actions undertaken to reach these goals; outcomes must be evaluated and mistakes corrected; and the costs and benefits of social action must be assessed and allocated. In a

simpler time, many human societies used essentially nonpolitical mechanisms for doing these things, for example, the price machinery of the free market, the town meeting, or the voluntary association. Now, however, the public interest requires a more authoritative mechanism for coordinating thousands of private decisions, attitudes, and behaviors. Government is the only agency yet devised that can do many of these things. How these tasks are performed is influenced by the human, environmental, and structural factors we have just enumerated. The ways in which these tasks are performed, in turn, determine the impact of public policies on private human values.

The significance of politics for human values varies from one world to another. In Western Europe, the principal factors seem to be the quality of leadership of the state (Is it creative and strong or indecisive and mediocre?); the vigor of the bureaucracy (Can it assume a leadership role when elected officials fail to rise to their challenge?); and the ability of leaders of interest groups (Can they penetrate the barriers surrounding the political system and influence public policy?) In the Communist Party states, the major political factors are the Marxist-Leninist ideology and the various national adaptations of it; the strong personal leadership of such men as Stalin and Mao, which was autocratic and cruel at times, but served the peculiar needs of revolutionary Russia and China; and the centralized structure of policy making in the one-party state. In the developing world, on the other hand, politics plays a key role primarily in the absence of certain crucial determinants. Power remains seriously fragmented, and few regimes have found a way to consolidate their power in the face of continued challenges both at home and abroad; institutions that could channel popular participation and mobilize resources are slow in emerging, and they frequently are not enduring; and the charismatic leader, so badly needed at the birth of the country, becomes self-defeating after the routine of politics sets in and the government must manage on a day-to-day basis.

[4]Seymour M. Lipset, "Some Social Requisites of Democracy: Economic Development and Political Legitimacy," *American Political Science Review*, 53 (1) (1959), pp. 69–105.

[5]Han S. Park, "Socio-Economic Development and Democratic Performance: An Empirical Study," *International Review of Modern Sociology*, 6, (2), (1976), pp. 349–361.

[6]Roger W. Benjamin and John H. Kautsky, "Communism and Economic Development," *American Political Science Review*, 62 (1) (1969), pp. 110–123.

[7]Thomas R. Dye, *Politics, Economics, and the Public* (Chicago: Rand McNally, 1966); Frederick C. Pryor, *Public Expenditures in Capitalist and Communist Nations* (Homewood, Ill.: Richard D. Irwin, 1968); Harold I. Wilensky, *The Welfare State and Equality* (Berkeley: University of California Press, 1975).

## POLITICS AND HUMAN VALUES: A LOOK TO THE FUTURE

Political scientists enjoy no special gifts to see into the future, so our forecasts must, like those of anyone else, be based on the perception of current trends and the projection of those trends into the years ahead.

There are some developments that give us cause for satisfaction and reason for optimism in our assessment of the state of human dignity in the coming years. In the West, the transition of Spain and Portugal to democracy and the steps taken in Canada and Belgium to respect their ethnic minorities show promise for the future. In most Communist Party states, the governments seem to be succeeding in improving the welfare of the common citizen. Better health care, social services, education, and a growing emphasis on mass consumption in most systems appear to be improving the quality of life and the material opportunities related to human dignity. In the Third World, India's step back from the brink of dictatorship and the police state was welcomed by democrats around the world.

There are, however, many causes for concern and reasons for pessimism. In Europe, the festering problem of Northern Ireland refuses to go away and joins an economic malaise to bedevil the political leaders of Great Britain. The economic and political problems in Italy, Greece, Spain, and Portugal might overwhelm the democratic regimes in those countries unless fragile balances between left and right can be maintained. In the Communist Party states, the denial of human rights continues to cause worldwide concern. Furthermore, the courageous expressions of frustrations, discontent, and desires for change in Poland call attention to festering problems in the Second World. The Third World offers few rays of hope. The area suffers generally from industrial and agricultural stagnation; political instability continues to plague most of the developing countries; and human rights are not notably protected.

In short, the future offers a mixed picture of positive and negative signs for the state of human dignity. We foresee several important tensions that will determine the kinds of problems faced by the world's 167 governments over the next decade.

**1.** The tension between the desire for affluence or at least material comfort, on the one hand, and the recognition of the material limits to growth (energy, food, pollution, population) on the other.

**2.** The tension between modernity and tradition. Can societies choose portions of each culture or must modernity be adopted as a whole?

**3.** The tension between the rights of the individual and the rights of the collectivity of which he or she is a member.

**4.** The tension between efficiency and freedom.

**5.** The tension over the correct jurisdiction to deal with certain kinds of problems. It is becoming apparent that the nation-state is not necessarily the correct unit to help people achieve many of their values. Some problems are handled better at a local level (education); others may be better treated at the regional, supranational, or international level (energy supplies).

There are no easy answers to these questions and no "right" solutions to these tensions. Politics can help people to achieve their goals, but political institutions cannot perform miracles. Many of the problems and tensions we have discussed have been with us for generations, and many will likely be with us in the future. Politics can mean, however, the difference between a society in which human values are respected and where human beings are helped to improve their lives or it can mean a society in which human beings are no more than an object of oppression for an autocratic ruler. We think that difference is important now and that it will become crucial in coming years.

# Glossary

**Actions** (6)—The strategies and tactics implemented by political leaders to achieve their expressed goals.

**Administrative courts** (166)—Tribunals in code-law countries that decide on the legality of administrative actions, that is, whether, in implementing the law, executive agents have faithfully carried out the will of the lawmakers.

**Administrative élites** (126)—High-ranking, university trained, civil servants involved in policy making as well as in overseeing the implementation of policy.

**Affluence** (67)—A material condition in which basic human needs are satisfied and one can afford a variety of nonessential consumer goods.

**Agenda** (166)—The set of goals to which the political leaders of a country assign high priority at a given time.

**Aggregate demand** (364)—The demand of individuals and groups for goods and services treated as a combined unit in an economy.

**Aggregate purchasing power** (364)—The purchasing power of all individuals and groups in an economy treated collectively.

**Agrarian economy** (26)—An economy in which the vast majority of the working population is engaged in agriculture or related pursuits.

**Allocation of values** (2)—Priority choices made among competing values, that is, policy making.

**Anticlericalism** (73)—Opposition to any church influence in political matters, usually found in Catholic countries.

**Apparatchiki** (280)—Paid Communist Party functionaries who serve in central, regional, and local party positions.

**Aristocracy** (German: *Junkers*) (26)—In Europe, a social class located at the top of the social stratification hierarchy whose economic, social, and (formerly) political positions are (were) based on the ownership of land.

**Artisans** (27)—An occupational type prevalent in pre-industrial towns and cities. Those who work with their hands, producing individually made goods primarily for a local market.

**Ascriptive** (404)—Refers to the belief that society should reward its members for some attribute (usually acquired at birth) other than performance in social roles.

**Associational interest groups** (140)—Interest groups based on economic functions or other specialized roles played by the members of the group.

**Autonomous behavior** (422)—Behavior intended to influence government decisions.

**Backbenchers** (119)—Rank-and-file British MPs of the majority and opposition parties who are not part of the party leadership and, therefore, are not entitled to sit on the front bench.

**Basic Law** (120)—The equivalent of a constitution for the Federal Republic of Germany. When drafted in 1949, it was intended to be a temporary instrument until the reunification of East and West Germany.

**Basic personality** (413)—That personality configuration shared by the bulk of a society's members as a result of the early experiences they have in common.

**Betrayal syndrome** (412)—Child-rearing practices that teach children to distrust their environment.

**Bolsheviks** (188)—Lenin's wing of the Russian Social Democratic Labor Party, comprising the more radical Marxist revolutionaries who took power after the October Revolution in 1917. Distinguished from the less revolutionary Mensheviks.

**Bourgeoisie** (middle class) (220)—The entrepreneurs or property-owning class in modern capitalist systems who control the means of production (according to Marxist theory).

**Bundesrat** (Federal Council) (120)—The upper house of the West German Parliament, made up of delegates from the *land* (state) governments.

**Bundestag** (Federal Diet) (106)—The lower (directly elected) house of the West German Parliament.

**Bureaucratization** (317)—A more rational organization of human work that involves hierarchical arrangement of specialized task-performing roles.

**Capitalism** (4)—Economic system characterized by private ownership of property whereby the owners derive profit from the production and sale of goods and services.

**Capitalists** (30)—Private owners of the means of industrial production in a capitalist economy.

**Central Committee** (273)—Large and powerful body in Communist parties that formally elects members of the Politburo and Secretariat.

**Centralism** (360)—A distribution of power in which all major decisions are made by individuals or organizations remote from local authorities who lack the real power to govern themselves.

**Charisma** (482)—The quality of being able to convince others of one's superior powers (bordering on the supernatural)—for example, a charismatic leader.

**Christian Democracy** (101)—Ideology, found in countries with large Catholic populations, that appeals to devout Catholics who combine political and cultural conservatism with social progressivism.

**Civic competence** (87)—The belief that one has the capacity, *in actuality*, to influence government decisions.

**Civic culture** (88)—Term coined by Gabriel Almond and Sidney Verba to denote a political culture in which political participation is highly valued but in which there is sufficient contentment with the political system that most people are not in fact motivated to participate very actively in politics.

**Class consciousness** (259)—Self-identification as a member of a social class that has interests in common with oneself. These interests are in conflict with those of another class or other classes.

**Coalition government** (115)—In a parliamentary system, a prime minister and cabinet comprised of, and resting on a parliamentary majority consisting of, more than one political party.

**Code law** (165)—System of law that prevails in continental European countries, among others, and derives from the Roman law tradition. Laws enacted by parliament are codified into complex bodies of categories and subcategories that contain the legal norms that apply in individual cases.

**Codetermination** (149)—West German system of worker participation in the management of industry whereby workers' representatives sit on the directing boards of private corporations.

**Cognition** (405)—The mental processes that have to do with the possession of information.

**Cognitive dissonance** (407)—An individual's awareness of contradictory information, attitudes, or behavior. The contradiction will be dealt with through some psychological mechanism.

**Colonialism** (362)—A system of governance and relationships characterized by dominance of a weak people by strong (and distant) nation states.

**Command economy** (212)—Economic system based on government control of the factors of production and centralized planning; the laws of supply and demand are of little importance in such a system.

**Common law** (165)—System of law, originating in medieval England, that consists of a body of precedents found in earlier court decisions defining the legal norms that apply in individual cases.

**Common Market** (44)—The popular term for the European Community (EC)—a customs union of ten Western European countries in which customs barriers to trade among the member states have been removed and a common external tariff is enforced vis-à-vis third countries.

**Commune** (132)—Term for the most basic unit of local government in France, Italy, Yugoslavia and some other countries. Applied to cities, towns, and villages.

**Communism** (4)—A term meaning many different things, including a theory, movement, or system envisaged in the writings of Karl Marx. Based on the principle, "From each according to his abilities, to each according to his needs." Communism presupposes economic abundance and a classless society.

**Comparison** (7)—A mode of analysis that involves a search for similarities and differences among units in a given category (*e.g.*, sovereign states).

**Comprehensive schools** (61)—British secondary schools promoted by the Labour Party that are designed to break down the three-tiered school system that reinforces social class divisions.

**Comradeship** (254)—Interpersonal relations based on a universalistic ethic whereby individuals treat others as equal members of a cooperative political community.

**Confidence mechanism** (505)—Any social practice or structure that permits tangible resources to be distributed unequally but that does so in such a way as to convince those who lose that the system is essentially fair and that they lost because of their own shortcomings.

**Conservatism** (99)—Ideological defense of the *status quo*, involving skepticism toward, but not closed-minded rejection of, reform proposals.

**Constitutional courts** (166)—High courts that have the power to determine whether the acts of legislative and executive agencies of government are in accord with a constitution (*e.g.*, the West German Federal Constitutional Court).

**Constructive vote of nonconfidence** (120)—Under the West German Basic Law, the Chancellor must resign only if defeated on a motion of nonconfidence in which a successor is named and which passes by a majority of the entire membership of the Bundestag (absolute majority).

**Cynicism** (87)—In a political sense, the belief that all politicians are corrupt and that one is best advised to

worry about one's own affairs, thus avoiding the disillusionment inevitably resulting from involvement in politics.

**De facto** (360)—A condition that exists in reality regardless of whether the law prescribes or prohibits it.

**De facto one-party systems** (434)—Political party systems that are dominated by only one party although others are legal.

**Democracy** (329)—A system of government in which the majority of the people rule either directly or through the medium of elected representatives.

**Democratic centralism** (266)—Vladimir Ilyich Lenin's formula whereby members of Communist parties are encouraged to speak freely until a decision is taken, then, unity is to prevail. In addition, decisions of higher party bodies are binding on lower ones.

**Democratic socialism** (99)—Ideology advocating a redistribution of well-being, enlightenment, and respect in favor of groups in society that are relatively deprived of these values, but the ideology is opposed to any fundamental alteration of the structure of power in a polyarchy.

**Demographic transition** (389)—The change in size and composition of a nation's population brought about by the uneven impacts of hygiene and medicine at first and the changing mores and values later. The effect is a rapidly growing population, owing to declining infant mortality, coupled with high birth rates.

**Departement (French) (Italian counterpart: province)** (132)—French unit of local government encompassing several towns or cities and surrounding territory. Larger than the average U.S. county but much smaller than the average state.

**Devolution** (134)—Within a unitary system, the downward transfer of legislative power from the central government to regional or local units.

**Dissolution** (115)—In a parliamentary system, the premature termination of the life of an elected parliamentary body. It is designed to test the respective strengths of the majority and opposition parties.

**Distributive well-being** (102)—The value placed on the equalization of material goods among members of a society.

**Division** (119)—The mode of voting on important questions in the British House of Commons. The MPs file into separate division lobbies to be counted by tellers as voting aye or no.

**Division of labor** (219)—The structure of jobs and occupational skills in a society.

**Doctrine of natural harmony** (386)—The belief that the interests of the poor are identical with those of the rich in the expansion and growth of the national and international economic systems.

**Early industrialization** (26)—Often called the rapid industrialization or take-off stage, it is the period of time when an economy converts from an essentially agrarian base to one in which industry occupies approximately one-half the work force.

**Economic enclaves** (367)—The system by which foreign economic entities, such as plantations or mines, operate on a country's territory without interacting with that country's economy.

**Ego structures** (402)—Core mental structures that provide the central regulatory mechanisms for individual personality.

**Embourgeoisement** (67)—The process whereby members of the working class came to identify themselves with middle-class interests, values, and life styles.

**Enlightenment** (4)—The process by which individuals learn about themselves and their world by means of formal education, acquisition of information from the mass media, or transmission of informal social mores through family, peer group, or neighborhood. Also, the value attached to this process.

**Environment** (17)—The social, economic, and cultural setting that surrounds the political process and influences goals, actions and outcomes and, in turn, is influenced by them.

**Ethnicity** (74)—Social differentiation based on racial or linguistic distinctiveness, often associated with particular regions within countries.

**Ethnocentrism** (481)—Tendency to judge foreign groups by reference to one's own customs, institutions, and standards.

**Ethnonationalism** (371)—The belief that people should be governed only by others of their own ethnic group.

**Eurocommunism** (201)—The tendency on the part of some Communist parties in First World countries (notably Italy and Spain) to depart from the Soviet blueprint for proletarian revolution and dictatorship of the proletariat in favor of the attainment of socialism through adherence to the rules of parliamentary democracy.

**Executive dominance** (449)—The dominant role played by the political executive in developing countries. This is in contrast to the relatively weak and submissive role played by legislative and judicial branches.

**Expansionist** (360)—A characteristic of nation states or colonial empires to expand their boundaries and the territory over which they exercise control.

**Extractive capabilities** (9)—The ability of governing elites to obtain resources from the citizenry, especially the ability to tax income and to conscript to military service.

**Extreme (reactionary) right** (40)—Political movement exhibiting ideological commitment to nationalism, aversion to big government and big business, and resistance to many of the features accompanying modernization.

**Factions** (120)—Stable, identifiable, subgroups within a political party that usually espouse somewhat different sets of policies from one another or from the official party line; they may also constitute a tight-knit social group in which personal favors play an important role.

**Failure-prone policy processes** (462)—A term coined by Albert O. Hirschman for a frequently observed tendency in Latin America for the policy-making process to increase rather than decrease the probability of failure.

**Fascism** (40)—Term applied to extreme right-wing political movements that exhibit strong nationalism and appeal to the authoritarian inclinations of their supporters. Usually headed by a strong leader, as Benito Mussolini, leader of the Italian *fascisti*.

**Fatalism** (402)—The belief that human beings can not control their lives or the world around them.

**Federalism** (114)—A system of vertical power distribution in which there is a constitutionally protected division of power between central and regional units of government.

**Feedback** (475)—Information about past performance of a political system that is used to correct mistakes or improve future performance.

**First World** (9)—Countries in North America and Western Europe, plus Australia, Israel, Japan, and New Zealand, that are both industrially advanced and politically pluralistic.

**Five-year plans** (208)—Government plans for coordinating the economic goals, policies, and programs of Communist and some Third World countries.

**Future shock** (406)—Individual psychological disorientation caused by rapid change.

**Gaullism** (102)—A pragmatic blend of strong French nationalism, political conservatism, and economic growth-oriented progressivism, which is characteristic of the followers of General Charles de Gaulle's philosophy.

**Goals** (17)—Objectives advanced by political elites for the allocation of values within their society.

**Grammar school** (61)—Élite British secondary school that prepares students for a university education.

**Great Leap Forward** (209)—Chinese economic strategy in 1958–1960 that resulted in failure but was intended to make China an economic power—based on loosening restraints, decentralization, and modern and traditional methods of development.

**Great Proletarian Cultural Revolution** (GPCR) (210)—Attempt to rejuvenate the revolutionary spirit of the Chinese populace in 1966–1969 that resulted in political and economic turmoil.

**Green Revolution** (492)—Major changes of a scientific and technological nature that were expected to help the Third World solve its food-shortage problems without making changes in the social or institutional structures in the countryside.

**Gross national product** (GNP) (381)—The money value of a nation's total output of goods and services for a year.

**Gross national product (GNP) per capita** (216)—The money value of a nation's output of goods and services divided by its population. This permits comparisons of countries that have different population sizes.

**Groupthink** (469)—A term coined by Irving Janis for a process in which the government restricts debate on a complex problem, thus, dissent is suppressed in the interest of loyalty to the group and serious error results.

**Guerrilla insurgency** (363)—A violent political struggle in which the challengers, because of their relative weakness, choose strategies and tactics that minimize their vulnerability and maximize the vulnerability of the opponent.

**Gymnasium** (61)—Élite West German secondary school that prepares students for a university education.

**Head of state** (117)—In a parliamentary system, the ceremonial, but essentially powerless, representative of the nation. Usually an hereditary monarch or an indirectly elected President of the Republic.

**Hectare** (491)—A metric measure of area, equal to 2.47 acres.

**Horizontal power distribution** (114)—Formal distribution of government power among units at the same level (national, regional, or local), for example, the separation of powers between the three branches of the U.S. Government.

**Human dignity** (5)—A preferred state of being that depends on the ideal mixture of the values of power, well-being, respect, and enlightenment desired by a given society.

**Human values** (4)—What people want for themselves and, by derivation, what they want from government.

**Imperialism** (384)—The expansion of an industrial nation's power and authority abroad to many less powerful countries or nations.

**Incremental policy making** (307)—A mode of policy making that involves *ad hoc*, short-term planning based on incomplete information and resulting in marginal changes in policy.

**Indicative planning** (157)—System of economic planning, that involves targets set by government planners in consultation with economic-sector representatives and state-provided incentives (carrots rather than sticks) to encourage goal fulfillment.

**Industrialization** (8)—The process of changing the ways in which society produces goods and services, through the increasing application of technology to allow people to manipulate the natural world.

**Industrial maturity** (34)—The phase that follows early, rapid industrialization; economic trends, begun in the preceding period, continue and include a growth in the industrial work force (now the majority), a decline in the agricultural work force, and an increase in the size of business firms.

**Industrial Revolution** (7)—The transformation from preindustrial to industrial society that took place in Western Europe and North America between the mid-eighteenth and the late nineteenth centuries.

**Inflation** (54)—An economic condition characterized by increasing prices for consumer goods. This results from increased production costs per unit and an expansion of the money supply at a rate faster than the increased supply of goods and services.

**Infrastructure** (363)—The underlying network of transportation, communication, and institutions that sustain a society, especially an industrial society.

**Interest groups** (140)—Groups of people, organized or unorganized, who make claims on other groups and on government for policy outcomes that correspond to the values they seek.

**Komsomol** (244)—Soviet youth organization that serves as an agent of political socialization for youth ages 14 to 26.

**Laissez faire** (146)—The belief that the minimum amount of government intervention in the economy is necessary for economic prosperity.

**Land (plural, länder)** (121)—Regional subdivisions of government in the West German system of federalism, similar to the states in the United States.

**Land-tenure system** (393)—The system by which ownership of land is organized.

**Lethality** (364)—The characteristic of a weapon or weapon system that measures its ability to kill persons or destroy physical structures.

**Liberalism** (99)—Ideology supporting steady political, social, and economic reform within the framework of capitalism.

**Lycée** (61)—Élite French secondary school that prepares students for a university education.

**Machismo** (413)—Latin American cultural characteristic that emphasizes masculinity.

**Major networks** (446)—The national political élite of a developing country. Includes the national-government leaders, the civil and military bureaucracy, and the industrial leadership.

**Marxism** (4)—Body of political and economic doctrines founded on the writings of Karl Marx. Calls for collective ownership, the abolition of bourgeois morality, and the withering away of the state.

**Marxism-Leninism** (192)—A body of doctrine based on the writings of Karl Marx and the writings and practical experience of Vladimir Ilyich Lenin. The doctrine establishes the Communist Party as a centralized institution for building socialism and Communism.

**Mass-line** (327)—Pattern of reciprocating communications between party members and masses in Mao Zedong's China.

**Metropolitan country** (363)—The dominant and distant state in a colonial relationship.

**Minifundia (opposite: latifundia)** (394)—Spanish term that means a parcel of agricultural land too small to be worked productively by its owner.

**Minority government** (110)—A prime minister and cabinet in a parliamentary system who belong to one or more parties that together hold 50 per cent or fewer of the seats in parliament but that enjoy the support of a party or parties not included in the cabinet, thus, enabling the government to stay in office.

**Minor networks** (446)—The middle-echelon political élites of developing countries, typically linked to the major networks by patron-client systems.

**Mobilized behavior** (422)—Behavior of an actor stimulated by others actors to achieve their goals.

**Modernization** (8)—The process of individual and societal change that involves the transformation of individual attitudes from fatalistic to activistic and the transformation of society from being relatively unorganized to being relatively highly organized.

**Modernization from within** (14)—Modernization that occurred in the countries that experienced industrialization earliest (First World countries). It involves little external stimulus in comparison with countries that industrialized in the twentieth century.

**Modernization from without** (15)—Modernization that accompanied industrialization in the past 100 years; external sources of investment play a major role in fostering industrialization in this kind of modernization.

**Modernizing élites** (406)—Political élites who seek industrialization, attitudinal modernization, and the development of political system capabilities. Opposed by traditional, anti-industrial groups.

**Mosaic societies** (396)—Societies made up of many different culturally distinct pieces (subcultures), each of which adds to the overall society without being absorbed by it.

**Motion of confidence** (120)—Government-sponsored motion designed to rally majority support behind the policies of the prime minister and cabinet. Defeat on such a motion will force the prime minister to resign or call for new elections. (Censure is an opposition-sponsored motion that has the same potential consequences if adopted.)

**MPs** (118)—Members of Parliament, that is, the elected members of the British House of Commons.

**Multinationals** (384)—Business firms whose operations and span of ownership and control cross national boundaries and exist in more than one nation.

**Multiparty system** (105)—A political party system that includes more that two parties, each consistently receiving more than 5 percent of the popular vote.

**Multiple societies** (430)—A divided social order that consists of two separate social systems bound together by a single set of economic, political, and legal bounds.

**Nation** (7)—An ethnic group whose members share a common identity and desire to create or maintain their own nation state.

**National front** (299)—Postwar strategy used by Soviet and East European Communists to unite various groups in antifascist coalitions that were subsequently replaced by Communist regimes.

**Nationalism** (7)—The belief that one's nation is especially deserving of praise or loyalty; sometimes developed into a political ideology or movement.

**National self-determination** (357)—The principle that all nations have the right to choose the system of government under which they live and the people who shall govern them.

**Negative corporatism** (139)—Cooperation between government and business involving government regulation of industry in return for control over trade union activity designed to restrict wage increases.

**Neocolonialism** (360)—A condition of economic domination that exists or persists even after formal legal colonialism has been abolished.

**Neo-Marxism** (139)—In postindustrial society, continued perception that the class struggle has not altered and that the proletariat must wage relentless war against capitalism. See also: Radical left.

**Neutral civil service** (126)—A system of government employment in which strict standards of nonpartisanship prevail in the recruitment and promotion of personnel and in which employees loyally serve the government in power at any given time regardless of its partisan coloration.

**Object loss** (407)—An individual's psychological deprivation owing to loss of some valued object or person.

**Oligopoly** (383)—Control of a particular sector of the economy by a small number of firms.

**Outcomes** (17)—The degree of actual success achieved by political leaders as a result of actions taken in pursuit of their goals.

**Parliamentary system** (115)—A system of government in which executive power is lodged in a prime minister and cabinet responsible to, and removable by, an elected legislative body (parliament).

**Particularism** (404)—Bestowing one's loyalty on nearby social organizations, such as clan, village, or tribe.

**Patron-client systems** (431)—A political system consisting of several patrons (or bosses), who control the majority of the country's or region's political resources, and their clients (or followers), who participate only rarely or incompletely in the political process.

**Peak organizations** (141)—National confederations of employers' (also farmers' and workers') organizations that serve as spokespersons for the member organizations in deliberations with other peak organizations and with the government.

**Peasants** (15)—A generic term for the bulk of the rural population in preindustrial society; excludes large landholders but includes small-farm owners, tenant farmers, sharecroppers, and farm laborers.

**Periphery nations** (386)—Those raw-materials-producing nations identified in the Prebisch thesis as suffering from the workings of the international system.

**Personality structure** (402)—The cluster of mental orientations that characterize individuals and guide their behavior.

**Petite bourgeoisie** (also middling class) (31)—Owners of small-scale businesses, popularly characterized as conservative and reluctant to take risks.

**Pluralism** (138)—Refers to a political system. A condition in which many distinct groups with conflicting interests compete for power, thus, ensuring that power will not be concentrated in the hands of an élite few.

**Policy** (6)—The expressed goals of political élites and the actions taken to implement them.

**Policymaking** (462)—The process by which goals of political élites are converted into actions and, in turn, into outcomes.

**Politburo** (273)—The small and most powerful policy-making body in Communist parties.

**Political culture** (78)—The pattern of attitudes and beliefs that people in a society hold about their political system.

**Political decay** (430)—Decreasing ability of political institutions to absorb rising numbers of mass participants in the political process.

**Political development** (9)—Changes in political structures and attitudes accompanying and supportive of modernization. Includes an accretion of power by political élites and the development of attitudes and institutions that favor popular participation.

**Political élites** (81)—Those members of a society who are involved in the determining of policy, either directly as occupants of policy-making roles or indirectly as wielders of influence over the policy-making process.

**Political immobility** (*immobilisme*) (120)—A condition in which government leaders are unable to make coherent policy because of the absence of requisite political support.

**Political orientations** (78)—The ways in which people think and feel about politics, that is, political attitudes and beliefs.

**Political participation** (421)—Activity by private citizens to influence government decisions.

**Political performance** (18)—The extent to which a political system's goals, actions, and outcomes contribute to enhancing human dignity.

**Political socialization** (17–18)—The process by which the prevailing political attitudes and beliefs of a society are transmitted to new members and these attitudes and beliefs undergo change.

**Political stability** (7)—The persistence of a given organization of public authorities on a given territory without violent upheaval or serious political discontinuity.

**Political subcultures** (79)—Groups within a society that are differentiated on the basis of certain common political orientations as well as more objective characteristics, such as race, religion, or age.

**Political system** (6)—Distinguished from the narrower concept of government, this concept incorporates all individuals and institutions involved in the political process visualized as interacting systemically.

**Polyarchy** (23)—The type of political system in which the many rule, at least in the sense that there is meaningful competition among groups contending for power, from among whom the many can choose their rulers.

**Positive corporatism** (139)—Economic policymaking in which government, business and organized labor cooperate in promoting economic growth with low unemployment while maintaining modest wage increases in order to keep inflation in check.

**Postindustrial society** (26)—An advanced industrial society in which knowledge has become the most important economic resource. Indicators include a high GNP per capita, a preponderance of service-sector employees in the work force, and a rapid increase in the number of employees in professional and technical occupations.

**Power** (3)—The ability to influence the behavior of others; in a political context, the capacity to change or influence policy outcomes. Also, the value placed on the above.

**Prebisch thesis** (385)—The theory, advanced by Argentine economist, Raul Prebisch, that the international trade system works automatically and inherently to the disadvantage of the raw-materials-producing countries.

**Prefect** (132)—The official of the Ministry of the Interior who is the administrative head of the French *departement* (or of the Italian province).

**Presidential system** (122)—A system of government in which the legislative body and the chief executive (president) are separately elected and exercise constitutionally separated powers.

**Prime Minister** (123)—The effective head of government in a parliamentary system. Leads the cabinet and is accountable to the majority in parliament. In West Germany: the Federal Chancellor (*Bundeskanzler*).

**Proletarian dictatorship** (190)—Transitional state that follows revolution when the proletariat or those acting in their interests rule. In Marx's words, "in order to establish equality, we must first establish inequality."

**Proletarian revolution** (187)—Based on the writings of Karl Marx, the idea that the proletariat will develop a political consciousness and overthrow the ruling class (bourgeoisie). In fact, the proletariat did not play a major role in most Marxist-Leninist takeovers.

**Proletariat** (34)—Propertyless wage earners who sell their labor in exchange for wages to employers.

**Proportional representation** (106)—A method of distributing seats among political parties on the basis of election results so that each party gets approximately the same proportion of seats as of popular votes.

**Radical left** (100)—Adherents to the goal of redistributing power, well-being, enlightenment, and respect; heavily criticizing both Western polyarchies and Soviet-style Communist systems for their failure to alter the *status quo*.

**Redistributive policies** (102)—Policies designed to make a change in the distribution of power, well-being, respect, and enlightenment, with greater equality as the intended outcome.

**Regional level of government** (134)—Government jurisdiction that encompasses an area comprising more than one city and a significant proportion of a country's population (*e.g.*, U.S. states).

**Regional separatism** (135)—Political movements seeking to detach particular ethnically distinct regions from a given sovereign state to create a separate nation state.

**Relative deprivation** (407)—Perception of a significant gap between individual expectations and capabilities.

**Respect** (3)—The value placed on enjoyment of secure and supportive relationships with others (including political authorities) in a community, based on honor and prestige, respect for human rights, affection, and loyalty.

**Revisionism** (38)—Late nineteenth century modification of Marxism, which abandoned revolutionary strategy in favor of the attainment of socialism through obedience to the rules of parliamentary democracy.

**Revolution** (15)—Violent change in the existing social and political organization of a country, brought about by internal forces.

**Scientific socialism** (186)—Theory developed by Karl Marx and Friedrich Engels that claims that a scientific analysis of the evolution of material forces in history leads to the conclusion that socialism is inevitable.

**Second World** (15)—Communist states wherein the pace of industrialization has been forced by modernizing élites guided by Marxist-Leninist ideology and employing a centralized state apparatus.

**Secretariat** (273)—Organizational arm of the Politburo in Communist parties. Coordinates the implementation and execution of party policies through a hierarchy of party secretaries.

**Self-managing socialism** (212)—Used by the Yugoslavs to identify their more decentralized system of socialism, which asserts that in economic firms and all other organizations (except the military) decisions are to be made by members of those groups.

**Service sector** (49)—Collective term for sectors of the economy that provide services rather than produce goods. Includes transportation, utilities, trade, finance, insurance, real estate, health, education, research, recreation, and government.

**Shatter zones** (385)—Geopolitical areas characterized by weak governments whose inability to control their internal affairs leads stronger powers to intervene.

**Single-member plurality system** (110)—An electoral system in which each election district (constituency) returns one member to parliament, the candidate elected in a given constituency being the one who receives more votes than any other single candidate (*i.e.*, a plurality).

**Social classes** (26)—Categories of members of a society based on occupation and relative economic advantage and arranged hierarchically from upper, through middle, to lower.

**Social faultlines (cleavages)** (397)—Those dividing lines or characteristics that separate one social group from another, for example, race, religion, language.

**Socialism** (99)—System of social and economic organization where the public (or government) controls the means of production and distribution. Also an ideology and political movement advocating such a system.

**Socialization** (17)—The process by which new members of a society are taught its rules, norms, and mores.

**Social mobility** (226)—The movement of individuals from one social class to another, as the result of educational, occupational, and other experiences.

**Social stratification** (221)—The vertical organization of a society based upon social class lines of division.

**Stagflation** (56)—Simultaneous occurrence of unacceptably high levels of unemployment (re: stagnant economic growth) and unacceptably high levels of inflation.

**Soft state** (472)—A term coined by Gunnar Myrdal to describe the political system of the typical developing country. The government's ability to achieve goals is undermined by corruption, administrative weakness, and refusal to obey the law.

**State socialism** (212)—Economic and political system in which state ministries and other governmental and political bodies manage the factors of production.

**Subculture** (261)—A group of people differentiated from others in a society on the basis of shared characteristics, such as class or ethnicity, and the holding of common beliefs and opinions.

**Supreme Soviet** (289)—Bicameral legislature in the USSR that ratifies the policies of the Communist Party.

**Syncratic politics** (443)—A style of political coalition that attempts to unite both modernizing élites and antimodern élites to govern a modernizing country without disturbing its premodern classes and forces.

**Synoptic policymaking** (309)—Rational-comprehensive mode of policymaking that involves careful and thorough planning based on systematic analysis of all available information.

**Technocrats** (129)—Government élites recruited on the basis of their specialized technical expertise who are said to be impatient with the conflicts and compromises endemic to politics.

**Technology** (363)—Knowledge and tools that are used to manipulate our natural environment.

**Terrorism** (41)—The application of violence by insurgents with the intent to frighten a particular target group.

**Third World** (16)—The independent nations of the world located in Latin America, Africa, the Middle East, and Asia that have not yet chosen unequivocally to follow the political models offered by either Western industrialized democracies or Soviet authoritarianism.

**Totalitarianism** (40)—Highly centralized and dictatorial political process in which individuals and groups outside the ruling élite have no influence over decisions affecting their daily lives.

**Trade unions (U.S. usage: labor unions)** (142)—Organizations of employees formed to promote the economic objectives of their members vis-à-vis employers and vis-à-vis the state.

**Traditional (premodern) society** (26)—Society that was characterized by relatively low standards of organization and in which people's lives were controlled by custom or by personal standards of the rulers rather than by the rules and standards of bureaucracy.

**Two-party system** (105)—A political party system in which two (and only two) parties consistently receive more than 5 per cent of the popular vote.

**Unitary system** (132)—A system of vertical power distribution in which a central unit of government determines what powers will be exercised by units of government at lower levels.

**Universalism** (404)—Giving one's primary loyalty to a social or political entity larger than one's own narrow parochial grouping.

**Utopian socialists** (186)—Term used by Marxists in criticism of earlier socialist theorists who did not base their theories on a study of material forces, which Marxists regard as the key to history.

**Vertical power distribution** (114)—Formal distribution of power among different levels of government: national, regional, and local (*e.g.*, federalism).

**Well-being** (4)—The value placed on the enjoyment by groups and individuals of income, goods, services, wealth, safety, and comfort.

**Wildcat strikes** (144)—Unauthorized strikes initiated locally by trade unionists against the wishes of the union leadership.

**Withering away of the state** (266)—Largely ignored in Communist Party states today, this concept from early Marxist-Leninist doctrine holds that once classes are abolished, the "rule over men" will give way to the "administration of things" during the transition to Communism and will lead to the end of the state.

# PHOTO CREDITS

## PART I

### Chapter 2
Page 40: Fritz Henle/Photo Researchers. Page 45: (*top*) Tom Hollyman/Photo Researchers; (*bottom*) R. Rapelye/Editorial Photocolor Archives. Page 51: Niepce/Rapho-Photo Researchers.

### Chapter 3
Page 76: Courtesy German Information Center. Page 79: Gilbert Uzan/Gamma-Liaison.

### Chapter 4
Page 87: J.A. Pavlovsky/Sygma. Page 92: Selwyn Tait/Sygma. Page 95: Jacob Sutton/Gamma-Liaison.

### Chapter 5
Page 105: Editorial Photocolor Archives. Page 109: Courtesy German Information Center.

### Chapter 6
Page 131: Wide World. Page 141: J. Pavlovsky/Sygma. Page 146: Alain Nogues/Sygma.

### Chapter 7
Page 155: Michel Philippot/Sygma. Page 164: Alain Nogues/Sygma.

## PART II

### Chapter 1
Page 14: Culver Pictures. Page 15: UPI. Page 18: Culver Pictures. Page 20: Hugues Vassal/Gamma-Liaison. Page 23: Daniel Simon/Gamma-Liaison. Page 31: Tass from Sovfoto.

### Chapter 2
Page 45: G. Lajos/Photoreporters, Inc. Page 46: Luis Villota/Photo Researchers. Page 53: Hugues Vassal/Gamma-Liaison.

### Chapter 3
Page 61: UPI. Page 62: Audrey Topping/Photo Researchers. Page 65: UPI. Page 66: Marc Riboud/Magnum. Page 67: Hugues Vassal/Gamma-Liaison.

Page 69: Courtesy Yugoslav Embassy, Washington, D.C. Page 72: Gamma-Liaison.

### Chapter 4
Page 99: Sygma.

### Chapter 5
Page 120: Eastfoto.

### Chapter 7
Page 151: Gamma-Liaison. Page 152: Courtesy Yugoslav Embassy, Washington, D.C. Page 160: (*top*) Tass from Sovfoto (*bottom*) Copyright Agephoto. Page 162: (*top*) Marc Riboud/Magnum (*bottom*) Paolo Koch/Rapho-Photo Researchers.

PART III

**Chapter 1**
Page 12: Costa Manos/Magnum. Page 26: H. Villalobos/Black Star.

**Chapter 2**
Page 43: Paolo Koch/Rapho-Photo Researchers. Page 46: James Pickerell for World Bank. Page 48: Stern Magazine/Black Star.

**Chapter 3**
Page 67: Ken Heyman. Page 70: UPI. Page 79: J.P. Laffont/Sygma.

**Chapter 4**
Page 89: D. Goldberg/Sygma.

**Chapter 5**
Page 108: UPI.

**Chapter 6**
Page 117: Courtesy United Nations.

**Chapter 7**
Page 149: Courtesy UNESCO, Photo by Mirza. Page 150: UPI.

# INDEX

Illiteracy, 70, 365, 498, 516

Imperialism, 192; Great Power theory of, 385; Marxist-Leninist theory of, 384

Income distribution, 396

Incomes policy, *see* Wage and price controls

Incrementalism, 307, 310, 321; of Communist policy, 309–310; forces of, 314; in post-Mao China, 322

India, 228, 451, 521; foreign aid to, 471; industrialization of, 489; languages of, 397; mass media, 416–417, 418; population growth, 390

Industrialization, 7; and agriculture, 215; costs of, 442, 444, 489; defined, 29; delayed, 442; and division of labor, 219; early period of, 29–34; factors of, 8; of First World, 14–15; goals for, 488; mature period of, 34–37; models of, 443; obstacles to, 443; of Second World, 15–16; in Soviet World, 321; stages of, 26; of Third World, 16. *See also* Postindustrial society; Preindustrial society

Industrial Relations Act of 1971, Great Britain, 151

Industrial Revolution, 7, 25, 27–31, 186, 207

Inequality, 381, 382; as central issue, 374; dependency theory of, 387; international sources theory, 383–388; Prebisch theory of, 387. *See also* Poverty

Inflation, 137, 144, 146, 156, 159, 370, 381, 387; costs of, 54; effects of, 180; in France, 175; in Great Britain, 176, 177; in Italy, 177; in Japan, 172; in postindustrial economies, 51; solution to, 55; as taxation substitute, 371; theories of, 54, 55; in West Germany, 172, 175

Institutions: lack of, 438–440, 476; role of, 483

Interest groups, 164, 406, 484; business associations, 140–141; economic, 137; effectiveness of, 476; farmers' associations, 140; and pluralism, 138; role of, 434–438; trade unions, 142

Internationalism: within socialist world, 228

International relations: as power maintenance policy, 484

Intersind, Italy, 154

Interstate relations: attitudes concerning, 334

Iran, 409, 410

Irish Republican Army (IRA), 514

Iron Curtain, 197

Islamic fundamentalism, 409

Isolationism, 38

Italian Communist Party (PCI), 72, 75, 100; compromise with Christian Democratic Party, 155; support for, 91, 154; and trade unions, 144

Italian Confederation of Workers' (CISL), 153

Italian Social Movement (MSI), 107

Italy: administrative élites, 128, 131; alienation in, 84; as centrifugal polyarchy, 25; class structure in, 56, 71; colonial holdings, 361, 371; early industrialization in, 30, 33; economic diversification of, 70–71; economic policy of, 177; education in, 164; farmers' associations, 140; gross domestic product per capita, 168; import/export balance, 170; inflation, 177; invasion of Ethiopa, 42; negative corporatism, 139; parliamentary system in, 115; party system in, 106, 118; political participation in, 87; as postindustrial society, 50; post-World War I, 38; post-World War II, 44; power distribution in, 163; trade unions in, 144, 153; unitary system of government, 132

Japan, 193, 397; colonial holdings, 361, 371; *de facto* military dictatorship, 39; energy consumption, 169; gross domestic product per capita, 168; import/export balance, 170; inflation in, 172; invasion of China, 42; as naval power, 38

Jaruzelski, Wojciech, 276

Jaurés, Jean, 37, 38

Jews, 40, 41

Johnson, Lyndon B., 124, 163


Kaase, Max, 89, 94

Kadar, Janos, 276

Kampuchea, 198–199; communication indicators, 351; education in, 227, 347; gross national product of, 209; land area, 227; population, 227; public expenditures, 337; quality of life in, 340

Kautsky, John H., 37, 359

Kennedy, John F., 86

Kenya: population growth in, 391

Kenyatta, Jomo, 482

Kerensky, Alexander, 188

Keynes, John Maynard, 128

Khomeini, Ruhollah (Ayatollah), 410

Khmer Rouge, 198

Khrushchev, Nikita S., 202, 268, 274; education reforms of, 260, 304, 344; policy of liberalization, 310; as policy maker, 304, 306; removal of, 276; on role of party, 284; and Stalin, 251; and wage differentials, 220

Kiesinger, Kurt Georg, 147

Korea: and Communism, 194

Kosygin, Aleksei N., 291, 292, 310


Labor: division of, 219

Labor force, 208

Labor unions, *see* Trade unions

Labour Party, Great Britain, 105, 115, 120, 175; corporatist policy, 151; in educational system, 61, 65; interventionist pluralism, 150; post-World War II power, 45; power struggle within, 152; and trade unions, 144

*Laissez faire*, 146, 147, 485, 486

Land: area, 228; improvement, 491; redistribution of, 209; reform, 445; tenure system, 393

Länder, 133–134

Land Reform Commission, Pakistan, 445

Language, 397

Laos, 199; communication indicators, 347; education in, 227, 347; gross national product, 209; land area, 227; population, 227; public expenditures, 339; quality of life indicators, 340

*Latifundia*, 394

Latin America: land-tenure problem, 394; languages of, 397; and *machismo*, 413; military intervention in, 453; population growth, 390, 391

Laws, 474, 475

Leadership: charismatic, 416, 504; importance of, 520; methods of, 483

League of Communists of Yugoslavia (LCY): Executive Committee, 304; reassertion of power, 311, 328; regional party

North Korea: communication indicators, 347; Communist ascendancy in, 194, 199; education in, 227, 347; ethnic homogeneity of, 207; gross national product, 209; population, 227; quality of life indicators, 340

North Vietnam, *see* Vietnam

Nyerere, Julius K., 451, 481, 482

Object loss, 407

Occupational roles, 221, 222

Organization for Economic Cooperation and Development (OECD), 69

Organization of Petroleum Exporting Countries (OPEC), 55

Ottoman Empire, 194, 461

Pacifism, 37, 38

Pakistan, 470; basic democracies experiment, 476–477; data-gathering in, 469; national goals, 465; syncratic politics in, 445–446

Pakistan Academy for Rural Development, Bangladesh, 415

Palestinian Liberation Organization (PLO), 486

Parliamentary systems, 115–126

Particularism, 404

Parties, 36, 104, 484; characteristics of, 447; coalition, 107–112, 121; competition among, 111; economic impact of, 181; effectiveness of, 476; elimination of, 40; emergence of, 431–434; and goal setting, 465; and human rights issue, 500; identification with, 84; and ideology, 79, 98; inflation theory of, 56; lack of, 475; left-wing, 101; and political participation, 104; post-World War II, 44–46; right-wing, 102, 106; role of, 433; systems, 105; types, 433

Partisanship: ideal of, 249

Pathet Lao, 199

Patron: defined, 447 élite, 448. *See also* Networks, patron-client

Patronage system, 126

Peasantry, 15, 27, 239, 359, 443

People's Liberation Army (PLA), 318; political role of, 280, 300; ranks abolished, 221

People's Republic of China, *see* China

Persian Gulf, 410

Personal income, 222–223

Personal leadership: impact on values distribution, 349

Peru: corruption in, 473; doctrine of *aprismo*, 481; land tenure system, 394

*Petite bourgeoisie*, 31, 33

Philippines, 409; elections in, 424; foreign debt of, 488; languages of, 397; martial law, 488

Planning: attitudes toward, 403–404; models of, 465

PLO, *see* Palestinian Liberation Organization

Pluralism, 14, 16, 137–138, 160, 166, 510; in Great Britain, 150, 152; model of Communist policy, 308; in post-Stalin era, 311. *See also* Democracy

Podgorny, Nikolai V., 279, 281, 291

Poland: anti-Soviet demonstrations in, 257, 334; Catholicism in, 241, 248; communication indicators, 347; Communist takeover in, 196; economic liberalization in, 213; education in, 227, 347; gross national product, 209; land

area, 227; 1980 demonstrations, 240; 1970 food riots in, 257; population, 227; public expenditures, 339; quality of life, 340; tension in, 251

Polarization, 78

Policy making: bureaucracies, 301–304; categories of, 467; centralized, 349; in China, 318–319; defined, 462; and dignity, 477–479; evaluation process, 475–477; examples of, 318–323; expertise in, 325; experts, 470; failures, 464; and goal setting, 312–314, 464, 469–470; for human rights, 501; implementation constraints, 470–475; industrial, 488; institutional actors and, 297–301; models of, 307–312; politics of, 314; and power, 315; process of, 312–318, 320; and producing outcomes, 316–318; project preparation and, 470; taking action and, 314–318

Politburo, *see* Communist parties

Political culture, 81, 98, 258–261; changes in, 239–245; defined, 78, 236; desired types of, 245–249; dominant, 248–249; and enlightenment, 258–261; and expenditure patterns, 348; and ideology, 237–238; nonparticipant, 239; participant, 249; and power, 81, 249–253; research on, 236–237; and respect, 253–255; and subcultures, 79, 98–100, 261–262; traditional, 239–245; and well-being, 255–258

Political elites, *see* Elites

Political participation, 516, 517; attitudes toward, 86–92; and civic competence, 87, 89–90, 91; and civic culture, 88; defined, 421; demographic factors, 91–92; and dignity, 440; in electoral process, 104; increasing level of, 325; and institutions, 438; limits of, 251; and party rule restrictions, 330; patterns of, 422; as power maintenance policy, 484; and socialization, 92–94; in Soviet Union, 326; unconventional modes of, 89, 92; voting, 423. *See also* Voting

Political performance: enlightenment, 344–348; human rights, 330–335; power, 325–330; well-being, 335–344

Political process, 9, 406

Political socialization, 80, 92, 245, 259–263; in China, 344; defined, 238; instruments of, 241, 242–245; tactics, 240; in United States, 240; in Yugoslavia, 345

Political systems, 6; classification of, 7; symbols within, 505–506

Politics: as authoritative process, 6; defined, 5; environmental factors of, 517, 519; function of, 5; impact of, 519

Pollution, 489

Polyarchy: defined, 23; economic ranking of, 25. *See also* Democracy

Pompidou, Georges, 111, 123, 159

Population, 227, 228–229, 234, 389; effect on per capita income, 391; working-age, 390–391; world, 375, 388

Portugal, 371, 521

Postindustrial society, 46–48; class structure, 56, 59; compared to industrial society, 49; indigent population, 64; occupational structure, 59; workers, 50. *See also* Industrialization; Preindustrial society

Postmaterialism, 95, 96

Potsdam conferences of 1945, 195

Poverty, 1; and agricultural production, 392–395; class causes of, 395–399; dependency theory of, 387; income distribution causes of, 395–397; and land tenure system, 392–395; national sources of, 388–400; and population growth, 388–392. *See also* Inequality

Power, 2, 249–253; abuse of, 486; acquisition methods, 482, 484–485; centralization of, 450; as commodity, 482; defined, 3; distribution of, 3, 162–164, 325, 474, 503, 513; within European Community, 179; formal versus informal, 114; horizontal distribution of, 115–126, 135, 163; and land ownership, 359; and policy, 325–332; realms of, 481; in Third World, 510; and values allocation, 7; vertical distribution of, 114, 131–135, 163; views of, 510

Prebisch, Raul, 385, 386, 387

Preindustrial society, 26–27. *See also* Industrialization; Post-industrial society

Price controls, *see* Wage and price controls

Price structure, 386

Prime Minister: election of, 115; function of, 123

Private property, 219

Proletariat, *see* Working class

Propaganda, 41, 244

Protestant Reformation, 73

Psychological modernization, 7, 26, 401; agents of, 411–419; aids to, 407; attitude changes, 403–404; cognitive-behavioral aspect of, 405–406; consequences of, 406; and coping mechanisms, 408; and dignity, 419; ego structure changes, 402–403; of First World, 14–15; object loss aspect, 407; process of, 7–8; of Second World, 15–16; of Third World, 16

Public policy: models of, 137–140

Quality of life indicators, 340–341

*Question of Imperialism, The* (Cohen), 384

Racism: in United States, 253

Radical Party, Italy, 101

*Radio Indigena*, Mexico, 418

Rákosi, Mátyás, 197, 276

Rational-comprehensive planning, 321

Reagan, Ronald, 180, 499

Recession: causes of, 53; of 1966–1967, 146, 147; pre-World War I, 36

Red Guards, 210, 271, 318; challenge to Chinese Communist Party, 326; dedication of, 345. *See also* Great Proletarian Cultural Revolution

Reform Act of 1832, Great Britain, 32

Religion: and cultural division, 397; and political socialization, 237, 241; as subculture, 263

Republic of South Africa, 166

Resource consumption, 391

Respect, *see* Human rights

Revolution of rising expectations, 426

*Rheinische Zeitung*, 185

Risk-taking, 403

Romania, 196, 203; communication indicators, 347; education in, 227, 347; gross national product, 209; land area, 227; population of, 227; public expenditures, 339; quality of life indicators, 340

Russia, 188–190; autocratic rule of, 329. *See also* Soviet Union

Russo-Japanese War of 1904–1905, 188

Sakarov, Andrei, 263

Saloth Sar, 200, 276

Samrin, Heng, 276

Schiller, Kurt, 147

Schmidt, Helmut, 172, 174

Science, 404

Scientific community, 301

Scotland, 134, 135

Second World, *see* Communist Party states

Self-determination, 7, 368, 369, 397

Self-management, *see* Yugoslavia

Separation of powers, 288, 449, 464; meaning of, 450, 452–453

Service sector, 49

Shagari, Shehu, 437

Shanghai, 191

Shatter zones, 385

Sihanouk, Norodom, Prince, 198

Sinai, I. R., 408; *The Challenge of Modernization*, 358

Singapore, 451

Sino-Japanese War of 1894-1895, 191, 193

Sino-Soviet conflict, 203, 229

Smith Adam, 385

Social class structure, *see* Class

Social Democratic Party, Great Britain, 152

Social Democratic Party (SDP), West Germany, 67, 105

Social indicators, 209, 339

Socialism, 99; construction of, 189, 250; economic challenges of, 216; evolution to Communism, 211; international movements of, 202; in nineteenth century, 187; scientific theory of, 186; worker attitudes under, 212. *See also* Communism

Social mobility, 226–228

Socialist Party, Italy, 108, 154

Social stratification, 221–226

Society: traditional, 358–359, 402

Socioeconomic change, 227

Soft state, *see* Third World

Solzhenitsyn, Alexander, 190

Southeast Asian states: authoritarianism of, 322; fractricidal warfare in, 352

South Korea, 487

Soviet Union: Academy of Sciences, 301; alcoholism in, 256, 319–320; and allocation of material goods, 256; citizens role, 249; Committee for State Security (KGB), 301; communication indicators, 347; Constitution, 266, 289, 331; consumption in, 218, 256; corruption in, 250; Council of Ministers, 292, 297, 298–299; discrimination in, 254; economy of, 207–208, 351; education in, 227, 347; environmental policy, 320–321; ethnic diversity of, 207, 229; federal political arrangement, 229; as first Marxist-Leninist state, 205; government, 6, 289–292; gross national product, 207, 209, 215; hooliganism in, 319–320; human rights violations